Cook Memorial Public Library
3 1122 01326 9969

P9-DLZ-671

The

AMERICAN HERITAGE®

Student Science *dictionary*

SECOND EDITION

Houghton Mifflin Harcourt

BOSTON • NEW YORK

Words are included in this dictionary on the basis of their usage. Words that are known to have current trademark registrations are shown with an initial capital and are also identified as trademarks. No investigation has been made of common-law trademark rights in any word, because such investigation is impracticable. The inclusion of any word in this dictionary is not, however, an expression of the publisher's opinion as to whether or not it is subject to proprietary rights. Indeed, no definition in this dictionary is to be regarded as affecting the validity of any trademark.

Visit our websites: hmhco.com *and* ahdictionary.com

Library of Congress Cataloging-in-Publication Data
The American Heritage student science dictionary. — Second edition.
pages cm
Audience: Age 12+
Audience: Grade 7+
ISBN 978-0-547-85731-2
1. Science — Dictionaries, Juvenile. I. Title: Student science dictionary.
Q123.A52 2014
503 — dc23
2014011076

Manufactured in the United States of America

1 2 3 4 5 6 7 8 9 10 – DOC – 20 19 18 17 16 15 14

4500470942

The
AMERICAN HERITAGE®
Student Science *dictionary*

CONTENTS

Editorial and Production Staff iv
Preface v
Entries with Notes vi
Pronunciation vii
Elements of the Dictionary ..... viii–ix
The American Heritage Student Science Dictionary 1
Picture Credits 373–374

Tables and Charts
Geologic Time 146–147
Measurement Table 208
Organic Compounds 240
Periodic Table of the Elements 254–255
Rock Types 292
Solar System 312–313
Taxonomy 333

A Closer Look
Atoms 28
Cells 63
Color 76
Fission/Fusion 130
Flowers 133
Meiosis/Mitosis 210
Photosynthesis 258
Skeleton 307
Star 321
Tectonic Boundaries 334
Volcanoes 360
Waves 364

Senior Vice President, Publisher, General Interest Group
Bruce Nichols

Executive Editor
Steven R. Kleinedler

Project Editor
Louise E. Robbins

Senior Editor
Peter Chipman

Editorial Associate
Emily A. Neeves

Consulting Editors
Stuart D. Anderson
Linda Bush
Nicholas A. Durlacher
Hanna Schonthal

Contributors to the First Edition
Benjamin W. Fortson IV
Uchenna Ikonné
Wade A. Ostrowski
Joseph P. Pickett
Jacquelyn Pope
Vali Tamm

Proofreaders
Diane Fredrick
Katherine M. Isaacs
Deborah M. Posner
David R. Pritchard

Database Production Supervisor
Christopher J. Granniss

Director of Production Technologies
David Futato

Art and Production Supervisor
Margaret Anne Miles

Editorial and Production Coordinator
Sarah Iani

Text Design
Symmetry
Barrington, Illinois

Pre-Press Development
Chakra Communications, Inc.
Lancaster, New York

Air is probably part of your everyday vocabulary, but it's a good bet that **zooxanthella** isn't. The A–Z vocabulary of science ranges from the basic to the obscure, from words that are easy to spell and pronounce to those that are long and hard to say. But learning these words involves much more than just learning how to say and spell them. Pick any word, and you'll be transported into the fascinating world of our universe as scientists understand it today. You'll also find that the simple words are not as simple as you think, and the complicated ones aren't so daunting after all. Look inside to find out what a complex mixture of elements makes up air. And zooxanthellae, you'll discover, are nothing more than small algae that live inside corals—but they play a crucial role in the functioning of coral reefs.

This dictionary will help you understand the language and concepts of science. The definitions are clear and up-to-date, and the entries give you additional information beyond the basic meaning of the term. The entry for **static electricity,** for example, not only tells you what it is but gives examples from your daily life. Many entries, such as **fossil,** provide extended definitions for related terms: in this case, **fossil fuel.** Over two hundred biographical entries describe the accomplishments of scientists from ancient times to the present day. Several kinds of cross-references help you fill out your vocabulary. "Compare" references send you to a corresponding term: at the geological term **extrusion,** you are directed to **intrusion.** "See more" references direct you to entries where you can learn more about a similar topic: the **cell division** entry informs you that you can find out more at **fission, meiosis,** and **mitosis.**

The dictionary contains over 150 notes that provide in-depth information on certain topics. *Usage* notes help you untangle the precise terminology of science, where words are not always used in the same way as they are in everyday life. The note at **fruit,** for example, tells you why botanists call a cucumber a fruit rather than a vegetable. *Word History* notes discuss the origins and often surprising history of scientific terms. You probably wouldn't guess that the word for an immature insect, **larva,** comes from a Latin word for an actor's mask. The people behind important scientific advances, such as the physicist Marie **Curie,** the biologist Charles **Darwin,** and the physician Abu **Ibn Sina,** come to life in *Biography* notes. Nearly one hundred *Did You Know?* notes provide lively, in-depth explanations of scientific terms such as **antibody, neutrino,** and **plate tectonics.**

Photographs, drawings, tables, and charts are essential scientific tools, and you'll find hundreds of them here to supplement the main entries. A dozen full-page *Closer Look* features present detailed explanations along with labeled drawings of basic terms such as **cell, star,** and **volcano.** Tables and charts include the **periodic table of the elements,** the **solar system,** and **geologic time.** Over 450 full-color photographs and drawings, together with their captions, clarify complicated ideas and structures in a way that a definition alone sometimes can't.

In preparing the second edition of the *American Heritage Student Science Dictionary,* the editorial staff has reviewed all the definitions and revised over half of them. Numerous illustrations have been replaced. Over 250 new words and senses have been added, including the terms **aquaculture, biofuel, celiac disease, cloud computing, exoplanet,** and **trans fat.** We've enjoyed exploring the components of air and the workings of coral reefs, and we hope that you, too, will be enchanted and excited by what science tells us about the universe, and curious about what remains to be discovered.

Louise E. Robbins
Project Editor

ENTRIES WITH NOTES

Did You Know...?

acceleration
acid rain
adaptation
aerodynamics
alchemy
allergy
amber
antibody
archaeon
aspirin
atomic clock
bat
battery
beetle
Big Bang
bird
black hole
blood type
brain
Burgess Shale
cactus
cancer
carbon
Celsius
centripetal force
charge
circadian rhythm
compound eye
conduction
current
cyclone
dark matter
DNA
Doppler effect
dwarf star
earthquake
eclipse
electromagnetic radiation
endorphin
enzyme
evolution
fat
fault
fiber optics
force
fungus
gene
glass
Gondwana
gravity
greenhouse effect
heavy water
hologram
hormone
influenza
infrared
Internet
iridium
keratin
laser
lightning
magnetism
mimicry
moon
nanotechnology
neutrino
nuclear reactor
oxidation
ozone
planet
plate tectonics
pollination
program
pulsar
quasar
radioactivity
radiocarbon dating
rare-earth element
red blood cell
relativity
sickle cell anemia
solar cell
solar system
solution
sound[1]
space-time
subatomic particle
sublimation
thermodynamics
transpiration
turbojet
ultrasound
vaccine
vitamin
wetland
whale
worm
zero
zooxanthella

USAGE

bug
byte
centigrade
deduction
disk
electronic
endemic
fruit
germ
light year
megabyte
metal
meteor
ocean
refraction
revolution
stalactite
temperature
velocity
weight

WORD HISTORY

algebra
amphibian
brontosaurus
calculus
dynamite
element
entomology
gastropod
helium
humor
larva
mercury
pahoehoe
Rigel
tadpole
triceratops

BIOGRAPHY

Archimedes
Bohr, Niels
Carson, Rachel
Carver, George Washington
Copernicus, Nicolaus
Curie, Marie
Darwin, Charles
Einstein, Albert
Franklin, Benjamin
Galileo Galilei
Herschel, William and Caroline
Hutton, James
Ibn Sina
Lavoisier, Antoine
Leeuwenhoek, Anton van
Lovelace, Ada
Mendel, Gregor
Newton, Isaac
Pasteur, Louis
Pauling, Linus
Tesla, Nikola

This dictionary provides pronunciations using standard pronunciation symbols as explained in the key below. The pronunciations appear in parentheses following boldface entry words. If an entry word has a variant spelling and the two words have the same pronunciation, the pronunciation follows the variant spelling. If the variant does not have the same pronunciation, pronunciations follow the forms to which they apply. If a word has multiple common pronunciations, the first pronunciation is generally more common than the other; however, they are often equally common.

Stress

Stress, the relative degree of emphasis with which a word's syllables are spoken, is indicated in three ways. An unmarked syllable has the weakest stress in the word. A bold mark (**′**) indicates the strongest stress. A lighter mark (′) indicates a secondary level of stress. Words of one syllable show no stress mark, since there is no other stress level to which the syllable is compared.

Pronunciation Key

A list of the pronunciation symbols used in this dictionary is given here in the column headed Symbol. The column headed Examples contains words chosen to illustrate how the symbols are pronounced. The letters that correspond in sound to the symbols are shown in boldface.

The nonalphabetical symbol (ə) is called *schwa*. It is used to represent a reduced vowel (a vowel that receives the weakest level of stress within a word). The schwa sound varies, sometimes according to the vowel it is representing and often according to the sounds surrounding it:

ab•a•cus (ăb**′**ə-kəs)
ab•do•men (ăb**′**də-mən)
ac•ti•nide (ăk**′**tə-nīd′)
cu•mu•lus (kyo͞om**′**yə-ləs)

PRONUNCIATION KEY

Symbol	Examples	Symbol	Examples	Symbol	Examples	Symbol	Examples
ă	pat	ĭ	pit	oi	noise	ûr	urge, term, firm, word, heard
ā	pay	ī	pie, by	o͝o	took	v	valve
âr	care	îr	deer, pier	o͞o	boot	w	with
ä	father	j	judge	ou	out	y	yes
b	bib	k	kick, cat, pique	p	pop	z	zebra, xylem
ch	church	l	lid, needle	r	roar	zh	vision, pleasure, garage
d	deed, milled	m	mum	s	sauce	ə	about, item, edible, gallop, circus
ĕ	pet	n	no, sudden	sh	ship, dish	ər	butter
ē	bee	ng	thing	t	tight, stopped		
f	fife, phase, rough	ŏ	pot	th	thin		
g	gag	ō	toe	*th*	this		
h	hat	ô	caught, paw, for	ŭ	cut		
hw	which						

ELEMENTS OF THE DICTIONARY

guideword

***Compare* cross-reference**
identifies contrasting terms in a subject area

adult

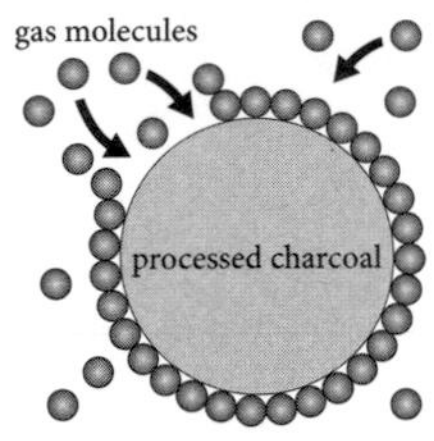

■ **adsorption**
Toxic gas molecules adhere to the processed charcoal in a gas mask, allowing the person wearing the mask to breathe nontoxic air.

of carbon cartridges that adsorb contaminants. *Compare* **absorption** (sense 2).

adult (ə-dŭlt′, ăd′ŭlt) An organism, especially an animal, that is fully grown and mature.

aerobic (â-rō′bĭk) Needing or using oxygen to live: *aerobic organisms.* ❖ **Aerobic exercise** increases the activity of the heart and lungs and improves the body's ability to use oxygen. *Compare* **anaerobic.**

aerodynamic (âr′ō-dī-năm′ĭk) **1.** Relating to objects, such as the wings of airplanes, that are designed to reduce wind drag. **2.** Relating to aerodynamics.

aerodynamics (âr′ō-dī-năm′ĭks) The study of the movement of air and other gases and of the forces involved in their movements. It is also the study of the way objects, such as cars and airplanes, interact with air when they are moving through it.

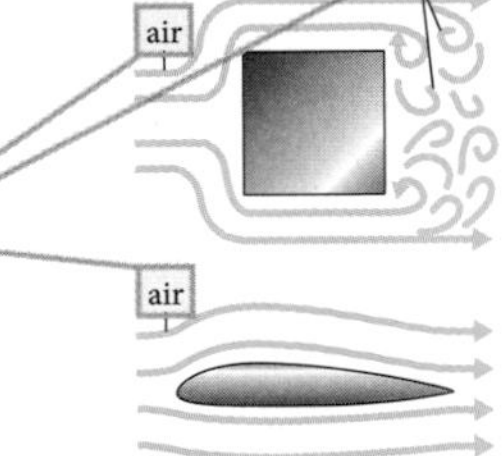

■ **aerodynamics**
top: *high wind drag on a less aerodynamic shape*
bottom: *low wind drag on a more aerodynamic shape*

aeronautics (âr′ə-nô′tĭks) **1.** The design and construction of aircraft. **2.** The study of the piloting and navigation of aircraft.

aerosol (âr′ə-sôl′) **1.** A substance consisting of very fine particles of a liquid or solid suspended in a gas. Mist, which consists of very fine droplets of water in air, is an aerosol. *Compare* **emulsion, foam. 2.** A substance, such as paint, an insecticide, or a hair spray, packaged under pressure for use in this form.

aerospace (âr′ō-spās′) **1.** Relating to the science and technology of flight. **2.** Relating to the Earth's atmosphere and the space beyond.

aestivation (ĕs′tə-vā′shən) Another spelling of **estivation.**

afferent (ăf′ər-ənt) Relating to nerves that carry sensory information toward the central nervous system. *Compare* **efferent.**

Did You Know...?

aerodynamics

The two primary forces in *aerodynamics* are lift and drag. *Lift* refers to forces perpendicular to the surface of an object (such as an airplane wing) that is traveling through the air. For example, airplane wings are designed so that when they move through the air, an area of low pressure is created above the wing; the low pressure produces a lift force that pulls the wing upward (in a direction perpendicular to the wing's broad surface), and the wing pulls the airplane up with it. *Drag* forces, which are parallel to the object's surface, are usually caused by friction. Drag makes it more difficult for airplane wings to slice through the air, and so drag forces push against the forward motion of the craft. Large wings usually generate a lot of lift, but they also produce a lot of drag. In designing airplane wings, engineers need to take into account such factors as the speed and altitude at which the plane will fly, so that they can find a wing shape that balances lift and drag as well as possible.

6

entry word

pronunciation
shows how to pronounce words; see key on page vii

art labels
identify key terms

art caption
provides additional information

Did You Know? note
provides more details about a topic. Other notes include Usage, Biography, and Word History; see list on page vi.

***See more* cross-reference**
shows you where to find additional information

irregular plural

crystal

sea animals, such as the sea lilies and feather stars, having a cup-shaped body, feathery arms, and a stalk by which they attach themselves to a surface. Crinoids are echinoderms.

crista (krĭs′tə) *Plural* **cristae** (krĭs′tē) One of the folds of the inner membrane of a mitochondrion. *See more at* **mitochondrion.**

crocodile (krŏk′ə-dīl′) Any of various large, meat-eating, aquatic reptiles native to tropical and subtropical regions. Crocodiles have a longer, more slender snout than alligators, and their teeth are visible when the jaw is closed.

crocodilian (krŏk′ə-dĭl′ē-ən) Any of various large meat-eating reptiles having a long jaw with sharp teeth, short legs, and a long tail, and mostly living in or near water. The crocodilians include the crocodiles, alligators, caimans (of South America), and gharial (of South Asia).

Crohn's disease (krōnz) Chronic inflammation of the digestive tract, characterized by abdominal pain and digestive problems such as diarrhea or constipation.

Crookes (krŏŏks), Sir **William** 1832–1919. British chemist and physicist who discovered thallium in 1861 and invented the radiometer in 1875. He also investigated cathode rays, demonstrating that they consisted of charged particles.

cross (krôs) *Noun* **1.** A plant or animal produced by crossbreeding. — *Verb* **2.** To crossbreed or cross-fertilize plants or animals.

crossbreed (krôs′brēd′) To produce offspring by

crevasse

crinoid

mating two animals or plants of different breeds, varieties, or species.

cross-fertilization The fertilization that occurs when a male sex cell from one individual joins to a female sex cell from another individual of the same species. In plants, cross-pollination is an example of cross-fertilization. — *Verb* **cross-fertilize.**

cross-pollination The transfer of pollen from the male reproductive organ (an anther or a male cone) of one plant to the female reproductive organ (a stigma or a female cone) of another plant. Insects and wind are agents of cross-pollination. — *Verb* **cross-pollinate.**

crucible (kro͞o′sə-bəl) A heat-resistant container used to melt ores, metals, and other materials.

crust (krŭst) The solid, outermost layer of the Earth. ❖ The crust that lies underneath the continents is called **continental crust,** and is approximately 22 to 37 miles (35 to 60 kilometers) thick. It consists mostly of rocks rich in silica and aluminum, with minor amounts of iron, magnesium, calcium, sodium, and potassium. ❖ The crust that lies underneath the oceans is called **oceanic crust,** and is approximately 3 to 6 miles (5 to 10 kilometers) thick. It has a similar composition to that of continental crust, but has higher concentrations of iron, magnesium, and calcium. It is denser than continental crust.

crustacean (krŭ-stā′shən) Any of a group of arthropods that usually live in water and have a segmented body, a hard shell, paired jointed limbs, and two pairs of antennae. Lobsters, crabs, shrimp, and barnacles are crustaceans.

cryogenics (krī′ə-jĕn′ĭks) The branch of physics that studies how matter behaves at very low temperatures.

crystal (krĭs′təl) A solid composed of atoms, molecules, or ions arranged in regular patterns that are repeated throughout the structure to form a characteristic network. Crystals have

87

run-on with part of speech

biographical entry

nested entries
define a closely related term that is derived from the entry word

parts of speech
are identified when there is more than one

A **1.** Abbreviation of **adenine. 2.** Abbreviation of **ampere. 3. Å** Abbreviation of **angstrom. 4.** Abbreviation of **area.**

a– A prefix meaning "without" or "not" when forming an adjective (such as *amorphous,* without form, or *atypical,* not typical), and "absence of" when forming a noun (such as *arrhythmia,* absence of rhythm). Before a vowel or *h* it becomes *an–* (as in *anhydrous, anoxia*).

aa (ä′ä) A type of lava having a rough, jagged surface composed of tumbled fragments. In its molten state, it is fairly viscous but flows relatively quickly. *See Note at* **pahoehoe.**

aardvark (ärd′värk′) A burrowing African mammal having a stocky body, large ears, a long tubular snout, and powerful claws used for digging. Aardvarks feed mostly on ants and termites.

abacus (ăb′ə-kəs) *Plural* **abacuses** *or* **abaci** (ăb′-ə-sī′) A computing device consisting of a frame holding parallel rods with sliding beads.

abalone (ăb′ə-lō′nē) Any of various edible mollusks that have a large, ear-shaped shell. The shell has a row of holes along the outer edge, and the interior is lined with mother-of-pearl.

abdomen (ăb′də-mən) **1.** In humans and other mammals, the portion of the body that lies between the chest and the pelvis. The abdomen contains the stomach, intestines, liver, spleen, and pancreas. **2.** A region similar to the abdomen in other vertebrates, such as a snake. **3.** In insects, arachnids, and other arthropods, the last, most posterior segment of the body. —*Adjective* **abdominal** (ăb-dŏm′ə-nəl).

abacus

On a Chinese abacus, the columns of beads go from right to left and present ones, tens, hundreds, thousands, and so on. The beads above the crossbar have a value of five; the beads below the crossbar have a value of one. The beads are totaled when moved down or up toward the crossbar.

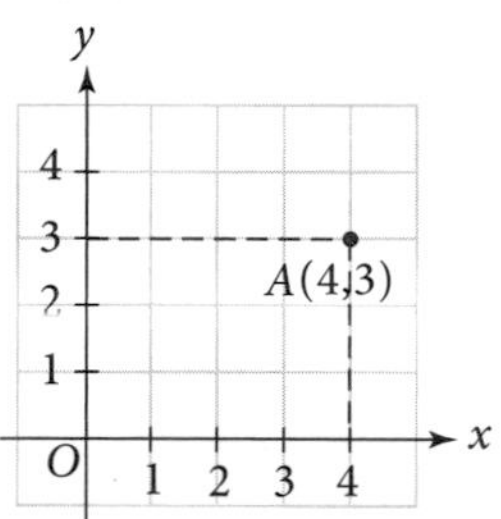

abscissa

The coordinates for A are (4,3); the abscissa is 4, and the ordinate is 3.

aberration (ăb′ə-rā′shən) **1.** The failure of a lens or mirror to bring light rays from a source, such as a star, to focus at a single point, causing a distorted or blurred image. **2.** A deviation in the normal structure or number of chromosomes in an organism.

ablation (ă-blā′shən) **1.** The wearing away or destruction of the outer or forward surface of an object, such as a meteorite or a spacecraft, as it moves very rapidly through the atmosphere. The friction of the air striking the object heats and often melts or burns its outer layers. **2.** The process by which snow and ice are removed from a glacier or other mass of ice. Ablation typically occurs through melting, sublimation, or wind erosion.

abomasum (ăb′ō-mā′səm) The fourth compartment of the stomach in ruminant animals, and the only one having glands that secrete acids and enzymes for digestion. It corresponds anatomically to the stomach of other mammals. *See more at* **ruminant.**

abrasion (ə-brā′zhən) **1.** The process of wearing away or rubbing down by means of friction. **2.** A scraped area on the skin.

abscess (ăb′sĕs′) A collection of pus that forms at one place in the body and is surrounded by inflamed tissue. An abscess is a sign of infection.

abscissa (ăb-sĭs′ə) The distance of a point from

the *y*-axis on a graph in the Cartesian coordinate system. It is measured parallel to the *x*-axis. For example, a point having coordinates (2,3) has 2 as its abscissa. *Compare* **ordinate.**

absolute humidity (ăb′sə-lo͞ot′) The amount of water vapor present in a unit volume of air, usually expressed in kilograms per cubic meter. *Compare* **relative humidity.**

absolute scale A temperature scale having absolute zero as the lowest temperature. The Kelvin scale is an absolute scale.

absolute temperature Temperature measured or calculated on an absolute scale.

absolute value The value of a number without regard to its sign. For example, the absolute value of +3 (written |+3|) and the absolute value of −3 (written |−3|) are both 3.

absolute zero The lowest possible temperature, at which atoms have the minimum amount of energy and almost all motion ceases. The Kelvin scale is defined as starting at absolute zero (0 K, which is equal to −459.67°F or −273.15°C).

absorption (əb-sôrp′shən) **1.** *Biology* The movement of a substance, such as a liquid or solute, through a cell membrane and into a cell by means of diffusion or osmosis. **2.** *Chemistry* The process of drawing a gas or liquid into a solid through the minute spaces between its parts. *Compare* **adsorption. 3.** *Physics* The taking up of energy, such as sound or light, by a material. The absorbed energy is usually converted into thermal energy, heating the material that absorbs it. Absorption is distinguished from reflection (where energy is turned back from the medium) and transmission (where energy goes through the medium).

absorption spectrum The pattern of dark lines in the spectrum of light that has passed through an absorbing medium, such as a gas. The dark lines indicate the wavelengths of light that were absorbed by the atoms of the medium rather than being transmitted through it. Every atomic element absorbs light only of certain wavelengths, and so produces a unique absorption spectrum. Scientists can determine the composition of the gaseous outer layer of a star by analyzing the absorption spectrum of the light coming from the star.

Ac The symbol for **actinium.**

AC Abbreviation of **alternating current.**

acceleration (ăk-sĕl′ə-rā′shən) The rate of change of the velocity (that is, the speed or direction) of a moving body with respect to time. A body accelerates if its speed changes, if the direction of its motion changes, or if both its speed and direction of motion change. *See more at* **gravity, relativity.**

acceleration of gravity The acceleration of

Did You Know...?

acceleration

Legend has it that one day in the 1500s, Galileo dropped a large cannonball and a small lead ball off the Leaning Tower of Pisa in Italy, and the two balls landed on the ground at the same time. Although he may never have done this exact experiment, Galileo did formulate the important principle that all objects fall to Earth at the same rate if you drop them—at least in a vacuum, where there's no air resistance. Why should this be? It seems as though the heavier ball should fall faster, as Aristotle and other Greek scientists had believed. You can understand why objects of different weights fall at the same rate if you know that when an object is accelerated by a force, the *acceleration* is related to the force and the object's mass according to the equation $F = ma$, where F is the force, m is the object's mass, and a is the resulting acceleration. Objects have weight because of the force of gravity, and the magnitude of that force depends on the mass of the object. Suppose the cannonball weighs ten times as much as the lead ball. Since the cannonball experiences ten times the gravitational force but also has ten times the mass of the lead ball, the larger force is just enough to accelerate the larger mass at the same rate of acceleration that the smaller force achieves acting on the smaller mass. In other words, the acceleration produced by gravity is independent of the mass of the object involved. All over the surface of the earth, all falling objects would accelerate at the same rate of 32 feet (9.8 meters) per second per second if it weren't for the effects of air resistance.

Did You Know...?

acid rain

We normally think of rain as a pure, life-giving substance, but in many parts of the world it is polluted with acids that can cause great harm to living things. How does this happen? When fossil fuels such as coal, gasoline, and oil are burned, they give off the gases sulfur dioxide and nitrogen oxide. In the atmosphere, these compounds react with water vapor to form highly corrosive sulfuric and nitric acids. Prevailing winds carry these acids away from the industrial areas where they originate, and they fall to Earth as acidic precipitation in the form of rain, snow, fog, or dew — commonly called *acid rain*. Acid rain is a serious environmental problem in parts of the United States, Canada, Europe, and Asia where there are many factories, power plants, and automobiles. It harms forests and soils and pollutes lakes and rivers, killing fish and other aquatic life. It can also damage buildings and monuments by eating away their stone and metal surfaces.

a body falling freely under the influence of the Earth's gravity, with no other forces acting on it. On the Earth at sea level, it is equal to approximately 32 feet (9.8 meters) per second per second.

–aceous A suffix used to form adjectives meaning "made of" or "resembling" a particular substance or material, such as *silicaceous,* containing silicon.

acetaldehyde (ăs′ĭ-tăl**′**də-hīd′) A colorless, flammable liquid, C_2H_4O, used to make acetic acid, perfumes, and drugs.

acetaminophen (ə-sē′tə-mĭn**′**ə-fən) A medicine used to relieve pain and reduce fever.

acetate (ăs**′**ĭ-tāt′) **1.** A salt, ester, or anion of acetic acid. **2.** Cellulose acetate or a product made from it, especially fibers or film. *See more at* **cellulose.**

acetic acid (ə-sē**′**tĭk) A clear, colorless, pungent acid, $C_2H_4O_2$, occurring naturally in vinegar and also produced commercially. It is used as a solvent and in making rubber, cellulose acetate plastics, paints, and dyes.

acetone (ăs**′**ĭ-tōn′) A colorless, extremely flammable liquid ketone, C_3H_6O, that is widely used as a solvent, for example in nail-polish remover.

acetylcholine (ə-sēt′l-kō**′**lēn′) A neurotransmitter that is present in most animals. It transmits nerve impulses from nerve cells to muscles or to other nerve cells. It was the first neurotransmitter discovered.

acetylene (ə-sĕt**′**l-ēn′) A colorless, highly flammable and explosive gas, C_2H_2. It is used in gas lighting and in cutting and welding metal. Also called *ethyne.*

acetylsalicylic acid (ə-sēt′l-săl′ĭ-sĭl**′**ĭk) The chemical name for aspirin.

Achilles tendon (ə-kĭl**′**ēz) A large tendon at the back of the leg connecting the calf muscles with the heel bone. The Achilles tendon is the strongest tendon in the body.

acid (ăs**′**ĭd) Any of a class of compounds that form hydrogen ions when dissolved in water. They also react, in solution, with bases and certain metals to form salts. Acids turn blue litmus paper red, have a sour taste, and have a pH of less than 7. *Compare* **base.** —*Adjective* **acidic.**

acid rain Rain or other precipitation that is highly acidic.

acne (ăk**′**nē) A skin disorder in which the oil glands become clogged and infected, often causing pimples to form, especially on the face. It is commonest during adolescence.

acoustics (ə-ko͞o**′**stĭks) **1.** *Used with a singular verb.* The scientific study of the generation, propagation, and reception of sound. **2.** *Used with*

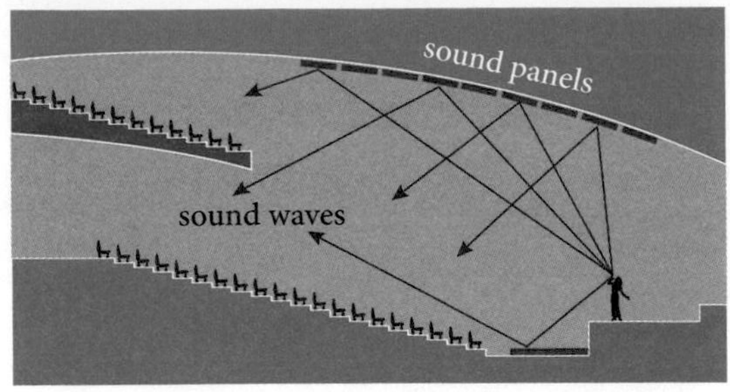

acoustics
Sound waves from a stage are deflected by sound panels and distributed throughout an auditorium.

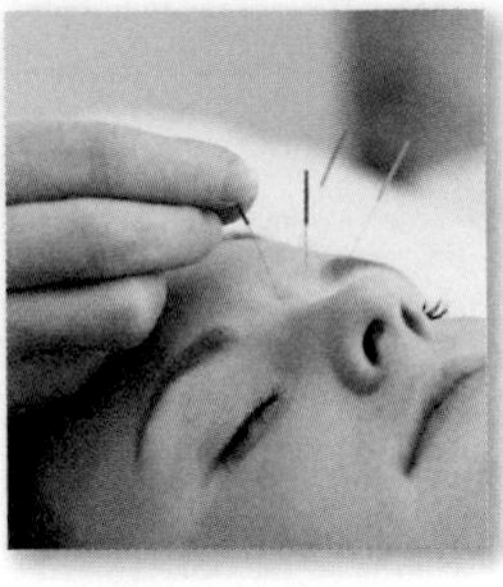

acupuncture

a plural verb. The total effect of sound, especially as produced in an enclosed space: *a concert hall with excellent acoustics.*

acquired immune deficiency syndrome (ə-kwīrd′) *See* **AIDS.**

acrylic acid (ə-krĭl′ĭk) A colorless, corrosive liquid, $C_3H_4O_2$, that readily forms polymers. It is used to make plastics, paints, synthetic rubbers, and textiles.

ACTH (ā′sē′tē-āch′) Short for *adrenocorticotropic hormone.* A hormone secreted by a lobe of the pituitary gland. ACTH stimulates the adrenal glands to produce cortisone and related hormones.

actinide (ăk′tə-nīd′) Any of a series of chemically similar metallic elements with atomic numbers ranging from 89 (actinium) to 103 (lawrencium). All of these elements are radioactive, and two of the elements, uranium and plutonium, are used to generate nuclear energy. *See* **Periodic Table,** pages 254–255.

actinium (ăk-tĭn′ē-əm) A silvery-white, highly radioactive metallic element of the actinide series that is found in uranium ores or produced artificially from radium. It is about 150 times more radioactive than radium and is used as a source of alpha particles and neutrons. Its most stable isotope has a half-life of about 22 years. *Symbol* **Ac.** *Atomic number* 89. *See* **Periodic Table,** pages 254–255.

activation energy (ăk′tə-vā′shən) The least amount of energy needed for a chemical reaction to occur. For example, striking a match on the side of a matchbox provides the activation energy, in the form of heat, necessary for the chemicals in the match to catch fire.

active site (ăk′tĭv) The part of an enzyme where the substance that the enzyme acts upon (called the substrate) is catalyzed. *See Note at* **enzyme.**

active transport The movement of ions or molecules across a cell membrane in the direction opposite that of diffusion, that is, from an area of lower concentration to one of higher concentration. The energy needed for active transport is chiefly supplied by ATP.

acupuncture (ăk′yo͝o-pŭngk′chər) The practice of inserting thin needles into the body at specific points to relieve pain, treat a disease, or numb a body part during surgery. Acupuncture has its origin in traditional Chinese medicine and has been in use for more than 5,000 years.

acute angle (ə-kyo͞ot′) An angle whose measure is between 0° and 90°. *Compare* **obtuse angle.**

adaptation (ăd′ăp-tā′shən) **1.** Change or adjustment in structure or habits by which the members of a species become better able to function in their environment. Adaptation occurs during evolution through the action of natural selection. **2.** A structure or habit that results from this process.

addend (ăd′ĕnd′) A number that is added to another number.

addiction (ə-dĭk′shən) **1.** A physical or psychological need for a habit-forming substance, such as drugs or alcohol. **2.** A habitual or

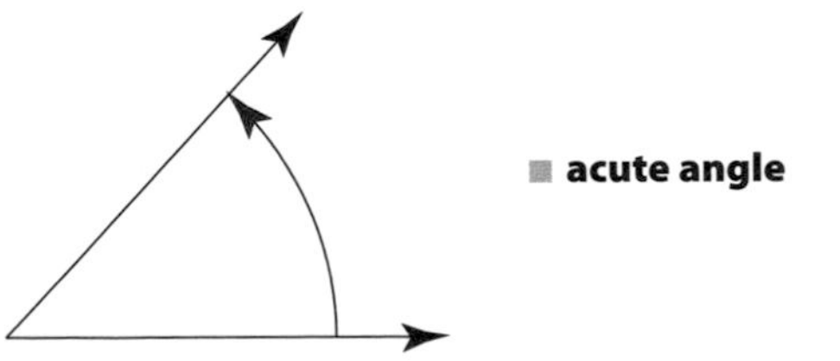

acute angle

Did You Know...?

adaptation

Orchids are stunning flowers that are favorites of florists and home decorators. Their beautiful and complex shapes aren't meant for our enjoyment, though. They are *adaptations* that developed over thousands of years, and the creatures they are designed to attract are not humans, but bees, flies, and other pollinators. Every organism has characteristics that are suited to its environment—the polar bear's thick fur, the snake's flexible jaws, the cat's sharp claws. According to the Darwinian theory of evolution, these adaptations are the result of a two-stage evolutionary process: random variation followed by natural selection. Slight genetic differences often result in variations among individuals. Perhaps the flowers on one orchid plant have a slightly different shape from those on other plants, and that shape happens to be more attractive to pollinating male wasps because it looks a little like a female wasp. That plant will produce more seeds, and those seeds will grow into plants with genes for that flower shape. Over many generations of variation and natural selection, the flowers will become more and more attractive to pollinators. Eventually, the result is an orchid species with flowers that look like a female wasp—an adaptation for pollination that provides an irresistible lure for male wasps and an exquisite bloom for humans to admire.

compulsive involvement in an activity, such as gambling.

addition (ə-dĭsh′ən) The act, process, or operation of adding two or more numbers to compute their sum.

additive (ăd′ĭ-tĭv) *Noun* **1.** A substance that is added in small amounts to something in order to improve its performance or quality, preserve its usefulness, or make it more effective. —*Adjective* **2.** Being any of the primary colors red, green, or blue, whose wavelengths may be mixed with one another to produce all other colors. *See more at* **color. 3.** *Mathematics* Marked by or involving addition.

adenine (ăd′n-ēn′) A base that is a component of DNA and RNA, forming a base pair with thymine in DNA and a base pair with uracil in RNA during transcription.

adenoids (ăd′n-oidz′) A mass of tissue located at the back of the nose in the upper part of the throat in children. Adenoids are part of the immune system, but if they become infected and swollen, they can obstruct normal breathing. They usually shrink by adulthood.

adenosine (ə-dĕn′ə-sēn′) An organic compound, $C_{10}H_{13}N_5O_4$, that is a component of several very important molecules in living things, including DNA, ADP, AMP, and ATP.

adenosine diphosphate (dī-fŏs′fāt′) *See* **ADP.**

adenosine monophosphate (mŏn′ō-fŏs′fāt′) *See* **AMP.**

adenosine triphosphate (trī-fŏs′fāt′) *See* **ATP.**

ADHD Abbreviation of **attention deficit hyperactivity disorder.**

adiabatic (ăd′ē-ə-băt′ĭk) Occurring without gain or loss of heat. The passage of sound through air is generally adiabatic.

adipose (ăd′ə-pōs′) Relating to or consisting of animal fat.

adjacent angle (ə-jā′sənt) Either of two angles having a common side and a common vertex.

ADP (ā′dē′pē′) Short for *adenosine diphosphate.* An organic compound, $C_{10}H_{15}N_5O_{10}P_2$, that is composed of adenosine and two phosphate groups. With the addition of another phosphate group, it is converted to ATP for the storage of energy during cell metabolism.

adrenal gland (ə-drē′nəl) Either of two endocrine glands, one located above each kidney, that produce several important hormones. ❖ The outer part of the adrenal gland, called the **adrenal cortex,** produces steroid hormones. ❖ The inner part of the adrenal gland, called the **adrenal medulla,** produces epinephrine.

adrenaline (ə-drĕn′ə-lĭn) *See* **epinephrine.**

adsorption (ăd-sôrp′shən) The process by which molecules of a substance, such as a gas or a liquid, collect on the surface of another substance, such as a solid. The molecules are attracted to the surface but do not enter the solid's minute spaces, as in absorption. Some drinking water filters consist

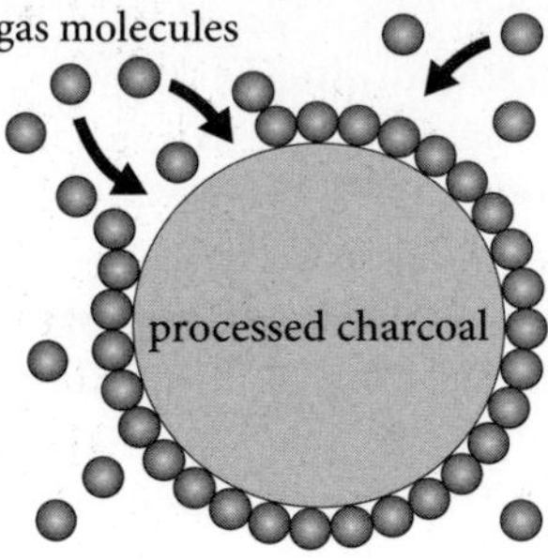

■ **adsorption**
Toxic gas molecules adhere to the processed charcoal in a gas mask, allowing the person wearing the mask to breathe nontoxic air.

of carbon cartridges that adsorb contaminants. *Compare* **absorption** (sense 2).

adult (ə-dŭlt′, ăd′ŭlt) An organism, especially an animal, that is fully grown and mature.

aerobic (â-rō′bĭk) Needing or using oxygen to live: *aerobic organisms.* ❖ **Aerobic exercise** increases the activity of the heart and lungs and improves the body's ability to use oxygen. *Compare* **anaerobic.**

aerodynamic (âr′ō-dī-năm′ĭk) **1.** Relating to objects, such as the wings of airplanes, that are designed to reduce wind drag. **2.** Relating to aerodynamics.

aerodynamics (âr′ō-dī-năm′ĭks) The study of the movement of air and other gases and of the forces involved in their movements. It is also the study of the way objects, such as cars and airplanes, interact with air when they are moving through it.

■ **aerodynamics**
top: *high wind drag on a less aerodynamic shape*
bottom: *low wind drag on a more aerodynamic shape*

aeronautics (âr′ə-nô′tĭks) **1.** The design and construction of aircraft. **2.** The study of the piloting and navigation of aircraft.

aerosol (âr′ə-sôl′) **1.** A substance consisting of very fine particles of a liquid or solid suspended in a gas. Mist, which consists of very fine droplets of water in air, is an aerosol. *Compare* **emulsion, foam. 2.** A substance, such as paint, an insecticide, or a hair spray, packaged under pressure for use in this form.

aerospace (âr′ō-spās′) **1.** Relating to the science and technology of flight. **2.** Relating to the Earth's atmosphere and the space beyond.

aestivation (ĕs′tə-vā′shən) Another spelling of **estivation.**

afferent (ăf′ər-ənt) Relating to nerves that carry sensory information toward the central nervous system. *Compare* **efferent.**

Did You Know...?

aerodynamics

The two primary forces in *aerodynamics* are lift and drag. *Lift* refers to forces perpendicular to the surface of an object (such as an airplane wing) that is traveling through the air. For example, airplane wings are designed so that when they move through the air, an area of low pressure is created above the wing; the low pressure produces a lift force that pulls the wing upward (in a direction perpendicular to the wing's broad surface), and the wing pulls the airplane up with it. *Drag* forces, which are parallel to the object's surface, are usually caused by friction. Drag makes it more difficult for airplane wings to slice through the air, and so drag forces push against the forward motion of the craft. Large wings usually generate a lot of lift, but they also produce a lot of drag. In designing airplane wings, engineers need to take into account such factors as the speed and altitude at which the plane will fly, so that they can find a wing shape that balances lift and drag as well as possible.

Louis Agassiz

Maria Agnesi

aftershock (ăf′tər-shŏk′) A less powerful earthquake that follows a more forceful one. Aftershocks usually originate in or near the same place as the main earthquakes they follow.

Ag The symbol for **silver.**

agar (ā′gär′, ä′gär′) A jellylike material obtained from marine algae, especially seaweed. It is used as a medium for growing bacterial cultures in the laboratory and as a thickener and stabilizer in food products.

Agassiz (ăg′ə-sē), **(Jean) Louis (Rodolphe)** 1807–1873. Swiss-born American geologist and zoologist whose fieldwork in Europe and the United States provided conclusive evidence that much of the Northern Hemisphere had once been covered by glaciers, thus confirming the hypothesis that Earth had undergone an ice age. Earlier in his career, Agassiz published a groundbreaking study of fossil fish and was known as the greatest ichthyologist of his day.

agate (ăg′ĭt) A type of very fine-grained quartz found in various colors that are arranged in bands or in cloudy patterns. The bands form when water rich with silica enters empty spaces in rock, after which the silica comes out of solution and forms crystals, gradually filling the spaces from the outside inward. The different colors are the result of various impurities in the water.

agate

agent (ā′jənt) A substance that can cause a chemical reaction or a biological effect. *Compare* **reagent.**

Agnesi (än-yā′zē), **Maria Gaetana** 1718–1799. Italian mathematician and philosopher whose major work, *Analytical Institutions* (1748), was the first comprehensive treatment of algebra and calculus. It brought together the work of authors writing in various languages, formulated new mathematical methods, and was widely used as a textbook. Agnesi spent the later part of her life as director of a nursing home in Milan that cared for poor women.

agonist (ăg′ə-nĭst) **1.** A muscle that actively contracts to produce a desired movement. **2.** A chemical substance, especially a drug, that combines with a receptor on a cell to produce a response. *Compare* **antagonist.**

AIDS (ādz) Short for *acquired immune deficiency syndrome.* A severe disease caused by HIV, in which the immune system is attacked and weakened, making the body susceptible to other infections. The virus is transmitted through bodily fluids such as semen and blood.

aileron (ā′lə-rŏn′) A small section of the back edge of an airplane wing that can be moved up or down to control the plane's degree of side-to-side tilt.

air (âr) The colorless, odorless, tasteless mixture of gases that surrounds the Earth. Air contains about 78 percent nitrogen and 21 percent oxygen, with the remaining part being made up of argon, carbon dioxide, neon, helium, and other gases.

air bladder 1. *See* **swim bladder. 2.** *See* **float.**

airfoil (âr′foil′) A part, such as an aircraft wing, designed to provide lift as air flows around its surface. Air passes over the airfoil faster than it passes beneath it, resulting in greater pressure below than above. Propellers are airfoils that are spun rapidly to provide propulsion.

airplane (âr′plān′) Any of various vehicles that are capable of flight, are held up by the force of air flowing around their wings, and are driven by jet engines or propellers.

air sac 1. An air-filled space in the body of a bird that forms a connection between the lungs and bone cavities and aids in breathing and temperature regulation. **2.** *See* **alveolus.**

Al The symbol for **aluminum.**

alanine (ăl′ə-nēn′) A nonessential amino acid. *See more at* **amino acid.**

albedo (ăl-bē′dō) The percentage of incoming light or other electromagnetic radiation reflected by a surface, especially by the surface of Earth or a celestial object. Dark-colored objects have low albedo and warm up more when exposed to sunlight than light-colored objects do.

albinism (ăl′bə-nĭz′əm) The condition of being born without pigmentation in the hair, skin, or eyes because of little or no production of melanin. People with albinism often have white hair, pale skin, and reddish or blue eyes and often have vision problems.

albino (ăl-bī′nō) A human or other animal with albinism.

albumen (ăl-byo͞o′mən) The white of the egg of certain animals, especially birds and reptiles, consisting mostly of the protein albumin dissolved in water. The albumen protects the growing embryo and supplies it with water and some nutrients.

albumin (ăl-byo͞o′mĭn) Any of a class of proteins found in egg white, milk, blood, and various other plant and animal tissues. Albumins dissolve in water and form solid or semisolid masses when heated.

alchemy (ăl′kə-mē) An early form of chemistry that was practiced from the Middle Ages through the early 1700s and included both a philosophical system and a set of experimental practices. Practitioners of alchemy studied the properties of matter and attempted to change common metals into gold.

Did You Know...?

alchemy

A popular image of a practitioner of *alchemy* might involve a bearded man in a tall hat hunched over a cauldron, vainly trying to create gold from lead or invent an elixir of eternal youth. Alchemy was a philosophical approach to nature that incorporated supernatural and mystical elements, and alchemists did attempt to find a "philosopher's stone" that could be used to turn other metals into gold. But it wasn't a foolish or useless approach to nature. In fact, alchemy attracted some of the greatest minds of the time, including Isaac Newton and Robert Boyle. Alchemists invented early forms of some kinds of laboratory equipment that are still in use today, including beakers, crucibles, filters, and stirring rods. They introduced methods to separate mixtures and purify compounds by distillation and extraction that are still important, and they developed various alloys, dyes, and metalworking techniques. Alchemical physicians pioneered the idea of treating diseases with chemicals, such as mercury. Modern chemistry owes much to its alchemical roots.

alcohol (ăl′kə-hôl′) **1.** Any of a large number of colorless, flammable organic compounds that contain the hydroxyl group (OH). Names of alcohols usually end in *–ol.* **2.** Ethanol.

alcoholism (ăl′kə-hô-lĭz′əm) The physical dependence on and excessive drinking of alcoholic beverages.

Aldebaran (ăl-dĕb′ər-ən) A very bright binary star in the constellation Taurus. *See Note at* **Rigel.**

aldehyde (ăl′də-hīd′) Any of a class of highly reactive organic chemical compounds containing the group CHO. Aldehydes are used in resins, dyes, and organic acids.

alga (ăl′gə) *Plural* **algae** (ăl′jē) Any of numerous green, red, or brown organisms that grow in water or in moist habitats, ranging in size from single cells to large seaweeds. Algae manufacture their own food through photosynthesis and are characterized by a lack of complex organs and tissues such as roots and leaves. Once classified as plants, the algae are now considered to include several unrelated groups belonging to different kingdoms.

algebra (ăl**′**jə-brə) A branch of mathematics dealing with the relations and properties of quantities. It uses letters and other symbols to represent numbers, especially in equations to solve problems or to express general mathematical relationships.

algorithm (ăl**′**gə-rĭ*th***′**əm) A step-by-step procedure for solving a problem, especially a mathematical rule or procedure used to compute a desired result.

Alhazen (ăl-hăz**′**ən) *See* **Ibn al-Haytham.**

alimentary canal (ăl′ə-mĕn**′**tə-rē) *See* **digestive tract.**

aliphatic (ăl′ə-făt**′**ĭk) Relating to organic compounds that do not contain a benzene ring; not aromatic. Alkanes are aliphatic compounds. *Compare* **aromatic.**

alkali (ăl**′**kə-lī′) *Plural* **alkalis** *or* **alkalies** A chemical that acts like a base and reacts strongly with acids, especially a hydroxide or carbonate of an alkali metal.

alkali metal Any of a group of soft metals that form alkaline solutions when they combine with water. They include lithium, sodium, potassium, rubidium, cesium, and francium. Except for cesium, which has a gold sheen, alkali metals are white. Because the alkali metals have only one electron in their outer shell, they react easily with other elements and are found in nature only in compounds. *See* **Periodic Table,** pages 254–255.

alkaline (ăl**′**kə-lĭn, ăl**′**kə-līn′) **1.** Capable of neutralizing an acid; basic. **2.** Relating to or containing an alkali. —*Noun* **alkalinity.**

alkaline-earth metal Any of a group of metallic elements that includes beryllium, magnesium, calcium, strontium, barium, and radium. Because the alkaline-earth metals have two electrons in their outer shell, they react easily with other elements and are found in nature only in compounds. *See* **Periodic Table,** pages 254–255.

alkaloid (ăl**′**kə-loid′) Any of a large class of complex organic compounds that contain nitrogen and mostly occur in plants. Alkaloids have a wide range of physiological effects and many uses in medicine, but they can also be toxic. Morphine, strychnine, caffeine, and nicotine are all alkaloids.

WORD HISTORY

algebra

For much of the Middle Ages, the center of scientific learning was not Europe, but the Islamic world of the Arabs. The Arabs studied the Greek classics of Plato and Aristotle while the Europeans nearly forgot about them. The Arabs were particularly interested in medicine and astronomy, and because astronomy requires making careful measurements and calculations, they became expert mathematicians. In the 800s, an Arabic mathematician named Muhammad al-Khwarizmi wrote a book called *The Book of Restoring and Balancing,* which explained the principles of algebra. Algebra had been developed earlier by mathematicians in Greece and India, but al-Khwarizmi's book, as the first comprehensive treatment of it, became a medieval bestseller. The Arabic word for "restoring" in the book's title is *al-jabr,* which is the source of our word *algebra.* Al-Khwarizmi's own name is the source of another mathematical term in English, *algorithm.*

alkane (ăl**′**kān′) Any of a group of saturated hydrocarbons whose carbon atoms form chains or rings linked by single bonds. Alkanes have the general formula C_nH_{2n+2} and include propane and butane.

alkene (ăl**′**kēn′) Any of a group of unsaturated hydrocarbons containing carbon atoms linked by one or more double bonds. Alkenes have the general formula C_nH_{2n} and include ethene. Also called *olefin.*

alkyne (ăl**′**kīn′) Any of a group of unsaturated hydrocarbons containing carbon atoms linked by one or more triple bonds. Alkynes have the general formula C_nH_{2n-2} and include acetylene.

allantois (ə-lăn**′**tō-ĭs) A membranous sac that develops from the lower end of the digestive tract in reptile, bird, and mammal embryos and that functions in waste storage and gas exchange. In mammals, the blood vessels of the allantois

Did You Know...?

allergies and allergens

Feeling miserable because of an allergic reaction? Perhaps you can find some comfort in knowing that your misery is an unhappy side effect of your immune system trying to protect you. The immune system recognizes that a particular substance, called an *allergen* (for example, dust, mold, or pollen), might be dangerous. Antibodies, special molecules whose job is to round up the invaders, charge into action. The immune system, however, can overreact, causing some people to develop unpleasant symptoms, such as a rash, a runny nose, or even a serious illness. People with severe symptoms can get a series of allergy shots that prevent or lessen the allergic reaction by training the immune system to accept the allergen. Oddly enough, many people develop allergies after repeated exposures to an allergen. The difference is that controlled, small exposures through shots prompt the immune system to grow accustomed to the allergen, while accidental, large exposures provoke the allergic reaction.

develop into the blood vessels of the umbilical cord.

allele (ə-lēl′) Any of the possible forms in which a gene can occur. Most animal and plant cells have two alleles for every trait, each of which is inherited from a different parent and is located on one of a pair of chromosomes. An individual is called homozygous for a particular gene if the two alleles for that gene are the same, and it is called heterozygous if the two alleles are different.

allergen (ăl′ər-jən) A substance, such as pollen, that causes an allergy.

allergy (ăl′ər-jē) A condition in which exposure to a particular substance or environmental influence, such as pollen, certain foods, or sunlight, causes an abnormal physiological reaction. The reaction may include difficulty in breathing, sneezing, skin rashes, and in severe cases, shock or death.

alligator (ăl′ĭ-gā′tər) A large, meat-eating, semiaquatic reptile having sharp teeth and powerful jaws. Alligators have a broader, shorter snout than crocodiles, and their teeth do not show when the jaws are closed. There are two species of alligators: one lives in the southeast United States, and one lives in China.

allosaurus (ăl′ə-sôr′əs) A very large meat-eating dinosaur of the Jurassic Period, having a massive head with narrow jaws, a pair of bony bumps above the eyes, large claws on the hands, and sturdy hind legs with clawed feet.

allotrope (ăl′ə-trōp′) Any of several molecular or crystalline forms of a chemical element. Charcoal, graphite, and diamond are some of the allotropes of carbon.

alloy (ăl′oi′) A metallic substance that is made by combining two or more metals, or a metal and a nonmetal, in order to obtain desirable qualities such as hardness, lightness, and strength. Brass, bronze, and steel are alloys.

alluvial fan (ə-lo͞o′vē-əl) A fan-shaped mass of silt, sand, gravel, or boulders deposited by a river where its flow slows suddenly as it pours out from a steep valley or ravine onto a flat plain. Unlike deltas, alluvial fans are not deposited into a body of standing water.

alluvium (ə-lo͞o′vē-əm) Sand, silt, gravel, or other matter deposited by flowing water, as in a riverbed, floodplain, or delta.

Alpha Centauri (ăl′fə sĕn-tôr′ē) A multiple star consisting of three stars in the constellation Centaurus. These stars are the closest of any stars to our sun, at a distance of a little over 4 light years,

alluvial fan

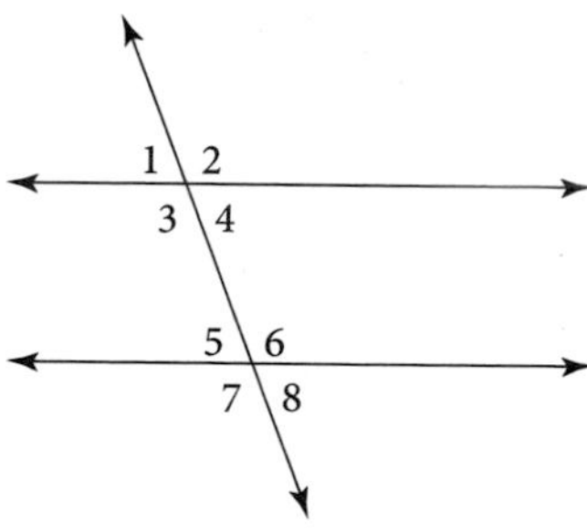

alternate angles

Angles 3 and 6 are alternate interior angles, as are angles 4 and 5. Angles 1 and 8 are alternate exterior angles, as are angles 2 and 7.

and together they appear as the third brightest object in the night sky. ❖ **Proxima Centauri** (prŏk′sə-mə) is the individual star in this system that is closest to Earth, but it is much fainter than its companions, Alpha Centauri A and B.

alpha particle A positively charged particle that consists of two protons and two neutrons bound together. Alpha particles are emitted by the nuclei of certain isotopes when they undergo radioactive decay and are identical to the nucleus of a helium atom. Alpha particles are the slowest and least penetrating form of nuclear radiation. ❖ The process of emitting an alpha particle is called **alpha decay.** When an atom undergoes alpha decay, its atomic number decreases by two and its mass number decreases by four. *See more at* **radiation, radioactive decay.**

Altair (ăl-tīr′, ăl-târ′) A very bright star in the constellation Aquila. It is a variable binary star. *See Note at* **Rigel.**

alternate angles (ôl′tər-nĭt) Two angles formed on opposite sides of a line that crosses two other lines. The angles are both exterior or both interior, but not adjacent.

alternating current (ôl′tər-nā′tĭng) An electric current that reverses its direction of flow at regular intervals. Because the voltage of alternating current can be easily controlled with transformers, this is the type of electricity generated by power stations. The transformers raise the voltage to make it easier to transmit over long distances, then lower the voltage for safer use in homes and buildings. *Compare* **direct current.** *See Notes at* **current, Tesla.**

alternative medicine (ôl-tûr′nə-tĭv) A health care practice that is generally not included in traditional Western medical teaching or practice and may not have a widely accepted scientific explanation for its effectiveness. Examples of alternative medicines are homeopathy and acupuncture.

alternator (ôl′tər-nā′tər) An electric generator that produces alternating current. In an alternator, a coil of wire rotates rapidly in a magnetic field, causing the coil's orientation to the magnetic field to shift rapidly from one direction to the other. As a result, the direction of the electric current produced in the wire rapidly alternates, first moving in one direction and then in the other.

altimeter (ăl-tĭm′ĭ-tər) An instrument that measures and indicates the height above sea level at which an object, such as an airplane, is located.

altiplano (äl′tĭ-plä′nō) A high mountain plateau, as in certain parts of the Andes Mountains.

altitude (ăl′tĭ-to͞od′) **1.** The height of a thing above a reference level, usually above sea level or the Earth's surface. **2.** *Astronomy* The vertical angle between a celestial object and the horizon, as seen by the observer. Altitude and azimuth are the coordinates used to navigate with respect to the stars. **3.** *Mathematics* The perpendicular distance from the base of a geometric figure, such as a triangle, to the opposite vertex, side, or surface.

altocumulus (ăl′tō-kyo͞o′myə-ləs) A fleecy white or gray cloud formation, usually occurring in wide patches or bands. Altocumulus clouds form at middle levels of the atmosphere.

altostratus (ăl′tō-străt′əs) A cloud formation that extends in flat, smooth sheets or layers of

altocumulus

varying thickness. Altostratus clouds form at middle levels of the atmosphere.

altricial (ăl-trĭsh′əl) Hatched or born with the eyes closed and requiring care from a parent or parents. The offspring of dogs, cats, and most birds are altricial. *Compare* **precocial.**

alum (ăl′əm) Any of various crystalline salts in which a metal such as aluminum or chromium is combined with another metal such as potassium or sodium, especially aluminum potassium sulfate. Alum is widely used in industry as a hardener and purifier, and in medicine to stop bleeding.

aluminum (ə-lo͞o′mə-nəm) A lightweight, silvery-white metallic element that is easily shaped and a good conductor of electricity. It is the most abundant metal in the Earth's crust and is used to make a wide variety of products, from soda cans to airplane components. *Symbol* **Al.** *Atomic number* 13. *See* **Periodic Table,** pages 254–255.

Alvarez (ăl′və-rĕz′), **Luis Walter** 1911–1988. American physicist who studied subatomic particles. Alvarez built a device called a hydrogen bubble chamber that made it possible to analyze the reactions occurring between atomic nuclei inside it. His observations led to the theory that protons, neutrons, and electrons are made of quarks. With his son, geologist **Walter Alvarez** (born 1940), he developed a theory that the extinction of dinosaurs was caused by climate changes resulting from a giant asteroid striking the Earth. *See Note at* **iridium.**

alveolus (ăl-vē′ə-ləs) *Plural* **alveoli** (ăl-vē′ə-lī′) Any of numerous tiny air-filled sacs in the lungs where the exchange of oxygen and carbon dioxide takes place. Oxygen enters the blood and carbon dioxide leaves the blood through capillaries that surround the alveoli. Also called *air sac.*

Alzheimer's disease (älts′hī-mərz) A disease that causes degeneration of parts of the brain. Symptoms include the gradual loss of memory and other mental abilities. Alzheimer's disease most commonly affects elderly people.

Am The symbol for **americium.**

AM Abbreviation of **amplitude modulation.**

amalgam (ə-măl′gəm) An alloy of mercury and another metal, especially silver, often used in dental fillings.

amber (ăm′bər) A hard, transparent or translucent, brownish-yellow substance that is the fossilized resin of ancient trees, often used as a gemstone.

ambergris (ăm′bər-grĭs′, ăm′bər-grēs′) A grayish, waxy material formed in the intestines of sperm whales, sometimes found floating at sea or washed ashore. It was formerly used to make perfume.

ameba (ə-mē′bə) Another spelling of **amoeba.**

americium (ăm′ə-rĭsh′ē-əm) A synthetic, silvery-white, radioactive metallic element of the actinide series that is produced artificially by bombarding plutonium with neutrons. Americium is used as a source of alpha particles for smoke detectors and gamma rays for industrial gauges. Its most stable isotope has a half-life of 7,370 years. *Symbol* **Am.** *Atomic number* 95. *See* **Periodic Table,** pages 254–255.

Did You Know...?

amber

Certain trees, especially conifers, produce a sticky substance called *resin* to protect themselves against insects and fungi. Resin normally decays, but under certain conditions, for example if it happens to fall to the ground and be covered by mud or sand, it can harden and eventually fossilize, becoming the yellowish, transparent or translucent substance known as *amber.* If insects or other organisms become trapped in the resin before it hardens, their bodies become preserved, often in amazing detail. Scientists have found preserved insects from as far back as the Cretaceous Period, 140 million years ago, before the dinosaurs went extinct. It has been speculated (as in the 1990 science-fiction novel *Jurassic Park* by Michael Crichton) that ancient mosquitoes preserved in amber might still contain DNA from the blood of dinosaurs. If that were so, could the DNA be used to clone dinosaurs and bring them back to life? Probably not. Although fragments of DNA have been found in amber, fossil mosquitoes would almost certainly not contain enough dinosaur DNA to actually create clones of dinosaurs — or even clones of the mosquitoes that dined on their blood.

amethyst (ăm′ə-thĭst) A purple or violet, transparent form of quartz used as a gemstone. The color is caused by the presence of iron compounds in the crystal structure.

amide (ăm′īd′) A compound containing the organic group $CONH_2$.

amine (ə-mēn′, ăm′ēn) Any of a group of organic nitrogen compounds containing a single nitrogen atom that is bonded to one or more hydrocarbon groups. Amines are alkaline, often pungent, and common in plant and animal tissues.

amino acid (ə-mē′nō) Any of a large number of compounds that contain carbon, oxygen, hydrogen, and nitrogen and join together in different combinations to form proteins in living cells. ❖ About 20 amino acids are needed by animal cells to produce proteins, but only about half, called **nonessential amino acids,** can be produced by animal cells. The remaining half, called **essential amino acids,** must be obtained from food.

ammeter (ăm′mē′tər) An instrument that measures an electric current and indicates its strength in amperes.

ammonia (ə-mōn′yə) A colorless alkaline gas, NH_3, that is lighter than air and has a strongly pungent odor. It is used as a refrigerant and in the manufacture of fertilizers, dyes, textiles, plastics, and explosives.

ammonite (ăm′ə-nīt′) Any of various extinct mollusks having a coiled shell resembling the shell of a nautilus. Ammonites were especially abundant during the Mesozoic Era and are often found as fossils.

ammonium (ə-mō′nē-əm) A positively charged univalent ion, NH_4, derived from ammonia and found in a wide variety of organic and inorganic compounds.

■ **ammonite**

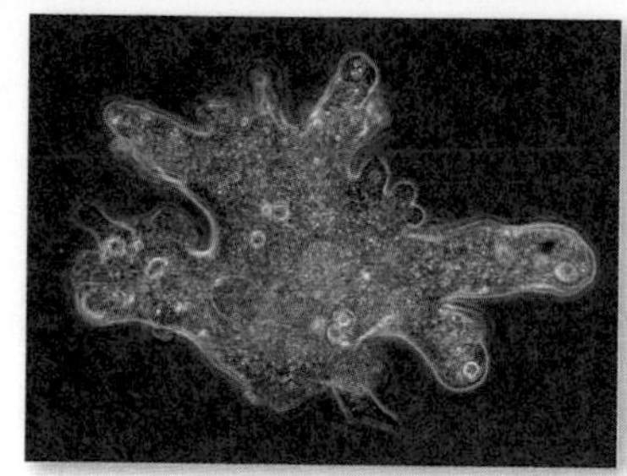

■ **amoeba**

amnesia (ăm-nē′zhə) A partial or total loss of memory, usually caused by shock or brain injury.

amnion (ăm′nē-ən) A thin, tough membrane that forms a sac containing a watery liquid in which the embryo of a reptile, bird, or mammal is suspended. ❖ The watery fluid in the amnion is called **amniotic fluid.**

amoeba (ə-mē′bə) *Plural* **amoebas** *or* **amoebae** (ə-mē′bē) A one-celled microscopic organism that constantly changes shape by forming pseudopods, temporary projections that are used for movement and for the ingestion of food. Amoebas are members of the group of organisms called protozoans.

amorphous (ə-môr′fəs) **1.** Not made of crystals. Glass is an amorphous substance. **2.** Lacking definite form or shape.

AMP (ā′ĕm-pē′) Short for *adenosine monophosphate.* An organic compound, $C_{10}H_{14}N_5O_7P$, that is composed of adenosine and one phosphate group and is formed by the breakdown of ATP or ADP during cell metabolism. It is also one of the nucleotides that make up RNA molecules.

ampere (ăm′pîr′) A unit used to measure electric current. Electric current is usually measured as the amount of electric charge passing through a point in an electric circuit in one second. One ampere is equal to the flow of one coulomb per second.

Ampère (ăm′pîr′, äm-pĕr′), **André Marie** 1775–1836. French mathematician and physicist. He is best known for his analysis of the relationship between magnetic force and electric current, including the formulation of Ampère's law, a mathematical description of the strength of the magnetic field produced by the flow of electricity

■ André Ampère

through a conductor. The ampere unit of electric current is named for him.

amphetamine (ăm-fĕt′ə-mēn′) Any of a group of drugs that stimulate the nervous system, causing heightened alertness and a faster heartbeat and metabolism. Amphetamines are highly addictive.

amphibian (ăm-fĭb′ē-ən) Any of various cold-blooded vertebrate animals having moist skin without scales. Most amphibians live in the water and breathe with gills when young but develop lungs and breathe air as adults. Frogs, salamanders, and caecilians are amphibians.

amphibole (ăm′fə-bōl′) Any of a large group of minerals composed of a silicate joined to various metals, such as calcium, magnesium, iron, or sodium. Hornblende is a mineral of the amphibole group.

amphioxus (ăm′fē-ŏk′səs) *See* **lancelet.**

amphoteric (ăm′fə-tĕr′ĭk) Having the characteristics of both an acid and a base and capable of reacting chemically as either an acid or a base. Water, ammonia, amino acids, and the hydroxides of certain metals are amphoteric.

amplification (ăm′plə-fĭ-kā′shən) An increase in the magnitude or strength of an electric current, a force, or another physical quantity, such as a radio signal.

amplitude (ăm′plĭ-to͞od′) One half the full range of motion of an oscillation or wave. For example, the amplitude of an ocean wave is the maximum height of the wave crest above the level of calm water or the maximum depth of the wave trough below the level of calm water. The amplitude of a pendulum that swings through an angle of 60° is 30°. *See more at* **wave.**

WORD HISTORY

amphibian

Amphibians are not quite fish and not quite reptiles. Like fish, they spend part of their lives living in water and breathing with gills; like reptiles, they typically spend another part of their lives breathing air with lungs and able to live on land. This double life is also at the root of their name, *amphibian,* which, like many scientific words, comes from Greek. It is made up of the Greek prefix *amphi–*, meaning "both" or "double," and the Greek word *bios,* meaning "life." Both these elements are widely used in other scientific words in English: *bios,* for example, is also seen in words like *biology, antibiotic,* and *symbiotic,* and *amphi–* appears in *amphibole.*

amplitude modulation A method of radio broadcasting in which the amplitude of the wave that carries the sound signal varies to correspond to the vibrations of the sounds that are to be reproduced, while the frequency of the wave remains the same. *Compare* **frequency modulation.**

amyl alcohol (ăm′əl, ā′məl) Any of various alcohols having the formula $C_5H_{11}OH$. Amyl alcohols are used to make solvents and esters.

amylase (ăm′ə-lās′) Any of various enzymes

■ **amphibian**
top: *green frog*
bottom: *spotted salamander*

that break down starches into their component sugars, such as glucose. Amylase is present in fluid secreted by the pancreas, in the saliva of some mammals, and in plants.

anabolism (ə-năb′ə-lĭz′əm) The phase of metabolism in which complex molecules, such as the proteins and fats that make up body tissue, are formed from simpler ones. *Compare* **catabolism.** —*Adjective* **anabolic.**

anaconda (ăn′ə-kŏn′də) A very large, mostly aquatic snake of tropical South America that is the largest snake known. Anacondas kill by coiling around and suffocating or drowning their prey.

anadromous (ə-năd′rə-məs) Relating to fish that migrate up rivers from the sea to breed in fresh water. Salmon and shad are anadromous.

anaerobic (ăn′ə-rō′bĭk) Occurring or living in the absence of oxygen: *anaerobic bacteria. Compare* **aerobic.** ❖ **Anaerobic exercise** involves short-duration, high-intensity activities in which the body generates energy primarily from ATP or from the breakdown of carbohydrates.

analgesic (ăn′əl-jē′zĭk) A drug that deadens the sense of pain; a painkiller.

analog (ăn′ə-lôg′) Relating to a device that uses continuously changing physical quantities to represent data. For example, the position of the hands of a clock is an analog representation of time.

analogous (ə-năl′ə-gəs) Similar in function but having different evolutionary origins, as the wings of a butterfly and the wings of a bird. *Compare* **homologous.**

analysis (ə-năl′ĭ-sĭs) *Plural* **analyses** (ə-năl′ĭ-sēz′) The separation of a substance into its parts, usually by chemical means, for the study and identification of each component. ❖ **Qualitative analysis** determines what substances are present in a compound. ❖ **Quantitative analysis** determines how much of each substance is present in a compound.

analytic geometry (ăn′ə-lĭt′ĭk) The use of algebra to solve problems in geometry. In analytic geometry, geometric figures are represented by algebraic equations and plotted using coordinates.

anaphase (ăn′ə-fāz′) The stage of cell division in which the chromosomes move to opposite ends of the cell. In mitosis, anaphase is preceded by metaphase and followed by telophase. *See more at* **meiosis, mitosis.**

■ **anadromous**
salmon swimming upstream

anatomy (ə-năt′ə-mē) **1.** The structure of an animal, plant, or other organism or of any of its parts. **2.** The scientific study of the shape and structure of living things. —*Adjective* **anatomical** (ăn′ə-tŏm′ĭ-kəl).

Anaxagoras (ăn′ăk-săg′ər-əs) 500?–428 BC. Greek philosopher and astronomer who was the first to explain eclipses correctly. He also stated that the sun and stars were glowing stones and that the moon took its light from the sun.

androgen (ăn′drə-jən) Any of several steroid hormones, such as testosterone, that control the development and maintenance of physical characteristics in males.

Andromeda (ăn-drŏm′ĭ-də) A constellation in the Northern Hemisphere near Perseus and Pegasus. It contains a spiral-shaped galaxy visible to the unaided eye.

-ane A suffix used to form the names of saturated hydrocarbons (hydrocarbons having only single bonds), such as *ethane. Compare* **-ene.**

anemia (ə-nē′mē-ə) A condition in which the blood does not carry enough oxygen to the body tissues. It can be caused too few red blood cells, not enough hemoglobin, or poorly formed red blood cells. *See also* **sickle cell anemia.** —*Adjective* **anemic.**

■ **anemometer**

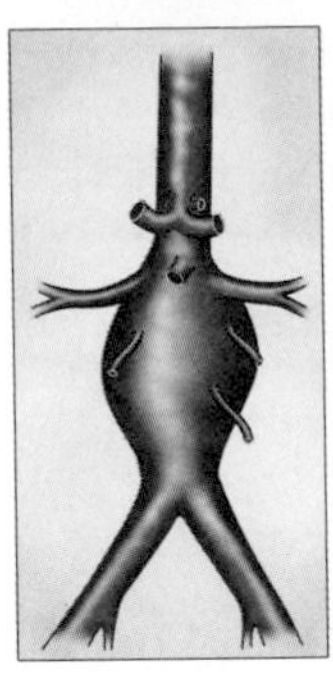

■ **aneurysm**
abdominal aortic aneurysm

anemometer (ăn′ə-mŏm**′**ĭ-tər) An instrument that measures the speed of the wind. One simple type of anemometer consists of a set of cups mounted at the end of arms that rotate in the wind at a rate proportional to the wind speed.

anemone (ə-nĕm**′**ə-nē) *See* **sea anemone.**

aneroid barometer (ăn**′**ə-roid′) A barometer that operates by measuring how the flexible lid of a vacuum chamber responds to changes in atmospheric pressure. When atmospheric pressure is high, the lid is pressed inward slightly; when the pressure drops, the lid bulges outward. These movements are transmitted to a pointer on a dial.

anesthesia (ăn′ĭs-thē**′**zhə) Loss of sensation to touch or pain, usually produced by nerve injury or by the administration of drugs, especially before surgery.

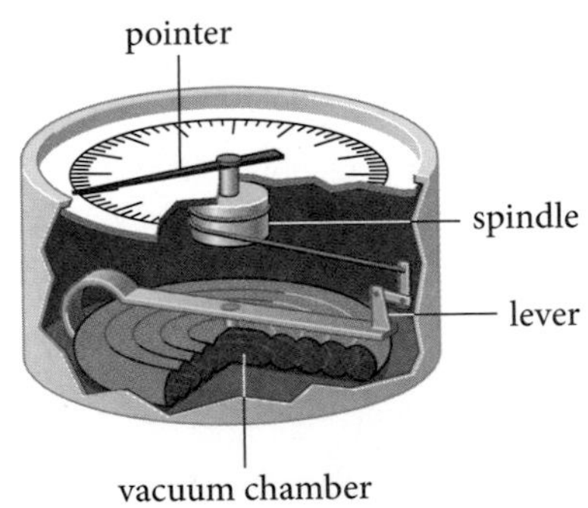

■ **aneroid barometer**
Expansion or contraction of the vacuum chamber, caused by a change in air pressure, forces the pointer to move.

aneurysm (ăn**′**yə-rĭz′əm) A swelling in the wall of an artery or vein that is caused by disease or injury.

angiosperm (ăn**′**jē-ə-spûrm′) Any of a large group of plants that have flowers and produce seeds that are enclosed in an ovary; a flowering plant. Most living plants are angiosperms. *Compare* **gymnosperm.**

angle (ăng**′**gəl) **1.** A geometric figure formed by two lines that begin at a common point or by two planes that begin at a common line. **2.** The space between such lines or planes, measured in degrees. *See also* **acute angle, obtuse angle, right angle.**

angle of incidence The angle formed by a ray or wave, as of light or sound, striking a surface and a line perpendicular to the surface at the point of impact. *See more at* **wave.**

angle of reflection The angle formed by a ray or wave reflected from a surface and a line perpendicular to the surface at the point of reflection. *See more at* **wave.**

angle of refraction The angle formed by the path of refracted light or other radiation and a line drawn perpendicular to the refracting surface at the point where the refraction occurred. *See more at* **wave.**

angstrom or **ångstrom** (ăng**′**strəm) A unit of length equal to one hundred-millionth (10^{-8}) of a centimeter. It is used mainly to measure wavelengths of light and shorter electromagnetic radiation.

Ångström (ăng**′**strəm), **Anders Jonas** 1814–

1874. Swedish physicist and astronomer who pioneered the use of the spectroscope in the analysis of radiation. By studying the spectrum of the sun's visible light, he discovered that there is hydrogen in the sun's atmosphere. The angstrom unit of measurement is named for him.

angular momentum (ăng′gyə-lər) A property of a body (or a system of bodies) in motion, especially one that is revolving or rotating. The angular momentum of a body revolving about a center depends on its mass, speed, and distance from the center. The angular momentum remains constant if there are no external rotational forces acting on the body. As an ice skater spinning with arms extended draws the arms in, the skater spins faster because the angular momentum must remain the same — pulling the arms in decreases the distance of the skater's mass from the center, so the skater's speed increases.

angular velocity The rate at which an object moving along a curved path changes its position. Angular velocity is expressed in units of angle per unit of time, such as revolutions per minute or radians per second.

anhydride (ăn-hī′drīd′) A chemical compound formed from another, especially an acid, by the removal of water.

anhydrous (ăn-hī′drəs) Not containing water.

animal (ăn′ə-məl) Any of a wide variety of multicellular organisms that cannot make their own food and are usually able to move around during at least part of their life cycle. Some animals, such as sponges, corals, and insects, do not have a spinal column (backbone) and are called invertebrates. Other animals, such as fish, birds, amphibians, reptiles, and mammals, do have a spinal column and are called vertebrates. Animals are grouped as a separate kingdom in taxonomy. *See Table at* **taxonomy.**

animal kingdom The category of living organisms that includes all animals. *See Table at* **taxonomy.**

anion (ăn′ī′ən) An ion that has a negative charge. Hydroxide and chloride ions are anions. *Compare* **cation.**

ankylosaurus (ăng′kə-lō-sôr′əs) A large, plant-eating dinosaur of the Cretaceous Period having a squat, heavily armored body and a clubbed tail.

annelid (ăn′ə-lĭd) Any of various worms or wormlike animals having soft, elongated bodies that are divided into ringlike segments. Earthworms and leeches are annelids.

annual (ăn′yo͞o-əl) *Botany. Adjective* **1.** Completing a life cycle in one growing season. —*Noun* **2.** An annual plant. Tomatoes and sunflowers are examples of annuals.

annual ring *See under* **growth ring.**

anode (ăn′ōd′) A positive terminal or positively charged electrode, which repels positively charged particles and attracts negatively charged particles. In an electric circuit, electrons (which are negatively charged) flow toward the anode (positive terminal) of a power supply. In an electrolytic cell or a vacuum tube, the anode is the electrode that is connected to the positive terminal of a power supply. *Compare* **cathode.**

anomaly (ə-nŏm′ə-lē) Something that is unusual or unexpected: *When they found anomalies in their data, the scientists decided to perform the experiment again.* —*Adjective* **anomalous.**

anopheles (ə-nŏf′ə-lēz′) Any of various mosquitoes that can transmit malaria to humans.

anorexia nervosa (ăn′ə-rĕk′sē-ə nûr-vō′sə) An eating disorder characterized by fear of gaining weight, revulsion toward food, and severe weight loss. It most commonly affects young women, who often stop menstruating, develop brittle bones, and experience other physical changes as a result.

ant (ănt) Any of numerous insects that live in large colonies composed of workers, soldiers, and a queen. Ants often tunnel in the ground or in wood. Only the males and the queen have wings. *See also* **queen, soldier, worker.**

antagonist (ăn-tăg′ə-nĭst) **1.** A muscle that resists or counteracts another muscle, as by relaxing while the opposite one contracts. **2.** A chemical substance, especially a drug, that interferes with the action of another substance, especially by blocking a receptor on a cell. *Compare* **agonist.**

Antarctic Circle (ănt-ärk′tĭk) The parallel of latitude approximately 66°34′ south, the northernmost latitude where the sun stays below the horizon all day on the Southern Hemisphere's

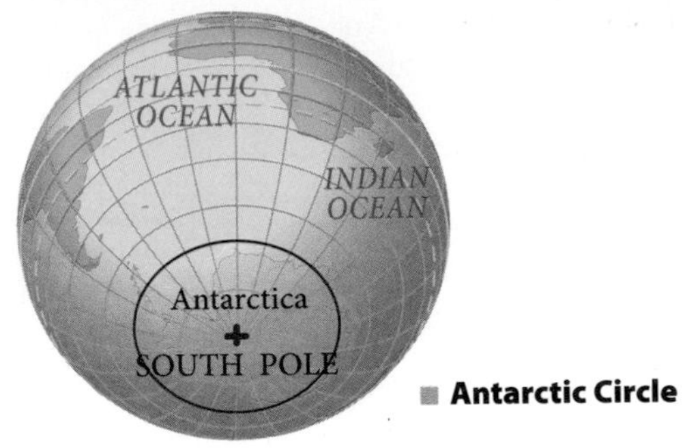

■ **Antarctic Circle**

winter solstice. It is considered the boundary of the South Frigid Zone.

Antares (ăn-târ′ēz) A reddish, very bright binary star in the constellation Scorpio. It is a supergiant.

antenna (ăn-tĕn′ə) *Plural* **antennae** (ăn-tĕn′ē) **1.** One of a pair of long, slender, segmented structures on the head of insects, centipedes, millipedes, and crustaceans. Antennae are sensory organs used for feeling and also for sensing chemicals such as pheromones. **2.** A metallic device for sending or receiving electromagnetic waves, such as radio waves or microwaves.

anther (ăn′thər) The pollen-bearing part at the tip of the stamen of a flower. *See more at* **flower.**

anthracite (ăn′thrə-sīt′) A hard, shiny coal that has a high carbon content. It is valued as a fuel because it burns with a clean flame and without smoke or odor, but it is much less abundant than bituminous coal. *Compare* **bituminous coal, lignite.**

anthrax (ăn′thrăks′) An infectious, usually fatal disease of mammals, especially cattle and sheep, caused by a bacterium. It can spread to people, causing symptoms ranging from blistering of the skin to potentially fatal infection of the lungs.

anthropology (ăn′thrə-pŏl′ə-jē) The scientific study of the origin, the behavior, and the physical, social, and cultural development of humans.

anti– A prefix whose basic meaning is "against." It is used to form adjectives that mean "counteracting" (such as *antiseptic,* preventing infection). It is also used to form nouns referring to substances that counteract other substances (such as *antihistamine,* a substance counteracting histamine), and nouns meaning "something that displays opposite, reverse, or inverse characteristics of something else" (such as *anticyclone,* a storm that circulates in the opposite direction from a cyclone). Before a vowel it becomes *ant–*, as in *antacid.*

■ **antenna**
left: *butterfly antennae*
right: *television antenna*

antibiotic (ăn′tĭ-bī-ŏt′ĭk) A substance, such as penicillin, that is capable of destroying or weakening certain microorganisms, especially disease-causing bacteria or fungi. Antibiotics are obtained from other microorganisms, especially molds.

antibody (ăn′tĭ-bŏd′ē) A protein produced in the blood or tissues in response to the presence of a specific foreign antigen. Antibodies provide immunity against certain microorganisms and toxins by binding with them and often by deactivating them. Also called *immunoglobulin.*

anticline (ăn′tĭ-klīn′) A fold of rock layers that slope downward on both sides of a common crest. Anticlines form when rocks are compressed by plate-tectonic forces. *Compare* **syncline.**

anticyclone (ăn′tē-sī′klōn′) A system of winds that spiral outward around a region of high atmospheric pressure, circling clockwise in the Northern Hemisphere and counterclockwise in the Southern Hemisphere. *Compare* **cyclone.**

antidote (ăn′tĭ-dōt′) A substance that counteracts the effects of poison.

antigen (ăn′tĭ-jən) A substance that when introduced into the body stimulates an immune response, such as the production of antibodies by B cells. Antigens include toxins, bacteria, viruses, and other foreign substances. *See Note at* **blood type.**

antihistamine (ăn′tē-hĭs′tə-mēn′) Any of vari-

Did You Know...?

antibodies

Antibodies are complex, Y-shaped protein molecules that guard our bodies against diseases. The immune system's B lymphocytes, or B cells, develop into plasma cells, which can produce a huge variety of antibodies, each one capable of grabbing an invading molecule at the top ends of the Y. The molecules that antibodies recognize can be quite specific—they might exist only on a particular bacterium or virus. When that bacterium or virus enters the body, the antibodies quickly recognize its molecules, as if a sentry recognized an enemy soldier from the soldier's uniform. Once the invader is caught, the antibodies may make it inactive or lead it to cells that can destroy it. High numbers of a particular antibody may persist for months after an invasion. The numbers may then get quite small, but the experienced B cells can quickly make more of that specific antibody if necessary. Vaccines work by training B cells to do just that.

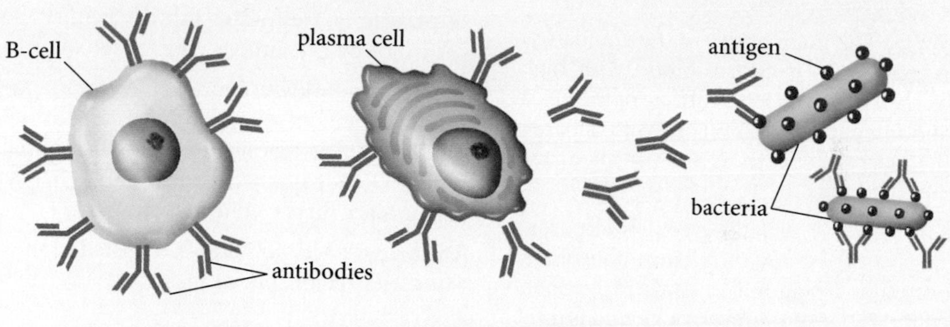

ous drugs that relieve cold or allergy symptoms by blocking the action of histamine in the body.

antilogarithm (ăn′tē-lô**′**gə-rĭ*th*′əm, ăn′tī-lô**′**gə-rĭ*th*′əm) The number whose logarithm is a given number. For example, the logarithm of 1,000 (or 10^3) is 3, so the antilogarithm of 3 is 1,000. In algebraic notation, if log $x = y$, then antilog $y = x$.

antimatter (ăn**′**tĭ-măt′ər) Matter that is made of the antiparticles corresponding to the particles that make up ordinary matter.

antimony (ăn**′**tə-mō′nē) A metallic element having many forms, the most common of which is a hard, very brittle, shiny, blue-white crystal. It is used in a wide variety of alloys, especially with lead in car batteries, and in making flameproofing compounds, semiconductors, and ceramics. *Symbol* **Sb.** *Atomic number* 51. *See* **Periodic Table,** pages 254–255.

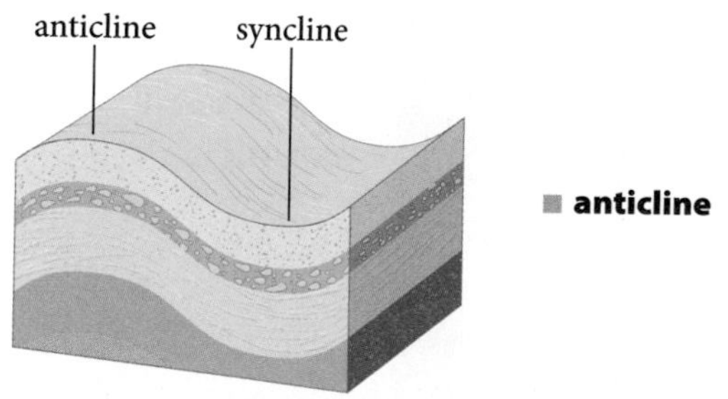

■ **anticline**

antinode (ăn**′**tĭ-nōd′) In a standing wave, the point of maximum amplitude between two adjacent nodes. *Compare* **node** (sense 3).

antioxidant (ăn′tē-ŏk**′**sĭ-dənt, ăn′tī-ŏk**′**sĭ-dənt) A chemical compound or substance that inhibits oxidation. Certain vitamins, such as vitamin E, are antioxidants and may protect body cells from damage due to oxidation.

antiparticle (ăn′tē-pär**′**tĭ-kəl, ăn′tī-pär**′**tĭ-kəl) A particle of antimatter that corresponds to a particle of ordinary matter. Many of the properties of an antiparticle, such as its mass and spin, have the same value as those of the corresponding ordinary matter particle, but its electric charge and certain other properties have the opposite value. The positron is the antiparticle of the electron.

antipodes (ăn-tĭp′ə-dēz′) Two places on directly opposite sides of the Earth, such as the North Pole and the South Pole.

antiseptic (ăn′tĭ-sĕp′tĭk) A substance that prevents infection or rot by preventing the growth of microorganisms.

antler (ănt′lər) A bony growth on the head of a deer, moose, elk, or other related animal, usually having one or more branches. Antlers typically grow only on males and are shed and grown again each year.

anus (ā′nəs) The opening at the lower end of the digestive tract through which solid waste is excreted. —*Adjective* **anal.**

aorta (ā-ôr′tə) The main artery of the circulatory system in mammals. It carries blood with high levels of oxygen from the left ventricle of the heart into the abdomen, where it branches into smaller arteries that carry blood to all the organs of the body except the lungs.

apatite (ăp′ə-tīt′) A usually green, transparent mineral consisting mainly of calcium phosphate. Apatite occurs as hexagonal crystals in igneous, metamorphic, and sedimentary rocks, and is used as a source of phosphate for making fertilizers. It is the mineral used to represent a hardness of 5 on the Mohs scale.

apatosaurus (ə-păt′ə-sôr′əs) A very large sauropod dinosaur of the late Jurassic Period, having a long neck and tail and a relatively small head. *See Note at* **brontosaurus.**

ape (āp) Any of various primates that have no tail and live in or evolved in Africa or Asia. Gibbons, orangutans, gorillas, chimpanzees, bonobos, and humans are apes. *Compare* **monkey.** ❖ In nonscientific contexts, *ape* is often used to mean "nonhuman ape."

apex (ā′pĕks) The highest point, especially the vertex of a triangle, cone, or pyramid.

aphelion (ə-fē′lē-ən) The point farthest from the sun in the orbit of a body, such as a planet or a comet, that travels around the sun.

aphid (ā′fĭd, ăf′ĭd) Any of various small, soft-bodied insects that feed by sucking sap from plants and sometimes damage crops or transmit plant viruses. Some ants feed on the sweet substances secreted by aphids.

apogee (ăp′ə-jē) The point in an orbit around Earth where the orbiting body is farthest from Earth. Sometimes this term is used informally to describe an analogous point in an orbit around a celestial object other than Earth. *Compare* **perigee.**

appendix (ə-pĕn′dĭks) *Plural* **appendixes** *or* **appendices** (ə-pĕn′-dĭ-sēz′) A tubular projection attached to the cecum of the large intestine in humans and some other mammals. ❖ Inflammation of the appendix is called **appendicitis** (ə-pĕn′dĭ-sī′tĭs). ❖ Surgical removal of the appendix is called an **appendectomy** (ăp′-ən-dĕk′tə-mē).

aquaculture (ăk′wə-kŭl′chər) The cultivation of marine or freshwater fish or shellfish, such as catfish or oysters, under controlled conditions.

aquarium (ə-kwâr′ē-əm) **1.** A tank, bowl, or other container filled with water for keeping and displaying fish or other aquatic animals and plants. **2.** A place where fish and other aquatic animals are displayed to the public.

Aquarius (ə-kwâr′ē-əs) A constellation in the Southern Hemisphere near the constellations Pisces and Aquila.

aquatic (ə-kwăt′ĭk) Relating to, living in, or growing in water.

aqueous (ā′kwē-əs) Relating to or dissolved in water.

aqueous humor The clear, watery fluid that fills the space between the cornea and the lens of the eye.

aquifer (ăk′wə-fər) An underground layer of sand, gravel, or porous rock that collects

■ **aphid**

Did You Know...?

archaea

When the single-celled organisms now known as *archaea* were first described in the 1970s, they were named *archaebacteria.* "Bacteria" because they looked a lot like bacteria, and "archae" (ancient) because scientists thought their ancestors were the first life forms on Earth. But new research brought a name change. It's true that archaea have no nucleus, like bacteria; however, their cell walls are made of different chemicals, and their genes are quite different, too. They are as different from bacteria as bacteria are from humans. And it turns out that archaea may have evolved from ancient bacteria rather than vice versa. Today they inhabit some of the most inhospitable places on the earth: boiling hot springs, super salty seas, ice-cold oceans, and the stomachs of cows.

water and holds it like a sponge. Much of the water we use is obtained by drilling wells into aquifers.

Aquila (ăk′wə-lə) A constellation in the Northern Hemisphere near Aquarius and Hercules.

Ar The symbol for **argon.**

Arabic numeral (ăr′ə-bĭk) One of the numerical symbols 1, 2, 3, 4, 5, 6, 7, 8, 9, or 0. They are called Arabic numerals because they were introduced into western Europe from sources of Arabic scholarship.

arachnid (ə-răk′nĭd) Any of a group of arthropods having eight legs, no wings or antennae, and a body divided into two parts. The front part of the body, consisting of the head and thorax joined together, is called the cephalothorax, and the back part of the body is the abdomen. Spiders, scorpions, ticks, and mites are arachnids.

arc (ärk) A segment of a circle.

archaebacterium (är′kē-băk-tîr′ē-əm) *See* **archaeon.**

archaeology or **archeology** (är′kē-ŏl′ə-jē) The scientific study of past human life and culture by the examination of physical remains, such as graves, tools, and pottery.

archaeon (är′kē-ŏn′) *Plural* **archaea** Any of a group of one-celled organisms that are similar to bacteria in some ways, as in lacking a nucleus, but are different from them genetically and biochemically. Archaea usually live in extreme environments, such as very hot or salty ones. Most biologists classify the archaea as one of the three domains of life, the other two being bacteria and eukaryotes. Also called *archaebacterium.*

archaeopteryx (är′kē-ŏp′tər-ĭks) A small extinct vertebrate of the Jurassic Period, having feathered wings with claws, a long snout with teeth, and a feathered bony tail. It is thought to have been one of the earliest birds. *See Note at* **bird.**

Archean (är-kē′ən) The earlier of the two divisions of the Precambrian Eon, from about 3.8 to 2.5 billion years ago. During this time, the Earth had an atmosphere with little free oxygen, and the first single-celled life appeared. *See Chart at* **geologic time,** pages 146–147.

Archimedes (är′kə-mē′dēz) 287?–212 BC. Greek mathematician, engineer, and inventor. He made numerous contributions to mathematics, including a method for calculating the value of pi as well as formulas for the areas and volumes of various geometric figures. Archimedes created the science of mechanics, devising the first general theory of levers and finding methods for

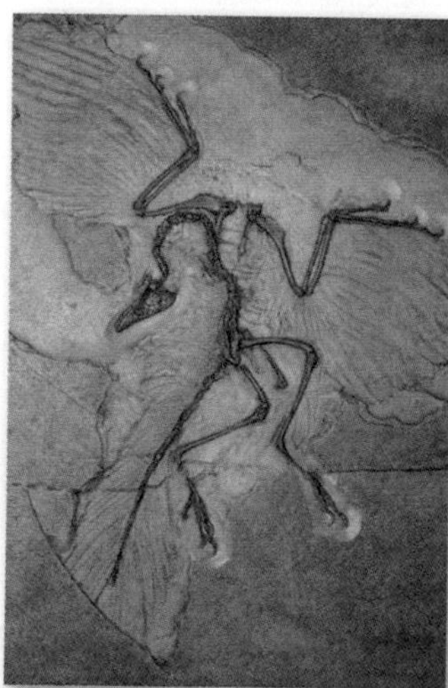

archaeopteryx

BIOGRAPHY

Archimedes

Archimedes was celebrated in his day for his many practical inventions as well as for his contributions to pure mathematics, but some of his greatest achievements lay in the application of mathematics to real-world physical phenomena such as floating and submerged objects. Everyday observation shows us that if you dump a pound of potatoes in a pot of water that's filled to the top, some water will overflow; that is, placing a solid object into a fluid causes some of that fluid to be displaced. Archimedes was able to show mathematically that the volume of fluid displaced is equal to the volume of the object immersed in it. Further, he found that dense objects seem lighter when they are immersed in water—their effective weight is reduced by an amount equal to the weight of the water they displace. He thus conceived of the principle of buoyancy: that all objects immersed in a fluid are subject to an upward force equal to the weight of the fluid they displace. If the object is less dense than the fluid, it will float on the surface with only as much of its volume submerged as is needed to produce a buoyant force equal to its weight.

determining the center of gravity of a variety of bodies.

Arctic Circle (ärk′tĭk) The parallel of latitude approximately 66°34′ north, the southernmost latitude where the sun stays below the horizon all day on the Northern Hemisphere's winter solstice. It is considered the boundary of the North Frigid Zone.

Arcturus (ärk-to͝or′əs) The brightest star in the Northern Hemisphere. It is in the constellation Boötes.

area (âr′ē-ə) The extent of a surface or plane figure as measured in square units.

arginine (är′jə-nēn′) An essential amino acid. *See more at* **amino acid.**

argon (är′gŏn′) A colorless, odorless element that is a noble gas and makes up about one percent of the atmosphere. It is used in electric light bulbs, fluorescent tubes, and radio vacuum tubes. *Symbol* **Ar.** *Atomic number* 18. *See* **Periodic Table,** pages 254–255.

arid (ăr′ĭd) Very dry, especially having less rainfall than is needed to support most trees or woody plants: *an arid climate; an arid region.*

Aries (âr′ēz) A constellation in the Northern Hemisphere near Taurus and Pisces.

Aristotle (ăr′ĭ-stŏt′l) 384–322 BC. Greek philosopher and scientist whose writings in a wide variety of fields profoundly influenced Western thought. Throughout his life he made careful observations, collected specimens, and summarized existing knowledge about the natural world. He wrote influential works on logic, the classification of animals, meteorology, ethics, and many other topics. His systematic approach later evolved into the basic scientific method in the Western world.

arithmetic (ə-rĭth′mĭ-tĭk) **1.** The mathematical

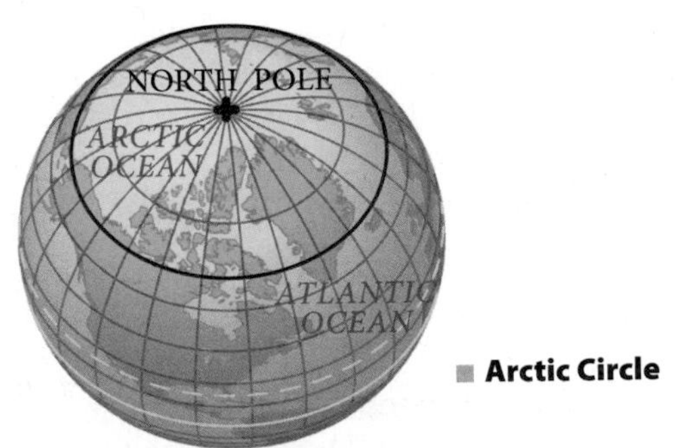

Arctic Circle

study of numbers and their properties under the operations of addition, subtraction, multiplication, and division. **2.** Calculation using these operations.

arithmetic mean (ăr′ĭth-mĕt**′**ĭk) The value obtained by dividing the sum of a set of quantities by the number of quantities in the set. For example, if there are three test scores, 70, 83, and 90, the arithmetic mean of the scores is their sum (243) divided by the number of scores (3), or 81. *See more at* **mean.** *Compare* **average, median, mode.**

arithmetic progression (ăr′ĭth-mĕt**′**ĭk) A sequence of numbers such as 1, 3, 5, 7, 9 . . . , in which each term after the first is formed by adding a constant to the preceding number (in this case, 2). *Compare* **geometric progression.**

armadillo (är′mə-dĭl**′**ō) Any of several toothless, burrowing mammals of South America, Central America, and southern North America. Armadillos have an armorlike covering of jointed bony plates and roll up into a ball when attacked.

armature (är**′**mə-chər) **1.** The usually rotating part of an electric motor or generator consisting of wire wound around an iron core. The armature carries the electric current. **2.** A piece of soft iron connecting the poles of a magnet. **3.** The part of an electromagnetic device, such as a relay or loudspeaker, that moves or vibrates.

aromatic (ăr′ə-măt**′**ĭk) Relating to an organic compound containing at least one benzene ring or similar ring-shaped component and having properties similar to benzene. Naphthalene and TNT are aromatic compounds. *Compare* **aliphatic.**

array (ə-rā**′**) **1.** *Mathematics* A rectangular arrangement of quantities in rows and columns. **2.** Numerical data ordered in a linear fashion, by magnitude. **3.** An arrangement of identical devices that function as a unit.

Arrhenius (ə-rē**′**nē-əs), **Svante August** 1859–1927. Swedish physicist and chemist who first explained the process by which certain compounds, such as salts, acids, and bases, dissociate into ions when they dissolve in water. He also did research on the relationship between carbon dioxide levels in the atmosphere and temperature at the surface of the Earth.

arrhythmia (ə-rĭ*th***′**mē-ə) An abnormal rhythm of the heart.

arsenic (är**′**sə-nĭk) A nonmetallic element most commonly occurring as a gray crystal, but also found as a yellow crystal and in other forms. Arsenic and its compounds are highly poisonous and are used to make insecticides, weed killers, semiconductors, and various alloys. *Symbol* **As.** *Atomic number* 33. *See* **Periodic Table,** pages 254–255.

arteriole (är-tîr**′**ē-ōl′) Any of the smaller branches of an artery, especially one that ends in the capillaries.

arteriosclerosis (är-tîr′ē-ō-sklə-rō**′**sĭs) A thickening and hardening of the walls of the arteries that interferes with the circulation of the blood. It can be caused by disease and is also associated with high blood pressure and diets that are rich in cholesterol and saturated fats. *See also* **atherosclerosis.**

artery (är**′**tə-rē) Any of the blood vessels that carry blood away from the heart. Arteries have muscular walls that pump blood with high levels of oxygen to the tissues of the body. —*Adjective* **arterial** (är-tîr**′**ē-əl).

artesian well (är-tē**′**zhən) A deep well that passes through hard, nonporous rock or sediment and reaches an aquifer in which the water is under enough pressure to rise to a height above the water table. ❖ In a **flowing artesian well** the water is under enough pressure to rise to the surface without being pumped.

arthritis (är-thrī**′**tĭs) Inflammation and stiffness

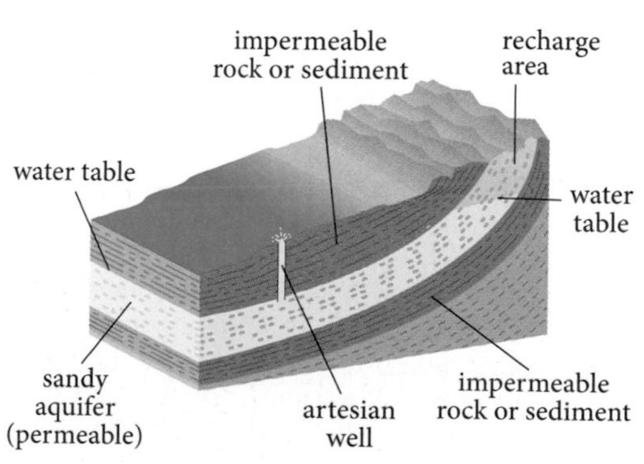

artesian well

If the water table in the recharge area is higher than the surface of a well, then the water will flow from the well without being pumped.

of a joint or joints. *See also* **osteoarthritis, rheumatoid arthritis.**

arthropod (är′thrə-pŏd′) Any of numerous invertebrate animals having a segmented body, jointed legs and other appendages, and an external skeleton. Crustaceans, insects, arachnids, and centipedes are all arthropods. There are more species of arthropods than of any other phylum in the animal kingdom.

artificial (är′tə-fĭsh′əl) Made by humans rather than occurring naturally: *artificial sweeteners; an artificial heart.*

artificial intelligence The ability of a computer or other machine to perform actions thought to require intelligence. Among these actions are logical deduction and inference, creativity, the ability to make decisions based on past experience or insufficient or conflicting information, and the ability to understand spoken language.

artificial selection The process by which humans choose individual plants or animals with certain genetically based characteristics for breeding, so that those characteristics will become more common in future generations.

artiodactyl (är′tē-ō-dăk′təl) Any of various hoofed mammals having an even number of toes, either two or four, on each foot. Artiodactyls include camels, pigs, hippopotamuses, and the ruminants, such as cattle, deer, sheep, and antelopes. Also called *even-toed ungulate. Compare* **perissodactyl.**

As The symbol for **arsenic.**

asbestos (ăs-bĕs′təs) Any of several fibrous mineral forms of magnesium silicate. Asbestos is resistant to heat, flames, and chemical action. Some forms have been shown to cause lung diseases. For this reason, asbestos is no longer used to make insulation, fireproofing material, and brake linings.

ASCII (ăs′kē) *Computers* A code that assigns numbers to the letters of the alphabet, the digits 0 through 9, and punctuation marks. For example, the capital letter A is coded as 65. (In the binary number system used by computers, 65 is written 1000001.) By standardizing the code used in representing written text, ASCII enables computers to exchange information.

ascorbic acid (ə-skôr′bĭk) *See* **vitamin C.**

–ase A suffix used to form the names of enzymes. It is often added to the name of the compound that the enzyme breaks down, as in *lactase*, an enzyme that breaks down lactose.

aseptic (ə-sĕp′tĭk, ā-) Free of microorganisms that cause disease; sterile.

asexual reproduction (ā-sĕk′sho͞o-əl) *See under* **reproduction.**

asparagine (ə-spăr′ə-jēn′) A nonessential amino acid. *See more at* **amino acid.**

aspartic acid (ə-spär′tĭk) A nonessential amino acid. *See more at* **amino acid.**

Asperger's syndrome (ăs′pər-gərz) A disorder of development, beginning in childhood, in which a person has difficulty socializing and communicating with others and may have a narrow range of interests.

asphalt (ăs′fôlt′) A thick, sticky, dark-brown mixture of petroleum tars used in paving, roofing, and waterproofing. Asphalt is produced as a byproduct in refining petroleum or is found in natural deposits.

asphyxia (ăs-fĭk′sē-ə) Suffocation resulting from a severe drop in the level of oxygen in the body, leading to loss of consciousness and sometimes death.

aspirate (ăs′pə-rāt′) **1.** To remove a liquid or gas from a body cavity, such as the chest, by suction. **2.** To inhale a foreign substance or object.

aspirin (ăs′pər-ĭn, ăs′prĭn) A compound derived from salicylic acid that is used as a drug to relieve fever and pain. Also called *acetylsalicylic acid.*

associative property (ə-sō′shə-tĭv) A property distinguishing some mathematical operations, such as addition and multiplication, when they are applied more than once. Operations with the associative property give the same result regardless of the order in which the operations are performed. For example, 3 + (4 + 5) is equal to (3 + 4) + 5. *See also* **commutative property, distributive property.**

astatine (ăs′tə-tēn′) A highly unstable, radioactive element that is the heaviest of the halogen elements. The most stable of its many isotopes has a half-life of only about eight hours. *Symbol* **At.** *Atomic number* 85. *See* **Periodic Table,** pages 254–255.

asteroid (ăs′tə-roid′) Any of numerous small solar system bodies that orbit the sun. Asteroids

Did You Know...?

aspirin

A forest may not look like a pharmacy, but many of the medical drugs we use now originally came from plants. Quinine, used to treat malaria, was derived from a South American tree; digitalis, used as a heart medicine, came from the foxglove plant; and *aspirin* was created from chemicals in willow bark. For thousands of years, people chewed the bark and leaves of willow trees when they had aches and pains. In the late 1800s, scientists isolated the pain-relieving chemical from willows and certain other plants. A German chemist figured out how to prepare this chemical so that it could be used as a drug, and aspirin tablets were patented in 1900. Today, aspirin is widely used to reduce pain, fevers, and inflammation, and to decrease the risk of heart disease, stroke, and some kinds of cancer. But willow trees and other living plants are no longer used as the raw material — it would be impractical and expensive to cultivate the vast amounts needed. The main ingredient in aspirin is now made from phenol, which comes from petroleum. Since petroleum and other fossil fuels are the remains of aquatic plants and other organisms that have been buried underground for millions of years, you might say that aspirin still ultimately comes from plants — very ancient plants.

range from several hundred miles in diameter to the size of a speck of dust. ❖ Most asteroids are found in the region between the orbits of Mars and Jupiter known as the **asteroid belt.** *See more at* **small solar system body.** *See Note at* **solar system.**

asthenosphere (ăs-thĕn**′**ə-sfîr′) A layer of the Earth's mantle lying beneath the lithosphere and consisting of several hundred miles of partially molten rock. Because it is partially molten, seismic waves passing through this layer have slow velocities. *Compare* **atmosphere, hydrosphere, lithosphere.**

asthma (ăz**′**mə) A chronic inflammatory disease of the lungs characterized by a narrowing of the airways and brought on by allergies, infection, or other factors. It results in attacks of wheezing, coughing, and shortness of breath, and is treated with medicines and avoidance of triggers.

astigmatism (ə-stĭg**′**mə-tĭz′əm) A defect of the eye in which the curvature of the cornea or lens is uneven. This prevents rays of light from being focused at a single point on the retina, resulting in indistinct or imperfect images.

astral (ăs**′**trəl) Relating to or coming from the stars; stellar: *astral distances.*

astringent (ə-strĭn**′**jənt) A substance, such as alum, that checks the flow of bodily secretions by causing tissue contraction.

astro– A prefix that means "star" (as in *astrophysics*), "celestial object" (as in *astronomy*), or "outer space" (as in *astronaut*).

astrometry (ə-strŏm**′**ĭ-trē) The scientific measurement of the positions and motions of celestial objects.

astronomical unit (ăs′trə-nŏm**′**ĭ-kəl) A unit of length equal to the average distance from Earth to the sun, approximately 93 million miles (150 million kilometers). It is used to measure distances within the solar system.

astronomy (ə-strŏn**′**ə-mē) The scientific study of the universe and the objects in it, including stars, planets, and nebulae. Astronomy deals with the position, size, motion, composition, and evolution of celestial objects. Astronomers analyze not only visible light but also radio waves, x-rays, and other types of electromagnetic radiation that come from sources outside the Earth's atmosphere.

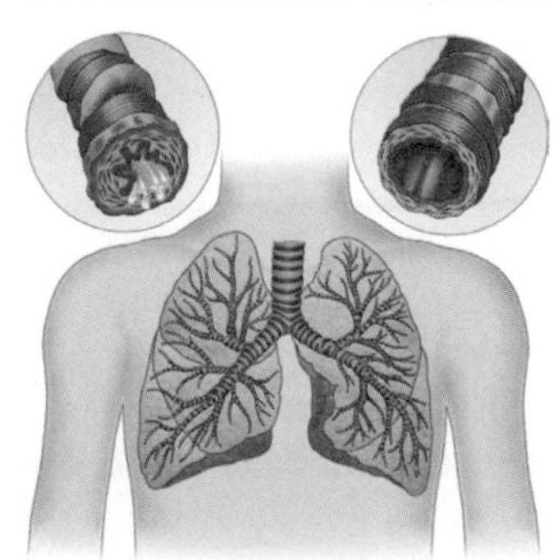

asthma
left: *inflamed bronchial tube with contracted muscles and mucus discharge*
right: *normal bronchial tube*

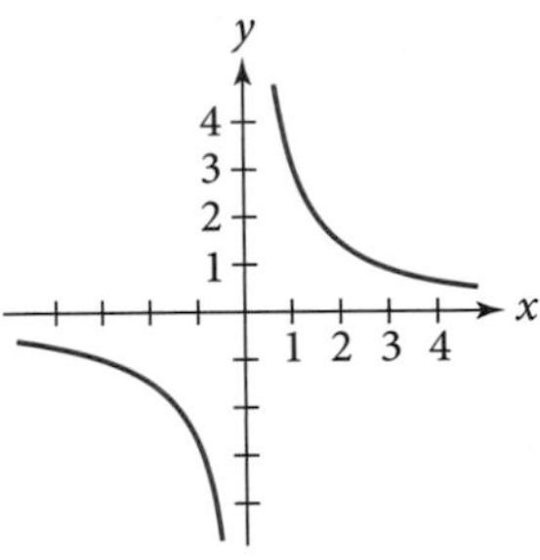

asymptote

The x-axis and y-axis are asymptotes of the hyperbola $xy = 3$.

astrophysics (ăs′trō-fĭz′ĭks) The branch of astronomy that deals with the physical processes that occur in stars, galaxies, and interstellar space.

asymmetry (ā-sĭm′ĭ-trē) Lack of symmetry. —*Adjective* **asymmetric** (ā′sĭ-mĕt′rĭk), **asymmetrical** (ā′sĭ-mĕt′rĭ-kəl).

asymptote (ăs′ĭm-tōt′) A line whose distance to a given curve gets closer and closer to zero. The curve may come closer and closer without ever touching the asymptote, or it may cross back and forth over the asymptote like ripples that get smaller and smaller without completely flattening out.

At The symbol for **astatine.**

ataxia (ə-tăk′sē-ə) Loss of muscular coordination as a result of damage to the nervous system.

-ate A suffix used to form the name of a salt, ester, or anion of an acid whose name ends in *-ic*. Such compounds or ions have one oxygen atom more than corresponding compounds or ions with names ending in *-ite.* For example, a sulfate is a salt of sulfuric acid and contains the group SO_4, while a sulfite contains SO_3. *Compare* **-ite** (sense 2).

atherosclerosis (ăth′ə-rō-sklə-rō′sĭs) Narrowing of the walls of the arteries caused by deposits of fatty substances (called plaques), especially cholesterol.

athlete's foot (ăth′lēts) A contagious infection of the feet that usually affects the skin between the toes, causing it to itch, blister, and crack. It is caused by a fungus.

atmosphere (ăt′mə-sfîr′) **1.** The mixture of gases that surrounds the Earth or some other celestial object. It is held by the force of gravity and forms various layers at different heights, including the troposphere, stratosphere, mesosphere, thermosphere, and exosphere. The Earth's atmosphere, called air, is rich in nitrogen and oxygen; that of Venus is mainly carbon dioxide. *Compare* **asthenosphere, hydrosphere, lithosphere. 2.** A unit of pressure equal to the pressure of the air at sea level, about 14.7 pounds per square inch or 1,013 millibars.

atmospheric pressure (ăt′mə-sfîr′ĭk) Pressure caused by the weight of the air. At sea level, it has an average value of one atmosphere, and it gradually decreases as the altitude increases. Slight variations in atmospheric pressure affect the weather. For example, low pressure often brings rain. In areas of low air pressure, the air is less dense and relatively warm, which causes it to rise. As the rising air cools, the water vapor in the air condenses, forming clouds and the drops that fall as rain.

atmosphere

The Earth's atmosphere is divided into layers primarily according to differences in temperature. In the troposphere and mesosphere, air temperature drops with altitude, while in the stratosphere and thermosphere it rises. Beyond the atmosphere lies the exosphere.

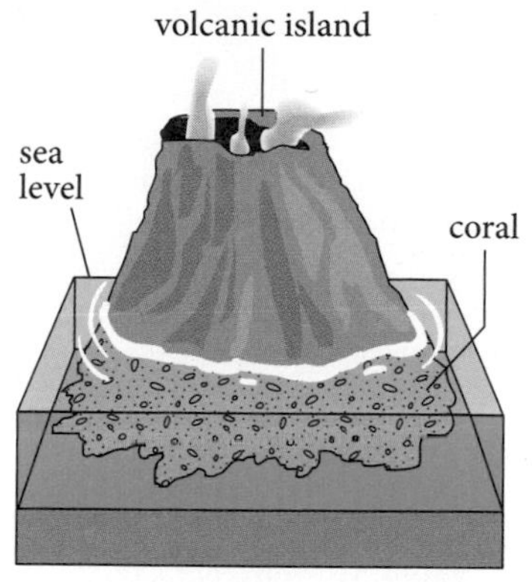

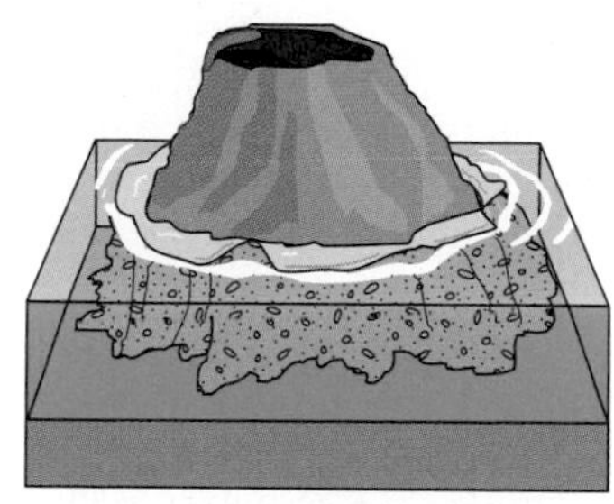
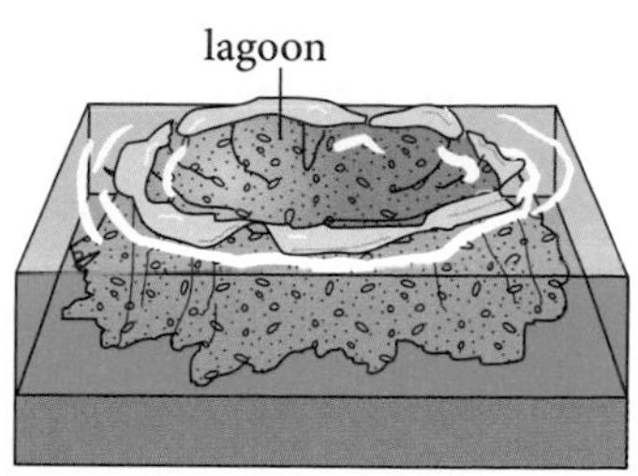

■ **atoll**

An atoll develops (from left to right) *when a volcanic island sinks below the surface of the ocean and a coral reef grows up around it, forming a lagoon.*

atoll (ăt′ôl′, ā′tôl′) An island or chain of islets connected by a coral reef that nearly or entirely encloses a lagoon.

atom (ăt′əm) The smallest unit of a chemical element. An atom consists of a dense central nucleus composed of protons and neutrons, surrounded by a cloud of rapidly orbiting electrons. All atoms of an element have the same number of protons in their nuclei, and each element has a different number; for example, every helium atom has two protons, and every carbon atom has six protons. In electrically neutral atoms, the number of electrons is the same as the number of protons. In a chemical reaction, an atom may lose, gain, or share electrons, but the nucleus remains unchanged. In a nuclear reaction, the number of protons or neutrons in the nucleus may change. *See Note at* **subatomic particle.** *See A Closer Look, on page 28.*

atomic (ə-tŏm′ĭk) **1.** Relating to an atom or atoms. **2.** Employing nuclear energy: *atomic weapons.*

atomic bomb A very destructive weapon that derives its explosive energy from the fission of atomic nuclei, usually uranium-235 or plutonium-239. Also called *atom bomb.*

atomic clock A device that measures time based on the frequency of the electromagnetic radiation emitted by electrons in the atoms of a certain element as they pass from a higher to a lower energy level. *See Note on page 29.*

atomic energy *See* **nuclear energy.**

atomic mass The mass of an atom, usually expressed in atomic mass units. *Compare* **atomic weight.**

atomic mass unit A unit of mass equal to $\frac{1}{12}$ the mass of an atom of the most common isotope of carbon (carbon-12), which is assigned a mass of 12.

atomic number The number of protons in the nucleus of an atom. In electrically neutral atoms, this number is also equal to the number of electrons surrounding the atom's nucleus. The atomic number of an element determines its position in the periodic table.

atomic weight The average mass of an atom of an element, usually expressed in atomic mass units.

■ **atomic bomb**

test at Frenchman Flat, Nevada, in 1951

A CLOSER LOOK

Atoms

Every atom consists of a nucleus containing protons and (except in the case of hydrogen) neutrons, with rapidly moving electrons surrounding it. The electrons occupy regions called shells that have different energy levels. Hydrogen (the lightest element) consists of one proton, located in the nucleus, and one electron, which moves around the nucleus in an electron shell.

Hydrogen

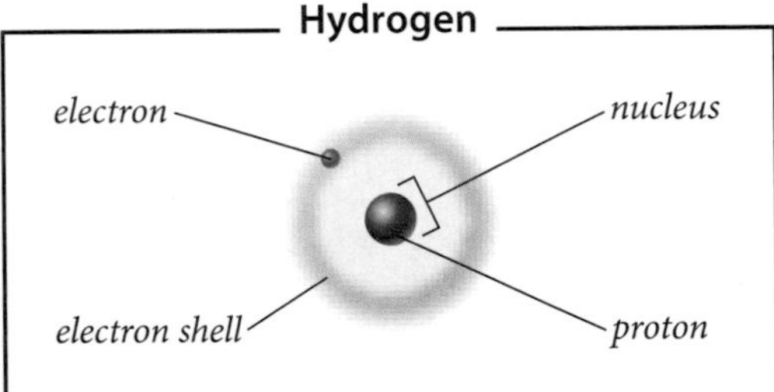

The second-lightest element, helium, has two protons and two neutrons in its nucleus, and two electrons in the lowest-energy electron shell.

Helium

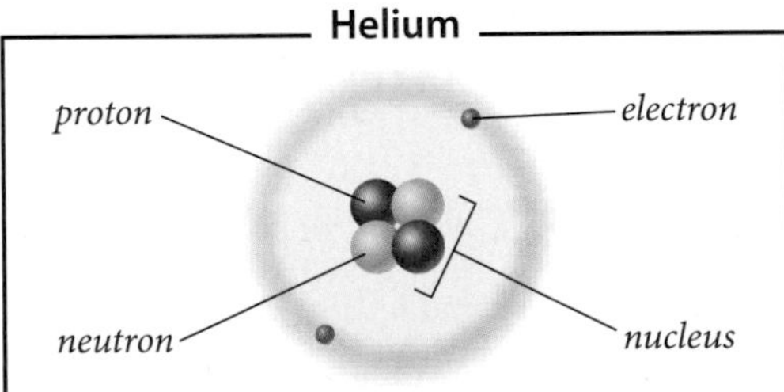

Lithium, the third-lightest element, has three protons, three or four neutrons, and three electrons. The inner electron shell can only hold two electrons, so lithium's third electron is in an outer electron shell. This outer shell can hold up to eight electrons.

Lithium

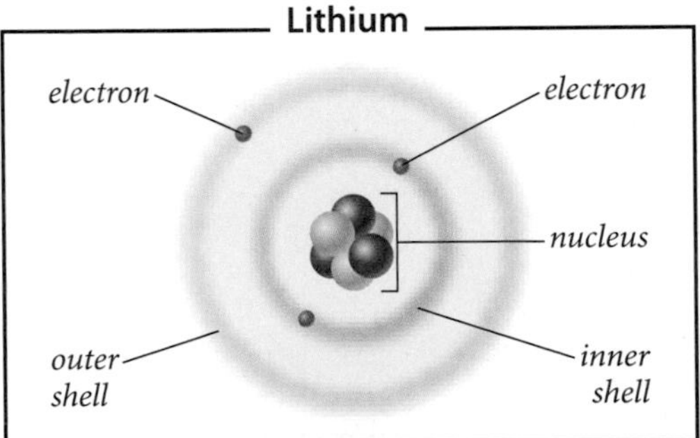

Heavier atoms have as many as seven electron shells, with outer shells having higher energy levels. The number of electrons occupying the outermost shell determines how easily the atoms of an element will react with other atoms to form compounds. Atoms whose outermost shell is full are inert; they do not normally combine with other atoms. Atoms whose outermost shell is only partially filled, however, react easily. Because a full outer shell is more stable, an atom tends to gain electrons from or share electrons with other atoms until its outer shell is full.

Oxygen

An oxygen atom, for example, has eight protons and eight neutrons in its nucleus, with eight electrons distributed throughout its two shells: two in the inner shell and six in the outer shell. Because the outer shell has room for two more electrons, oxygen often reacts with other elements to gain or share two more electrons.

A water molecule is formed in this way, when an atom of oxygen combines with two atoms of hydrogen. The oxygen atom fills its outermost (second) shell by sharing two electrons with the hydrogen atoms. Each hydrogen atom fills its outermost (first) shell by sharing two electrons with the oxygen atom.

Water (H_20)

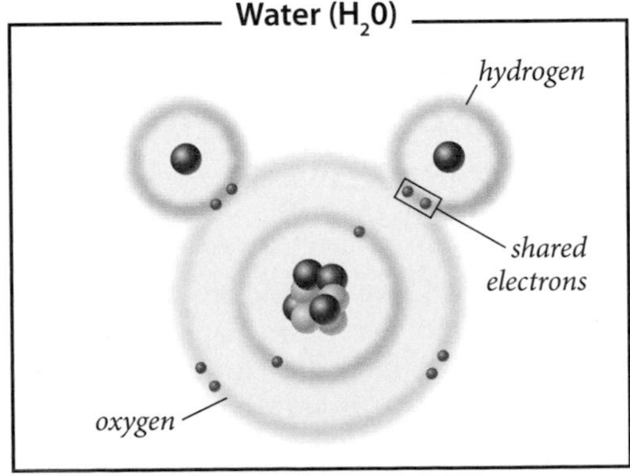

Did You Know...?

atomic clock

The standard unit of time, the second, is no longer defined as one sixtieth of one sixtieth of one twenty-fourth of a day. Instead, it is defined as 9,192,631,770 cycles of a device, an *atomic clock,* that measures the frequency of radiation emitted by atoms of cesium-133 as their electrons pass from a higher energy level to a lower one. This may sound like an arbitrary definition, but in fact it's very useful, because the behavior of cesium atoms is much more unchanging than the length of a day. The best atomic clocks gain or lose less than a second in 20 million years; this accuracy makes them extremely useful in telecommunications technologies such as the Global Positioning System (GPS). Other applications include measuring variability in the Earth's rotation period and navigating in outer space.

The atomic weight of an element having more than one naturally occurring isotope is calculated both from the atomic masses of the isotopes and from the relative abundance of each isotope. For example, the atomic weight of the element chlorine is 35.453, determined by averaging the atomic masses and relative abundances of its two main naturally occurring isotopes, which have atomic masses of about 35 and 37. *Compare* **atomic mass.**

ATP (ā′tē′pē′) Short for *adenosine triphosphate.* An organic compound, $C_{10}H_{16}N_5O_{13}P_3$, that is composed of adenosine and three phosphate groups. It serves as a source of energy for metabolic processes in cells. ATP releases energy during hydrolysis when it loses one of its phosphate groups and is converted into ADP.

atrium (ā′trē-əm) *Plural* **atria** A chamber of the heart that receives blood from the veins and pumps it into a ventricle. Mammals, birds, reptiles, and amphibians have two atria; fish have one. —*Adjective* **atrial.**

atrophy (ăt′rə-fē) The wasting away of a body part, most commonly caused by disease or nerve damage.

attention deficit hyperactivity disorder (ə-tĕn′shən) A condition whose symptoms most commonly include impulsiveness, a short attention span, and hyperactivity. It is usually diagnosed in childhood and can interfere with performance at school, in the workplace, and in social situations. ❖ When symptoms include problems with focus and attention more than hyperactivity, the condition is sometimes called **attention deficit disorder (ADD).**

Au The symbol for **gold.**

AU Abbreviation of **astronomical unit.**

auditory (ô′dĭ-tôr′ē) Relating to hearing or the organs of hearing: *the auditory canal of the ear.*

auditory nerve The nerve that carries sensory information relating to sound and balance from the ear to the brain. The auditory nerve is a cranial nerve.

Audubon (ô′də-bŏn′), **John James** 1785–1851. Haitian-born American ornithologist and artist who spent years traveling around the United States painting birds and mammals. His collection of 435 life-size engravings of the birds of eastern and central North America was published as *The Birds of America* (1827–1838). The engravings are noted for their naturalistic detail and artistic sensibility.

auricle (ôr′ĭ-kəl) **1.** The visible part of the outer ear. **2.** An atrium of the heart.

John James Audubon
"Snowy Owl," from The Birds of America, *by John James Audubon*

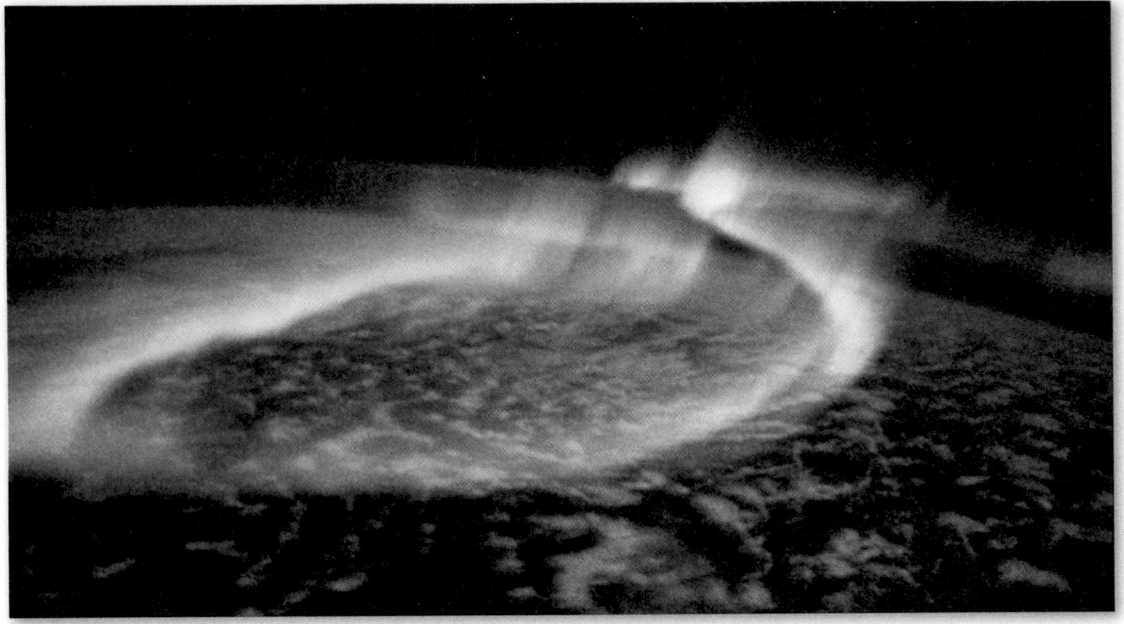

aurora australis
view from a satellite

aurora (ə-rôr′ə) *Plural* **auroras** *or* **aurorae** (ə-rôr′ē) A brilliant display of bands of often green, blue, or red light in the sky at night, especially in polar regions. The light is thought to be caused by charged particles from the sun entering the Earth's magnetic field and causing molecules in the atmosphere to release photons.

aurora australis (ô-strā′lĭs) An aurora that occurs in southern regions of the Earth. Also called *southern lights.*

aurora borealis (bôr′ē-ăl′ĭs) An aurora that occurs in northern regions of the Earth. Also called *northern lights.*

australopithecine (ô-strā′lō-pĭth′ĭ-sēn′) Any of several early hominids of eastern and southern Africa, known from fossils dating from about four million to about one million years ago. The most complete australopithecine skeleton found so far, named Lucy by its discoverers, is estimated to be just over three million years old. While many scientists believe that australopithecines are ancestors of modern humans, not enough fossils have yet been found to establish any direct descent.

autism (ô′tĭz′əm) A disorder of development, beginning in early childhood, in which a person's ability to interact with others is severely limited. People with autism usually have difficulty communicating and often exhibit repetitive movements or focus intently on certain objects. —*Adjective* **autistic.**

auto– **1.** A prefix that means "oneself," as in *autoimmune,* producing antibodies or immunity against oneself. **2.** A prefix that means "by itself" or "spontaneously," as in *autonomic,* operating by itself.

autoimmune (ô′tō-ĭ-myo͞on′) Relating to a reaction of the immune system in which antibodies are produced that attack the body's own cells and tissues, often causing illness.

autonomic nervous system (ô′tə-nŏm′ĭk) The part of the nervous system of a vertebrate animal that regulates involuntary action, as of the intestines, heart, or glands. It is composed of two parts, the sympathetic nervous system and the parasympathetic nervous system.

autopsy (ô′tŏp′sē) A medical examination of a dead body to determine the cause of death.

autotrophic (ô′tə-trŏf′ĭk) Relating to an organism that manufactures its own food from inorganic substances, such as carbon dioxide and nitrogen, using light or chemical energy. Green plants, algae, and some bacteria are autotrophic.

❖ An organism capable of producing food from inorganic substances is called an **autotroph** (ô′tə-trŏf′). *Compare* **heterotrophic.**

autumnal equinox (ô-tŭm′nəl) **1.** The moment of the year when the sun crosses the celestial equator while moving from north to south. It occurs on or about September 23. In the Northern Hemisphere, this marks the beginning of autumn. **2.** The point on the celestial sphere where this crossing occurs. *Compare* **vernal equinox.**

auxin (ôk′sĭn) Any of various plant hormones that regulate growth and development. Auxins are produced in tissues where new cells are forming, such as shoot tips and young leaves. Auxins are also produced artificially in laboratories and are used as herbicides and to control fruit development or promote rooting.

avalanche (ăv′ə-lănch′) A fall or slide of a large mass of material, especially of snow, down a mountainside.

average (ăv′ər-ĭj) A number, especially the arithmetic mean, that is derived from and considered typical or representative of a set of numbers. *Compare* **arithmetic mean, median, mode.**

Avery (ā′və-rē) **Oswald Theodore** 1877–1955. Canadian-born American bacteriologist who determined that DNA was the material that caused genetic changes in bacteria. His work was vital to scientists who later established that DNA is the carrier of genetic information in all living organisms.

avian (ā′vē-ən) Relating to birds.

aviary (ā′vē-ĕr′ē) A large cage or enclosure for birds, as in a zoo.

Avicenna (ăv′ĭ-sĕn′ə) *See* **Ibn Sina, Hakim.**

Avogadro (ä′və-gä′drō), **Amedeo** 1776–1856. Italian chemist and physicist who formulated the hypothesis known as Avogadro's law, which states that equal volumes of gases, under equal conditions of temperature and pressure, contain equal numbers of atoms or molecules. From this hypothesis, other physicists were able to calculate Avogadro's number.

Avogadro's number The number of items, especially atoms or molecules, in a mole of a substance, equal to approximately 6.0221×10^{23}. *See more at* **mole³.**

avoirdupois weight (ăv′ər-də-poiz′) A system of weights based on a pound of 16 ounces, used in the United States to weigh everything except gems, precious metals, and drugs.

axil (ăk′sĭl) The angle between the upper side of a leaf and the stem it is attached to. Each axil contains a bud.

axiom (ăk′sē-əm) A principle that is accepted as true without proof; a postulate.

axis (ăk′sĭs) *Plural* **axes** (ăk′sēz′) **1.** An imaginary line around which an object rotates. In a rotating sphere, such as the Earth and other planets, the two ends of the axis are called poles. **2.** *Mathematics* A line, ray, or line segment with respect to which a figure or object is symmetrical. **3.** *Mathematics* In the Cartesian coordinate system, one of the reference lines from which or along which distances or angles are measured: *the x-axis.* **4.** *Anatomy* The second cervical vertebra on which the head turns. **5.** *Botany* The main stem or central part of a plant, about which plant parts, such as branches, are arranged. —*Adjective* **axial.**

axon (ăk′sŏn′) The long portion of a nerve cell that carries impulses away from the body of the cell. Also called *nerve fiber.*

azimuth (ăz′ə-məth) The horizontal angle measured clockwise between the northern point of the horizon and the point directly below a celestial object, as seen by the observer. Azimuth and altitude are the coordinates used to navigate with respect to the stars.

azurite (ăzh′ə-rīt′) A dark-blue copper carbonate mineral having a glassy luster and occurring in various forms. It is often found together with malachite. Azurite is used as a source of copper, as a gemstone, and as a pigment.

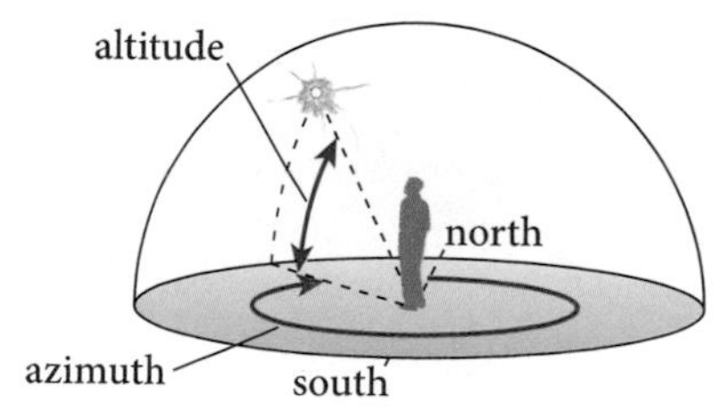

■ **azimuth**

B

B The symbol for **boron.**

Ba The symbol for **barium.**

Babbage (băb′ĭj), **Charles** 1791–1871. British mathematician, inventor, and pioneer of machine computing. Between 1820 and 1822, Babbage built a model of a mechanical device, called a difference engine, which was used to make repetitive calculations. Later he designed a much larger machine, called an analytical engine, which could be programmed with punched cards. Although the analytical engine was never finished, it is recognized as the forerunner of the modern computer. *See Note at* **Lovelace.**

baboon (bă-bo͞on′) Any of several large monkeys of Africa and Arabia that have a projecting muzzle like that of a dog and thick pads of hairless skin on the buttocks. Baboons spend most of their time on the ground rather than in trees.

bacillus (bə-sĭl′əs) *Plural* **bacilli** (bə-sĭl′ī′) Any of various bacteria that are shaped like a rod.

backbone (băk′bōn′) *See* **spinal column.**

Bacon (bā′kən), **Roger** 1214?–1292. English philosopher who wrote on a wide range of scientific topics. Bacon asserted that mathematics is fundamental to science and that experimentation is essential for testing scientific theories. He did important work in the field of optics, explaining the principles of reflection and refraction and describing the use of lenses to observe very small and very distant objects.

bacteriology (băk-tîr′ē-ŏl′ə-jē) The scientific study of bacteria and bacterial diseases.

bacterium (băk-tîr′ē-əm) *Plural* **bacteria** Any of a large group of one-celled organisms that lack a cell nucleus and reproduce by fission or by forming spores. Bacteria are found in all of the Earth's environments, including inside the bodies of other organisms, where they sometimes cause disease. Bacteria and archaea together make up the group called the prokaryotes. —*Adjective* **bacterial.**

badlands (băd′lăndz′) An area of heavily eroded land with numerous gullies or streambeds between ridges of variously colored sand, silt, and clay. Badlands usually form in dry regions where sudden, heavy rains wash away soil and keep most vegetation from becoming established.

Baily's beads (bā′lēs) Dots or patches of sunlight visible along the edge of the moon's disk in the seconds before and after the moon completely blocks the sun during a total solar eclipse, caused by sunlight passing through valleys on the moon's surface. This phenomenon is named for the British astronomer Francis Baily (1774–1844), who first described it in 1836.

baking soda (bā′kĭng) A white crystalline compound, $NaHCO_3$, chemically known as sodium bicarbonate. It is used especially in beverages and as a leavening agent to make baked goods.

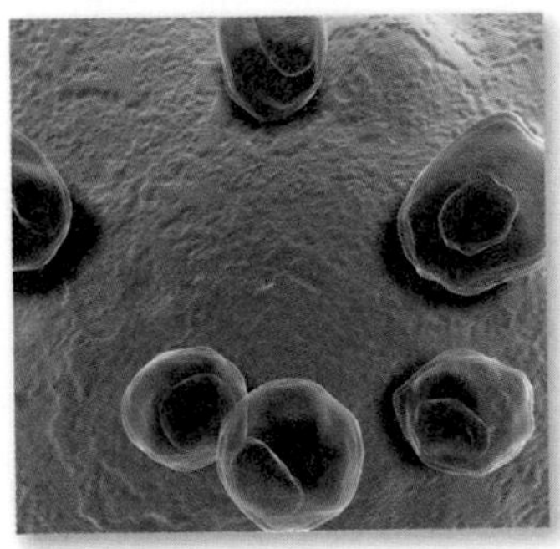
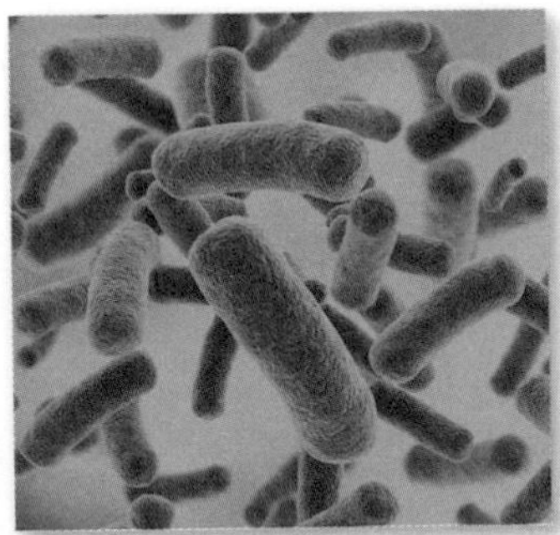
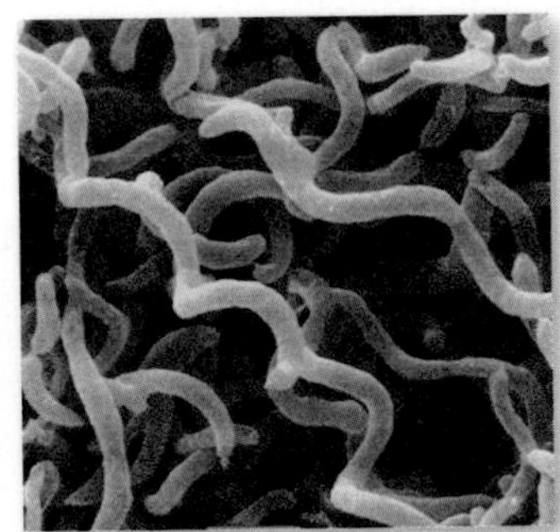

■ **bacterium**

Bacteria are divided into three main types by shape. From left to right: *cocci (sphere-shaped), bacilli (rod-shaped), and spirilla (spiral-shaped).*

Baily's beads

bamboo

balance (băl′əns) To adjust a chemical equation so that the number of each type of atom, and the total charge, on the reactant (left-hand) side of the equation matches the number and charge on the product (right-hand) side of the equation.

baleen (bə-lēn′) A flexible horny substance that hangs in plates from the upper jaw of certain whales, such as the humpback whale. These whales feed on plankton that they collect by filtering large amounts of seawater through the baleen plates. Also called *whalebone.*

ballistics (bə-lĭs′tĭks) The scientific study of the motion of projectiles, such as bullets and missiles.

Baltimore (bôl′tə-môr′), **David** Born 1938. American microbiologist who discovered the enzyme known as reverse transcriptase, which is capable of passing information from RNA to DNA. Prior to this discovery, it was assumed that information could flow only from DNA to RNA. Baltimore's work led to increased understanding of viruses that cause AIDS and certain forms of cancer.

bamboo (băm-bo͞o′) Any of various grasses that have jointed, woody, hollow stems and can grow very tall. Bamboo stems are widely used as building materials, and the young shoots of some types of bamboo are used as food.

band (bănd) A specific range of frequencies of electromagnetic radiation, such as the VHF (very high frequency) radio band, part of which is used in FM (frequency modulation) radio broadcasting.

Banks (băngks), Sir **Joseph** 1743–1820. British botanist who took part in Captain James Cook's voyage around the world (1768–1771), during which he discovered and cataloged many species of plant and animal life.

Banneker (băn′ĭ-kər), **Benjamin** 1731–1806. American mathematician and astronomer. He correctly predicted a solar eclipse in 1789. Banneker published an almanac from 1792 to 1797 that contained tide tables, future eclipses, and medicinal information.

Banting (băn′tĭng), Sir **Frederick Grant** 1891–1941. Canadian physiologist who isolated the hormone insulin, used in the treatment of diabetes. Banting conducted research into the secretions of the pancreas, including insulin. With Charles Best, he experimented with diabetic dogs, demonstrating that insulin lowered their blood sugar. Insulin was tested and proven effective on humans within months of the first experiments with dogs.

baobab (bā′ō-băb′) An African tree having a large trunk, bulbous branches, and hard-shelled

Benjamin Banneker

■ baobab

fruit with edible pulp. The baobab has spongy wood that holds large amounts of water, and the bark can be used to make rope, mats, paper, and other items. Baobabs can live for over 1,000 years.

bar (bär) A unit used to measure atmospheric pressure. It is equal to a force of 100,000 newtons per square meter, or about 0.987 atmosphere.

barb (bärb) **1.** A sharp point projecting backward, as on the stinger of a bee. **2.** One of the hairlike branches on the shaft of a feather.

barbel (bär′bəl) A slender feeler extending from the head of certain fish, such as catfish. It is used for sensing the environment, especially for tasting.

barbiturate (bär-bĭch′ər-ĭt) Any of a group of drugs that reduce the activity of the nervous system and are used as sedatives. Barbiturates are highly addictive.

barbule (bär′byo͞ol) A small barb or pointed projection, especially one that fringes the edges of the barbs of feathers.

Bardeen (bär-dēn′), **John** 1908–1991. American physicist who was one of the inventors of the transistor (1947) and later helped to develop the theory of superconductivity. Bardeen's research explained why the electrical resistance of certain materials disappears at temperatures close to absolute zero, thereby allowing a current to flow through them.

barite (bâr′īt) A usually white or clear mineral consisting of barium sulfate and occurring as flattened blades. Barite also occurs in a circular pattern of crystals that looks like a flower and, when colored red by iron stains, is called a desert rose. Barite is used as a source of barium.

barium (bâr′ē-əm) A soft, silvery-white metallic alkaline-earth element that only occurs combined with other elements, especially in barite. Barium compounds are used in x-raying the stomach and intestines and in making fireworks and various pigments. *Symbol* **Ba.** *Atomic number* 56. *See* **Periodic Table,** pages 254–255.

barium sulfate A fine, white powder, $BaSO_4$. It is used in making textiles, rubber, and plastic and in taking x-rays of the digestive tract.

bark (bärk) The protective outer covering of the trunk, branches, and roots of trees and other woody plants. Bark is usually divided into inner bark, consisting of phloem (tissue that carries dissolved sugars to all parts of the plant), and outer bark, consisting chiefly of layers of dead cells. The outer bark protects the tree from heat, cold, insects, and other dangers.

barnacle (bär′nə-kəl) Any of various small, hard-shelled crustaceans that have feathery structures used for filtering food particles from the water. Barnacles attach themselves to underwater objects such as rocks, pilings, and the bottoms of ships.

barometer (bə-rŏm′ĭ-tər) An instrument for measuring atmospheric pressure. Barometers are used to determine height above sea level and in weather forecasting. ❖ Important kinds of barometers include the **aneroid barometer** and the **mercury barometer.** —*Adjective* **barometric** (băr′ə-mĕt′rĭk).

barrier island (băr′ē-ər) A long, narrow sand island that is parallel to the mainland and serves to protect the coast from erosion.

barrier reef A long, narrow ridge of coral deposits parallel to the mainland and separated from it by a deep lagoon.

basalt (bə-sôlt′, bā′sôlt′) A dark, fine-grained, igneous rock consisting largely of feldspar, iron, and magnesium. Basalt makes up most of the ocean floor. It commonly forms when lava solidifies. *See Table at* **rock.**

base (bās) **1.** *Chemistry* Any of a class of compounds that contain hydroxide ions (OH^-), or that yield hydroxide ions when dissolved in water, and are capable of neutralizing acids.

■ **basalt**
basalt columns at Yellowstone National Park, Wyoming

They react with acids and certain metals to form water and salts. Bases turn red litmus paper blue, have a bitter taste, and have a pH of greater than 7. *Compare* **acid.** **2.** *Biology* One of the purines (adenine or guanine) or pyrimidines (cytosine, thymine, or uracil) found in DNA or RNA. **3.** *Mathematics* **a.** The side or face of a geometric figure to which an altitude can be drawn. The base is often, but not always, the bottom part of the figure. **b.** The number that is raised to various powers to generate the principal counting units of a number system. The base of the decimal system, for example, is 10. **c.** The number that is raised to a particular power in a given mathematical expression. In the expression a^n, a is the base.

base pair Any of certain pairs of nitrogen-containing bases, consisting of a purine linked by hydrogen bonds to a pyrimidine, that connect complementary strands of nucleic acid molecules. Base pairs link together the two strands in a DNA molecule, a DNA strand with a messenger RNA strand during transcription, and in some cases, two strands of RNA with each other. The base pairs in DNA are adenine-thymine and guanine-cytosine. In RNA, thymine is replaced with uracil.

basic (bā′sĭk) Having the chemical characteristics of a base; alkaline.

basin (bā′sĭn) **1.** An enclosed area filled with water. **2.** A region drained by a river and the streams that flow into it. **3.** A low-lying area on the Earth's surface in which thick layers of sediment have accumulated. Some basins are bowl-shaped, and others are shaped like long valleys that have been filled in. Basins are important because they are often a source of valuable oil.

Did You Know...?

bat

Bats are the only mammals that can truly fly, and they have been very successful: there are over 1,000 different species. Many eat insects or fruit, but some species have evolved to feed on nectar, small vertebrates, or blood. Most bats navigate using a form of natural radar called *echolocation.* The bat emits a series of very high-pitched squeaks, inaudible to human ears, which reflect off objects in its path. Relying on the pattern of echoes it hears, the bat can then avoid obstacles or head for a specific target, such as a tasty moth.

bat (băt) Any of various flying mammals that have thin wings consisting of skin that extends from the forelimbs to the hind limbs and tail. Bats are usually active at night and use echolocation to navigate.

bathyscaphe (băth′ĭ-skăf′, băth′ĭ-skāf′) A free-diving vessel used to explore the ocean at great depths. Bathyscaphes have a large buoyant hull attached to a round observation capsule.

battery (băt′ə-rē) A device that uses chemical energy stored in a single electric cell or a series of

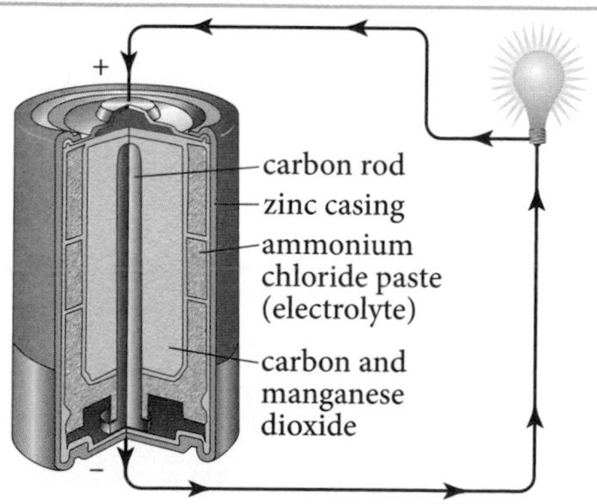

■ **battery**
Electrons flow from the zinc casing through the light bulb to the carbon rod, making the bulb glow. The zinc casing acts as a negative electrode, and the carbon rod acts as a positive electrode.

Did You Know...?

battery

You wouldn't guess from looking at a *battery* that there are chemical reactions going on inside it. But that's what's happening: a battery enables chemical energy to be converted into electrical energy. The substances inside a battery are arranged so that when they react with each other they pull electrons away from the battery's positive terminal and push them toward the negative terminal. If the battery is not connected to anything, the reaction doesn't go on very long because the electrons gathered at the negative terminal repel any additional ones that further reactions would carry there. But if you connect the two terminals with a wire, electrons will flow along the wire from negative to positive. On the way, they give up some of their energy to power whatever device you've connected to the wire — a light bulb, for instance. Eventually, the chemical reactions inside the battery change the nature of the positive and negative terminals and of the chemicals between them, making them unable to produce any more electricity. In rechargeable batteries, you can restore the power-generating capacity of the terminals and the chemicals by using another power source to run an electric current through the battery backward.

electric cells to produce electricity in the form of direct current. Each cell consists of two electrodes with a chemical electrolyte between them. In dry cells, such as flashlight batteries, the electrolyte is in the form of a paste. In wet cells, such as car batteries, the electrolyte is in liquid form.

bauxite (bôk′sīt′) A soft, whitish to reddish-brown rock composed mainly of hydrous aluminum oxides. Bauxite forms from the breakdown of clays and is a major source of aluminum.

bay (bā) A body of water partially enclosed by land but having a wide outlet to the sea. A bay is usually smaller than a gulf.

bayou (bī′o͞o) A sluggish, marshy or swampy stream connected with a river, lake, or gulf. Bayous are common in the southern United States.

B cell Any of the lymphocytes that develop into plasma cells in the presence of a specific antigen, such as a bacterium or virus. The plasma cells then produce antibodies that attack or neutralize the antigen. In mammals, B cells mature in the bone marrow and are then released into the blood. *See Note at* **antibody.**

B complex *See* **vitamin B complex.**

Be The symbol for **beryllium.**

beach (bēch) The area of accumulated sand, gravel, or stones deposited along a shore by the action of waves and tides. Beaches usually slope gently toward the body of water they border.

beak (bēk) **1.** The bill of a bird. **2.** A similar, often horny part forming the mouth of other animals, such as turtles and octopuses.

beaker (bē′kər) A wide, cylindrical glass container with a pouring lip, used especially in laboratories.

bear (bâr) Any of various large mammals that have a shaggy coat and a very short tail and that walk with the entire lower surface of the foot touching the ground. Bears usually eat both plants and animals, such as insects and small rodents.

Beaufort scale (bō′fərt) A scale for classifying the force of the wind, ranging from 0 (calm) to 12 (hurricane). The scale was devised in 1805 as a means of describing the effect of different wind velocities on ships at sea.

beaver (bē′vər) Either of two rodents, one species native to North America and the other native to Eurasia, having thick fur, a flat broad tail,

beak

top to bottom: *black skimmer, pileated woodpecker, and American goldfinch*

and large front teeth. Beavers live in and near lakes and streams and feed on bark, twigs, and roots. They use their sharp teeth to cut down trees, which they use for building dams and lodges.

becquerel (bĕ-krĕl′, bĕk′ə-rĕl′) A unit used to measure the rate of radioactive decay, the process by which the nuclei of the atoms of a radioactive substance disintegrate by emitting subatomic particles or gamma rays. One becquerel is equal to one of these nuclear disintegrations per second.

Becquerel (bĕ-krĕl′, bĕk′ə-rĕl′) Family of French physicists, including **Antoine César** (1788–1878), one of the first investigators of electrochemistry; his son **Alexandre Edmond** (1820–1891), noted for his research on phosphorescence; and his grandson **Antoine Henri** (1852–1908), who discovered spontaneous radioactivity in uranium.

bed (bĕd) **1.** A layer of sediments or rock that extends under a large area and has other layers below and sometimes above it: *a bed of coal.* **2.** The bottom of a body of water: *the bed of a stream.*

bedbug (bĕd′bŭg′) A small wingless insect with a flat reddish body that feeds on human blood. Bedbugs are found in bedding, upholstery, and other places where humans sleep or rest.

bedrock (bĕd′rŏk′) The solid rock that lies beneath the soil and other loose material on the Earth's surface.

bee (bē) Any of a numerous winged, hairy-bodied, usually stinging insects that gather pollen and nectar from flowers. Bees are important pollinators of flowering plants. Most bees are solitary, but some, such as honeybees, live in colonies. ❖ Bees that produce honey from nectar and pollen are called **honeybees.** Honeybees live in large colonies with an organized social structure, consisting of workers, drones, and a queen. The Western honeybee, native to Eurasia and Africa, was domesticated several thousand years ago and is raised commercially as a source of honey and beeswax and for pollinating crops. *See also* **drone, queen, worker.**

■ **bedbug**

beetle (bēt′l) Any of numerous insects that have biting or chewing mouthparts and hard forewings that fold over the delicate hind wings when at rest. Most beetles eat plants or fungi, but some are predatory, and others are scavengers, feeding on decaying matter.

Did You Know...?

beetle

How many kinds of *beetles* can you name? Perhaps you can think of the red-and-black spotted ladybird beetle, and maybe a firefly, a dung beetle, or a destructive pest like the boll weevil. If you wanted to name all known beetle species, you'd still have 399,996 to go — about 400,000 species have been described so far by scientists. The biologist J.B.S. Haldane was reportedly once asked if the study of life on Earth had given him any insights into the nature of the Creator, and he replied that God must have "an inordinate fondness for beetles." Beetles are thought to represent about 40 percent of all species of insects, and insects themselves make up about half of all known species of eukaryotes (all organisms excluding bacteria and archaea). Beetles constitute the insect order Coleoptera and are also called *coleopterans.* The order name comes from the Greek word *koleopteros,* meaning "sheath-wing," which refers to the main distinguishing feature of beetles, their hardened forewings (called *elytra*). Beetles first evolved during the Permian Period, about 265 million years ago, before the dinosaurs and mammals. Many new beetle groups appeared during the Mesozoic Era, and today they can be found everywhere from rainforests to deserts, ranging in size from the featherwing beetles, which are smaller than a pinhead, to the horned Hercules beetles, which can be as large as a human hand.

Alexander Graham Bell

behavior (bĭ-hāv′yər) **1.** The actions displayed by an organism in response to either internal or external stimuli. **2.** One of these actions. Feeding and mating are examples of animal behaviors. **3.** The manner in which a physical system, such as a gas, a subatomic particle, or a wave, acts under specific conditions.

Bell (bĕl), **Alexander Graham** 1847–1922. British-born American scientist and inventor. Bell's lifelong interest in the education of deaf people led him to conceive the idea of transmitting speech by electric waves. In 1876 he received the first patent for an electric telephone. Bell also invented many other devices, including the metal detector and a telephone that transmitted speech by means of light rays.

belladonna (bĕl′ə-dŏn′ə) Any of several toxic alkaloids produced by the plant known as deadly nightshade. Drugs derived from these alkaloids are often used in medicine, for example to increase the heart rate.

Bell Burnell (bĕl′ bûr′nĕl′), **(Susan) Jocelyn** Born 1943. British astronomer. In 1967, working with astronomer Antony Hewish, she discovered the first pulsar.

bell curve A symmetrical bell-shaped curve that represents the typical distribution and frequency of the values of a set of random data. It slopes downward from a point in the middle corresponding to the mean.

benign (bĭ-nīn′) Not likely to spread or get worse; not malignant: *a benign tumor.*

benthic (bĕn′thĭk) Relating to the bottom of a sea or lake, especially to the organisms living there.

benzene (bĕn′zēn′) A clear, colorless, toxic, flammable liquid, C_6H_6. It is derived from petroleum and used to make detergents, insecticides, motor fuels, and many other chemical products. ❖ The six carbon atoms of benzene are arranged in a hexagon-shaped ring, called a **benzene ring.** Benzene rings and the compounds that contain them are called **aromatic compounds** and are particularly stable.

benzoic acid (bĕn-zō′ĭk) An aromatic, white, crystalline acid, $C_7H_6O_2$, used in preserving food, as a cosmetic, and in medicine.

beriberi (bĕr′ē-bĕr′ē) A disease caused by a lack of thiamine in the diet. It causes nerve damage and circulatory problems.

berkelium (bər-kē′lē-əm, bûrk′lē-əm) A synthetic, radioactive metallic element of the actinide series that is produced from americium, curium, or plutonium. Its most stable isotope has a half-life of about 1,400 years. *Symbol* **Bk.** *Atomic number* 97. *See* **Periodic Table,** pages 254–255.

Berners-Lee (bûr′nûrz-lē′), Sir **Timothy John** Born 1955. British computer scientist. He proposed the World Wide Web and developed the first website (1989–1991) while working at the European Particle Physics Laboratory (CERN) in Geneva, Switzerland.

Bernoulli (bər-no͞o′lē) Family of Swiss mathematicians. **Jacques** (or **Jakob**) (1654–1705) made important contributions to calculus and probability theory. His brother **Jean** (or **Johann**) (1667–1748) also helped to develop calculus and contributed to the study of complex numbers and trigonometry. Jean's son **Daniel** (1700–1782) is noted for his work in the field of hydrodynamics.

berry (bĕr′ē) **1a.** A fruit that develops from

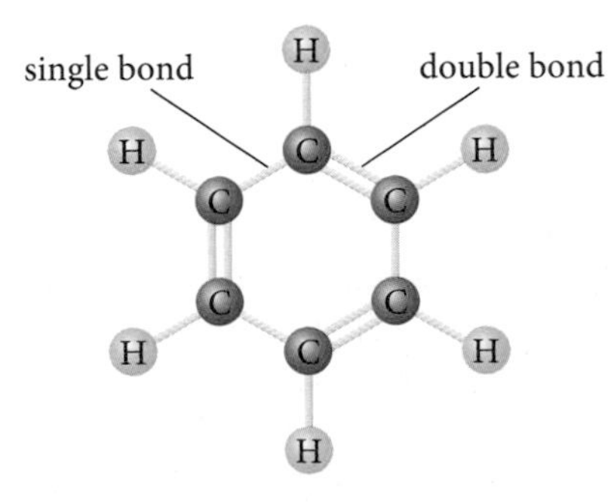

benzene ring

■ Timothy Berners-Lee

a single ovary and has one or more seeds and fleshy pulp. Grapes, tomatoes, blueberries, and avocados are berries in this technical sense. **b.** Any small, juicy, fleshy fruit, such as a raspberry or strawberry, regardless of its botanical structure. **2.** A seed or dried kernel of certain kinds of grain or other plants such as wheat, barley, or coffee.

beryl (bĕr′əl) A usually green or bluish-green mineral that is a silicate of beryllium and aluminum. Beryl occurs as transparent to translucent prisms in igneous and metamorphic rocks. Transparent varieties, such as emeralds, are valued as gems. Beryl is the main source of the element beryllium.

beryllium (bə-rĭl′ē-əm) A hard, lightweight, steel-gray metallic element that is an alkaline-earth metal and is found in various minerals, especially beryl. It has a high melting point and resists corrosion. Beryllium is used to make sturdy, lightweight alloys and to control the speed of neutrons inside the core of nuclear reactors. *Symbol* **Be.** *Atomic number* 4. *See* **Periodic Table,** pages 254–255.

Berzelius (bər-zē′lē-əs), Baron **Jöns Jakob** 1779–1848. Swedish chemist who is regarded as one of the founders of modern chemistry. Berzelius developed the concepts of the ion and of ionic compounds and made extensive determinations of atomic weights. He also introduced the classical system of chemical symbols, in which the names of elements are identified by one or two letters.

Bessemer process (bĕs′ə-mər) A method for making steel by forcing compressed air through molten iron to reduce the amount of carbon and burn out impurities.

Best (bĕst), **Charles Herbert** 1899–1978. American-born Canadian physiologist noted for his work with Frederick Banting on the isolation and use of insulin. Later in his career, Best discovered the vitamin choline and the enzyme histaminase, which breaks down histamine.

beta carotene (bā′tə) A form of carotene that is found in many plants, especially in yellow or orange fruits and vegetables and in leafy green vegetables. Beta carotene is converted to vitamin A in the liver.

beta particle An electron emitted by certain atomic nuclei when they undergo radioactive decay. A beta particle is created when a neutron changes into a proton. Beta particles have greater speed and penetrating power than alpha particles. ❖ The process of emitting a beta particle is called **beta decay.** When an atom undergoes beta decay, its atomic number increases by one and its mass number stays the same. *See more at* **radiation, radioactive decay.**

Betelgeuse (bēt′l-jo͞oz′) A reddish, very bright variable star in the constellation Orion. It is a supergiant. *See Note at* **Rigel.**

Bethe (bā′tə), **Hans Albrecht** 1906–2005. German-born American physicist who helped to develop quantum physics and described the nuclear reactions that produce energy in the sun and other stars. Bethe played an important role in the development of the atomic bomb, later working to educate the public about the threat of nuclear weapons.

Bh The symbol for **bohrium.**

Bhaskara (bäs′kə-rə) 1114–1185? Indian math-

■ Hans Bethe

Did You Know...?

Big Bang

It's a chilling thought: In the 1920s, astronomers found that wherever they looked in space, distant galaxies were rapidly moving away from Earth. In other words, the universe was getting larger and larger. By calculating the speed of several galaxies and working back from there, astronomers calculated that this expansion must have begun about 14 billion years ago, when the entire universe was smaller than a dime and almost infinitely dense. According to the widely accepted *Big Bang* theory, a massive explosion kicked off the expansion and was the origin of space and time. Now scientists must figure out how much mass the universe contains in order to see what lies ahead. If there is enough mass, the gravity attracting all the pieces to each other will eventually stop the expansion and pull all the pieces of the universe back together in a "big crunch" that would reduce all matter to a single point. Scientists call this model of the universe a "closed universe." If there is not enough mass, then we would be inhabiting what's called an "open universe" that would expand forever. All the galaxies and stars would continue to fly away from each other and eventually become dark and cold.

ematician who is noted for his contributions to the study of algebra and trigonometry and for his speculations on the relationship between zero and infinity.

Bi The symbol for **bismuth.**

bi– A prefix meaning "two." It is often used to form adjectives meaning "having two of" or "having double" something, such as in *bilateral,* having two sides.

bicarbonate (bī-kär**′**bə-nāt′) The anion HCO_3^- or a compound containing it, such as sodium bicarbonate.

bicarbonate of soda *See* **sodium bicarbonate.**

biceps (bī**′**sĕps′) The muscle at the front of the upper arm that bends the elbow. The biceps has two points of origin.

bicuspid (bī-kŭs**′**pĭd) A tooth having two points or cusps, especially a premolar.

biennial (bī-ĕn**′**ē-əl) *Botany. Adjective* **1.** Having a life cycle that normally takes two growing seasons to complete. —*Noun* **2.** A biennial plant. Carrots, parsnips, and sugar beets are some examples of biennials.

Big Bang The violent explosion of an extremely small, hot, and dense body of matter about 14 billion years ago. According to the Big Bang theory, the entire universe began with this explosion.

Big Dipper A group of seven stars in the constellation Ursa Major. Four stars form the bowl and three form the handle in the outline of a dipper.

bilateral symmetry (bī-lăt**′**ər-əl) An arrangement of parts, such as the structures of an organism, such that the body can be divided into mirror-image left and right halves by only one plane. *Compare* **radial symmetry.**

bile (bīl) A bitter, alkaline, greenish or brownish fluid that is produced by the liver, stored in the gallbladder, and released into the small intestine, where it helps to digest fats and neutralize acids.

bill (bĭl) A structure projecting from the head of a bird, consisting of the upper and lower jaws and their horny covering; a beak.

binary (bī**′**nə-rē) **1.** Having two parts. **2.** *Mathematics* Based on the number 2 or the binary number system.

binary digit Either of the digits 0 or 1, used in the binary number system.

binary fission *See* **fission** (sense 1).

binary number system A method of represent-

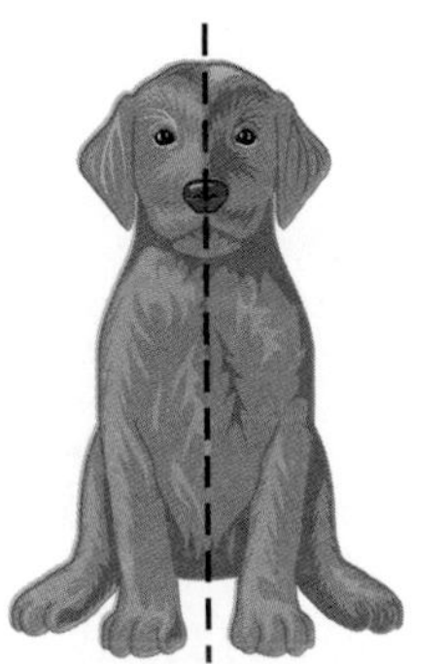

bilateral symmetry

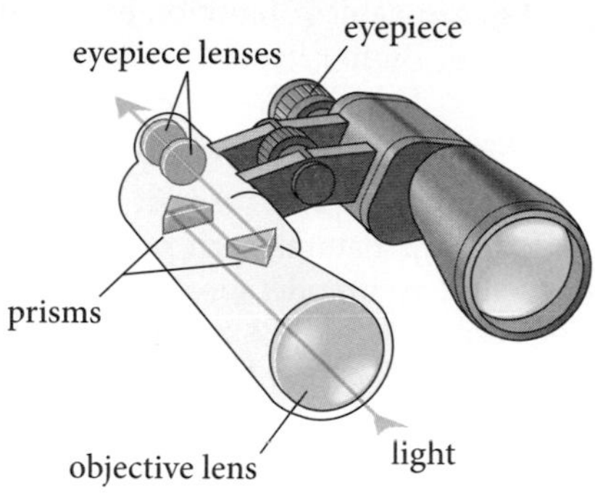

■ **binoculars**

ing numbers that has 2 as its base and uses only the digits 0 and 1. Each successive digit represents a power of 2. For example, 10011 represents $(1 \times 2^4) + (0 \times 2^3) + (0 \times 2^2) + (1 \times 2^1) + (1 \times 2^0)$, or $16 + 0 + 0 + 2 + 1$, or 19.

binary star A system of two stars that orbit a common center of mass. The pair often appears as a single star to the unaided eye.

binocular (bə-nŏk′yə-lər) Relating to or involving both eyes at once: *binocular vision.*

binoculars (bə-nŏk′yə-lərz) A device used to view objects that are far away, consisting of two small telescopes mounted next to each other. Binoculars are designed for use by both eyes at the same time.

binomial (bī-nō′mē-əl) A mathematical expression consisting of the sum or difference of two monomials, such as $3a^2 + 2b$.

binomial nomenclature The system used in science to name an organism, consisting of two terms, the first indicating the genus and the second indicating the species. *Mus musculus,* the scientific name of the common house mouse, is an example of binomial nomenclature.

biochemistry (bī′ō-kĕm′ĭ-strē) The scientific study of the chemical composition of substances that form living matter and of the chemical processes that go on in living organisms.

biocomputing (bī′ō-kŏm-pyōō′tĭng) The use of cells or biological molecules such as DNA to perform the functions of an electronic computer.

biodegradable (bī′ō-dĭ-grā′də-bəl) Capable of being decomposed by the action of biological agents, especially bacteria: *biodegradable packaging.*

biodiversity (bī′ō-dĭ-vûr′sĭ-tē) The number and variety of different organisms found within a specified geographic region.

bioethics (bī′ō-ĕth′ĭks) The study of the ethics surrounding medical research and health-care practices.

biofuel (bī′ō-fyōō′əl) Fuel that is produced from renewable resources, especially corn and other plants, vegetable oils, or treated municipal and industrial wastes.

biogeography (bī′ō-jē-ŏg′rə-fē) The scientific study of the geographic distribution of plant and animal life.

biological clock (bī′ə-lŏj′ĭ-kəl) An internal mechanism in organisms that controls the cycle of various functions, such as sleep cycles in mammals and photosynthesis in plants. *See Note at* **circadian rhythm.**

biology (bī-ŏl′ə-jē) The scientific study of life and of living organisms. Botany, zoology, microbiology, and genetics are all branches of biology.

bioluminescence (bī′ō-lōō′mə-nĕs′əns) Emission of light by living organisms, such as fireflies and certain fish, squids, jellyfish, fungi, and bacteria. It occurs when chemical compounds react and give off light.

biomass (bī′ō-măs′) **1.** The total amount of living material in a given area. **2.** Plants, residue

■ **bioluminescence**
a bioluminescent squid

biome

top to bottom: *desert in Arizona, rainforest in Hawaii, and taiga in the Altai Mountains region of Russia*

from paper mills, agricultural waste, or other organic materials used as a fuel or energy source. Biomass fuels produce less carbon dioxide than some fossil fuels, such as petroleum.

biome (bī′ōm′) A large community of plants, animals, and other organisms that occupies a distinct region defined by its climate and dominant vegetation. Grassland, tundra, desert, and tropical rainforest are all examples of biomes.

biomechanics (bī′ō-mĭ-kăn′ĭks) The scientific study of the mechanics of motion in humans and other animals. Biomechanics is sometimes used by athletes to help analyze and improve their performance.

bionics (bī-ŏn′ĭks) The use of a system or design found in nature, such as the design of insects' wings, as a model for designing artificial systems, especially mechanical or electronic systems. —*Adjective* **bionic.**

biophysics (bī′ō-fĭz′ĭks) The scientific study of biological systems and processes using the methods of physics.

biopsy (bī′ŏp′sē) A sample of tissue removed by a surgeon from a living body for examination and diagnosis.

biorhythm (bī′ō-rĭ*th*′əm) A recurring biological process, such as sleep, that is controlled by the circadian rhythms of an organism.

biosphere (bī′ə-sfîr′) The parts of the Earth and its atmosphere in which living organisms exist, along with all those organisms.

biotechnology (bī′ō-tĕk-nŏl′ə-jē) **1.** The use of techniques involving the modification of genes in living organisms to develop useful products or substances, as when genes for herbicide resistance are inserted into the cells of corn plants. *See more at* **genetic engineering. 2.** The use of living organisms to solve an engineering problem or perform an industrial task. Using bacteria that feed on hydrocarbons to clean up an oil spill is one example of biotechnology.

biotic (bī-ŏt′ĭk) Relating to living organisms: *the biotic components of an ecosystem.*

biotin (bī′ə-tĭn) A vitamin belonging to the vitamin B complex that is necessary for the action of many enzymes and is important in the metabolism of carbohydrates, fats, and proteins. It is found in liver, egg yolks, milk, and yeast.

biotite (bī′ə-tīt′) A dark-brown to black mica found in igneous and metamorphic rocks.

biped (bī′pĕd′) An animal having two feet, such as a bird or human.

bipedal (bī-pĕd′l) Standing or walking on two feet. ❖ The use of two feet for standing and walking is known as **bipedalism** or **bipedal locomotion.** Humans are the only primates that are strictly bipedal. Anthropologists believe that the first human ancestors to exhibit bipedalism lived about four million years ago.

bipolar disorder (bī-pō′lər) A mental disorder characterized by periods of sadness and lack of energy alternating with periods of happiness and energetic activity.

bird (bûrd) Any of numerous warm-blooded, egg-laying vertebrate animals that have wings for forelimbs, a body covered with feathers, a hard bill covering the jaws, no teeth, and a four-chambered heart.

bird of prey Any of various birds, such as a hawk, eagle, owl, or vulture, that hunt and kill other animals for food or that feed on dead animals.

bismuth (bĭz′məth) A brittle, pinkish-white, crystalline metallic element that occurs in nature as a free metal and in various ores. Bismuth has the greatest resistance to being magnetized of all metals and has the highest atomic number of all stable elements. It is used to make low-melting alloys for fire-safety devices. *Symbol* **Bi.** *Atomic number* 83. *See* **Periodic Table,** pages 254–255.

Did You Know...?

birds: modern-day dinosaurs?

The discovery of the first archaeopteryx fossil in Germany in 1861 was a triumph for Darwin's theory of evolution, which had appeared in print just two years before. The ancient creature, about the size of a crow, had wings and feathers, like a bird, but it also had a long bony tail, claws at the end of its fingers, and teeth, like a dinosaur. Archaeopteryx dates from the Jurassic Period, about 150 million years ago. It is regarded as the earliest known *bird* and is widely thought to represent a transitional stage in the evolution of birds from some sort of dinosaur-like ancestor. How exactly that evolution occurred, however, is not known. How did limbs evolve into wings, and scales into feathers? Most scientists believe that birds developed from small meat-eating dinosaurs similar to the velociraptor. Paleontologists in China have made exciting fossil finds showing that some of these dinosaurs were covered with feathers. The feathers might have served as insulation, as camouflage, or for gliding. Over millions of years, natural selection may have favored gliders that had more and more powerful wings—until eventually birds became fully adapted to flying through the air with great ease.

bisphenol A (bĭs′fē′nôl′) A synthetic chemical that is used to make certain kinds of plastics. It is suspected of causing health problems by interfering with the body's hormones.

bit (bĭt) The smallest unit of computer memory. A bit holds one of two possible values, either of the binary digits 0 or 1. *See Note at* **byte.**

bitmap (bĭt′măp′) *Computers* A set of bits that represents a graphic image, with each bit or group of bits corresponding to a pixel in the image.

bitumen (bĭ-to͞o′mən) Any of various flammable mixtures of hydrocarbons that occur naturally or are produced from petroleum and coal. Bitumens are a component of asphalt pavement and are used for surfacing roads and for waterproofing.

bituminous coal (bĭ-to͞o′mə-nəs) A soft type of coal that burns with a smoky, yellow flame. Bituminous coal is the most abundant form of coal, but because of its high sulfur content its use can contribute to air pollution and acid rain. *Compare* **anthracite, lignite.**

bivalent (bī-vā′lənt) *Chemistry* Divalent.

bivalve (bī′vălv′) Any of numerous freshwater or marine mollusks having a shell that consists of two parts connected by a hinge. Clams, mussels, oysters, and scallops are all bivalves. *Compare* **univalve.**

Bk The symbol for **berkelium.**

Black (blăk), **Joseph** 1728–1799. British chemist. In 1756 he discovered carbon dioxide, which he called "fixed air." In addition to further studies of carbon dioxide, Black formulated the concepts of latent heat and specific heat.

black dwarf A celestial object that consists of the remains of a white dwarf after it has used up all of its energy and no longer gives off detectable radiation. *See Note at* **dwarf star.**

black hole A massive star in the last phase of its evolution, in which the star collapses, creating a

Did You Know...?

black hole

One of the strangest objects in the universe is the burnt-out remnant of a large star, known as a *black hole.* The name comes from the fact that the star collapses into itself, becoming so dense that its gravitational pull keeps even light from escaping. And if light can't get out, then nothing that enters the black hole would ever escape. A rocket that propels a spacecraft to the moon or Mars needs to achieve what is called *escape velocity,* the speed necessary to overcome the Earth's gravity. But since nothing can go faster than the speed of light, nothing could go fast enough to reach the escape velocity necessary to emerge from a black hole. If black holes emit no light, how do astronomers know about them? They detect them by observing the behavior of nearby material, such as dust particles that emit x-rays as they heat up while being sucked into a black hole.

gravitational field that is so strong that nothing can escape, not even light. *See more at* **star.**

black lung A lung disease of coal miners that is caused by the long-term inhalation of coal dust.

Blackwell (blăk′wĕl′), **Elizabeth** 1821–1910. British-born American physician who was the first woman to be awarded a medical doctorate in modern times (1849). She founded an infirmary for women and children in New York City that her sister **Emily Blackwell** (1826–1910), also a physician, directed. Emily Blackwell was the first woman doctor to perform major surgeries on a regular basis.

Elizabeth Blackwell

black widow Any of several spiders with a black shiny body, the female of which is venomous and often has red markings in the shape of an hourglass on the underside.

bladder (blăd′ər) **1.** A sac-shaped organ that stores the urine secreted by the kidneys, found in most vertebrates except birds and some reptiles. In mammals, the bladder is connected to each kidney by a ureter. **2.** A swim bladder.

blastula (blăs′chə-lə) *Plural* **blastulas** *or* **blastulae** (blăs′chə-lē′) An embryo at the stage immediately following the division of the fertilized egg cell, consisting of a ball-shaped layer of cells around a fluid-filled cavity. *Compare* **gastrula.**

blight (blīt) **1.** Any of numerous plant diseases that cause leaves, stems, or fruits to wither and die. **2.** The bacterium, fungus, or virus that causes such a disease.

block and tackle (blŏk) A device consisting of a fixed pulley and a movable one, used to reduce the amount of force needed to move heavy loads. One pulley is attached to the load, and a rope connects this pulley to the fixed pulley. Pulling on the rope draws the load-bearing pulley, along with the load, toward the fixed pulley. The more times the rope is passed around the two pulleys, the less effort is needed to raise the load.

blood (blŭd) **1.** The fluid that circulates through blood vessels in the body of a vertebrate animal by the action of the heart, carrying oxygen and nutrients to the body's cells and removing waste products. In humans and other mammals, blood

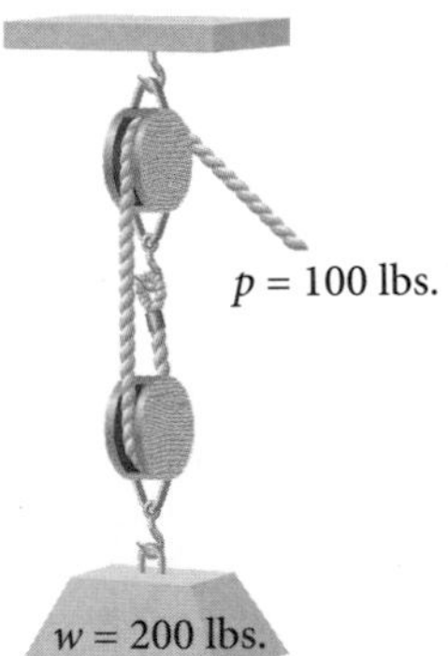

block and tackle

With a two-pulley block and tackle unit, the amount of pull (p) required to lift a weight (w) is half the amount of the weight.

consists of a liquid (called plasma) in which red blood cells, white blood cells, and platelets are suspended. **2.** A fluid in many invertebrate animals that is similar in function.

blood cell Any of the cells contained in blood, especially a red blood cell or a white blood cell.

blood clot A group of blood cells and platelets that clump together to form a clot, usually in a blood vessel. Blood clots can interfere with the circulation of blood.

blood gas The concentration of a gas, especially oxygen or carbon dioxide, in the blood. Analysis of blood gases is used in medicine to help diagnose disease and monitor a person's response to treatment.

blood group *See* **blood type.**

blood plasma *See* **plasma** (sense 1).

blood pressure The pressure that the blood exerts on the walls of the arteries or other blood vessels. Blood pressure varies with the strength of the heartbeat, the volume of the blood, the elasticity of the arteries, and the individual's health, age, and physical condition. *See more at* **high blood pressure.**

Did You Know...?

blood types

Blood transfusions were once a big problem—they often caused people to become sick and die. But in the 1890s, a scientist named Karl Landsteiner began to solve the transfusion puzzle. He found that all human blood could be divided into four groups, or *blood types,* which he named A, B, AB, and O. The letters A and B refer to substances, called *antigens,* that are found on the surface of red blood cells. Antibodies circulating in a person's blood normally recognize the antigens in that same person's blood cells and don't react with them. If a person receives a transfusion of blood of the wrong type, the person's antibodies bind to the antigens on the mismatched red blood cells, causing clumping of the cells. So the key to the puzzle is to give a person blood that matches his or her blood type. Because the red blood cells in type O blood have no antigens on the surface, anyone can receive a transfusion with type O blood.

blowhole
of a beluga whale

blood serum Blood plasma, especially blood plasma from which factors that cause clotting of the blood have been removed.

blood type Any of the four main types into which human blood is divided: A, B, AB, and O. Blood types are based on the presence or absence of certain substances, called antigens, on red blood cells. Also called *blood group.*

blood vessel An elastic tubular structure in the body through which blood circulates; an artery, vein, or capillary.

blowhole (blō′hōl′) **1.** An opening or one of a pair of openings used for breathing and located on the top of the head of a whale, porpoise, or dolphin. **2.** A hole in the ice to which marine mammals such as seals and whales come to breathe.

blubber (blŭb′ər) The thick layer of fat lying between the skin and the muscle layers of whales and other marine mammals. Blubber insulates the animal from heat loss and serves as a food reserve.

blue-green alga (blo͞o′grēn′) *See* **cyanobacterium.**

blue supergiant A supergiant star with surface temperature ranging from 10,000 to 40,000 kelvin (17,540° to 71,540°F), making the star appear blue-white.

bog (bôg) A wetland in which the ground consists mainly of wet, partly decayed mosses or other plant material. Many of the plants that live in bogs

BIOGRAPHY

Niels Bohr

In the early 1900s, scientists thought that atoms consisted of electrons scattered evenly throughout a positively charged blob. In 1911, Ernest Rutherford discovered that atoms have a very small, positively charged nucleus, and he developed a different model of the atom, in which negatively charged electrons orbit a central nucleus, like planets orbiting the sun. Niels Bohr became interested in Rutherford's model, but it puzzled him because according to the laws of physics known at the time, it should be very unstable. To explain the atom's stability, Bohr proposed that electrons could travel around the nucleus only in certain orbits at specific energy levels. If an electron's energy increased or decreased, it could jump to a higher or lower orbit. In Bohr's model, an electron jumps from a lower energy orbit to a higher energy orbit by absorbing a photon of light whose energy is equal to the difference between the energy levels of the two orbits. Similarly, an electron jumps down from a higher energy orbit to a lower energy orbit by emitting a photon with an energy equal to the difference in energy between the two orbits. Bohr's model explained why hydrogen (which has only one proton and one electron) emits and absorbs light only of certain frequencies, corresponding to the difference in energy levels of orbits that the electron can occupy. Bohr was awarded a Nobel Prize in physics in 1922 for his theory, which led to the development of quantum mechanics.

have adaptations that allow them to survive in an acidic environment with few available nutrients.

Bohr (bôr), **Niels Henrik David** 1885–1962. Danish physicist who investigated the structure of atoms and the nature of radiation. He proposed that electrons orbit the nucleus of an atom only at certain energy levels. When an electron changes levels, it gains or loses an amount of energy, in the form of electromagnetic radiation, that equals the difference between those two levels. His concepts were fundamental to the theory of quantum mechanics and to the understanding of nuclear fission.

bohrium (bôr′ē-əm) A synthetic, radioactive element that can be produced by bombarding bismuth with chromium atoms. Its most stable isotope has a half-life of 1.3 seconds. *Symbol* **Bh.** *Atomic number* 107. *See* **Periodic Table,** pages 254–255.

boil (boil) To change from a liquid to a gaseous state by heating or being heated to the boiling point.

boiling point (boi′lĭng) The temperature at which a liquid changes to a vapor or gas. As the temperature of a liquid rises, the pressure of escaping vapor also rises, and at the boiling point the pressure of the escaping vapor is equal to that exerted on the liquid by the surrounding air, causing bubbles to form. Typically boiling points are measured at sea level. At higher altitudes, where atmospheric pressure is lower, boiling points are lower. The boiling point of water at sea level is 212°F (100°C); that of mercury is 673.84°F (356.58°C).

Boltzmann (bôlts′män′), **Ludwig** 1844–1906. Austrian physicist who developed statistical mechanics, the branch of physics that explains how the properties of atoms (such as mass and structure) determine the visible properties of matter (such as viscosity and heat conduction). Through his investigations of thermodynamics, Boltzmann developed numerous theories about the laws governing atomic motion and energy.

bond (bŏnd) A force of attraction that holds atoms or ions together in a molecule or crystal. Bonds are usually created by a sharing or transfer of one or more electrons. Single, double, and triple bonds are most common. *See also* **covalent bond, ionic bond, metallic bond.**

bone (bōn) **1.** The hard, dense, calcified tissue

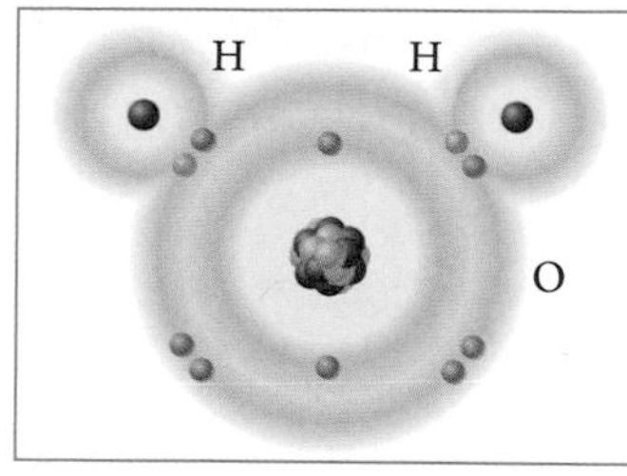

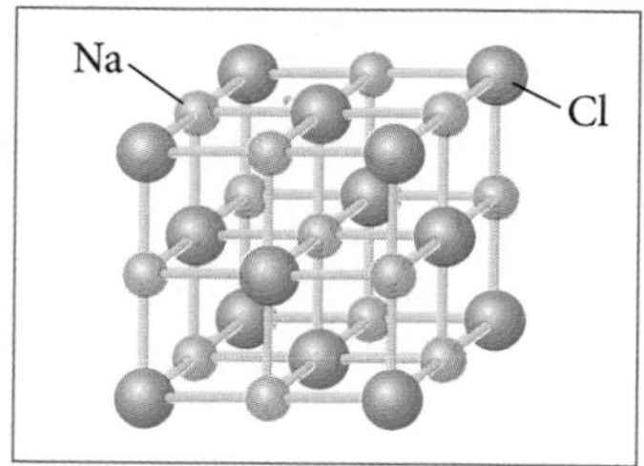

bond

In a water molecule (left), *each hydrogen atom (H) shares an electron (yellow) with the oxygen atom (O), forming covalent bonds. In silver* (center), *a metal, the negatively charged electrons (e) "float" around positively charged silver ions (Ag), illustrating metallic bonding. In sodium chloride, or salt* (right), *the sodium atom (Na) donates an electron to the chlorine atom (Cl), forming an ionic bond.*

that forms the skeleton of most vertebrates. Bone serves as a framework for the attachment of muscles and protects vital organs, such as the brain. It also contains large amounts of calcium, a mineral that is essential for proper cell function. *See more at* **osteoblast, osteoclast, osteocyte.** **2.** Any of the bones in a skeleton, such as the femur in the leg of a mammal.

bone marrow The spongy tissue that fills the bone cavities of most vertebrates. In mammals, red blood cells, platelets, and the majority of white blood cells are produced by the bone marrow.

bonobo (bə-nō′bō) *Plural* **bonobos** A dark-haired African ape that is closely related to and resembles the chimpanzee but has a more slender build. Bonobos are found only in the Democratic Republic of the Congo, south of the Congo River.

bony fish (bō′nē) A fish having a skeleton composed chiefly of bone rather than cartilage. Most living species of fish are bony fish. *Compare* **cartilaginous fish, jawless fish.**

book lung (bo͝ok) One of the paired organs used for breathing by spiders, scorpions, and some other arachnids. Book lungs are located on the underside of the abdomen and consist of membranes arranged in several parallel folds like the pages of a book.

Boole (bo͞ol), **George** 1815–1864. British mathematician who wrote important works on many different areas of mathematics. He developed a method to describe reasoning using algebra that is now known as Boolean algebra.

Boolean algebra (bo͞o′lē-ən) A mathematical system dealing with the relationship between sets, used to solve problems in logic and engineering. Variables consist of 0 and 1, and operations are expressed as AND, OR, and NOT. Boolean algebra has been important in the development of modern computers and programming.

Boötes (bō-ō′tēz) A constellation in the Northern Hemisphere near Virgo and Corona Borealis. It contains the bright star Arcturus.

borate (bôr′āt′) **1.** A salt, ester, or anion of boric acid. **2.** Any of a family of compounds or ions composed of boron and oxygen.

borax (bôr′ăks′) A white, powdery boron compound, $Na_2B_4O_7{\cdot}10H_2O$, that is used as a household cleaner and in making insulation and heat-resistant glass.

boreal (bôr′ē-əl) Relating to the forest areas of the northern hemisphere that are dominated by coniferous trees such as spruces, firs, and pines.

boric acid (bôr′ĭk) A white or colorless crystalline compound, H_3BO_3, either naturally occurring or made from borax. It is used as an antiseptic and preservative, and in cements, enamels, and cosmetics.

boron (bôr′ŏn′) A shiny, brittle, black nonmetallic element extracted chiefly from borax. It conducts electricity well at high temperatures but poorly at low temperatures. Boron is necessary for the growth of land plants and is used to make soaps, abrasives, control rods for nuclear reactors, and hard alloys. *Symbol* **B.** *Atomic number* 5. *See* **Periodic Table,** pages 254–255.

Bose (bōs, bōz), **Satyendra Nath** 1894–1974. Indian physicist known for his work in quantum theory, especially the development of a method used to describe the behavior of subatomic particles.

botany (bŏt**′**n-ē) The scientific study of plants, including their growth and structure.

botulism (bŏch**′**ə-lĭz′əm) A severe, sometimes fatal form of food poisoning caused by eating food contaminated with a bacterium that produces a powerful nerve toxin. The bacterium is usually found in food that has been improperly preserved. ❖ The nerve toxin produced by this bacterium is called **botulin** (bŏch**′**ə-lĭn).

bovine (bō**′**vīn′) *Adjective* **1.** Relating to cows and closely related ruminant mammals, such as yaks. —*Noun* **2.** A cow or a closely related ruminant mammal.

bovine spongiform encephalopathy (spŭn**′**jĭ-fôrm′ ĕn-sĕf′ə-lŏp**′**ə-thē) *See* **mad cow disease.**

bowel (bou**′**əl) The intestine, especially of a human. Often used in the plural as *bowels.*

Boyle (boil), **Robert** 1627–1691. English physicist and chemist whose book, *The Sceptical Chemist* (1661), marked the beginning of modern chemistry. Boyle rejected the traditional theory that all matter was composed of four elements and defined an element as a substance that cannot be reduced to other, simpler substances or produced by combining simpler substances. Boyle also conducted important physics experiments with Robert Hooke that led to the development of Boyle's law.

Boyle's law A physical law stating that the volume of a given amount of a gas increases as its pressure decreases and decreases as its pressure increases, as long as the temperature remains constant. *Compare* **Charles's law.**

BPA Abbreviation of **bisphenol A.**

Br The symbol for **bromine.**

brachial (brā**′**kē-əl) Relating to or resembling the arm or a similar part.

brachiopod (brā**′**kē-ə-pŏd′) Any of various invertebrate sea animals having paired shells attached to a stalk and a ring of hollow tentacles covered with cilia that sweep food particles into the mouth. Brachiopods were much more common during the Paleozoic Era than they are now, and they are often found as fossils.

brachiosaurus (brā′kē-ə-sôr**′**əs) A massive sauropod dinosaur of the Jurassic Period. It had forelegs that were longer than the hind legs, and nostrils and eyes set high up on the head.

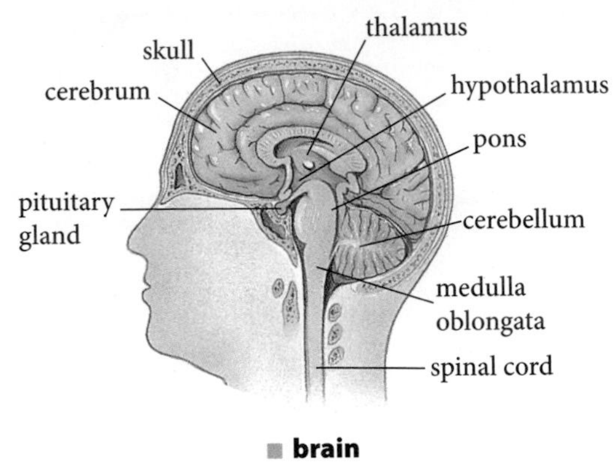

■ **brain**

brackish (brăk**′**ĭsh) Containing a mixture of seawater and fresh water; somewhat salty.

bract (brăkt) A small plant part resembling a leaf and growing at the base of a flower or a flower cluster. Most bracts are small and inconspicuous, but some, as in the poinsettia, are showy or brightly colored and resemble petals.

Bragg (brăg), Sir **William Henry** 1862–1942. British physicist who invented a device used to measure x-ray wavelengths. With his son, the physicist Sir **William Lawrence Bragg** (1890–1971), he developed the technique of x-ray crystallography, used to determine the atomic structure of crystals.

Brahe (brä, brä**′**hē), **Tycho** 1546–1601. Danish astronomer who made the most accurate and extensive observations of the planets and stars in the age before the telescope. Brahe determined the position of 777 stars, demonstrated that comets follow regular paths, and observed the supernova of 1572, which became known as Tycho's star.

brain (brān) **1.** The part of the nervous system in vertebrates that is enclosed within the skull, is connected with the spinal cord, and is composed of gray matter and white matter. It receives and interprets impulses from sense organs, and it coordinates and controls body functions and activities such as walking and talking. The brain is also the center of memory, thought, and emotion. **2.** A bundle of nerves in many invertebrate animals that is similar to the vertebrate brain in function and position.

brainstem (brān**′**stĕm′) The part of the

Did You Know...?

brain

At this very moment, while you are reading this note, your *brain* is performing thousands of complex activities. Light rays reaching your eyes are being transformed into nerve impulses in your optic nerves. Squiggles on the page or screen are being translated into words. Your auditory nerves are transmitting sound waves that hit your eardrums. Without even realizing it, you are continuing to breathe and to pump blood through your body. All of these activities are taking place in very specific regions of the brain. The *brainstem* is where involuntary processes like breathing and heart rate are controlled. The back part of your brain, the *cerebellum,* controls balance and posture. Most conscious thinking takes place in the *cerebrum.* The right half, or *hemisphere,* of the cerebrum is responsible for musical and artistic ability and the ability to recognize faces. The left hemisphere is where mathematical and logical analysis takes place, as well as most language processing. Each hemisphere is in turn divided into four *lobes* (frontal, occipital, parietal, and temporal) that have their own special functions. Perhaps the best proof of the brain's power is that it can think about itself!

vertebrate brain located at the base of the brain and important in the control of many voluntary and involuntary body functions. In humans and other mammals, the brainstem is composed of the pons, medulla oblongata, and midbrain.

brass (brăs) A yellowish alloy of copper and zinc, usually 67 percent copper and 33 percent zinc. It sometimes includes small amounts of other metals. Brass is characterized by being strong and ductile, and by being resistant to many forms of corrosion.

breast (brĕst) **1.** One of a pair of milk-producing mammary glands in human females. Breasts are present but undeveloped in human males. **2.** The upper part of the front surface of the human body, extending from the neck to the abdomen, or a similar part of other animals.

breastbone (brĕst′bōn′) *See* **sternum.**

breed (brēd) *Verb* **1.** To produce offspring: *Mosquitoes breed rapidly.* **2.** To raise animals or plants, often to produce new or improved types: *breed a new type of corn.* —*Noun* **3.** A group of organisms having common ancestors and sharing certain traits that are not shared with other members of the same species. Breeds are usually produced by mating selected parents.

brine (brīn) **1.** Water saturated with or containing large amounts of a salt, especially sodium chloride. **2.** The water of a sea or an ocean.

British thermal unit (brĭt′ĭsh) The amount of heat that is needed to raise the temperature of one pound of water by one degree Fahrenheit. This unit is used mainly to measure heat, but it can be applied to other forms of energy.

brittle (brĭt′l) Likely to break, snap, or crack. *Compare* **ductile.**

bromate (brō′māt′) A chemical compound containing the group BrO_3.

bromeliad (brō-mē′lē-ăd′) Any of various tropical plants of the Western Hemisphere, usually having long stiff leaves, colorful flowers, and showy bracts. Many species of bromeliad grow on trees as epiphytes. The pineapple and Spanish moss are bromeliads.

bromide (brō′mīd′) An anion of bromine or a compound containing this anion, such as potassium bromide.

bromine (brō′mēn) A reddish-brown halogen element that can be found in combined form in ocean water. The pure form is a nonmetallic corrosive liquid that gives off a highly irritating vapor. It is used to make dyes, sedatives, and

bromeliad

photographic film. *Symbol* **Br.** *Atomic number* 35. *See* **Periodic Table,** pages 254–255.

bronchial tube (brŏng′kē-əl) A bronchus or any of the tubes branching from a bronchus. The bronchial tubes decrease in size as they descend into the lungs.

bronchiole (brŏng′kē-ōl′) Any of the small, thin-walled tubes that branch from the bronchi of the lungs. At the ends of the bronchioles are the small air sacs called alveoli.

bronchitis (brŏng-kī′tĭs) Inflammation of the bronchial tubes, often resulting from infection with a virus.

bronchus (brŏng′kəs) *Plural* **bronchi** (brŏng′-kī′, brŏng′kē′) Either of the two main tubular structures that branch off from the trachea and lead to the lungs, where they divide into smaller branches.

brontosaurus (brŏn′tə-sôr′əs) *An earlier name for* **apatosaurus.**

bronze (brŏnz) **1.** An alloy of copper and tin, sometimes with small amounts of other metals. Bronze is harder than brass and is used both in industry and in art. **2.** An alloy of copper and certain metals other than tin, such as aluminum.

WORD HISTORY

brontosaurus

Take a little deception, add a little excitement, stir them with a century-long mistake, and you have the mystery of the brontosaurus. Specifically, you have the mystery of its name. For 100 years this 70-foot-long, 30-ton vegetarian giant had two names. This case of double identity began in 1877, when bones of a large dinosaur were discovered. The creature was dubbed *Apatosaurus,* a name that meant "deceptive lizard" or "unreal lizard." Two years later, bones of a larger dinosaur were found, and in all the excitement, scientists named it *Brontosaurus,* or "thunder lizard." This name stuck until scientists decided it was all a mistake—the two sets of bones actually belonged to the same type of dinosaur. Since it is a rule in taxonomy that the first name given to a newly discovered organism is the one that must be used, scientists have had to use the name *Apatosaurus.* But "thunder lizard" had popular appeal, and many people still prefer to call the beast a brontosaurus.

brown dwarf (broun) A celestial object that is more massive than a gas giant such as Jupiter but not massive enough to sustain the hydrogen fusion reactions that produce radiant energy in stars. *See Note at* **dwarf star.**

Brownian motion (brou′nē-ən) The random movement of microscopic particles suspended in a liquid or gas, caused by collisions between these particles and the molecules of the liquid or gas.

browser (brou′zər) A computer program that accesses and displays files and other data available on the Internet.

bryophyte (brī′ə-fīt′) Any of a large group of plants that live on land, reproduce by spores, and do not have vascular tissues to circulate water and food. Bryophytes include the mosses and liverworts.

bryozoan (brī′ə-zō′ən) Any of various small aquatic animals that reproduce by budding and form mosslike or branching colonies attached to stones or seaweed.

Btu Abbreviation of **British thermal unit.**

bubble chamber (bŭb′əl) A particle detector that records the tracks of charged subatomic particles, such as electrons. A bubble chamber consists of a container filled with a liquid that is nearly boiling and vaporizing. The path of a charged particle is revealed as a trail of tiny bubbles of vapor in the liquid. Bubble chambers replaced cloud chambers and have in turn been replaced by more modern particle detectors. *Compare* **cloud chamber.**

bubo (bo͞o′bō) A swelling of a lymph node, especially of the armpit or groin. Buboes are characteristic of bubonic plague.

bubonic plague (bo͞o-bŏn′ĭk) The most common form of plague, with symptoms including fever, vomiting, diarrhea, and inflamed lymph nodes (called buboes). It is transmitted by fleas from infected rats or other rodents. The Black Death, which killed around one third of the population of Europe and parts of Asia and Africa in the 1300s, was an epidemic of bubonic plague.

bud (bŭd) *Noun* **1.** A small swelling on a branch or stem containing an undeveloped flower, shoot,

USAGE

bug

In everyday language, people use the word *bug* to refer to all kinds of small creatures, including insects such as aphids, mosquitoes, and cockroaches, as well as other many-legged animals that are not insects, such as spiders, ticks, and centipedes. But for scientists, the word has a much narrower meaning. In strictest terms, bugs are insects with mouthparts that are used for piercing and sucking and are contained in a beak-shaped structure. Entomologists often call these insects "true bugs," to distinguish them better from what everyone else calls "bugs." Examples of true bugs are bedbugs, which feed on blood, and aphids and cicadas, which suck plant juices.

or leaf. **2.** A partly opened flower or leaf. **3.** A small outgrowth on a simple organism, such as a yeast or hydra, that grows into a complete new organism of the same species. **4.** A tiny part or organ, such as a taste bud, that is shaped like a bud. — *Verb* **5.** To form or produce a bud or buds.

buffer (bŭf′ər) **1.** *Chemistry* A solution that maintains a nearly constant pH even when small amounts of an acid or base are added to it. **2.** *Computers* A device or an area of a computer that temporarily stores data that is being transferred between two machines that process data at different rates, such as a computer and a printer.

Buffon (bo͞o-fôɴ′), Comte **Georges Louis Leclerc de** 1707–1788. French naturalist whose popular *Histoire Naturelle* (36 volumes published between 1749 and 1788) provided encyclopedic coverage of vertebrate biology, geology, and mineralogy and was renowned for its elegant style.

bug (bŭg) **1.** *Zoology* An insect having mouthparts used for piercing and sucking, such as an aphid or bedbug. Informally, the word *bug* is applied more widely. **2.** *Computers* An error or defect in a computer program.

bulb (bŭlb) **1.** A rounded underground stem surrounded by fleshy modified leaves, from which a shoot emerges that will grow into a new plant. Tulips and onions grow from bulbs. *Compare* **corm, rhizome, runner, tuber. 2.** The part of an incandescent or fluorescent device that gives off light. The bulb of an incandescent light contains a filament inside a usually rounded piece of glass. The bulb of a fluorescent light is a glass tube or chamber containing a mixture of gases without a filament.

bulimia (bo͞o-lē′mē-ə) An eating disorder in which episodes of binge eating are followed by fasting, self-induced vomiting, or other measures to prevent weight gain. It is most common among young women of normal or nearly normal weight.

Bunsen (bŭn′sən) **Robert Wilhelm** 1811–1899. German chemist who with Gustav Kirchhoff discovered the elements cesium and rubidium. Bunsen also explained the action of geysers and invented various kinds of laboratory equipment, including the Bunsen burner.

Bunsen burner A small gas burner used in laboratories. It consists of a vertical metal tube connected to a gas fuel source, with adjustable holes at its base. These holes allow air to enter the tube and mix with the gas in order to make a very hot flame.

buoyancy (boi′ən-sē) The upward force exerted on an object by a fluid in which it is immersed. Archimedes' Principle states that the buoyant force equals the weight of the fluid displaced by the object. If the buoyant force is equal to or greater than the weight of the object, the object floats; otherwise, it sinks. *See Note at* **Archimedes.**

burette (byo͞o-rĕt′) A glass tube with fine

Bunsen burner

gradations and with a tapered bottom that has a valve. It is used especially in laboratories to pour a measured amount of liquid from one container into another.

Burgess Shale (bûr′jĭs) A rock formation in the western Canadian Rockies that contains numerous fossilized invertebrates from the Cambrian Period.

burl (bûrl) A large, rounded outgrowth on the trunk or branch of a tree.

burn (bûrn) *Verb* **1.** To be on fire; undergo combustion. A substance burns if it is heated up enough to react chemically with oxygen. *See Note at* **oxidation.** —*Noun* **2.** *Medicine* An injury produced by fire, heat, radiation, electricity, or a chemical. Burns are classified according to the degree of damage done to the tissues.

Did You Know...?

Burgess Shale

Many of the invertebrate animals that evolved during the Cambrian Period would look very odd to us now. These animals had bizarre combinations of legs, spines, segments, and heads found in no animals since. The rapid evolution of such a diversity of life is known as the Cambrian Explosion. Many of these species became extinct and left no descendants, but others evolved into groups, such as the insects, that are familiar to us today. Most of our knowledge about these early life forms comes from the *Burgess Shale,* a 505-million-year-old formation of black shale in the Rocky Mountains of British Columbia. The unusual process of fossilization that occurred in this formation preserved the soft parts of organisms that are normally rotted away (by reacting with oxygen) before animals become fossils. The animals in the Burgess Shale were killed instantly by a mudslide deep in the ocean, where there is very little oxygen. After the mud buried the animals, it hardened into shale, which eventually was pushed up far above sea level by tectonic forces. Thanks to this event, we know a lot about the diversity of forms that filled the world's oceans before any living creatures had colonized the land.

■ **butte**
West Mitten Butte, Monument Valley Navajo Tribal Park, Utah

bursa (bûr′sə) *Plural* **bursae** (bûr′sē) *or* **bursas** A flattened sac containing a lubricating fluid that reduces friction between a muscle or tendon and a bone. ❖ Inflammation of a bursa is called **bursitis** (bər-sī′tĭs).

butane (byo͞o′tān′) An alkane, C_4H_{10}, found in natural gas and produced from petroleum. Butane is used as a fuel, refrigerant, and propellant in aerosol cans. —*Adjective* **butyl** (byo͞ot′l).

butte (byo͞ot) A steep-sided hill with a flat top, often standing alone in an otherwise flat area. A butte is smaller than a mesa.

butterfly (bŭt′ər-flī′) Any of numerous insects having four broad, often colorful wings, a narrow body, and slender antennae with knobs at the tips. Unlike moths, butterflies tend to hold their wings upright and together when at rest. *Compare* **moth.**

butyric acid (byo͞o-tîr′ĭk) A colorless organic acid, $C_4H_8O_2$, found in butter and certain plant oils. It has an unpleasant odor and is used in disinfectants and drugs.

bypass (bī′păs′) An alternative pathway for the flow of blood or other body fluid, created by a surgeon as a detour around a blocked or diseased organ.

byproduct or **by-product** (bī′prŏd′əkt) Something produced in the process of making something else. For example, oxygen is released as a byproduct of photosynthesis, and asphalt and paraffin are byproducts of the process of refining crude oil into gasoline.

Byrd (bûrd), **Richard Evelyn** 1888–1957. American naval officer and explorer who established a base for scientific discovery in Antarctica.

Byron (bī′rən), **Augusta Ada.** *See* **Lovelace, Ada.**

byte (bīt) A sequence of adjacent bits operated on as a unit by a computer. A byte usually consists of eight bits. Amounts of computer memory are often expressed in terms of megabytes (1,048,576 bytes) or gigabytes (1,073,741,824 bytes).

Richard Byrd

USAGE

byte/bit

The word *bit* is short for *bi*nary digi*t*. A bit consists of one of two values, usually 0 or 1. Computers use bits because their system of counting is based on two options: switches on a microchip that are either *on* or *off*. Thus, a computer counts to seven in bits as follows: 0, 1, 10 [2], 11 [3], 100 [4], 101 [5], 110 [6], 111 [7]. Notice that the higher you count, the more adjacent bits you need to represent the number. For example, it requires two adjacent bits to count from 0 to 3, and it takes three adjacent bits to count from 0 to 7. A sequence of bits can represent not just numbers, but other kinds of data, such as the letters and symbols on a keyboard. The sequence of 0s and 1s that make up data are usually counted in groups of 8, and these groups of 8 bits are called *bytes*. The word *byte* is short for *b*inar*y* digi*t* *e*ight. To transmit one keystroke on a typical keyboard requires one byte of information (or 8 bits). To transmit the three-letter word *the* requires three bytes of information (or 24 bits).

C

c The symbol for the speed of light in a vacuum.

C 1. The symbol for **carbon. 2.** Abbreviation of **Celsius. 3.** Abbreviation of **coulomb. 4.** Abbreviation of **cytosine.**

Ca The symbol for **calcium.**

cactus (kăk′təs) *Plural* **cacti** (kăk′tī′) *or* **cactuses** Any of numerous plants having thick, spiny stems and often brightly colored flowers with many stamens. Cacti grow in hot, dry places, and all but one of the almost 2,000 known species are native to North, Central, and South America and the West Inies.

cadmium (kăd′mē-əm) A rare, bluish-white metallic element that occurs mainly in small amounts in zinc ores. It is soft and easily cut with a knife. Cadmium is plated onto other metals and alloys to prevent corrosion, and it is used to make rechargeable batteries and nuclear reactor shields. *Symbol* **Cd.** *Atomic number* 48. *See* **Periodic Table,** pages 254–255.

caecilian (sə-sĭl′yən) Any of various legless, burrowing amphibians that have numerous grooved rings encircling the body. Caecilians are found mostly in tropical regions.

caffeine (kă-fēn′) A bitter alkaloid found in many plants and in products derived from them, such as tea, coffee, and chocolate. It is a mild stimulant.

calcareous (kăl-kâr′ē-əs) Composed of or containing calcium or calcium carbonate. Many carbonate rocks are calcareous.

calcification (kăl′sə-fĭ-kā′shən) **1.** *Medicine* The accumulation of calcium or calcium salts in a body tissue. Calcification normally occurs in the formation of bone. **2.** *Geology* **a.** The replacement of organic material, especially original hard material such as bone, with calcium carbonate during the process of fossilization. **b.** The accumulation of calcium in certain soils, especially soils of cool temperate regions where leaching takes place very slowly.

calcine (kăl-sīn′) To heat a substance to a high temperature without melting it, in order to turn it into a powder, oxidize it, or cause it to change in some other way. Liquid radioactive waste is sometimes calcined to produce a powder that can be stored more safely.

calcite (kăl′sīt′) A usually white, clear, or pale-yellow mineral consisting of calcium carbonate. It occurs in many different forms and is the main component of chalk, limestone, and marble. Cal-

Did You Know...?

cactus

The deserts of the southwest United States and northern Mexico are extremely hot and dry, yet many *cactus* plants thrive there. Cacti can live in this climate because they have adaptations for conserving water. Most cacti lack leaves and carry out photosynthesis in their stems. The stems are thick and succulent, storing large amounts of water but having a waxy cuticle that reduces evaporation. Pores called *stomata,* which let in the carbon dioxide needed for photosynthesis, open at night to reduce water loss. The characteristic spines help the plant gather scarce water. Water vapor in the air condenses on the spines and then drips to the ground, where it is taken up by the shallow roots. The spines also help to protect cacti from herbivores. Despite the spines, cactus fruits and stems have long been an important food source for many Native American peoples.

cite is the mineral used to represent a hardness of 3 on the Mohs scale.

calcium (kăl′sē-əm) A silvery-white, moderately hard metallic element that is an alkaline-earth metal and occurs in limestone and gypsum. It is a basic component of leaves, bones, teeth, and shells, and is essential for the normal growth and development of most animals and plants. Calcium is used to make plaster, cement, and alloys. *Symbol* **Ca.** *Atomic number* 20. *See* **Periodic Table,** pages 254–255.

calcium carbonate A white or colorless crystalline compound, $CaCO_3$, occurring naturally in chalk, limestone, and marble. It is used to make toothpaste, white paint, and cleaning powder.

calcium chloride A white crystalline salt, $CaCl_2$, that attracts water very strongly. It is used in food preservation and is spread on roads to melt ice and control dust.

calcium oxide A white, lumpy powder, CaO. It is made by heating limestone, bones, or shells, and is used to make glass, paper, steel, and building plaster. It is also used to neutralize the acids in sewage and other acidic waste. Also called *lime.*

calculus (kăl′kyə-ləs) The branch of mathematics that finds the maximum or minimum values of functions by means of differentiation and integration. Calculus can be used to calculate such things as rates of change, the area bounded by curves, and the volume bounded by surfaces. *See more at* **differentiation, integration.**

calibrate (kăl′ə-brāt′) To check, adjust, or standardize a measuring instrument, usually by comparing it with an accepted model: *calibrate an oven thermometer.*

californium (kăl′ə-fôr′nē-əm) A synthetic, radioactive metallic element of the actinide series that is produced from curium or berkelium. Californium emits a large number of neutrons and is used in the analysis of chemical components of substances. Its most stable isotope has a half-life of nearly 900 years. *Symbol* **Cf.** *Atomic number* 98. *See* **Periodic Table,** pages 254–255.

caliper (kăl′ə-pər) An instrument having two legs that can pivot or slide relative to each other, used to measure thickness and distance. Often used in the plural as *calipers.*

calorie (kăl′ə-rē) **1.** A unit of heat equal to the amount of heat needed to raise the temperature of one gram of water by one degree Celsius. Also called *small calorie.* **2a.** A unit of heat equal to the amount of heat needed to raise the temperature of 1,000 grams of water by one degree Celsius. Also called *kilocalorie, large calorie.* **b.** This unit used as a measure of the amount of heat energy released by food as it is digested by the body.

WORD HISTORY

calculus

The branch of mathematics called *calculus* deals with problems that simple arithmetic or algebra cannot solve, such as finding areas and volumes of unusual shapes and solids, and measuring rates of change. The word *calculus* comes from Latin, in which it originally meant "little stone, pebble." How did a word meaning "little stone" come to refer to a branch of mathematics? The answer comes from the counting practices of the ancient Romans over 2,000 years ago. They would add things up by using little pebbles or stones that represented particular numbers, as on an abacus. Later, the word *calculus* came to mean not just the pebble used in counting, but a counting system itself. Adopted into English, it eventually came to refer to the modern branch of mathematics, which was invented in the 17th century. The related Latin verb *calculare,* "to add up," is the source of our word *calculate.*

calyx (kā′lĭks, kăl′ĭks) The sepals of a flower considered as a group.

cambium (kăm′bē-əm) A plant tissue in the stems and roots of most woody seed plants, consisting of cells that divide rapidly to form new layers of tissue. Monocotyledons, like grasses and palm trees, do not usually have any cambium. ❖ The **vascular cambium** forms tissues that carry water and nutrients throughout the plant. Toward the outside of the plant, the vascular cambium forms new layers of phloem; to the inside, it forms new layers of xylem. The growth of these new tissues causes the diameter of the stem to increase. ❖ The **cork cambium** forms the cork cells of the outer bark toward the outside of the plant; toward the inside, it forms cells that add to the cortex.

Cambrian (kăm′brē-ən, kām′brē-ən) The first period of the Paleozoic Era, from about 542 to

488 million years ago, characterized by warm seas and desert land areas. During the Cambrian Period, animal life diversified rapidly and almost all modern animal phyla arose. *See Chart at* **geologic time,** pages 146–147.

Cambrian Explosion The rapid diversification of multicellular animal life that took place around the beginning of the Cambrian Period. It resulted in the appearance of almost all modern animal phyla. *See Note at* **Burgess Shale.**

camouflage (kăm′ə-fläzh′) Body form or coloration, often accompanied by certain behavior, that causes an organism to blend in with its surroundings.

camphor (kăm′fər) A white, gumlike, crystalline compound, $C_{10}H_{16}O$, having a strong odor and evaporating easily. It is used as an insect repellent and in making plastics and explosives.

cancer (kăn′sər) **1.** A disease in which cells in a part of the body become abnormal and multiply without limit. Cells of some cancers may spread to and damage tissues in other parts of the body. **2.** A tumor, especially a malignant one.

Cancer A constellation in the Northern Hemisphere near Leo and Gemini.

candela (kăn-dĕl′ə) A unit used to measure the brightness of a source of light. *See Table at* **measurement.**

canine (kā′nīn) *Adjective* **1.** Relating to the family of meat-eating mammals that includes the dogs, wolves, foxes, and coyotes. **2.** Relating to any of the four pointed teeth located behind the incisors in most mammals. In carnivores, the canine teeth are used for cutting and tearing meat. —*Noun* **3.** An animal belonging to the canine family of mammals. **4.** A canine tooth.

camouflage
frogfish on the ocean floor

Did You Know...?

cancer

The word *cancer* refers to diseases that are caused when abnormal cells multiply out of control. Often this runaway process is caused by changes called *mutations* in the parts of a cell's DNA that control cell division. These mutations can be triggered by exposure to certain viruses, chemicals, or radiation. People can also inherit mutated genes that increase their risk of developing cancer. Cancer cells that keep dividing can produce lumps, called *tumors,* in a particular area of the body. Sometimes cancer cells break free from one area and travel through the bloodstream or lymph to other parts of the body, in a process called *metastasis.* Treatments for cancer include surgery, to remove the tumors, and chemotherapy and radiation, to kill cancer cells. Scientists are now developing drugs that target and block the specific molecules responsible for the growth and survival of cancer cells.

Canis Major (kā′nĭs) A constellation in the Southern Hemisphere near Orion. It contains Sirius, the brightest star in the night sky.

Canis Minor A constellation in the Northern Hemisphere near Hydra and the celestial equator. It contains the bright star Procyon.

canyon (kăn′yən) A long, deep, narrow valley with steep cliff walls, cut into the earth by running water and often having a stream at the bottom.

capacitor (kə-păs′ĭ-tər) A device used to store electric charge. A capacitor typically consists of two conducting metal plates separated by an electrical insulator, and it is charged by connecting the plates to the terminals of an electric power supply. Positive charge is stored on the plate connected to the positive terminal, and an equal amount of negative charge is stored on the plate connected

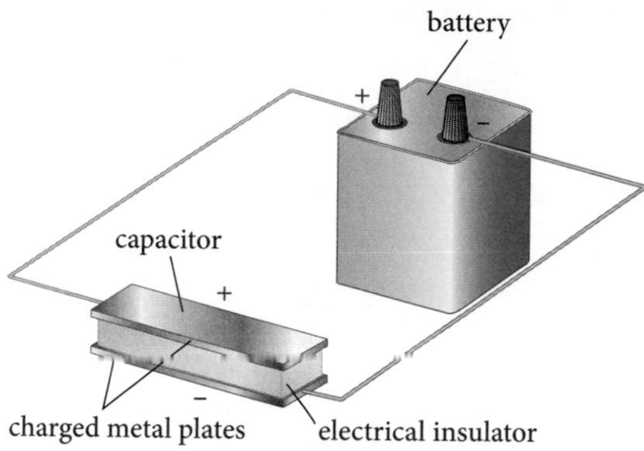

capacitor

A capacitor is charged when electrons from a power source, such as a battery, flow to one of the two plates. Because the electrons cannot pass through the insulating layer, they build up on the first plate, giving it a negative charge. Electrons on the other plate are attracted to the positive terminal of the battery, causing that plate to become positively charged.

to the negative terminal. Capacitors are used to regulate the flow of charge in electric circuits. ❖ The ability of a capacitor to store electric charge is called its **capacitance** (kə-păs′ĭ-təns). The capacitance depends on the area of the plates, the width of their separation, and the type of insulator between them.

cape (kāp) A point of land projecting into a body of water.

capillary (kăp′ə-lĕr′ē) Any of the tiny blood vessels that connect the smallest arteries to the smallest veins and form a network throughout the tissues of the body. The exchange of oxygen, nutrients, metabolic waste products, and carbon dioxide between the tissues and the blood takes place in the capillaries.

capillary action The movement of a liquid along the surface of a solid as a result of the attraction of the molecules of the liquid to the molecules of the solid. The liquid's molecules adhere to the solid surface and also to each other, so that each molecule of liquid pulls the next one along. Water moves into the pores of a sponge or the fibers of a paper towel by capillary action.

Capricornus (kăp′rĭ-kôr′nəs) or **Capricorn** (kăp′rĭ-kôrn′) A constellation in the Southern Hemisphere near Aquarius and Sagittarius.

carapace (kăr′ə-pās′) A hard outer covering made of bone or chitin on the back of an animal such as a turtle, armadillo, lobster, or crab.

carbide (kär′bīd′) A binary chemical compound consisting of carbon combined with another element such as calcium or tungsten. Some carbides, such as those consisting of carbon and silicon or boron, are very hard and are used to make abrasives and tools that cut metal.

carbohydrate (kar′bō-hī′drāt′) Any of a large class of organic compounds that contain only carbon, hydrogen, and oxygen, usually with twice as many hydrogen atoms as carbon or oxygen atoms. Carbohydrates are produced chiefly by photosynthesis and serve as a major energy source for living things. Sugars, starches, and cellulose are all carbohydrates.

carbolic acid (kär-bŏl′ĭk) *See* **phenol.**

carbon (kär′bən) An abundant, nonmetallic element that occurs in all organic compounds and can be found in all living things. Diamonds

Did You Know...?

carbon

Proteins, sugars, fats, and DNA all contain many carbon atoms. The element *carbon* is also important, however, outside the chemistry of living things. The two most familiar forms of carbon, diamond and graphite, differ greatly because of the arrangement of their atoms. In diamond, each carbon atom bonds to four others in a dense network that makes the material the hardest substance known. But in graphite, each carbon atom bonds only to three others in a much looser arrangement of layers, each of which is weakly bonded to neighboring layers. Because individual layers of carbon in graphite are so loosely connected, they are easily scraped away, which is why graphite is used in pencils. In 1985 an entirely new form of carbon was discovered in which carbon atoms join to make microscopic spheres or tubes. These structures are called *fullerenes* after Buckminster Fuller, who created geodesic domes with a similar form. Synthetic fullerenes have many potential uses due to their unusual physical properties.

and graphite are pure forms, and carbon is a major part of coal, limestone, petroleum, and natural gas. Carbon can bond to itself in rings and chains and forms an enormous number of important molecules, many of which are essential for life. *Symbol* **C.** *Atomic number* 6. *See* **Periodic Table,** pages 254–255.

carbon-12 A stable isotope of carbon that has six protons and six neutrons in the nucleus. Carbon-12 makes up most naturally occurring carbon.

carbon-14 A naturally occurring radioactive isotope of carbon that is important in dating archaeological and biological remains by the technique known as radiocarbon dating. *See more at* **radiocarbon dating.**

carbonate (kär′bə-nāt′) *Noun* **1.** A compound containing the group CO_3. Carbonates include minerals such as calcite and rocks such as limestone. — *Verb* **2.** To add carbon dioxide to a substance, such as a beverage.

carbon cycle The continuous process by which carbon is exchanged between organisms and the environment. Carbon dioxide is absorbed from the atmosphere or from water by plants, algae, and certain bacteria and is converted to carbohydrates by photosynthesis. Carbon is then passed into the food chain and returned to the environment by the respiration and decay of animals, plants, and other organisms. The burning of fossil fuels also releases carbon dioxide into the atmosphere.

carbon dating *See* **radiocarbon dating.**

carbon dioxide A colorless, odorless gas, CO_2, that is present in the atmosphere and is formed when any fuel containing carbon is burned. It is breathed out of an animal's lungs during respiration, produced by the decay of organic matter, and used by plants in photosynthesis. Carbon dioxide is also used in refrigeration, fire extinguishers, and carbonated drinks.

carbon fixation The process by which carbon from the environment is converted into carbon compounds, such as carbohydrates, in plants, algae, and certain bacteria, primarily by photosynthesis.

Carboniferous (kär′bə-nĭf′ər-əs) The fifth period of the Paleozoic Era, from about 359 to 299 million years ago. It comprises the Missis-

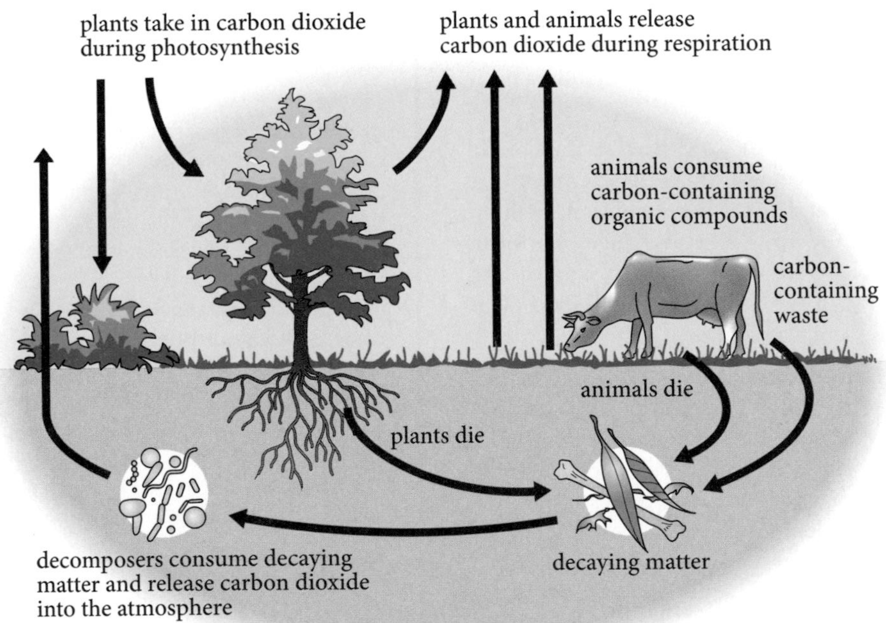

carbon cycle

sippian (or Lower Carboniferous) and Pennsylvanian (or Upper Carboniferous) subdivisions, which have traditionally been classified in North America as full geologic periods. During the Carboniferous, widespread swamps formed in which plant remains accumulated and later hardened into coal. *See Chart at* **geologic time,** pages 146–147.

carbon monoxide A colorless, odorless gas, CO, formed when a compound containing carbon burns incompletely because there is not enough oxygen. It is present in the exhaust gases of automobile engines and is very poisonous.

carcinogen (kär-sĭn′ə-jən) A substance or agent that can cause cancer. Asbestos and tobacco products are examples of carcinogens.

carcinoma (kär′sə-nō′mə) A malignant tumor that begins on the surface of the skin, blood vessels, or other organ or structure.

cardiac (kär′dē-ăk′) Relating to the heart: *a cardiac disorder.*

cardinal number (kär′dn-əl) A number, such as 3, 11, or 412, used in counting to indicate quantity but not order. *Compare* **ordinal number.**

cardinal point One of the four principal directions on a compass; north, south, east, or west.

cardiology (kär′dē-ŏl′ə-jē) The branch of medicine that deals with the heart, its diseases, and their treatment.

cardiopulmonary resuscitation (kär′dē-ō-pŏŏl′mə-nĕr′ē) *See* **CPR.**

cardiovascular (kär′dē-ō-văs′kyə-lər) Relating to the heart and blood vessels: *cardiovascular fitness.*

carnivore (kär′nə-vôr′) **1a.** An animal that feeds chiefly on the flesh of other animals. Carnivores include predators such as lions and alligators, and scavengers such as hyenas and vultures. *Compare* **herbivore. b.** Any of various mammals belonging to the order Carnivora, most of which have large, sharp canine teeth and eat meat. Dogs, cats, bears, racoons, and seals all belong to this order. **2.** A plant that eats insects, such as a Venus flytrap or a pitcher plant. —*Adjective* **carnivorous.**

Carnot (kär-nō′), **Nicolas Léonard Sadi** 1796–1832. French physicist and engineer who founded the science of thermodynamics. He was the first to analyze the working cycle and efficiency of the steam engine according to scientific principles. Through his experiments Carnot developed what would become the second law of thermodynamics and laid the foundation for work by Kelvin, Joule, and others.

carotene (kăr′ə-tēn′) An organic compound that occurs as an orange-yellow to red pigment in many plants and in animal tissue. In animals, it is converted to vitamin A by the liver. Carotenes give carrots and pumpkins their characteristic color.

carotid artery (kə-rŏt′ĭd) Either of the two large arteries in the neck that carry blood to the head.

carpal (kär′pəl) Any of the eight bones of the wrist lying between the forearm bones and the metacarpals. *See more at* **skeleton.**

carpal tunnel syndrome Pain, numbness, or tingling in the hand, caused by compression of a nerve in the wrist. The syndrome is a type of repetitive strain injury and may be caused by excessive texting or typing.

carpel (kär′pəl) The part of a flowering plant that encloses the ovules. A pistil may consist of a single carpel or of several carpels joined together. *See more at* **flower.**

carrier (kăr′ē-ər) **1.** An organism that serves as a host for a disease-causing agent and can transmit it to others, but does not have symptoms of the disease. Mosquitoes are carriers of malaria, for example. **2.** An organism that carries a gene for a trait but does not show the trait itself. Carriers can produce offspring that express the trait by mating with another carrier of the same gene.

Carson (kär′sən), **Rachel Louise** 1907–1964. American marine biologist and writer whose best-known book, *Silent Spring* (1962), identified the dangerous effects of synthetic pesticides. Public reaction to the book led to stricter controls on pesticide use and shaped the ideas of the modern environmental movement. *See Note on next page.*

Cartesian coordinate system (kär-tē′zhən) A system in which the location of a point is given by a set of numbers called coordinates that represent its distances from perpendicular lines that intersect at a point called the origin. A Cartesian coordinate system in a plane has two

BIOGRAPHY

Rachel Carson

Rachel Carson's highly influential book *Silent Spring* shows how combining scientific knowledge with powerful writing ability can bring about important changes. Carson studied literature and biology in college, then went on to do research in marine biology. She completed a master's degree at Johns Hopkins University in 1932. She got a job with the US Fish and Wildlife Service, where she wrote and edited reports while doing her own writing on the side. In 1951, she left her job to devote herself full-time to writing. She published three popular books on the ecology of oceans and coastlines: *Under the Sea-Wind* (1941), *The Sea Around Us* (1951), and *The Edge of the Sea* (1955). At the same time, she was becoming more and more aware of the harmful effects of pollution and especially of chemical pesticides such as DDT. In *Silent Spring,* published in 1962, Carson laid out in detail the damage these pesticides were doing to the natural environment and to human health. The deaths of multitudes of birds, she contended, had resulted in "strangely silent" spring mornings. Although the chemical industry vigorously criticized Carson, her powerful book caught the attention of the general public and resulted in stricter regulations against toxic chemicals and the banning of DDT in the United States.

y
P(4, 2)
x
O

z
P(3, 2, 4)
y
O
4
3
2
x

Cartesian coordinate system
top: *two-dimensional coordinate system*
bottom: *three-dimensional coordinate system*

perpendicular lines (the x-axis and y-axis); in three-dimensional space, it has three (the x-axis, y-axis, and z-axis). *Compare* **polar coordinate system.**

cartilage (kär′tl-ĭj) A strong, flexible connective tissue that in most vertebrates forms the major part of the skeleton of the embryo but changes largely to bone as the individual matures. It is more flexible than bone but not as hard. In adult humans, cartilage is found in the joints, the outer ear, the nose, and the larynx. —*Adjective* **cartilaginous** (kär′tl-ăj′ə-nəs)

cartilaginous fish A fish whose skeleton is made mainly of cartilage rather than bone. Sharks, rays, and skates are cartilaginous fish. *Compare* **bony fish, jawless fish.**

Carver (kär′vər), **George Washington** 1864?–1943. American botanist, agricultural chemist, and educator noted for his efforts to improve agricultural efficiency in the United States. Carver taught farmers in the South, where the soil was depleted from growing cotton, the importance of soil-improving techniques such as growing different crops from season to season.

To encourage them to use these techniques, he researched hundreds of uses for soil-enriching crops such as peanuts, soybeans, and sweet potatoes.

Cassiopeia (kăs′ē-ə-pē′ə) A W-shaped constellation in the Northern Hemisphere near Andromeda and Perseus.

caste (kăst) A group of social insects carrying out a specific function within a colony. In an ant colony, members of the caste of workers forage for food outside the colony or tend eggs and larvae, while members of the caste of soldiers defend the colony from attack.

cat (kăt) **1.** Any of various meat-eating mammals including the lion, tiger, jaguar, lynx, and cheetah. Most cats are solitary animals. All species except the cheetah have fully retractable claws. **2.** The house cat, domesticated since ancient times and widely kept as a pet or a killer of rodents.

catabolism (kə-tăb′ə-lĭz′əm) The phase of metabolism in which energy in the form of ATP is produced by the breakdown of complex molecules, such as proteins and fats, into simpler ones. *Compare* **anabolism.** —*Adjective* **catabolic.**

catalyst (kăt′l-ĭst) A substance that speeds up a chemical reaction while undergoing no permanent change itself. All enzymes are catalysts. The enzymes in saliva, for example, are catalysts of digestion. —*Verb* **catalyze.**

cataract (kăt′ə-răkt′) **1.** A cloudiness in the lens of an eye or the membrane that covers it, causing partial or total blindness. **2.** A large, steep waterfall.

caterpillar (kăt′ər-pĭl′ər) The wormlike larva of a butterfly or moth, often having fine hairs or brightly colored patterns. Caterpillars feed on plants.

catfish (kăt′fĭsh′) Any of numerous scaleless, usually freshwater fish having whiskerlike feelers on the upper jaw.

catheter (kăth′ĭ-tər) A thin, flexible tube inserted into a duct of the body to remove a blockage or to drain fluid.

cathode (kăth′ōd′) A negative terminal or negatively charged electrode, which repels negatively charged particles and attracts positively charged particles. In an electric circuit, electrons (which are negatively charged) flow away from the cathode (negative terminal) of a power supply. In an electrolytic cell or a vacuum tube, the cathode is the electrode that is connected to the negative terminal of a power supply. The cathode in a vacuum tube is usually made of a metal that releases electrons when heated. *Compare* **anode.**

BIOGRAPHY

George Washington Carver

After the Civil War, Southern farmers had a big problem: many of them grew nothing but cotton, and their cotton crops were becoming smaller every year. George Washington Carver, who headed the agriculture department at the Tuskegee Institute in Alabama, discovered that crops such as peanuts and sweet potatoes, both of which grow well in Alabama, could restore the vitality of the soil by replenishing nutrients and organic materials. To make these crops economically beneficial to farmers, he researched and developed hundreds of uses for peanuts, sweet potatoes, soybeans, and other plants—uses ranging from foods to industrial products such as plastics, synthetic rubber, shaving cream, and paper. Carver also introduced movable schools that brought practical agricultural knowledge directly to farmers.

cathode ray A stream of electrons emitted by the cathode (that is, the negative electrode) of a vacuum tube. These electrons are attracted to the anode (the positive electrode) of the vacuum tube. When high-energy cathode rays collide with the anode, x-rays are generated.

cathode-ray tube A kind of vacuum tube designed to produce cathode rays, especially to form images on older television or computer screens.

cation (kăt′ī′ən) An ion that has a positive charge. Hydrogen and ammonium ions are cations. *Compare* **anion.**

catkin (kăt′kĭn) A dense, often drooping cluster of very small flowers without petals, found especially in willows, birches, and oaks. The flowers on a catkin are either all male or all female. *See more at* **flower.**

CAT scan (kăt) Short for *computerized axial tomography.* A CT scan.

caudal (kôd′l) Of or near the tail or hind parts of an animal: *the caudal fin of a fish.*

cave (kāv) A hollow or natural passage under the earth or in the side of a hill or mountain with an opening to the surface. Caves can form in many ways, but the largest caves are formed by groundwater gradually dissolving limestone bedrock.

Cavendish (kăv′ən-dĭsh), **Henry** 1731–1810. British chemist and physicist who discovered hydrogen. He also showed that it was the lightest of all the gases and established that water is a compound of hydrogen and oxygen.

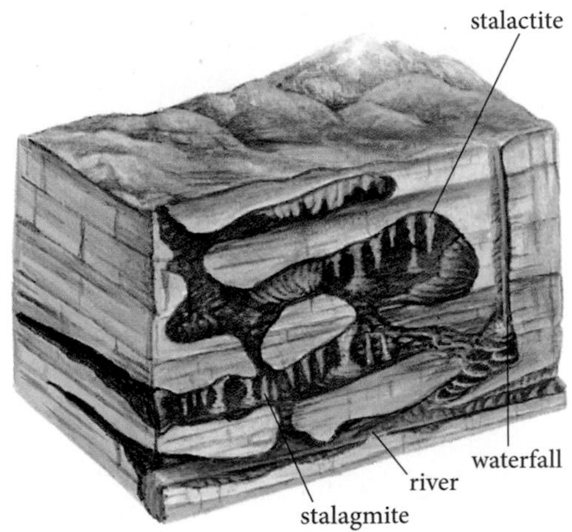

cave

Caves form in limestone or similar rock when water moving through rock wears it away.

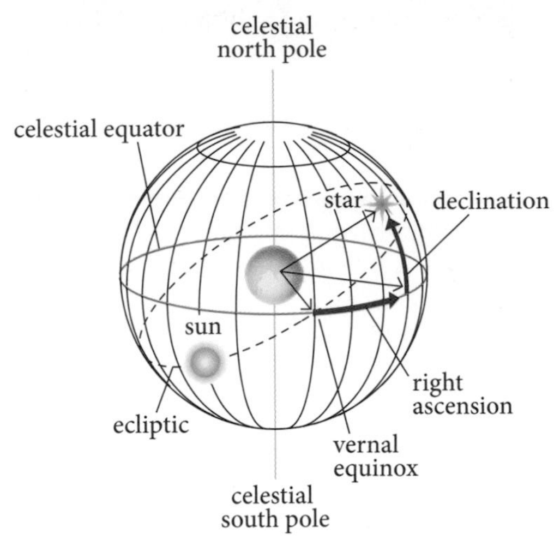

celestial sphere

cavitation (kăv′ĭ-tā′shən) The sudden formation and collapsing of bubbles in a liquid caused by mechanical forces, such as the moving blades of a ship's propeller.

cc Abbreviation of cubic centimeter.

Cd The symbol for **cadmium.**

CD (sē′dē′) A compact disc.

Ce The symbol for **cerium.**

cecum (sē′kəm) A large pouch that forms the beginning of the large intestine. The cecum attaches to the ileum.

celestial (sə-lĕs′chəl) Relating to the sky or the universe. Stars and planets are celestial objects.

celestial equator A great circle on the celestial sphere in the same plane as the Earth's equator.

celestial pole Either of the two points where Earth's axis would intersect the celestial sphere if the axis were extended into space in both directions.

celestial sphere An imaginary sphere with Earth at its center. The stars, planets, sun, moon, and other celestial objects appear to be located on this sphere.

celiac disease (sē′lē-ăk′) A long-lasting disease of the stomach and intestines that is characterized by sensitivity to gluten and poor absorption of nutrients.

cell (sĕl) **1.** *Biology* The basic unit of living matter in all organisms, made up of cytoplasm,

A CLOSER LOOK

Cells

The cell is the basic structural unit of all organisms. From single-celled algae to complex multicellular animals, cells perform all of the chemical processes needed to sustain life. The cells of eukaryotes—which include all organisms except bacteria and archaea—are made up of the same basic elements: a protective cell membrane, cytoplasm, a distinct nucleus that carries most of the organism's DNA, and small bodies called organelles. Cells vary in shape and form depending on the tasks they perform.

Typical Animal Cell

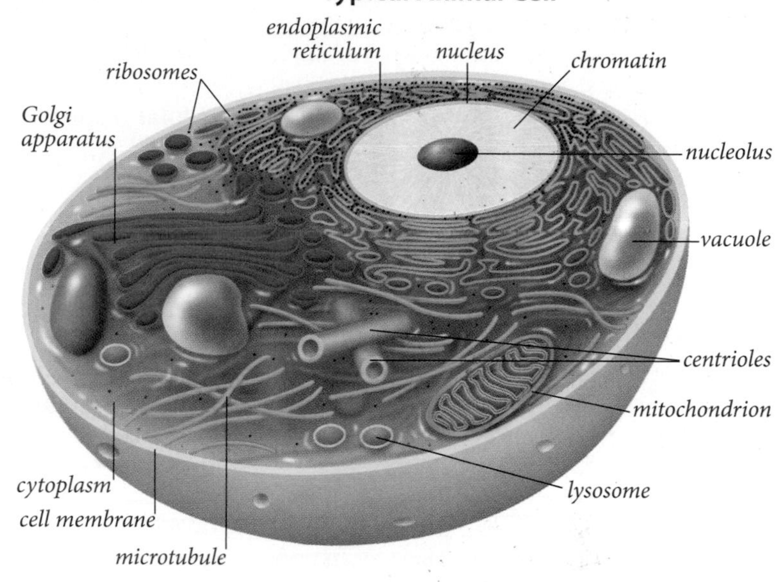

Typical Plant Cell

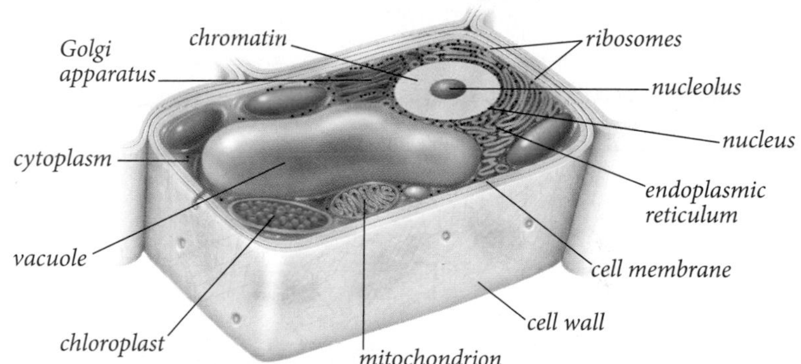

Specialized Cells

Nerve cell (neuron)

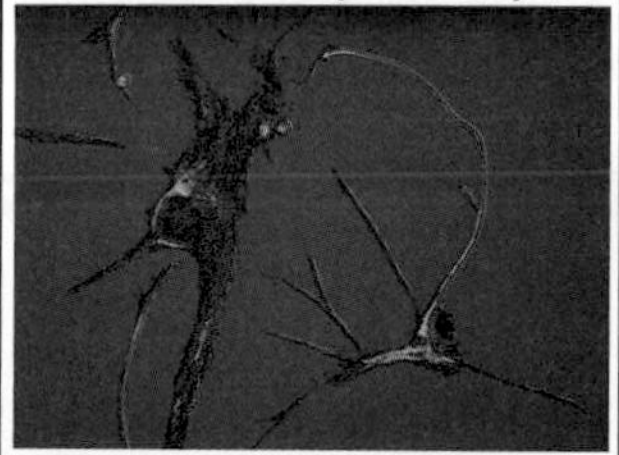

Nerve cells transmit electrical impulses within the nervous system.

Red blood cell

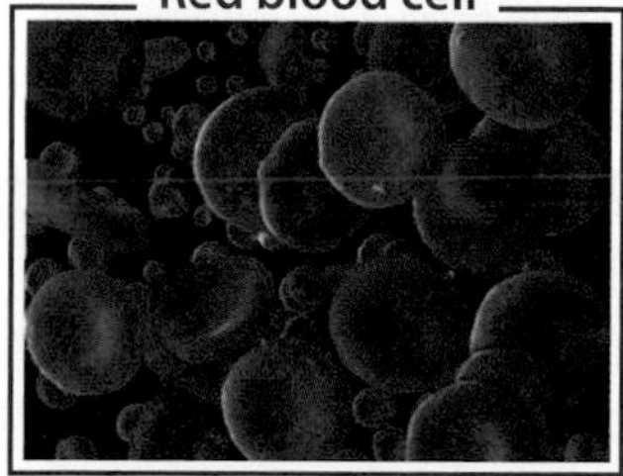

Red blood cells transport oxygen to the tissues of the body. They get their color from an iron-containing compound called hemoglobin.

Guard cell

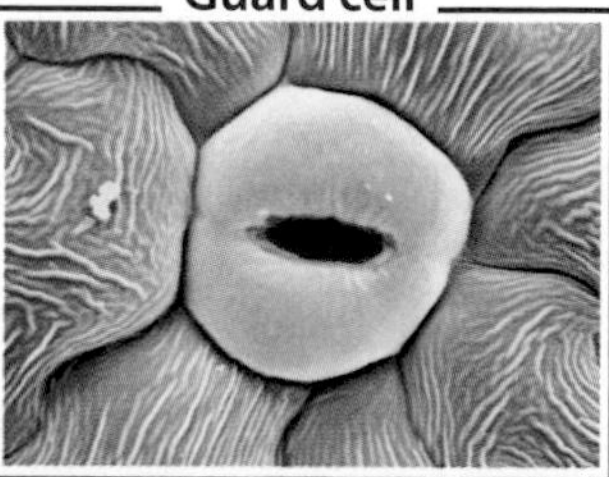

Guard cells open and close pores (called stomata) in leaves, letting air in and water vapor out.

various organelles, such as mitochondria, and an enclosing membrane. All cells except bacteria and archaea have a distinct nucleus that contains the cell's DNA. Some organisms consist of single cells, while others consist of vast numbers of cells. *See more at* **eukaryote, prokaryote. 2.** *Physics* Any of various devices or units within such devices that are capable of converting some form of energy into electricity. Solar cells convert sunlight into electricity, and car batteries contain cells that convert chemical energy into electricity. —*Adjective* **cellular.**

cell division The process by which a cell divides into two or more cells. Division by fission occurs in one-celled organisms. In multicellular organisms, new body cells are produced by mitosis, a process that results in two identical cells, and sex cells are produced by meiosis, a process that results in four daughter cells, each with half as much genetic material as the parent cell. *See more at* **fission, meiosis, mitosis.**

Did You Know...?

Celsius, Fahrenheit, and Kelvin scales

In the United States, a forecast of 30° might get you to wear a coat and hat. In Canada, however, 30° would call for shorts and sandals. Do Canadians simply enjoy the cold more? Well, possibly, but more importantly, the two forecasts are very different because the United States generally uses the *Fahrenheit* scale, in which 30° is below freezing, while Canadians, along with most of the world, use the *Celsius* scale, in which 30° is quite warm—equivalent to 86° Fahrenheit! The Celsius scale is convenient for scientists, because in Celsius water freezes at 0° (32°F) and boils at 100° (212°F). (To convert between scales, see the table of measurements at the entry for measurement.) Scientists also use the *Kelvin* scale, in which 0 is as cold as anything could ever get, about −273° Celsius. Each Kelvin degree equals one Celsius degree, so the only difference between the Kelvin and Celsius scales is which point on the scale is labeled as zero.

cell membrane The thin membrane that forms the outer surface of the cytoplasm of a cell and regulates the passage of materials in and out of the cell. Cell membranes are made up of proteins and lipids.

cellular respiration (sĕl**′**yə-lər) *See* **respiration.**

cellular slime mold *See under* **slime mold.**

cellulose (sĕl**′**yə-lōs′) A carbohydrate that is formed from hundreds of linked glucose molecules and is the main component of the cell walls of plants. Cellulose is insoluble in water and is used to make paper, cellophane, textiles, explosives, and other products. ❖ An important compound derived from cellulose is **cellulose acetate,** forming a durable material that is used in making movie film, magnetic tape, plastic film for wrapping and packaging, and textile fibers. It is often called *cellulose* or *acetate* for short.

cell wall The rigid outer layer that surrounds the cell membrane in plants, fungi, and most bacteria and algae. In plants, the cell wall is made up mostly of cellulose. Animal cells do not have a cell wall outside the cell membrane.

Celsius (sĕl**′**sē-əs) Relating to a temperature scale on which the freezing point of water is 0° and the boiling point of water is 100° under normal atmospheric pressure. *See Note at* **centigrade.**

Celsius, Anders 1701–1744. Swedish astronomer who devised the Celsius scale in 1742.

Cenozoic (sĕn′ə-zō**′**ĭk) The most recent era of geologic time, from about 66 million years ago to the present. The Cenozoic Era is characterized by the formation of modern continents and the diversification of mammals and plants. *See Chart at* **geologic time,** pages 146–147.

Centaurus (sĕn-tôr**′**əs) A constellation in the Southern Hemisphere near the Southern Cross and Libra. It contains Alpha Centauri, the star nearest Earth.

center of gravity (sĕn**′**tər) The point in a body around which its weight is evenly distributed. In a uniform gravitational field, as on or near the Earth's surface, a body's center of gravity is the same as its center of mass.

center of mass The point in a body or a system of bodies around which the mass is evenly distributed. For many calculations in physics, a

USAGE

centigrade

Because of confusion over the prefix *centi–*, which originally meant 100 but developed the meaning $\frac{1}{100}$, scientists agreed to stop using the term *centigrade* in 1948. They use the term *Celsius* instead.

body or system of bodies can be treated as if all of its mass were concentrated at that point.

centi– A prefix meaning "a hundredth," as in *centigram*, a hundredth of a gram.

centigrade (sĕn′tĭ-grād′) *See* **Celsius.**

centigram (sĕn′tĭ-grăm′) A unit of mass in the metric system equal to 0.01 gram. *See Table at* **measurement.**

centiliter (sĕn′tə-lē′tər) A unit of volume in the metric system equal to 0.01 liter. *See Table at* **measurement.**

centimeter (sĕn′tə-mē′tər) A unit of length in the metric system equal to 0.01 meter. *See Table at* **measurement.**

centipede (sĕn′tə-pēd′) Any of various small arthropods having a body divided into many segments, each with a pair of legs. A pair of clawlike appendages on the first segment behind the head are used for injecting venom into prey. *Compare* **millipede.**

central angle (sĕn′trəl) An angle formed by two rays from the center of a circle, with the center forming the vertex.

central nervous system In vertebrate animals, the part of the nervous system that consists of the brain and spinal cord. *Compare* **peripheral nervous system.**

central processing unit The part of a computer that interprets and carries out instructions. It also transfers information to and from other components, such as a hard drive or the keyboard.

centrifugal force (sĕn-trĭf′yə-gəl) An apparent force that seems to cause a body moving in a curving path to be pushed away from the center of the curve. Centrifugal force is not a true force but is actually the effect of inertia, which causes a body in motion to continue moving in a straight line if there are no forces acting on it. For example, a passenger sitting in a car that is turning sharply will be pressed against the door. If the car door were to suddenly open, the passenger would continue moving straight ahead and would be thrown out of the car. *See Note at* **centripetal force.**

centrifuge (sĕn′trə-fyo͞oj′) A machine that separates substances of different densities by rotating them at very high speed. The denser substances are thrown farther outward than the less dense ones. A centrifuge can be used to separate cream from milk, or bacteria from a fluid.

centriole (sĕn′trē-ōl′) Either of a pair of cylinder-shaped bodies found in the centrosome of an animal cell. During mitosis, the centrioles move apart to help form the spindle, which then distributes the chromosomes in the dividing cell. *See more at* **cell, meiosis, mitosis.**

centripetal force (sĕn-trĭp′ĭ-tl) A force on a moving body that is directed toward the center of a circle and causes the body to follow a curving path. For example, Earth's gravity exerts a centripetal force on the moon, causing it to orbit in a

Did You Know...?

centripetal force

In a popular carnival ride, people stand with their backs against the wall of a cylindrical chamber. The chamber spins rapidly and then the floor drops out, but the riders remain pressed against the wall and don't fall down. Why? Most people on the ride would say that an outward force — a *centrifugal force* — was pushing them against the wall. In reality, though, the only force acting on the people is an inward force — a *centripetal force.* As the ride spins, it forces the riders to travel in a circle. According to the law of inertia, objects in motion tend to travel in a straight line at constant speed unless acted on by an external force. To make an object travel along a curved path, you have to keep forcing it toward the inside of the curve. The wall of the ride's cylindrical chamber accomplishes this by pushing the riders toward the center (with the friction between the riders and the wall holding the riders up).

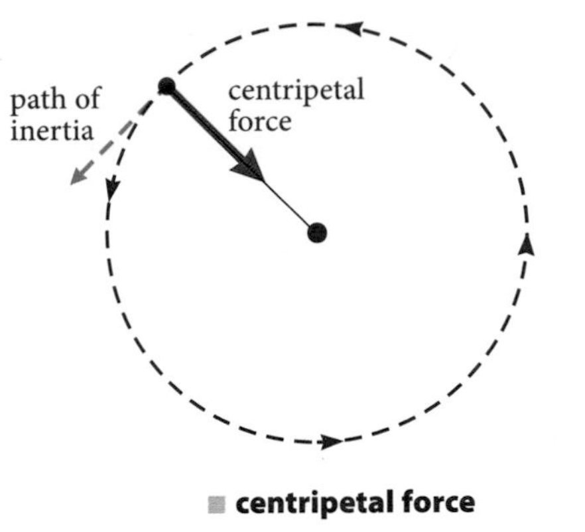

centripetal force

nearly circular path around the Earth rather than moving in a straight line.

centromere (sĕn′trə-mîr′) The region of the chromosome to which the spindle fiber is attached during cell division. The centromere is the constricted point at which the two chromatids forming the chromosome are joined together. *See more at* **meiosis, mitosis.**

centrosome (sĕn′trə-sōm′) In animal cells, a specialized region of the cytoplasm that contains the centrioles and is involved in organizing the microtubules that form the spindle during cell division.

cephalic (sə-făl′ĭk) Relating to or located on or near the head.

cephalopod (sĕf′ə-lə-pŏd′) Any of various ocean mollusks, such as an octopus, squid, or nautilus, having long arms or tentacles around the mouth, a large head, a pair of large eyes, and a sharp beak. Cephalopods have the most complex nervous system of all invertebrates. If attacked, they squirt a cloud of dark inky liquid to confuse predators.

cephalothorax (sĕf′ə-lə-thôr′ăks′) The front body part of arachnids, such as spiders, and many crustaceans, such as crabs. It consists of the fused head and thorax and is one of the two divisions of the body, the other being the abdomen.

ceratopsian (sĕr′ə-tŏp′sē-ən) Any of various plant-eating dinosaurs of the Cretaceous Period, having a beaked mouth, usually a bony plate on the back of the skull, and sometimes horns on the head. The triceratops is an example of a ceratopsian.

cereal (sîr′ē-əl) A grass, such as corn or wheat, whose starchy grains are used as food.

cerebellum (sĕr′ə-bĕl′əm) The part of the vertebrate brain that is located below the cerebrum at the rear of the skull and coordinates balance and muscle activity. In humans and other mammals, the cerebellum is divided into left and right sides, with a small part connecting them.

cerebral (sĕr′ə-brəl, sə-rē′brəl) Relating to the cerebrum or the brain.

cerebral cortex The outer layer of gray matter that covers the cerebral hemispheres in the brain of many vertebrate animals and is composed of folds of nerve cells and fibers. The cerebral cortex is responsible for voluntary muscle movement and the senses of hearing, vision, and touch. In humans, it is the center of thought, language, and memory.

cerebral hemisphere Either of the two symmetrical halves of the cerebrum. *See Note at* **brain.**

cerebral palsy A disability caused by brain injury usually at or before birth, resulting in symptoms that affect a person's ability to move the muscles in a coordinated way. Symptoms of cerebral palsy vary widely and can be mild or severe, depending on the type and amount of brain injury.

cerebrospinal fluid (sĕr′ə-brō-spī′nəl, sə-rē′-brō-spī′nəl) The clear fluid that fills the cavities of the brain and spinal cord, serving to lubricate the tissues and to absorb shock.

cerebrum (sĕr′ə-brəm, sə-rē′brəm) The largest part of the vertebrate brain, filling most of the skull and consisting of two hemispheres divided by a deep groove and joined by a mass of nerve fibers. It consists of gray matter (the cerebral cortex) on the outside and white matter on the inside. Each hemisphere is divided into four sections, called the frontal, occipital, parietal, and temporal lobes. The cerebrum controls voluntary activity, processes complex sensory information, and is responsible for mental functions.

Ceres (sîr′ēz) A dwarf planet that orbits the sun and lies in the asteroid belt between Mars and Jupiter. Ceres is the closest dwarf planet to the sun, and it was the first object in the asteroid belt to be discovered. Its diameter at its equator is 597 miles (960 kilometers).

cerium (sîr′ē-əm) A shiny, gray metallic element of the lanthanide series. It is easily shaped and in pure form will ignite if scratched with a knife. It is used in glass polishing and as a catalyst in self-cleaning ovens. *Symbol* **Ce.** *Atomic number* 58. *See* **Periodic Table,** pages 254–255.

cervical (sûr′vĭ-kəl) **1.** Relating to the cervix of the uterus. **2.** Located at or near the part of the spine that forms the neck: *cervical vertebrae.*

cervix (sûr′vĭks) The narrowed, lower end of the uterus, projecting into the vagina.

cesium (sē′zē-əm) A soft, easily shaped, silvery-white element that is an alkali metal. It is liquid near room temperature and is the most reactive of all metals. Cesium is used to make photoelectric cells, electron tubes, and atomic clocks. *Symbol* **Cs.** *Atomic number* 55. *See* **Periodic Table,** pages 254–255.

cetacean (sĭ-tā′shən) Any of various marine mammals having an almost hairless body that is shaped like that of a fish. Cetaceans have a flat horizontal tail, one or two blowholes for breathing, and forelimbs modified into broad flippers. Whales, dolphins, and porpoises are cetaceans.

Cf The symbol for **californium.**

CFC Abbreviation of **chlorofluorocarbon.** *See under* **fluorocarbon.**

Chadwick (chăd′wĭk), Sir **James** 1891–1974. British physicist who discovered the neutron in 1932.

Chain (chān), Sir **Ernst Boris** 1906–1979. German-born British biochemist who developed and purified penicillin with Howard Florey. Chain also helped to develop a way to manufacture the drug in large quantities and was involved in the first tests of its effects on humans.

chain reaction 1. *Physics* A continuous series of nuclear fissions in which neutrons released from the splitting of one atomic nucleus collide with nearby nuclei, which in turn split and release more neutrons to collide with other nuclei, thus keeping the reaction going. *See more at* **fission.** *See Note at* **nuclear reactor. 2.** *Chemistry* A chemical reaction or process that occurs as a series of steps in which each intermediate step produces an unstable compound that becomes the starting material for the next step, and the final step occurs when a stable product or result is formed.

chalcedony (kăl-sĕd′n-ē) A type of quartz that has a waxy luster and varies from transparent to translucent. It is used as a gemstone. Agate and onyx are forms of chalcedony.

chalk (chôk) A soft, white, gray, or yellow limestone formed primarily from fossil seashells and consisting mainly of calcium carbonate. Chalk is used in making lime, cement, and fertilizers, and as a whitening pigment in ceramics, paints, and cosmetics. The chalk used in classrooms, however, is usually made mostly of calcium sulfate, which is also called gypsum.

■ **chameleon**

chameleon (kə-mēl′yən) Any of various tropical lizards chiefly of Africa and Madagascar, having a grasping tail, eyes that can move independently of each other, and the ability to change color.

chaos (kā′ŏs′) *Mathematics* A system, such as the weather, that develops from a set of often simple initial conditions but behaves very differently if the initial conditions are changed even slightly. Chaotic systems often appear random and unpredictable, but in fact have regular patterns that are repeated at any scale of observation. *See more at* **fractal.**

characteristic (kăr′ək-tə-rĭs′tĭk) *Mathematics* The part of a logarithm to the base ten that is to the left of the decimal point. For example, if 2.749 is a logarithm, 2 is the characteristic. *Compare* **mantissa.**

charcoal (chär′kōl′) A black porous form of carbon produced by heating wood in little or no air. Charcoal is used as a fuel, for drawing, and in air and water filters.

charge (chärj) **1.** The electrical property of particles of matter that determines whether they are attracted to or repelled by other charged particles. The sign of a charge is designated as positive or negative. Particles with charges of the same sign repel each other, and particles with charges of the opposite sign attract each other.

Did You Know...?

charge

Electric *charge* is a basic property of elementary particles of matter. Protons have a positive charge, while electrons have a negative charge of the same magnitude. In an ordinary atom, the number of protons equals the number of electrons, so the atom is electrically neutral. If an atom gains some electrons, it becomes negatively charged. If it loses some electrons, it becomes positively charged. Atoms that become charged are called *ions*. A charged particle creates around itself an *electric field* that exerts a force on any other charged particle that enters that space. Because of their electric fields, particles with opposite charges attract each other, while those with the same charges repel each other. *Static electricity* consists of charged particles at rest. Electric *current* consists of charged particles, especially electrons or ions, that are moving. The movement of electrical charges is essential not only for our computers and other electronic devices, but for the transmission of signals in our nerve cells.

The greater the amount of a particle's charge, the greater the force of attraction or repulsion. Also called *electric charge*. **2.** The total amount of charge in an object or region of space. If an object contains equal amounts of positive and negative charges, then the overall charge is zero and the object is electrically neutral.

Charles (chärlz), **Jacques Alexandre César** 1746–1823. French physicist and inventor who formulated Charles's law in 1787. In 1783 he became the first person to use hydrogen in balloons for flight.

Charles's law (chärl**′**zĭz) A physical law stating that the volume of a given amount of a gas increases as its temperature increases and decreases as its temperature decreases, as long as the pressure remains constant. *Compare* **Boyle's law.**

checksum (chĕk**′**sŭm′) A number used to test whether digital data has changed during transmission or while stored. Usually, the checksum is the sum of the series of bits that make up the data. If the data has changed, the checksum will not match the result of the calculation.

chemical (kĕm**′**ĭ-kəl) *Adjective* **1.** Relating to or produced by means of chemistry: *a chemical discovery; a chemical change.* —*Noun* **2.** A substance obtained by or used in a chemical process; a chemical compound.

chemical engineering The branch of engineering that deals with the development and manufacture of products involving chemicals.

chemical name The name of a chemical compound that shows the names of each of its elements or subcompounds. For example, the chemical name of baking soda is sodium bicarbonate.

chemistry (kĕm**′**ĭ-strē) **1.** The scientific study of the structure, properties, and reactions of the chemical elements and the compounds they form. **2.** The composition, structure, properties, and reactions of a substance.

chemosynthesis (kē′mō-sĭn**′**thĭ-sĭs) The formation of carbohydrates using energy obtained from chemical reactions rather than energy obtained from light, as in photosynthesis. Certain bacteria and archaea, especially those that live deep in the ocean, use chemosynthesis for making their own food. They obtain energy by oxidizing chemicals such as hydrogen, sulfide, or methane.

chemotherapy (kē′mō-thĕr**′**ə-pē) The treatment of disease, especially cancer, with chemicals that have a specific poisonous effect on the cancerous or disease-causing cells.

chert (chûrt) A hard, brittle, reddish-brown to green sedimentary rock consisting of very small crystals of quartz.

chickenpox (chĭk**′**ən-pŏks′) A highly contagious infection, usually of young children, that is caused by a virus. Symptoms include an itchy skin rash and fever. Also called *varicella*.

chimpanzee (chĭm′păn-zē**′**) A dark-haired ape that is smaller than a gorilla and is found in central and western Africa north of the Congo River. Chimpanzees and bonobos are the closest living relatives of humans.

chip (chĭp) *See* **integrated circuit.**

chiropractic (kī**′**rə-prăk′tĭk) A system for

treating disorders of the body, especially disorders of the bones, muscles, and joints, by manipulating the vertebrae of the spine and other structures.

chitin (kīt′n) A tough substance that is the main component of the exoskeletons of arthropods, such as the shells of crustaceans and the outer coverings of insects and spiders, and of the cell walls of fungi.

chlamydia (klə-mĭd′ē-ə) A sexually transmitted disease caused by a bacterium, often resulting in inflammation of the reproductive organs. If untreated, it can lead to infertility in women.

chlorate (klôr′āt′) A chemical compound containing the group ClO_3.

chloride (klôr′īd′) An anion of chlorine or a compound containing this anion, such as sodium chloride.

chlorinate (klôr′ə-nāt′) To add chlorine or one of its compounds to a substance. Water and sewage are chlorinated to be disinfected, and paper pulp is chlorinated to be bleached.

chlorine (klôr′ēn′) A greenish-yellow, gaseous halogen element that can combine with most other elements and is found chiefly in combination with sodium as common salt. Chlorine is very poisonous, being highly irritating to the nose, throat, and lungs, and causing suffocation. It is used in purifying water, as a disinfectant and bleach, and in making many important compounds such as chloroform. *Symbol* **Cl.** *Atomic number* 17. *See* **Periodic Table,** pages 254–255.

chlorofluorocarbon (klôr′ō-flo͝or′ō-kär′bən) *See under* **fluorocarbon.**

chloroform (klôr′ə-fôrm′) A colorless, toxic, sweet-tasting liquid, $CHCl_3$, used chiefly as a solvent. It was also once widely used as an anesthetic.

chlorophyll (klôr′ə-fĭl) Any of several green pigments that are found in green plants, algae, and certain bacteria. Chlorophyll captures light energy, which is used in photosynthesis to convert carbon dioxide and water into food molecules. Chlorophyll molecules are composed of carbon, hydrogen, magnesium, nitrogen, and oxygen. *See more at* **photosynthesis.**

chloroplast (klôr′ə-plăst′) A structure in the cells of green plants and algae that contains chlorophyll and is the site where photosynthesis takes place. *See more at* **cell, photosynthesis.**

cholera (kŏl′ər-ə) An infectious, sometimes fatal disease of the small intestine caused by a bacterium. It is contracted from contaminated water and food and causes severe diarrhea, vomiting, and dehydration.

cholesterol (kə-lĕs′tə-rôl′) A fatty substance found in animals that is a main component of cell membranes and is important in metabolism and hormone production. In vertebrate animals, cholesterol is a major component of the blood. Higher than normal amounts of cholesterol in the blood, which can occur from eating too many fatty foods, may lead to diseases of the arteries such as atherosclerosis.

chordate (kôr′dāt′) Any of a large group of animals having at some stage of development a flexible rodlike structure (called a notochord) and a hollow nerve cord running along the back, and gill-like openings in the pharynx. Chordates include all vertebrates and certain marine animals, such as the lancelets and the tunicates.

chorion (kôr′ē-ŏn′) The outer membrane that encloses the embryo of a reptile, bird, or mammal. In mammals, the chorion contributes to the development of the placenta.

chromate (krō′māt′) A chemical compound containing the group CrO_4.

chromatic (krō-măt′ĭk) Relating to color or colors.

chromatid (krō′mə-tĭd) Either of the two strands formed when a chromosome duplicates itself during cell division. The chromatids are joined together by a single centromere and later separate to become individual chromosomes. *See more at* **meiosis, mitosis.**

chromatin (krō′mə-tĭn) A substance in the nucleus of a cell that consists mainly of DNA and proteins called histones. During cell division, the chromatin becomes dense and compact, forming individual chromosomes.

chromatography (krō′mə-tŏg′rə-fē) A technique used to separate the components of a chemical mixture by moving the mixture along a stationary material, such as gelatin or paper. Different components of the mixture are separated from each other because they move at different rates through the material.

chromium (krō′mē-əm) A hard, shiny, steel-gray metallic element that does not rust or become dull easily. It is used to plate other metals, to harden steel, and to make stainless steel and other alloys. *Symbol* **Cr.** *Atomic number* 24. *See* **Periodic Table,** pages 254–255.

chromosome (krō′mə-sōm′) A structure in all living cells that carries the genes that determine heredity. In all cells except those of bacteria and archaea, the chromosomes are threadlike strands of DNA and protein that are contained in the nucleus. In eukaryotes, they occur in pairs in all of the cells except the sex cells. In bacteria and archaea, which have no nucleus, the chromosome is a circular strand of DNA located in the cytoplasm.

chromosphere (krō′mə-sfîr′) A glowing, transparent layer of gas surrounding the photosphere of a star, especially the sun. The sun's chromosphere is several thousand miles thick and is composed mainly of hydrogen.

chronometer (krə-nŏm′ĭ-tər) An extremely accurate clock or other timepiece. Chronometers are used in scientific experiments, navigation, and astronomical observations.

chrysalis (krĭs′ə-lĭs) **1.** The pupa of certain kinds of insects, especially butterflies. A chrysalis has a hard case from which the adult eventually emerges. **2.** The hard case of a chrysalis.

cicada (sĭ-kā′də) Any of various insects having a broad head and transparent wings. Male cicadas produce a high-pitched droning sound from specialized organs on the abdomen. Cicadas live underground as nymphs for anywhere from 1 to 17 years before emerging to live for a short time as adults.

–cide A suffix that means "a killer of." It is used to form the names of substances that kill a specified organism, such as *insecticide,* a substance that kills insects.

cilium (sĭl′ē-əm) *Plural* **cilia** One of usually many hairlike projections found on the outside of certain cells and capable of a whipping motion. Some microorganisms use cilia to move themselves. The respiratory tract in humans is lined with cilia that remove foreign matter from air before it reaches the lungs.

cinchona (sĭng-kō′nə, sĭn-chō′nə) Any of several evergreen trees and shrubs of South America whose bark is the source of quinine and certain other drugs used to treat malaria.

circadian rhythm (sər-kā′dē-ən) A daily cycle

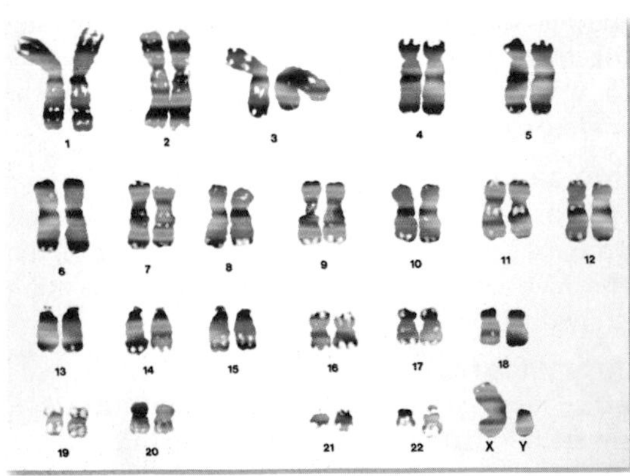

■ **chromosome**

color-enhanced photomicrograph of a complete set of chromosomes from a human male

Did You Know...?

circadian rhythm

Why do you sometimes wake up on time even if your alarm doesn't ring? What causes nocturnal animals to become active at dusk, and some flowers to open at dawn? The answer is that you — and many other organisms — have a kind of internal clock that controls the cycle of the day's biological activities. These daily biological activities are known as *circadian rhythms* because they are influenced by the regular intervals of light and dark in each 24-hour day. While the process underlying circadian rhythm is not completely understood, it is thought to be controlled in animals mainly by the release of hormones. The brain regulates the amount of hormone released in response to the information it gets from light-sensitive cells in the eye, called *photoreceptors.* Circadian rhythms can be disrupted by changes in this daily schedule. For example, birds exposed to artificial light for a long time sometimes build nests in the fall instead of the spring. In humans who travel long distances by air, the local time of day no longer matches the body's internal clock, causing a condition known as *jet lag.*

of biological activity based on a 24-hour period and influenced by regular variations in the environment, such as the alternation of night and day.

circle (sûr′kəl) A closed curve whose points are all on the same plane and at the same distance from a fixed point (the center).

circuit (sûr′kĭt) **1.** A closed path through which an electric current flows or may flow. Circuits in which a power supply is connected to two or more components (such as light bulbs) can be arranged in different ways. In a **series circuit,** the components are connected to the power source one after the other in a single path. If a break occurs in one part of the circuit, no current flows through any of the components. In a **parallel circuit,** each component is directly connected with the power source along its own branch. If a break occurs in one branch, the component in that branch stops receiving current, but current can still flow through the other components. **2.** A system of electrically connected components: *a microchip containing all the circuits of a computer.*

circuit board In a computer, an insulated board on which interconnected circuits and components such as microchips are mounted or etched.

circuit breaker A switch that automatically interrupts the flow of an electric current if the current becomes too strong.

circulation (sûr′kyə-lā′shən) The flow of blood through the circulatory system.

circulatory system (sûr′kyə-lə-tôr′ē) The system that circulates blood throughout the body in vertebrates, consisting of the heart and blood vessels. Blood that is rich in oxygen is carried away from the heart by the arteries, and blood that is low in oxygen is returned to the heart by the veins. Nutrients and waste products are exchanged between the blood and the tissues of the body as the blood circulates. The lymphatic system is often considered part of the circulatory system. Many invertebrates have a similar system, often without distinct vessels to contain the fluid.

circum– A prefix meaning "around," as in

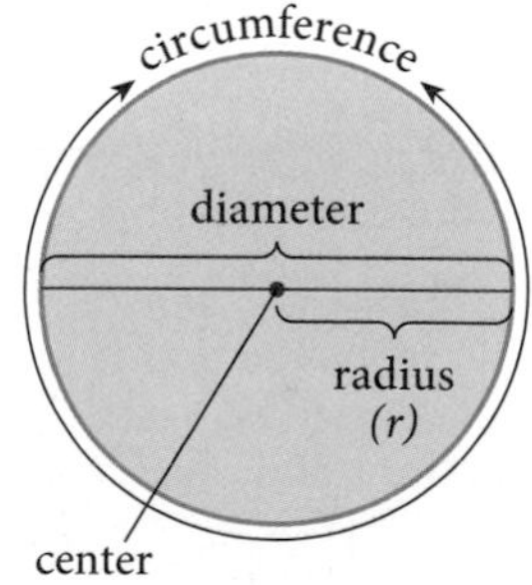

■ **circle**
The area of a circle is πr^2. The length of the circumference is $2\pi r$.

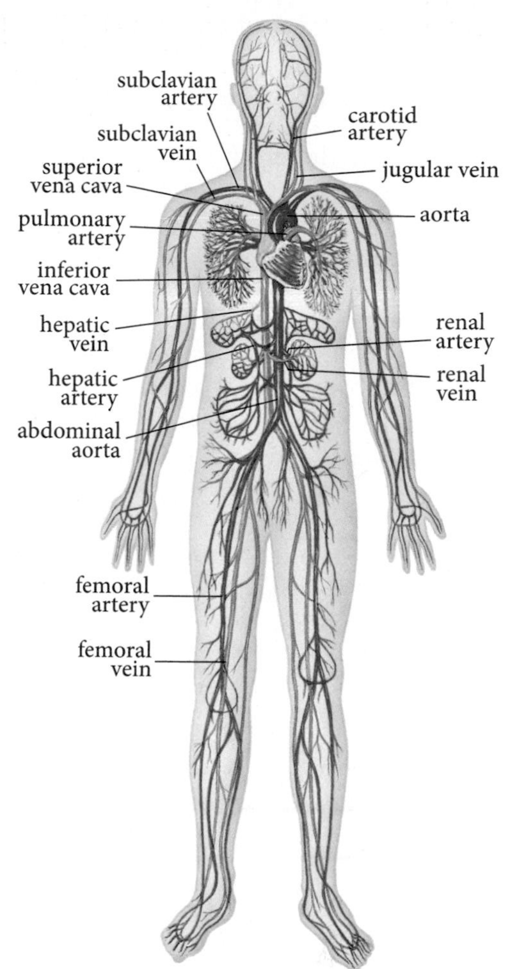

■ **circulatory system**
In the diagram above, the blood vessels of the circulatory system are colored according to whether they carry blood that is high in oxygen (red) or low in oxygen (blue). Most arteries, which carry blood away from the heart, are colored red; most veins, which carry blood back toward the heart, are colored blue.

circumscribe, to draw a figure around another figure.

circumference (sər-kŭm′fər-əns) **1.** The boundary line of a circle or of another closed curve, such as an ellipse. **2.** The length of such a boundary. The circumference of a circle is computed by multiplying the diameter by pi.

circumscribe (sûr′kəm-skrīb′) *Geometry* To draw a figure around another figure so as to touch as many points as possible. A circle that is circumscribed around a triangle touches it at each of the triangle's three vertices.

cirque (sûrk) A steep bowl-shaped hollow occurring at the upper end of a mountain valley, especially one carved out by a former or existing glacier.

cirrhosis (sĭ-rō′sĭs) A liver disease in which normal liver cells are gradually replaced by scar tissue, causing the organ to shrink, harden, and lose its function. Cirrhosis is commonly caused by chronic alcohol abuse or severe infection.

cirrocumulus (sîr′ō-kyo͞om′yə-ləs) A grainy or rippled cloud formation, usually occurring in sheets or bands. Cirrocumulus clouds form at upper levels of the atmosphere.

cirrostratus (sîr′ō-străt′əs) A thin, hazy cloud formation made up of ice crystals, often covering the sky in sheets and producing a halo effect around the sun. Cirrostratus clouds form at upper levels of the atmosphere.

cirrus (sîr′əs) A cloud formation made up of feathery white patches, bands, or streamers of ice crystals. Cirrus clouds form at upper levels of the atmosphere.

citrate (sĭt′rāt′) A salt, ester, or anion of citric acid.

citric acid (sĭt′rĭk) A white, odorless acid, $C_6H_8O_7$, having a sour taste and occurring widely in plants, especially in citrus fruit. It is used in medicine and as a flavoring.

citric acid cycle *See* **Krebs cycle.**

citrus (sĭt′rəs) **1.** Any of various evergreen trees or shrubs bearing fruit with juicy flesh and a thick rind. Citrus trees are native to South and Southeast Asia but are grown in warm climates around the world. Many species have spines. The orange, lemon, lime, and grapefruit are citrus trees. **2.** The usually edible fruit of one of these trees or shrubs.

civil engineering (sĭv′əl) The branch of engineering that deals with the design and construction of structures such as bridges, roads, and dams.

Cl The symbol for **chlorine.**

clam (klăm) Any of various saltwater or freshwater bivalve mollusks that burrow into sand or mud. Many kinds of clams are edible.

class (klăs) A taxonomic category of organisms that share certain characteristics, ranking above an order and below a phylum. *See Table at* **taxonomy.**

classical physics (klăs′ĭ-kəl) Physics that is based on Newton's laws of motion and does not make use of quantum mechanics or the theory of relativity. ❖ **Classical mechanics** refers to Newton's laws of motion and other principles of mechanics based on them. Classical mechanics does not correctly describe the behavior of objects that are very small, such as atoms and subatomic particles, or objects that are moving at speeds close to the speed of light. Quantum mechanics is needed to describe the behavior of very small particles, and the theory of relativity for rapidly moving objects.

classification (klăs′ə-fĭ-kā′shən) In biology, the systematic grouping of organisms by similarity of characteristics, often thought to reflect evolutionary relationships. The traditional system of classification is called the Linnaean system. *See Table at* **taxonomy.**

clavicle (klăv′ĭ-kəl) Either of two slender bones in humans and other primates that extend from the upper part of the sternum to the shoulder. Also called *collarbone. See more at* **skeleton.**

claw (klô) **1.** A sharp, curved nail at the end of a toe of a vertebrate animal. **2.** A pincer, as of a lobster or crab, used for grasping.

clay (klā) A stiff, sticky, earthy material that is soft and flexible when wet and consists mainly of various silicates of aluminum. It is widely used to make bricks, pottery, and tiles.

cleavage (klē′vĭj) **1.** *Geology* The breaking of certain minerals along specific planes, making smooth surfaces. These surfaces are parallel to the faces of the molecular crystals that make up the minerals. A mineral that exhibits cleavage breaks into smooth pieces with the same pattern of parallel surfaces regardless of how many times it is broken. Some minerals, like quartz, do not have a cleavage and break into uneven pieces with rough surfaces. **2.** *Biology* In an embryo, the series of cell divisions by which a single fertilized egg cell becomes a many-celled blastula.

cleft palate (klĕft) Incomplete closure of the palate during development of an embryo, resulting in a split along part or all of the roof of the mouth. ❖ A vertical split or cleft in the upper lip that can occur with or without a cleft palate is called a **cleft lip.**

climate (klī′mĭt) The general or average weather conditions of a certain region, including temperature, rainfall, and wind.

climatology (klī′mə-tŏl′ə-jē) The scientific study of climates, including the causes and long-term effects of variation in regional and global climates.

climax community (klī′măks′) An ecological community in which there is little change in the kinds and numbers of organisms present until a disturbance such as a fire or flood occurs. A climax community is the final stage of ecological succession. *See more at* **succession.**

clitoris (klĭt′ər-ĭs, klĭ-tôr′ĭs) A sex organ that forms part of the external reproductive system in female mammals and some other animals. The clitoris is composed largely of erectile tissue.

cloaca (klō-ā′kə) The common body cavity that serves as the opening for the intestinal, genital, and urinary tracts in amphibians, reptiles, birds, some fish, and the mammals known as monotremes.

clone (klōn) *Noun* **1.** A cell, group of cells, or organism produced asexually from a single ancestor and genetically identical to it. Cloning can occur naturally, as by fission in one-celled organisms, or can be performed artificially, as by taking the nucleus from the cell of an adult organism and placing it into an egg cell so that it grows into an adult with the same genes as the original organism. **2.** A copy of a DNA sequence, as produced by genetic engineering. — *Verb* **3.** To produce or grow a cell, group of cells, or organism from a single original cell. **4.** To make identical copies of a DNA sequence. *See more at* **genetic engineering.**

closed circuit (klōzd) **1.** An electric circuit through which current can flow in an uninterrupted path. **2.** A television system in which the signal is usually sent by cable to a limited number of receivers, as in a video camera surveillance system.

closed universe A model of the universe in which there is enough matter, and therefore enough gravitational force, to stop the expansion started by the Big Bang. *See Note at* **Big Bang.**

clot (klŏt) A thickened or solid mass formed from a liquid, such as blood.

cloud (kloud) **1.** *Meteorology* A visible mass of condensed water droplets or ice particles floating in the atmosphere. Clouds take various shapes depending on the conditions under which they form and their height in the atmosphere, ranging from ground or sea level to several miles above the Earth. **2.** *Physics* A distinguishable mass of particles or gas, such as the collection of gases and dust in a nebula. **3.** *Computers* The collection of data and services available through the Internet.

cloud chamber A particle detector that records the tracks of charged subatomic particles, such as electrons. A cloud chamber consists of a container

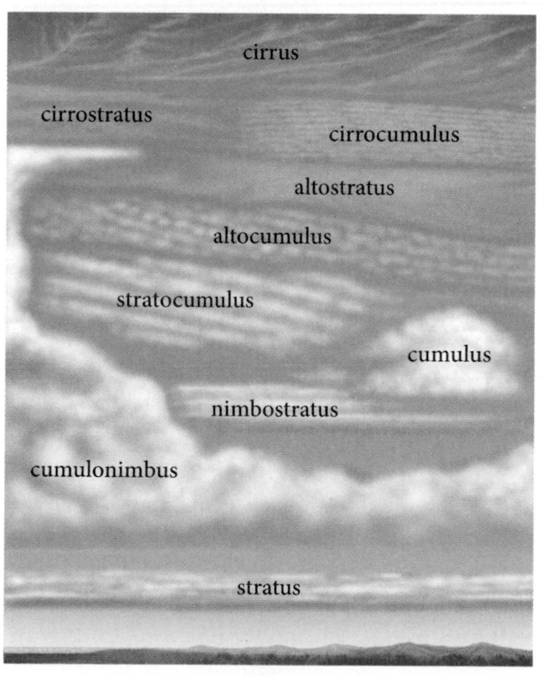

■ **cloud**

filled with a vapor that is nearly condensing and liquefying. The path of a charged particle is revealed as a trail of tiny droplets of liquid in the vapor. Cloud chambers were replaced by bubble chambers, which have in turn been replaced by other more modern particle detectors. *Compare* **bubble chamber.**

cloud computing The use of services made available on the Internet for storing data and running software programs. Cloud computing replaces many of the traditional functions of the personal computer.

cloud seeding A method of making a cloud give up its moisture as rain, especially by releasing particles of dry ice or silver iodide into the cloud.

club moss (klŭb) Any of various small evergreen plants that have vascular tissue for conducting fluids and that reproduce by spores. Club mosses have small, narrow leaves, and the spores are contained in clublike structures, often on stalks.

cm Abbreviation of **centimeter.**

Cm The symbol for **curium.**

Cn The symbol for **copernicium.**

cnidarian (nī-dâr′ē-ən) Any of various aquatic invertebrate animals that have a body with radial symmetry, stinging tentacles, and a saclike internal cavity. They have a single opening for ingesting food and eliminating wastes. Cnidarians include the jellyfishes, hydras, sea anemones, and corals.

Co The symbol for **cobalt.**

coagulate (kō-ăg′yə-lāt′) To change or thicken from a liquid into a solid or nearly solid mass: *Blood coagulates when exposed to the air.*

coal (kōl) A dark-brown to black, natural solid substance formed from fossilized plants under conditions of great pressure, high humidity, and lack of air. Coal consists mainly of carbon and is widely used as a fuel and raw material. *See more at* **anthracite, bituminous coal, lignite.**

coal tar A thick, sticky, black liquid obtained by heating coal in the absence of air. It is used as a component of roofing and waterproofing materials and as a raw material for many dyes, drugs, and paints.

cobalamin (kō-băl′ə-mĭn) *See under* **vitamin B complex.**

cobalt (kō′bôlt′) A silvery-white, hard, brittle metallic element that occurs widely in ores containing other metals. It is used to make magnetic alloys, heat-resistant alloys, and blue pigment for ceramics and glass. *Symbol* **Co.** *Atomic number* 27. *See* **Periodic Table,** pages 254–255.

cobra (kō′brə) Any of several venomous snakes that are capable of spreading out the skin of the neck to form a flattened hood. Cobras are native to Asia and Africa.

coccus (kŏk′əs) *Plural* **cocci** (kŏk′sī, kŏk′ī) Any of various bacteria that are shaped like a sphere and are usually grouped together in chains or clusters.

coccyx (kŏk′sĭks) A small triangular bone found at the base of the spinal column in humans and other apes. It is composed of several fused vertebrae. Also called *tailbone. See more at* **skeleton.**

cochlea (kŏk′lē-ə) The part of the inner ear of vertebrates that contains the nerve endings necessary for hearing. In mammals it has a spiral shape, like a snail shell.

Cockcroft (kŏk′krôft′), Sir **John Douglas** 1897–1967. British physicist. With the physicist Ernest Walton, he developed the particle accelerator. Their experiments with it led to the first successful splitting of an atom in 1932.

cockroach (kŏk′rōch′) Any of numerous brownish or black insects that have a flat body and lay their eggs in hardened cases. Certain species are common household pests.

cocoon (kə-ko͞on′) **1.** A case of silky strands spun by the larvae of moths and certain other insects as a protective covering for the pupa. **2.** A similar protective covering or structure, such as the egg case of a spider.

coefficient (kō′ə-fĭsh′ənt) A number or symbol multiplied with a variable or an unknown quantity in an algebraic term. For example, 4 is the coefficient in the term $4x$, and x is the coefficient in $x(a + b)$.

coelacanth (sē′lə-kănth′) Any of various fish having lobed, fleshy fins and several characteristics not found in other vertebrate animals. Coelacanths were known only from fossil remains until a living specimen was caught off the coast of southern Africa in 1938. A second species was discovered in 1999 in Indonesia.

coelenterate (sĭ-lĕn′tə-rĭt) A jellyfish or similar marine invertebrate. Scientists now use the term *cnidarian* for most species that were formerly classified as coelenterates. *See more at* **cnidarian.**

coevolution (kō′ĕv-ə-lo͞o′shən) The process by which two or more interacting species evolve together, each changing as a result of changes in the other or others. Coevolution occurs, for example, between predators and prey and between insects and the flowers that they pollinate.

cohesion (kō-hē′zhən) The force of attraction that holds molecules of a given substance together. It is strongest in solids, less strong in liquids, and least strong in gases. Cohesion allows the formation of drops in liquids, and clouds in the atmosphere.

cold-blooded (kōld′blŭd′ĭd) Having a body temperature that is maintained by external rather than internal sources of heat. Most fish, amphibians, and reptiles are cold-blooded.

cold front (kōld) The forward edge of an advancing mass of cold air that pushes under a mass of warm air. A cold front is often accompanied by heavy showers or thunderstorms. *See more at* **front.**

collagen (kŏl′ə-jən) The tough, fibrous protein found in bone, cartilage, skin, and other connective tissue.

collarbone (kŏl′ər-bōn′) *See* **clavicle.**

collinear (kə-lĭn′ē-ər) *Mathematics* **1.** Sharing a common line, such as two intersecting planes. **2.** Lying on the same line, such as a set of points.

collision zone (kə-lĭzh′ən) *See* **convergent plate boundary.**

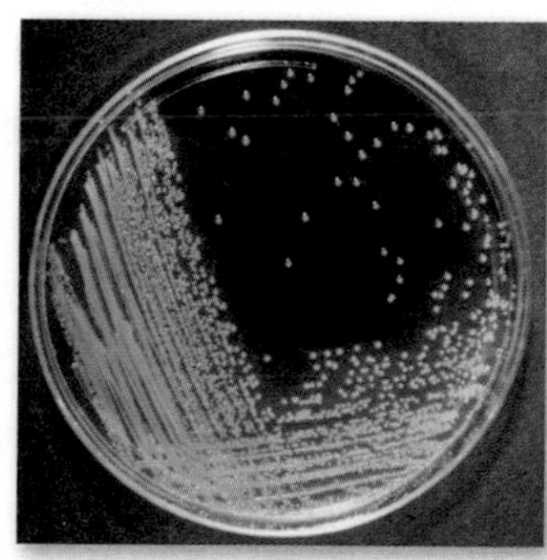

■ **colony**
colony of cholera bacteria in a petri dish

colloid (kŏl′oid′) A mixture in which very small particles of one substance are distributed evenly throughout another substance. The particles are generally larger than those in a solution, and smaller than those in a suspension. Paints, milk, and fog are examples of colloids. *Compare* **solution, suspension.**

colon (kō′lən) The longest part of the large intestine, extending from the cecum to the rectum. Food waste received from the small intestine is solidified and prepared for elimination from the body in the colon.

colonization (kŏl′ə-nĭ-zā′shən) *Ecology* The spreading of a species into a geographic area where it did not exist before.

colony (kŏl′ə-nē) A group of the same kind of organisms living or growing together: *a colony of ants; a colony of bacteria.*

color (kŭl′ər) The sensation produced by the effect of light waves striking the retina of the eye. The color of something depends mainly on which wavelengths of light it emits, reflects, or transmits. *See A Closer Look, on page 76.*

colorblind (kŭl′ər-blīnd′) Unable to distinguish certain colors. Humans who are colorblind usually cannot distinguish red from green. Colorblindness is usually inherited, and it is more common in men than in women.

coma[1] (kō′mə) A state of deep unconsciousness resulting from disease or injury, from which a person cannot be aroused. A person in a coma usually is unable to respond to events taking place outside the body.

coma[2] The brightly shining cloud of gas that surrounds a comet's nucleus. The coma is made of material that evaporates from the nucleus when the comet is close to the sun or other star that it orbits.

combustion (kəm-bŭs′chən) A heat-producing chemical reaction in which a fuel combines with oxygen or with some other substance that behaves chemically like oxygen. Burning wood is an example of combustion. *See also* **spontaneous combustion.**

comet (kŏm′ĭt) A celestial object composed of ice, frozen gases, and dust that orbits the sun along an elongated path. When a comet comes close to the sun, it develops a gaseous coma around the

A CLOSER LOOK

Color

When beams of colored light are mixed, or added, their wavelengths combine to form other colors. Colors of any hue can be formed by mixing wavelengths corresponding to the additive primaries red, green, and blue. When two of the additive primaries are mixed in equal proportion, they form the complement of the third. Thus cyan (a mixture of green and blue) is the complement of red; magenta (a mixture of blue and red) is the complement of green; and yellow (a mixture of red and green) is the complement of blue. Mixing the three additive primaries in equal proportions produces white light.

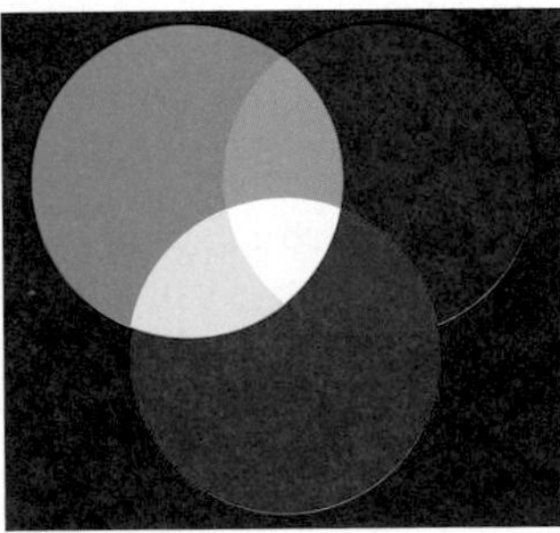

Additive Primaries

Subtractive Primaries

When light passes through a color filter, certain wavelengths are absorbed, or subtracted, while others are transmitted. The subtractive primaries cyan, magenta, and yellow can be combined using overlapping filters to form colors of any hue. Thus overlapping filters of cyan (blue and green) and magenta (blue and red) filter out all wavelengths except blue; magenta (blue and red) and yellow (red and green) filter out all except red; and yellow (red and green) and cyan (blue and green) filter out all except green. Combining all three subtractive primaries in equal proportions filters out all wavelengths, producing black.

We often describe different shades of color as being dark, light, bright, or pale. A particular color can be described scientifically in terms of its hue (red, green, blue, and so forth), its value (how light or dark it is), and its saturation (how intense or vivid it is). The diagram below organizes these aspects of color into three dimensions: a central disk or ring displaying the range of hues, a vertical axis representing the values from light to dark, and a radius representing the degree of saturation from pale to bright.

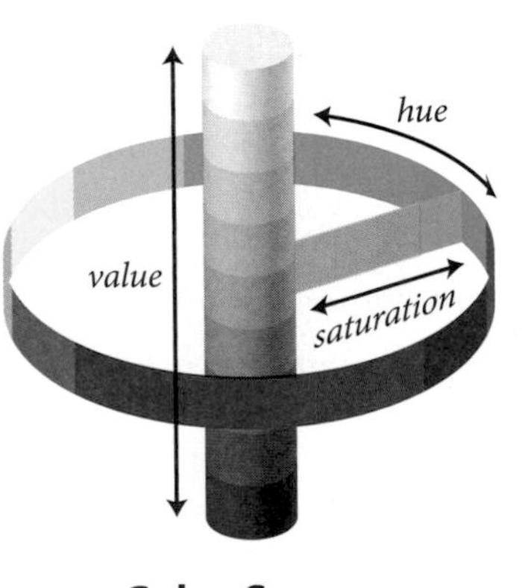

Color Space

nucleus and a long, bright tail of gas and dust. *See Note at* **solar system.**

commensalism (kə-mĕn′sə-lĭz′əm) A relationship between two organisms of different species in which one benefits while the other is unaffected, as when an orchid uses a tree branch for support.

common cold (kŏm′ən) An infection caused by a virus, in which the membranes lining the mouth, nose, and throat become inflamed. Its symptoms are fever, sneezing, and coughing.

common denominator A quantity into which all the denominators of a set of fractions may be divided without a remainder. For example, the fractions $\frac{1}{3}$ and $\frac{2}{5}$ have a common denominator of 15.

common divisor A number that is a factor of two or more numbers. For example, 3 is a common divisor of both 9 and 15. Also called *common factor.*

common logarithm A logarithm having 10 as its base. *Compare* **natural logarithm.**

common multiple A number that is divisible by each of two or more numbers without a remainder. For example, 12 is a common multiple of 2, 3, 4, and 6.

common name An ordinary, everyday name as distinguished from a scientific name. For example, "sugar maple" is the common name for the tree *Acer saccharum.*

common salt *See under* **salt.**

communicable (kə-myo͞oʹnĭ-kə-bəl) Capable of being transmitted from one individual to another; contagious. Chickenpox is a communicable disease.

communications satellite (kə-myo͞o′nĭ-kāʹ-shənz) An artificial space satellite used to transmit signals, such as television and telephone signals, from one ground station to another.

community (kə-myo͞oʹnĭ-tē) A group of organisms that interact with one another and with the environment in a specific place. A community can be small and local, as in a pond or city park, or it can be regional or global, as in a rainforest or the ocean.

commutative property (kə-myo͞oʹtə-tĭv, kŏmʹ-yə-tā′tĭv) A property distinguishing some mathematical operations on two objects, such as the addition or multiplication of two numbers, where the order of the objects may be reversed without affecting the result. For example, 2 + 3 gives the same sum as 3 + 2, and 2 × 3 gives the same product as 3 × 2. *See also* **associative property, distributive property.**

compass
left: *directional compass*
right: *drawing compass*

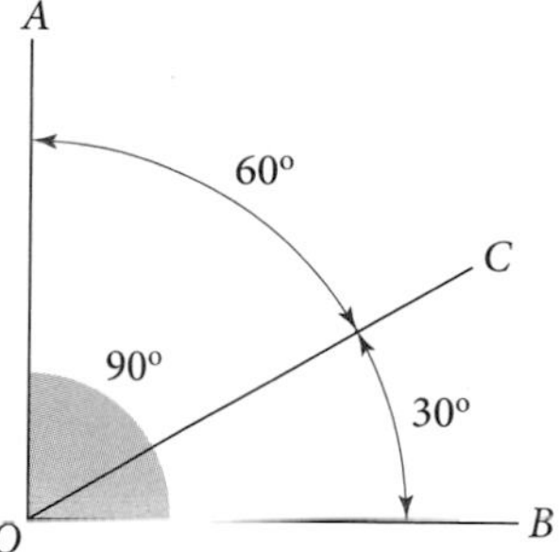

complementary angles
angles AOC + COB = 90°

compact disc or **compact disk** (kŏmʹpăkt′) A small optical disc on which data such as music, text, or graphic images is digitally encoded. *See Note at* **disk.**

compass (kŭmʹpəs) **1.** A device used to determine geographical direction, usually consisting of a magnetic needle mounted on a pivot, aligning itself naturally with the Earth's magnetic field so that it points to the Earth's geomagnetic north or south pole. **2.** A device used for drawing circles and arcs and for measuring distances, consisting of two legs hinged together at one end.

complement (kŏmʹplə-mənt) **1.** A system of proteins found in normal blood plasma that combines with antibodies to destroy disease-causing bacteria and other foreign cells. **2.** A complementary color.

complementary angles (kŏm′plə-mĕnʹtə-rē) Two angles whose sum is 90°.

complementary color A secondary color that, when combined with the primary color whose wavelength it does not contain, produces white light. *See more at* **color.**

complete metamorphosis (kəm-plētʹ) *See under* **metamorphosis.**

complex number (kŏmʹplĕks′) A number that can be expressed in terms of *i* (the square root of −1). Mathematically, such a number can be written $a + bi$, where a and b are real numbers. An example is $4 + 5i$.

composite number (kəm-pŏzʹĭt) A positive integer that can be divided by at least one other positive integer besides itself and 1 without leaving a remainder. 24 is a composite number since it can be divided by 2, 3, 4, 6, 8, and 12. No prime numbers are composite numbers. *Compare* **prime number.**

compost (kŏm′pōst′) A mixture of decayed organic matter used to fertilize soil. Compost is usually made by gathering plant material, such as leaves, grass clippings, and food waste, into a pile or bin and letting it rot. Manure and other substances are often added to enrich the mixture or to speed its decomposition.

compound (kŏm′pound′) A substance made up of atoms or ions of two or more different elements joined by chemical bonds into a unit such as a molecule. The elements are combined in a definite ratio. Water, for example, is a compound having two hydrogen atoms and one oxygen atom in each molecule.

compound eye An eye, as of an insect or crustacean, consisting of many small light-sensitive units, each of which forms part of an image.

compound leaf A leaf that is composed of two or more leaflets on a common stalk. Clover, roses, sumac, and walnut trees have compound leaves.

compound lens *See* **lens** (sense 2b).

compression (kəm-prĕsh′ən) **1.** *Physics* A force that tends to shorten or squeeze something, decreasing its volume. **2.** *Computers* The process by which data is encoded to minimize the amount of space required for storage or transmission.

Compton (kŏmp′tən), **Arthur Holly** 1892–1962. American physicist who proved Albert Einstein's statement that a particle of light has momentum even though it has no mass. Compton's experiments showed that when particles of light (called photons) collide with other particles, such as electrons, they lose energy and momentum and the light's wavelength increases. This phenomenon is known as the Compton effect.

computer (kəm-pyo͞o′tər) An electronic device capable of processing information according to a set of instructions stored within the device. *See Note at* **program.**

computer science The study of the design and operation of computers and their application to science, business, and the arts.

concave (kŏn′kāv′) Curved inward, like the inside of a circle or sphere. *Compare* **convex.**

concentration (kŏn′sən-trā′shən) The amount of a particular substance in a given amount of another substance, especially a solution or mixture.

conception (kən-sĕp′shən) The formation of a cell capable of developing into a new organism by the union of a sperm and egg cell; fertilization.

concussion (kən-kŭsh′ən) An injury to the brain usually resulting from a violent blow to the head

Did You Know...?

compound eye

Swatting a housefly is not an easy task. The fly usually sees you coming and buzzes off. Flies are master motion detectors thanks to their *compound eyes.* The compound eye, found in insects and many other arthropods, consists of a cluster of many identical units, called *ommatidia.* Each ommatidium is like a miniature vertebrate eye, with its own lens and light receptors. Compared with human eyes, compound eyes are not very good at seeing fine detail—that fly might see your swatting hand as just a blur. For many arthropods, though, it's more important to detect motion than to see a sharp image. It can also be important to see ultraviolet light, which is invisible to humans. Dragonflies have over 25,000 ommatidia in each eye and pigments that detect ultraviolet light. As a result, a dragonfly can see a rapidly flying mosquito against the glare of the sky and catch it in a flash.

Did You Know...?

conduction, convection, and radiation

Heat energy can be transferred by conduction, convection, or radiation. In *conduction,* heat spreads through a substance when atoms and molecules that are moving fast collide with neighboring ones that are moving more slowly, transferring some of their kinetic energy to them. This is how the handle of a teaspoon sticking out of a cup of hot tea eventually gets hot, though the handle itself is not touching the hot liquid. *Convection* refers to the transfer of heat by the movement of a substance's molecules. When a fluid is heated, for example, portions of the fluid near the source of the heat tend to become less dense and expand outward. When these less dense regions rise, cooler portions flow in to take their place, and are then heated in turn. Many ocean currents are convection currents caused by the uneven heating of the ocean waters by the sun. *Radiation* transmits heat in the form of electromagnetic waves, especially infrared waves. A hot wire in a heat lamp gives off infrared rays that travel through space. When the rays strike an object, like your face, its molecules absorb the rays' energy and vibrate faster, so the object becomes hotter.

and causing a temporary disruption in the brain's ability to function normally. Symptoms include short-term memory loss.

condensation (kŏn′dən-sā′shən) The change of a gas or vapor to a liquid, either by cooling or by being subjected to increased pressure. When water vapor cools in the atmosphere, for example, it condenses into drops of water that form clouds.

condenser (kən-dĕn′sər) An apparatus that is used to condense vapor.

conductance (kən-dŭk′təns) A measure of the ability of a material to carry an electric charge.

conduction (kən-dŭk′shən) The transfer of energy, such as heat or an electric charge, through a substance. In heat conduction, energy flows by direct contact of the substance's molecules with each other; the molecules vibrate more or less quickly but do not change position. In electrical conduction, energy flows by the movement of electrons or ions. ❖ **Conductivity** (kŏn′dŭk-tĭv′-ĭ-tē) is the ability to transfer heat, electricity, or sound by conduction.

conductor (kən-dŭk′tər) A material or an object that transmits heat, electricity, light, or sound. Copper is a good conductor of electricity.

cone (kōn) **1.** A three-dimensional surface or solid object whose surface rises from a circular base in a continuous series of smaller circles, narrowing to a point (the vertex) at the top. A cone can be defined as the surface covered by a line segment with one end fixed at the vertex, and the other end rotated in a circle. **2.** A rounded or elongated cluster of woody scales enclosing the reproductive structures of most gymnosperms, such as pines, spruces, and other conifers. Cones are either male, producing pollen, or female, producing ovules. Male cones are usually much

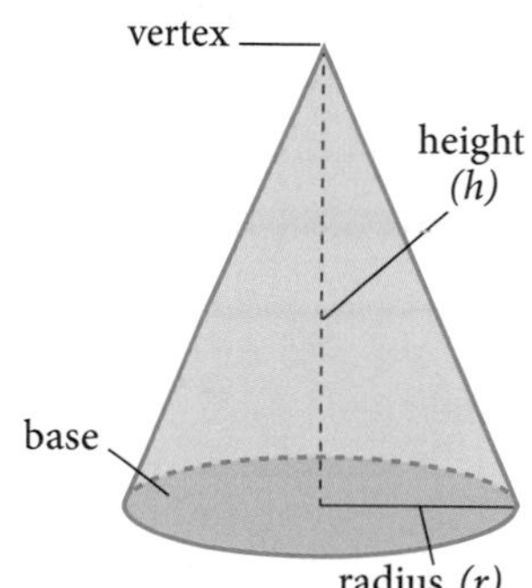

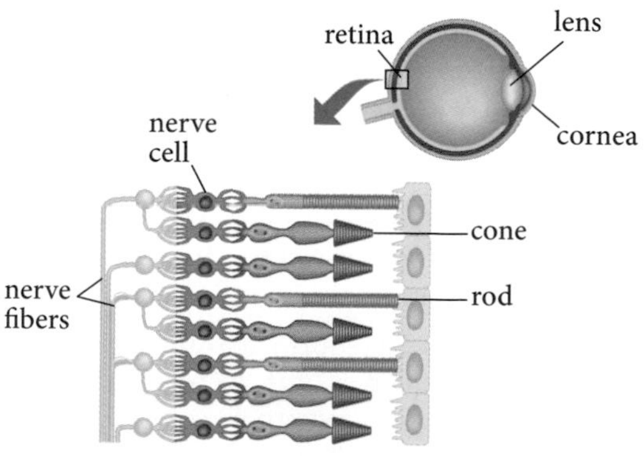

cone

top: *The volume (V) of a cone can be calculated using the following equation:* $V = \frac{1}{3}\pi r^2 h$.

bottom: *detail of the retina showing cones and rods*

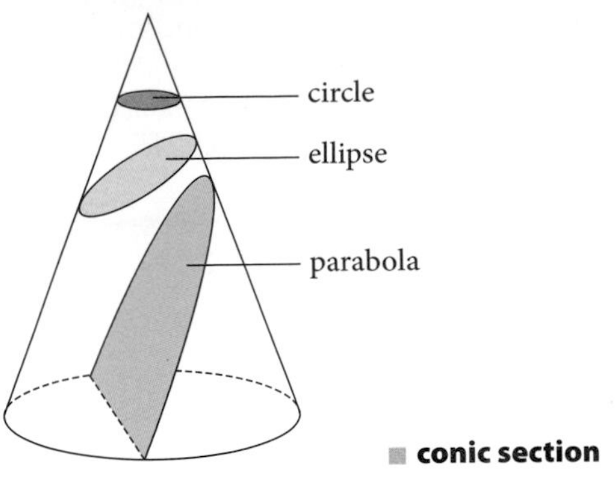

conic section

smaller than female cones. **3.** One of the cone-shaped cells in the retina of the eye of humans and many other vertebrate animals. Cones are responsible for daylight vision and color vision. *Compare* **rod.**

congenital (kən-jĕn′ĭ-tl) Relating to a condition that is present at birth, as a result of either environmental or genetic causes. Spina bifida is an example of a congenital condition.

congestive heart failure (kən-jĕs′tĭv) Inability of the heart to circulate blood adequately to the lungs and outer body tissues, resulting in congestion in the lungs, weakness, and shortness of breath.

conglomerate (kən-glŏm′ə-rāt′) A coarse-grained sedimentary rock that consists of pebbles, gravel, or seashells cemented together by hardened silt, clay, calcium carbonate, or a similar material. *See Table at* **rock.**

congruent (kŏng′gro͞o-ənt, kən-gro͞o′ənt) *Geometry* Having the same size and shape; matching exactly: *congruent triangles.*

conic projection (kŏn′ĭk) A method of making a flat map of the Earth by projecting its surface features onto a cone, which is then flattened out so that parallels appear as arcs of circles. *Compare* **homolosine projection, Mercator projection, sinusoidal projection.**

conic section A curve formed by the intersection of a plane with a cone. Conic sections can appear as circles, ellipses, hyperbolas, or parabolas, depending on the angle of the intersecting plane relative to the cone's base.

conifer (kŏn′ə-fər) Any of various trees or shrubs that bear cones. Conifers are usually evergreen, often have needle-shaped or scalelike leaves, and include pines, firs, spruces, hemlocks, and yews. Conifers bear two kinds of cones, usually on the same tree. Male cones produce pollen that is blown by the wind to the female cones, where the seeds develop.

conjugation (kŏn′jə-gā′shən) A process in certain bacteria, algae, and fungi in which genetic material is exchanged between two cells of the same species. Conjugation is often considered a type of sexual reproduction.

conjunctiva (kŏn′jŭngk-tī′və) The mucous membrane that lines the inside of the eyelid and covers the surface of the eyeball. ❖ Inflammation of the conjunctiva is called **conjunctivitis** (kən-jŭngk′tə-vī′tĭs).

connective tissue (kə-nĕk′tĭv) Tissue that forms the framework and supporting structures of the body, including bone, cartilage, mucous membrane, and fat.

conservation (kŏn′sûr-vā′shən) **1.** The protection, preservation, management, or restoration of wildlife, forests, fisheries, and other elements of the natural environment. **2.** The careful use of something, such as energy, so as to minimize waste. **3.** The absence of change in the amount of a physical quantity, such as mass, during a physical or chemical transformation.

constant (kŏn′stənt) **1.** A quantity that is unknown but assumed to have a fixed value in a specified mathematical context. **2.** A theoretical or experimental quantity, condition, or factor that does not vary in specified circumstances. Avogadro's number and Planck's constant are examples of constants.

constellation (kŏn′stə-lā′shən) **1.** A group of stars seen as forming a figure or design in the sky, especially one of 88 recognized groups. **2.** An area of the celestial sphere occupied by one of the 88 recognized constellations.

constrictor (kən-strĭk′tər) Any of various snakes that tightly coil around and suffocate their prey. Boa constrictors, pythons, and anacondas are constrictors.

consumer (kən-so͞o′mər) An organism that feeds on other organisms or particles of organic matter. ❖ Organisms that feed on producers in a food chain are called **primary consumers,** and animals that feed on primary consumers are called **secondary consumers.** An animal that eats animals that eat animals is a **tertiary consumer.** *Compare* **producer.**

contact (kŏn′tăkt′) **1.** *Physics* **a.** A connection between two conductors that allows an electric current or heat to flow. **b.** A part or device that makes or breaks such a connection. **2.** *Geology* The place where two different geological layers or rocks come together.

contagion (kən-tā′jən) **1.** The transmission of disease resulting from contact between individuals: *Lack of sanitary conditions may lead to widespread contagion.* **2.** A disease that is transmitted in this way: *The flu is a common contagion of the winter months.*

contagious (kən-tā′jəs) Capable of being transmitted by direct or indirect contact; communicable: *a contagious disease.*

contaminate (kən-tăm′ə-nāt′) **1.** To introduce a dangerous or unwanted substance, such as a toxin or a bacterium, by mixture or contact. **2.** To deposit radioactive material on or in something, causing it to be exposed to potentially harmful radiation. ❖ Something that contaminates is called a **contaminant.**

continent (kŏn′tə-nənt) One of the great landmasses of the Earth. The continents are usually considered to include Africa, Antarctica, Asia, Australia, Europe, North America, and South America. Some geographers consider Asia and Europe to constitute a single continent, called Eurasia.

continental divide (kŏn′tə-nĕn′tl) A region of high ground, from each side of which the river systems of a continent flow in opposite directions. ❖ In North America, the **Continental Divide** separates rivers flowing to the Pacific from those flowing to the Atlantic and Arctic Oceans on either side of a series of mountain ridges that run from Alaska to Mexico.

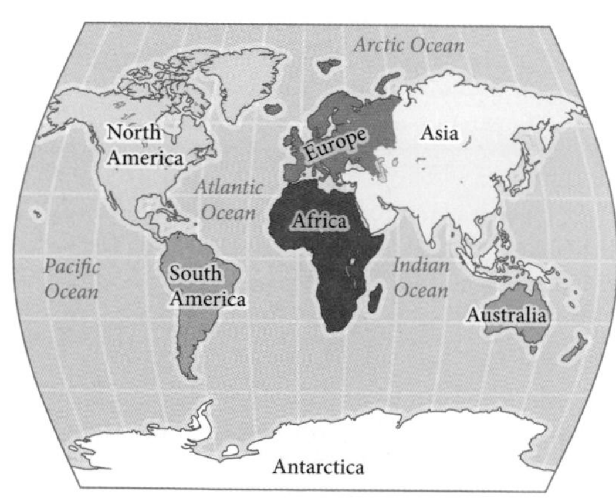

■ **continent**

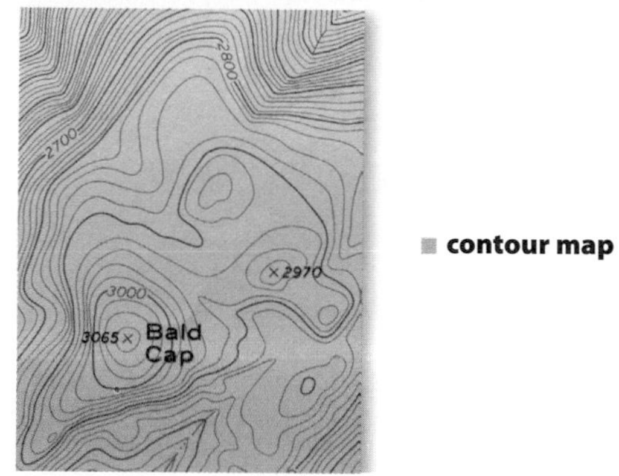

■ **contour map**

continental drift The gradual movement of the Earth's continents toward or away from each other. *See more at* **plate tectonics.** *See Note at* **Gondwana.**

continental rise A wide, gentle incline from the ocean bottom to the continental slope. The continental rise consists mainly of silts, muds, and sand, and can be several hundreds of miles wide.

continental shelf The part of the edge of a continent covered by shallow ocean waters and extending to the continental slope.

continental slope The sloping region between the continental shelf and the continental rise. The continental slope is typically about 12.5 miles (20 kilometers) wide, consists of muds and silts, and is often crosscut by submarine canyons.

contour line (kŏn′to͝or′) A line on a map joining points of the same elevation.

contour map A map that shows elevations above sea level and surface features of the land by means of contour lines.

contraceptive (kŏn′trə-sĕp′tĭv) A substance or device capable of preventing pregnancy.

contraction (kən-trăk′shən) The shortening and thickening of a muscle in action. Contraction of the biceps of the arm causes the elbow to bend.

control (kən-trōl′) Something used as a standard of comparison in a scientific experiment. In an

■ **convection**
When water in a pot is heated on a stove, warmer water rises to the surface, while cooler water sinks to the bottom where it is reheated.

experiment to test the effectiveness of a new drug, for instance, the control is an inactive substance (such as a sugar pill) that is given to one group of people, so that the data from that group can be compared with those of a group who actually took the drug. ❖ An experiment designed to test the effects of a single condition or factor on a system is called a **controlled experiment.** Only the condition being studied is allowed to vary, and all other conditions are kept constant. The group that does not receive the experimental treatment is called the **control group.**

convection (kən-vĕk′shən) Transfer of heat energy in a liquid or gas by movement of the substance's molecules. *See Note at* **conduction.**

convection zone A region of turbulent plasma within the sun and other stars where energy travels outward to the photosphere through convection. In this layer, plasma heats up and rises, cools as it nears the surface, and then falls to be heated and rise again.

converge (kən-vûrj′) **1.** To tend toward or approach an intersecting point. **2.** In calculus, to approach a limit.

convergence (kən-vûr′jəns) **1.** The act or process of converging; the tendency to meet in one point. **2.** *Mathematics* The property or manner of approaching a limit, such as a point, line, or value. **3.** *Biology* The evolution of superficially similar forms or structures in species that are not closely related to each other as a result of adapting to similar environments. An example of convergence is the independent development of fins in both fish and whales. Also called *convergent evolution. Compare* **divergence.**

convergent plate boundary (kən-vûr′jənt) A tectonic boundary where two plates are moving toward each other. If the two plates are of equal density, they usually push up against each other to form a mountain chain. If they are of unequal density, one plate usually sinks (subducts) beneath the other. Also called *collision zone. See more at* **tectonic boundary.** *Compare* **divergent plate boundary.**

converter (kən-vûr′tər) **1.** A device that changes electric current from one form to another, such as from alternating to direct current or from a higher to a lower voltage. **2.** An electronic device that changes the frequency of a radio or other electromagnetic signal.

convex (kŏn′vĕks′) Curving outward, like the outer boundary of a circle or sphere. *Compare* **concave.**

coordinate (kō-ôr′dn-ĭt) One of a set of numbers that determines the position of a point. Only one coordinate is needed if the point is on a line, two if the point is in a plane, and three if it is in space.

coordinate bond A type of covalent bond in which both the shared electrons are contributed by one of the two atoms. Also called *dative bond. See more at* **covalent bond.**

coordinated universal time (kō-ôr′dn-ā′tĭd) An international time standard that is calculated by atomic clock and serves as the basis for standard time around the world.

copepod (kō′pə-pŏd′) Any of numerous very small crustaceans that are abundant in both salt and fresh water. Some copepods are parasitic, and others are free-living.

copernicium (kō′pər-nē′sē-əm, kō′pər-nē′shē-əm) An artificially produced radioactive element that has only been produced in trace amounts. Its most stable isotope has a half-life of about 34 seconds. *Symbol* **Cn.** *Atomic number* 112. *See* **Periodic Table,** pages 254–255.

Copernicus (kō-pûr′nə-kəs), **Nicolaus** 1473–1543. Polish astronomer whose theory that Earth and other planets revolve around the sun provided the foundation for modern astronomy. He also proposed that the Earth turns once daily on its own axis.

copper (kŏp′ər) A reddish-brown, malleable metallic element that is an excellent conductor of heat and electricity. It is widely used for electrical wiring, water piping, and rust-resistant parts, either in its pure form or in alloys such as brass

BIOGRAPHY

Nicolaus Copernicus

Nicolaus Copernicus was a doctor by profession, but he had received a thorough education in the astronomical theories of his day, including the Earth-centered (or geocentric) model of the universe devised by the Greek astronomer Ptolemy. The geocentric model, with its motionless Earth, made intuitive sense, since we do not directly perceive our planet as moving, but it failed to account accurately for the observed movements of the other planets. This shortcoming led Copernicus to propose a sun-centered (or heliocentric) model of the universe, in which all the planets and stars revolve in circles around the sun. The heliocentric model as Copernicus devised it was not perfect either, since the orbital paths of the planets are actually elliptical rather than circular. Almost all of his contemporaries doubted that his system could be true, and they kept working with the older, geocentric model. In the years after Copernicus's death, a few astronomers, such as Johannes Kepler and Galileo Galilei, adopted and improved Copernicus's model, replacing the circular orbits with elliptical orbits that more closely matched actual observations. But it took almost 150 years for the heliocentric model to win widespread acceptance, when Sir Isaac Newton published his theory of gravitation.

and bronze. *Symbol* **Cu.** *Atomic number* 29. *See* **Periodic Table,** pages 254–255.

coral (kôr′əl) **1.** Any of numerous small, sedentary animals that often form massive colonies in shallow sea water. Many corals secrete a hard skeleton of calcium carbonate. Corals are cnidarians and have stinging tentacles around their mouth opening, which they use for catching prey. Many corals obtain nutrients from one-celled algae called zooxanthellae that live within their cells. *See Note at* **zooxanthella. 2.** A hard, usually white, stony substance consisting of the skeletons of these animals, often forming large reefs that support an abundance of marine life. Some kinds of coral are pink or reddish and are used in jewelry.

coral reef A mound or ridge of coral skeletons and calcium carbonate deposits. Coral reefs form especially in warm, shallow sea waters and provide food and shelter to a wide variety of fish and invertebrates. They also protect shores against erosion by causing large waves to break and lose some of their force before reaching land.

cordillera (kôr′dl-yâr′ə) A long and wide chain of mountains, especially the main mountain range of a large landmass.

core (kôr) **1.** The hard central part of certain fruits, such as apples and pears, that contains the seeds. **2a.** The central part of the Earth, below the mantle, probably consisting of iron and nickel. It is divided into a liquid outer core, which begins at a depth of about 1,800 miles (2,890 kilometers), and a solid inner core, which begins at a depth of about 3,200 miles (5,150 kilometers). **b.** The central part of any celestial object. **3.** A long, cylindrical sample of rock, ice, or other material, collected with a drill to study details that are not visible from the surface. **4.** A piece of magnetizable material, such as a rod of soft iron, that is placed inside an electrical coil or transformer to intensify and provide a path for the magnetic field produced by the current running through the wire windings. **5.** The central part of a nuclear reactor, where atomic fission occurs.

Coriolis effect (kôr′ē-ō′lĭs) The deflection of a freely moving object as viewed from a rotating object such as a planet. For example, to observers on Earth's surface, objects moving due north from the equator appear to curve toward the east. This effect explains why hurricanes and other storm systems rotate clockwise in the Southern Hemisphere and counterclockwise in the Northern Hemisphere.

cork (kôrk) **1.** A nonliving, water-resistant protective tissue that constitutes most of the outer bark of the woody stems and roots of many seed plants. It is formed on the outside of the cork cambium. Also called *phellem.* **2.** The lightweight, elastic outer bark of the cork oak, which grows near the Mediterranean Sea. Cork is used for bottle stoppers, insulation, and other products.

cork cambium The cambium that is found near the outer edge of the stems of woody plants. It produces cork to the outside and cortex (called phelloderm) to the inside. Also called *phellogen. See more at* **cambium.**

corm (kôrm) A short, thick, underground stem in which food is stored in the form of starch, often surrounded by papery scales. Crocus and gladiolus plants produce corms. *Compare* **bulb, rhizome, runner, tuber.**

cornea (kôr′nē-ə) The tough transparent membrane of the outer layer of the eyeball that covers the iris and the pupil. *See more at* **eye.**

corolla (kə-rŏl′ə, kə-rō′lə) The petals of a flower considered as a group. *See more at* **flower.**

corollary (kôr′ə-lĕr′ē) A statement that follows with little or no proof required from an already proven statement.

■ **corona**
top: *corona of the sun during a solar eclipse*
bottom: *corona of a daffodil*

■ **corrosion**

corona (kə-rō′nə) **1.** The luminous, irregular layer of gas outside the chromosphere of a star, especially the sun. During a solar eclipse, the sun's corona is visible as a halo of light. **2.** A faintly colored luminous ring that appears to surround a celestial object, especially the moon or sun, when seen through a haze or thin cloud. **3.** *Botany* A crown-shaped or trumpet-shaped structure in the center of certain flowers, such as a daffodil.

Corona Borealis (bôr′ē-ăl′ĭs) A constellation in the Northern Hemisphere between Hercules and Boötes.

coronary (kôr′ə-nĕr′ē) **1.** Relating to the heart. **2.** The two arteries that branch from the aorta to supply blood directly to the heart are called the **coronary arteries.**

corpuscle (kôr′pə-səl) Any of various cells or cell-shaped structures in the body, especially a blood cell.

corrosion (kə-rō′zhən) The breaking down or destruction of a material, especially a metal, through chemical reactions. An example of corrosion is rusting, which occurs when iron combines with oxygen and water.

cortex (kôr′tĕks′) **1.** The outer layer of an organ or body part, such as the cerebrum or the adrenal glands. **2.** The region of tissue next to the outermost layer of plant stems and roots. The cortex lies between the epidermis (the outermost layer) and the vascular tissue. In roots the cortex transfers water and minerals from the epidermis to the vascular tissue, which distributes them to other parts of the plant. The cortex also stores food manufactured in the leaves.

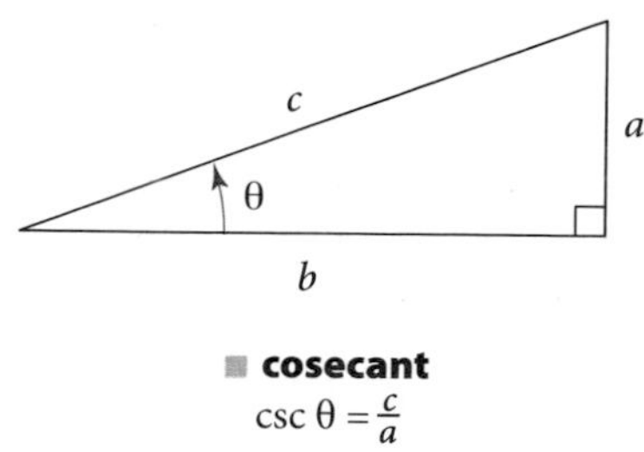

cosecant
$\csc\theta = \frac{c}{a}$

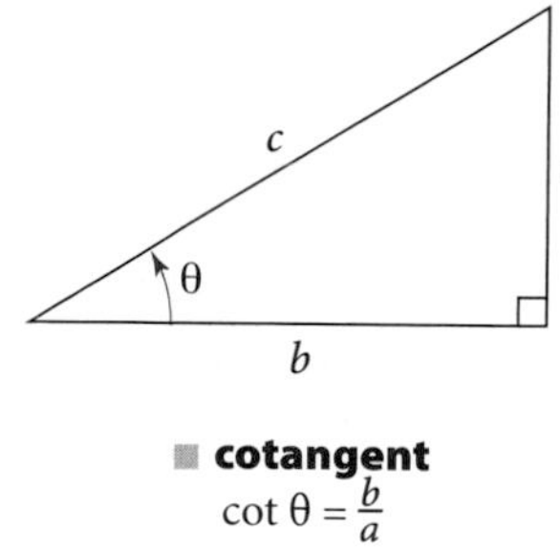

cotangent
$\cot\theta = \frac{b}{a}$

corundum (kə-rŭn′dəm) An extremely hard mineral composed mainly of aluminum oxide. It occurs in gem varieties such as ruby and sapphire and in a dark-colored variety that is used for polishing and scraping. Corundum is the mineral used to represent a hardness of 9 on the Mohs scale.

corymb (kôr′ĭmb, kôr′ĭm) A flat-topped flower cluster in which the outer flowers have longer stalks than the inner flowers.

cos Abbreviation of **cosine.**

cosecant (kō-sē′kănt′) The ratio of the length of the hypotenuse in a right triangle to the length of the side opposite an acute angle; the inverse of the sine.

cosine (kō′sīn′) The ratio of the length of the side adjacent to an acute angle of a right triangle to the length of the hypotenuse.

cosmic (kŏz′mĭk) Relating to the universe or the objects in it.

cosmology (kŏz-mŏl′ə-jē) The branch of astronomy that deals with the origin, evolution, and structure of the universe.

cosmos (kŏz′məs, kŏz′mōs′) The universe, especially when considered as an orderly and harmonious whole.

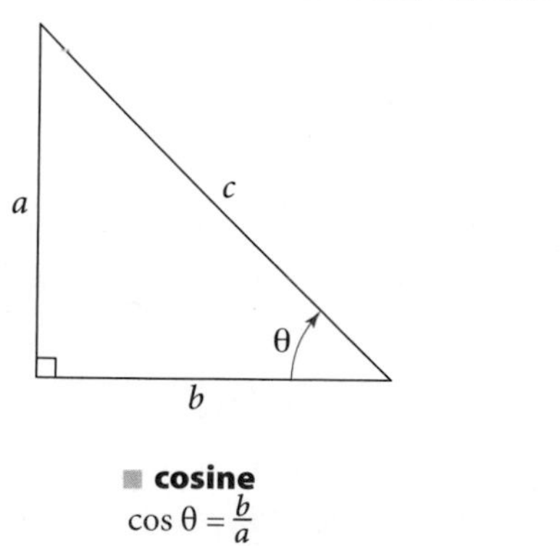

cosine
$\cos\theta = \frac{b}{a}$

cot Abbreviation of **cotangent.**

cotangent (kō-tăn′jənt) The ratio of the length of the adjacent side of an acute angle in a right triangle to the length of the opposite side; the inverse of a tangent.

cotyledon (kŏt′l-ēd′n) A leaf of the embryo of a seed plant. Most cotyledons emerge, enlarge, and become green after the seed has germinated, but some remain underground. Cotyledons supply stored food to the growing seedling. Also called *seed leaf. See more at* **dicotyledon, monocotyledon.**

coulomb (ko͞o′lŏm′, ko͞o′lōm′) A unit used to measure electric charge. One coulomb is equal to the quantity of charge that passes a point in an electric circuit in one second when a current of one ampere is flowing through the circuit.

Coulomb, Charles Augustin de 1736–1806. French physicist who pioneered research on magnetism and electricity. He is best known for the formulation of Coulomb's law, which he developed as a result of his investigations of Joseph Priestley's work on electrical repulsion. Coulomb also established a law governing the attraction and repulsion of magnetic poles. The coulomb unit of electric charge is named for him.

Coulomb's law A physical law stating that the strength of the force between two charged objects depends on the strength of the charges and the distance between them. The force increases as the strengths of the charges increase and as the distance between them decreases. If the two charges are both positive or both negative, they will repel each other, while if one is positive and the other is negative, they will attract each other.

Cousteau (ko͞o-stō′), **Jacques Yves** 1910–1997. French underwater explorer, film producer, and author. Cousteau invented scuba equipment,

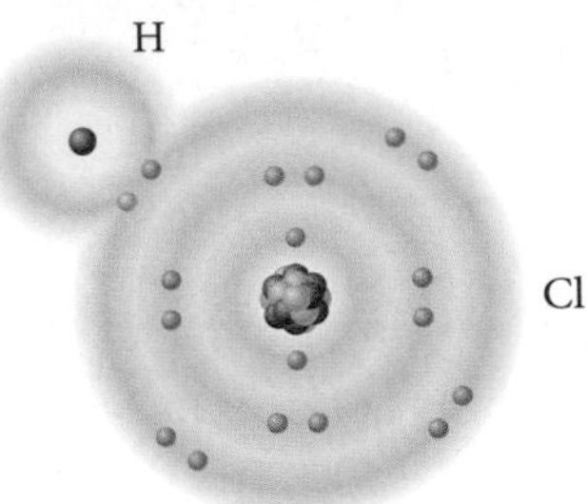

covalent bond
Covalent bonding as seen in a hydrogen chloride molecule. The hydrogen atom (H) and the chloride atom (Cl) share two electrons.

structures that permit humans to live underwater for prolonged periods of time, and a small submarine known as a diving saucer. He made three feature films and several television series about marine life and later in his career became increasingly involved in biological research and marine conservation.

covalent bond (kō-vā′lənt) A chemical bond formed when electrons are shared between two atoms. Usually each atom contributes one electron to form a pair of electrons that are shared by both atoms. *See more at* **bond, coordinate bond, double bond, ionic bond.**

CPR (sē′pē-är′) Short for *cardiopulmonary resuscitation.* An emergency procedure in which the heart and lungs are made to work by compressing the chest overlying the heart and forcing air into the lungs. CPR is used to maintain circulation when the heart has stopped pumping on its own.

CPU Abbreviation of **central processing unit.**

Cr The symbol for **chromium.**

cranial (krā′nē-əl) Relating to the skull or cranium.

cranial nerve Any of the 12 pairs of nerves in humans and other mammals that arise from the underside of the brain and exit through openings in the skull. The cranial nerves receive sensory information from the eyes, ears, nose, and mouth and send impulses to the muscles of the head and neck, as well as to the digestive organs and the heart.

cranium (krā′nē-əm) The part of the skull of a vertebrate animal that encloses and protects the brain. *See more at* **skeleton.**

crater (krā′tər) **1.** A bowl-shaped depression created by the activity of a volcano. Craters are formed when a large amount of lava is thrown out from a volcano, leaving a hole, or when the roof of rock over an underground magma pool collapses after the magma has flowed away. **2.** A shallow, bowl-shaped depression in a surface, formed by an explosion or by the impact of a body, such as a meteorite.

crescent (krĕs′ənt) Partly but less than half illuminated. Used to describe the moon or a planet. *Compare* **gibbous.**

crest (krĕst) **1.** The highest part of a wave. *See more at* **wave. 2.** A projecting tuft or outgrowth on the head of a bird or other animal.

Cretaceous (krĭ-tā′shəs) The third and last period of the Mesozoic Era, from about 146 to 66 million years ago, characterized by the development of flowering plants. The Cretaceous Period ended with the sudden mass extinction of dinosaurs and many other forms of life. *See Chart at* **geologic time,** pages 146–147.

crevasse (krĭ-văs′) A deep fissure in a glacier, caused by the cracking of the ice as it speeds up or passes over uneven terrain.

Crick (krĭk), **Francis Harry Compton** 1916–2004. British biologist who with James D. Watson identified the structure of DNA. By analyzing the patterns cast by x-rays striking DNA molecules, they discovered that DNA has the structure of a double helix, two spirals linked together by bases, forming ladderlike rungs. Their discovery formed the basis of molecular genetics.

crinoid (krī′noid′) Any of various invertebrate

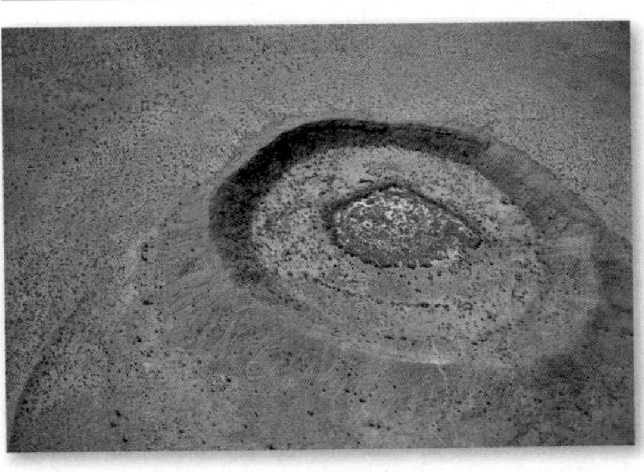

crater
Wolf Creek Crater, Australia

sea animals, such as the sea lilies and feather stars, having a cup-shaped body, feathery arms, and a stalk by which they attach themselves to a surface. Crinoids are echinoderms.

crista (krĭs′tə) *Plural* **cristae** (krĭs′tē) One of the folds of the inner membrane of a mitochondrion. *See more at* **mitochondrion.**

crocodile (krŏk′ə-dīl′) Any of various large, meat-eating, aquatic reptiles native to tropical and subtropical regions. Crocodiles have a longer, more slender snout than alligators, and their teeth are visible when the jaw is closed.

crocodilian (krŏk′ə-dĭl′ē-ən) Any of various large meat-eating reptiles having a long jaw with sharp teeth, short legs, and a long tail, and mostly living in or near water. The crocodilians include the crocodiles, alligators, caimans (of South America), and gharial (of South Asia).

Crohn's disease (krōnz) Chronic inflammation of the digestive tract, characterized by abdominal pain and digestive problems such as diarrhea or constipation.

Crookes (kro͝oks), Sir **William** 1832–1919. British chemist and physicist who discovered thallium in 1861 and invented the radiometer in 1875. He also investigated cathode rays, demonstrating that they consisted of charged particles.

cross (krôs) *Noun* **1.** A plant or animal produced by crossbreeding. —*Verb* **2.** To crossbreed or cross-fertilize plants or animals.

crossbreed (krôs′brēd′) To produce offspring by mating two animals or plants of different breeds, varieties, or species.

■ **crevasse**

■ **crinoid**

cross-fertilization The fertilization that occurs when a male sex cell from one individual joins to a female sex cell from another individual of the same species. In plants, cross-pollination is an example of cross-fertilization. —*Verb* **cross-fertilize.**

cross-pollination The transfer of pollen from the male reproductive organ (an anther or a male cone) of one plant to the female reproductive organ (a stigma or a female cone) of another plant. Insects and wind are agents of cross-pollination. —*Verb* **cross-pollinate.**

crucible (kro͞o′sə-bəl) A heat-resistant container used to melt ores, metals, and other materials.

crust (krŭst) The solid, outermost layer of the Earth. ❖ The crust that lies underneath the continents is called **continental crust,** and is approximately 22 to 37 miles (35 to 60 kilometers) thick. It consists mostly of rocks rich in silica and aluminum, with minor amounts of iron, magnesium, calcium, sodium, and potassium. ❖ The crust that lies underneath the oceans is called **oceanic crust,** and is approximately 3 to 6 miles (5 to 10 kilometers) thick. It has a similar composition to that of continental crust, but has higher concentrations of iron, magnesium, and calcium. It is denser than continental crust.

crustacean (krŭ-stā′shən) Any of a group of arthropods that usually live in water and have a segmented body, a hard shell, paired jointed limbs, and two pairs of antennae. Lobsters, crabs, shrimp, and barnacles are crustaceans.

cryogenics (krī′ə-jĕn′ĭks) The branch of physics that studies how matter behaves at very low temperatures.

crystal (krĭs′təl) A solid composed of atoms, molecules, or ions arranged in regular patterns that are repeated throughout the structure to form a characteristic network. Crystals have

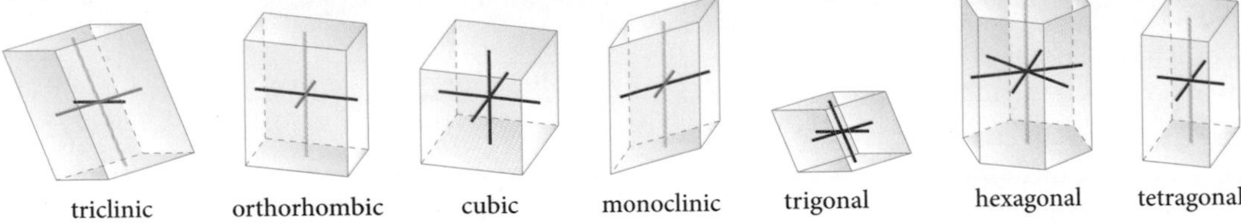

crystal

Imaginary axes of symmetry in the seven main crystal systems are depicted using different colors. Within each crystal, axes having the same color are of equal length.

straight edges and flat surfaces, and can occur in many sizes and shapes. ❖ The particular arrangement in space of these atoms, molecules, or ions, and the way in which they are joined is called a **crystal lattice.** There are seven crystal groups or systems. Each is defined on the basis of the geometrical arrangement of the crystal lattice. —*Adjective* **crystalline.**

crystallize (krĭs′tə-līz′) To take on the form of crystals or cause to form crystals.

Cs The symbol for **cesium.**

csc Abbreviation of **cosecant.**

CT scan (sē′tē′) Short for *computed tomography scan.* A view of an internal body part made by a computer that assembles a series of x-rays taken at different angles into a three-dimensional image. CT scans are used in medicine to help diagnose a disease or disorder.

Cu The symbol for **copper.**

cube (kyo͞ob) *Verb* **1.** To multiply a number or a quantity by itself three times; raise to the third power. For example, five cubed is $5 \times 5 \times 5$. —*Noun* **2.** The product that results when a number or quantity is cubed. **3.** A three-dimensional geometric figure having six equal square faces or sides.

culm

cube root The number whose cube is equal to a given number. For example, the cube root of 125 is 5, since $5^3 = 125$.

cubewano (kyo͞o′bē′wŏn′ō) *Plural* **cubewanos** A Kuiper belt object that is far enough away from Neptune that its orbit around the sun is not strongly affected by Neptune's gravity. The first object of this kind that was found (after Pluto and its satellite Charon) was given the temporary name *(15760) 1992 QB1,* and the name *cubewano* came from *QB1.*

cubic (kyo͞o′bĭk) **1.** Referring to a volume unit of measurement: *cubic meter.* **2.** Involving a number or a variable that has been raised to the third power. **3.** Relating to a crystal having three axes of equal length intersecting at right angles. The mineral pyrite has cubic crystals. Also called *isometric. See more at* **crystal.**

cud (kŭd) Food that has been partly digested and brought up from the first stomach to the mouth again for further chewing by ruminants, such as cattle and sheep.

culm (kŭlm) The stem of a grass or similar plant.

culture (kŭl′chər) *Noun* **1.** A growth of microorganisms, viruses, or tissue cells in a sterile nutrient medium. —*Verb* **2.** To grow microorganisms, viruses, or tissue cells in a nutrient medium.

cumulonimbus (kyo͞om′yə-lō-nĭm′bəs) A very large cloud with a low, dark base and fluffy masses that billow upward to great heights. Cumulonimbus clouds usually produce heavy rains, thunderstorms, or hailstorms.

cumulus (kyo͞om′yə-ləs) A white, fluffy cloud often having a flat base. Cumulus clouds form at

cumulonimbus

lower levels of the atmosphere and are generally associated with fair weather. However, large cumulus clouds that billow to higher levels can produce rain showers.

curie (kyo͝or′ē, kyo͝o-rē′) A unit used to measure the rate of radioactive decay, the process by which the nuclei of the atoms of a radioactive substance disintegrate by emitting subatomic particles or gamma rays. One curie is equal to 37 billion (3.7×10^{10}) of these disintegrations per second. Many scientists now measure radioactive decay in becquerels rather than curies.

Curie, Marie Skłodowska 1867–1934. Polish-born French chemist noted for her pioneering research in radioactivity and her discovery and study of radium and polonium.

curium (kyo͝or′ē-əm) A synthetic, silvery-white, radioactive metallic element of the actinide series that is produced artificially from plutonium or americium. Curium isotopes are used to provide electricity for satellites and space probes. Its most stable isotope has a half-life of 15.6 million years. *Symbol* **Cm.** *Atomic number* 96. *See* **Periodic Table,** pages 254–255.

current (kûr′ənt) **1.** A flowing movement in a fluid, such as a liquid or gas, especially when the movement is steady and continuous. **2.** A flow of electric charge. The strength of current flow in a material is related to the electrical properties of that material and to the voltage difference within it. Electric current is measured in amperes. *See Note on next page. See Note at* **charge.**

curve (kûrv) **1.** A line or surface that bends in a smooth, continuous way without sharp angles. **2.** The graph of a function on a coordinate plane. In this technical sense, straight lines, circles, and waves are all curves.

cutaneous (kyo͞o-tā′nē-əs) Relating to the skin.

cuticle (kyo͞o′tĭ-kəl) **1.** A protective covering that is secreted by the epidermis of many invertebrates, such as the transparent membrane that covers an earthworm or the hardened exoskeleton of a beetle. **2.** A waxy layer that covers the outermost layer of leaves and other plant parts. The cuticle is secreted by the epidermis and helps prevent water loss and infection by fungi and bacteria. **3.** The hard skin around the sides and base of a fingernail or toenail.

BIOGRAPHY

Marie Curie

Marie Curie was the first woman to win a Nobel prize (in 1903) and the first person to win a second Nobel prize (1911). The first award, which she shared with her husband Pierre (1859–1906) and the French physicist Antoine Henri Becquerel, was for her investigation of radioactivity (a word she coined). This work changed scientists' view of the nature of the atom, showing that it was made of small particles that could be emitted as powerful rays. The second award was for her discovery of the elements polonium (named for her native country, Poland) and radium. Marie Curie later founded the Radium Institute in France and advocated the use of radium for medical purposes. The dark side of radiation cut short her own life, however; she died at the age of 67 from the effects of years of exposure to radium.

Did You Know...?

current: direct and alternating

You operate a flashlight thanks to direct current, but you turn on a desk lamp thanks to alternating current. *Direct current,* or *DC,* is electricity that flows at a constant voltage directly from a source, such as a battery with a stored electric charge. Batteries are great when you're on the move, but DC has a fundamental problem: it tends to waste a significant portion of its current as heat. *Alternating current,* or *AC,* on the other hand, is what flows from outlets in your walls. It can be transmitted at very high voltage over long distances with little heat loss, and the voltage can be efficiently reduced to a low, safe level for home use. AC's name reflects the fact that the current alternates its direction of flow. One complete period of flow first in one direction and then in the reverse direction is called a *cycle.* On average, the power system in the United States operates at 60 cycles per second and delivers about 120 volts from an ordinary outlet. Other countries have different AC standards. That's why when you travel abroad, you often need to use an adapter when you plug in electric appliances.

Cuvier (kyo͞o′vē-ā′), Baron **Georges Léopold** 1769–1832. French anatomist who is considered the founder of comparative anatomy. He originated a system of zoological classification that grouped animals according to the structures of their skeletons and organs. Cuvier extended his system to fossils, and his reconstructions of the way extinct animals looked, based on their skeletal remains, greatly advanced the science of paleontology.

cyanide (sī′ə-nīd′) Any of a large group of chemical compounds containing the univalent anion CN^-, especially the very poisonous salts sodium cyanide and potassium cyanide. Cyanides are used to make plastics and to extract and treat metals.

cyanobacterium (sī′ə-nō-băk-tîr′ē-əm) Any of various bacteria that are capable of photosynthesis and are usually found in water. Many cyanobacteria are able to convert nitrogen into chemical compounds used in cell metabolism. A combination of pigments, including chlorophyll, gives these bacteria their characteristic blue-green color. Also called *blue-green alga.*

cyber– A prefix that means "computer" or "computer network," as in *cyberspace,* the electronic medium in which online communication takes place.

cybernetics (sī′bər-nĕt′ĭks) The study of communication and control processes in biological, mechanical, and electronic systems. Research in cybernetics often involves the comparison of these processes in biological and artificial systems.

cycad (sī′kăd′) Any of various tropical evergreen plants that bear cones and have large leaves resembling those of a palm tree.

cyclone (sī′klōn′) **1.** A system of winds that spiral in toward a region of low atmospheric pressure. On Earth, these winds circle counterclockwise in the Northern Hemisphere and clockwise in the Southern Hemisphere. *Compare* **anticyclone. 2.** A violent rotating windstorm, such as a hurricane or tornado.

cyclotron (sī′klə-trŏn′) A particle accelerator in which charged subatomic particles, such as protons and electrons, are accelerated in a path that spirals outward. The cyclotron gradually increases the speeds and energies of these particles to high values. The high-energy particles that are produced can be caused to collide with other particles so that scientists can study their structure. *Compare* **linear accelerator, synchrotron.**

Cygnus (sĭg′nəs) A constellation in the Northern Hemisphere near Lyra and Draco. It contains the supergiant Deneb.

cylinder (sĭl′ən-dər) A three-dimensional surface or solid object bounded by a curved surface and two parallel circles of equal size at the ends. The curved surface is formed by all the line segments joining corresponding points of the two parallel circles.

cyme (sīm) A flower cluster in which the main stem and each branch end in a flower that opens before the flowers below or to the side of it. Tomato flowers are arranged in cymes.

cyst (sĭst) An abnormal sac in the body, composed

Did You Know...?

cyclone

Technically, a *cyclone* is nothing more than a region of low pressure around which air flows. In the Northern Hemisphere, the air moves counterclockwise around the low-pressure center, while in the Southern Hemisphere, the air travels clockwise. Meteorologists also refer to *tropical cyclones,* which develop over warm water and can be huge, severe storms. Strong tropical cyclones that form in the Atlantic Ocean, the Gulf of Mexico, or the northeastern Pacific Ocean are known as hurricanes; those that form in the western Pacific Ocean are called typhoons. Such storms can be extremely devastating: Cyclone Nargis, which hit the coast of Myanmar (Burma) in May 2008, killed over 100,000 people. Because the word *cyclone* broadly defines a kind of air flow, cyclones are also found on other planets in our solar system.

of a membrane surrounding a fluid or a soft solid material.

cysteine (sĭs′tə-ēn′) A nonessential amino acid. *See more at* **amino acid.** *See Note at* **keratin.**

cystic fibrosis (sĭs′tĭk fī-brō′sĭs) An inherited disease that causes thick mucus to build up in certain organs of the body, such as the lungs and pancreas. It results in problems with breathing and digestion and leads to frequent infections.

cyto– A prefix meaning "cell," as in the word *cytoplasm,* the material inside a cell.

cytochrome (sī′tə-krōm′) Any of a class of proteins that are important in cell metabolism and respiration.

cytology (sī-tŏl′ə-jē) The scientific study of the formation, structure, and function of cells.

cytometry (sī-tŏm′ə-trē) The counting and measuring of cells, especially cell size and shape. Cytometry is usually performed using a standardized glass slide or small glass chamber of known volume.

cytoplasm (sī′tə-plăz′əm) The jellylike material that makes up much of a cell inside the cell membrane, and, in eukaryotic cells, surrounds the nucleus. The organelles of the cell, such as mitochondria and (in green plants) chloroplasts, are contained in the cytoplasm. *See more at* **cell.**

cytosine (sī′tə-sēn′) A base that is a component of DNA and RNA, forming a base pair with guanine.

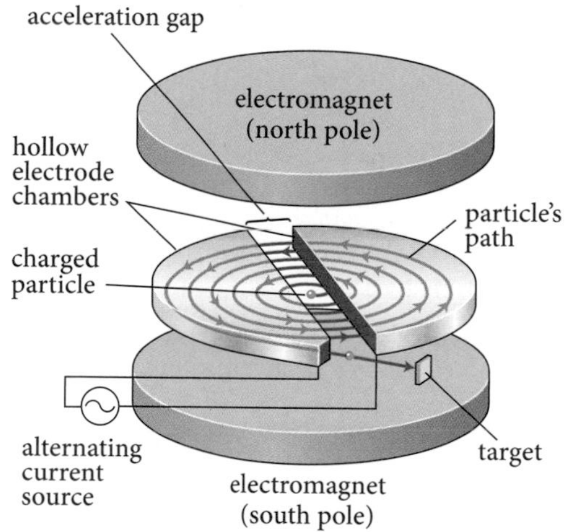

cyclotron

An alternating electric field attracts the particles from one side of the cyclotron to the other. The cyclotron's magnetic field, generated by the two electromagnets, bends each particle's path into a horizontal spiral, forcing it to accelerate in order to keep up with the alternating electric field. When the particle reaches its peak acceleration it is released to collide with the desired target.

d Abbreviation of **diameter.**

Dalton (dôl′tən), **John** 1766–1844. British chemist. His pioneering work on the properties of the atmosphere and gases led him to formulate the atomic theory. It stated that all matter is made up of combinations of atoms and that chemical reactions take place through the rearrangement of atoms.

dark matter (därk) Matter that gives off little or no detectable radiation. Astronomers have proposed that dark matter exists because the amount of visible matter in the universe is not enough to generate the gravitational forces that are observed.

darmstadtium (därm′shtät′ē-əm) A synthetic, radioactive element, first produced by bombarding lead atoms with nickel atoms. The most stable isotope has a half-life of about 10 seconds. *Symbol* **Ds.** *Atomic number* 110. *See* **Periodic Table,** pages 254–255.

Darwin (där′wĭn), **Charles Robert** 1809–1882. British naturalist who proposed the theory of evolution based on natural selection (1859). Darwin's theory revolutionized the study of biology.

data (dā′tə, dăt′ə) *Used with a singular or plural verb.* **1.** Information, especially when it is to be analyzed or used as the basis for a decision. **2.** Information, usually in numerical form, suitable for processing by a computer.

data mining The search for useful information in large sets of data by using computer programs to find meaningful patterns, usually without much prior knowledge of the data's content or relationships.

dative bond (dā′tĭv) *See* **coordinate bond.**

daughter cell (dô′tər) Either of the two cells formed when a cell undergoes cell division.

Davy (dā′vē), Sir **Humphry** 1778–1829. British chemist who was a pioneer of electrochemistry, which is concerned with the interaction of electric and chemical phenomena. Davy used its methods to isolate sodium and potassium (1807) and barium, boron, calcium, and magnesium (1808). He also proved that diamonds are a form of carbon.

dB Abbreviation of **decibel.**

Db The symbol for **dubnium.**

DC Abbreviation of **direct current.**

DDT (dē′dē-tē′) Short for *dichlorodiphenyltrichloroethane.* A powerful insecticide that is also poisonous to humans and many other animals. It remains active in the environment for many years and has been banned in the United States for most uses since 1972. *See Note at* **Carson.**

Did You Know...?

dark matter

What is the universe made of? We know that galaxies contain planets, stars, and huge clouds of gas and dust, because all of these objects give off radiation (radio waves, infrared light, visible light, ultraviolet light, x-rays, or gamma rays) that we can observe using various kinds of telescopes. But astronomers suspect that the universe contains much more matter that we can't observe directly. One sign that such *dark matter* exists is the fact that stars at the outer edges of galaxies rotate much faster than expected based on the observed mass of the galaxy. Perhaps galaxies have much more mass than we can see. Various theories of the composition of dark matter have been proposed. One early suggestion was that it consists of planet-sized objects made of ordinary matter that are too small or far away for our instruments to observe, but recent calculations indicate that such objects could make up only a small fraction of the dark matter that is believed to exist. Astronomers now think that most dark matter consists of some kind of yet-to-be-discovered particle. But nobody has come up with a convincing explanation of what that particle might be, so the fundamental question of what makes up most of the universe remains unanswered.

de Broglie (də broi′, də brô′yə), **Louis Victor** 1892–1987. French physicist who was the first to theorize that subatomic particles can behave as waves. Influenced by Albert Einstein's concept that waves can behave as particles, de Broglie proposed that the opposite was also true: that electrons, for example, exhibit wavelike properties. De Broglie's work led to the development of wave mechanics, which was important in the development of quantum physics.

deca– A prefix that means "ten," as in *decahedron,* a polygon having ten faces.

decagon (dĕk′ə-gŏn′) A polygon having ten sides.

decapod (dĕk′ə-pŏd′) **1.** A crustacean characteristically having ten legs joined to the thorax. Crabs, lobsters, and shrimp are decapods. **2.** A cephalopod mollusk, such as a squid or cuttlefish, having eight arms and two tentacles.

decay (dĭ-kā′) *Verb* **1.** *Biology* To break down into component parts through the action of bacteria or fungi; decompose. **2.** *Physics* To undergo radioactive decay. —*Noun* **3.** *Biology* The breaking down or rotting of organic matter through the action of bacteria or fungi; decomposition. **4.** *Physics* Radioactive decay.

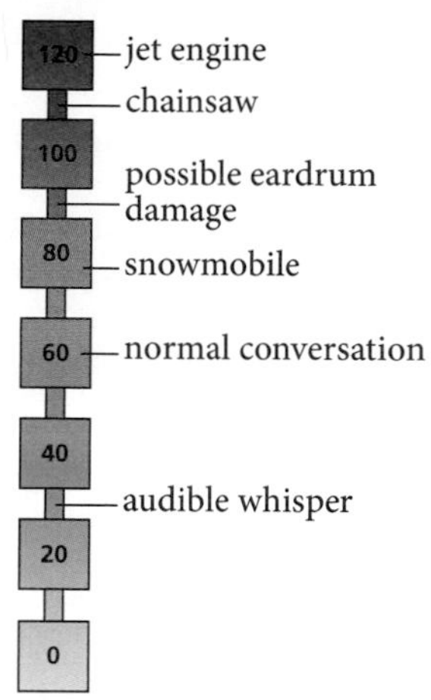

decibel
range of human hearing in decibels

deci– A prefix that means "one tenth," as in *deciliter,* one tenth of a liter.

decibel (dĕs′ə-bəl) A unit used to measure the loudness or intensity of a sound. The speaking

BIOGRAPHY

Charles Darwin

When Charles Darwin was 22 years old, he was appointed the ship's naturalist on the HMS *Beagle* and spent five years traveling the world. The observations he made during that voyage laid the groundwork for his theory of evolution by natural selection. He was especially intrigued by the birds of the Galápagos Archipelago, a group of islands in the Pacific Ocean 650 miles west of Ecuador. Every island had its own species of finch with a slightly different bill shape that suited the bird's diet. Darwin suspected that the finches (now called "Darwin's finches") had a common ancestor that colonized the island millions of years ago. But what process caused the original birds' descendants to change and adapt to the conditions on the various islands? In 1859, Darwin laid out his theory of evolution in *On the Origin of Species.* He included many examples, including that of the finches. His argument is simple: variations among individual organisms are often inherited, and those organisms best suited to their environment will produce the most offspring. Over millions of years this "selection" of the best-adapted individuals will result in the evolution of new species, or, in Darwin's own words, "endless forms most beautiful and most wonderful."

voice of most people ranges from 45 to 75 decibels. *See Note at* **sound¹.**

deciduous (dĭ-sĭj′o͞o-əs) **1.** Shedding leaves at the end of a growing season and developing new leaves at the beginning of the next growing season: *Maple trees are deciduous. Compare* **evergreen. 2.** Falling off or shed at a particular season or stage of growth: *Deer have deciduous antlers.*

decimal (dĕs′ə-məl) **1.** A representation of a real number using the base ten and decimal notation, such as 201.4, 3.89, or 0.0006. **2.** A decimal fraction.

decimal fraction A number, such as 0.57, written in decimal notation and having only a zero to the left of the decimal point. A decimal fraction can be written as a fraction with a denominator that is a power of 10 (for example, $\frac{57}{100}$).

decimal notation A representation of a fraction or other real number using the base ten and consisting of any of the digits 0, 1, 2, 3, 4, 5, 6, 7, 8, 9, and a decimal point. Each digit to the left of the decimal point indicates a multiple of a positive power of ten, while each digit to the right indicates a multiple of a negative power of ten. For example, the number $26\frac{37}{100}$ can be written in decimal notation as 26.37, where 2 represents 2 × 10, 6 represents 6 × 1, 3 represents $3 \times \frac{1}{10}$ or $\frac{3}{10}$, and 7 represents $7 \times \frac{1}{100}$ or $\frac{7}{100}$.

decimal place The position of a digit to the right of the decimal point in a number written in decimal notation. In 0.079, for example, 0 is in the first decimal place, 7 is in the second decimal place, and 9 is in the third decimal place.

decimal point A period used in decimal notation to separate whole numbers from fractions, as in the number 1.3, which represents $1 + \frac{3}{10}$.

decimal system A number system based on units of 10 and using decimal notation.

declination (dĕk′lə-nā′shən) **1.** The position of a celestial object above or below the celestial equator. It is measured as a vertical angle from 0° at the celestial equator to 90° at the north celestial pole or −90° at the south celestial pole. Declination and right ascension are the measurements used to map objects on the celestial sphere. *See more at* **celestial sphere. 2.** *See* **magnetic declination.**

decomposer (dē′kəm-pō′zər) An organism, often a bacterium or fungus, that feeds on and breaks down dead plant or animal matter. Decomposers make essential nutrients available to plants and other organisms in the ecosystem.

USAGE

deduction/induction

The logical processes known as deduction and induction work in opposite ways. When you use *deduction,* you apply general principles to specific instances. Thus, if you know that diamond is the hardest mineral, meaning that it can't be scratched by any other mineral, and you find by experiment that a particular pebble can be scratched by a piece of quartz, you can use deduction to conclude that the pebble is not a diamond. By contrast, when you use *induction,* you examine a number of specific instances of something and make a generalization based on them. Thus, if you observe hundreds of examples in which a certain chemical kills plants, you might conclude by induction that the chemical is toxic to all plants. Inductive generalizations are often revised as more examples are studied and more facts are known. Certain plants that you have not tested, for instance, may turn out to be unaffected by the chemical, and you might have to revise your thinking. In this way, an inductive generalization is much like a hypothesis.

decomposition (dē-kŏm′pə-zĭsh′ən) **1.** The separation of a substance into simpler substances as the result of a chemical reaction. **2.** The process of decaying or rotting. Decomposition of dead organic matter is brought about mainly by the activity of bacteria and fungi.

deduction (dĭ-dŭk′shən) **1.** The process of reasoning in which a conclusion follows necessarily from the premises; reasoning from the general to the specific. **2.** A conclusion reached by this process.

deep-sky object (dēp′skī′) Any of various celestial objects, such as nebulae, galaxies, and star clusters, that appear faint and diffuse, unlike objects within the solar system or individual stars. Usually a deep-sky object can only be seen with a telescope.

deforestation (dē-fôr′ĭ-stā′shən) The cutting down and removal of all or most of the trees in a forested area. Deforestation leads to erosion of soils and decreases biodiversity by destroying the habitats of forest species.

deglaciation (dē-glā′shē-ā′shən) The uncovering of land because of the melting of a glacier.

degree (dĭ-grē′) **1.** A unit division of a temperature scale. *See Note at* **Celsius. 2a.** A unit for measuring an angle or an arc of a circle. One degree is $\frac{1}{360}$ of the circumference of a circle. **b.** This unit used to measure latitude or longitude on the Earth's surface. **3.** In a polynomial, the degree of the term that has the highest degree. For example, $x^3 + 2xy + x$ is of the third degree.

dehydration (dē′hī-drā′shən) **1.** The process of losing or removing water or moisture from a substance or compound. **2.** Excessive loss of water and often salts from the tissues of an animal, plant, or other organism.

Delbrück (dĕl′bro͝ok′), **Max** 1906–1981. German-born American biologist who was a pioneer in the study of molecular genetics. He discovered that viruses can exchange genetic material to create new types of viruses.

delta (dĕl′tə) A usually triangular mass of sediment, especially silt and sand, deposited at the mouth of a river. Deltas form when a river flows into a body of standing water, such as a sea or lake.

Democritus (dĭ-mŏk′rĭ-təs) 460?–370? BC. Greek philosopher who developed one of the first atomist theories of the universe, which held that the world consists of an infinite number of very small indivisible particles.

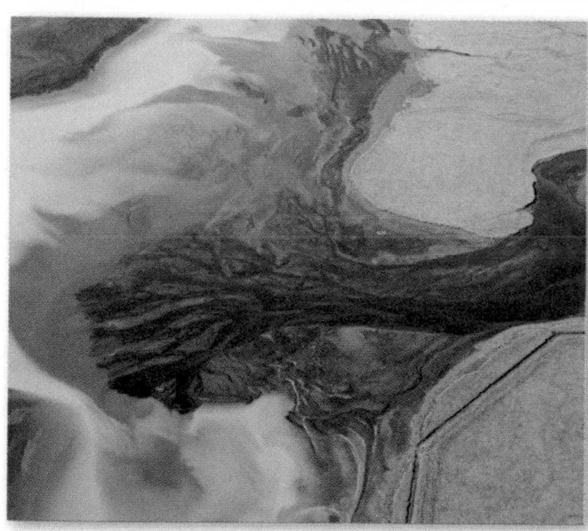

delta
aerial view

dendrite (dĕn′drīt′) **1.** *Biology* A structure that extends out from the body of a nerve cell and receives information from other cells. A single nerve cell usually has many dendrites branching from it. **2.** *Geology* A mineral that has a branching crystal pattern. Dendrites often form within or on the surface of other minerals.

dendrochronology (dĕn′drō-krə-nŏl′ə-jē) The study of annual rings in trees in order to analyze past climate conditions or to determine the date of past events. Trees grow more slowly and produce smaller annual rings during periods of drought or other environmental stress than they do during periods with more favorable conditions. By observing the sequence of narrow and wide rings in a sample taken from a tree trunk, scientists can learn about the environmental conditions that existed during the tree's lifetime.

Deneb (dĕn′ĕb′) The brightest star in the constellation Cygnus. It is a supergiant. *See Note at* **Rigel.**

denitrifying bacterium (dē-nī′trə-fī′ĭng) Any of various bacteria that convert nitrate or nitrite into nitrogen gas in the absence of oxygen and play an important role in the nitrogen cycle.

denominator (dĭ-nŏm′ə-nā′tər) The number below or to the right of the line in a fraction, indicating the number of equal parts into which one whole is divided. For example, in the fraction $\frac{2}{7}$, 7 is the denominator.

density (dĕn′sĭ-tē) A measure of the compactness of a substance. Density is equal to the amount of mass per unit of volume. In general, density increases as pressure increases and temperature decreases.

dentin (dĕn′tĭn) The hard, bonelike material that forms most of a tooth and lies beneath the enamel.

dentistry (dĕn′tĭ-strē) The branch of medicine that deals with the diagnosis, prevention, and treatment of diseases of the teeth, gums, and other structures of the mouth.

dentition (dĕn-tĭsh′ən) The type, number, and arrangement of the teeth in an animal species. Mammals have complex dentitions, with several different types of teeth, including incisors, canines, and molars. The teeth of toothed fish and reptiles are usually of only one type.

deoxyribonucleic acid (dē-ŏk′sē-rī′bō-nōō-klē′ĭk) *See* **DNA.**

dependent variable (dĭ-pĕn′dənt) In mathematics, a variable whose value is determined by the value of some other variable. For example, in the function $y = x + 5$, y is the dependent variable because its value is determined by the value of x.

deposit (dĭ-pŏz′ĭt) *Verb* **1.** *Chemistry* To transform or be transformed directly from a gas to a solid without becoming a liquid. **2.** *Geology* To leave or lay down material such as sand or debris. —*Noun.* **3.** *Geology* A mass or layer of solid material deposited by a natural process. In geology, deposits can include layers of sand and mud left by streams, an accumulation of stones and debris left by a melting glacier, or a layer of coal formed over many years as decomposing plant material became fossilized.

deposition (dĕp′ə-zĭsh′ən) **1.** *Geology* The process of leaving or laying down material such as sand or debris. **2.** *Chemistry* The process of changing from a gas to a solid without passing through an intermediate liquid phase. Deposition of water vapor from the air on a very cold morning results in a layer of frost on exposed surfaces. *Compare* **sublimation.**

depression (dĭ-prĕsh′ən) A mental disorder characterized by extreme sadness, difficulty concentrating, changes in eating habits and sleep patterns, feelings of guilt or hopelessness, and the inability to experience pleasure.

derivative (dĭ-rĭv′ə-tĭv) In calculus, the slope of the tangent line at a particular point on a curve graphing a variable y as a function of some other variable x. The derivative can also be thought of as the function's rate of change at that point. Derivatives are computed using differentiation.

dermal (dûr′məl) Relating to the skin.

dermis (dûr′mĭs) The innermost layer of the skin in vertebrate animals, lying under the epidermis and containing nerve endings and blood and lymph vessels. In mammals, the dermis also contains hair follicles and sweat glands.

desalination (dē-săl′ə-nā′shən) The removal of dissolved salts from something, such as seawater. —*Verb* **desalinate.**

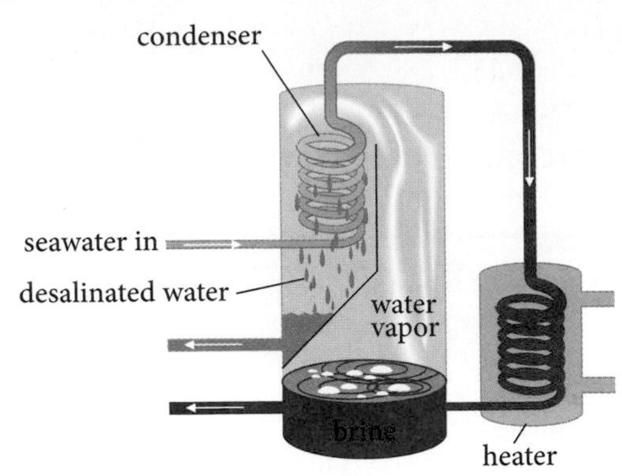

desalination
desalination of seawater

Descartes (dā-kärt′), **René** 1596–1650. French mathematician and philosopher. He invented the method of using coordinates to define the position of a point, thus laying the foundation for analytic geometry.

desert (dĕz′ərt) A dry region that has little or no vegetation. Most deserts receive less than 10 inches (25 centimeters) of precipitation each year. Deserts occur in hot climates, as in western Australia, and also in cold climates, as in Antarctica.

desertification (dĭ-zûr′tə-fĭ-kā′shən) The transformation of land once suitable for agriculture into desert. Desertification can result from climate change or from human practices such as cutting down forests or allowing too many animals to graze in a particular area.

desiccate (dĕs′ĭ-kāt′) To remove the moisture from something or dry it thoroughly.

detergent (dĭ-tûr′jənt) A cleaning agent that increases the ability of water to penetrate fabric and break down greases and dirt. Detergents act like soap but are made of chemicals obtained from petroleum products. Their molecules surround particles of grease and dirt, allowing them to be carried away. *Compare* **soap.**

detritus (dĭ-trī′təs) Loose fragments, such as sand or gravel, that have been worn away from rock.

deuterium (dōō-tîr′ē-əm) An isotope of hydrogen whose nucleus has one proton and one neu-

■ **desert**
top: *Wright Valley, Antarctica*
bottom: *Death Valley, California*

tron and whose atomic mass is 2. Deuterium is used widely as a tracer for analyzing chemical reactions, and it combines with oxygen to form heavy water. Also called *heavy hydrogen. See more at* **hydrogen.** *See Note at* **heavy water.**

deviation (dē′vē-ā′shən) *Mathematics* The difference between a particular number in a set and the mean of the set.

Devonian (dĭ-vō′nē-ən) The fourth period of the Paleozoic Era, from about 416 to 359 million years ago, characterized by the appearance of forests, amphibians, and insects. *See Chart at* **geologic time,** pages 146–147.

dew (do͞o) Water droplets that condense from the air onto cool surfaces. Dew usually forms at night, when air near the ground cools and cannot hold as much water vapor as warmer air.

dewlap (do͞o′lăp′) A loose fold of skin hanging from the neck of certain animals, such as some dogs, cattle, and lizards. Lizards can extend their dewlaps.

dew point The temperature at which air becomes saturated with water vapor and dew forms. The dew point varies depending on how much water vapor is in the air.

dextrose (dĕk′strōs′) A sugar that is the naturally occurring form of glucose, found in all living organisms.

di– A prefix that means "two," "twice," or "double." It is used commonly in chemistry, as in *dioxide,* a compound having two oxygen atoms.

dia– A prefix meaning "through" or "across," as in *diameter,* the length of a line going through a circle.

diabetes (dī′ə-bē′tĭs, dī′ə-bē′tēz) A disease marked by abnormally high levels of sugar in the blood, caused by the body's inability to produce or use insulin properly. If untreated, it can cause circulatory problems and nerve damage. ❖ **Type 1 diabetes** occurs when not enough insulin is produced by the cells of the pancreas, resulting in high sugar levels in the blood and urine. People with type 1 diabetes need insulin injections to control their blood glucose levels. ❖ **Type 2 diabetes** is a disease linked to obesity and an inactive lifestyle. It often has no symptoms and is diagnosed by tests that show problems with the body's ability to process and use insulin. Type 2 diabetes can often be prevented or treated with changes in diet and an exercise program.

diagnosis (dī′əg-nō′sĭs) *Plural* **diagnoses** (dī′-əg-nō′sēz) The identification by a doctor or other medical professional of a disease or injury, made

■ **dewlap**
extended dewlap on a male lizard

by examining and taking the medical history of a patient.

diagonal (dī-ăg′ə-nəl) *Adjective* **1.** Connecting two nonadjacent corners in a polygon or two nonadjacent corners in a polyhedron that do not lie in the same face. *—Noun* **2.** A diagonal line segment.

dialysis (dī-ăl′ĭ-sĭs) **1.** The separation of the smaller molecules in a solution from the larger molecules by passing the solution through a membrane that does not allow the large molecules through. **2.** The removal of wastes from the bloodstream by a machine that performs dialysis when the kidneys do not function properly.

diameter (dī-ăm′ĭ-tər) **1.** A straight line segment that passes through the center of a circle or sphere from one side to the other. **2.** The length of such a line segment.

diamond (dī′ə-mənd) A form of pure carbon that occurs naturally as a clear crystal and is the hardest of all known minerals. It is used as a gemstone in its finer varieties. Poorly crystallized diamonds are used in abrasives and in industrial cutting tools. *See Note at* **carbon.**

diaphragm (dī′ə-frăm′) **1.** A muscle that separates the chest cavity from the abdominal cavity. As the diaphragm contracts and expands, it causes air to move into and out of the lungs. **2.** A thin, flexible disk, especially in a microphone or telephone receiver, that vibrates in response to sound waves to produce electrical signals, or that vibrates in response to electrical signals to produce sound waves.

diastole (dī-ăs′tə-lē) The period during the normal beating of the heart in which relaxation occurs and the heart's chambers fill with blood. *Compare* **systole.**

diatom (dī′ə-tŏm′) Any of numerous one-celled algae that live in water, make their own food by photosynthesis, and have hard, two-part shells containing silica. Diatoms often live in colonies, and they are an important component of plankton.

diatom
photomicrograph of a variety of diatoms

dicotyledon (dī′kŏt′l-ēd′n) or **dicot** (dī′kŏt′) A flowering plant having two cotyledons that emerge from the seed when it germinates. Dicotyledons have leaves with netlike rather than parallel veins, flower parts in multiples of four or five, and a tissue layer known as cambium that enables them to grow in width. *Compare* **monocotyledon.**

dielectric (dī′ĭ-lĕk′trĭk) *Noun* **1.** A material, such as glass, ceramic, or rubber, that does not conduct an electric current but does become polarized (with a positive charge on one side and a negative charge on the opposite side) when in an electric field. *—Adjective* **2.** Having the properties or function of a dielectric.

diesel engine (dē′zəl) An internal-combustion engine in which the fuel is ignited by the heat of air that has been highly compressed in the cylinder.

difference (dĭf′ər-əns) **1.** The amount by which one number or quantity is greater or less than another. The difference between 10 and 15, for example, is 5. **2.** The amount remaining after one number or quantity is subtracted from another. In the equation $15 - 10 = 5$, 5 is the difference.

differentiation (dĭf′ə-rĕn′shē-ā′shən) **1.** *Mathematics* In calculus, the process of computing the derivative of a function. *Compare* **integration. 2.** *Biology* The process by which cells or tissues undergo a change toward a more specialized form or function, especially during embryonic development.

diffraction (dĭ-frăk′shən) The bending or turning of the path of a wave, such as a light wave or an ocean wave, when it encounters an obstacle. Waves that pass through openings create patterns called interference patterns, which can be used to study the structure of the object through which the waves are passing. *See more at* **wave, x-ray diffraction.**

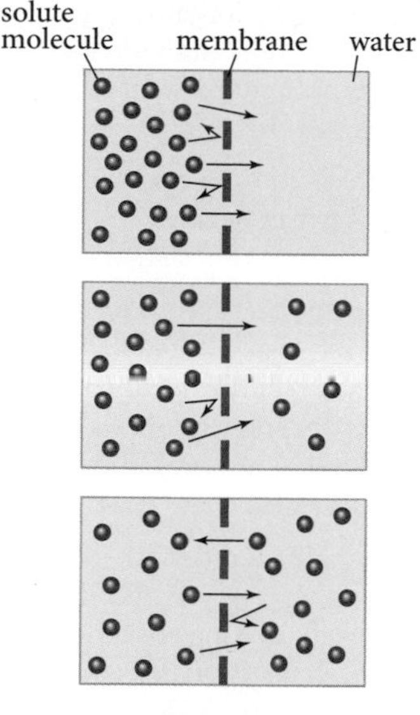

■ **diffusion**

When the concentration of a solute is greater on one side of a membrane than on the other (top), *solute molecules will move through the membrane* (center) *until the concentration of the solute is the same on both sides* (bottom).

diffusion (dĭ-fyo͞o′zhən) **1.** The movement of ions or molecules from an area of higher concentration to an area of lower concentration. Ions and small molecules can move across a cell membrane by diffusion. *Compare* **osmosis. 2.** The gradual spreading out of particles from a small area to a large area as a result of random thermal motions. **3a.** The scattering of light by a rough reflective surface. **b.** The scattering of light as it passes through a translucent material.

digestion (dī-jĕs′chən) **1.** The process by which food is broken down into simple chemical compounds that can be absorbed and used as nutrients or eliminated by the body. In most animals, nutrients are obtained from food by the action of digestive enzymes. In humans, digestion takes place mainly in the small intestine. **2.** The decomposition of sewage by bacteria.

digestive system (dī-jĕs′tĭv) The system of organs that breaks down and absorbs food as nourishment in the body of an animal. In humans, it consists of the digestive tract and the glands, such as the salivary glands, liver, and pancreas, that produce secretions necessary for digestion.

digestive tract The tube of the digestive system through which food passes, in which digestion takes place, and from which wastes are eliminated. In humans, it extends from the mouth to the anus and includes the pharynx, esophagus, stomach, and small and large intestines. Also called *alimentary canal, gastrointestinal tract.*

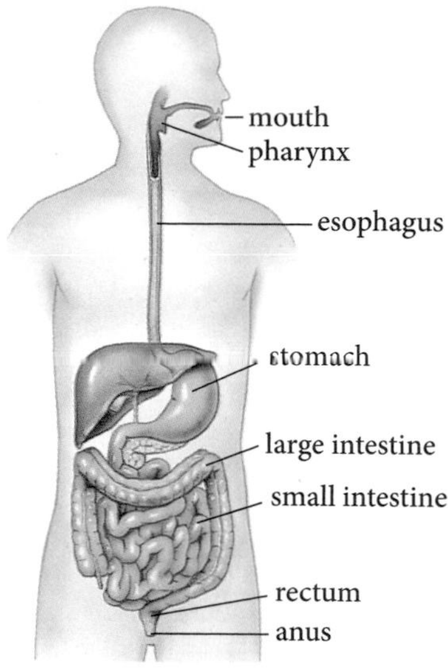

■ **digestive tract**

digit (dĭj′ĭt) **1.** A finger or toe. **2.** One of the ten Arabic numerals, 0 through 9.

digital (dĭj′ĭ-tl) **1.** *Anatomy* Relating to or resembling a digit, especially a finger. **2.** Expressed in numerical form, especially for use by a computer: *converted the image to a digital form.* **3.** *Computers* Relating to a device that can read, write, or store information represented in numerical form: *a digital computer.*

dihedral (dī-hē′drəl) Formed by a pair of planes or sections of planes that intersect: *a dihedral angle.*

dike (dīk) A long mass of igneous rock that cuts across the structure of adjoining rock. It is often of a different composition than the rock it cuts across and can be useful in determining the age relationship between rocks.

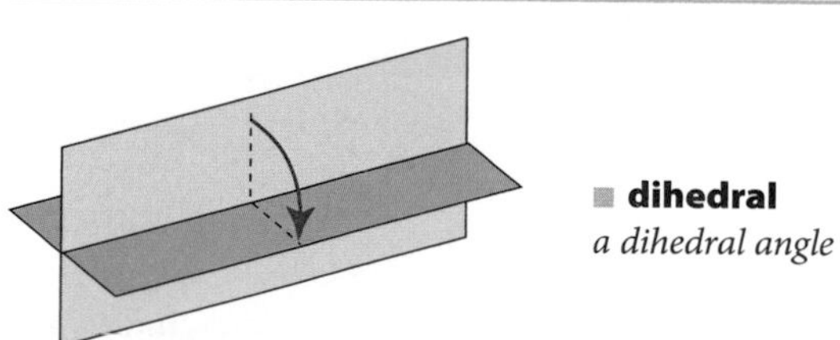

■ **dihedral**
a dihedral angle

dilate (dī-lāt′, dī′lāt′) To widen or become wider: *Some medications dilate blood vessels. The pupils of the eye dilate in the dark.*

dilute (dī-lo͞ot′) To make a substance less concentrated by adding a liquid such as water.

dimension (dĭ-mĕn′shən) **1a.** *Mathematics* Any one of the three physical or spatial properties of length, area, and volume. In geometry, a point is said to have zero dimension; a figure having only length, such as a line, has one dimension; a plane or surface, two dimensions; and a figure having volume, three dimensions. The fourth dimension is often said to be time, as in the theory of general relativity. Higher dimensions can be dealt with mathematically but cannot be represented visually. **b.** The measurement of a length, width, or thickness: *The dimensions of the window are 2 feet by 4 feet.* **2.** A unit, such as mass, time, or charge, associated with a physical quantity and used as the basis for other measurements, such as acceleration.

dimer (dī′mər) Any of various chemical compounds made of two smaller, identical molecules (called monomers) that are linked together.

dimetrodon (dī-mĕt′rə-dŏn′) An extinct meat-eating animal of the Permian Period, having long spines on the back that supported a saillike structure, and powerful jaws with sharp teeth. Dimetrodons lived millions of years before the dinosaurs. They had some features similar to reptiles, and some similar to mammals.

dinoflagellate (dī′nō-flăj′ə-lĭt) Any of numerous protozoans found mostly in the ocean, usually having two flagella and an outer covering of cellulose. Dinoflagellates are one of the main components of plankton.

dinosaur (dī′nə-sôr′) One of a large group of extinct meat-eating or plant-eating reptiles that lived on land during the Mesozoic Era. The smallest dinosaurs were the size of chickens, and the largest were the largest land animals that have ever lived. *See more at* **ornithischian, saurischian.** *See Note at* **bird.**

diode (dī′ōd′) An electronic device, such as an electron tube or a component containing a semiconductor, that allows electric current to flow in only one direction. A diode can be used to convert an AC current into a DC current.

dioecious (dī-ē′shəs) Having the male and female reproductive organs, especially flowers or cones, on different individuals. Ginkgo trees and asparagus plants are dioecious. *Compare* **monoecious.**

dioxide (dī-ŏk′sīd) A compound containing two oxygen atoms per molecule.

diphtheria (dĭf-thîr′ē-ə, dĭp-thîr′ē-ə) A contagious disease caused by a bacterium and characterized by fever, swollen glands, and the formation of a membrane in the throat that prevents breathing. Diphtheria was once a leading cause of death in children, but now children are routinely immunized against it.

diplodocus (dĭ-plŏd′ə-kəs) A very large plant-eating dinosaur of the Jurassic Period. Diplodocus had a long neck and tail and a small head, and its hind legs were longer than its front legs. Adults could grow to be 90 feet (27 meters) in length.

diploid (dĭp′loid′) Being a cell or composed of cells in which each different chromosome occurs in pairs. In most animals and vascular plants, all cells except the sex cells are diploid. *Compare* **haploid.** *See more at* **meiosis, sporophyte.**

dipole (dī′pōl′) **1.** A pair of equal and opposite electric charges or magnetic poles, separated by a small distance. **2.** A molecule having two such charges or poles.

Dirac (dĭ-răk′), **Paul Adrien Maurice** 1902–1984. British mathematician and physicist. He developed a mathematical interpretation of electron behavior that reconciled the theory of relativity with quantum mechanics and that correctly predicted the existence of antimatter.

direct current (dĭ-rĕkt′) An electric current flowing in one direction only, as in a battery. *Compare* **alternating current.** *See Notes at* **current, Tesla.**

directrix (dĭ-rĕk′trĭks) A straight line used in constructing a curve such as a parabola.

disaccharide (dī-săk′ə-rīd′) Any of a class of sugars, including lactose and sucrose, that are composed of two monosaccharides.

discharge (dĭs′chärj) A release of matter or energy, especially electrical energy, as from a battery or in a flash of lightning.

disinfectant (dĭs′ĭn-fĕk′tənt) A substance that

USAGE

disk/disc

Disk and *disc* are both acceptable spellings. The two variants have the same basic meaning, but historically *disc* has generally been preferred in the context of audio recording, where it appears in such words as *compact disc* and *disc jockey*. In the context of digital data storage for computers, the *disk* spelling is usually preferred, as in the terms *disk drive* and *hard disk*. In the context of anatomy, the spelling *disk* is becoming more common, as in the term *intervertebral disk.*

kills or prevents the growth of microorganisms that cause disease.

disk or **disc** (dĭsk) **1.** *Computers* A magnetic disk, such as a hard disk, or an optical disc, such as a compact disc. **2.** *Anatomy See* **intervertebral disk.**

disk drive *Computers* A device that reads data stored on an optical or magnetic disk and writes data onto the disk for storage.

dislocation (dĭs′lō-kā′shən) Displacement of a bone from its normal position, especially in a joint.

dispersion (dĭ-spûr′zhən) The separation of light or other radiation into the individual wavelengths that it is composed of. Dispersion occurs, for example, when a beam of white light passes through a prism. The white light, which contains many different wavelengths of light, fans out into a spectrum containing all the colors of the rainbow.

dissect (dĭ-sĕkt′, dī′sĕkt′) To cut apart or separate organs or parts of an organism for study. *—Noun* **dissection** (dĭ-sĕk′shən, dī-sĕk′shən).

dissociation (dĭ-sō′sē-ā′shən) The separation of a substance into two or more simpler substances, or of a molecule into atoms or ions, by the action of heat or a chemical process. Dissociation is usually reversible.

dissolve (dĭ-zŏlv′) To become mixed with another substance so that a solution forms. For example, salt dissolves in water, and limestone dissolves in acid.

distillation (dĭs′tə-lā′shən) A method of separating a substance that is in solution from its solvent or of separating a liquid from a mixture of liquids having different boiling points. The liquid to be separated is evaporated (as by boiling), and its vapor is then collected after it condenses. Distillation is used to separate fresh water from a salt solution and gasoline from petroleum. ❖ The condensed vapor, which is the purified liquid, is called the **distillate.**

distributive property (dĭ-strĭb′yə-tĭv) A property distinguishing some pairs of mathematical operations, according to which applying one operation (such as multiplication) to a set of objects combined by another operation (such as addition) gives the same result as applying the first operation to each object in the set individually, and then combining those results using the second operation. Thus $2 \times (3 + 4) = (2 \times 3) + (2 \times 4)$, meaning that multiplication is distributive relative to addition. *See also* **associative property, commutative property.**

diurnal (dī-ûr′nəl) **1.** Occurring in a 24-hour cycle; daily. **2.** Most active during the daytime rather than at night. Apes, most monkeys, and many other animals are diurnal. **3.** Opening in daylight and closing at night. Morning glory flowers are diurnal. *Compare* **nocturnal.**

divalent (dī-vā′lənt) *Chemistry* Having a valence of 2.

divergence (dĭ-vûr′jəns) **1.** *Mathematics* The property or manner of failing to approach a limit,

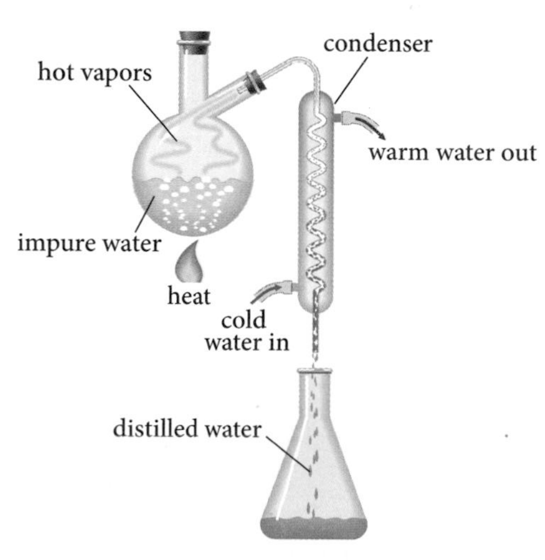

distillation
simple distillation of water

such as a point, line, or value. **2.** *Biology* The evolution of different forms or structures in groups of related organisms, resulting in new species that become more and more different from each other. An example of divergence is the development of wings in bats from the same bones that developed into the arm and hand or paw in most other mammals. Also called *divergent evolution. Compare* **convergence.**

divergent plate boundary (dĭ-vûr′jənt) A tectonic boundary where two plates are moving away from each other and new crust is forming from magma that rises to the Earth's surface between the two plates. Also called *spreading zone. See more at* **tectonic boundary.** *Compare* **convergent plate boundary.**

dividend (dĭv′ĭ-dĕnd′) A number divided by another. In the equation 15 ÷ 3 = 5, 15 is the dividend.

division (dĭ-vĭzh′ən) **1.** The act, process, or operation of dividing one number or quantity by another; the process of finding out how many times one number or quantity is contained in the other. **2.** The highest taxonomic category within the plant kingdom, made up of one or more related classes and roughly corresponding to a phylum in animal classification. *See Table at* **taxonomy.**

divisor (dĭ-vī′zər) A number used to divide another. In the equation 15 ÷ 3 = 5, 3 is the divisor.

Djerassi (djĕ-rä′sē), **Carl** Born 1923. Austrian-born American chemist who pioneered the development of a contraceptive pill and many commonly used drugs, including antihistamines.

DNA (dē′ĕn-ā′) Short for *deoxyribonucleic acid.* A nucleic acid that is found in all living cells and certain viruses, has a spiral structure resembling a twisted ladder, and forms the main part of chromosomes. DNA contains genes that determine or influence many of an organism's traits and that are passed on to the next generation when the organism reproduces. When a cell divides, its DNA replicates to produce two exact copies, one for each daughter cell. *Compare* **RNA.** *See Note at* **gene.**

DNA profiling The determination of the structure of certain regions of a DNA molecule that are known to vary among individuals. One technique involves analyzing the number of short repeated DNA segments at a particular location. DNA profiling can be used to help identify individuals, as by analyzing DNA-containing evidence (such as hair) left at a crime scene. Also called *DNA fingerprinting.*

dodecagon (dō-dĕk′ə-gŏn′) A polygon having 12 sides.

Did You Know...?

DNA

One of the wonders of nature is that the complexity and diversity of life can be contained in a molecule with a relatively simple structure. *Deoxyribonucleic acid,* commonly called *DNA,* exists in all organisms. In eukaryotes, it is found inside the nucleus of almost every cell. A DNA molecule consists of two long strands of subunits called *nucleotides* that are linked together in a structure known as a *double helix,* which resembles a ladder twisted into a spiral. Each rung is made up of two chemical bases that are joined together by hydrogen bonds. There are four kinds of bases in a DNA molecule: cytosine, guanine, adenine, and thymine—C, G, A, and T, for short. Specific sequences of these bases, known as *genes,* form codes that contain all of an organism's genetic information. Most of these codes provide instructions for the production of proteins. The codes are "read" by the processes of *transcription* and *translation.*

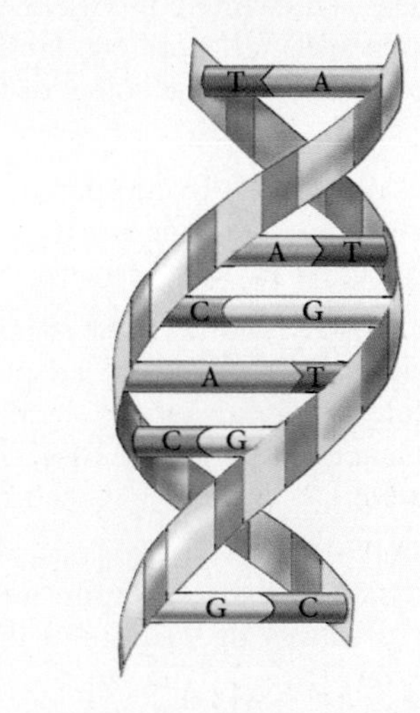

dodecahedron (dō′dĕk-ə-hē′drən) A three-dimensional geometric figure having 12 faces. The faces of a regular dodecahedron are pentagonal.

dog (dôg) **1.** Any of various meat-eating mammals having a long muzzle and nonretractable claws. Many species hunt in packs that have complex social structures. Dogs include the wolves, foxes, jackals, and dingo. **2.** The domesticated dog, kept as a pet or work animal since ancient times and probably descended from the wolf. Domesticated dogs are bred in many varieties, though they all belong to the same species.

doldrums (dōl′drəmz′) A region of the globe found over the oceans near the equator, having weather characterized by calm air and light winds, with occasional squalls and thunderstorms. Hurricanes originate in this region.

dolomite (dō′lə-mīt′, dŏl′ə-mīt′) **1.** A gray, pink, or white mineral consisting mainly of a carbonate of calcium and magnesium. Dolomite occurs as trigonal crystals with a pearly to glassy luster. It is a common rock-forming mineral. **2.** A sedimentary rock containing more than 50 percent of the mineral dolomite by weight.

dolphin (dŏl′fĭn) Any of various aquatic mammals having a snout shaped like a beak, forelimbs shaped like flippers, and horizontal tail flukes. Most dolphins live in the ocean, but a few species inhabit rivers. Dolphins, like porpoises and whales, are cetaceans.

domain (dō-mān′) **1.** *Mathematics* The set of all values that an independent variable of a function can have. In the function $y = 2x$, the set of values that x (the independent variable) can have is the domain. *Compare* **range. 2.** *Biology* A division of organisms that ranks above a kingdom in systems of classification that are based on similarities in DNA sequences. In these systems, there are three domains: the archaea, the bacteria, and the eukaryotes.

dominant (dŏm′ə-nənt) Relating to an allele (a form of a gene) that produces its characteristic effect if it is present on either or both of a pair of chromosomes. For example, if a plant has one allele for purple flowers and one allele for white flowers, and the purple allele is dominant, then that plant will have purple flowers. *Compare* **recessive.** *See more at* **inheritance.**

dopamine (dō′pə-mēn′) A neurotransmitter that is essential for normal brain function. Decreased concentrations of dopamine are associated with Parkinson's disease.

Doppler effect (dŏp′lər) The change in the observed frequency of sound or light waves as a result of the motion of the wave source or the observer, either toward or away from each other. *See Note on next page.*

dormant (dôr′mənt) **1.** *Biology* In an inactive state in which growth stops and metabolism is slowed. Many seeds are dormant until the arrival of favorable conditions that prompt germination. Hibernating animals are also in a dormant state. **2.** *Geology* Not active but capable of renewed activity: *a dormant volcano.*

dorsal (dôr′səl) Of or on the back or upper surface of an animal: *the dorsal fin of a fish.*

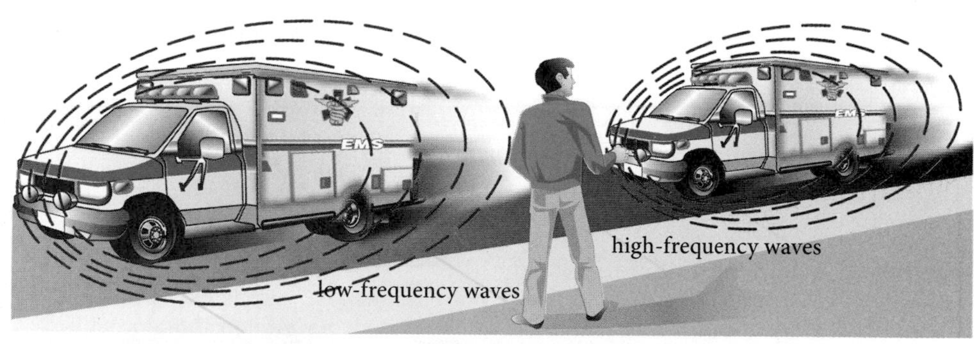

Doppler effect

As the source of sound waves (the ambulance) moves closer to the observer, the frequency of the sound waves and pitch of the sound become higher. As the source moves away from the observer, the frequency and pitch become lower.

Did You Know...?

Doppler effect

When a car rushes past you on the road with the driver holding down the horn, you hear the horn change tone: it's higher pitched than normal as the car approaches and lower pitched as it departs. That's because of the *Doppler effect.* Sound waves spread outward in all directions from the horn. The forward motion of the car compresses the sound waves traveling ahead of the car, making the crests of the waves closer together. Sound having shorter wavelengths has higher frequency and therefore higher pitch—what you hear if the car is moving toward you. Behind the car, however, the crests of the sound waves are farther apart. Longer wavelengths mean lower frequency and lower pitch, which is what you hear once the car rushes past. The Doppler effect occurs with light waves, too; in fact, this was how scientists determined that the universe is expanding. Astronomers observed that the light from galaxies and other distant celestial objects is shifted toward longer wavelengths, that is, toward the red end of the spectrum (a phenomenon called *red shift*). In the 1920s, the astronomer Edwin Hubble proposed that the red shift was due to the Doppler effect: the galaxies are speeding away from us, drawing out the wavelengths of the light emitted behind them, and the universe as a whole is expanding.

double bond (dŭb′əl) A chemical bond in which two covalent bonds are formed between two atoms. *See more at* **covalent bond.**

down (doun) Soft, fluffy feathers that cover a young bird and lie under the outer feathers of certain adult birds. Down feathers are fluffy because, unlike adult outer feathers, they do not have interlocking barbules.

Down syndrome A congenital disorder caused by the presence of an extra 21st chromosome. People with Down syndrome have mild to moderate intellectual disability, short stature, and a flattened facial profile.

Draco (drā′kō) A constellation in the polar region of the Northern Hemisphere near Cepheus and Cygnus.

drag (drăg) A force that acts on an object moving through a fluid such as air or water. Drag acts in a direction opposite the object's direction of motion and slows the object down. It can be reduced by smooth, streamlined designs. *Compare* **lift.** *See Note at* **aerodynamics.**

dragonfly (drăg′ən-flī′) Any of various flying insects having a long slender body and two pairs of clear wings with fine networks of veins.

Draper (drā′pər), **Henry** 1837–1882. American astronomer who developed methods for astronomical photography and was the first to photograph a stellar spectrum (1872) and a nebula (1880).

drone (drōn) A male bee, especially a honeybee whose only function is to fertilize the queen. Drones lack stingers, do not work, and do not produce honey.

drosophila (drə-sŏf′ə-lə) Any of various small fruit flies, one species of which *(Drosophila melanogaster)* is used extensively in scientific research.

drought (drout) A long period of abnormally low rainfall.

drug (drŭg) Any substance that is taken or administered in order to cause physiological changes, especially one prescribed by a doctor to treat or prevent a medical condition. Drugs that affect the central nervous system are often addictive.

drumlin (drŭm′lĭn) An elongated oval hill or ridge consisting of debris deposited by a glacier, sometimes over a core of bedrock. Drumlins have one steep and one gentle slope along their longest axis.

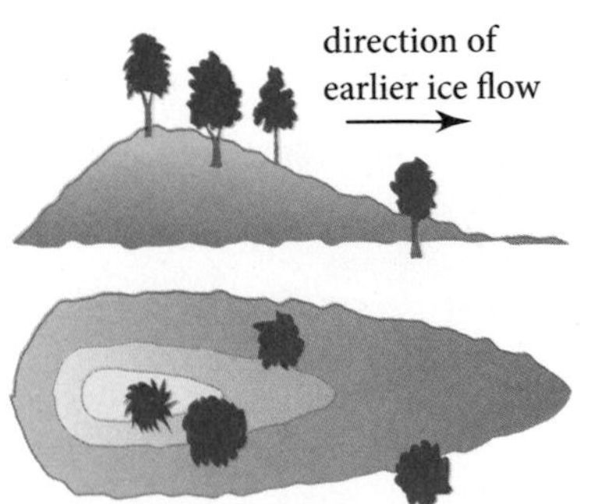

drumlin

Émilie du Châtelet

drupe (dro͝op) A fleshy fruit, such as a cherry, plum, or peach, whose seed is contained in a hard pit or stone surrounded by soft pulpy flesh.

dry cell (drī) An electric cell, such as a flashlight battery, in which the chemicals producing the current are made into a paste so that they cannot spill from their container.

dry ice Solid carbon dioxide. Dry ice evaporates without first passing through a liquid state, by a process known as sublimation. It is used for refrigeration. *See Note at* **sublimation.**

Ds The symbol for **darmstadtium.**

dubnium (do͞ob′nē-əm) A synthetic, radioactive element that is mainly produced by nuclear bombardment reactions of californium, americium, or berkelium. Its most stable isotope has a half-life of 35 seconds. *Symbol* **Db.** *Atomic number* 105. *See* **Periodic Table,** pages 254–255.

du Châtelet (do͞o shä-tə-lā′), Marquise. *Title of* (Gabrielle) Émilie Le Tonnelier de Breteuil. 1706–1749. French mathematician and physicist. She wrote several essays and books and translated Newton's major work, *Principia Mathematica,* from Latin into French.

duck-billed dinosaur (dŭk′bĭld′) *See* **hadrosaur.**

duct (dŭkt) A tube or tubelike structure through which something flows, especially a tube in the body for carrying a fluid secreted by a gland.

ductile (dŭk′təl) **1.** Easily drawn out into a fine strand or wire. Gold and silver are ductile metals. *Compare* **brittle. 2.** Relating to rock or other materials that are capable of withstanding a certain amount of force by changing form before fracturing or breaking.

dune (do͞on) A hill or ridge of wind-blown sand. Dunes are capable of moving (by the motion of their individual grains) but usually keep the same shape.

duodecimal (do͞o′ə-dĕs′ə-məl) Relating to or based on the number 12; having 12 as the base. In the duodecimal number system, each digit represents a multiple of a power of 12 instead of 10. Thus the duodecimal number 24 represents $(2 \times 12^1) + (4 \times 12^0)$, or 28.

duodenum (do͞o′ə-dē′nəm) The beginning part of the small intestine, starting at the lower end of the stomach and extending to the jejunum.

dwarf planet A celestial object that orbits the sun, is not a moon, and has enough gravity to have assumed a nearly spherical shape but not enough to pull most objects in nearby orbits into orbit around it. Pluto is a dwarf planet. *See Note at* **planet.**

dwarf star (dwôrf) A small star of low mass that

dune
top: *sandstone cliff formed from the sand of ancient dunes, Canyon de Chelly, Arizona*
bottom: *sand dunes in the desert of Algeria*

gives off an average or below average amount of light. The sun is a dwarf star.

Dy The symbol for **dysprosium.**

dynamic (dī-năm′ĭk) **1a.** Relating to energy or to objects in motion. *Compare* **static. b.** Relating to the study of dynamics. **2.** Characterized by continuous change or activity.

dynamics (dī-năm′ĭks) The branch of physics that deals with the effects of forces on the motion of bodies. *Compare* **kinematics.**

dynamite (dī′nə-mīt′) A powerful explosive used in blasting and mining. It typically consists of nitroglycerin and a nitrate, combined with an absorbent material that makes it safer to handle.

Did You Know...?

dwarf star

In the world of stars, even a dwarf is quite large. At 864,000 miles in diameter and more than 330,000 times the mass of Earth, our sun is still classified as a *dwarf star.* But a dwarf star is indeed small compared with certain other kinds of stars, such as red giants, which have a diameter of 10 to 100 times that of the sun. Dwarf stars come in several varieties. The type of star known as a *white dwarf* is the remnant of a red giant that has burned nearly all its fuel. Because of the gravitational attraction of its atoms for each other, the star starts to collapse in on itself. After it contracts and blows its outer layers away, the red giant ends up as a white dwarf. A *black dwarf* is a burned-out white dwarf that no longer gives off detectable radiation. A *red dwarf* is a star that has a relatively cool surface temperature, which makes it appear reddish-orange. Typically, red dwarfs have a mass of one-tenth to one-half that of the sun. Astronomers also refer to *brown dwarfs,* which are not stars. A brown dwarf is bigger than Jupiter, but too small to carry on the sustained nuclear reactions that are needed to become a true star.

WORD HISTORY

dynamite

The Nobel Prizes were established by the Swedish chemist and industrialist Alfred Nobel (1833–1896) with funds from the personal fortune he had amassed in part as a manufacturer of explosives and weapons. Nobel was the inventor of dynamite—he had discovered that the highly explosive chemical compound nitroglycerine could be made safer to transport and handle if it was mixed with an inert substance. Nobel called such a mixture *dynamit,* combining the Greek *dunamis,* "power," and the Swedish suffix *-it,* which corresponds to the English suffix *-ite* used to form the names of rocks, minerals, commercial products, and other substances. Greek *dunamis* also gave us words such as *dynamic* and *dynamo.*

dynamo (dī′nə-mō′) An electric generator, especially one that produces direct current. *See more at* **generator.**

dyne (dīn) A unit of force equal to the amount of force required to give a mass of one gram an acceleration of one centimeter per second for each second the force is applied.

dysentery (dĭs′ən-tĕr′ē) A disease of the lower intestines characterized by severe diarrhea, usually caused by infection with bacteria or parasites.

dyslexia (dĭs-lĕk′sē-ə) A learning disability that interferes with a person's ability to recognize and understand written words. *—Adjective* **dyslexic.**

dysplasia (dĭs-plā′zhə) Abnormal development or growth of tissues, organs, or cells.

dysprosium (dĭs-prō′zē-əm) A soft, silvery metallic element of the lanthanide series. Because it has a high melting point and absorbs neutrons well, dysprosium is used to help control nuclear reactions. *Symbol* **Dy.** *Atomic number* 66. *See* **Periodic Table,** pages 254–255.

e (ē) An irrational number with a numerical value of 2.718281828459 . . . . It is mathematically defined as the limit of $(1 + 1/n)^n$ as n grows infinitely large. It has many applications in science as a natural base for expressions involving exponential growth and decay.

E The symbol for **energy.**

eagle (ē′gəl) Any of various large birds of prey having a hooked bill, sharp claws, and long, broad wings.

ear[1] (îr) The organ of hearing in humans and other vertebrate animals. The ear also plays an important role in maintaining balance. In many mammals, the ear is composed of three parts: the outer ear, the middle ear, and the inner ear.

ear[2] The seed-bearing spike of a cereal plant, such as corn or wheat.

eardrum (îr′drŭm′) The thin, oval-shaped membrane that separates the middle ear from the outer ear. It vibrates in response to sound waves, which are then transmitted to the three small bones of the middle ear. Also called *tympanic membrane.*

Earth (ûrth) **1.** The third planet from the sun and the fifth largest. Earth is the only planet known to support life. It is also the only planet known to have large amounts of water in liquid form. Water covers more than 70 percent of the Earth's surface. *See Table at* **solar system,** pages 312–313. **2. earth** Dry land; the ground.

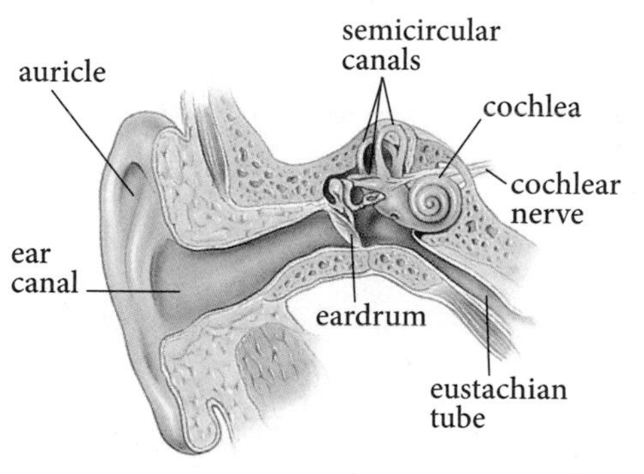

ear[1]

earthquake (ûrth′kwāk′) A sudden movement of the Earth's crust. Earthquakes are caused by the release of built-up stress within rocks along geologic faults or by the movement of magma in volcanic areas. They are usually followed by aftershocks. *See Note on next page. See Note at* **fault.**

earth science Any of several sciences, such as geology, oceanography, or meteorology, that deal with the origin, composition, and physical features of the Earth.

earthworm (ûrth′wûrm′) Any of various segmented worms that burrow into the ground. Earthworms are annelids. *See Note at* **worm.**

Eastern Hemisphere (ē′stərn) The half of the Earth that includes Europe, Africa, Asia, and Australia.

eating disorder A psychological disorder characterized by a disturbance in eating behavior. Anorexia nervosa and bulimia are types of eating disorders.

ebb tide (ĕb) The period between high tide and low tide, during which water flows away from the shore. *Compare* **flood tide.** *See more at* **tide.**

Ebola virus (ĭ-bō′lə) A highly contagious virus that causes fever, bleeding, loss of consciousness, and usually death.

echidna (ĭ-kĭd′nə) Any of several burrowing, egg-laying mammals having a spiny coat, slender snout, and long sticky tongue used for catching ants and termites. Echidnas are toothless and have claws used for digging. They are found in Australia, Tasmania, and New Guinea.

echinoderm (ĭ-kī′nə-dûrm′) Any of numerous invertebrate sea animals that are radially symmetrical, have a hard internal skeleton, and are often covered with spines. Starfish, sea urchins, and sea cucumbers are echinoderms.

echo (ĕk′ō) **1.** A repeated sound that is caused by the reflection of sound waves from a surface. The sound is heard a second time because of the time difference between the initial production of the sound waves and their return from the reflecting

Did You Know...?

earthquake

If all the dishes fall out of your cabinet, you may honestly be able to say, "It's the Earth's fault!" Indeed, the Earth has faults, cracks where sections of its outer shell (the lithosphere) slip past each other, causing an *earthquake* when subjected to great forces. Three kinds of waves accompany earthquakes. Primary (P) waves have a push-pull type of vibration. Secondary (S) waves have a side-to-side type of vibration. Both P and S waves travel deep into the Earth, reflecting off the surfaces of its various layers. S waves cannot travel through the liquid outer core. By contrast, surface (L) waves—a third type of wave, named after British mathematician A.E.H. Love (1863–1940)—travel along the Earth's surface and do most of the damage associated with an earthquake. The total amount of energy released by an earthquake is measured on the Richter scale. On this scale, each increase by 1 corresponds to a tenfold increase in earthquake strength. Thus an earthquake measuring 5.0 on the Richter scale is 10 times stronger than one measuring 4.0. Earthquakes above 7 on the Richter scale are severe. The famous earthquake that flattened San Francisco in 1906 measured 7.8.

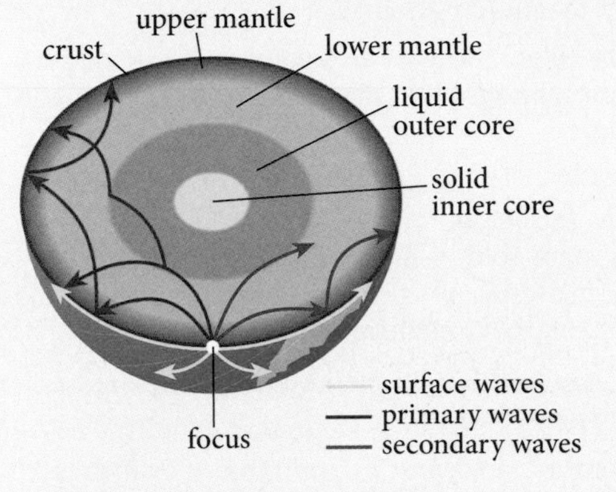

surface. **2.** A reflected radio wave. Echoes of radio waves are the basis for radar.

echolocation (ĕk′ō-lō-kā**′**shən) A sensory system in certain animals, such as bats and dolphins, in which the animal sends out high-pitched sounds and uses the echoes to determine the position of objects. *See Note at* **bat.**

eclipse (ĭ-klĭps**′**) The partial or total blocking of light from one celestial object as it passes in front of another celestial object. ❖ In a **solar eclipse** the moon comes between the sun and Earth. ❖ In a **lunar eclipse** the moon enters Earth's shadow.

eclipsing binary (ĭ-klĭp**′**sĭng) A binary star in which the two stars periodically pass in front of each other from the point of view of an observer on Earth, thereby causing alternating eclipses and regular changes in brightness.

ecliptic (ĭ-klĭp**′**tĭk) The great circle on the celestial sphere that is made by the plane containing Earth's orbit around the sun. The ecliptic traces the sun's apparent path in the sky in one year, as viewed from Earth. *See more at* **celestial sphere.**

E. coli (ē kō**′**lī) A bacterium *(Escherichia coli)* that is normally found in the intestines of humans and other mammals and is widely used in biological research. Some strains can cause disease.

ecology (ĭ-kŏl**′**ə-jē) **1.** The scientific study of the relationships between living things and their environments. **2.** A system of such relationships: *the fragile ecology of the desert.*

ecosystem (ē**′**kō-sĭs′təm) An interacting community of organisms together with their environment, considered as a unit. A lake and a grassland are examples of ecosystems.

ectothermic (ĕk′tō-thûr**′**mĭk) Cold-blooded: *ectothermic vertebrates. Compare* **endothermic.**

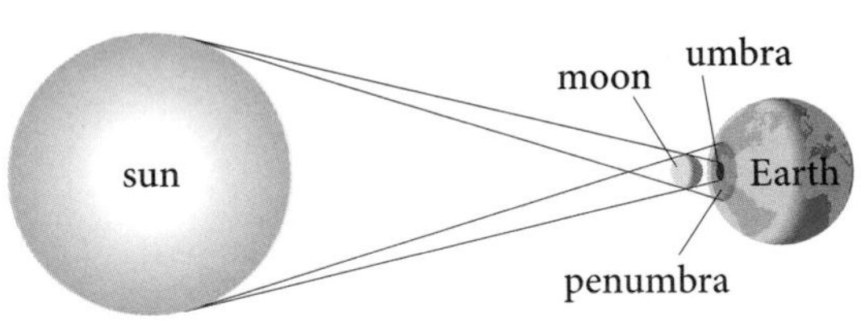

eclipse

A solar eclipse occurs when the moon passes between the sun and the Earth. An observer within the umbra will witness a total solar eclipse, while someone within the penumbra will observe a partial solar eclipse.

Did You Know...?

eclipse

The sun is about 400 times wider than the moon, and it also happens to be about 400 times farther from Earth. For this reason, the sun and moon appear to be almost exactly the same size in the sky. Our unique vantage point makes for the spectacular phenomenon of a *total solar eclipse,* when the moon blocks out the sun. A total solar eclipse reveals the beautiful and delicate corona, wispy tendrils of charged gases that surround the sun but are invisible to the unaided eye in normal sunlight. The orbits of Earth around the sun and of the moon around Earth are not perfect circles. Therefore the sun and moon may vary slightly in how big they appear to us, and the length of total solar eclipses can also vary. The longest solar eclipses, which occur when Earth is farthest from the sun and the moon is nearest to Earth, last only seven and a half minutes. Since looking at the sun can cause blindness, it is safest to view any solar eclipse indirectly. A good method is to project the image through a pinhole in a piece of paper onto another piece of paper.

eczema (ĕk′sə-mə) Inflammation of the skin, often caused by an allergy to a particular substance. Symptoms include itching, scaling, and blistering.

Eddington (ĕd′ĭng-tən), Sir **Arthur Stanley** 1882–1944. British mathematician, astronomer, and physicist who conducted research on the evolution, structure, and motion of stars. He was one of the first scientists to promote Einstein's theory of relativity.

eddy (ĕd′ē) A current, as of water or air, moving in a direction that is different from that of the main current. Eddies often move in a circular motion.

edema (ĭ-dē′mə) An excessive accumulation of fluid in body tissue that results in swelling.

Edison (ĕd′ĭ-sən), **Thomas Alva** 1847–1931. American inventor and physicist who took out more than 1,000 patents in his lifetime. His inventions include the phonograph (1877), the microphone (1878), and an improved incandescent light bulb (1879).

EEG Abbreviation of **electroencephalogram.**

eel (ēl) **1.** Any of various fish having long, snakelike bodies without scales. Eels typically migrate from fresh to salt water to spawn. **2.** Any of several similar fish, such as the lamprey.

efferent (ĕf′ər-ənt) Relating to nerves that carry motor impulses from the central nervous system to the muscles. *Compare* **afferent.**

effervescence (ĕf′ər-vĕs′əns) The bubbling of a solution due to the escape of gas. The gas may form by a chemical reaction, as in a fermenting liquid, or by coming out of solution after having been under pressure, as in a carbonated drink.

efflorescence (ĕf′lə-rĕs′əns) A whitish, powdery deposit on the surface of rocks or soil in dry regions. It is formed as mineral-rich water rises to the surface through capillary action and then

■ **ecosystem**
A pond ecosystem includes the water in the pond, the surrounding environment, and the plants and animals that live there.

evaporates. Efflorescence usually consists of gypsum, salt, or calcite.

egg (ĕg) **1.** The female sex cell of humans and other animals, from which an embryo develops after fertilization with a sperm. An egg carries half as many chromosomes as the other cells of the body. Also called *ovum.* **2.** In many animals, such as birds, turtles, frogs, fish, and insects, a structure consisting of this sex cell together with nourishment for the developing embryo and often a protective covering. It is laid or deposited outside the body of the female. **3.** In plants and most algae, the sex cell whose nucleus is capable of fusing with the nucleus of a male sex cell to form a new organism. An egg has half as many chromosomes as the other cells of the organism. In gymnosperms and angiosperms, eggs are enclosed within ovules.

egg tooth A hard toothlike projection on the beak of an embryonic bird or on the snout of an embryonic reptile that is used to break through the eggshell upon hatching and that later falls off.

Ehrlich (âr′lĭk), **Paul** 1854–1915. German bacteriologist who was a pioneer in the study of the blood and the immune system, and in the development of drugs to fight specific disease-causing agents. Ehrlich theorized that the interactions between cells, antibodies, and antigens were chemical responses, and he developed systematic techniques to search for chemicals that would attack and destroy microorganisms without harming human cells. In the process, he discovered a compound that was effective in combating sleeping sickness and another drug that cured syphilis.

Einstein (īn′stīn′), **Albert** 1879–1955. German-born American physicist whose theories revolutionized the scientific understanding of space, time, matter, energy, and gravity. His theory of special relativity, published in 1905, showed that bodies moving at speeds close to the speed

BIOGRAPHY

Albert Einstein

By around 1900, the field of physics had fallen into confusion. Scientists had discovered phenomena that the laws of classical mechanics established by Galileo and Newton were unable to explain. For example, the observed orbit of the planet Mercury differed slightly from that predicted by Newton's laws. And laws describing the motion of electromagnetic waves did not work under certain conditions. In 1905, an unknown 26-year-old patent office clerk named Albert Einstein published four papers that not only solved these problems but revolutionized physics. Two of these papers presented his special theory of relativity, which broke away from the Newtonian view that space and time are identical in all frames of reference. Einstein posited that the speed of light is the same for all observers and showed that as a consequence, measurements of space and time must differ in frames of reference that are moving relative to each other. The theory also predicted the equivalence of mass and energy, expressed by the famous equation $E = mc^2$, which later became the basis for the development of nuclear energy and nuclear weapons. A third paper showed that light consists of particles, now called photons, which explained phenomena such as the photoelectric effect. A fourth paper explained Brownian motion, the random movement of particles suspended in a fluid. In 1915, Einstein introduced his general theory of relativity, which described gravity as a warping of space and time caused by the presence of matter or energy. Einstein's new conception of gravity correctly predicted Mercury's observed orbit. In his later years, Einstein unsuccessfully attempted to find a theory that would combine all four basic forces of nature.

of light appear to increase in mass, decrease in length, and experience time more slowly. His theory of general relativity, published in 1915, stated that the force of gravity is a result of the curvature of space-time. Einstein also showed that light is composed of indivisible units of electromagnetic energy, later called photons, and that energy and mass can be converted into each other. *See more at* **relativity.**

einsteinium (īn-stī′nē-əm) A synthetic, radioactive metallic element of the actinide series that is usually produced by bombarding plutonium or another element with neutrons. The most stable isotope of einsteinium has a half-life of 1.3 years. *Symbol* **Es.** *Atomic number* 99. *See* **Periodic Table,** pages 254–255.

EKG Abbreviation of **electrocardiogram.**

elasticity (ĭ-lă-stĭs′ĭ-tē) The ability of a solid to return to its original shape or form after being stretched or compressed by a force. Elasticity is a property of most solid materials, including rubber, steel, and many tissues of the body. —*Adjective* **elastic.**

electric (ĭ-lĕk′trĭk) also **electrical** (ĭ-lĕk′trĭ-kəl) Relating to or operated by electricity: *electric power; an electrical appliance. See Note at* **electronic.**

electrical engineering The branch of engineering that deals with the design, construction, and practical uses of electrical systems.

electric cell A device, such as a battery, that is capable of changing some form of energy, such as chemical energy or radiant energy, into electricity.

electric charge *See* **charge** (sense 1).

electric field A region of space in which force is exerted on a charged particle. At every point in an electric field, the force has a strength and a direction. An electric field can be created by an electric charge or by a changing magnetic field.

electricity (ĭ-lĕk-trĭs′ĭ-tē) **1.** The collection of physical effects relating to electrically charged particles, especially electrons, including the forces they generate when at rest or in motion. *See more at* **charge. 2.** The electric current generated by the flow of electrons around a circuit and used as a source of power.

electric potential The potential energy per unit of electric charge at a specific point in an electric field, the standard unit of which is the volt. An electric potential difference, which is the difference between the voltages at two points, is the work per unit of charge required to move a charged particle from one point to the other.

electrocardiogram (ĭ-lĕk′trō-kär′dē-ə-grăm′) A recording of the electrical activity of the heart. The electrocardiogram is used by doctors to analyze how well the heart is working and to diagnose abnormal heart rhythms. ❖ The machine used to record an electrocardiogram is called an **electrocardiograph.**

electrochemistry (ĭ-lĕk′trō-kĕm′ĭ-strē) The scientific study of the use of electric currents to cause chemical reactions and the use of chemical reactions to generate electric currents.

electrode (ĭ-lĕk′trōd′) A conductor, often made of metal or carbon, through which an electric current flows into or out of a device such as a battery or vacuum tube. The positive electrode is called the anode, and the negative electrode is called the cathode.

electrodynamics (ĭ-lĕk′trō-dī-năm′ĭks) The scientific study of electric charges and currents, the electric and magnetic fields they produce, and the forces generated by their interactions.

electroencephalogram (ĭ-lĕk′trō-ĕn-sĕf′ə-lə-grăm′) A recording of the electrical activity of the brain. It is used to diagnose abnormalities of the brain. ❖ The machine used to record an electroencephalogram is called an **electroencephalograph.**

electrolysis (ĭ-lĕk-trŏl′ĭ-sĭs) A process in which a chemical change, especially decomposition, is brought about by passing an electric current through a solution of electrolytes so that the ions in solution move toward the negative and positive electrodes and react with them.

electrolyte (ĭ-lĕk′trə-līt′) **1.** A substance that when dissolved or melted becomes electrically conductive by breaking apart into ions. The movement of ions carries the current. An electrolyte solution is also called an electrolyte. Electrolytes of this type are used in batteries. **2.** A substance that conducts electricity by permitting the movement of ions, especially ions of a particular charge. Electrolytes of this type are used in fuel cells. **3.** Any of several electrically

Did You Know...?

electromagnetic radiation

One of the most significant and intriguing advances of modern physics was the realization that light, along with all other forms of electromagnetic radiation, has properties of both waves and particles. First, consider light as waves. In the late 1800s, physicists discovered that a changing electric field (created, for example, when a charged particle such as an electron moves up and down) generates a changing magnetic field, which in turn generates a changing electric field, and so on, producing an electromagnetic wave that travels through space. Electromagnetic radiation with longer wavelengths, like radio waves, has less energy than electromagnetic radiation with shorter wavelengths, like x-rays. Now, consider light as particles. The smallest possible unit, or quantum, of electromagnetic radiation is called a photon. A beam of electromagnetic radiation can be understood as a stream of photons, with each photon carrying a quantum of energy. The quantum character of light is apparent when light is emitted or absorbed. When an electron in an atom drops from a higher energy level to a lower energy level, a single photon is emitted, carrying the energy difference between the two levels. Physicists sometimes say that electromagnetic radiation is emitted or absorbed like a particle but travels like a wave.

conductive ions found in body fluids. Electrolytes play an important role in many cellular processes.

electrolytic cell (ĭ-lĕk′trə-lĭt′ĭk) A device containing two electrodes immersed in an electrolyte solution, used to bring about a chemical reaction. Electrolytic cells require an outside source of electricity to initiate the movement of ions between the two electrodes, where the chemical change takes place. They have many practical uses, including the recovery of pure metal from alloys and the coating of surfaces with a layer of metal. *Compare* **voltaic cell.**

electromagnet (ĭ-lĕk′trō-măg′nĭt) A device that consists of a coil of insulated wire wrapped around an iron core that becomes magnetized when an electric current flows through the wire. *See Note at* **magnetism.**

electromagnetic force (ĭ-lĕk′trō-măg-nĕt′ĭk) The force of attraction or repulsion that arises from the interactions between electric charges and electric fields or between electric currents and magnetic fields. The electromagnetic force is one of the four basic forces of nature. It is weaker than the strong nuclear force but stronger than the weak nuclear force and gravity.

electromagnetic radiation Energy that moves in the form of magnetic and electric waves and also has some of the properties of particles. A particle of electromagnetic radiation is called a photon. In a vacuum, electromagnetic radiation moves at the highest possible speed, known as the speed of light. It moves more slowly through a material medium such as air or glass.

electromagnetic spectrum The entire range of

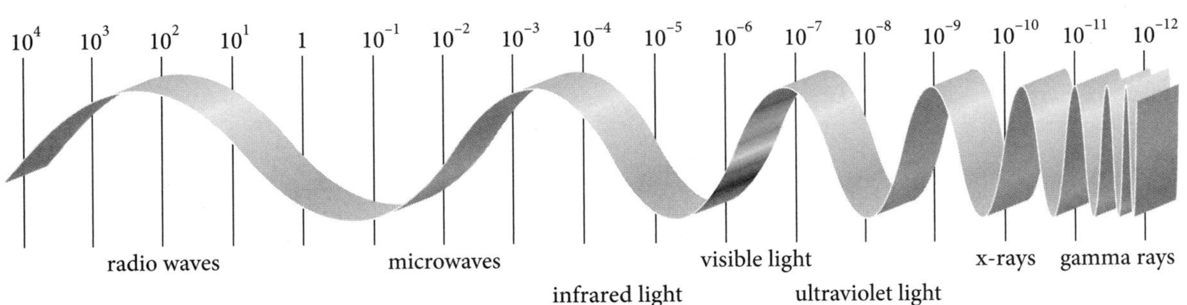

electromagnetic spectrum

The electromagnetic spectrum can be measured in frequencies or in wavelengths. This diagram shows wavelengths in meters, ranging from the longest wavelengths (radio waves) to the shortest (gamma rays). Visible light, which is a band of colors from red to violet, is the only portion of the spectrum that can be seen by the human eye.

electromagnetic radiation. The electromagnetic spectrum is divided into seven major segments. From the lowest frequencies (with the longest wavelengths) to the highest frequencies (with the shortest wavelengths), these segments are radio waves, microwaves, infrared light, visible light, ultraviolet light, x-rays, and gamma rays.

electromagnetic wave A wave that consists of oscillating electric and magnetic fields. All forms of electromagnetic radiation, such as radio waves, visible light, and x-rays, travel as electromagnetic waves.

electromagnetism (ĭ-lĕk′trō-măg**′**nĭ-tĭz′əm) The natural phenomena of electricity, magnetism, and the interactions between them, or the study of these phenomena. *See Note at* **magnetism.**

electromotive (ĭ-lĕk′trō-mō**′**tĭv) Relating to or producing electric current.

electromotive force A difference in electric potential that appears to be a force because it causes a current to flow in an electric circuit. Electromotive force is provided by a power supply such as a battery or generator. It is measured in volts.

electron (ĭ-lĕk**′**trŏn′) A stable subatomic particle with a negative electric charge that is opposite to that of a proton but is equal in magnitude. Electrons spin on their axes as they revolve about an atom's nucleus in orbits called shells. Electrons behave both as particles and as waves, and their motion generates electric and magnetic fields. Protons and neutrons are more than 1,800 times more massive than electrons. *See more at* **atom.**

electronic (ĭ-lĕk′trŏn**′**ĭk) Relating to devices that operate by controlling the flow of electric charge carriers, such as electrons, especially through a vacuum or gas or a semiconducting material. ❖ The study and development of electronic components for use in devices such as radios, televisions, telephones, and computers is called **electronics.**

electron microscope An instrument that uses a beam of electrons to view objects that are too small to be seen with an ordinary microscope. As the electrons hit the object being viewed, other electrons are knocked loose from its surface and are picked up by a detector that converts them into a black and white image.

electron tube A sealed glass tube containing either a vacuum or a small amount of gas, in which electrons move from a negatively charged electrode to a positively charged one. With the application and varying of an electric or magnetic field, the direction and number of electrons in the tube can be controlled. Electron tubes are used to amplify signals and change AC currents to DC currents. They have mostly been replaced by transistors. *Compare* **vacuum tube.**

USAGE

electronic/electric

All electronic devices are electric, but not all electric devices are electronic. An *electric* device is simply one that is powered by electricity. An electric fan usually consists of an electric motor that moves fan blades in a circle. An *electronic* device has special components that control the movement of electrons, as across a vacuum (for example in a vacuum tube) or a semiconductor. These components allow a great range of capabilities, from tuning in to radio and television channels, to performing complicated calculations on a computer, to controlling the operations of a vehicle such as a car or airplane.

electron volt A unit used to measure the energy of subatomic particles. It is equal to the energy gained by an electron that is accelerated until its electric potential is one volt greater than it was before being accelerated.

electrophoresis (ĭ-lĕk′trō-fə-rē**′**sĭs) The migration of electrically charged particles through a fluid that is under the influence of an electric field. Electrophoresis is used especially to separate colloids for the purpose of studying their components.

electrostatic (ĭ-lĕk′trō-stăt**′**ĭk) Relating to or caused by electric charges that do not move. *See more at* **static electricity.**

element (ĕl**′**ə-mənt) **1.** A substance that cannot be broken down into simpler substances by chemical means. An element is composed of atoms that have the same atomic number; that is, each atom has the same number of protons in its nucleus as all other atoms of that element. Today 118 elements are known, of which 92 are known to occur in nature, while the remaining ones have

WORD HISTORY

element symbols

The symbols scientists use for the chemical elements often seem like straightforward abbreviations of the elements' names in English. The symbol for uranium, for example, is U, and the symbol for arsenic is As. But some symbols are nothing like an element's English name, such as Sn for tin. Why is this? The answer is that scientists usually assign chemical symbols based on the elements' names not in English but in either ancient or modern Latin. Often, the elements' Latin names are identical or very similar to their English names: uranium is *uranium* in Latin, for instance, while arsenic is *arsenicum*. But in several cases an element's Latin name is entirely different from its English name. This is especially true of well-known elements that already had English names before the scientific naming system was adopted, such as iron, silver, gold, tin, and lead. The symbols for these metals—Fe, Ag, Au, Sn, and Pb—were taken from their ancient Latin names: *ferrum, argentum, aurum, stannum,* and *plumbum.*

only been made with particle accelerators. **2.** *Mathematics* A member of a set.

elementary particle (ĕl′ə-mĕn′tə-rē) Any of the smallest known units of matter, such as quarks and neutrinos. Elementary particles are not made up of smaller units. *See Note at* **subatomic particle.**

elephant (ĕl′ə-fənt) **1.** A large mammal having thick, nearly hairless skin, a long flexible trunk, and long ivory tusks. Two species of elephants are found in Africa, and one is found in Asia. African elephants have large fan-shaped ears. Elephants can live over 60 years and display complex social behavior. **2.** Any of various similar animals that are extinct, such as the mammoths.

elevation (ĕl′ə-vā′shən) The vertical distance between a standard reference point, such as sea level, and an object or point on the Earth, such as the summit of a mountain. Mount Everest, the highest point on Earth, has an elevation of 29,029 feet (8,848 meters).

ellipse (ĭ-lĭps′) A closed, symmetric curve shaped like an oval, which can be formed by intersecting a cone with a plane that is not parallel or perpendicular to the cone's base. The sum of the distances of any point on an ellipse from two fixed points (called the foci) remains constant no matter where the point is on the curve.

ellipsoid (ĭ-lĭp′soid′) A three-dimensional geometric figure resembling a flattened sphere. Any cross section of an ellipsoid is an ellipse or a circle.

El Niño (ĕl nēn′yō) A climate event occurring every two to seven years in which the surface water of the eastern Pacific Ocean becomes warmer than usual, resulting in decreased abundance of fish and plankton. El Niños also influence jet stream winds, altering storm tracks and affecting the climate over much of the world. *Compare* **La Niña.**

elytron (ĕl′ĭ-trŏn′) *Plural* **elytra** Either of the thick, hard forewings of a beetle that encase the thin hind wings used in flight.

embryo (ĕm′brē-ō′) **1.** An animal in its earliest stages of development, especially before it hatches or, in mammals, before it has reached

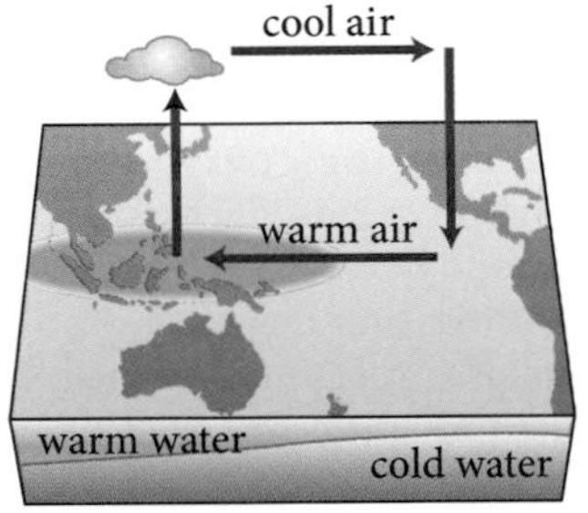

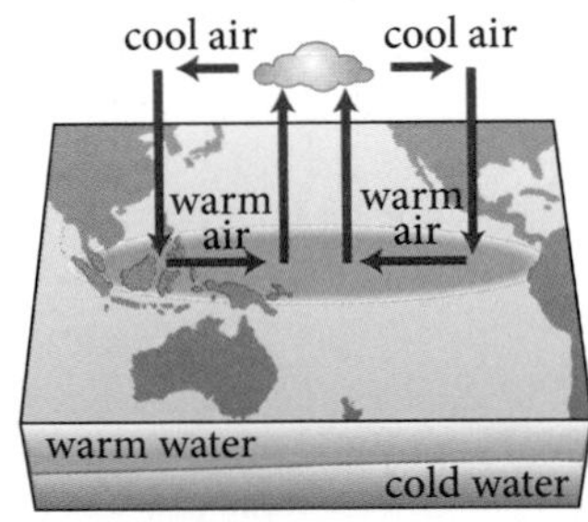

El Niño

top: *normal water temperatures, with warm water concentrated in the western Pacific Ocean*
bottom: *El Niño conditions, with warm water extending from the western Pacific Ocean to the eastern Pacific Ocean*

a distinctively recognizable form. **2.** A plant in its earliest stages of development, especially the partially developed plant contained within a seed. —*Adjective* **embryonic** (ĕm′brē-ŏn′ĭk).

embryology (ĕm′brē-ŏl′ə-jē) The branch of biology that deals with the formation and early development of living organisms.

embryo sac A small structure containing the egg cell in a flowering plant. It is contained within the ovule.

emerald (ĕm′ər-əld) A transparent, green form of the mineral beryl. It is valued as a gem.

emission (ĭ-mĭsh′ən) **1.** The act or process of giving off or discharging: *the emission of light from a tungsten filament; regulating the emission of greenhouse gases.* **2.** Something that is given off or discharged: *harmful emissions from automobiles.*

emission spectrum The radiation, such as light, given off by a substance whose atoms have been excited by heat or other radiation. The atoms of different elements give off radiation at specific frequencies as they return to their normal energy level. The radiation can then be passed through a prism, forming a pattern of colored bars (one bar for each frequency). By analyzing these bars, scientists can determine what kinds of atoms the substance is made of. *See more at* **spectroscope.**

emphysema (ĕm′fĭ-sē′mə) A chronic disease in which the small air sacs of the lungs (called alveoli) become enlarged and eventually collapse, causing blockage to the flow of air. Symptoms include difficulty breathing and loss of physical endurance. Emphysema can be caused by excessive smoking.

empirical (ĕm-pîr′ĭ-kəl) Relying on or derived from observation or experiment rather than theory: *an empirical test of the hypothesis.*

■ **emission**
emissions from a coal-burning power plant

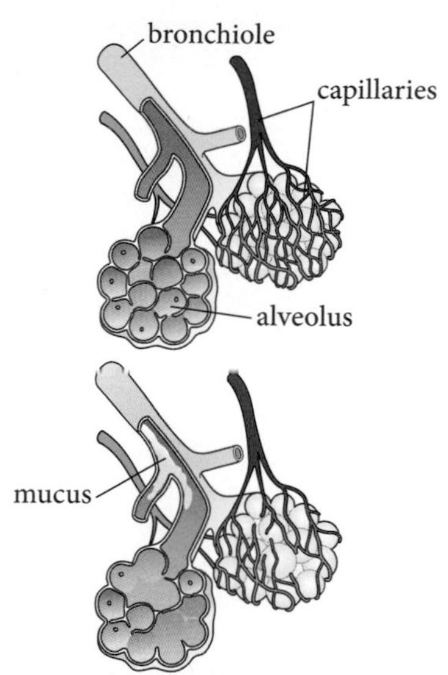

■ **emphysema**
top: *normal bronchiole and alveoli*
bottom: *diseased bronchiole with mucus, enlarged alveoli, and fewer capillaries*

empty set *Mathematics* The set that has no members or elements.

emu (ē′myo͞o) A large, flightless Australian bird related to and resembling the ostrich but smaller in size.

emulsion (ĭ-mŭl′shən) A suspension of tiny droplets of one liquid in a second liquid. By making an emulsion, one can mix two liquids that ordinarily do not mix well, such as oil and water. *Compare* **aerosol, foam.** —*Verb* **emulsify.**

enamel (ĭ-năm′əl) The hard substance covering the exposed portion of a tooth.

encephalitis (ĕn-sĕf′ə-lī′tĭs) Inflammation of the brain, usually caused by a virus.

endangered species (ĕn-dān′jərd) A plant or animal species existing in such small numbers that it is in danger of becoming extinct. An organism often becomes endangered because of destruction of its native habitat.

endemic (ĕn-dĕm′ĭk) **1.** *Ecology* Native to a particular region or environment and not occurring naturally anywhere else. Hawaii, for example, has many endemic species of birds. **2.** *Medicine* Con-

USAGE

endemic/epidemic

A disease that occurs regularly in a particular area, as malaria does in many tropical countries, is said to be *endemic*. The word *endemic*, built from the prefix *en–*, "in or within," and the Greek word *demos*, "people," means "within the people (of a region)." A disease that affects many more people than usual in a particular area or that spreads into regions in which it does not usually occur is said to be *epidemic*. This word, built from the prefix *epi–*, meaning "upon," and *demos*, "people," means "upon the people." In order for a disease to become epidemic it must be highly contagious, that is, easily spread through a population. Influenza, better known as the flu, has been the cause of many epidemics throughout history. Epidemics of waterborne diseases such as cholera often occur after natural disasters such as earthquakes and severe storms that disrupt or destroy sanitation systems and supplies of fresh water.

stantly present in a particular place or group of people, often at a low rate. Malaria, for example, is endemic to tropical regions.

endo– A prefix that means "inside" or "within," as in *endometrium*, a membrane inside the uterus.

endocrine gland (ĕn′də-krĭn, ĕn′də-krēn′) Any gland of the body that produces hormones and secretes them directly into the bloodstream. In mammals, the thyroid gland, adrenal glands, and pituitary gland, as well as the ovaries, testes, and pancreas are all endocrine glands. *Compare* **exocrine gland.** ❖ The group of endocrine glands together with the hormones they secrete is known as the **endocrine system.** *See Note at* **hormone.**

endocrinology (ĕn′də-krə-nŏl′ə-jē) The branch of biology or medicine that deals with endocrine glands, their functions, and their diseases.

endocytosis (ĕn′dō-sī-tō′sĭs) A process by which a cell takes in substances such as proteins and other large molecules. The cell membrane folds around the substance, forming a pocket that is then brought into the cell.

endometrium (ĕn′dō-mē′trē-əm) The membrane that lines the uterus of a female mammal. A fertilized egg must attach itself to the endometrium to continue to develop.

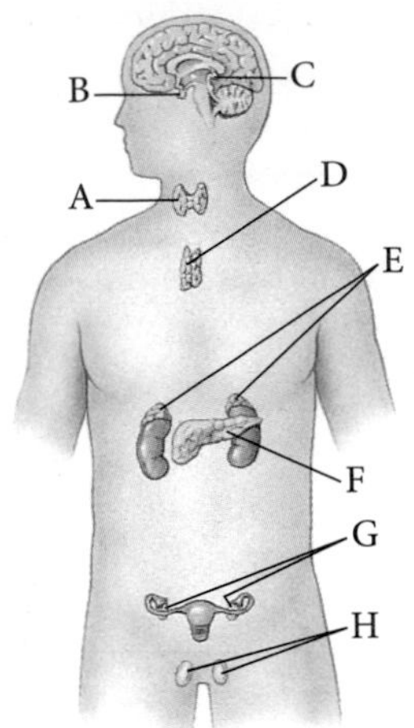

■ **endocrine glands**
A. *thyroid gland*
B. *pituitary gland*
C. *pineal gland*
D. *thymus*
E. *adrenal glands*
F. *pancreas*
G. *ovaries (female)*
H. *testes (male)*

endoplasmic reticulum (ĕn′də-plăz′mĭk) A network of membranes within the cytoplasm of many cells that is important in protein synthesis and involved in the transport of cellular materials. There is no endoplasmic reticulum in bacteria or archaea. *See more at* **cell.**

endorphin (ĕn-dôr′fĭn) Any of a group of small molecules that are produced in the body and regulate pain perception. Endorphins are made up of chains of amino acids.

endoskeleton (ĕn′dō-skĕl′ĭ-tn) A supporting framework in an animal that is contained inside the body. Humans and many other vertebrate animals have bony endoskeletons. Certain invertebrate animals, such as sponges and starfish, have endoskeletons made up of calcium carbonate or other minerals. *Compare* **exoskeleton.**

endosperm (ĕn′də-spûrm′) The tissue that surrounds and provides nourishment to the embryo in plant seeds.

endothermic (ĕn′dō-thûr′mĭk) **1.** Causing or characterized by absorption of heat: *an endothermic chemical reaction. Compare* **exothermic. 2.** Warm-blooded: *endothermic vertebrates. Compare* **ectothermic.**

–ene A suffix used to form the names of hydrocarbons having one or more double bonds, such as *ethene. Compare* **–ane.**

energy (ĕn′ər-jē) **1.** The capacity to do work, which is defined as the amount of force multiplied by the distance over which it is applied. Energy exists in a variety of forms, such as kinetic, thermal, electrical, mechanical, chemical, and nuclear, and can be converted from one form to another. The standard unit is the joule. *Compare* **power, work. 2.** Usable power: *The company reduced its energy consumption.*

engine (ĕn′jĭn) A machine that turns energy into mechanical force or motion, especially one that gets its energy from a source of heat, such as steam. *See more at* **internal-combustion engine, jet engine, steam engine.**

engineering (ĕn′jə-nîr′ĭng) The application of science to practical uses such as the design of structures, machines, and systems. *See more at* **chemical engineering, civil engineering, electrical engineering, mechanical engineering.**

enthalpy (ĕn′thăl′pē) The total amount of energy in a system, equal to its internal energy (the energy due to the physical state and motion of its molecules) plus the pressure exerted on the system multiplied by its volume. At constant pressure, enthalpy increases when heat flows into a system and decreases when heat flows out.

entomology (ĕn′tə-mŏl′ə-jē) The scientific study of insects.

entropy (ĕn′trə-pē) A measure of how evenly spread out the energy of a system is. According to the second law of thermodynamics, the entropy in an isolated system always tends to increase until it reaches equilibrium. For instance, if you pour a cup of hot water into a bowl that contains a cup of cold water, the result will be lukewarm water, in which the heat energy is evenly spread out. But a bowl of lukewarm water will not spontaneously sort itself out into separate areas of hot and cold water. *See Note at* **thermodynamics.**

environment (ĕn-vī′rən-mənt) **1.** All of the physical, chemical, and biological conditions that together affect an organism and influence its growth and development. Soil, air, water, climate, plant and animal life, and noise level are all components of an environment. **2.** The natural world or a particular region of the natural world: *an oil spill that had a devastating effect on the coastal environment.*

enzyme (ĕn′zīm) Any of the proteins produced in the cells of living organisms that act as catalysts in biochemical processes. For example, enzymes

WORD HISTORY

entomology

Scientists who study insects (there are millions of species out there to study!) are called entomologists. Why are they not called "insectologists"? Well, in a way they are. The word *insect* comes from the Latin word *insectum,* meaning "cut up or divided into segments." (The plural of *insectum,* namely *insecta,* is used by scientists as the name of the taxonomic class that insects belong to.) This Latin word was created in order to translate the Greek word for "insect," which is *entomon.* This Greek word also literally means "cut up or divided into segments," and it is the source of the word *entomology.* The Greeks had coined this term for insects because of the clear division of insect bodies into three segments, now called the head, thorax, and abdomen.

Did You Know...?

endorphins

Painkillers such as morphine work by binding to molecules called receptors on the surface of certain cells, especially cells in the brain and the spinal cord. But cell receptors usually respond to chemicals produced within the body, not to substances from outside the body, like morphine, which comes from a poppy plant. Scientists reasoned that there must be chemicals in the body that bind to the same receptors. In the 1970s a group of these chemicals was identified and called *endorphins,* for *endogenous* (meaning "naturally occurring within the body,") and *morphine.* Endorphins are produced when the body is under stress. They allow people to function in otherwise unbearable situations by reducing the amount of pain that is felt. Many long-distance runners, for example, claim that after they run for a long time they start to feel exceptionally happy, a condition sometimes called a *runner's high.* High levels of endorphins in response to the strain of running seem to be responsible for this state of mind.

Did You Know...?

enzymes

Even if you don't know much about biochemistry, your body is performing complex biochemistry every minute. Many of the chemical reactions that take place inside our bodies depend on the proteins known as *enzymes.* These large, globular proteins catalyze chemical reactions, speeding them up by as much as a million times. The shape of an enzyme enables it to bind with the molecule undergoing the reaction, called the *substrate.* The substrate binds to a specific place on the enzyme called the *active site,* where it is modified or is joined to another substrate to form a new molecule. The enzyme itself is not changed by the reaction. Enzymes perform a vast array of duties, from breaking down the proteins, fats, and carbohydrates that we eat, to regulating nerve impulses, to repairing DNA strands. People have found uses for enzymes outside our bodies as well. For example, detergents often include enzymes that break down organic stains on clothing, and enzymes have long been used in making cheese.

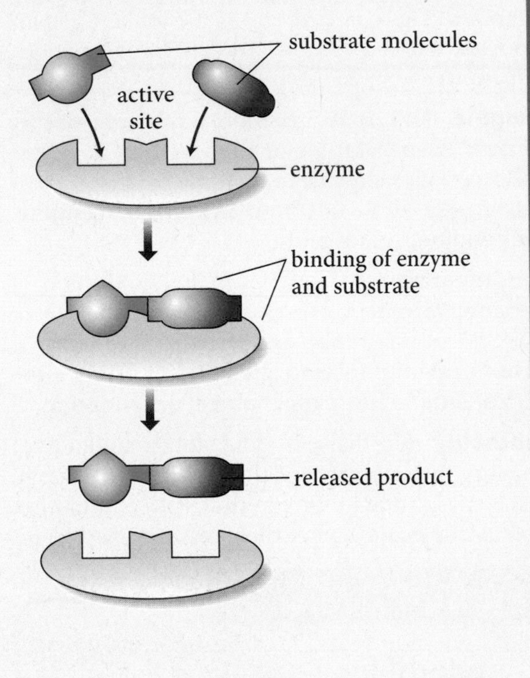

break down the large molecules found in food into smaller molecules so they can be digested.

Eocene (ē′ə-sēn′) The second epoch of the Tertiary Period, from about 56 to 34 million years ago, characterized by warm climates, the rise of most modern families of mammals, and the formation of the Himalayas. *See Chart at* **geologic time,** pages 146–147.

eohippus (ē′ō-hĭp′əs) *See* **hyracotherium.**

eon (ē′ŏn′) The longest division of geologic time, containing two or more eras.

epicenter (ĕp′ĭ-sĕn′tər) The point on the Earth's surface directly above the point from which an earthquake originates. *Compare* **focus.**

epidemic (ĕp′ĭ-dĕm′ĭk) *Noun* **1.** An outbreak of a contagious disease that spreads rapidly and widely. *—Adjective* **2.** Spreading rapidly and widely among the individuals in an area. *See Note at* **endemic.**

epidemiology (ĕp′ĭ-dē′mē-ŏl′ə-jē) The branch of medicine that deals with the study of the causes, spread, and control of disease in populations.

epidermis (ĕp′ĭ-dûr′mĭs) **1.** The protective outer layer of the skin of an animal. In invertebrate animals, the epidermis is made up of a single layer of cells. In vertebrates, the epidermis is made up of several layers of cells and overlies the dermis. Hair and feathers grow from the epidermis. **2.** The outer layer of cells of the stems, roots, and leaves of plants. The epidermis protects the plant from invasion by pathogens and physical damage. It often secretes a waxy cuticle that helps prevent water loss.

epiglottis (ĕp′ĭ-glŏt′ĭs) A thin, triangular plate of cartilage at the base of the tongue that covers the glottis during swallowing to keep food and liquid from entering the trachea.

epilepsy (ĕp′ə-lĕp′sē) A disorder characterized by a tendency to have seizures. It is caused by an abnormal discharge of electrical activity in the brain.

epinephrine (ĕp′ə-nĕf′rĭn) A hormone secreted by the adrenal gland in response to physical or mental stress, as from fear or injury. The release of epinephrine causes the heart to beat faster and more strongly, the pupils to dilate, and the rate of breathing to increase. Epinephrine also causes the release of additional sugar into the blood, which can be used by the body as fuel when more alertness or greater physical effort is needed. Also called *adrenaline.*

epiphyte (ĕp′ə-fīt′) A plant that grows on another plant and depends on it for support but not food. Epiphytes get moisture and nutrients from the air, from rainfall, and from organic material that accumulates around their roots. Spanish moss and many orchids are epiphytes.

epithelium (ĕp′ə-thē′lē-əm) Tissue consisting of a thin, protective layer of cells that covers most of the outer surface of an animal body and lines the inner surface of many body parts. In vertebrate animals, the outer layer of the skin, called the epidermis, is composed of epithelium.

epoch (ĕp′ək, ē′pŏk′) A unit of geologic time that is a subdivision of a period.

epoxide (ĕ-pŏk′sīd) A ring-shaped chemical structure or compound consisting of an oxygen atom bonded to two other atoms, usually of carbon, that are already bonded to each other.

epoxy (ĭ-pŏk′sē) Any of various artificial resins that are tough, very adhesive, and resistant to chemicals.

equation (ĭ-kwā′zhən) **1.** *Mathematics* A written statement indicating the equality of two expressions. It consists of a sequence of symbols that is split into left and right sides joined by an equal sign. For example, $2 + 3 + 5 = 10$ is an equation. **2.** *Chemistry* A written representation of a chemical reaction, in which the symbols and amounts of the reactants are separated from those of the products by an arrow, a set of opposing arrows, or an equal sign. For example, $NaOH + HCl \rightarrow NaCl + H_2O$ is an equation.

equator (ĭ-kwā′tər) **1.** The imaginary line forming a great circle around the Earth's surface halfway between the North and South Poles. It divides the Earth into the Northern Hemisphere and the Southern Hemisphere. **2.** A similar circle on the surface of any celestial object.

equi– A prefix that means "equal" or "equally," as in *equidistant.*

equidistant (ē′kwĭ-dĭs′tənt) Equally distant: *two points that are equidistant from a third point.*

equilateral (ē′kwə-lăt′ər-əl) Having all sides of equal length, as a square or as a triangle that is neither scalene nor isosceles.

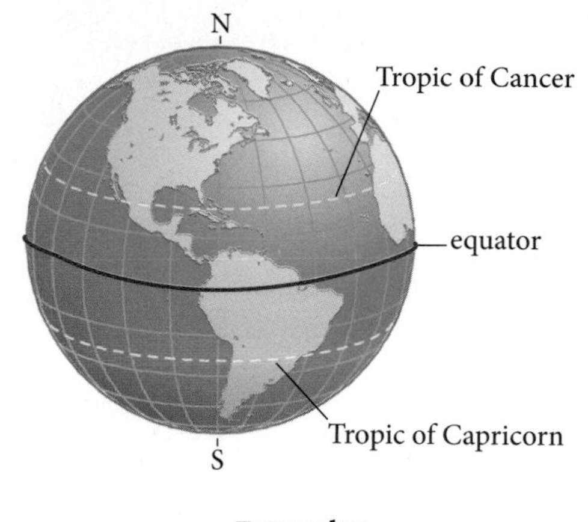

equator

equilibrium (ē′kwə-lĭb′rē-əm) **1.** *Physics* **a.** In mechanics, the state of a body or a system of bodies that is either at rest or in steady motion. At equilibrium the sum of all forces acting on a body is zero (because any opposing forces balance each other), and the state of rest or motion does not change. **b.** In thermodynamics, the state of a system in which no heat flows occur and the entire system is at the same temperature. **2.** *Chemistry* The state of a reversible chemical reaction in which the forward and reverse reactions occur at equal rates so that the concentration of the reactants and products remains constant.

equine (ē′kwīn′, ĕk′wīn′) Relating to horses and closely related animals, such as zebras.

equinox (ē′kwə-nŏks′) **1.** Either of the two moments of the year when the sun crosses the celestial equator. The vernal equinox occurs on or about March 20, and the autumnal equinox occurs on or about September 23. The days on which an equinox falls have about equal periods of sunlight and darkness. **2.** Either of the two points on the celestial sphere where the apparent

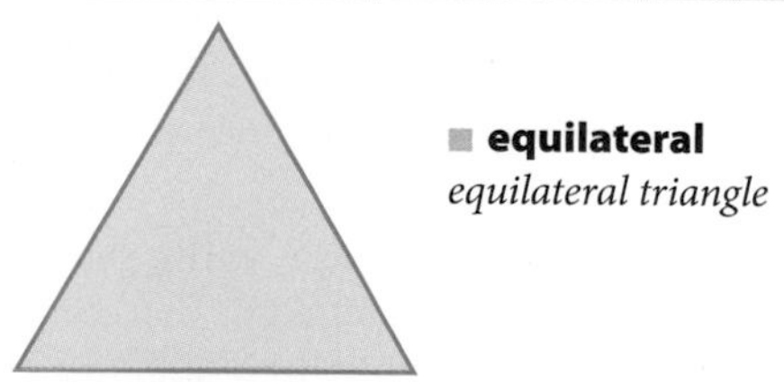

equilateral
equilateral triangle

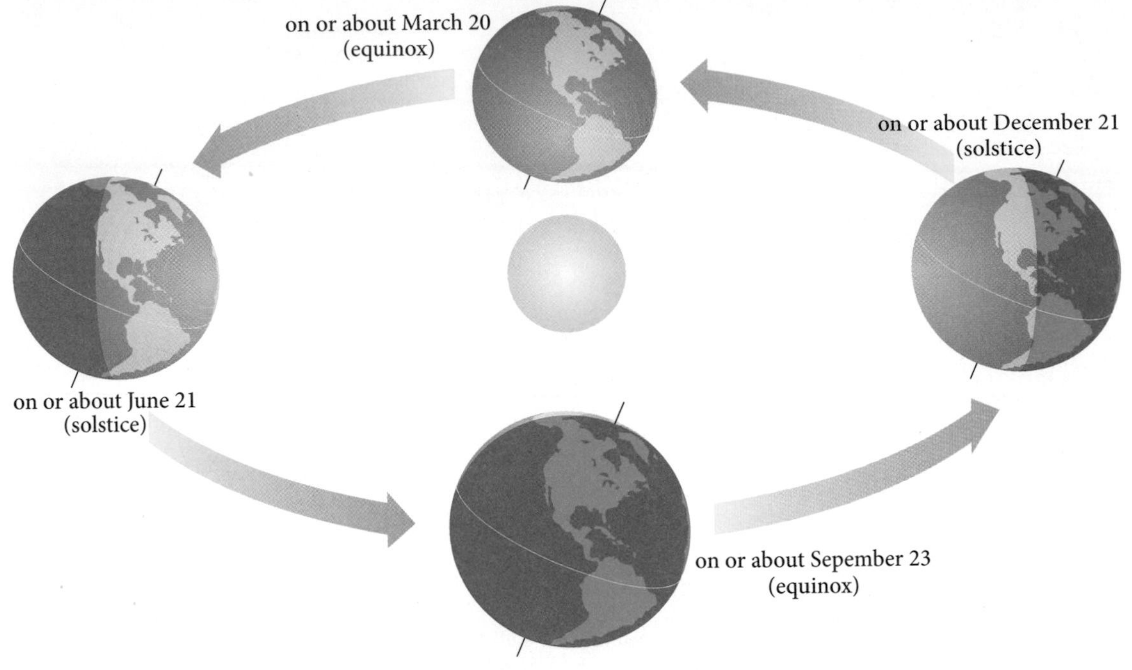

equinox

Changes in seasons occur as the position of the Earth in relation to the sun changes. Equinoxes and solstices mark the beginning of opposite seasons in the Northern and Southern Hemispheres. For example, the June solstice marks the beginning of summer in the Northern Hemisphere and of winter in the Southern Hemisphere. The September equinox marks the beginning of fall in the Northern Hemisphere and of spring in the Southern Hemisphere.

path of the sun (known as the ecliptic) crosses the celestial equator. *Compare* **solstice.**

equivalent (ĭ-kwĭv′ə-lənt) **1.** Equal, as in value, meaning, or force. **2.** Having a one-to-one correspondence, as between parts: *equivalent geometric figures.*

Er The symbol for **erbium.**

era (îr′ə) A division of geologic time, longer than a period and shorter than an eon.

Eratosthenes (ĕr′ə-tŏs′thə-nēz′) Third century BC. Greek mathematician and astronomer. He is best known for making an accurate estimate of the circumference of the Earth by measuring the angle of the sun's rays at two different locations at the same time. Eratosthenes also invented a method for listing the prime numbers that are less than any given number.

erbium (ûr′bē-əm) A soft, silvery, easily shaped metallic element of the lanthanide series. It is used in lasers and other light-amplification equipment, in certain alloys, in optical filters, and as a colorant for glass. *Symbol* **Er.** *Atomic number* 68. *See* **Periodic Table,** pages 254–255.

erectile (ĭ-rĕk′təl, ĭ-rĕk′tīl′) **1.** Capable of being raised to an upright position, as the spines in the dorsal fin of a fish. **2.** Relating to tissue that is capable of filling with blood and becoming rigid.

erection (ĭ-rĕk′shən) The stiffening or enlargement of certain body parts, especially the penis or the clitoris, when the tissues within them fill with blood.

erg (ûrg) A unit used to measure energy or work, equal to the force of one dyne over a distance of one centimeter. This unit has been mostly replaced by the joule.

ergot (ûr′gət) A fungus that infects rye, wheat, and other grain plants, forming black masses among the seeds. Grain infected with ergot is poisonous and can cause serious illness. Drugs derived from ergot are sometimes used in medicine.

erosion (ĭ-rō′zhən) The gradual wearing away of land surface materials, especially rocks, sediments, and soils, by the action of water, wind, or a glacier. Usually erosion also involves the transfer of eroded material from one place to another, as from the top of a mountain to an adjacent valley, or from the upstream portion of a river to the downstream portion.

erupt (ĭ-rŭpt′) To release gas, ash, molten materials, or hot water into the atmosphere or onto the Earth's surface.

erythrocyte (ĭ-rĭth′rə-sīt′) *See* **red blood cell.**

Es The symbol for **einsteinium.**

escape velocity (ĭ-skāp′) The velocity that a body, such as a rocket, must achieve to overcome the gravitational pull of the Earth or another celestial object.

escarpment (ĭ-skärp′mənt) A steep slope or long cliff formed by erosion or by vertical movement of the Earth's crust along a fault.

esker (ĕs′kər) A long, narrow ridge of coarse sand and gravel deposited by a stream flowing in or under a melting sheet of glacial ice.

esophagus (ĭ-sŏf′ə-gəs) The part of the digestive tract that consists of a muscular tube connecting the throat to the stomach.

ester (ĕs′tər) An organic compound formed when an acid and an alcohol combine and release water. Animal and vegetable fats and oils are esters.

esker

aerial photograph of an esker near Whitefish Lake, Northwest Territories, Canada

estivation (ĕs′tə-vā′shən) *Zoology* An inactive state, resembling deep sleep, in which some animals pass the summer or another hot, dry period. *Compare* **hibernation.**

estrogen (ĕs′trə-jən) **1.** Any of a group of steroid hormones that primarily regulate the growth, development, and function of the female reproductive system. The main sources of estrogen in the body are the ovaries and the placenta. **2.** Any of several synthetic compounds that are similar to naturally produced estrogen in their effects on the body. Synthetic estrogens are used primarily in oral contraceptives.

estrous cycle (ĕs′trəs) The recurring set of physiological and behavioral changes that take place in a female mammal from one period of estrus to another. The estrous cycle often occurs during a specific breeding period, and the young are then born at a time of year when the conditions are best for their survival.

estrus (ĕs′trəs) A regularly recurring period during which most female mammals, excluding humans and some other primates, are ready to mate. Also called *heat.*

estuary (ĕs′cho͞o-ĕr′ē) **1.** The wide lower course of a river where it flows into the sea. The water in estuaries is a mixture of fresh water and salt water. **2.** An arm of the sea that extends inland to meet the mouth of a river.

ethane (ĕth′ān′) A colorless, odorless, flammable gas, C_2H_6, occurring in natural gas. It is used as a fuel and in refrigeration.

ethanol (ĕth′ə-nôl′) An alcohol, C_2H_5OH, obtained from the fermentation of sugars and starches and also made artificially. It is the intoxicating ingredient of alcoholic beverages, and it is also used as a solvent. Also called *ethyl alcohol, grain alcohol.*

ethene (ĕth′ēn′) A colorless, flammable gas, C_2H_4, obtained from petroleum and natural gas. It is used as a fuel, in making plastics, and in ripening and coloring fruits. Also called *ethylene.*

ether (ē′thər) **1.** An organic compound in which two hydrocarbon groups are linked by an oxygen atom. **2.** A colorless, volatile, flammable liquid, $C_4H_{10}O$. It is used as a solvent and was formerly used as an anesthetic. **3.** A hypothetical medium formerly believed to permeate all space and to be the medium through which light and other electromagnetic radiation move. The existence of ether was disproved by the American physicists Albert Michelson and Edward Morley in 1887.

ethyl (ĕth′əl) The organic group C_2H_5, derived from ethane, and occurring as a radical, as an ion, or as a component of many important chemical compounds.

ethyl alcohol *See* **ethanol.**

ethylene (ĕth′ə-lēn′) *See* **ethene.**

ethyne (eth′īn′) *See* **acetylene.**

etiology (ē′tē-ŏl′ə-jē) The cause or origin of a disease.

Eu The symbol for **europium.**

eucalyptus (yo͞o′kə-lĭp′təs) Any of numerous tall trees that are native to Australia. Eucalyptus trees have wood valued as timber and aromatic leaves containing an oil used in medicinal preparations.

Euclid (yo͞o′klĭd) Third century BC. Greek mathematician whose book, *Elements*, was used continuously until the 19th century. In it, he organized and systematized all that was known about geometry. Euclid's systematic use of deductions and axioms was widely regarded as a model working method and influenced mathematicians and scientists for over two thousand years.

euglena (yo͞o-glē′nə) Any of various green, one-celled water organisms that move by means of a whiplike structure called a flagellum. Euglenas produce their own food through photosynthesis. They are protozoans.

Euclid

eukaryote (yo͞o-kăr′ē-ōt) Any of numerous organisms whose cells contain a nucleus surrounded by a membrane. All organisms except bacteria and archaea are eukaryotes. The eukaryotes include animals, plants, fungi, and protists. *Compare* **prokaryote.**

Euler (oi′lər), **Leonhard** 1707–1783. Swiss mathematician who made important contributions to calculus, trigonometry, and the theory of imaginary numbers. Euler introduced much of the basic mathematical notation still used today.

europium (yo͞o-rō′pē-əm) A silvery-white metallic element that is the softest member of the lanthanide series. It is used in making color television tubes and lasers and in scientific research. *Symbol* **Eu.** *Atomic number* 63. *See* **Periodic Table,** pages 254–255.

eustachian tube (yo͞o-stā′shən) A slender tube that connects the middle ear with the upper part of the pharynx, serving to equalize air pressure on the two sides of the eardrum.

eutrophic (yo͞o-trŏf′ĭk) Having large amounts of mineral and organic nutrients that promote the growth of algae and aquatic plants, resulting in a reduction of dissolved oxygen and often the death of fish and other aquatic organisms. Lakes and ponds often become eutrophic as a result of the runoff of fertilizers.

evaporation (ĭ-văp′ə-rā′shən) The change of a liquid into a vapor at a temperature below the boiling point.

even (ē′vən) Divisible by 2 with a remainder of 0, such as 12 or 876.

even-toed ungulate *See* **artiodactyl.**

evergreen (ĕv′ər-grēn′) *Adjective* **1.** Having green leaves or needles all year. *Compare* **deciduous.** —*Noun* **2.** An evergreen plant, such as a pine tree or a rhododendron.

evolution (ĕv′ə-lo͞o′shən) Change in the genes of a group of organisms over many generations, such that descendants are different from their ancestors. In time, one or more new species may form from an ancestral species. Evolution is caused by natural selection and certain other processes, such as mutation. *See also* **natural selection.** *See Note at* **Darwin.**

evolve (ĭ-vŏlv′) **1.** To undergo evolution: *Whales evolved from ancient land mammals.* **2.** To develop a characteristic through the process

Did You Know...?

evolution

Before Charles Darwin developed the theory of *evolution* by natural selection, other naturalists, including Darwin's grandfather Erasmus Darwin, had suggested that organisms might slowly change over long periods of time. But how did that change come about, and how did plants and animals come to be so exquisitely adapted to their environments? Darwin came up with the idea of *natural selection* at about the same time as another naturalist, Alfred Russel Wallace. Both of them realized that if an organism had many offspring that differed slightly from each other, and those offspring that had certain heritable characteristics survived and reproduced more than the others did, then little by little, as each generation differed from the previous one, huge changes could occur over millions of years.

of evolution: *Cats have evolved an extraordinary sense of balance.*

excrement (ĕk′skrə-mənt) Waste matter that is passed from the body after digestion.

excretion (ĭk-skrē′shən) The elimination by an organism of waste products resulting from metabolic processes. Vertebrates have specific organs of excretion, such as the kidneys. In plants and many invertebrate organisms, waste is eliminated by diffusion to the outside environment. —*Verb* **excrete.**

exo– A prefix that means "outside" or "external," as in *exoskeleton,* a covering on the outside of an animal's body.

exocrine gland (ĕk′sə-krĭn, ĕk′sə-krēn) A gland of the body that discharges its secretions through a duct to an internal or external surface, rather than directly into the bloodstream. In mammals, the sweat glands and salivary glands are exocrine glands. *Compare* **endocrine gland.**

exocytosis (ĕk′sō-sī-tō′sĭs) A process by which a cell secretes or excretes a substance by enclosing the substance in a vesicle. The vesicle fuses with the cell membrane and discharges its contents outside the cell.

exoplanet (ĕk′sō-plăn′ĭt) A planet orbiting around a star other than the sun.

exoskeleton (ĕk′sō-skĕl′ĭ-tn) A hard outer covering, such as the shell of a grasshopper or a crab, that provides protection and support. The exoskeletons of insects and crustaceans are largely made of chitin. *Compare* **endoskeleton.**

exosphere (ĕk′sō-sfîr′) The transitional zone between the thermosphere (the outermost region of the Earth's atmosphere) and outer space. The gasses in the exosphere get thinner and thinner until the lightest particles, such as hydrogen atoms, begin to escape Earth's gravity.

exothermic (ĕk′sō-thûr′mĭk) Causing or characterized by release of heat: *an exothermic chemical reaction. Compare* **endothermic.**

expanding universe (ĭk-spăn′dĭng) A model of the universe in which the volume of the universe is expanding. It is based on the idea that the red shift in light from distant galaxies is evidence that all galaxies are moving away from one another. *See Notes at* **Big Bang, Doppler effect.**

expansion (ĭk-spăn′shən) **1.** An increase in size, volume, or quantity, usually due to heating. When substances are heated, the molecular bonds between their particles are weakened, and the particles move faster, causing the substance to expand. **2.** A number or other mathematical expression written in an extended form; for example, $a^2 + 2ab + b^2$ is the expansion of $(a + b)^2$.

expectorant (ĭk-spĕk′tər-ənt) A drug that helps discharge phlegm or mucus from the respiratory tract.

experiment (ĭk-spĕr′ə-mənt) A test or procedure that is designed to determine either the validity of a hypothesis or the effects of something and is carried out under carefully controlled conditions.

explosion (ĭk-splō′zhən) A violent blowing apart or bursting caused by energy released from a very fast chemical reaction, a nuclear reaction, or the escape of gases under pressure.

exponent (ĕk′spō′nənt, ĭk-spō′nənt) A number or symbol, placed above and to the right of the expression to which it applies, that indicates the number of times the expression is used as a factor. For example, the exponent 3 in 5^3 indicates $5 \times 5 \times 5$; the exponent 2 in $(a + b)^2$ indicates $(a + b) \times (a + b)$.

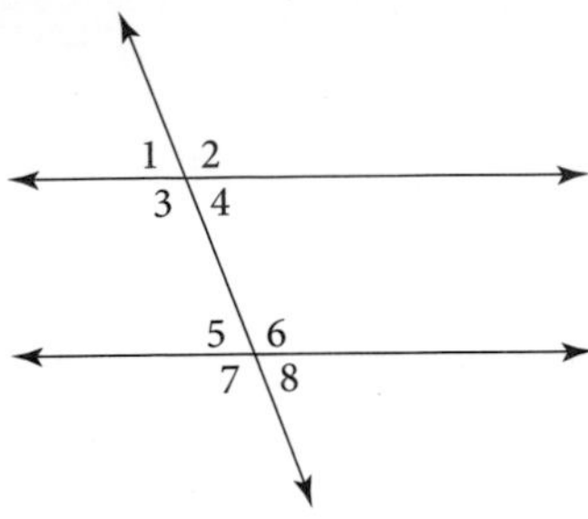

■ **exterior angle**
Angles 1, 2, 7, and 8 are exterior angles.

exponential (ĕk′spə-nĕn′shəl) Relating to a mathematical expression containing one or more exponents. ❖ Something is said to increase **exponentially** if its rate of change must be expressed using exponents. A graph of such a rate would appear not as a line, but as a curve that becomes steeper and steeper.

extensor (ĭk-stĕn′sər) A muscle that extends or straightens a limb or joint. *Compare* **flexor.**

exterior angle (ĭk-stîr′ē-ər) **1.** Any of the four angles formed on the outside of two straight lines when these lines are intersected by a third straight line. **2.** The angle formed between a side of a polygon and an extended adjacent side. *Compare* **interior angle.**

extinct (ĭk-stĭngkt′) **1.** No longer existing or living. Species become extinct for many reasons, including climate change, destruction of habitat, and natural disasters. The great majority of species that have ever lived are now extinct. **2.** No longer active: *an extinct volcano.* —*Noun* **extinction.**

extrapolate (ĭk-străp′ə-lāt′) To estimate the value of a quantity that falls outside the range in which its values are known.

extraterrestrial (ĕk′strə-tə-rĕs′trē-əl) Originating, located, or occurring outside the Earth or its atmosphere: *searching for evidence of extraterrestrial life.*

extreme (ĭk-strēm′) Either the first or fourth term of a proportion of four terms. In the proportion $\frac{2}{3} = \frac{4}{6}$, the extremes are 2 and 6. *Compare* **mean** (sense 2).

extrusion (ĭk-stro͞o′zhən) The emission of lava onto the surface of the Earth. ❖ Rocks that formed from the cooling of lava are called **extrusive rocks.** *Compare* **intrusion.**

eye (ī) **1.** An organ by means of which an animal is able to see or sense light. In vertebrate animals, eyes occur in pairs, each one consisting of a spherical structure filled with fluid. Incoming light is refracted by the cornea and transmitted through the pupil to the lens, which focuses the image onto the retina. Cephalopods, such as octopuses, have eyes with a very similar structure. *See more at* **compound eye, eyespot. 2.** The relatively calm area at the center of a hurricane or similar storm. *See more at* **hurricane.**

eyepiece (ī′pēs′) The lens or group of lenses closest to the eye in an optical instrument such as a telescope.

eyespot (ī′spŏt′) **1.** An area that is sensitive to light and functions somewhat like an eye, found in certain single-celled organisms and many invertebrate animals. **2.** A round marking resembling an eye, as on a butterfly's wing.

eyestalk (ī′stôk′) A movable structure having a compound eye on its tip, found on crabs, lobsters, and certain other crustaceans.

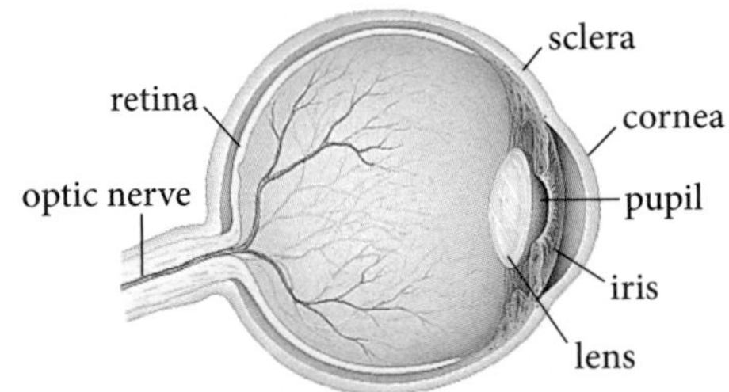

■ **eye**
top: *cross section of a human eye*
bottom: *satellite view of a hurricane; the eye is the dark area in the center of the large white cloud formation*

F **1.** Abbreviation of **farad. 2.** The symbol for **fluorine. 3.** Abbreviation of **Fahrenheit.**

factor (făk′tər) *Noun* **1.** One of two or more numbers or expressions that are multiplied to obtain a given product. For example, 2 and 3 are factors of 6, and $a + b$ and $a - b$ are factors of $a^2 - b^2$. **2.** A substance found in the body, such as a protein, that is essential to a biological process. For example, growth factors are needed for proper cell growth and development. —*Verb* **3.** To find the factors of a number or expression. For example, the number 12 can be factored into 2 and 6, or 3 and 4, or 1 and 12.

factorial (făk-tôr′ē-əl) The product of all of the positive integers from 1 to a given positive integer. It is written as the given integer followed by an exclamation point. For example, the factorial of 4 (written 4!) is 1 × 2 × 3 × 4, or 24.

Fahrenheit (făr′ən-hīt′) Relating to or based on a temperature scale that indicates the freezing point of water as 32° and the boiling point of water as 212° under standard atmospheric pressure. *See Note at* **Celsius.**

Fahrenheit, Daniel Gabriel 1686–1736. German-Dutch physicist. He invented the mercury thermometer in 1714 and devised the Fahrenheit temperature scale.

falcon (făl′kən, fôl′kən) Any of various birds of prey having a short curved beak, sharp claws, and long pointed wings.

fallopian tube (fə-lō′pē-ən) Either of a pair of tubes found in female mammals that carry egg cells from the ovaries to the uterus.

fallout (fôl′out′) **1.** The tiny particles of debris discharged into the atmosphere by an explosion, especially radioactive debris from a nuclear explosion. **2.** The fall of such particles back to the Earth.

false color (fôls) Color that does not appear in a digital image as originally produced, for example by a telescope or a CT scanner, but is applied later in order to enhance certain details.

family (făm′ə-lē) A taxonomic category of organisms that share certain characteristics, ranking above a genus and below an order. *See Table at* **taxonomy.**

fang (făng) A long pointed structure that an animal uses to seize prey or to inject venom. The fangs of a venomous snake, for example, are teeth with a hollow groove that venom flows through. A spider's fangs are made of chitin and are also used to inject venom.

farad (făr′əd) A unit used to measure electric capacitance. A capacitor in which a charge of one coulomb can produce a difference of one volt between its two storage plates has a capacitance of one farad.

faraday (făr′ə-dā′) A unit of electric charge, equal to about 96,494 coulombs, used to express the amounts of electric charge used in electrochemical reactions. One faraday is equal to the electric charge of a mole of protons.

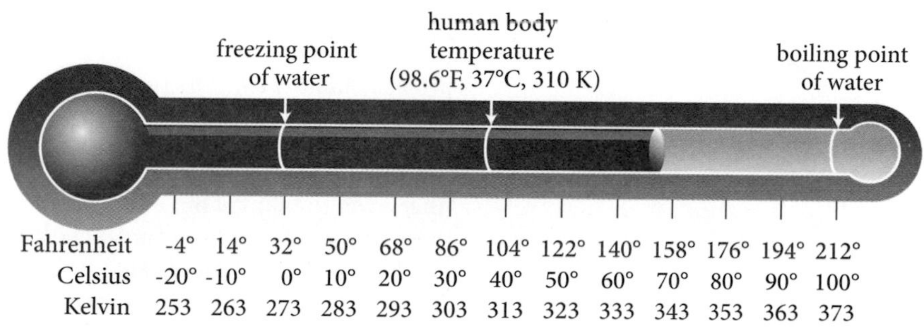

Fahrenheit

Faraday (făr′ə-dā′, făr′ə-dē), **Michael** 1791–1867. British physicist and chemist whose experiments into the connections between electricity, magnetism, and light laid the foundation for modern physics. In addition to discovering electromagnetic induction and inventing the electric motor, generator, and transformer, Faraday discovered benzene and performed the first scientific study of the properties of gold nanoparticles.

farsightedness (fär′sī′tĭd-nĭs) The ability to see distant objects better than objects at close range. It is caused by the eye focusing incoming light behind the retina rather than directly on it. Also called *hyperopia*. *Compare* **nearsightedness.**

fat (făt) Any of a large class of oily compounds that are widely found in animal tissues and in nuts, seeds, and some fruits and serve mainly as a reserve source of energy. In mammals, fat is deposited beneath the skin and around the internal organs, where it also protects and insulates against heat loss. Fats are made chiefly of triglycerides, each molecule of which contains glycerol and three fatty acids. *See more at* **saturated fat, unsaturated fat.**

fathom (făth′əm) A unit of length equal to six feet (about 1.8 meters), used to measure the depth of water.

fatty acid (făt′ē) Any of a large group of organic acids, especially those found in animal and vegetable fats and oils. Fatty acids are mainly composed of long chains of carbon atoms linked to hydrogen atoms. A fatty acid is saturated when the bonds between carbon atoms are all single bonds. It is unsaturated when any of these bonds is a double or triple bond.

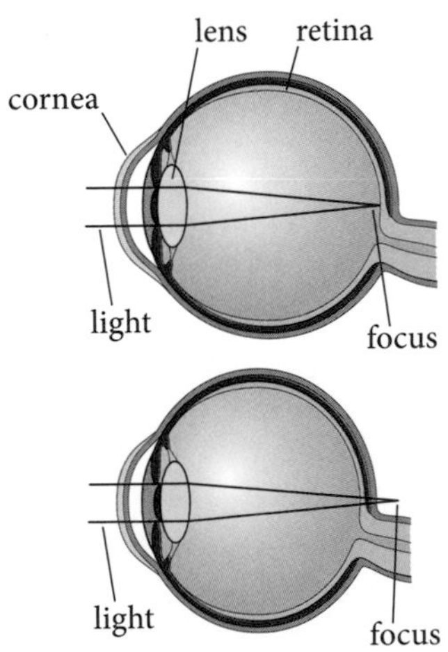

farsightedness
top: *normal eye*
bottom: *farsighted eye*

Did You Know...?

fat

Many people choose "fat-free" or "reduced fat" foods in an attempt to limit the amount of *fat* in their diets. Fatty foods are hard to resist, though, because they taste good. Many of the chemicals that give food pleasant flavors dissolve easily in fats, so fatty foods often contain more of these flavorful compounds. Fat is also satisfying, which means that if you eliminate it from your diet, you can feel hungry. And some fat is necessary for your body. A gram of fat contains more than twice as much stored energy—calories—as does a gram of either protein or carbohydrate, so it's the most efficient way to store excess food. This reserve not only provides energy in times of scarcity, but insulates as well. Sea mammals, such as whales and seals, have thick layers of fat, called *blubber,* that protect them from the cold and serve as a reserve supply of food. A whale's blubber may be up to two feet thick!

fault (fôlt) A crack in a rock mass along which there has been movement. The rock on one side of the crack moves relative to the rock on the other side of the crack. Faults are caused by plate-tectonic forces. *See Note at* **earthquake.**

fauna (fô′nə) *Used with a singular or plural verb.* The animals of a particular region or time period: *tropical fauna; prehistoric fauna.*

Fe The symbol for **iron.**

feather (fĕth′ər) One of the light, flat structures that cover the skin of birds. A feather is formed of numerous slender, closely arranged parallel barbs forming a vane on either side of a hollow shaft. The barbs of outer feathers are formed of even smaller structures (called barbules) that interlock. The barbs of down feathers do not interlock.

Did You Know...?

faults

Bedrock is often cracked along surfaces known as planes. In some places the cracks extend only a tiny distance; in others they can run for hundreds of miles. When the rocks separated by a crack move past each other, the cracks are known as *faults.* The rocks move because they are pushed or pulled by the forces of plate tectonics. This movement often occurs in sudden jerks known as earthquakes. Geologists study faults to learn the history of the forces that have acted on rocks. *Normal faults* occur when rocks are pulled apart. In this case, the rocks above the fault plane move down relative to the rocks below it. When rocks are pushed together, the opposite happens—the rocks above the plane move upward relative to the rocks below the plane; these faults are called *reverse faults. Strike-slip faults* occur when rocks slide past each other; rocks on either side of the crack slide parallel to the fault plane between them. *Transform faults* are a special category of strike-slip faults in which the crack is actually part of a boundary between two enormous tectonic plates. This is the nature of the famous San Andreas Fault in California.

feces (fē′sēz) Waste matter excreted from the large intestine.

feedback (fēd′băk′) The return of a part of the output of a system or process to the input, especially when used to regulate an electrical system or an electronic process. Computers use feedback to regulate their operations.

feeler (fē′lər) A slender body part used for touching or sensing. The antennae of insects and the barbels of catfish are feelers.

feldspar (fĕld′spär′, fĕl′spär′) Any of a group of abundant minerals consisting of silicates of aluminum with potassium, sodium, and calcium. Feldspars range from white, pink, or brown to grayish blue in color. They occur in igneous, sedimentary, and metamorphic rocks and make up more than 60 percent of the Earth's crust.

feline (fē′līn′) *Adjective* **1.** Relating to the family of meat-eating mammals that includes the lions, tigers, leopards, and other cats. *—Noun* **2.** An animal belonging to this family.

female (fē′māl′) *Adjective* **1.** Relating to or being the sex that produces eggs or gives birth to offspring: *female frogs.* **2.** Relating to or being the sex cell that is larger and less mobile than the other corresponding sex cell: *female gametes.* **3.** Relating to or being a reproductive organ that produces female sex cells: *female flower parts. —Noun* **4.** A female organism.

femur (fē′mər) The long bone of the thigh in humans, or the corresponding bone in other vertebrates. *See more at* **skeleton.**

Fermat (fĕr-mä′), **Pierre de** 1601–1665. French mathematician who is best known for his work on probability and on the properties of numbers. He formulated Fermat's last theorem, which remained unproved for over three hundred years.

Fermat's last theorem (fĕr-mäz′) A theorem stating that the equation $a^n + b^n = c^n$ has no solution if *a, b,* and *c* are positive integers and if *n* is an integer greater than 2. The theorem was

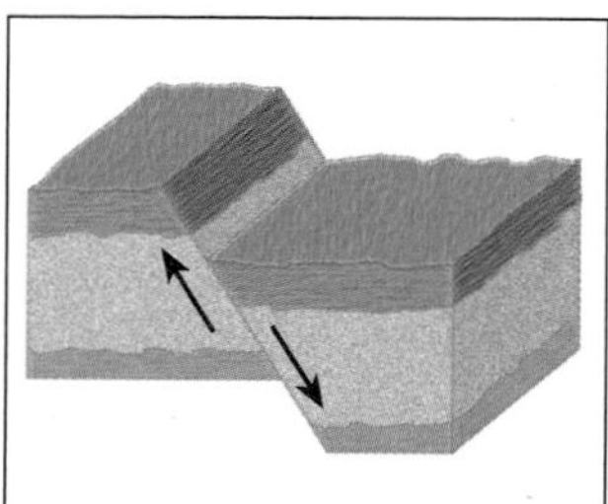

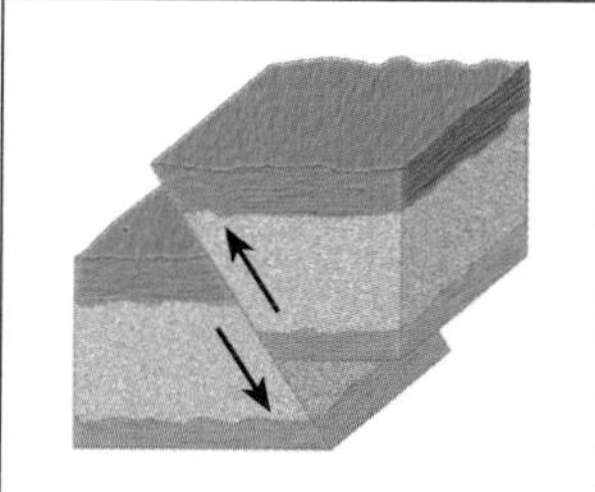

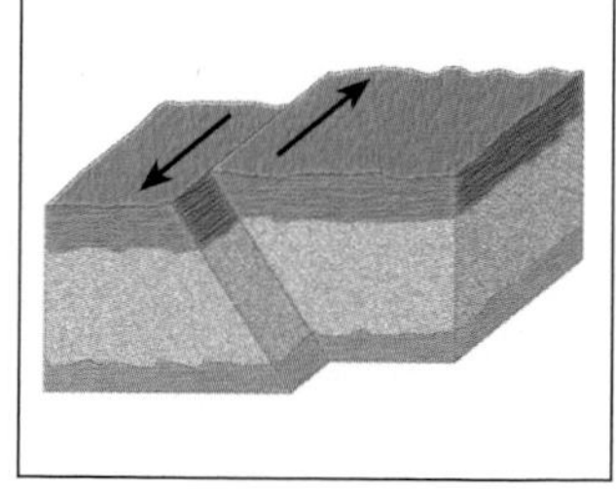

■ **fault**
left to right: *normal, reverse, and strike-slip faults*

first stated by the French mathematician Pierre de Fermat around 1630, but not proved until 1994.

fermentation (fûr′mĕn-tā′shən) Any of several chemical reactions by which sugar or other complex organic compounds are broken down by enzymes without the use of oxygen, resulting in the release of energy. Yeasts and many bacteria obtain energy from fermentation, and muscle cells use fermentation when they lack oxygen. Fermentation is used to produce many kinds of food and drink, including wine, beer, cheese, soy sauce, and pickles.

Fermi (fĕr′mē), **Enrico** 1901–1954. Italian-born American physicist who is best known for his work on nuclear physics. He discovered over 40 new isotopes and predicted the existence of the neutrino. In 1942, with Leo Szilard, Fermi built the world's first atomic reactor. Fermi also helped to develop the atomic bomb.

fermium (fûr′mē-əm) A synthetic, radioactive metallic element of the actinide series that is produced from plutonium or uranium. Its most stable isotope has a half-life of about 100 days. *Symbol* **Fm.** *Atomic number* 100. *See* **Periodic Table,** pages 254–255.

fern (fûrn) Any of numerous plants usually having feathery fronds divided into many leaflets. Ferns have vascular tissue, like seed plants, but they reproduce by means of spores instead of seeds.

ferrate (fĕr′āt′) An anion containing iron and oxygen, most commonly FeO_4^{2-}, or a compound containing such an anion.

ferric (fĕr′ĭk) Containing iron, especially iron with a valence of 3. *Compare* **ferrous.**

Enrico Fermi

ferric oxide A reddish-brown to silver or black compound, Fe_2O_3, which occurs naturally as the mineral hematite, or as rust. It is often used as a pigment and a metal polish.

ferrous (fĕr′əs) Containing iron, especially iron with a valence of 2. *Compare* **ferric.**

fertile (fûr′tl) **1.** Capable of producing offspring; able to reproduce. **2.** Capable of developing into a complete organism; fertilized: *a fertile egg.* **3.** Capable of supporting plant life; favorable to the growth of crops or other plants: *fertile soil.* —*Noun* **fertility.**

fertilization (fûr′tl-ĭ-zā′shən) **1.** The process by which a female sex cell becomes capable of developing into a new organism by uniting with a male sex cell. In mammals, fertilization occurs inside the body of the female. In most fish, eggs are fertilized in the water. In flowering plants, fertilization occurs in the ovule, following pollination. *See Note at* **pollination. 2.** The process of making soil more productive of plant growth. —*Verb* **fertilize.**

fetus (fē′təs) The unborn young of a mammal at the later stages of its development, especially a human embryo from its eighth week of development to its birth. —*Adjective* **fetal.**

fever (fē′vər) A body temperature higher than normal. Fever is usually a response of the body's immune system to infection, as by a virus.

Feynman (fīn′mən), **Richard Phillips** 1918–1988. American physicist who developed many new aspects of quantum theory, especially as applied to the interactions between photons and electrons. He also devised a method of using diagrams to indicate the interactions of subatomic particles.

fiber (fī′bər) **1.** Any of the elongated, thick-walled cells that give strength and support to plant tissue. **2.** The part of vegetable foods such as grains, fruits, and vegetables that contains cellulose and other substances that cannot be digested by humans. Eating foods with fiber helps the intestines function properly. **3a.** A single skeletal muscle cell; a muscle fiber. **b.** The axon of a nerve cell. —*Adjective* **fibrous.**

fiberglass (fī′bər-glăs′) A material made up of very fine fibers of glass. Fiberglass is resistant to heat and fire and is used to make various products, such as building insulation and boat hulls. It is often used to strengthen plastics. Because the

Did You Know...?

fiber optics

In an optical fiber, a beam of light travels within a thin strand of glass or plastic. The light stays within the strand, even if the strand is curved or twisted. That's because of the materials the optical fiber is made of and the way in which the light is aimed into the fiber: when the light beam reaches the strand's outer edge, it reflects back into the strand rather than escaping through the wall. Generally, when a beam of light traveling in one material strikes the boundary of another material, some light travels through the boundary and some is reflected back into the original material. But if the speed of light in the material the beam starts out in (the glass) is lower than the speed of light in the other material (the air or insulating material surrounding the fiber), and if the light strikes the boundary of the other material at a shallow enough angle, then all of the light is reflected and none escapes.

fibers in fiberglass are capable of transmitting light around curves, fiberglass is an important component of fiber optics.

fiber optics The technology based on the use of fine glass or plastic fibers that are capable of transmitting light around curves. Fiber optics is used in medicine and for long-distance telephone and computer lines.

Fibonacci (fē′bə-nä′chē), **Leonardo** 1170?–1250? Italian mathematician who promoted the use of Arabic numerals in Europe and described the Fibonacci sequence of integers.

Fibonacci sequence The sequence of numbers, 1, 1, 2, 3, 5, 8, 13, 21, . . . , in which each successive number is equal to the sum of the two preceding numbers. Many shapes occurring in nature, such as certain spirals, have proportions that can be described in terms of the Fibonacci sequence.

fibrillation (fĭb′rə-lā′shən) A rapid twitching of muscle fibers, as of the heart, caused by the abnormal discharge of electrical nerve impulses.

fibrin (fī′brĭn) A tough, insoluble protein that is produced in response to bleeding and is the main component involved in blood clotting.

fibula (fĭb′yə-lə) The smaller of the two bones of the lower leg in humans, or the corresponding bone in other vertebrates. *See more at* **skeleton.**

field (fēld) **1.** A region of space in which an object experiences the effects of a physical force, such as magnetism or gravity. **2.** The area in which an image is visible to the eye or to an optical instrument.

field magnet A magnet used to produce a magnetic field for the operation of an electrical device such as a motor or generator.

filament (fĭl′ə-mənt) **1.** A fine or slender thread, wire, or fiber. **2.** The slender stalk that bears the anther in the stamen of a flower. *See more at* **flower. 3.** A fine wire that is enclosed in an incandescent light bulb and gives off light when an electric current is passed through it. **4.** A wire that acts as the cathode in some electron tubes when it is heated with an electric current.

filter (fĭl′tər) *Noun* **1.** A material that has very tiny holes and is used to separate out solid particles contained in a liquid or gas that is passed through it. **2.** A device used to block signals, vibrations, or electromagnetic waves of certain frequencies while allowing others to pass. For example, filters on photographic lenses allow only some frequencies of light to enter the camera. —*Verb* **3.** To pass something through a filter.

filter feeder An aquatic animal that feeds by filtering tiny organisms or particles of organic material from the water. Sponges and clams are filter feeders, as are many whales and some sharks.

fin (fĭn) One of the movable parts that extends from the body of a fish, whale, or other aquatic

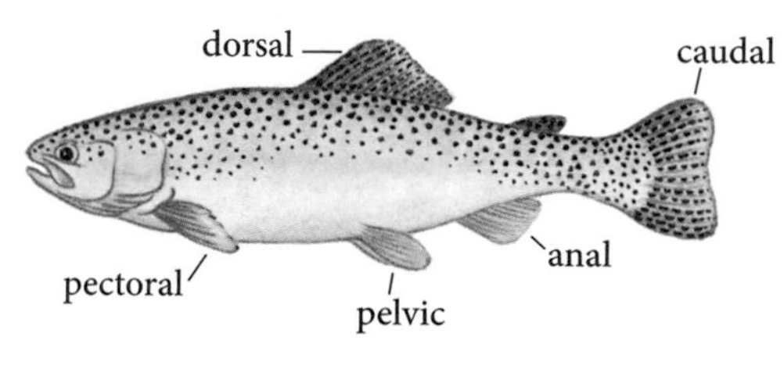

fin
fins on a typical bony fish

A CLOSER LOOK

Fission/Fusion

Fission

Nuclear fission occurs when a heavy, unstable atomic nucleus splits into two (or sometimes three) lighter nuclei and releases neutrons and a large amount of energy. Fission can occur spontaneously, or it can be caused when a free neutron collides with the nucleus. For example, if the nucleus of the U-235 isotope of uranium is struck by a neutron, it splits into two smaller nuclei and releases energy along with three neutrons. Where does the energy come from? The combined mass of the nuclei and neutrons produced by the reaction is less than the mass of the original nucleus and neutron that started the reaction. The missing mass is converted into energy in the form of heat and gamma rays.

The free neutrons released by the fission of one nucleus may collide with other U-235 nuclei, causing them in turn to undergo fission. The result is a nuclear chain reaction, in which the number of fission events multiplies rapidly within a tiny fraction of a second. In a nuclear reactor, the chain reaction is controlled by material that slows down or absorbs some of the neutrons. In a nuclear weapon, such as an atomic bomb, the chain reaction is allowed to continue uncontrolled and produces tremendous amounts of energy.

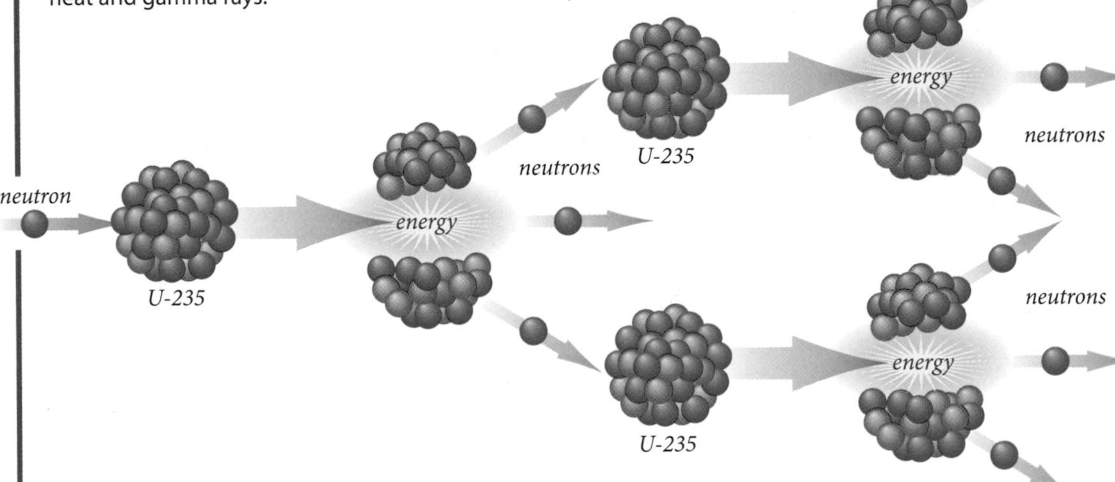

Fusion

Nuclear fusion is basically the opposite of fission: it unites nuclei instead of breaking them apart.

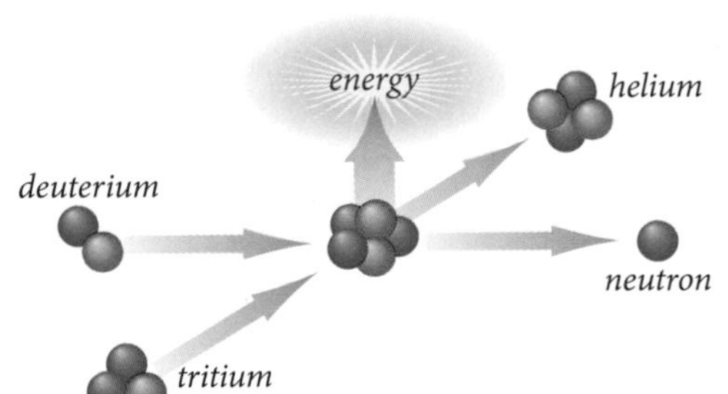

Nuclear fusion occurs when two rapidly moving nuclei of low mass collide and merge to form a single heavier nucleus and release a large amount of energy. For example, when two heavy isotopes of hydrogen (deuterium and tritium) collide, they form a helium nucleus, an extra neutron, and energy. This is what happens when a hydrogen bomb explodes. Nuclear fusion also powers the sun and other stars.

animal and is used for propelling, steering, and balancing in water.

finite (fī′nīt′) Having a bound or limit; not infinite or unbounded: *a finite sum; a finite line segment.*

fir (fûr) Any of various evergreen trees that have flat needles and bear cones. Firs are found in the Northern Hemisphere, especially in cool regions or at high altitudes.

firefly (fīr′flī′) Any of various beetles that are active at night and produce a flashing light in the abdomen. The flash, which is used for communication, is an example of bioluminescence.

firewall (fīr′wôl′) A software program or hardware device that restricts communication between a private network or computer system and outside networks.

fish (fĭsh) *Plural* **fish** *or* **fishes** Any of numerous cold-blooded vertebrate animals that live in water. Fish have gills for obtaining oxygen and a lateral line for sensing pressure changes in the water. Most fish have fins and are covered with scales. *See more at* **bony fish, cartilaginous fish, jawless fish.**

fission (fĭsh′ən) **1.** *Physics* The splitting of a massive atomic nucleus into two or more nuclei. Fission occurs spontaneously in certain isotopes, but it usually results from the collision of a freely moving neutron with the nucleus. The fission of a nucleus releases a great amount of energy and one or more neutrons, which can induce further fissions, initiating a nuclear chain reaction. *Compare* **fusion. 2.** *Biology* A reproductive process in which a single cell splits to form two independent cells that later grow to full size. Bacteria and other single-celled organisms usually reproduce by means of fission. Also called *binary fission.*

fissure (fĭsh′ər) A long, narrow crack or opening in the face of a rock. Fissures are often filled with minerals of a different type from those in the surrounding rock.

fjord (fyôrd) A long, narrow inlet from the sea between steep mountainous slopes. Fjords occur where ocean water fills valleys that have been deepened by the erosive effects of past glaciers.

Fl The symbol for **flerovium.**

flagellate (flăj′ə-lāt′) A protozoan, such as a euglena or a dinoflagellate, that moves by means of a flagellum or flagella.

flagellum (flə-jĕl′əm) *Plural* **flagella** A slender part extending from certain cells or single-celled organisms that moves rapidly back and forth to produce movement. Dinoflagellates have flagella, and so do the male sex cells of many species.

flame (flām) The hot, glowing mixture of burning gases and tiny particles that is produced by rapid combustion.

flash memory (flăsh) Computer memory that uses transistors to store data and that can be erased and rewritten many times. Flash memory requires less physical space than a hard disk or optical disc.

flash point The lowest temperature at which a combustible liquid or solid gives off enough vapor that the resulting mixture of vapor and air can catch fire.

flash tube A device that generates a short, strong burst of light or other electromagnetic radiation by discharging a high voltage of electricity through a substance such as xenon or quartz.

flask (flăsk) A glass container with a wide round bottom and a narrow neck, used in laboratories.

flatfish (flăt′fĭsh′) Any of numerous bottom-dwelling fish, such as flounder, halibut, and sole, that have a flattened body. During a flatfish's larval stage, one eye migrates to the other side, so that both eyes in the adult are on the same side of the body. In some species both eyes are always on the right side, and in others they are always on the left.

flatworm (flăt′wûrm′) Any of numerous unsegmented worms that have a flat body and chiefly live in water or as parasites in humans or other animals. Tapeworms are parasitic flatworms.

flea (flē) Any of various small, wingless, jumping insects that live as parasites on the bodies of humans and other animals, where they feed on blood.

fledgling (flĕj′lĭng) A young bird that has just grown the feathers needed to fly and can survive outside the nest.

Fleming (flĕm′ĭng), Sir **Alexander** 1881–1955. British bacteriologist who discovered penicillin in 1928. The drug was developed and purified 11

■ **Sir Alexander Fleming**

years later by Howard Florey and Ernst Chain. Fleming was also the first to administer typhoid vaccines to humans.

Fleming, Sir **John Ambrose** 1849–1945. British physicist and electrical engineer who invented the vacuum tube in 1904. His invention was essential to the development of radio.

flerovium (flə-rō′vē-əm) An artificially produced radioactive element that has only been produced in trace amounts. Its most stable isotope has a half-life of about 2.7 seconds. *Symbol* **Fl.** *Atomic number* 114. *See* **Periodic Table,** pages 254–255.

flexor (flĕk′sər) A muscle that bends or flexes a joint. *Compare* **extensor.**

flint (flĭnt) A very hard, gray to black sedimentary rock that makes sparks when it strikes against steel. Flint is a type of chert.

flipper (flĭp′ər) A wide, flat limb used for swimming, found on aquatic animals such as whales, seals, and sea turtles.

float (flōt) An air-filled sac in certain aquatic organisms, such as kelp, that helps maintain buoyancy. Also called *air bladder.*

floe (flō) A mass or sheet of floating ice.

floodplain (flŭd′plān′) Flat land bordering a river and made up of sediments such as sand, silt, and clay deposited during floods.

flood tide (flŭd) The period between low tide and high tide, during which water flows toward the shore. *Compare* **ebb tide.** *See more at* **tide.**

flora (flôr′ə) *Used with a singular or plural verb.* The plants of a particular region or time period: *desert flora; prehistoric flora.*

Florey (flôr′ē), Sir **Howard Walter.** Baron Florey. 1898–1968. Australian-born British pathologist who developed and purified penicillin, with Ernst Chain. Florey also helped to develop a way to manufacture the drug in large quantities and was involved in the first tests of its effects on humans.

flow chart (flō) A diagram of a sequence of operations, as in a manufacturing process or computer program.

flower (flou′ər) *Noun* **1.** The reproductive structure of the seed-bearing plants known as angiosperms. A complete flower contains both female reproductive parts (the pistil, including the ovary, style, and stigma) and male reproductive parts (the stamen, including the filament and anther), enclosed by an outer envelope of petals and sepals. **2.** A flowering plant that is grown mainly for its brightly colored petals. —*Verb* **3.** To produce flowers; bloom.

flowering plant (flou′ər-ĭng) A plant that produces flowers and fruit; an angiosperm.

fl. oz. Abbreviation of **fluid ounce.**

flu (flo͞o) *See* **influenza.**

fluid (flo͞o′ĭd) A substance, such as air or water, in which the atoms or molecules can freely move past one another. Fluids flow easily and take on the shape of their containers. All liquids and gases are fluids. —*Noun* **fluidity** (flo͞o-ĭd′ĭ-tē).

fluid dram A unit equal to $\frac{1}{8}$ of a fluid ounce (about 3.70 milliliters).

fluid ounce A liquid measure equal to $\frac{1}{16}$ of a pint (about 29.57 milliliters). *See Table at* **measurement.**

fluke (flo͝ok) Either of the two flattened fins of a whale's tail.

fluorescence (flo͝o-rĕs′əns) The giving off of light by a substance while it is exposed to electromagnetic radiation, such as ultraviolet light or x-rays. The emission of light stops as soon as the source of radiation is removed. *Compare* **phosphorescence.**

fluorescent light (flo͝o-rĕs′ənt) A device that produces light by exciting the atoms of a mixture of argon gas and mercury vapor with electric current. Ultraviolet rays produced by the excited atoms strike a phosphor coating on the interior

A CLOSER LOOK

Flowers

Most flowers, like the lily shown here, have both male and female organs. The anther of the male organ releases pollen that is transferred to the stigma of the female organ, usually on a flower of another plant, by the wind or by pollinating animals such as insects.

Certain species, such as corn plants and birch trees, have flowers with only male organs and flowers with only female organs growing on the same plant. Some other species, such as ginkgo trees, have flowers with male organs growing on one plant, and flowers with female organs growing on another.

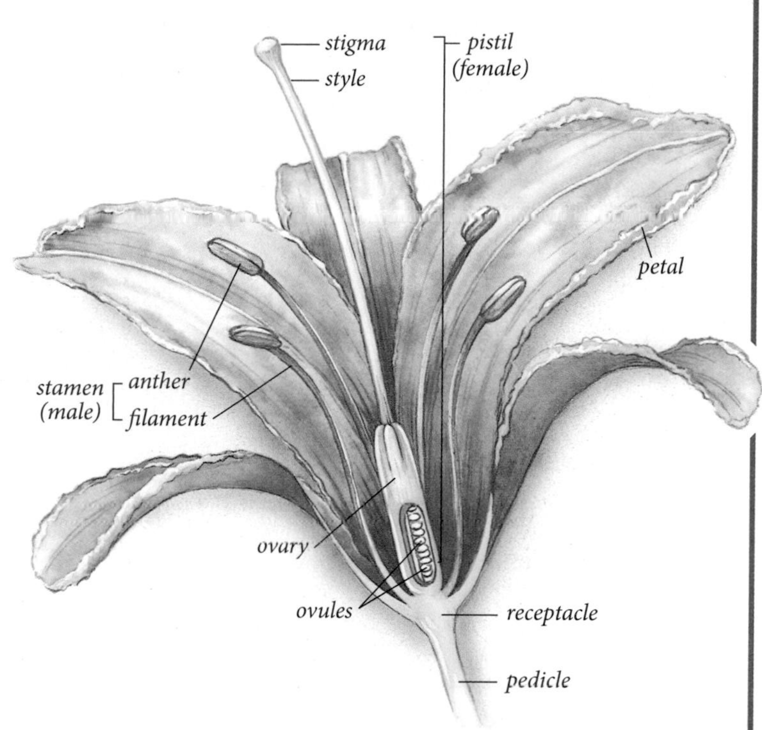

clematis

wild rye

Not all flowers occur as large individual blooms attached to a stem, as in the lily and clematis. The flowers of rye grass, for example, are very small. Some plants, such as clover, have groups of flowers growing in clusters as flower heads. Certain trees, like alders, produce blossoms in elongated clusters known as catkins. The sausage-like part of the cattail is actually a head of densely packed female flowers. The cattail's male flowers grow on the more slender tip or "tail" that extends at the top.

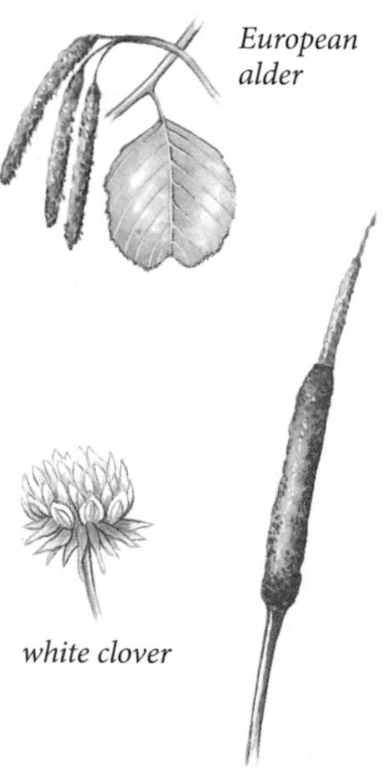

European alder

white clover

cattail

surface of the bulb, causing it to emit visible light. Fluorescent lights are much more efficient than incandescent lights because the excited atoms give off little of their energy as heat. *Compare* **incandescent light.**

fluoridate (flo͝or′ĭ-dāt′) To add fluorine or a fluoride to something, especially to drinking water in order to prevent tooth decay.

fluoride (flo͝or′īd′) An anion of fluorine or a compound containing this anion, such as sodium fluoride.

fluorine (flo͝or′ēn′) A pale-yellow, poisonous, gaseous halogen element that is highly corrosive. It is used to separate certain isotopes of uranium and to make refrigerants and high-temperature plastics. It is also added in fluoride form to the water supply to prevent tooth decay. *Symbol* **F.** *Atomic number* 9. *See* **Periodic Table,** pages 254–255.

fluorite (flo͝or′īt′) A mineral consisting of calcium fluoride. Fluorite occurs in many colors (especially yellow and purple), usually in crystals shaped like cubes or octahedrons, and is often fluorescent in ultraviolet light. It is the mineral used to represent a hardness of 4 on the Mohs scale.

fluorocarbon (flo͝or′ō-kär′bən) An inert, liquid or gaseous organic compound similar to a hydrocarbon but having fluorine atoms in the place of some or all of the hydrogen atoms. Fluorocarbons are used in aerosol propellants and refrigerants. ❖ Fluorocarbons containing chlorine, known as **chlorofluorocarbons**, are destructive to the Earth's ozone layer. For this reason, the production and use of chlorofluorocarbons has been sharply reduced in recent years.

fluoroscopy (flo͝o-rŏs′kə-pē) A technique for viewing internal organs in which x-rays are directed through the body toward a device containing fluorescent material that generates images that can be viewed on a monitor or recorded by a video camera. Fluoroscopy makes it possible to see moving images of the body system being examined.

flux (flŭks) **1.** A substance used in a smelting furnace to make metals melt more easily. **2.** The rate of flow of matter or energy through a given surface area.

fly (flī) Any of numerous insects having one pair of wings and large compound eyes. Flies include the houseflies, horseflies, and mosquitoes. Most flies have sucking, lapping, or piercing mouthparts. Adults typically feed on nectar, decaying matter, or blood.

Fm The symbol for **fermium.**

FM Abbreviation of **frequency modulation.**

foam (fōm) **1.** A mass of small, frothy bubbles formed in or on the surface of a liquid, as from fermentation or shaking. **2.** A colloid in which particles of a gas are dispersed throughout a liquid or solid. *Compare* **aerosol, emulsion.**

focal length (fō′kəl) The distance from the center of a lens or mirror to its focal point.

focal point The point at which all rays of light or other radiation coming from a single direction and passing through a lens or striking a mirror come together or from which they appear to spread apart. Also called *focus.*

focus (fō′kəs) *Plural* **focuses** *or* **foci** (fō′sī′, fō′kī′) **1.** *See* **focal point. 2.** The degree of clarity with which an eye or optical instrument produces an image: *a telescope with excellent focus.* **3.** The point inside the Earth from which an earthquake originates. *Compare* **epicenter. 4.** *Mathematics* A fixed point or one of a pair of fixed points used in constructing a curve such as an ellipse, a parabola, or a hyperbola.

fog (fôg) A dense layer of cloud lying close to the surface of the ground or water.

fold (fōld) A bend in a layer or in several layers of rock. Folds occur in rocks when they are compressed by plate-tectonic forces.

folic acid (fō′lĭk, fŏl′ĭk) A vitamin belonging to the vitamin B complex that is important in cell

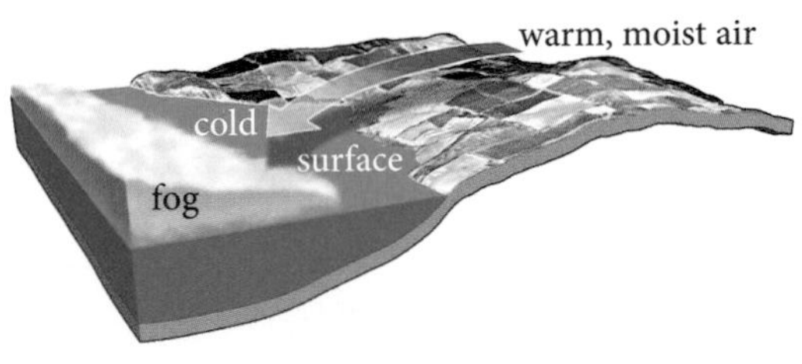

■ **fog**

Fog forms when warm, moist air travels over a warm surface, such as land, and then encounters a cold surface, such as a body of water.

food web
arrows show which organism is eaten by another

growth and metabolism. It is found especially in green leafy vegetables, citrus fruit, legumes, and wheat products such as bread. Folic acid is necessary for the production of blood cells and for the normal development of fetuses.

follicle (fŏl′ĭ-kəl) **1.** A small, protective sac in the body. In most vertebrate animals, unfertilized eggs develop in follicles located in the ovaries. In mammals, hair develops and grows from follicles in the skin. **2.** A dry fruit that has a single chamber and splits open along only one seam to release its seeds, as in a milkweed plant.

food chain (fo͞od) A succession of organisms in an ecological community that are linked to each other through the transfer of energy and nutrients, beginning with an organism, such as a plant, that makes its own food and continuing with each organism being eaten by one higher in the chain. Because many organisms in an ecological community feed on more than one kind of food, several food chains are usually joined together in a food web. *See more at* **consumer, producer.**

food web A complex system of interrelated food chains in a particular ecological community.

fool's gold (fo͞olz) Any of several minerals, especially pyrite, that are sometimes mistaken for gold.

foot (fo͝ot) *Plural* **feet** (fēt) A unit of length equal to $\frac{1}{3}$ of a yard or 12 inches (30.48 centimeters). *See Table at* **measurement.**

foot-and-mouth disease A highly contagious disease of cattle and other hoofed animals that is caused by a virus. Symptoms include fever and the presence of blisters around the mouth and hooves.

foot-pound A unit of work equal to the work or energy needed to lift a one-pound weight a distance of one foot against the force of the Earth's gravity.

force (fôrs) **1.** Any of various factors that cause a body to change its speed, direction, or shape. If a body is acted on by several forces that counteract and balance each other, then it experiences no net force. **2.** Any of the four natural phenomena that involve interactions between particles of matter. From the strongest to the weakest, the four basic forces are the strong nuclear force, the electromagnetic force, the weak nuclear force, and gravity.

Did You Know...?

force

In physics, *force* has less to do with muscles and military might than with motion. Force is at work even when a feather falls gently to the ground. In the mid-1600s, the English scientist Isaac Newton figured out that the amount of force needed to move an object is directly related to both the mass of the object and how much it is accelerated. This might seem obvious: pushing a boulder takes more force than pushing a pebble, and pushing a boulder quickly takes more force than pushing it slowly. But Newton set this relationship down quantitatively in what is now known as Newton's second law of motion: *Force* equals *mass* times *acceleration,* or $F = ma$. Acceleration here means a change in direction or in speed, either faster or slower. If a boat bumps into a dock, you can determine the force of the impact by multiplying the decrease in the boat's speed by the boat's mass. If you swing a ball around your head on a string, the ball is constantly accelerating as its direction changes, and your hand is exerting a force. The heavier the ball, the more force is needed!

forebrain (fôr′brān′) The front part of the brain in vertebrate animals. In humans, it consists of the thalamus, the hypothalamus, and the cerebrum. *Compare* **hindbrain, midbrain.**

forest (fôr′ĭst) A dense growth of trees and usually bushes or other plants covering a large area. Forests exist in all regions of the Earth except for regions of extreme cold or dryness. ❖ The science of cultivating and managing forests is called **forestry.**

formaldehyde (fôr-măl′də-hīd′) A colorless gas, CH_2O, having a sharp, suffocating odor. It is used in making plastics and is mixed with water to form a solution used to preserve biological specimens.

formation (fôr-mā′shən) A set of sediments or rocks that look alike and were formed at the same time, usually as an extensive layer or series of layers. Different formations are shown in different colors on geological maps.

formic acid (fôr′mĭk) A colorless, caustic, fuming liquid, CH_2O_2, that occurs naturally as the poison of ants and stinging nettles. It is used in making textiles and paper and in insecticides.

formula (fôr′myə-lə) **1.** A set of symbols showing the composition of a chemical compound. A formula lists the elements contained within it and indicates the number of atoms of each element with a subscript numeral if the number is more than 1. For example, H_2O is the formula for water, where H_2 indicates two atoms of hydrogen and O indicates one atom of oxygen. **2.** A set of symbols that expresses a mathematical rule or principle; for example, the formula for the area of a rectangle is $a = lw$, where a is the area, l the length, and w the width.

Fossey (fŏs′ē), **Dian** 1932–1985. American zoologist who studied gorillas in Rwanda, Africa, and was very active in conservation efforts. Her research led to a better understanding of the gorilla's behavior and habitat.

fossil (fŏs′əl) The hardened remains or imprint of a living thing that lived long ago. Fossils are often found in layers of sedimentary rock and along the beds of rivers that flow through them. Other sources of fossils include tar pits, ice, and amber. ❖ Petroleum, coal, and natural gas, which are derived from the accumulated remains of ancient living things, are called **fossil fuels.** —*Verb* **fossilize.**

Foucault (fo͞o-kō′), **Jean Bernard Léon** 1819–1868. French physicist who measured the velocity of light (1850) and proved that light moves more slowly in water than in air. He also used the apparent shift in the path of a swinging pendulum to demonstrate that the Earth rotates on its axis (1851).

fowl (foul) **1.** A bird, such as a chicken, duck, or dove, that is raised or hunted for food. **2.** In scientific usage, any of various birds having large heavy bodies, short wings, and legs built for running and scratching the ground. Most fowl nest on the ground. The turkey, pheasant, quail, grouse, partridge, and chicken are fowl.

Fr The symbol for **francium.**

fracking (frăk′ĭng) *See* **hydraulic fracturing.**

fractal (frăk′təl) A geometric pattern repeated at ever smaller scales to produce irregular shapes and surfaces that cannot be represented by standard geometry. Even the most minute details of a fractal's pattern repeat elements of the overall geometric pattern. Fractals are widely used in computer modeling of irregular patterns and structures in nature, such as the patterns of seasonal weather. They are also considered to be a visual representation of chaos. *See more at* **chaos.**

fraction (frăk′shən) A number that compares part of an object or a set with the whole, especially the quotient of two whole numbers written in the form $\frac{a}{b}$. The fraction $\frac{1}{2}$, which means 1 divided by 2, can represent such things as 10 pencils out of a box of 20, or 50 cents out of a dollar. *See also* **decimal fraction, improper fraction, proper fraction.**

■ **fractal**

BIOGRAPHY

Benjamin Franklin

On one of his many voyages to Europe by ship, Benjamin Franklin observed a strong current of warm water running north and east across the Atlantic Ocean. He later learned from his cousin Timothy Folger, a captain of a whaling ship, that this current was well known to whalers and that it formed a narrow band running much of the way from North America to Europe. Realizing that ships could save sailing time by remaining within the band of current on the voyage from America to England and by avoiding that band on the return voyage, Franklin and Folger produced a map of the current, then known as the "Gulph Stream." On later voyages Franklin systematically measured the water temperature at regular intervals, and he even invented a device for collecting water samples from a depth of up to 100 feet, to determine how the water temperature dropped off with increasing depth. His systematic collection, interpretation, and publication of these data make him one of the founders of the science of oceanography.

fractionation (frăk′shə-nā′shən) The separation of a chemical compound into components, as by distillation or crystallization.

fracture (frăk′chər) A break or crack in a bone, usually also involving injury to surrounding structures. A fracture occurs when a force greater than the strength of the bone is applied, as in a fall.

frame of reference (frām) A set of coordinate axes that are used as a reference for indicating the position and motion of bodies.

francium (frăn′sē-əm) An extremely unstable, radioactive element that is the heaviest alkali metal. Francium occurs in nature, but less than one ounce (30 grams) is present in the Earth's crust at any time. The most stable of its several isotopes has a half-life of 22 minutes. *Symbol* **Fr.** *Atomic number* 87. *See* **Periodic Table,** pages 254–255.

Franklin (frăngk′lĭn), **Benjamin** 1706–1790. American public official, scientist, inventor, and writer. He experimented with electricity and studied the movements of storms and ocean currents, publishing the first map of the Gulf Stream. Franklin also invented bifocals, the lightning rod, and a wood-burning stove that was more efficient than fireplaces of his day.

Franklin, Rosalind 1920–1958. British chemist whose diffraction images, made by directing x-rays at DNA, provided crucial information that led to the discovery of DNA's structure as a double helix.

freeze (frēz) To change from a liquid to a solid state by cooling or being cooled to the freezing point.

freeze-dry To preserve something by freezing it rapidly and then placing it in a vacuum chamber. The ice is then forced out, through sublimation, in the form of water vapor.

freezing point (frē′zĭng) The temperature at which a liquid becomes a solid. For a given substance, the freezing point of its liquid form is the same as the melting point of its solid form. The freezing point of water is 32°F (0°C); that of liquid nitrogen is −345.75°F (−209.89°C).

frequency (frē′kwən-sē) **1.** *Physics* The number of complete cycles of a repeating phenomenon,

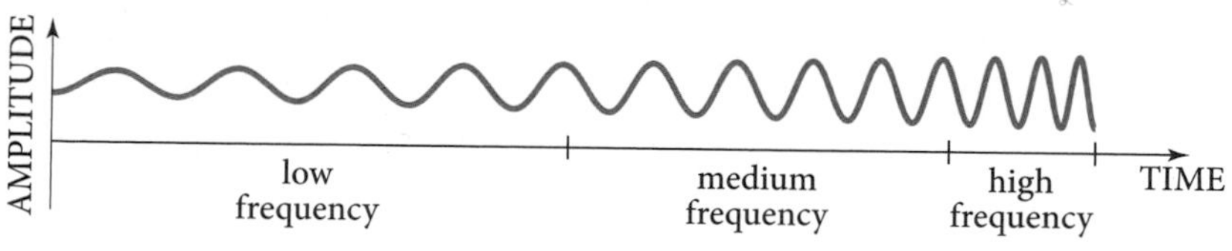

■ **frequency**

such as a wave, over a specified time interval. Frequencies are often measured in cycles per second (hertz). *See more at* **wave. 2.** *Mathematics* The ratio of the number of occurrences of some event to the number of opportunities for its occurrence.

frequency modulation A method of radio broadcasting in which the frequency of the wave that carries the sound signal varies slightly to correspond to the vibrations in the sounds that are to be reproduced, while the amplitude of the wave remains the same. Frequency modulation reduces static in radio transmission. *Compare* **amplitude modulation.**

freshwater (frĕsh′wô′tər) Consisting of or living in water that is not salty: *a freshwater pond; freshwater fish.*

Fresnel (frā-nĕl′), **Augustin Jean** 1788–1827. French physicist whose investigations of the properties of light were fundamental to the establishment of the theory that light moves in a wavelike motion. Fresnel also made great contributions to the field of optics, including the development of a lightweight lens for use in lighthouses.

friction (frĭk′shən) The resistance to movement that occurs when two objects are in contact. It is friction, for example, that slows down a ball rolling on grass and causes the blade of a saw cutting wood to get hot. There is less friction between smooth surfaces than between rough surfaces. Friction can be reduced by using a lubricant such as oil or silicone.

Frigid Zone (frĭj′ĭd) Either of two zones of the Earth of extreme latitude, the **North Frigid Zone,** extending north of the Arctic Circle, or the **South Frigid Zone,** extending south of the Antarctic Circle. Because the sun's light hits the Frigid Zones at a very low angle, they have a very cold climate.

frog (frôg) Any of numerous amphibians that have a short body, large head, long hind legs used for leaping, webbed feet, and no tail when fully grown. Technically, toads are a kind of frog, but informally, "frog" is often used for species with smoother skin that spend more time in the water, and "toad" is used for species with drier, rougher skin that spend more time on land.

frond (frŏnd) **1.** A leaf of a fern or a palm tree, usually divided into smaller leaflets. **2.** A part of a seaweed or a lichen that resembles a leaf.

front (frŭnt) The boundary between two air masses that have different temperatures. Fronts are often accompanied by rain or unsettled weather. *See more at* **cold front, warm front.**

frontal (frŭn′tl) **1.** *Anatomy* Relating to the forehead. **2.** *Meteorology* Relating to a front.

frontal lobe The largest part of each cerebral hemisphere, located in the front of the brain. In humans, it controls voluntary muscle activity, decision-making, and planning and contains, usually on the left side, the area that controls the ability to produce speech.

frost (frôst) A deposit of tiny ice crystals on a surface. Frost is formed when water vapor in the air condenses at a temperature below freezing.

frostbite (frôst′bīt′) Damage to a part of the

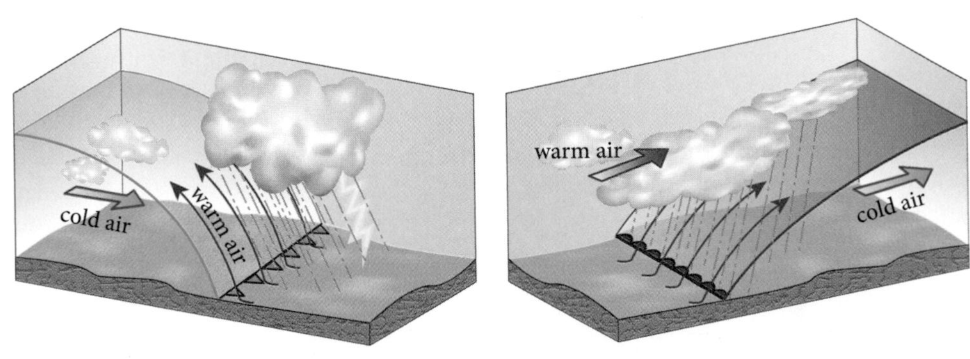

front

In a cold front (left), *a mass of colder, denser air pushes into a mass of warmer, lighter air, forcing the warmer air up. In a warm front* (right), *a mass of warmer air is forced upward as it pushes into a mass of colder air.*

USAGE

fruit/vegetable

To most of us, a *fruit* is a plant part that is eaten as a dessert or snack because it is sweet. But to a botanist, a fruit is a mature ovary of a plant that may or may not taste sweet. All species of flowering plants produce fruits that contain seeds. Apples are the fruits of apple trees, for example, and acorns are the fruits of oak trees. To a botanist, apples, peaches, peppers, tomatoes, cucumbers, acorns, and winged maple seeds are all fruits. The word *vegetable* is not a scientific term. We use it to refer to any part of a plant that is used primarily for food and isn't sweet. The leaf of spinach, the root of a carrot, the flower of broccoli, and the stalk of celery are all called vegetables. In everyday, nonscientific talk we speak of peppers and tomatoes and cucumbers as vegetables, but to botanists they are all fruits.

body as a result of exposure to freezing temperatures. It is caused by a loss of blood supply and the formation of ice crystals in the affected body part.

fructose (frŭk′tōs′) A simple sugar found in honey, many fruits, and some vegetables. ❖ Many soft drinks and processed foods are sweetened with **high-fructose corn syrup,** a syrup that is made from cornstarch and contains a higher proportion of fructose (usually 42% or 55%) than does regular corn syrup.

fruit (fro͞ot) The ripened ovary of a flowering plant that contains the seeds. Fruits can be dry or fleshy. Berries, nuts, grains, pods, and drupes are fruits.

fruit fly Any of various small flies whose larvae feed on ripening or decaying plant material, especially fruit.

fruiting body (fro͞o′tĭng) A specialized spore-producing structure, especially of a fungus. The part of a mushroom that is above ground is the fruiting body.

ft. Abbreviation of **foot.**

fuel (fyo͞o′əl) A substance that produces useful energy when it undergoes a chemical or nuclear reaction. Fuel such as coal, wood, oil, or gas provides energy when burned. Compounds in the body such as glucose are broken down into simpler compounds to provide energy for metabolic processes. Some radioactive substances, such as plutonium and tritium, provide energy by undergoing nuclear fission or fusion.

fuel cell A device that produces electricity by combining a fuel (usually hydrogen gas) with oxygen. A fuel cell consists of two electrodes, one in contact with the fuel and one with the oxygen, separated by an electrolyte. Chemical reactions that occur at the electrodes generate an electric current. Fuel cells are used in portable and emergency power systems, in some passenger vehicles, and in spacecraft.

fuel rod A metal tube that contains the fuel used in a nuclear reactor. *See picture at* **nuclear reactor.**

fulcrum (fo͝ol′krəm) The point or support on which a lever turns.

fullerene (fo͝ol′ə-rēn′) Any of various carbon molecules that are spherical or tubular in shape and whose atoms are usually arranged in hexagons and pentagons. Fullerenes constitute the

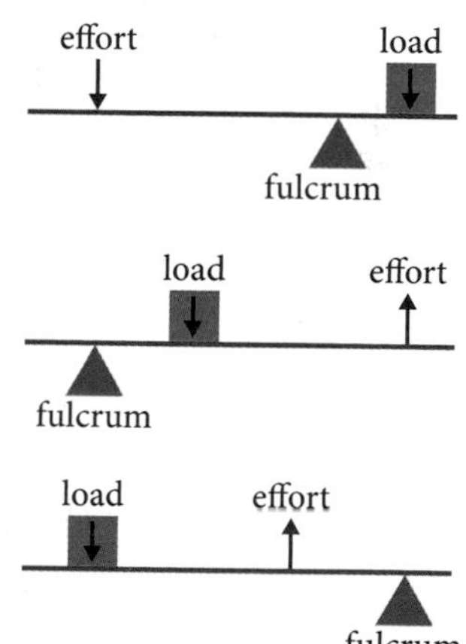

fulcrum

This diagram shows the relative position of the fulcrum in three basic types of levers. Top: *The effort and the load are on opposite sides of the fulcrum, as in a crowbar.* Middle: *The load is between the fulcrum and the effort, as in a wheelbarrow.* Bottom: *The effort is between the load and the fulcrum, as in the human forearm.*

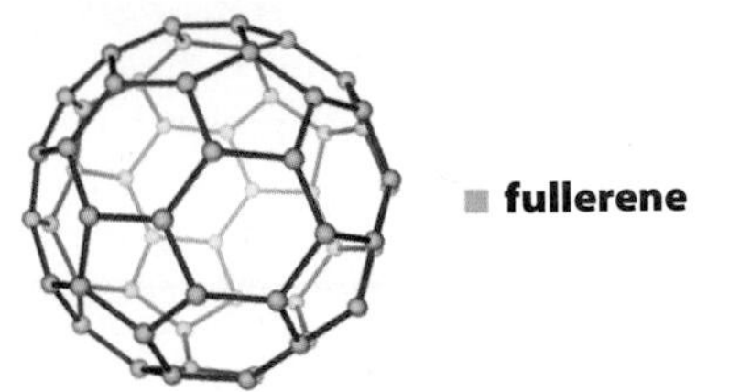

fullerene

third form of pure carbon after diamond and graphite. *See Note at* **carbon.**

full moon (fo͝ol) The phase of the moon in which it is visible as a fully illuminated disk. This phase occurs when the moon is on the opposite side of Earth as the sun and is not in Earth's shadow. *See more at* **moon.** *Compare* **new moon.**

Fulton (fo͝ol′tən), **Robert** 1765–1815. American engineer and inventor who developed one of the first submarines (1800) and the first commercially successful steamboat (1807).

fumarole (fyo͞o′mə-rōl′) A hole in the surface of the Earth from which hot smoke and gases escape. Fumaroles are found on or near volcanoes.

function (fŭngk′shən) **1.** A relationship between two sets that matches each member of the first set with a unique member of the second set. Functions are often expressed as an equation, such as $y = x + 5$, meaning that y is a function of x such that for any value of x, the value of y will be 5 greater than x. **2.** A quantity whose value depends on the value given to one or more related quantities. For example, the area of a square is a function of the length of its sides.

fungicide (fŭn′jĭ-sīd′, fŭng′gĭ-sīd′) A substance used to destroy or prevent the growth of fungi, especially disease-causing fungi in animals and plants.

fungus (fŭng′gəs) *Plural* **fungi** (fŭn′jī, fŭng′gī) Any of a large group of organisms, including mushrooms, molds, yeasts, and mildews, that reproduce by spores and obtain their nourishment from other organisms. The spores of most fungi grow into a network of slender filaments called hyphae. Fungi are grouped as a separate kingdom in taxonomy. *See Table at* **taxonomy.** —*Adjective* **fungal.**

funnel (fŭn′əl) A utensil with a wide opening at one end and a tube at the other, used to pour liquids or other substances into a container with a small mouth.

furcula (fûr′kyə-lə) *Plural* **furculae** (fûr′kyə-lē′) *See* **wishbone.**

fuse (fyo͞oz) *Noun* **1.** A safety device that protects an electric circuit from becoming overloaded. Fuses contain a length of thin wire that melts and breaks the circuit if too much current flows through it. Fuses have largely been replaced by circuit breakers. —*Verb* **2.** To melt something, such as metal or glass, by heating. **3.** To blend two or more substances by melting: *Bronze is made by fusing copper and tin.*

fusion (fyo͞o′zhən) The joining together of light atomic nuclei, especially hydrogen nuclei, to form a heavier nucleus, especially a helium nucleus. Fusion occurs when light nuclei are heated to extremely high temperatures, forcing them to collide at great speed. The collision releases one or more neutrons and energy in the form of radiation. Fusion reactions power the sun and other stars. *See more at* **fission.**

Did You Know...?

fungi

You probably know that mushrooms are *fungi,* but you might not know about all the different kinds of fungi that affect your daily life. Yeasts that make bread dough rise are fungi, and so are the molds that grow on old bread. Fungi cause athlete's foot and other infections in animals, as well as serious plant diseases, like Dutch elm disease. But fungi also help to cure disease: some of them produce substances that kill bacteria, and these substances can be made into antibiotics. Some fungi live in plant roots and help the plants absorb nutrients. Fungi cannot make their own food. Instead, they grow on living or dead organisms and break down large molecules into smaller molecules that they can absorb. Fungi are neither plants nor animals—they are different enough to be classified by scientists into their own unique kingdom.

G

g 1. The symbol for **acceleration of gravity. 2.** A symbol for **g-force. 3.** Abbreviation of **gram.**

G 1. A symbol for **g-force. 2.** The symbol for **gravitational constant. 3.** Abbreviation of **guanine.**

Ga The symbol for **gallium.**

gabbro (găb′rō) A usually dark, coarse-grained igneous rock composed mostly of plagioclase and pyroxene. It is mineralogically similar to basalt but has larger crystals. *See Table at* **rock.**

gadolinium (găd′l-ĭn′ē-əm) A silvery-white, easily shaped metallic element of the lanthanide series that occurs in nature as a mix of seven isotopes. It is used to improve the heat and corrosion resistance of iron, chromium, and various alloys. Certain compounds of gadolinium are also used to improve contrast in magnetic resonance imaging. *Symbol* **Gd.** *Atomic number* 64. *See* **Periodic Table,** pages 254–255.

gal. Abbreviation of **gallon.**

galaxy (găl′ək-sē) Any of the numerous large-scale collections of stars, gas, and dust that make up the universe. Galaxies are held together by gravity and can contain hundreds of billions of stars. Our solar system is located in the Milky Way galaxy.

Galen (gā′lən) AD 130?–200? Greek anatomist, physician, and writer. He developed numerous theories about the structures and functions of the human body, many of which were based on information he gained from dissecting animals. Galen's theories formed the basis of European medicine until the Renaissance.

galaxy
spiral galaxy Messier 74

galena (gə-lē′nə) A gray, metallic mineral consisting of lead and sulfur. Galena usually occurs in cube-shaped crystals within veins of igneous rock or in sedimentary rocks. It is the main ore of lead.

Galileo Galilei (găl′ə-lā′ō găl′ə-lā′) 1564–1642. Italian astronomer and physicist who, using one of the first telescopes, discovered that Jupiter has moons and that Venus has phases like those of Earth's moon. He also studied the mathematics behind the motions of pendulums and falling bodies. *See Note on next page.*

gall (gôl) An abnormal swelling of plant tissue, usually caused by organisms, such as bacteria, insects, or mites, or by an injury.

gallbladder (gôl′blăd′ər) A small, pear-shaped muscular sac in which bile is stored. The gallbladder is located beneath the liver and secretes bile into the small intestine.

gallium (găl′ē-əm) A rare, silvery metallic element that is found as a trace element in coal, bauxite, and several minerals. It melts just above room temperature and is used in thermometers, semiconductors, and blue light-emitting diodes. *Symbol* **Ga.** *Atomic number* 31. *See* **Periodic Table,** pages 254–255.

gallon (găl′ən) A unit of volume or capacity used for measuring liquids, equal to 4 quarts (about 3.79 liters). *See Table at* **measurement.**

galvanic (găl-văn′ĭk) Relating to electricity that is produced by a chemical reaction.

galvanometer (găl′və-nŏm′ĭ-tər) An instrument that detects, measures, and determines the direction of small electric currents.

gamete (găm′ēt′) *See* **sex cell.**

gametophyte (gə-mē′tə-fīt′) In plants and most algae, the phase or generation that produces sex cells (gametes). The gametophyte is haploid (each cell has only one set of chromosomes). The sex cells produced by the gametophyte unite to form the sporophyte, which in turn produces spores that develop into the gametophyte. In nonvascular plants like mosses, the gametophyte is the main plant form and the sporophyte is a small structure that usually grows from the main plant. In ferns, the gametophyte is a very small independent plant and the main plant form is the sporophyte. In seed plants, the gametophyte phase consists of only a few cells, including the pollen grains and embryo sac. *Compare* **sporophyte.**

gamma globulin (găm′ə) **1.** A component of the blood plasma of humans and other mammals consisting of certain proteins, most of which function as antibodies in the body's immune system. **2.** A solution of these proteins prepared from human blood and used in the prevention or treatment of certain diseases.

gamma ray A stream of electromagnetic radiation having wavelengths shorter than those of x-rays and therefore greater energy. Gamma rays are emitted during the radioactive decay of certain unstable atomic nuclei. Gamma rays are the fastest and most penetrating form of nuclear radiation. ❖ The process of emitting gamma rays is called **gamma decay.** When an atom undergoes gamma decay, its atomic number and mass number stay the same, but its mass decreases slightly. *See more at* **radiation, radioactive decay.**

ganglion (găng′glē-ən) *Plural* **ganglia** A cluster of nerve cells having a specific function. In invertebrate animals, pairs of ganglia occur at intervals along the axis of the body. In vertebrates, ganglia are usually located outside the brain or spinal cord and control the functioning of the body's internal organs.

gangrene (găng′grēn′) Death of tissue in a living body, especially in a limb, caused by a bacterial infection resulting from a stoppage of the blood supply to the affected area.

garnet (gär′nĭt) Any of several common red, brown, black, green, or yellow minerals consisting of silicates of aluminum or calcium. Garnets occur in igneous, metamorphic, and sedimentary rocks, and are used as gemstones and industrial abrasives.

gas (găs) One of the basic forms of matter, composed of atoms or molecules in constant random motion. Unlike a solid, a gas has no fixed shape and will take on the shape of the space

BIOGRAPHY

Galileo Galilei

In 1609, Galileo heard of a newly invented device consisting of a tube with a lens at each end that made objects appear closer and larger when you looked through it. He set about making his own. One night Galileo used his telescope (as they began to be called) to look up at the moon. After careful observation of the dark and light spots on its surface, he concluded that he was viewing mountains and valleys like those on Earth. This was an astonishing claim, since the moon was believed to be perfectly smooth. Galileo continued to observe the heavens, and a few months later he discovered Jupiter's four largest moons. As he studied them, he realized that they were orbiting Jupiter, not Earth. Galileo's observations convinced him that Copernicus had been right when he stated that Earth and all the planets orbit the sun. Many people feared Copernicus's theory, which overthrew the long-held belief that Earth was the center of the universe. Because he openly supported Copernicus's theory, Galileo was called before authorities of the Catholic Church and forced to declare that the theory was false. He was then put under house arrest on his own farm, where he was nonetheless allowed to continue his scientific work until the end of his life.

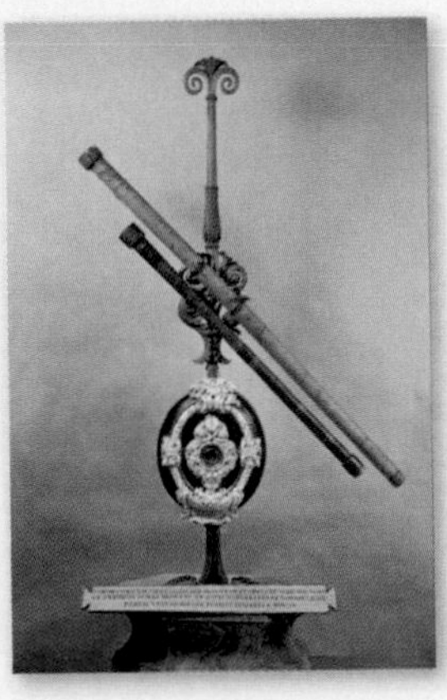

available. Unlike a liquid, it has no fixed volume and will expand to fill the space available. —*Adjective* **gaseous** (găs′ē-əs, găsh′əs).

gas exchange The movement of gases from an area of higher concentration to an area of lower concentration, especially the exchange of oxygen and carbon dioxide between an organism and its environment.

gas giant A large planet that has an atmosphere made of thick gases and does not have a solid surface, although it may have a small solid core. Jupiter, Saturn, Uranus, and Neptune are gas giants.

gasoline (găs′ə-lēn′) A highly flammable mixture of liquid hydrocarbons that are derived from petroleum. Gasoline is used as a fuel for internal-combustion engines in automobiles, motorcycles, and small trucks.

gastric (găs′trĭk) Relating to the stomach.

gastric juice A fluid secreted by glands lining the inside of the stomach. It contains hydrochloric acid and enzymes, such as pepsin, that aid in digestion.

gastrointestinal tract (găs′trō-ĭn-tĕs′tə-nəl) *See* **digestive tract.**

gastropod (găs′trə-pŏd′) Any of various mollusks having a head with eyes and tentacles, usually a single coiled shell, and a muscular foot on the underside of the body with which it moves. Gastropods include both land-dwelling forms, like land snails and slugs, and aquatic species, like conchs, cowries, and whelks.

gastrula (găs′trə-lə) *Plural* **gastrulas** *or* **gastrulae** (găs′trə-lē′) An embryo at the stage following the blastula, in which the cells are distributed into layers that eventually develop into the different tissues and organs of the body. *Compare* **blastula.**

Gauss (gous), **Karl Friedrich** 1777–1855. German mathematician, astronomer, and physicist. He brought about significant and rapid advances to mathematics with his contributions to algebra, geometry, statistics, and number theory.

Gay-Lussac (gā′lə-săk′), **Joseph Louis** 1778–1850. French chemist and physicist who discovered a law governing the combination of gases. He discovered boron, with Louis Jacques Thénard, in 1808.

WORD HISTORY

gastropod

Snails, conchs, whelks, and many other similar animals with shells are all called *gastropods* by scientists. The word *gastropod* comes from Greek and means "stomach foot," a name that owes its existence to the unusual anatomy of snails. While they don't have feet like ours, exactly, snails have a broad flat "foot" used for support and for forward movement. This foot runs along the underside of the animal—essentially along its belly. The Greek elements *gastro–*, "stomach," and *–pod*, "foot," are found in many other scientific names, such as *gastritis* (an inflammation of the stomach) and *sauropod* ("lizard foot," a type of dinosaur).

Gd The symbol for **gadolinium.**

Ge The symbol for **germanium.**

gear (gîr) A wheel with teeth around its rim that mesh with the teeth of another wheel to transmit motion. Gears are used to transmit power (as in a car transmission) or change the direction of motion in a mechanism (as in a differential axle). Speed in various parts of a machine is usually determined by the arrangement of gears.

Geiger (gī′gər), **Hans Wilhelm** 1882–1945. German physicist who was a pioneer in nuclear physics. He invented numerous instruments and techniques used to detect charged particles, including the Geiger counter (1908).

Geiger counter An electronic instrument that detects and measures nuclear radiation, such as x-rays or gamma rays. A Geiger counter consists of a gas-filled tube with an electrode connected to a counter. As radiation passes through the gas, ions are produced, making pulses of electric current that are registered by the counter.

gelatin (jĕl′ə-tn) An odorless, colorless protein substance obtained by boiling a mixture of water and the skin, bones, and tendons of animals. The preparation forms a gel when allowed to cool. It is used in foods, drugs, glue, and photographic film.

Gell-Mann (gĕl′măn′), **Murray** Born 1929.

American physicist who studied the interactions of subatomic particles and helped develop a system for classifying them. He also introduced the concept of quarks.

Gemini (jĕm′ə-nī′) A constellation in the Northern Hemisphere near Cancer and Orion.

gene (jēn) A segment of DNA, occupying a specific place on a chromosome, that is the basic unit of heredity. Genes act by directing the production of RNA, which controls the synthesis of proteins. Different forms of the same gene are called alleles. Many physical traits, such as the texture of a tree's bark, the color of an animal's coat, and the shape of a person's chin, are determined largely by genes. *See also* **dominant, recessive.** *See Notes at* **DNA, Mendel.**

generator (jĕn′ə-rā′tər) A device that converts motion (kinetic energy) into electrical energy. A generator contains a coil of wire that rotates within a magnetic field, producing an electric current in the wire.

gene therapy A medical treatment in which specific genes produced by genetic engineering are inserted into a person's cells. Gene therapy has been used experimentally to treat diseases caused by defective genes and to help destroy cells, such as cancer cells, that cause disease.

Did You Know...?

genes

Are you the way you are because of your genes? Yes and no. Each *gene* is a specific segment of DNA occupying a certain place on a chromosome. Genes contain the chemical information needed to create proteins, which are essential to the functioning of all living cells. Scientists now know the DNA sequence of the entire human genome—all of the approximately 20,000 genes that are found in each of our cells. The vast majority of any person's genes are identical to those found in all other humans. We also share genes with other species, such as mice and flies. The more closely related we are evolutionarily to another species, the more genes we share. Our genes make us human, but what makes each of us unique is a complex interaction of our genes with environmental factors like where we were born and what we eat.

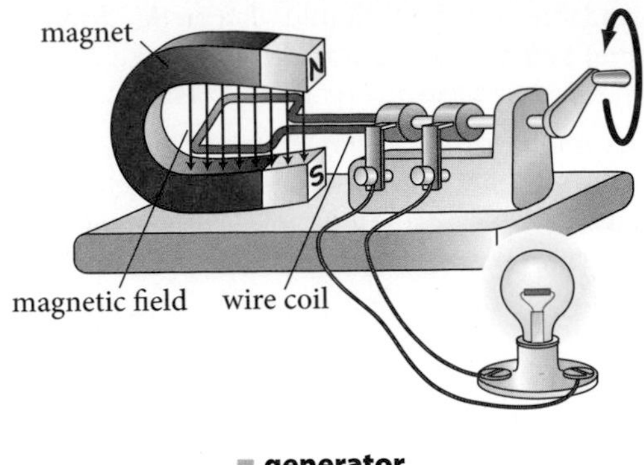

generator

genetically modified organism An organism whose genetic characteristics have been altered by inserting a modified gene or a gene from another organism into its genome. Most of the corn and soybean varieties grown in the United States are genetically modified.

genetic code (jə-nĕt′ĭk) The sequence of bases in DNA or RNA that determines the order of amino acids when a protein is made. A group of three bases specifies a particular amino acid or designates the beginning or end of a protein.

genetic engineering The alteration of the genetic material of an organism, usually by inserting a gene from another organism. Genetic engineering is used to create genetically modified organisms (GMOs) that have desired traits such as resistance to herbicides or that can be used to produce biological substances, such as a proteins or hormones.

genetic map or **gene map** A graphic representation of the arrangement of genes on a chromosome. A genetic map is used to locate and identify the gene or genes that determine a particular inherited trait. ❖ Locating and identifying genes in a genetic map is called **genetic mapping.**

genetics (jə-nĕt′ĭks) The branch of biology that deals with genes, especially their inheritance and expression and their distribution among different individuals and species.

genitals (jĕn′ĭ-tlz) The organs of reproduction in animals, especially the external sex organs and associated structures in humans and other mammals.

genome (jē′nōm) The total genetic content in the chromosomes of an organism or in the DNA or RNA of viruses. The human genome consists of 23 pairs of chromosomes found within the nucleus of every cell (except the sex cells, which have just one pair), containing about 20,000 genes that code for proteins, along with large amounts of DNA having other functions.

genomics (jə-nō′mĭks) The scientific study of the entire genome of an organism.

genotype (jē′nə-tīp′, jĕn′ə-tīp′) The genetic makeup of an organism, as distinguished from its physical characteristics. *Compare* **phenotype.**

genus (jē′nəs) *Plural* **genera** (jĕn′ər-ə) A taxonomic category of organisms that are closely related and share many characteristics, ranking below a family and above a species. *See Table at* **taxonomy.**

geo– or **ge–** A prefix that means "earth," as in *geochemistry,* the study of the Earth's chemistry.

geocentric (jē′ō-sĕn′trĭk) **1.** Relating to or measured from the Earth's center. **2.** Relating to a model of the solar system or universe having the Earth as the center. *Compare* **heliocentric.**

geochemistry (jē′ō-kĕm′ĭ-strē) The study of the chemistry of the Earth, including its layers, waters, and atmosphere.

geode (jē′ōd′) A small, hollow, usually rounded rock lined on the inside with inward-pointing crystals. Geodes form when mineral-rich water entering a cavity in a rock undergoes a change in pressure or temperature, causing crystals to form from the solution and line the cavity's walls.

geodesic dome (jē′ə-dĕs′ĭk, jē′ə-dē′sĭk) A structure having the shape of a dome or partial sphere but made of flat triangular pieces that fit rigidly together.

geographic north (jē′ə-grăf′ĭk) The direction from any point on Earth toward the North Pole. Also called *true north. Compare* **magnetic north.**

geography (jē-ŏg′rə-fē) The scientific study of the Earth's surface and its various climates, countries, peoples, and natural resources.

geologic time (jē′ə-lŏj′ĭk) The period of time covering the formation and development of the Earth, from about 4.6 billion years ago to today. *See Chart,* pages 146–147.

geology (jē-ŏl′ə-jē) **1.** The scientific study of the history, composition, and structure of the Earth, including its rocks, minerals, and landforms. **2.** The history, composition, and structure of the rocks, minerals, and landforms in a specific region of the Earth.

geomagnetism (jē′ō-măg′nĭ-tĭz′əm) The magnetic properties of the Earth. ❖ The magnetic field surrounding the Earth is called the **geomagnetic field.**

geometric progression (jē′ə-mĕt′rĭk) A sequence of numbers in which each number is multiplied by the same factor to obtain the next number in the sequence; a sequence in which the ratio of any two adjacent numbers is the same. An example is 5, 25, 125, 625, . . . , where each number is multiplied by 5 to obtain the following number, and the ratio of any number to the next number is always 1 to 5. *Compare* **arithmetic progression.**

geometry (jē-ŏm′ĭ-trē) The mathematical study of the properties, measurement, and relationships of points, lines, planes, surfaces, angles, and solids.

geophysics (jē′ō-fĭz′ĭks) The application of physics to the scientific study of the Earth and its environment.

geothermal (jē′ō-thûr′məl) Relating to the internal heat of the Earth. The water of hot springs and geysers is heated by geothermal sources. ❖ Power that is generated using the Earth's internal heat is called **geothermal energy.**

geotropism (jē-ŏt′rə-pĭz′əm) *See* **gravitropism.** —*Adjective* **geotropic** (jē′ə-trō′pĭk).

germ (jûrm) **1.** A microscopic organism or agent, especially a bacterium or a virus that causes disease. **2.** The earliest living form of an organism; a seed, spore, or bud: *wheat germ. See Note on page 148.*

Germain (zhĕr-măn′), **Sophie** 1776–1831. French mathematician who made significant advances in theoretical mathematics.

germanium (jər-mā′nē-əm) A brittle, crystalline, grayish-white nonmetallic element that is found in coal, zinc ores, and other minerals. It is used as a semiconductor and in wide-angle lenses. *Symbol* **Ge.** *Atomic number* 32. *See* **Periodic Table,** pages 254–255.

German measles (jûr′mən) A contagious disease caused by a virus in which symptoms, such as skin rash and fever, are usually mild. German

GEOLOGIC TIME

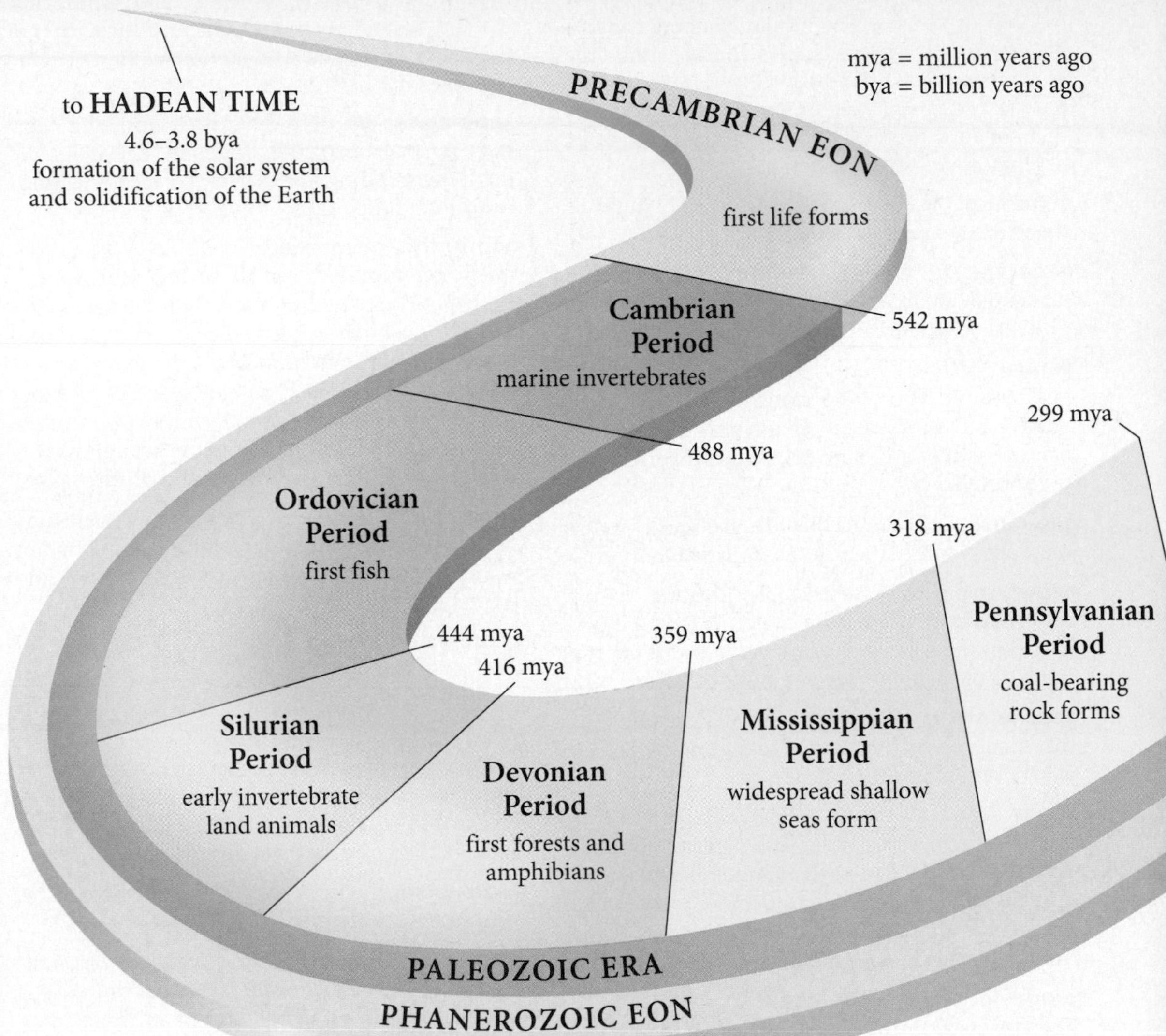

The Earth formed approximately 4.6 billion years ago. For the purpose of studying its history, scientists have separated these 4.6 billion years into a set of divisions, much as a year is divided into months, weeks, and days. The first 800 million years of the Earth's history are referred to as Hadean Time. During this time the solar system was forming and the Earth was solidifying. The 3.8 billion years after Hadean time are subdivided into eons, eras, periods, and epochs. Eons are the longest divisions of time, and epochs are the shortest. Most of the boundaries between the divisions correspond to visible changes in the types of life forms preserved as fossils in the corresponding rocks.

We know a lot more about the Earth's recent history than we do about its earlier history because most younger rocks have not yet been destroyed by weathering, earthquakes, and other forces, the way most older rocks have. This is why most of the geologic time divisions correspond to the last 540 million years (the Phanerozoic Eon), even though most of the Earth's history occurred before that time.

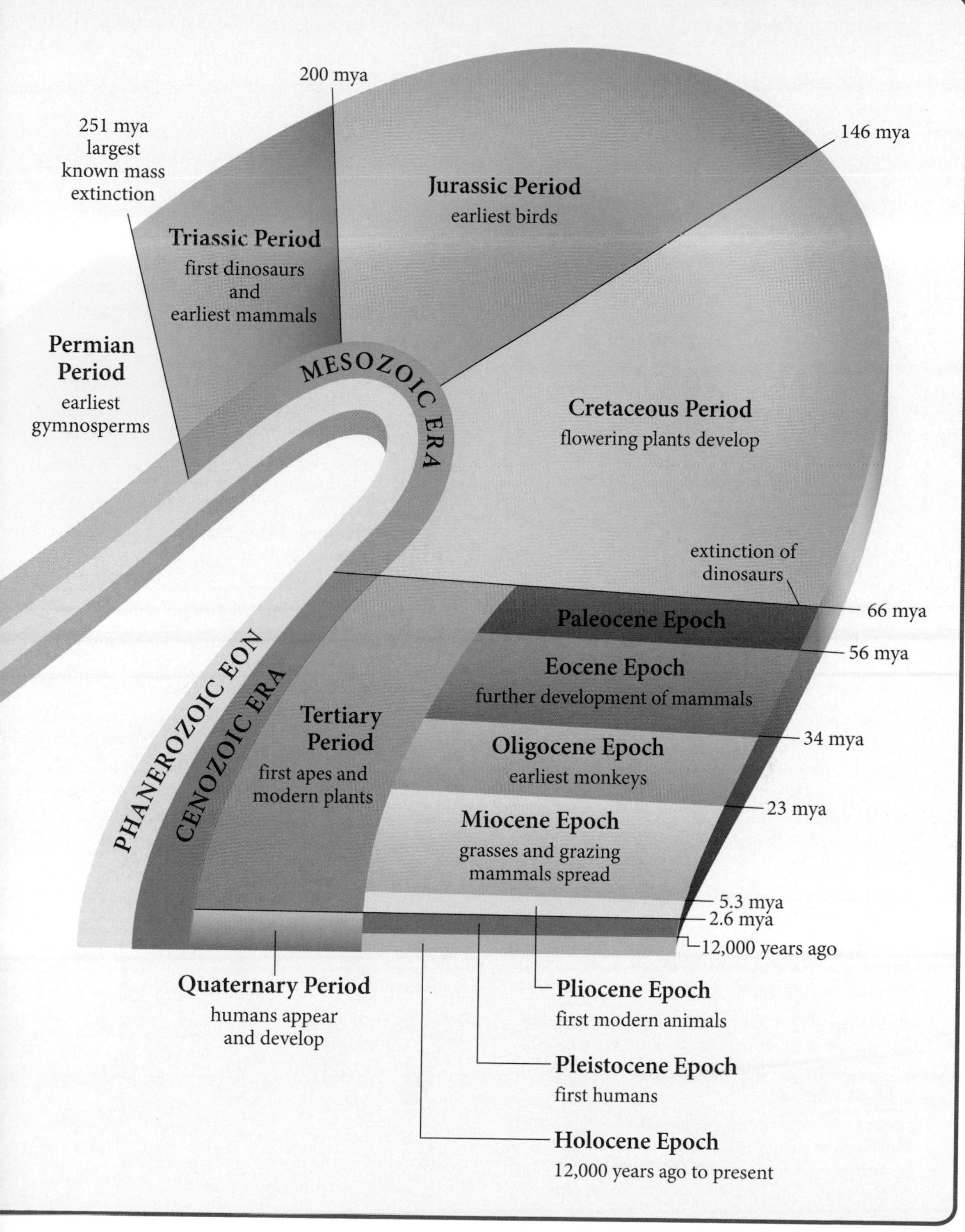
200 mya
251 mya
largest
known mass
extinction
146 mya
Jurassic Period
earliest birds
Triassic Period
first dinosaurs
and
earliest mammals
Permian
Period
earliest
gymnosperms
MESOZOIC ERA
Cretaceous Period
flowering plants develop
extinction of
dinosaurs
66 mya
Paleocene Epoch
56 mya
Eocene Epoch
further development of mammals
PHANEROZOIC EON
CENOZOIC ERA
Tertiary
Period
first apes and
modern plants
34 mya
Oligocene Epoch
earliest monkeys
23 mya
Miocene Epoch
grasses and grazing
mammals spread
5.3 mya
2.6 mya
12,000 years ago
Quaternary Period
humans appear
and develop
Pliocene Epoch
first modern animals
Pleistocene Epoch
first humans
Holocene Epoch
12,000 years ago to present

USAGE

germ/microbe/pathogen

If someone sneezes on you, you might accuse them of spraying you with germs. The term *germ* has been used to refer to invisible agents of disease since the 1700s, and it became more popular in the late 1800s when scientists like Louis Pasteur championed the idea that infections and contagious diseases are caused by microscopic organisms. In 1878 a French biologist invented a new word for these tiny creatures: *microbe*, from the Greek prefix *mikro–*, "small," and the Greek word *bios*, "life." Today, scientists usually use the terms *germ* and *microbe* only informally. To refer generally to agents of disease, whether bacteria, parasites, fungi, or viruses, they use the term *pathogen*, from the Greek *pathos*, "suffering," and the suffix *gen–*, "producer." They use *microorganism* to refer to any unicellular organism, whether it causes disease or not.

measles can cause congenital defects if contracted by a woman during early pregnancy. Also called *rubella.*

germ cell A sex cell of a multicellular organism; a gamete. Eggs and sperm are germ cells.

germination (jûr′mə-nā′shən) The beginning of growth of a seed or spore. Most seeds require water for germination. Some seeds also require specific conditions such as low temperatures or mechanical breakdown of the seed coat. —*Verb* **germinate.**

gestation (jĕ-stā′shən) The carrying and development of young in the uterus from conception to birth; pregnancy. The gestation period is about three weeks in rats, nine months in humans, and twenty-two months in elephants.

geyser (gī′zər) A natural hot spring that regularly ejects a spray of steam and boiling water into the air. The water is heated by coming in contact with hot rock underground.

g-force A measure of force acting on a body, expressed as a multiple of the force that the Earth's gravity at sea level (equal to 1 g) would exert on the body. The force of gravity on Jupiter, for example, is 2.5 g. A person in an airplane feels a force of more than 1 g when the plane accelerates for takeoff.

giant star (jī′ənt) A bright star that is very massive or very large in diameter or both.

gibbon (gĭb′ən) Any of several small tree-dwelling apes of Southeast Asia, having a slender body, long arms, and no tail.

gibbous (gĭb′əs) More than half but less than fully illuminated. Used to describe the moon or a planet. *Compare* **crescent.**

Gibbs (gĭbz), **Josiah Willard** 1839–1903. American mathematician and physicist known especially for his investigations of thermodynamics. He developed methods for analyzing the thermodynamic properties of substances, and his findings established the basic theory for physical chemistry.

giga– **1.** A prefix that means "one billion," as in *gigahertz,* one billion hertz. **2.** A prefix that means 2^{30} (that is, 1,073,741,824, which is the power of 2 closest to a billion), as in *gigabyte. See Table at* **measurement.**

gigabit (gĭg′ə-bĭt′) *Computers* **1.** One billion bits. **2.** 1,073,741,824 (2^{30}) bits. *See Note at* **megabyte.**

gigabyte (gĭg′ə-bīt′) **1.** A unit of computer memory or data storage capacity equal to 1,024 megabytes (2^{30} bytes). **2.** One billion bytes. *See Note at* **megabyte.**

Gilbert (gĭl′bərt), **William** 1544–1603. English court physician and physicist whose book *De Magnete* (1600), a systematic explanation of magnetism and static electricity, was the first com-

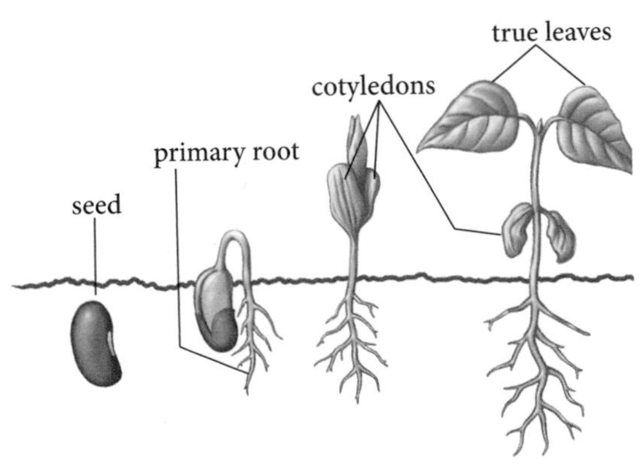

germination
a bean seed germinating

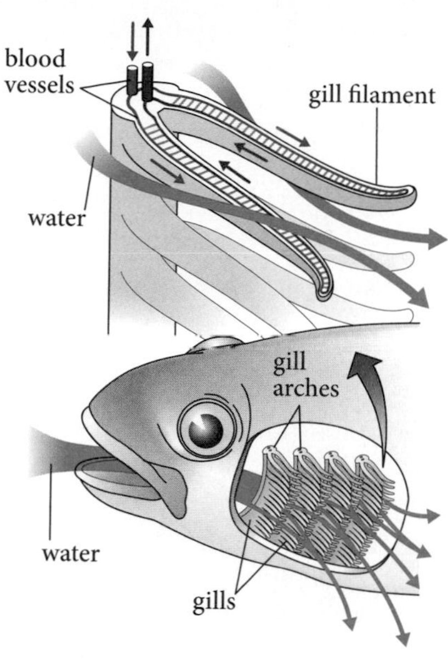

■ **gill**

A fish breathes by swallowing water and passing it through gill slits on each side of its head. Blood-filled filaments on the gills extract oxygen from the water as it flows through.

prehensive scientific work published in England. Gilbert demonstrated that the Earth itself is a magnet, with lines of force running between the North and South Poles.

gill (gĭl) **1.** The organ that enables fish and many other aquatic animals to take oxygen from the water. A gill consists of a series of thin membranes that are full of small blood vessels. As water flows across the membranes, oxygen passes into the blood vessels and carbon dioxide passes out of them. **2.** One of the thin structures on the underside of the cap of a mushroom.

gingiva (jĭn′jə-və) The gums of the mouth. ❖ Inflammation of the gums is called **gingivitis** (jĭn′jə-vī′tĭs).

ginkgo (gĭng′kō) A deciduous tree originally native to China, having fan-shaped leaves and seeds with a fleshy yellow coat. Ginkgoes are gymnosperms and do not have flowers.

gizzard (gĭz′ərd) A muscular pouch behind the stomach in birds. It has a rough, thick lining and contains pieces of grit or sand that the bird has swallowed. The gizzard functions to grind up hard pieces of food.

glacier (glā′shər) A large mass of ice flowing very slowly through a valley or spreading outward from a center. Glaciers form over many years from packed snow in areas where snow accumulates faster than it melts. A glacier is always moving, but when its forward edge melts faster than the ice behind it advances, the glacier as a whole shrinks backward.

gland (glănd) An organ or group of cells in the body of an animal that produces and secretes a specific substance, such as a hormone or enzyme. *See also* **endocrine gland, exocrine gland.**

glass (glăs) A transparent or translucent material that has no crystalline structure and that usually breaks or shatters easily. It is typically made by melting a silicate, such as sand, with other ingredients to give it desired properties such as strength, hardness, or index of refraction.

glaucoma (glou-kō′mə, glô-kō′mə) An eye disease in which the pressure of fluid inside the eyeball becomes abnormally high. The pressure can damage the optic nerve and lead to partial or complete loss of vision.

Global Positioning System (glō′bəl) A system that determines latitude and longitude of a particular location on the Earth by calculating

Did You Know...?

glass

You may sometimes hear fine *glass* referred to as "crystal," and it is true that glass, like many kinds of crystals, is typically hard and transparent. Indeed, the main ingredient in most glass is silicon dioxide, which is also the main component of quartz crystals. But glass is not actually a crystal; some scientists describe it as a sort of frozen liquid, whereas others describe it as a disordered kind of solid. When glass is made, it begins as a melted mixture of silicon dioxide and other ingredients. This mixture is formed into the desired shape and then allowed to cool quickly, becoming harder and harder until its molecules become fixed in place before they have a chance to form crystals. Rather than having the orderly arrangement of molecules that is typical of most solids, glass thus resembles a liquid, stuck in time.

the difference in the time it takes for signals sent from different satellites to reach a receiver at that location.

global warming An increase in the average temperature of the Earth's atmosphere, especially when occurring over a significant period of time. The Earth has been in a period of global warming since at least the early 1900s, with effects that include melting glaciers and rising sea levels. Most scientists believe that this warming has been caused chiefly by the increased production of greenhouse gases related to human activity. *See Note at* **greenhouse effect.**

globular cluster (glŏb′yə-lər) A dense system of ten thousand to a million stars that has a roughly spherical structure and orbits a galaxy. Most known galaxies have numerous globular clusters. *Compare* **open cluster.**

globulin (glŏb′yə-lĭn) Any of a class of simple proteins found in the seeds of plants and in the blood, muscle, and milk of animals. *See also* **gamma globulin.**

glottis (glŏt′ĭs) The space between the vocal cords at the upper part of the larynx.

glucose (glo͞o′kōs′) A crystalline sugar having the formula $C_6H_{12}O_6$, produced in plants by photosynthesis and essential for metabolism in most living things. In humans it is transported by blood and lymph to all the cells of the body, where it is broken down to produce ATP, the main source of energy for cellular processes.

glutamic acid (glo͞o-tăm′ĭk) A nonessential amino acid. *See more at* **amino acid.**

glutamine (glo͞o′tə-mēn′) A nonessential amino acid. *See more at* **amino acid.**

gluten (glo͞ot′n) Any of various plant proteins found in cereal grains, especially certain ones in wheat, rye, and barley that can cause digestive disorders.

glycerin also **glycerine** (glĭs′ər-ĭn) *See* **glycerol.**

glycerol (glĭs′ə-rôl′) A sweet, syrupy liquid obtained from animal fats and oils or by the fermentation of glucose. It is used as a solvent, sweetener, and antifreeze and in making explosives and soaps. Also called *glycerin.*

glycine (glī′sēn′, glī′sĭn) A nonessential amino acid. *See more at* **amino acid.**

glycogen (glī′kə-jən) A carbohydrate stored in the liver and muscles of animals that is converted to glucose for energy when glucose levels in the blood are low or when the muscles need fuel.

glycolysis (glī-kŏl′ə-sĭs) The process in cell metabolism by which glucose is broken down in a series of steps, producing ATP and pyruvic acid.

GMO Abbreviation of **genetically modified organism.**

gneiss (nīs) A type of metamorphic rock consisting of light-colored layers, usually of quartz and feldspar, alternating with dark-colored layers of other minerals. The layers are often folded into curves. *See Table at* **rock.**

gnetophyte (nē′tə-fīt′) Any of various seed plants that are gymnosperms (like conifers) but have some similarities to angiosperms (flowering plants).

Goddard (gŏd′ərd), **Robert Hutchings** 1882–1945. American physicist who developed and launched the first successful liquid-fueled rocket, in 1926. He also invented numerous rocketry devices.

Gödel (gŭd′l), **Kurt** 1906–1978. Austrian-born American mathematician who is noted for developing the incompleteness theorem, which states that in any finite mathematical system, there will always be statements that cannot be proved or disproved. His proof of this theorem ended efforts by mathematicians to find a mathematical system that was entirely consistent in itself.

Goeppert-Mayer (gŭp′ûrt-mā′ər), **Maria** 1906–1972. German-born American physicist. She developed a model of the atomic nucleus that explained why certain nuclei were stable and had an unusual number of stable isotopes.

goiter (goi′tər) An enlarged thyroid gland, visible as a swelling at the front of the neck. It is often associated with a diet that contains too little iodine.

gold (gōld) A soft, shiny, yellow element that is the most easily shaped metal. It occurs in veins and in alluvial deposits. Because it is very durable, resistant to corrosion, and a good conductor of heat and electricity, gold is used as a plating on electrical and mechanical components. It is also an international monetary standard and is used to make jewelry and decoration. *Symbol* **Au.** *Atomic* *number* 79. *See* **Periodic Table,** pages 254–255. *See Note at* **element.**

Goldberger (gōld′bər-gər), **Joseph** 1874–1929. Hungarian-born American physician. He investigated the cause of pellagra, which was a widespread and often fatal disease. Goldberger demonstrated that it was caused by a poor diet and introduced an effective method of prevention.

Golgi apparatus or **Golgi complex** (gōl′jē) A structure within most cells that is composed of a series of sacs and plays a role in the storage, modification, and transport of proteins and other large molecules. There is no Golgi apparatus in bacteria or archaea. *See more at* **cell.**

Did You Know...?

Gondwana

Sometimes a suggested solution to a scientific problem can raise more questions than it answers. So it was with Austrian geologist Eduard Suess's hypothesis explaining why identical groups of fossil plants occur in India, South America, southern Africa, Australia, and Antarctica. These plants, known as the *Glossopteris flora,* had seeds that were too large to have blown across wide oceans. In 1885 Suess proposed that the plant fossils were common to all of the landmasses because when the plants first developed, the landmasses were actually connected in one huge continent. He named this continent *Gondwanaland* (now usually called just *Gondwana*) after the region of Gondwana in central India. Few believed Suess's idea, because it was hard to see how such distant continents could have been connected. In the early 1900s, Alfred Wegener, a German meteorologist, noticed that if the shapes of the continents of the Southern Hemisphere were fit together like puzzle pieces, adjacent regions on the different landmasses had similar geological features. Wegener used this evidence to propose the idea of *continental drift,* which says that the continents are always moving toward or away from one another. But Wegener's ideas and the concept of Gondwanaland weren't accepted until the 1960s, when the theory of *plate tectonics* was put forward to explain how the internal workings of the Earth could cause continents to move about.

Jane Goodall

gonad (gō′năd′) An organ, such as an ovary or testis, that produces sex cells in an animal.

Gondwana (gŏnd-wä′nə) A supercontinent of the Southern Hemisphere comprising the landmasses that currently correspond to India, Australia, Antarctica, and South America. According to the theory of plate tectonics, Gondwana formed at the end of the Paleozoic Era and broke up in the middle of the Mesozoic Era. *Compare* **Laurasia.**

gonorrhea (gŏn′ə-rē′ə) A sexually transmitted disease caused by a bacterial infection that causes inflammation of the genitals and urinary tract.

Goodall (go͝od′ôl), **Jane** Born 1934. British zoologist whose study of the behavior and habitat of the chimpanzee has greatly increased understanding of primate behavior. She established a research center in Tanzania, Africa, and has been a leader in international conservation efforts.

googol (go͞o′gôl′, go͞o′gəl) The number 10 raised to the 100th power, written as 10^{100} or as 1 followed by 100 zeros.

gorge (gôrj) A deep, narrow valley with steep sides, often with a stream flowing through it.

gorilla (gə-rĭl′ə) Either of two species of large apes of the central African forests and mountains. Gorillas have a stocky body and dark hair, dwell on the ground, and feed on plants.

gout (gout) A kind of arthritis characterized by

painful deposits of crystals in the joints, especially of the big toe, knee, or elbow. It is caused by abnormally high levels of uric acid in the blood.

GPS Abbreviation of **Global Positioning System.**

gradient (grā′dē-ənt) **1.** The degree to which something inclines; a slope. A mountain road with a gradient of 10 percent rises 1 foot for every 10 feet of horizontal length. **2.** The rate at which a physical quantity, such as temperature or pressure, changes over a distance.

graduated (grăj′o͞o-ā′tĭd) Divided into or marked with intervals indicating measures, as of length, volume, or temperature. A graduated cylinder, for example, is used to measure the volume of a liquid.

graft (grăft) *Noun* **1.** A shoot or bud of one plant that is inserted into or joined to the stem, branch, or root of another plant so that the two grow together as a single plant. Grafts are often used for fruit trees and ornamental plants. **2.** A transplant of body tissue, especially skin or bone, from one part to another. —*Verb* **3.** To join a graft to another plant. **4.** To transplant tissue from one part of the body to another.

grain (grān) **1.** A small, dry, one-seeded fruit, such as an individual rice seed in its hull. Many of the plants that bear such fruit, such as the cereal grasses wheat, rye, corn, and rice, are also called grains. **2.** A small particle of something, such as salt, pollen, or sand. **3.** A unit of weight equal to about 0.0023 ounce (0.065 gram). *See Table at* **measurement.**

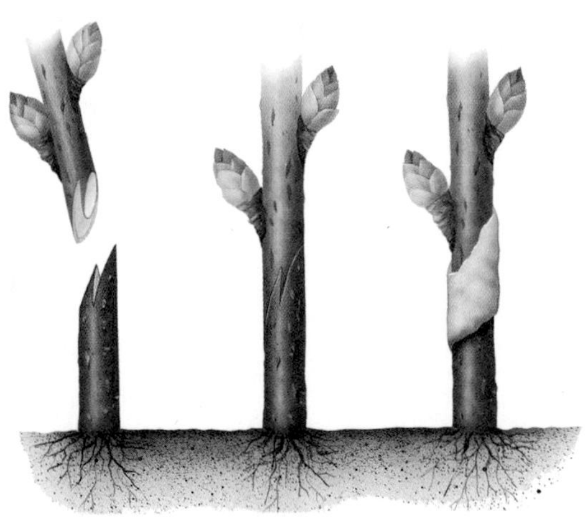

graft

One kind of grafting involves cutting a stem with buds from one plant and fitting it tightly into a rooted stem of another plant.

grain alcohol *See* **ethanol.**

gram (grăm) A unit of mass in the metric system, equal to about 0.04 ounces. *See Table at* **measurement.**

gram-negative Relating to a group of bacteria that do not change color when subjected to the Gram stain. Gram-negative bacteria have relatively thin cell walls and are more resistant to antibiotics and the body's immune cells than are gram-positive bacteria.

gram-positive Relating to a group of bacteria that turn a dark-blue color when subjected to the Gram stain. Gram-positive bacteria have relatively thick cell walls, and they are more easily destroyed by antibiotics and by the body's immune cells than are gram-negative bacteria.

Gram stain A staining technique using a purplish-blue dye that is used to classify bacteria into one of two groups. Because of differences in cell wall structure, some bacteria, called gram-positive, retain the dye when it is applied to them, while others, called gram-negative, do not. The Gram stain is named for the Danish physician Hans Christian Gram (1853–1838), who developed the technique.

grand unified theory (grănd) Any of various theories that attempt to unite three of the four basic forces in nature—the electromagnetic force, the weak nuclear force, and the strong nuclear force—by showing that they are all aspects of one force. No such theory has yet been generally accepted.

granite (grăn′ĭt) A usually light-colored, coarse-grained igneous rock composed mostly of quartz, feldspar, and mica. It is one of the most common rocks in the crust of continents. *See Table at* **rock.**

granulocyte (grăn′yə-lō-sīt′) Any of several kinds of white blood cells that contain granular material in the cytoplasm and are important in the body's defense against infection. Granulocytes are the most numerous of the white blood cells in humans.

graph (grăf) **1.** A diagram showing the relationship of quantities, especially such a diagram in which lines, bars, or proportional areas represent how one quantity depends on or changes with another. **2.** A curve or line showing a mathematical

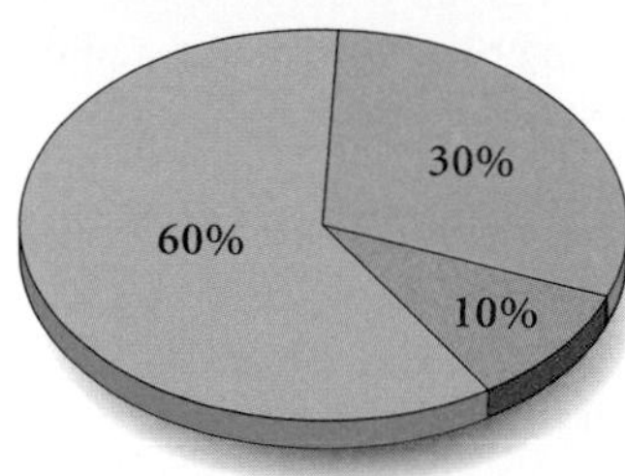

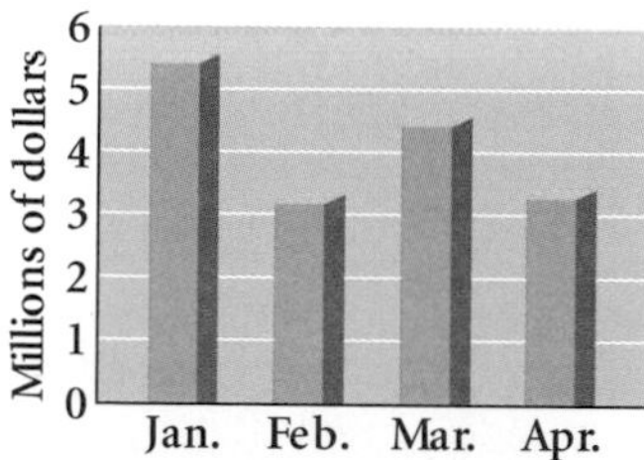

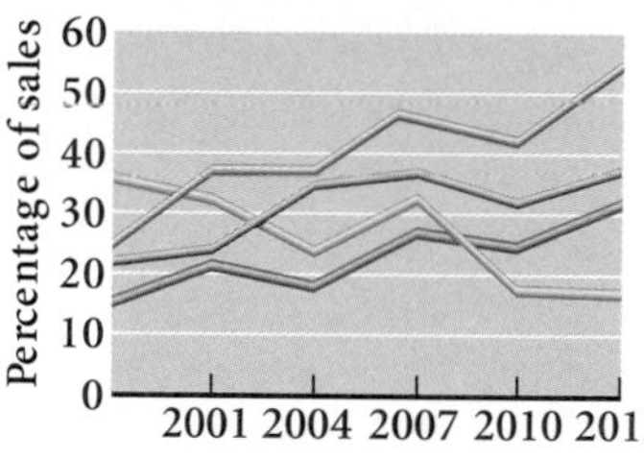

■ **graph**

top to bottom: *a pie chart, a bar graph, and a line graph*

function or equation, typically drawn in a Cartesian coordinate system.

graphical user interface (grăf′ĭ-kəl) *See* **GUI.**

graphics (grăf′ĭks) **1.** The representation of data in a way that includes images in addition to text. Computer-aided design, typesetting, and video games, for example, involve the use of graphics. **2.** The process by which a computer displays information in the form of images.

graphite (grăf′īt′) A naturally occurring, steel-gray to black, crystalline form of carbon. The carbon atoms in graphite are strongly bonded together in sheets. Because the bonds between the sheets are weak, other atoms can easily fit between them, causing the graphite to be soft and slippery to the touch. Graphite is used in pencils and paints and as a lubricant and electrode. It is also used to control chain reactions in nuclear reactors because of its ability to absorb neutrons. *See Note at* **carbon.**

grass (grăs) Any of numerous plants having narrow leaves, hollow stems, and clusters of very small flowers. Grasses include wheat, corn, sugar cane, and bamboo, as well as many plants grown for pastures and lawns.

grasshopper (grăs′hŏp′ər) Any of numerous insects having two pairs of wings and long hind legs used for jumping. Grasshoppers feed on plants and sometimes destroy crops.

grassland (grăs′lănd′) An area, such as a prairie or steppe, that is covered with grasses.

gravimeter (gră-vĭm′ĭ-tər) **1.** An instrument used to measure specific gravity. **2.** An instrument used to measure variations in a gravitational field.

gravitation (grăv′ĭ-tā′shən) Gravity.

gravitational constant (grăv′ĭ-tā′shə-nəl) A number used in Newton's law of gravitation to calculate the force of the gravity between two bodies. The gravitational constant *G* equals 6.67 × 10^{-11} cubic meters per kilogram per second squared. *See more at* **Newton's law of gravitation.**

gravitropism (gră-vĭt′rə-pĭz′əm) Growth or movement of an organism in response to the Earth's gravity. Examples of gravitropism include the downward growth of plant roots and the upward growth of new shoots on a plant. —*Adjective* **gravitropic** (grăv′ĭ-trō′pĭk).

gravity (grăv′ĭ-tē) **1.** The force of attraction between any two objects in the universe. Gravity increases as the masses of the objects increase and as their distance from each other decreases. Gravity is the weakest of the four basic forces of nature, being weaker than the strong nuclear force, the electromagnetic force, and the weak nuclear force. *See more at* **relativity. 2.** The gravitational force as it acts near the Earth and

■ **grasshopper**

Did You Know...?

gravity

With his law of universal gravitation, Isaac Newton described *gravity* as the mutual attraction between any two objects in the universe. He formulated an equation that expresses the strength of gravity in terms of the masses of the objects and the distance between them: the more massive the objects, and the closer they are, the greater the force. Newton's theory explained both the trajectory of a falling apple and the motion of the planets—previously completely unconnected phenomena—using the same equation. Centuries later, Albert Einstein realized that Newton's theories were inadequate. In Newton's theories, the effects of gravity happen instantaneously, meaning that gravity travels at almost infinite velocity. But that is impossible according to Einstein's theory of special relativity, since nothing can travel faster than the speed of light. Einstein's theory of general relativity solved this problem by connecting gravity, mass, and acceleration in a new way. Imagine, he said, that you are standing in a stationary rocket on Earth: because of Earth's gravity, your feet are pressed against the rocket's floor with a force equal to your weight. Now imagine you are in the same rocket in outer space, far from any gravitational pull, and the rocket is accelerating. The rocket floor pushes against your feet, creating a force that feels the same as if you were being acted upon by gravity. From this realization that acceleration and gravity are equivalent, Einstein showed that mass itself forms curves in space and time that affect even entities without mass, such as light. In most situations, Einstein's and Newton's theories predict the same results; but where they differ, the predictions from Einstein's are more accurate.

other very massive objects, such as stars and planets.

gray (grā) A unit used to measure the energy absorbed from radiation. One gray is equal to one joule per kilogram, or 100 rads.

gray matter The brownish-gray tissue of the brain and spinal cord in vertebrate animals, made up chiefly of the cell bodies of neurons. *Compare* **white matter.**

great circle (grāt) A circle on the surface of a sphere whose plane passes through the center of the sphere. The Earth's equator is a great circle on the sphere of the globe.

greenhouse effect (grēn′hous′) The effect by which greenhouse gases in the atmosphere absorb energy given off by the sun-warmed surface of the Earth in the form of infrared radiation and then radiate part of that energy back downward toward the Earth.

greenhouse gas Any of the atmospheric gases that contribute to the greenhouse effect. Greenhouse gases include carbon dioxide, water vapor, methane, and nitrous oxide.

Greenwich Mean Time (grĕn′ĭch) Coordinated universal time, used as the standard time in the United Kingdom.

ground (ground) **1.** The solid surface of the Earth; land. **2.** A connection between an electrical conductor and the Earth. **3.** A point in an electrical system where the voltage is zero.

ground state The state of a system, such as an atom or subatomic particle, that has the lowest possible energy. A system that is not in its ground state, such as an atom with an electron excited to a higher energy level, returns to its ground state by emitting a photon of electromagnetic radiation.

groundwater (ground′wô′tər) Water that flows or collects beneath the Earth's surface. Groundwater originates from rain and from melting snow and ice. It sinks into the ground, filling the small empty spaces in soil, sediment, and porous rocks. Aquifers, springs, and wells are supplied by the flow of groundwater.

group (gro͞op) **1.** Two or more atoms bound together that act as a unit in a number of chemical compounds: *a hydroxyl group.* **2.** In the periodic table, a vertical column that contains elements having the same number of electrons in the outermost shell of their atoms. Elements in the same group have similar chemical properties. *See* **Periodic Table,** pages 254–255.

growth (grōth) An increase in size, amount, or volume, usually as a result of an increase in the number of cells. Growth of an organism may stop at maturity, as in the case of humans and other

Did You Know...?

greenhouse effect

Greenhouses and the greenhouse effect both provide warmth by retaining solar energy rather than letting it escape, but they operate by very different processes. In the greenhouse effect, the shorter wavelengths of light in sunlight pass through the atmosphere and warm the Earth's surface, which then radiates energy back upward in the form of longer-wavelength infrared radiation. Although some of this energy escapes into space, much of it is absorbed by water vapor, carbon dioxide, and other gases in the atmosphere. This absorption of energy warms the atmosphere, which then re-radiates some of the energy back toward the surface. By contrast, actual greenhouses retain solar energy mostly by preventing warm air from flowing away rather than by keeping infrared radiation from escaping.

mammals, or it may continue throughout life, as in many plants.

growth ring A layer of wood formed in a plant during a single period of growth. Growth rings are visible as concentric circular bands of varying width when a tree is cut crosswise. Each ring contains the xylem cells that were produced during one growing period by the tissue known as vascular cambium. ❖ Most growth rings reflect a full year's growth and are called **annual rings.** But abrupt changes in the environment, especially in the availability of water, can cause a plant to produce more than one growth ring in a year. *See more at* **dendrochronology.**

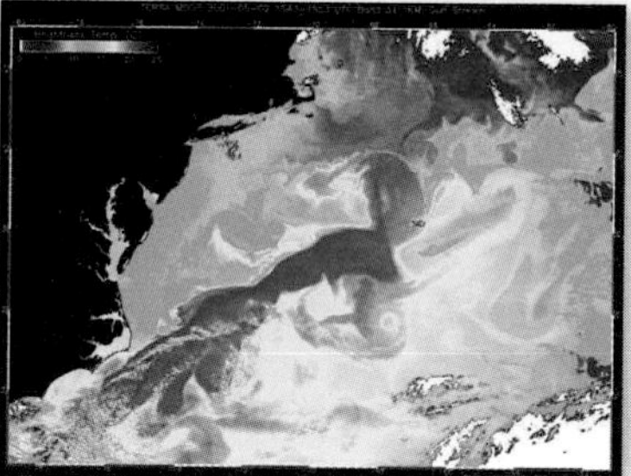

Gulf Stream

A satellite image showing the temperature of the ocean and the overlying atmosphere off the East Coast of the United States. The warm temperatures of the Gulf Stream appear in red.

guanine (gwä′nēn′) A base that is a component of DNA and RNA, forming a base pair with cytosine.

guano (gwä′nō) The excrement of certain seabirds or bats that has accumulated along sea coasts or in caves. It contains nitrogen, phosphorus, and other nutrients and is used as a fertilizer.

guard cell (gärd) One of the paired cells that border each pore, called a stoma, in a leaf or other plant part. When the guard cells are swollen with water, they pull apart and the stoma opens, allowing gas exchange and the escape of water vapor. When they lose water, they move close together and the stoma closes, preventing the loss of water vapor from the plant. *See more at* **cell.**

GUI (go͞o′ē) Short for *graphical user interface.* An interface that is used to issue commands to a computer by means of a device such as a mouse that manipulates and activates onscreen images.

gulf (gŭlf) A large body of ocean or sea water that is partly surrounded by land.

Gulf Stream A warm ocean current of the northern Atlantic Ocean off eastern North America. It flows northward and eastward from the Gulf of Mexico, eventually dividing into several branches. A major branch continues eastward to warm the coast and moderate the climate of northwest Europe.

gully (gŭl′ē) A narrow, steep-sided channel formed in loose earth by running water. A gully is usually dry except after periods of heavy rainfall or after the melting of snow or ice.

gum[1] (gŭm) A sticky substance that is produced by certain plants and trees and dries into a brittle solid that dissolves in water.

gum[2] The firm connective tissue that surrounds and supports the bases of the teeth.

gut (gŭt) The digestive tract, especially of an invertebrate animal or an embryo of a vertebrate animal.

GUT Abbreviation of **grand unified theory.**

gymnosperm (jĭm′nə-spûrm′) Any of a group of plants, including the conifers, the cycads, and the ginkgo, that produce seeds that are not enclosed in an ovary. In cone-bearing gymnosperms, the seeds develop on the surface of the scales of the female cones. *Compare* **angiosperm.**

gynecology (gī′nĭ-kŏl′ə-jē) The branch of medicine that deals with the female reproductive system, its diseases, and their treatment.

gypsum (jĭp′səm) A colorless, white, or pinkish mineral consisting of calcium sulfate. Gypsum occurs as individual blade-shaped crystals or as massive beds in sedimentary rocks. It is used in manufacturing plasterboard, cement, and fertilizers. It is the mineral used to represent a hardness of 2 on the Mohs scale.

gyroscope (jī′rə-skōp′) An instrument consisting of a disk or wheel that spins rapidly about an axis like a top. The spinning motion keeps the axis fixed even if the base is turned in any direction, making the gyroscope an accurate navigational instrument and an effective stabilizing device in ships and airplanes.

■ **gyroscope**

h Abbreviation of **hour.**

H 1. Abbreviation of **henry. 2.** The symbol for **hydrogen.**

Haber (hä′bər), **Fritz** 1868–1934. German chemist who was the first to produce ammonia synthetically, in 1908–1909.

habit (hăb′ĭt) **1.** The characteristic shape of a crystal: *the cubic habit of pyrite.* **2.** The characteristic manner of growth of a plant: *a low plant with a creeping habit.*

habitat (hăb′ĭ-tăt′) The natural environment in which a species or group of species normally lives, such as a desert, coral reef, or freshwater lake. A lake, for example, is a suitable habitat for a frog but not for a whale.

Hadean Time (hā-dē′ən) The period of time between 4.6 and 3.8 billion years ago, when the solar system was forming and the Earth was solidifying. No rocks are known from this time, probably because they have eroded or they were drawn deep into the Earth and melted through the processes of plate tectonics. *See Chart at* **geologic time,** pages 146–147.

hadrosaur (hăd′rə-sôr′) Any of various medium-sized to large plant-eating dinosaurs of the Cretaceous Period that had a ducklike bill, numerous teeth in the back of the jaw, a stiff tail, and sometimes a crest on the head. Also called *duck-billed dinosaur.*

hafnium (hăf′nē-əm) A bright, silvery metallic element that occurs in zirconium ores. Because hafnium absorbs neutrons better than any other metal and is resistant to corrosion, it is used to control nuclear reactions. *Symbol* **Hf.** *Atomic number* 72. *See* **Periodic Table,** pages 254–255.

hagfish (hăg′fĭsh′) Any of various long, thin ocean fish that lack jaws and vertebrae, have a skeleton made of cartilage, and have a sucking mouth with sharp toothlike projections. Hagfish feed on other fish and on large worms and have glands that produce large amounts of slime.

Hahn (hän), **Otto** 1879–1968. German chemist who discovered several new radioactive isotopes and in 1938 was the first scientist to experimentally observe nuclear fission.

hail (hāl) Precipitation in the form of rounded pellets of ice that usually falls during thunderstorms. Hail forms when water droplets are lifted by an updraft within a cloud, freezing as they rise into colder air and collecting layers of ice until they are too heavy for the winds to keep them from falling.

hair (hâr) **1.** One of the fine strands that grow from the skin of humans and other mammals. Hair provides insulation against the cold in most mammals. Specialized hairs, such as porcupine quills, provide protection. **2.** A slender growth resembling a mammalian hair, found on insects and other animals. **3.** *Botany* A fine strand growing from the outer layer of a plant.

half-life (hăf′līf′) The time it takes for half the nuclei in a sample of a radioactive substance to undergo radioactive decay. For example, if you start with 100 grams of strontium-90, whose half-life is 29 years, then after 29 years, 50 grams of strontium-90 will be left in the sample (the rest will have decayed to yttrium-90); after 58 years, 25 grams will be left; after 87 years, 12.5 grams will be left, and so on. Each radioactive substance has a different half-life.

halide (hăl′īd′, hā′līd′) An anion of one of the elements called halogens, or a compound containing such an anion. Salts such as sodium

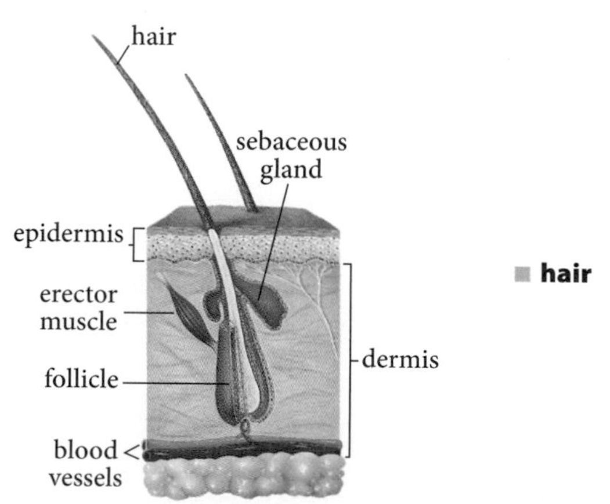

hair

chloride (NaCl) and potassium fluoride (KF) are examples of halide compounds.

halite (hăl′īt′, hā′līt′) A colorless or white mineral consisting of sodium chloride and occurring as cubic crystals. Halite is found in dried lakebeds in arid climates and in underground deposits. It is used to melt ice on roads and is ground up to use as table salt.

Halley (hăl′ē), **Edmund** 1656–1742. English astronomer who is best known for his study of comets. He accurately predicted that a comet observed in 1583 would return in 1758, 1835, and 1910. This comet is now named for him. Halley was also the first to catalog the stars in the Southern Hemisphere (1679).

Halley's comet (hăl′ēz, hā′lēz) A comet that makes one complete orbit around the sun in approximately 76 years. It is visible to the unaided eye and last appeared in 1986.

hallucinogen (hə-lo͞o′sə-nə-jən) A drug or chemical that causes a person to see, hear, or otherwise sense something that is not real.

halo (hā′lō) A hazy ring of colored light in the sky around the sun, the moon, or a similar bright object. It is caused by the reflection and refraction of light through ice crystals suspended in the upper atmosphere of the Earth.

halogen (hăl′ə-jən) Any of a group of five nonmetallic elements with similar properties. The halogens are fluorine, chlorine, bromine, iodine, and astatine. Because they are missing an electron from their outermost shell, they react readily with most metals to form salts. The halogens are located in the column of the periodic table that is second from the right. *See* **Periodic Table,** pages 254–255.

halo

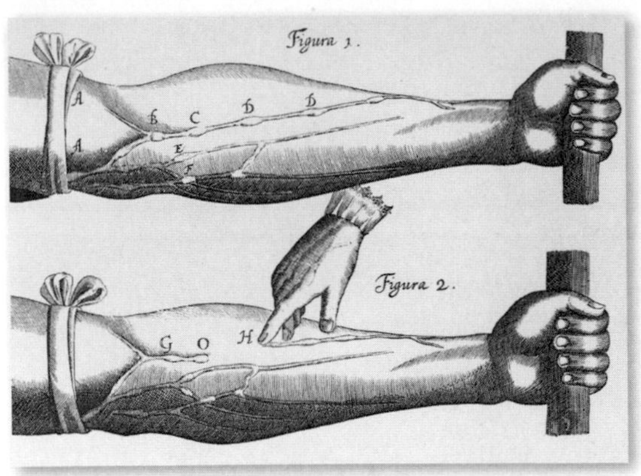

William Harvey

This engraving, from William Harvey's 1628 treatise "On the Motion of the Heart and Blood in Animals," shows the blood vessels in the arm.

halophyte (hăl′ə-fīt′) A plant that lives in salty soil, as along the seashore. Mangroves and grasses that grow in salt marshes are halophytes.

hamstring (hăm′strĭng′) A powerful group of muscles with strong tendons at the back of the thigh in humans or the hind leg in other animals.

Hansen's disease (hăn′sənz) *See* **leprosy.**

haploid (hăp′loid′) Being a cell or composed of cells in which there is only one of each different chromosome. In animals and plants, sex cells are haploid. *Compare* **diploid.** *See more at* **gametophyte, meiosis.**

hard disk (härd) A rigid magnetic disk fixed within a disk drive and used for storing computer data.

hard drive A disk drive that reads data stored on hard disks.

hardness (härd′nĭs) A measure of how easily a mineral can be scratched. Hardness is measured on the Mohs scale.

hard palate *See under* **palate.**

hardware (härd′wâr′) A computer, its components, and its related equipment. Hardware includes drives, integrated circuits, display screens, cables, modems, speakers, and printers. *Compare* **software.**

Harvey (här′vē), **William** 1578–1657. English

physician who demonstrated (1628) how blood circulates through the human body and showed that the heart acts as a pump.

hassium (hä′sē-əm) A synthetic, radioactive element that is mainly produced in particle accelerators during collisions between two relatively heavy atoms, such as iron and lead or magnesium and curium. Its most stable isotope has a half-life of 16.5 minutes. *Symbol* **Hs.** *Atomic number* 108. *See* **Periodic Table,** pages 254–255.

hawk (hôk) Any of various birds of prey having a short hooked bill, broad wings, and strong claws for seizing prey.

Hawking (hô′kĭng), **Stephen William** Born 1942. British physicist noted for his study of black holes and the origin of the universe, especially the Big Bang theory. His work has provided much of the mathematical basis for scientific explanations of the physical properties of black holes.

hay fever (hā) An allergic reaction to pollen that results in sneezing, itching, and watery eyes. Hay fever is usually caused by the pollen of plants, such as certain trees and grasses, that are pollinated by the wind and produce large amounts of pollen.

hazardous waste (hăz′ər-dəs) A used or discarded material that can damage the environment and be harmful to health. Certain chemicals left over from industrial processes, and the radioactive remains of fuel used in nuclear power plants, are examples of hazardous waste.

He The symbol for **helium.**

heart (härt) **1.** The hollow, muscular organ in a vertebrate animal that pumps blood throughout the body by contracting and relaxing. In humans and other mammals, it has four chambers, consisting of two atria and two ventricles. The right side of the heart collects blood with low oxygen levels from the veins and pumps it to the lungs. The left side receives blood with high oxygen levels from the lungs and pumps it into the aorta, which carries it to all of the arteries of the body. The heart in other vertebrates functions similarly but often has fewer chambers. **2.** A similar but less complex organ in invertebrate animals.

Stephen Hawking

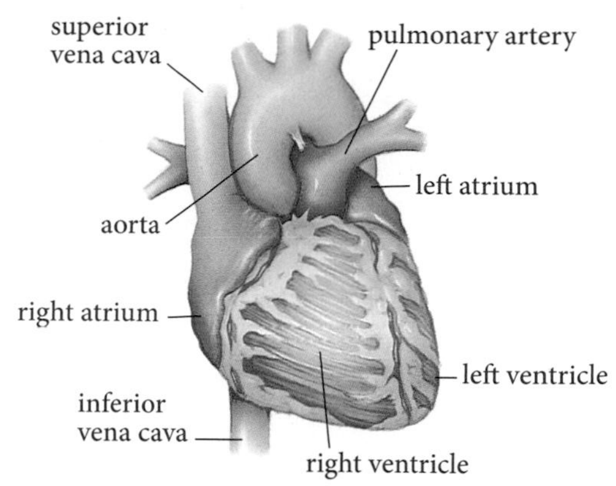

heart
adult human heart

heart attack A sudden interruption in the normal functioning of the heart that is often accompanied by severe pain. Heart attacks are usually caused by an insufficient supply of blood to part of the heart muscle resulting from blockage of a coronary artery.

heat (hēt) **1.** *Physics* Energy that is transferred from one system or body to another as a result of a difference in temperature between the two. Heat can be transferred by conduction, convection, or radiation. In physics, *heat* is not considered a property of a body. *See Notes at* **conduction, temperature. 2.** *Biology See* **estrus.**

heat exchanger A device used to transfer heat from one fluid to another without direct contact of the fluids. Heat exchangers contain a hot fluid that flows through one part of the exchanger, which transfers heat to a cool fluid in another part of the exchanger or to air or water outside of the exchanger in the environment. For example, a car radiator is a heat exchanger that transfers heat

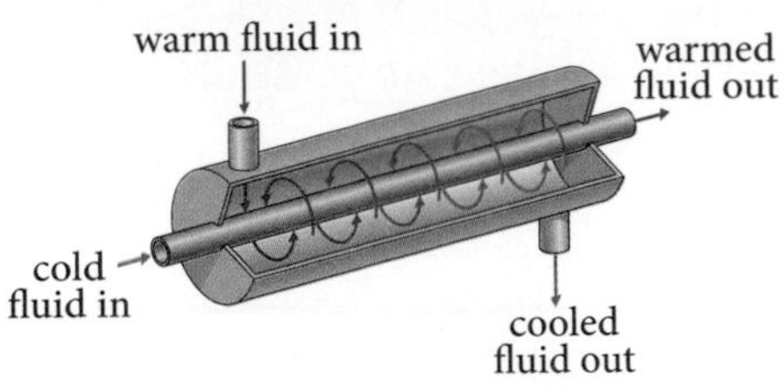

heat exchanger

from a hot liquid that has circulated through the engine to the cooler air outside.

heavy hydrogen (hĕv′ē) *See* **deuterium.**

heavy water Water formed of oxygen and deuterium. Heavy water is much like ordinary water but has higher freezing and boiling points. It is used in certain nuclear reactors to help promote fission reactions and to prevent the reactor core from overheating.

Heisenberg (hī′zən-bûrg′), **Werner Karl** 1901–1976. German physicist who was a founder of quantum mechanics. He formulated the uncertainty principle, which states that for certain pairs of properties of a particle, it is impossible to measure both properties with equally great precision. For example, the more precisely one knows the position of an electron, the less precisely one can know its momentum (that is, its mass multiplied by its velocity), and, conversely, the more precisely one knows its momentum, the less precisely one can know its position.

Did You Know...?

heavy water

How can one molecule of water be heavier than another, when both consist of a single oxygen atom and two hydrogen atoms? The answer lies at the atomic level. Normal hydrogen has a nucleus consisting entirely of one proton. However, in the variety of hydrogen called *deuterium,* a neutron accompanies the proton in the nucleus. Deuterium thus weighs about twice as much as standard hydrogen. The substance we call *heavy water* is H_2O in which many of the hydrogen atoms are deuterium. Heavy water has many applications in nuclear energy. Most importantly, it tends to slow down neutrons that result from nuclear fission reactions without absorbing them. For this reason it is used in some nuclear power plants to encourage fission. When a fuel atom absorbs a neutron, it splits, releasing energy and more neutrons. But these neutrons are moving too fast to be absorbed by other fuel atoms. The heavy water slows the neutrons down so that they are more easily absorbed, adding to the chain reaction.

heliocentric (hē′lē-ō-sĕn′trĭk) Relating to a model of the solar system or universe having the sun as the center. *Compare* **geocentric.** *See Note at* **Copernicus.**

heliotropism (hē′lē-ŏt′rə-pĭz′əm) Growth or movement of an organism, especially a plant, toward or away from the sunlight. *—Adjective* **heliotropic** (hē′lē-ə-trō′pĭk).

helium (hē′lē-əm) A very lightweight, colorless, odorless element that is a noble gas and occurs in natural gas, in radioactive ores, and in small amounts in the atmosphere. It has the lowest boiling point of any substance and is the second most abundant element in the universe, after hydrogen. Helium is used to provide lift for balloons and blimps and in cooling systems for magnetic resonance imaging equipment. *Symbol* **He.** *Atomic number* 2. *See* **Periodic Table,** pages 254–255.

helix (hē′lĭks) **1.** A three-dimensional spiral curve. In mathematical terms, a helix can be described as a curve turning about an axis on the surface of a cylinder or cone while rising at a constant upward angle from a base. **2.** Something, such as a strand of DNA, having a spiral shape.

Helmholtz (hĕlm′hōlts′), **Hermann Ludwig Ferdinand von** 1821–1894. German physicist and physiologist who formulated the law of conservation of energy and also did pioneering research on vision, inventing an instrument for examining the interior of the eye in 1851.

hematite (hē′mə-tīt′) A reddish-brown to silver-gray mineral consisting of iron oxide. Hematite occurs in igneous, metamorphic, and sedimentary rocks and is the most abundant iron ore. It is usually slightly magnetic.

hematoma (hē′mə-tō′mə) The abnormal buildup of blood in an organ or other tissue of the

WORD HISTORY

helium

A lot of elements are named after places, and in many cases the origin of the name is obvious, like germanium for Germany and californium for California. But in some cases, like that of *helium,* the connection is not so clear. Helium was discovered in 1868, when astronomers were studying a solar eclipse with a spectroscope, an instrument that breaks up light into a spectrum. When a chemical element is heated hot enough to glow, and the light emitted is refracted through a prism, it produces a unique spectrum. The astronomers noticed that the spectrum of the sun's corona, which is only visible during an eclipse, contained some lines produced by an unknown element. The element was then named *helium,* from *helios,* the Greek word for "sun." We now know that helium was produced abundantly in the first few moments after the Big Bang and continues to be produced by nuclear fusion in stars, and that it is found in small amounts on Earth. The Greek word *helios* gives us many other words pertaining to the sun, such as *heliocentric* and *perihelion.*

body, caused by a break in a blood vessel. A bruise is a type of hematoma.

hemi– A prefix meaning "half," as in *hemisphere,* half a sphere.

hemiplegia (hĕm′ĭ-plē′jə) Paralysis of one side of the body, usually resulting from injury to the brain.

hemisphere (hĕm′ĭ-sfîr′) **1.** One half of a sphere, formed by a plane that passes through the center of the sphere. **2.** Either the northern or southern half of the Earth as divided by the equator, or the eastern or western half as divided by a meridian. **3.** One half of the celestial sphere. **4.** *See* **cerebral hemisphere.**

hemlock (hĕm′lŏk′) **1.** Any of various evergreen trees of North America and eastern Asia, having small cones and short, flat, needle-shaped leaves with two white bands underneath. **2.** Any of several poisonous European plants that have small, white flowers.

hemo– A prefix meaning "blood," as in *hemophilia,* a disorder in which blood fails to clot.

hemoglobin (hē′mə-glō′bĭn) The iron-containing protein in the blood of vertebrate animals that binds to oxygen and carries it from the lungs to the body tissues. Hemoglobin is contained in the red blood cells and gives these cells their characteristic color. Hemoglobin is also found in some invertebrates, where it circulates freely in the blood. *See Note at* **red blood cell.**

hemophilia (hē′mə-fĭl′ē-ə) An inherited disease in which the blood does not clot properly, causing excessive bleeding. Hemophilia usually only affects males.

hemorrhage (hĕm′ər-ĭj) Bleeding, especially in excessive amounts.

henry (hĕn′rē) A unit used to measure electrical inductance. When a current varies at the rate of one ampere per second and induces an electromotive force of one volt, the circuit has an inductance of one henry.

Henry, Joseph 1797–1878. American physicist who studied electromagnetic phenomena. He constructed one of the first electromagnetic motors in 1831. The henry unit of inductance is named for him.

hepatic (hĭ-păt′ĭk) Relating to the liver.

hepatitis (hĕp′ə-tī′tĭs) Inflammation of the liver, usually caused by infection with a virus. It is characterized by jaundice, fever, and weakness.

heptagon (hĕp′tə-gŏn′) A polygon having seven sides.

herbicide (hûr′bĭ-sīd′, ûr′bĭ-sīd′) A substance used to destroy or reduce the growth of plants, especially weeds.

herbivore (hûr′bə-vôr′, ûr′bə-vôr′) An animal that feeds mainly or only on plants. *Compare* **carnivore.** —*Adjective* **herbivorous.**

Hercules (hûr′kyə-lēz′) A constellation in the Northern Hemisphere near Lyra and Corona Borealis.

hereditary (hə-rĕd′ĭ-tĕr′ē) Passed or capable of being passed from parent to offspring by means of genes: *a hereditary trait.*

heredity (hə-rĕd′ĭ-tē) The passage of biological traits or characteristics from parents to offspring through the inheritance of genes.

heritable (hĕr′ĭ-tə-bəl) Capable of being passed from one generation to the next through the genes. Cystic fibrosis is an example of a heritable disease.

hermaphrodite (hər-măf′rə-dīt′) **1.** An organism, such as an earthworm or a flowering plant, that typically has both male and female reproductive organs in a single individual. **2.** A person who has both male and female reproductive organs and secondary sexual characteristics.

hernia (hûr′nē-ə) A condition in which an organ or other structure of the body protrudes through an abnormal opening in the body structure that normally contains it.

Hero (hē′rō) First century AD. Greek mathematician who invented many water-driven and steam-driven machines and developed a formula for determining the area of a triangle.

herpes (hûr′pēz) Any of several infections caused by a virus, characterized by the eruption of painful blisters on the skin or a mucous membrane.

herpetology (hûr′pĭ-tŏl′ə-jē) The scientific study of reptiles and amphibians.

Herschel (hûr′shəl) Family of British astronomers. Sir **William Herschel** (1738–1822) discovered Uranus (1781) and cataloged more than 800 binary stars and 2,400 nebulae. His sister **Caroline Herschel** (1750–1848) discovered numerous comets, nebulae, and star clusters, and she published a star catalog in 1798. His son Sir **John Frederick William Herschel** (1792–1871) cataloged nearly 2,000 deep-sky objects and pioneered celestial photography. *See Note at* **infrared.**

hertz (hûrts) A unit used to measure the frequency of vibrations and waves. One hertz is equal to one cycle per second. The hertz is named after the German physicist Heinrich Hertz (1857–1894).

heterotrophic (hĕt′ər-ə-trŏf′ĭk) Relating to an organism that cannot manufacture its own food and instead obtains its food and energy by eating other organisms or by taking in parts or remains of other organisms. Animals, fungi, protozoans, and most bacteria are heterotrophic. ❖ An organism that consumes organic matter or other organisms for food is called a **heterotroph** (hĕt′ər-ə-trŏf′). *Compare* **autotrophic.**

heterozygous (hĕt′ər-ə-zī′gəs) Having two different forms of the same gene for a trait such as eye color (for example, brown and blue) at corresponding positions on a pair of chromosomes. *Compare* **homozygous.**

Hewish (hyo͞o′ĭsh), **Antony** Born 1924. British astronomer. In 1967, working with the astronomer Jocelyn Bell Burnell, he discovered the first pulsar.

BIOGRAPHY

William and Caroline Herschel

Both William and Caroline Herschel began their professional careers as musicians. They were born in Germany and later moved to England, where Caroline became a soprano soloist in performances conducted by her brother. William's background in music theory spurred him to study mathematics and astronomy, and he taught his sister in turn. Each produced a string of important discoveries. William was the first astronomer to study binary stars. His careful observations and his skill at mapping the stars led him to discover the planet Uranus in 1781. It was the first new planet to be discovered since ancient times. He further discovered two satellites of Uranus, Titania and Oberon (1787), and two of Saturn, Mimas and Enceladus (1789). King George III appointed William to the post of King's Astronomer in 1782, and Caroline was made his assistant. Caroline observed her first comet in 1786 and later discovered seven others, as well as nebulae and star clusters. After her brother's death in 1822, Caroline reorganized and published his catalog of nebulae. She also continued her own observations up to the end of her life.

hexagon (hĕk′sə-gŏn′) A polygon having six sides.

hexagonal (hĕk-săg′ə-nəl) **1.** Having six sides. **2.** Relating to a crystal having three axes of equal length intersecting at angles of 60° in one plane, and a fourth axis of a different length that is perpendicular to this plane. The mineral calcite has hexagonal crystals. *See more at* **crystal.**

Hf The symbol for **hafnium.**

Hg The symbol for **mercury.**

hibernation (hī′bər-nā′shən) An inactive state resembling deep sleep in which certain animals, such as rodents and bears, pass the winter in cold climates. During hibernation, the body temperature is lowered and breathing and heart rates slow down. Hibernation protects the animal from cold and reduces the need for food during the season when food is scarce. *Compare* **estivation.**

hiccup (hĭk′əp) A sudden and uncontrolled contraction of the diaphragm and throat muscles, followed by a closing of throat with a short, sharp sound. Hiccups usually occur repeatedly, once every few seconds.

high blood pressure (hī) A condition in which the pressure of the blood, especially in the arteries, is abnormally high. High blood pressure can increase the risk of heart attack or stroke. Also called *hypertension.*

high-fructose corn syrup *See under* **fructose.**

high-tension Having a high voltage: *high-tension wires.*

high tide The time at which the tide reaches the highest level in its regular rising and falling. There are usually two high tides per day.

hilum (hī′ləm) A mark or scar on a seed, such as a bean, showing where it was formerly attached to the plant.

hindbrain (hīnd′brān′) The rear part of the brain in vertebrate animals. In humans, it consists of the pons and the medulla oblongata. *Compare* **forebrain, midbrain.**

hipbone (hĭp′bōn′) Either of two large, flat bones that consist of three fused bones—the ilium, ischium, and pubis—and form the outer borders of the pelvis.

Hipparchus (hĭ-pär′kəs) Second century BC. Greek astronomer who discovered the precession of the equinoxes, developed the techniques of trigonometry, and cataloged the positions of 850 stars in the earliest known star chart.

Hippocrates (hĭ-pŏk′rə-tēz′) 460?–377? BC. Greek physician who helped develop a theory of medicine that attributed disease primarily to natural causes such as nutrition and environment rather than to supernatural forces.

hippopotamus (hĭp′ə-pŏt′ə-məs) A large, heavy African mammal having dark, almost hairless thick skin, short legs, a broad snout, and a wide mouth. Hippopotamuses live in and near rivers and lakes. They eat plants and stay under water for long periods of time. ❖ A related, smaller animal, called the **pygmy hippopotamus,** lives only in parts of western Africa.

histamine (hĭs′tə-mēn′) A chemical compound found in fungi, plants, and animal tissue. In humans, histamine is released as part of the immune response during allergic reactions, causing expansion of blood vessels, tightening of the airways, and faster beating of the heart, as well as itching and sneezing.

histidine (hĭs′tĭ-dēn′) An essential amino acid. *See more at* **amino acid.**

histology (hĭ-stŏl′ə-jē) The scientific study of the microscopic structure of plant and animal tissues.

histone (hĭs′tōn′) Any of several proteins that are closely associated with DNA in the nucleus of a eukaryotic cell. DNA molecules are very long, and they fit inside a nucleus by wrapping around histones to form a complex called chromatin.

HIV (āch′ī-vē′) Short for *human immunodeficiency virus.* The virus that causes AIDS by infecting cells of the body's immune system.

hive (hīv) **1.** A structure for housing honeybees. **2.** A colony of honeybees living in such a structure.

hives (hīvz) Itchy welts on the skin caused by an allergic response to a substance, such as food or a drug, or to a condition, such as an infection. Hives occur as a result of the release of histamine as part of the body's immune response.

Ho The symbol for **holmium.**

Hodgkin (hŏj′kĭn), **Dorothy Mary Crowfoot** 1910–1994. British chemist. Using x-ray techniques, she determined the structure of several

Dorothy Crowfoot Hodgkin

complex molecules, including penicillin and vitamin B_{12}.

holmium (hōl′mē-əm) A soft, silvery, easily shaped metallic element of the lanthanide series. When exposed to a magnetic field, holmium becomes highly magnetic. It is mainly used in scientific research but has also been used to make electronic devices. *Symbol* **Ho.** *Atomic number* 67. *See* **Periodic Table,** pages 254–255.

Holocene (hŏl′ə-sēn′, hō′lə-sēn′) The more recent of the two epochs of the Quaternary Period, beginning at the end of the last Ice Age, about 12,000 years ago. It is characterized by the development of human civilizations. Also called *Recent. See Chart at* **geologic time,** pages 146–147.

hologram (hŏl′ə-grăm′, hō′lə-grăm′) A three-dimensional image of an object made by holography.

holography (hō-lŏg′rə-fē) A method of making a three-dimensional image of an object by using a beam of light from a laser. The laser light beam is split into two beams that are directed by mirrors so that one beam reflects off the object onto a photographic plate while the other beam is aimed directly at the plate. When the two beams come back together, they create an interference pattern that is recorded on the plate. When this pattern, called the hologram, is illuminated and viewed, the observer sees a three-dimensional image of the object.

homeopathy (hō′mē-ŏp′ə-thē) A system for treating disease in which patients are given tiny doses of a drug that, when given in large amounts to healthy people, produces symptoms like those of the disease itself. Homeopathy is a kind of alternative medicine.

homeostasis (hō′mē-ō-stā′sĭs) The tendency of an organism or cell to maintain stable internal conditions regardless of changing outside conditions. The ability of warm-blooded animals to maintain a steady body temperature is an example of homeostasis.

hominid (hŏm′ə-nĭd) Any of a group of large primates that includes modern humans, orangutans, gorillas, chimpanzees, and bonobos, as well as their extinct relatives. Scientists formerly defined this group as including only humans and their extinct ancestors, and the word *hominid* is still sometimes used in this way.

hominin (hŏm′ĭ-nĭn′) Any of various primates belonging to a group that includes modern humans and their extinct relatives from the Pliocene and Pleistocene Epochs. The hominins were formerly classified as hominids.

Homo erectus (hō′mō ĭ-rĕk′təs) An extinct species of humans that lived during the Pleistocene Epoch from about 1.9 million years ago

Did You Know...?

hologram

If you tear an ordinary photograph in two, each piece shows only a part of the original image. If you break a *hologram* in two, each piece shows the entire original scene, although from slightly different points of view. That's because each spot on a hologram contains enough information to show how the entire scene would look if it were viewed from a particular point of view. Imagine looking at a room through a peephole set in a solid door. What you see depends on where in the door the peephole is placed. Each piece of the hologram is a "peephole" view, and that's what makes the image look three-dimensional: as you move the hologram around or look at different parts of it, you see the original object from different angles, just as if you were walking around it. For this reason, holograms are much harder to copy than simple two-dimensional images, because to forge one you'd have to know what the original object looked like from many angles. That's why credit cards and other objects that are targets of counterfeiting include holographic stickers as indicators of authenticity.

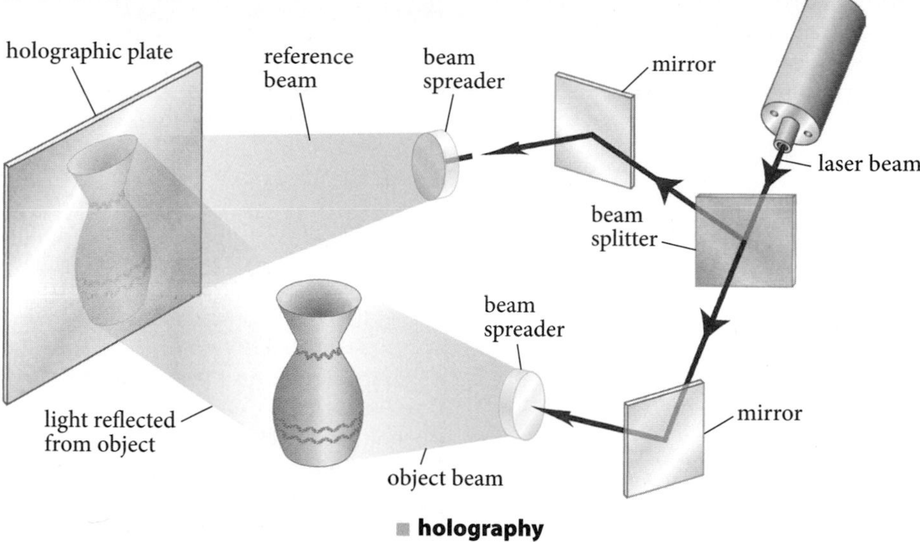

■ **holography**

to 100,000 years ago. *Homo erectus* was the first species of humans to master fire, and its remains have been found in Africa, Europe, and Asia. It is widely thought to be the direct ancestor of modern humans.

Homo habilis (hăb′ə-ləs) An extinct species of humans that may have been an ancestor of modern humans, existing from about 2.0 to 1.5 million years ago. Fossils of *Homo habilis* are often found together with stone tools.

homologous (hə-mŏl′ə-gəs) **1.** Similar in structure and evolutionary origin, though not necessarily in function, as the arm of a human and the flipper of a seal. *Compare* **analogous. 2.** Being one of a pair of chromosomes, one from the female parent and one from the male parent, that have the same structure, with genes for the same traits arranged in the same order. Genes on homologous chromosomes are not necessarily identical. For example, one chromosome in a pair of homologous chromosomes may contain an allele for brown eyes, and the other an allele for blue eyes.

homolosine projection (hō-mŏl′ə-sīn′) A method of making a flat map of the Earth with breaks in the oceans in order to show the correct relative sizes of the landmasses with only slight distortion of shapes. *Compare* **conic projection, Mercator projection, sinusoidal projection.**

Homo sapiens (sā′pē-ənz) The modern species of humans. *Homo sapiens* evolved probably between 200,000 and 100,000 years ago in Africa. The closest living relatives of *Homo sapiens* are the other hominids: the chimpanzee, bonobo, gorillas, and orangutans.

homozygous (hō′mō-zī′gəs) Having two identical forms of the same gene for a trait such as eye color at corresponding positions on a pair of chromosomes. *Compare* **heterozygous.**

honeybee (hŭn′ē-bē′) *See under* **bee.**

Hooke (ho͝ok), **Robert** 1635–1703. English physicist, inventor, and mathematician. He studied elasticity in solid bodies, observed the motions of the planets, and made detailed observations of natural objects using a microsope.

Hooke's law A law in physics stating that the extent to which an elastic material will change size and shape under stress is directly proportional to the amount of stress applied to it. If a spring is stretched to a certain length by a force of 1 newton, for example, it will be stretched to twice that length by a force of 2 newtons.

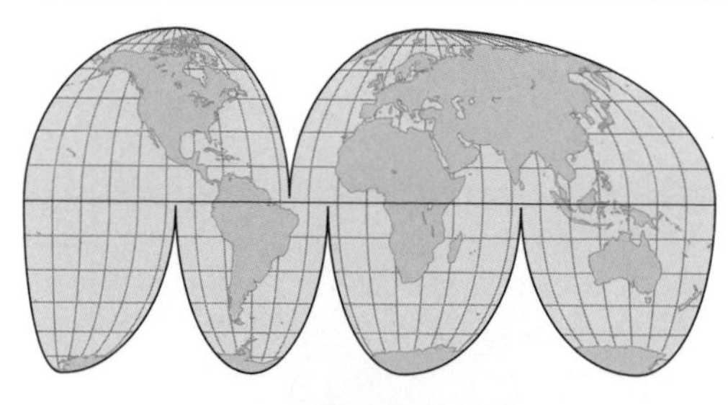

■ **homolosine projection**

hookworm (ho͝ok′wûrm′) Any of numerous parasitic worms that have hooked mouthparts by which they fasten themselves to the inside wall of the intestines of various animals, including humans.

Hopper (hŏp′ər), **Grace Murray** 1906–1992. American mathematician and computer programmer who is noted for her development of programming languages.

horizon (hə-rī′zən) **1.** The circle on the celestial sphere along which the Earth and the sky appear to meet. **2.** A layer of soil that has a different color, texture, structure, or chemical composition from the layers adjacent to it.

hormone (hôr′mōn′) A substance produced in one part of the body, especially in an endocrine gland, that has an effect on another part of the body, to which it is usually carried in the bloodstream. Hormones regulate many biological processes, including growth and metabolism.

horn (hôrn) **1.** Either of the bony growths projecting from the upper part of the head of cattle and related mammals, such as sheep, goats, and antelopes. The horns of these animals are never shed, and they consist of bone covered by a hard substance made of the protein keratin. This outer covering itself is also called horn. *See Note at* **keratin. 2.** A hard growth on the head of certain other animals, such as a giraffe or rhinoceros. These horns have a different structure.

hornblende (hôrn′blĕnd′) A common, green to black mineral found in many metamorphic and igneous rocks. It is composed of iron, calcium, magnesium, and other metals.

Grace Murray Hopper

Did You Know...?

hormones

On the inside, humans are bathing in a sea of *hormones,* chemical compounds that regulate many essential activities in the body. *Endocrine glands,* such as the thyroid and pituitary glands, produce many hormones, which are carried by the bloodstream to their target sites of action. The variety of different functions hormones have is astounding. Insulin, secreted by the pancreas, regulates sugar absorption. Estrogen and testosterone control sexual development. Some hormones limit the secretions of other hormones. If your body produces too much or too little of a hormone, you can become sick. People whose thyroids produce too much thyroxine, for example, can suffer from weight loss and high blood pressure. Too little insulin causes diabetes. Some of these medical conditions can be treated by synthetic hormones.

horology (hô-rŏl′ə-jē) The science of measuring time.

horse (hôrs) A large hoofed mammal having a short-haired coat, a long mane, and a long tail. Horses have been domesticated for riding and for pulling or carrying loads since ancient times. ❖ Most horses called "wild horses" are domesticated horses that have escaped captivity and become feral. The only true **wild horse** species that still exists is found in Mongolia.

horse latitudes Either of two regions of the globe found over the oceans about 30 degrees north and south of the equator. Because winds are generally light and unsteady in the horse latitudes, sailing ships were often caught in them for days without enough wind to move.

horsepower (hôrs′pou′ər) A unit used to measure the power of engines and motors. One unit of horsepower is equal to the power needed to lift 550 pounds one foot in one second. This unit has been widely replaced by the *watt* in scientific usage.

horseshoe crab (hôrs′sho͞o′) Any of various marine arthropods that have a large rounded shell, a stiff pointed tail, and several pairs of eyes, including a pair of compound eyes on the sides of the shell. Horseshoe crabs are more closely related to spiders than they are to crustaceans like lobsters, shrimp, and the typical crabs found at the seashore.

horticulture (hôr′tĭ-kŭl′chər) The science of raising and tending fruits, vegetables, flowers, or ornamental plants.

host (hōst) **1.** An organism or cell that another organism lives or feeds on or that is infected by a virus. For example, a cat with fleas is the host for those fleas, which feed on the cat's blood. **2.** A computer that holds data or programs that another computer can access by network or modem.

hot spot (hŏt) A volcanic area, usually about 60 to 120 miles (100 to 200 kilometers) across, believed to lie above a rising plume of hot magma within the Earth. The Hawaiian Islands may have formed as a tectonic plate moved slowly over a hot spot; the islands at the northwest end of the chain are millions of years older than those at the southeast end. *See more at* **tectonic boundary.**

hot spring A spring of water heated by passing through underground rocks deep in the Earth or shallower rocks close to a body of magma. Hot springs usually have a temperature greater than that of the human body.

HPV Abbreviation of **human papillomavirus.**

Hs The symbol for **hassium.**

Hubble (hŭb′əl), **Edwin Powell** 1889–1953. American astronomer. He demonstrated that there are galaxies beyond our own, that they are receding from ours, and that the velocity with which they are receding increases the farther away they are. This observation bolstered the theory that the universe is expanding. Hubble also established the first measurements for the age and radius of the known universe. *See Note at* **Doppler effect.**

hue (hyo͞o) The property of colors by which they are seen as ranging from red through yellow, green, and blue, as determined by the dominant wavelengths of the light being reflected, transmitted, or emitted. *See more at* **color.**

hull (hŭl) **1.** The dry outer covering of a fruit, seed, or nut; a husk. **2.** The enlarged calyx of a fruit, such as a strawberry, that is usually green and easily detached.

human (hyo͞o′mən) **1.** A human being; a member of the primate species *Homo sapiens*, distinguished from other apes by a large brain and the ability to speak. **2.** A member of any of the extinct species of the genus *Homo*, such as *Homo erectus* or *Homo habilis*, that are considered ancestral or closely related to modern humans.

human immunodeficiency virus *See* **HIV.**

human papillomavirus (păp′ə-lō′mə-vī′rəs) Any of various viruses that can cause genital warts and several types of cancer, especially cervical cancer.

Humboldt (hŭm′bōlt′), Baron **(Friedrich Heinrich) Alexander von** 1769–1859. German naturalist and writer. He undertook scientific expeditions in South America, Asia, and Europe and published works recording his observations. Humboldt made important contributions to the study of volcanoes, mountain ranges, ocean currents, and the relation of climate to plant growth.

humerus (hyo͞o′mər-əs) The bone of the upper arm in humans, or the corresponding bone in other vertebrates. *See more at* **skeleton.**

humidity (hyo͞o-mĭd′ĭ-tē) *See* **absolute humidity, relative humidity.**

humor (hyo͞o′mər) Any of the four fluids of the body—blood, phlegm, black bile, and yellow

WORD HISTORY

humor

Doctors in ancient times and in the Middle Ages thought the human body contained a mixture of four substances, called humors, that determined a person's health and character. The humors were fluids (*humor* means "fluid" in Latin), namely blood, phlegm, black bile, and yellow bile. Illnesses were thought to be caused by an imbalance in the humors, as were defects in personality. Too much black bile, for example, was thought to make one gloomy, and too much yellow bile was thought to make one short-tempered. Modern English has words referring to these moods that come from the Greek words for the relevant humors. We call a gloomy person *melancholic,* from the Greek term for "black bile," and we call a short-tempered person *choleric,* from the Greek word for "yellow bile." Our word *humorous,* in fact, once meant "having changeable moods due to the influence of different humors."

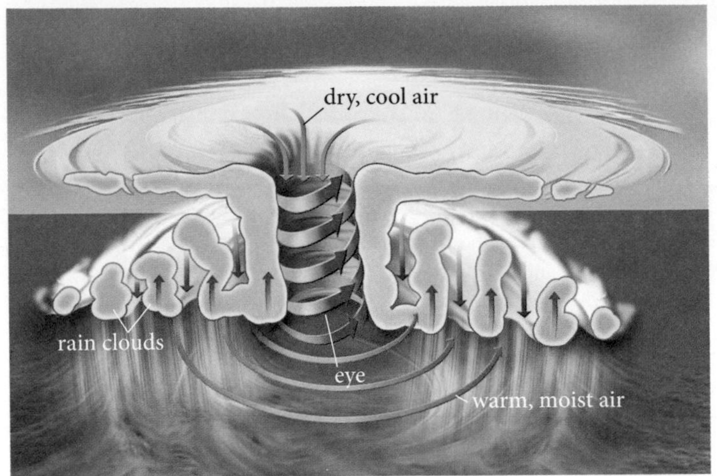

hurricane
In a hurricane, warm, moist air rotates as it rises around a column of cool, dry air, creating powerful winds.

bile—whose relative proportions were thought in ancient and medieval medicine to determine general health and character.

humus (hyo͞o′məs) A dark-brown or black organic substance made up of decayed plant or animal matter. Humus provides nutrients for plants and increases the ability of soil to retain water.

hurricane (hûr′ĭ-kān′) A severe, rotating tropical storm with heavy rains and cyclonic winds exceeding 74 miles (119 kilometers) per hour. Hurricanes originate in the tropical parts of the Atlantic Ocean, the Gulf of Mexico, or the northeastern Pacific Ocean and move generally northward. They lose force when they move over land or colder ocean waters. *See Note at* **cyclone.**

husk (hŭsk) The dry outer covering of certain seeds or fruits, as of an ear of corn or a nut.

Hutton (hŭt′n), **James** 1726–1797. British geologist whose theories of rock and land formation laid the foundation for modern geology. By observing the erosion of soil and the deposition of sediments and by analyzing structures in outcrops, Hutton concluded that the Earth was extremely old and that the geologic processes that created its landforms are still going on.

Huygens (hī′gənz, hoi′gĕns), **Christiaan** 1629–1695. Dutch physicist and astronomer. In 1655 he discovered Saturn's rings and its largest satellite, Titan, using a telescope he made himself. He built the first pendulum clock in 1657. Huygens also proposed that light consists of waves, a theory that contradicted Newton's proposal that light consists of particles.

hybrid (hī′brĭd) An organism that is the result of the mating of individuals of different species or varieties. A mule, which is the offspring of a male donkey and a female horse, is an example

BIOGRAPHY

James Hutton

As a gentleman farmer in late 18th-century Scotland, James Hutton noticed that farmers' soil is carried away, ultimately to the oceans, by wind and rain. Hutton was a religious man, and he reasoned that a God who was benevolent would have arranged for this lost soil to be replaced somehow. He theorized that soil must be replaced when older rocks are pushed upward, forming new mountains, which are then eroded by the weather into soil. Hutton proposed heat as the source of this mountain-building: as it built up inside the Earth, it forced rocks to move upward and created newer rocks from lava. He called this process Plutonism, in honor of Pluto, the Roman god of the underworld. Because the cycle of uplift and erosion had to take a very long time, Hutton concluded the Earth must be very old. It was not until the 20th century that geologists confirmed Hutton's conjecture, using radiometric dating to demonstrate that the Earth is in fact over four billion years old.

of a hybrid. Hybrid animals are usually unable to reproduce.

hydra (hī′drə) Any of several small freshwater animals having a tubular body and a mouth opening surrounded by stinging tentacles. Hydras reproduce by budding or by sexual reproduction. They are cnidarians, like jellyfish and corals.

hydrate (hī′drāt′) A compound that contains water or that is produced by the reaction of a substance with water. Many minerals and crystalline substances are hydrates that contain water molecules as part of their structure.

hydraulic (hī-drô′lĭk) **1.** Operated by or involving the pressure of water or other liquids in motion, especially when forced through an opening: *a hydraulic brake; a hydraulic jack.* **2.** Relating to hydraulics.

hydraulic fracturing The process of extracting oil or natural gas from deep underground rock formations by drilling a well and injecting a mixture of water, sand, and chemical additives under high enough pressure to create fractures in the rock. The oil or gas escapes through the fractures, which are held open by the sand. Also called *fracking.*

hydraulics (hī-drô′lĭks) The scientific study and engineering applications of liquids, such as water, and the forces and pressures associated with them.

hydride (hī′drīd′) An anion of hydrogen or a compound containing this anion, such as lithium hydride.

hydro– **1.** A prefix that means "water," as in *hydroelectric.* **2.** A prefix that means "hydrogen," as in *hydrocarbon.*

hydrocarbon (hī′drə-kär′bən) Any of numerous organic compounds, such as propane and benzene, that contain only carbon and hydrogen.

hydrochloric acid (hī′drə-klôr′ĭk) A solution of hydrogen chloride in water. It is a very strong, poisonous, and corrosive acid with a sharp odor and is used in food processing, metal cleaning, and dyeing. Small amounts of hydrochloric acid are also secreted by the stomachs of animals for digestion.

hydrochloride (hī′drə-klôr′īd′) A salt resulting from the combination of hydrogen chloride with an amine or other organic base.

hydrodynamics (hī′drō-dī-năm′ĭks) The scientific study of the mechanical properties of fluids in motion.

hydroelectric (hī′drō-ĭ-lĕk′trĭk) Generating electricity through the use of the energy of running water: *a hydroelectric power station.*

hydrogen (hī′drə-jən) A colorless, odorless, highly flammable gaseous element that is the lightest and most abundant element in the

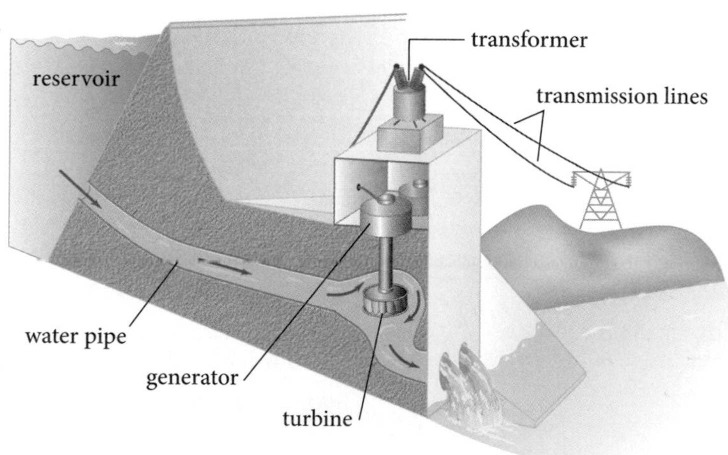

hydroelectric

Hydroelectric power uses the force of moving water to turn turbines. The turbines drive generators that convert the mechanical energy of moving water to electrical energy. Electricity is then changed by a transformer to the appropriate voltage and sent along transmission lines to consumers.

universe. It occurs in water in combination with oxygen, in most organic compounds, and in small amounts in the atmosphere as a gaseous mixture of its three isotopes (protium, deuterium, and tritium). In the sun and other stars, the conversion of hydrogen into helium by nuclear fusion produces heat and light. Hydrogen is used to make rocket fuel, synthetic ammonia, and methanol, to hydrogenate fats and oils, and to refine petroleum. *Symbol* **H.** *Atomic number* 1. *See* **Periodic Table,** pages 254–255.

hydrogenate (hī′drə-jə-nāt′, hī-drŏj′ə-nāt′) To treat or combine chemically with hydrogen. Liquid unsaturated vegetable oils are often hydrogenated to turn them into saturated solids.

hydrogen bomb An extremely destructive weapon that derives its explosive energy from the fusion of hydrogen nuclei to form helium nuclei. A hydrogen bomb has two main stages. First, a fission explosion like that of an atomic bomb occurs, heating and compressing the hydrogen fuel. Then, the hydrogen nuclei undergo fusion. Hydrogen bombs are much more powerful than atomic bombs.

hydrogen bond A chemical bond in which a hydrogen atom that is already bonded to an atom in a molecule forms a second bond with another atom, either in the same molecule or in a different one. The atoms that bond with the hydrogen atom are ones that strongly attract electrons, such as nitrogen or oxygen atoms.

hydrogen chloride A colorless, corrosive, suffocating gas, HCl, used in making plastics and in many industrial processes. When mixed with water, it forms hydrochloric acid.

hydrogen cyanide A colorless, flammable, extremely poisonous liquid, HCN, that vaporizes at or near room temperature. It is used to make dyes, poisons, and plastics. A solution of hydrogen cyanide in water forms a colorless acid that has a strong, irritating odor.

hydrogen peroxide A colorless, dense liquid, H_2O_2, that is often used as a bleach or is diluted with water for use as an antiseptic.

hydrogen sulfide A colorless, poisonous gas, H_2S, that smells like rotten eggs. It is formed naturally by decaying organic matter and is found in volcanic gases. It has many industrial uses.

hydrology (hī-drŏl′ə-jē) The scientific study of the properties, distribution, and effects of water on the Earth's surface, in the soil and underlying rocks, and in the atmosphere.

■ **hydroponics**

hydrolysis (hī-drŏl′ĭ-sĭs) The splitting of a chemical compound into two or more new compounds by reacting with water. Hydrolysis plays a role in the breakdown of food in the body, as in the conversion of starch to glucose.

hydrometer (hī-drŏm′ĭ-tər) An instrument used to measure the density of a liquid as compared with that of water. Hydrometers consist of a calibrated glass tube ending in a weighted glass bulb that makes the tube stand upright when placed in a sample of liquid. The lower the density of the liquid, the deeper the tube sinks.

hydrophyte (hī′drə-fīt′) A plant that grows wholly or partly submerged in water. Water lilies and cattails are hydrophytes.

hydroponics (hī′drə-pŏn′ĭks) The growing of plants in water supplied with nutrients rather than in soil. —*Adjective* **hydroponic** (hy′dropon′ic).

hydrosphere (hī′drə-sfîr′) All of the Earth's water, including surface water (water in oceans, lakes, and rivers), groundwater (water beneath the Earth's surface), ice, and water vapor in the atmosphere. *Compare* **asthenosphere, atmosphere, lithosphere.**

hydrostatics (hī′drə-stăt′ĭks) The scientific study of the mechanical properties of fluids at rest.

hydrothermal (hī′drə-thûr′məl) Relating to hot water, especially water heated by the Earth's internal heat. ❖ Hot springs on the ocean floor, called **hydrothermal vents,** support communities of organisms that derive their energy not from sunlight but from chemicals dissolved in the hot water that comes out of the springs.

■ **hyena**

hydrous (hī′drəs) *Chemistry* Containing water: *a hydrous salt.*

hydroxide (hī-drŏk′sīd′) The anion of the hydroxyl group or a compound containing this anion, such as potassium hydroxide. Metal hydroxides are bases and nonmetal hydroxides are acids.

hydroxyl (hī-drŏk′sĭl) The chemical group OH. It has a valence of 1 and is the characteristic group present in alcohols.

hyena (hī-ē′nə) Any of several meat-eating mammals of Asia and Africa having coarse, sometimes spotted or striped hair. Hyenas have powerful jaws used for stripping flesh from dead animals and a piercing cry resembling a laugh.

hygrometer (hī-grŏm′ĭ-tər) An instrument that measures the humidity of the air.

hymenopteran (hī′mə-nŏp′tər-ən) Any of numerous insects, including the bees, wasps, and ants, that characteristically have two pairs of membranous wings and that often live in complex social groups.

Hypatia (hī-pā′shə) AD 370?–415. Greek philosopher, mathematician, and astronomer whose writings on mathematics and astronomy were used as textbooks. She also invented instruments used to view the stars.

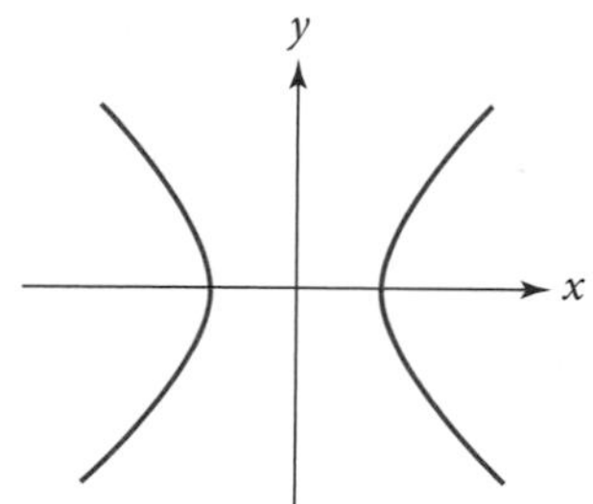

■ **hyperbola**
The equation for this hyperbola is $x^2 - y^2 = 1$.

hyper– A prefix that means "excessively," as in *hypertension,* excessively high blood pressure.

hyperactivity (hī′pər-ăk-tĭv′ĭ-tē) **1.** A condition of greater than normal activity. **2.** An abnormally high level of activity or excitement shown by a person, especially a child, that interferes with the ability to concentrate or interact with others.

hyperbola (hī-pûr′bə-lə) A plane curve having two separate parts or branches, formed when two cones that point toward one another are intersected by a plane that is parallel to the axes of the cones.

hyperopia (hī′pə-rō′pē-ə) *See* **farsightedness.**

hypertension (hī′pər-tĕn′shən) *See* **high blood pressure.**

hypertext (hī′pər-tĕkst′) A computer-based text retrieval system that enables a user to access particular locations in webpages or other electronic documents by clicking on links within specific webpages or documents.

hypha (hī′fə) *Plural* **hyphae** (hī′fē) One of the long slender filaments that form the structural parts of the body of a fungus. Masses of hyphae make up the mycelium.

hypnosis (hĭp-nō′sĭs) A trancelike state resembling sleep in which a person becomes very responsive to suggestions from another. Hypnosis is brought on by having one fix one's attention on a particular object, and it can be self-induced through concentration and relaxation.

hypo– or **hyp–** A prefix that means "beneath" or "below," as in *hypodermic,* below the skin. It also means "less than normal," as in *hypoglycemia,* a lower-than-normal level of sugar in the blood.

hypochondria (hī′pə-kŏn′drē-ə) A condition in which a person often believes that he or she is ill without actually being ill, or worries so much about becoming ill that it affects his or her life. ❖ A person with hypochondria is called a **hypochondriac.**

hypodermic needle (hī′pə-dûr′mĭk) A hollow needle used in medical syringes to inject a fluid beneath the skin.

hypoglycemia (hī′pō-glī-sē′mē-ə) An abnormally low level of sugar in the blood, usually caused by too much insulin and resulting in weakness and dizziness.

hypotenuse (hī-pŏt′n-o͞os′) The side of a right triangle opposite the right angle. It is the longest side, and the square of its length is equal to the sum of the squares of the lengths of the other two sides.

hypothalamus (hī′pō-thăl′ə-məs) The part of the brain in vertebrate animals that lies below the thalamus. It regulates many biological processes, including body temperature, thirst, hunger, and sleeping. The hypothalamus releases hormones that control the pituitary gland.

hypothermia (hī′pə-thûr′mē-ə) Abnormally low body temperature, often caused by prolonged exposure to cold.

hypothesis (hī-pŏth′ĭ-sĭs) *Plural* **hypotheses** (hī-pŏth′ĭ-sēz′) A statement that appears to explain a set of facts and that can become the basis for scientific testing. The results of the tests may support the hypothesis, or they may cause it to be modified or rejected.

hypothesize (hī-pŏth′ĭ-sīz′) To form a hypothesis.

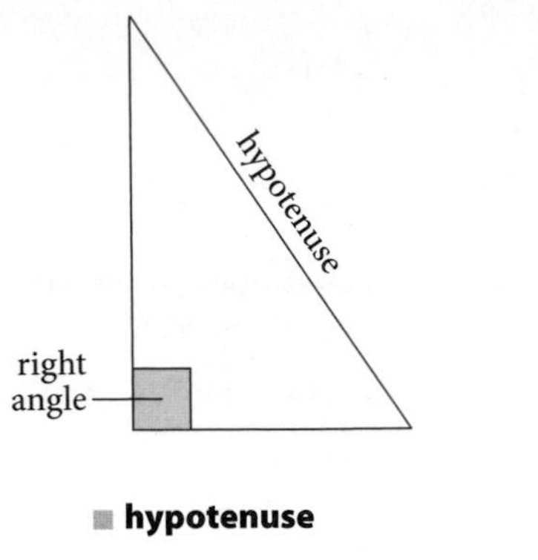

hypotenuse

hypothetical (hī′pə-thĕt′ĭ-kəl) Relating to or based on a hypothesis: *a hypothetical elementary particle that has not yet been observed.*

hyracotherium (hī′rə-kō-thîr′ē-əm) *Plural* **hyracotheria** A small horse that lived about 50 million years ago during the early Eocene Epoch. It had a short neck and three or four hoofed toes on each foot. It is sometimes called the "dawn horse," a translation of its earlier scientific name, *Eohippus.*

Hz Abbreviation of **hertz.**

I

i (ī) **1.** The square root of −1. Numbers expressed in terms of *i* are called imaginary or complex numbers. **2.** The symbol for **electric current.**

I The symbol for **iodine.**

Ibn al-Haytham (ĭb′ən ĕl-hī′thəm), **Abu Ali al-Hasan** Also known as **Alhazen** (ăl-hăz′ən) 965?–1040? Arab mathematician who is best known for his book on optics, which became very influential in Europe after it was translated in the 12th century. It contained a detailed description of the eye and disproved the older Greek idea that vision is the result of the eye sending out rays to the object being looked at.

Ibn Sina (ĭb′ən sē′nä), **Abu Ali al-Husain** Also known as **Avicenna** (ăv′ĭ-sĕn′ə) 980–1037. Persian physician and philosopher whose medical textbook, *Canon of Medicine,* greatly influenced European medical studies in the Middle Ages.

BIOGRAPHY

Ibn Sina

One of the most influential physicians and philosophers of the early Middle Ages was Abu Ali al-Husain Ibn Sina, often known in the West by his Latinized name Avicenna. Ibn Sina was born in 980 near the Central Asian town of Bukhara (now in Uzbekistan). Bukhara was a hub of commerce and a major center of Islamic learning. Ibn Sina began serious study of religious and medical texts at a young age. After becoming a physician he moved several times, finally settling in Isfahan (now in Iran). He wrote dozens of books, mostly in Arabic, on philosophy, mathematics, physics, astronomy, and medicine. One of the most famous is a medical textbook known in English as the *Canon of Medicine,* which combined a survey of all medical and pharmacological knowledge of the time with his own original observations. Ibn Sina's medical and philosophical works were translated into Latin and widely studied in Europe from the 1200s through the 1600s.

ibuprofen (ī′byo͞o-prō′fən) A medicine used to reduce fever, pain, or inflammation.

ice (īs) Water frozen solid, normally at or below a temperature of 32°F (0°C).

ice age 1. Any of several cold periods during which glaciers covered much of the Earth. **2. Ice Age.** The most recent glacial period, which occurred during the Pleistocene Epoch and ended about 12,000 years ago. During the Pleistocene Ice Age, great sheets of ice up to two miles thick covered most of Greenland, Canada, and the northern United States as well as northern Europe and Russia.

iceberg (īs′bûrg′) A massive body of floating ice that has broken away from a glacier. Most of an iceberg lies underwater, but because ice is not quite as dense as water, about one-ninth of it remains above the surface.

icecap (īs′kăp′) **1.** A glacier spreading out from a raised center and covering an area smaller than an ice sheet. **2.** A polar cap.

ice sheet A glacier spreading out from a center and covering a very large area, sometimes to such a depth that the continental crust is pushed below sea level. The only remaining ice sheets are in Greenland and Antarctica, but ice sheets also covered much of North America and Eurasia during the ice ages.

ichthyology (ĭk′thē-ŏl′ə-jē) The scientific study of fish.

ichthyosaur (ĭk′thē-ə-sôr′) Any of various extinct marine reptiles of the Mesozoic Era having a long toothed snout, four flippers, a dolphinlike body, and a large tail fin.

–ide A suffix used to form the names of various chemical compounds, especially the second part of the name of a compound that has two members (such as sodium *chloride*) or the name of a general type of compound (such as *polysaccharide*).

ideal gas (ī-dē′əl) A gas in which there is no interaction between the individual molecules. Such a gas would obey the gas laws (such as Charles's law) exactly. No known gas qualifies as an ideal gas.

igneous (ĭg′nē-əs) Relating to rocks formed by the cooling and hardening of magma or molten lava. Basalt and granite are examples of igneous rocks. *See Table at* **rock.**

iguana (ĭ-gwä′nə) Any of various large plant-eating lizards that have a ridge of spines along the back and are found in the American tropics.

ileum (ĭl′ē-əm) The lower part of the small intestine, connecting the jejunum to the cecum of the large intestine.

ilium (ĭl′ē-əm) The uppermost of the three bones that fuse together to form each of the hipbones in many vertebrate animals. *See more at* **skeleton.**

imaginary number (ĭ-măj′ə-nĕr′ē) A type of complex number in which the multiple of *i* (the square root of −1) is not equal to zero. Examples of imaginary numbers include $4i$ and $2 - 3i$, but not $3 + 0i$ (which is just 3). *See more at* **complex number.**

imago (ĭ-mā′gō) An insect in its sexually mature adult stage after metamorphosis. *Compare* **larva, nymph, pupa.**

immiscible (ĭ-mĭs′ə-bəl) Incapable of being mixed or blended together. Immiscible liquids that are shaken together eventually separate into layers. Oil and water are immiscible.

immune response (ĭ-myo͞on′) A response of the body to a foreign substance, especially to a bacterium, virus, or fungus that can cause disease. The immune response works to destroy or inactivate these foreign substances and occurs in several stages, usually involving a nonspecific response followed by a specific response targeted to the particular invader. The components of the immune response include white blood cells, such as phagocytes and lymphocytes, and antibodies.

immune system The system in humans and other animals that provides immunity by protecting against disease-causing agents, such as bacteria, viruses, parasites, and fungi. The immune system is composed of the skin and mucous membranes, which provide an external barrier to infection, and the cells involved in the body's immune response, such as lymphocytes.

immunity (ĭ-myo͞o′nĭ-tē) Resistance of the body to infection by a disease-causing agent, such as a bacterium or virus. Immunity is provided by some elements that are present in the body from birth and others that are acquired after exposure to disease-causing pathogens. Immunity can also be induced artificially, especially by vaccination.

immunization (ĭm′yə-nĭ-zā′shən) **1.** The production of immunity to an infectious disease in an individual through inoculation or vaccination. **2.** A specific inoculation or vaccination. —*Verb* **immunize.**

immunodeficiency (ĭm′yə-nō-dĭ-fĭsh′ən-sē, ĭ-myo͞o′nō-dĭ-fĭsh′ən-sē) The inability to produce a normal immune response, usually as a result of a disease or inherited disorder.

immunoglobulin (ĭm′yə-nō-glŏb′yə-lĭn, ĭ-myo͞o′nō-glŏb′yə-lĭn) *See* **antibody.**

immunology (ĭm′yə-nŏl′ə-jē) The scientific study of the structure and function of the immune system.

impedance (ĭm-pēd′ns) A measure of the opposition to the flow of electric current in an alternating current circuit. Impedance is measured in ohms.

impermeable (ĭm-pûr′mē-ə-bəl) Relating to a material through which substances, such as liquids or gases, cannot pass: *an impermeable cell wall.*

impetigo (ĭm′pĭ-tī′gō) A contagious skin disease caused by bacteria, characterized by pimples with thick yellow crusts, often on the face. It most commonly affects children.

improper fraction (ĭm-prŏp′ər) A fraction in which the numerator is greater than or equal to the denominator, such as $\frac{3}{2}$. *Compare* **proper fraction.**

impulse (ĭm′pŭls′) **1.** A sudden flow of electric current in one direction, typically occurring as a single event rather than as a series of pulses. **2.** An electrical signal traveling along the axon of a nerve cell. Nerve impulses excite or inhibit activity in other nerve cells or in the tissues of the body, such as muscles and glands.

in. or **in** Abbreviation of **inch.**

In The symbol for **indium.**

inbreeding (ĭn′brē′dĭng) The breeding or mating of closely related individuals, especially over several generations. *Compare* **outbreeding.**

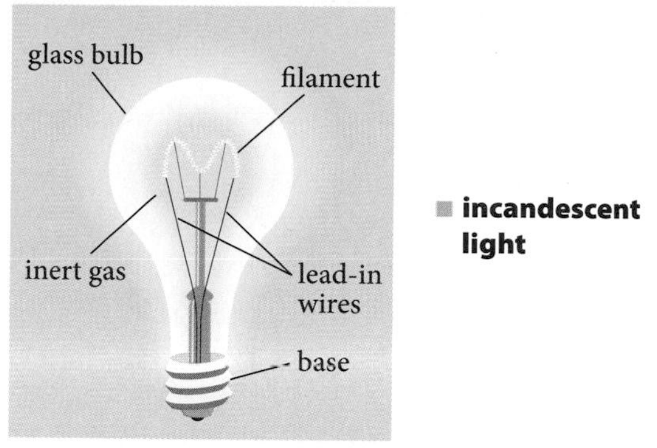

■ **incandescent light**

incandescence (ĭn′kən-dĕs**′**əns) The giving off of light by a substance when it is heated. *Compare* **luminescence.**

incandescent light (ĭn′kən-dĕs**′**ənt) A device that produces light by heating up a filament of wire inside a bulb with an electric current. Because the filament, usually made of tungsten, would burn from the heat, the bulb is filled with a nonreactive gas, such as argon, which prevents the wire from burning. *Compare* **fluorescent light.**

inch (ĭnch) A unit of length equal to $\frac{1}{12}$ of a foot (2.54 centimeters). *See Table at* **measurement.**

incisor (ĭn-sī**′**zər) A tooth usually having a sharp edge used for cutting or gnawing. In mammals, the incisors are located in the front of the mouth between the canine teeth.

inclined plane (ĭn**′**klīnd′) A plane surface, such as a ramp, set at an acute angle to a horizontal surface. An inclined plane is a simple machine because less force is needed to slide or roll a body up the plane than to raise the body vertically. Many tools are based on the principle of the inclined plane, such as the ax, screw, wedge, and chisel.

incomplete metamorphosis (ĭn′kəm-plēt**′**) *See under* **metamorphosis.**

incubate (ĭn**′**kyə-bāt′) **1.** To warm and hatch eggs by bodily heat; to brood. **2.** To keep eggs, cells, or other living tissue in conditions favorable for growth and development. **3.** To be infected with a pathogen, such as a bacterium or virus, before showing symptoms of an infectious disease. ❖ The **incubation period** of a disease is the amount of time that usually occurs between infection and the development of symptoms. ❖ An **incubator** is a device in which temperature and humidity can be controlled, used for growing or maintaining organisms or cells.

incus (ĭng**′**kəs) One of the three small bones, called ossicles, in the middle ear. The incus is also called the anvil.

independent variable (ĭn′dĭ-pĕn**′**dənt) *Mathematics* A variable whose value determines the value of other variables. For example, in the function $y = x - 4$, x is the independent variable because its value determines the value of y.

index of refraction (ĭn**′**dĕks′) The ratio of the speed of light in a vacuum to the speed of light in a particular medium, such as water or glass.

indicator (ĭn**′**dĭ-kā′tər) A substance that changes color when exposed to certain conditions and is therefore useful for chemical tests. Litmus, for example, becomes red in the presence of acids and blue in the presence of bases.

indicator species A species whose abundance in a given area is considered to be a sign of certain environmental or ecological conditions, such as the level of pollution.

indigenous (ĭn-dĭj**′**ə-nəs) **1.** Native to a particular place or region. The common dandelion, for example, is indigenous to Eurasia. **2.** Originally inhabiting a particular place or region. The Maya, for example, are indigenous people of Mexico and Central America.

indium (ĭn**′**dē-əm) A soft, easily shaped, silvery-white metallic element that occurs mainly in ores of zinc and lead. It is used in the manufacturing of semiconductors and bearings for aircraft engines and as a reflective coating that resists corrosion. *Symbol* **In.** *Atomic number* 49. *See* **Periodic Table,** pages 254–255.

indricotherium (ĭn′drə-kō-thîr**′**ē-əm) *Plural* **indricotheria** A very large, extinct land mammal of the Oligocene and Miocene Epochs, resembling a rhinoceros with a long neck. The largest animals stood 16 feet (4.9 meters) high at the shoulder and weighed 3 times as much as an elephant. The indricotherium is thought to be the largest land mammal that has ever lived.

inductance (ĭn-dŭk**′**təns) The property of an electric circuit by which voltage is produced because of a change in the current in a nearby circuit or in the circuit itself.

induction (ĭn-dŭk**′**shən) **1a.** The process of deriving general principles from particular

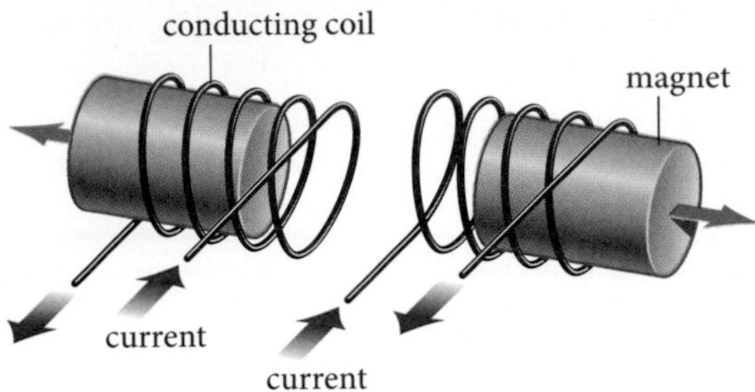

induction

When a magnet is passed through a coil of wire, it produces an electric current. The direction of the current depends on the direction in which the magnet moves. In the diagram on the left, the current flows from right to left. In the diagram on the right, the current flows from left to right.

facts or instances. **b.** A conclusion reached by this process. *See Note at* **deduction. 2a.** The generation of an electric current in a conductor, such as a copper wire, by exposing it to a changing magnetic field. The conductor can be moved through a magnetic field, or a magnetic field that is already affecting the conductor can be moved or varied. **b.** The building up of an electric charge on a conductive material by bringing a charged object near the material and then connecting the material to a ground. **3.** *See* **magnetic induction.**

induction coil A type of transformer that changes a low-voltage direct current to a high-voltage alternating current. Induction coils are used for many purposes, such as firing spark plugs in automobile engines and starting oil burners.

inert (ĭn-ûrt′) Not chemically reactive.

inert gas A gas that is not chemically reactive, especially a noble gas.

inertia (ĭ-nûr′shə) A property of matter by which a body at rest remains at rest, and a body in motion continues in motion at the same speed in the same direction, as long as no external force is applied to it. The mass of a body is a measure of its inertia.

infection (ĭn-fĕk′shən) The invasion of the body by microorganisms that can cause disease or by a virus. Microorganisms that can cause infection include bacteria, fungi, and protozoans.

infectious (ĭn-fĕk′shəs) Capable of causing infection: *an infectious disease.*

infertile (ĭn-fûr′tl) **1.** Not capable of producing offspring; unable to reproduce: *an infertile cow.* **2.** Not capable of developing into a complete organism; unfertilized: *infertile eggs.* **3.** Not capable of supporting plant life; unfavorable to the growth of crops or other plants: *infertile soil.* —*Noun* **infertility.**

infinity (ĭn-fĭn′ĭ-tē) A space, extent of time, or quantity that has no limit.

inflammation (ĭn′flə-mā′shən) The reaction of a part of the body to injury or infection, characterized by swelling, heat, and pain. Inflammation increases the amount of blood flow to the injured area, bringing in more white blood cells and often healing the damaged tissue.

inflorescence (ĭn′flə-rĕs′əns) A cluster of flowers arranged in a characteristic way on a stem.

influenza (ĭn′flo͞o-ĕn′zə) **1.** A contagious disease of humans that is caused by a virus and is characterized by fever, inflammation of the airways, and muscle pain. It often occurs in epidemics and can kill many thousands of people. **2.** Any of various contagious diseases of domestic or wild animals, such as pigs, chickens, and seals, caused by the

Did You Know...?

influenza

Why do people of all ages get vaccinated every year against *influenza,* commonly called the *flu,* when vaccines against most diseases are given only during childhood? Influenza is caused by a virus that was first isolated in the 1930s, after a worldwide epidemic killed over 20 million people between 1917 and 1919. The virus spreads quickly through the air and survives longer in cold weather, which is why flu outbreaks occur in the winter. There are three types and many different strains of the flu virus, and the virus's genes are constantly changing. Even if your body develops antibodies to a certain strain, those antibodies might not recognize a new strain. Every year scientists make vaccines from the newest strains of the virus, hoping to avert a dangerous flu outbreak.

Did You Know...?

infrared

Electromagnetic radiation in the infrared range is often called *infrared light,* even though it's invisible to humans. It was discovered in 1800 by the astronomer William Herschel when he was exploring the relationship between heat and light. Herschel used a prism to split a beam of sunlight into a spectrum of colors (red, orange, yellow, green, blue, indigo, and violet) and measured how hot a thermometer got when it was placed in each of the bands. When he placed the thermometer just beyond the red band, where there was no visible color, the temperature rose, just as if light were shining on the thermometer. Further experiments showed that this invisible radiation behaved like visible light in many ways; for example, it could be reflected by a mirror. Infrared radiation is simply electromagnetic radiation with longer wavelengths than visible light. Another kind of invisible light, ultraviolet light, is found just beyond the violet end of the spectrum and has shorter wavelengths than visible light.

same virus that causes human influenza. Some strains of the virus occur only in certain species, and others can be transmitted from one species to another.

information technology (ĭn′fər-mā′shən) The development, installation, and use of computer systems and applications.

infrared (ĭn′frə-rĕd′) Relating to electromagnetic radiation having wavelengths longer than those of visible light but shorter than those of microwaves. *See more at* **electromagnetic spectrum.**

infrasound (ĭn′frə-sound′) Sound waves that have frequencies lower than 20 hertz, which are too low for humans to hear.

inheritance (ĭn-hĕr′ĭ-təns) The process by which traits or characteristics pass from parents to offspring through the genes.

inner ear (ĭn′ər) The innermost part of the ear in most vertebrate animals, consisting of the cochlea and the semicircular canals. It transmits sound vibrations to the brain and is also the organ of balance. Also called *labyrinth. See more at* **ear.**

inoculation (ĭ-nŏk′yə-lā′shən) **1.** The production of immunity in an individual through injection with a vaccine. **2.** An injection of a specific vaccine. —*Verb* **inoculate.**

inorganic (ĭn′ôr-găn′ĭk) **1.** Not involving organisms or the products of their life processes. **2.** Relating to chemical compounds that occur mainly outside of living or once living organisms, such as those in rocks and minerals. Most inorganic compounds, such as salt (NaCl), lack carbon. A few, such as carbon dioxide (CO_2), do contain carbon, but they never contain carbon atoms attached to hydrogen atoms, as in hydrocarbons.

inorganic chemistry The branch of chemistry that deals with inorganic compounds.

input (ĭn′po͝ot′) *Noun* **1.** The energy, power, or work put into a system or device. **2.** The data or

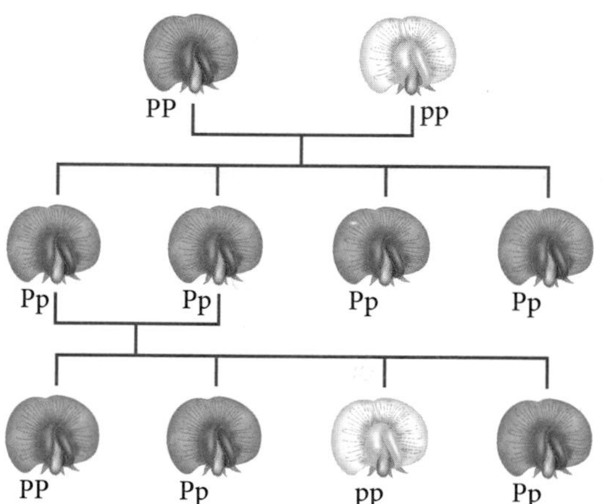

inheritance

The allele for pink pea flowers (P) *is dominant to the allele for white pea flowers* (p). *When plants with two dominant alleles are mated with plants with two recessive alleles* (top row), *all of the offspring in the first generation* (middle row) *will have one dominant and one recessive allele* (Pp). *Because dominant alleles suppress recessive alleles, all the flowers of the first-generation plants are pink. When first-generation plants are mated with each other, one-quarter of their offspring in the second generation* (bottom row) *will have two recessive alleles and will produce white flowers, half will have one dominant and one recessive allele and will produce pink flowers, and one-quarter will have two dominant alleles and will produce pink flowers.*

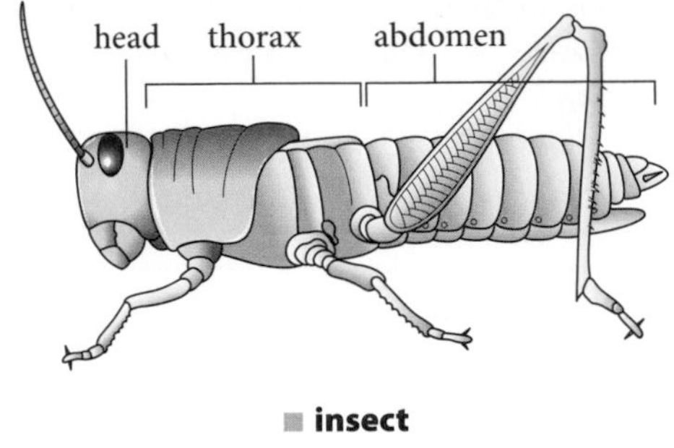

insect

programs put into a computer. —*Verb* **3.** To enter data or a program into a computer.

insect (ĭn′sĕkt′) Any of a large group of arthropods that in the adult stage have six legs and a body divided into three parts. The three parts are the head, thorax, and abdomen, and the thorax often has one or two pairs of wings. Flies, bees, grasshoppers, beetles, and butterflies are all insects. Over a million species are known, and scientists believe that millions more have yet to be described. *See Notes at* **beetle, bug, entomology.**

insecticide (ĭn-sĕk′tĭ-sīd′) A substance used to kill insects and certain other arthropods, such as spiders.

insectivore (ĭn-sĕk′tə-vôr′) An animal or plant that feeds mainly on insects. —*Adjective* **insectivorous.**

insoluble (ĭn-sŏl′yə-bəl) Not capable of being fully dissolved; not soluble.

instinct (ĭn′stĭngkt′) An inherited tendency of an organism to behave in a certain way. An instinct is usually characteristic of a species and does not have to be learned. Examples of behaviors based largely on instinct are nest-building in birds, web-spinning in spiders, and spawning in fish.

insulate (ĭn′sə-lāt′) To cover or surround with a material that prevents the loss or transfer of heat, electricity, or sound. —*Noun* **insulation.**

insulator (ĭn′sə-lā′tər) A material or an object that does not easily allow heat, electricity, or sound to pass through it. Air, cloth, and plastic are good electrical insulators; feathers and wool make good thermal insulators.

insulin (ĭn′sə-lĭn) **1.** A hormone produced in the pancreas that acts to regulate the amount of sugar in the blood by causing cells, especially liver and muscle cells, to absorb glucose from the bloodstream. If there is too little insulin or it is not working properly, the level of glucose in the blood becomes too high. **2.** A drug containing this hormone, obtained from the pancreas of animals or produced synthetically and used in treating diabetes.

integer (ĭn′tĭ-jər) A positive or negative whole number or zero. The numbers 4, –876, and 5,280 are all integers.

integral (ĭn′tĭ-grəl) **1.** Involving or expressed as an integer or integers. **2.** In calculus, the result of integration.

integrated circuit (ĭn′tĭ-grā′tĭd) A device made of interconnected electronic components that are etched or imprinted onto a tiny slice of a semiconducting material, such as silicon or germanium. An integrated circuit smaller than a fingernail can hold millions of circuits. Also called *chip.*

integration (ĭn′tĭ-grā′shən) In calculus, the inverse of differentiation. Integrating a given function results in a function whose derivative is the given function. Integration is used to compute such things as the areas and volumes of irregular shapes and solids. *Compare* **differentiation.**

integument (ĭn-tĕg′yo͝o-mənt) A natural outer covering of an animal or a plant, such as skin, a seed coat, or a shell.

inter– A prefix meaning "between" or "among," as in *interplanetary,* located between planets.

intercellular (ĭn′tər-sĕl′yə-lər) Located or occurring between or among cells: *intercellular fluid; intercellular communication.*

intercept (ĭn′tər-sĕpt′) In a Cartesian coordinate system, the coordinate of a point at which a line, curve, or surface intersects a coordinate axis. If

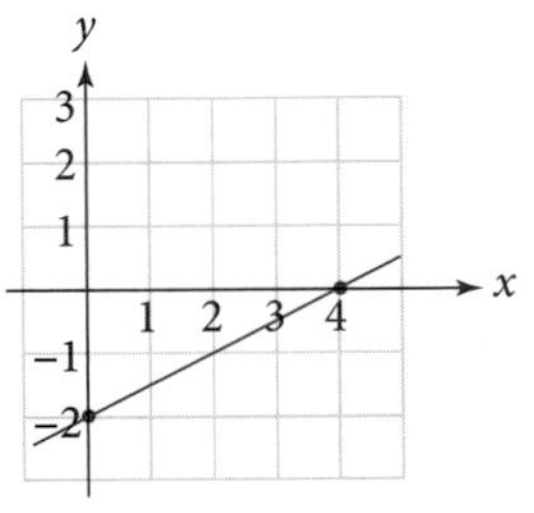

intercept

The x-intercept of this line is 4, and the y-intercept is –2.

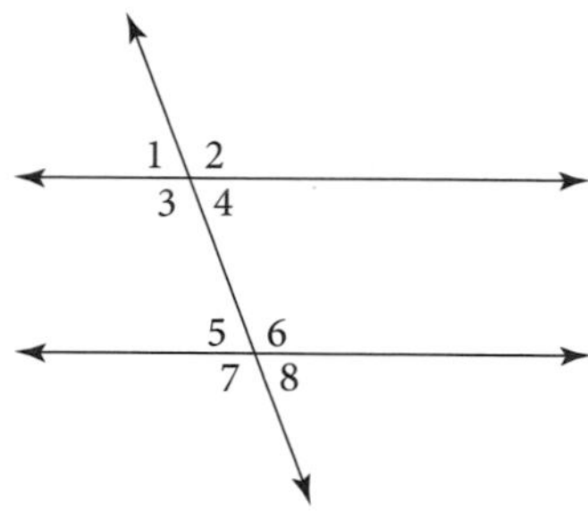

interior angle
Angles 3, 4, 5, and 6 are interior angles.

a curve intersects the x-axis at (4,0), then 4 is the curve's x-intercept; if the curve intersects the y-axis at (0,–2), then –2 is its y-intercept.

intercourse (ĭn′tər-kôrs′) *See* **sexual intercourse.**

interference (ĭn′tər-fîr′əns) **1.** The phenomenon that occurs when two or more waves come together. The amplitude of the resulting wave will be larger or smaller than the amplitudes of the individual waves, depending on whether or not the crests and troughs of the individual waves match up. ❖ If the crests and troughs of the waves match up, then the amplitude of the resulting wave will be larger than that of the individual waves. This is called **constructive interference.** ❖ If the crests and troughs of the waves do not match up, then the amplitude of the resulting wave will be smaller than that of the individual waves. This is called **destructive interference.** *See more at* **wave. 2.** In electronics, the distortion or disruption of one broadcast signal by others.

interferon (ĭn′tər-fîr′ŏn′) Any of a group of proteins that are produced by animal cells in response to infection by a virus and that, in many cases, prevent replication of the virus. Some interferons trigger an immune response in the body. Interferons produced in the laboratory are used as treatment for many diseases, including certain cancers.

interior angle (ĭn-tîr′ē-ər) **1.** Any of the four angles formed inside two straight lines when these lines are intersected by a third straight line. **2.** An angle formed by two adjacent sides of a polygon and included within the polygon. *Compare* **exterior angle.**

internal-combustion engine (ĭn-tûr′nəl-kəm-bŭs′chən) An engine whose fuel is burned inside the engine itself rather than in a separate furnace or burner. Gasoline and diesel engines are internal-combustion engines; a steam engine is not.

internal medicine The branch of medicine that deals with the diagnosis and nonsurgical treatment of diseases in adults.

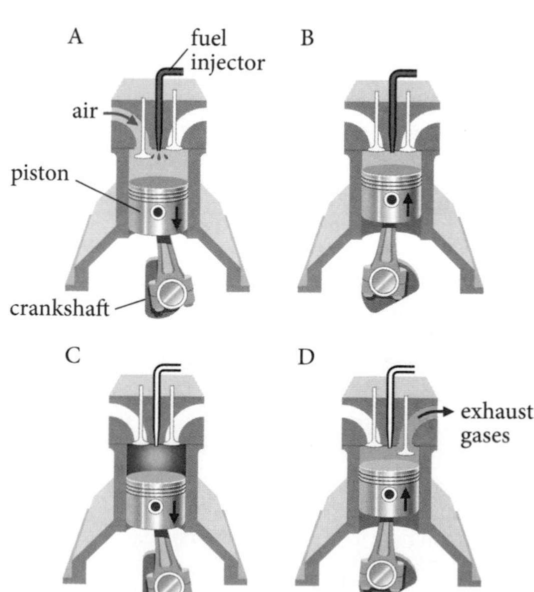

internal-combustion engine
one cycle of a four-stroke diesel engine
A. intake stroke: *the piston moves down, drawing air and fuel into the cylinder*
B. compression stroke: *the piston moves up, compressing and heating the air and fuel mixture*
C. power stroke: *the hot air and fuel mixture ignites, forcing the piston down*
D. exhaust stroke: *the piston moves up, forcing the exhaust gases out of the cylinder*

International Date Line (ĭn′tər-năsh′ə-nəl) An imaginary line through the Pacific Ocean roughly along the 180th meridian, agreed upon as the place where each new calendar day begins. The calendar day to the east of the line is one day earlier than it is to the west of the line.

International System of Units A decimal system of units used mainly in scientific work, in which the basic quantities are length, mass, time, electric current, temperature, amount of substance, and luminous intensity. The International System unit of length is the meter; the unit of mass is the kilogram. *See Table at* **measurement.**

international unit A unit for the measurement of a biologically active substance such as a vitamin. The amount in one unit of a substance is established by international agreement.

Internet (ĭn′tər-nĕt′) A system connecting computers around the world using a common software protocol for transmitting and receiving data. This protocol is known as TCP/IP, which stands for *Transmission Control Protocol/Internet Protocol.*

interphase (ĭn′tər-fāz′) The phase in the development of a cell between cell divisions, when the cell is carrying out its regular functions or preparing to divide.

intersection (ĭn′tər-sĕk′shən) **1.** *Geometry* The point or set of points where one line, surface, or solid crosses another. **2.** *Mathematics* The set that contains only those elements shared by two or more sets. The intersection of the sets {3,4,5,6} and {4,6,8,10} is the set {4,6}.

intervertebral disk or **intervertebral disc** (ĭn′tər-vûr′tə-brəl) A broad, flat pad of cartilage that separates adjacent vertebrae and acts as a shock absorber during movement.

intestine (ĭn-tĕs′tĭn) The part of the digestive tract that extends from the stomach to the anus, consisting of the small intestine and large intestine.

intra– A prefix meaning "inside" or "within," as in *intravenous,* within a vein.

intravenous (ĭn′trə-vē′nəs) Within or into a vein: *an intravenous injection.*

intrusion (ĭn-tro͞o′zhən) The movement of magma through underground rocks, usually in an upward direction. ❖ Rocks that formed from the underground cooling of magma are called **intrusive rocks.** *Compare* **extrusion.**

invasive (ĭn-vā′sĭv) **1.** Relating to a species that has a tendency to spread widely in a habitat or ecosystem. Invasive species are usually introduced from another region either intentionally or accidentally, and they sometimes cause serious ecological or agricultural harm. **2a.** Relating to a disease or condition that has a tendency to spread, especially a malignant cancer that spreads into healthy tissue. **b.** Relating to a medical procedure that involves entry into the body, as by a needle, scalpel, or tube.

inverse *Adjective* (ĭn-vûrs′) **1.** Relating to a mathematical operation whose nature or effect is the opposite of another operation. For example, addition and subtraction are inverse operations, as are multiplication and division. —*Noun* (ĭn′vûrs′) **2.** An inverse operation. Subtraction is the inverse of addition. **3.** Either of two numbers or quantities that cancel each other out under a given mathematical operation. For example, the inverse of 5 under multiplication is $\frac{1}{5}$, since 5 × $\frac{1}{5}$

Did You Know...?

Internet

Although the *Internet* is an immense global network that reaches billions of users, it began as a relatively simple computer network called ARPANET, funded by a Department of Defense research agency. ARPANET linked educational institutions and research facilities. Users could transfer files, send email, and post messages in a forum called USENET. Later, the development of HTTP (hypertext transfer protocol) allowed users to make connections from one electronic document to others by using hyperlinks. Such hyperlinked electronic documents (called *webpages*) can consist of text, pictures, and sound and video files. Over a billion of these webpages form the World Wide Web. The transmission of webpages, emails, files, and similar electronic data takes place on the massive network known as the Internet. What began as a simple way for military and educational researchers to communicate has developed into a new way of life.

= 1. The inverse of 5 under addition is −5, since 5 + −5 = 0.

inverse-square law A general principle in physics dealing with influences that spread out equally in all directions from a source. According to this principle, the influence weakens as the distance from the source increases. The strength of the influence at any given point is proportional to the reciprocal (or "inverse") of the square of the distance from the source. For example, compared to an observer one meter away from a source, an observer three meters away will experience only one-ninth ($\frac{1}{3^2}$) as strong an effect. Among the phenomena that obey inverse-square laws are sound waves; light and other forms of electromagnetic radiation; and electric, magnetic, and gravitational fields.

invertebrate (ĭn-vûr′tə-brĭt, ĭn-vûr′tə-brāt′) Any of numerous animals that do not have a spinal column (backbone). Sponges, octopuses, lobsters, snails, and insects are invertebrates.

in vitro (ĭn vē′trō) In an artificial environment, such as a test tube; not inside a living organism: *grow tissue in vitro. Compare* **in vivo.**

in vitro fertilization The production of an embryo or embryos by combining egg and sperm cells together outside the body.

in vivo (ĭn vē′vō) Inside a living organism rather than in an artificial environment: *test a new drug in vivo. Compare* **in vitro.**

involuntary (ĭn-vŏl′ən-tĕr′ē) Not under conscious control. Most of the biological processes in animals that are vital to life, such as contraction of the heart, blood flow, breathing, and digestion, are involuntary and are controlled by the autonomic nervous system.

iodide (ī′ə-dīd′) An anion of iodine or a compound containing this anion.

iodine (ī′ə-dīn′) A shiny, purple-black halogen element that is corrosive and poisonous. It occurs in very small amounts in nature but is abundant in seaweed. Iodine compounds are used in medicine, antiseptics, and dyes. *Symbol* **I.** *Atomic number* 53. *See* **Periodic Table,** pages 254–255.

ion (ī′ən, ī′ŏn′) An atom or a group of atoms that has an electric charge. Positive ions, or cations, are formed by the loss of electrons; negative ions, or anions, are formed by the gain of electrons. *See Note at* **charge.**

ionic bond (ī-ŏn′ĭk) A chemical bond formed between two ions with opposite charges. Ionic bonds can form between two individual atoms or between two groups of atoms and are the type of bond found in salts. See more at **bond, coordinate bond, covalent bond.**

ionize (ī′ə-nīz′) **1.** To add an electron to, or remove an electron from, an atom or group of atoms so as to give it an electric charge. **2.** To form ions in a substance. Lightning ionizes air, for example.

ionosphere (ī-ŏn′ə-sfîr′) A region of the Earth's atmosphere in which atoms are often ionized (electrically charged) by radiation from the sun. The ionosphere lies mostly in the lower thermosphere, from about 50 to 250 miles (80 to 400 kilometers) above the Earth. Radio waves, which normally travel in a straight line, can be transmitted long distances over the curved surface of the Earth because they bounce off certain layers of the ionosphere and return to Earth instead of continuing into space.

Ir The symbol for **iridium.**

iridium (ĭ-rĭd′ē-əm) A rare, whitish-yellow element that is the most corrosion-resistant metal known. It is very dense, hard, and brittle. Iridium is used to make hard alloys of platinum for jewelry, pen points, and electrical contacts. *Symbol* **Ir.** *Atomic number* 77. *See* **Periodic Table,** pages 254–255. *See Note on next page.*

iris (ī′rĭs) The colored part around the pupil of the eye in vertebrate animals, located between the cornea and lens. Contraction and expansion of the muscular iris controls the size of the pupil, thereby regulating the amount of light reaching the retina.

iron (ī′ərn) A silvery-white, hard, brittle metallic element that occurs abundantly in minerals such as hematite and magnetite. It can be magnetized and is used to make steel and other alloys important in construction and manufacturing. Iron is a component of hemoglobin, which allows red blood cells to carry oxygen and carbon dioxide through the body. *Symbol* **Fe.** *Atomic number* 26. *See* **Periodic Table,** pages 254–255. *See Note at* **element.**

irradiate (ĭ-rā′dē-āt′) To expose to radiation in order to cause a chemical or biological change. For example, meat sold as food is often irradiated with x-rays or gamma rays to kill bacteria.

irrational number (ĭ-răsh′ə-nəl) A number

Did You Know...?

iridium

In 1978 geologist Walter Alvarez found an unusually high concentration of the element *iridium* in a layer of clay. This layer formed at the time dinosaurs and many other organisms went extinct. The iridium deposits were a great surprise, since iridium is very rare at the Earth's surface. Most surface iridium is believed to come from outer space—from dust left over after meteors disintegrate in the atmosphere or smash into the Earth. Walter's father, the physicist Luis Alvarez, suggested that the iridium came from the impact of a meteor about 6 miles (10 kilometers) across. He argued that such an impact would have caused an enormous explosion, sending huge clouds of dust into the atmosphere. The dust, blocking out the sun and causing acid rain for years, would have caused a worldwide ecological disaster. Many scientists think that such a disaster caused the extinction of dinosaurs and at least 70 percent of all other species alive at the time, including most of the Earth's land plants. Geologists have since found iridium deposits in rocks of a similar date in over 100 places worldwide. In the early 1990s, a large impact crater of the same age as the iridium deposits was identified in the Yucatan peninsula of central Mexico. It is over 110 miles (180 kilometers) wide and may well have been caused by the impact hypothesized by Alvarez.

that cannot be expressed as a ratio between two integers and is not an imaginary number. If written in decimal notation, an irrational number would have an infinite number of digits to the right of the decimal point, without repetition. Pi and the square root of 2 ($\sqrt{2}$) are irrational numbers.

ischium (ĭs′kē-əm) The lowest or rearmost of the three bones that fuse together to form each of the hipbones in many vertebrate animals. *See more at* **skeleton.**

island arc (ī′lənd) A usually curved chain of volcanic islands occurring at a subduction zone. The chain occurs in the plate that rides over the subducting plate. It is curved because of the curvature of the Earth.

islets of Langerhans (ī′lĭts əv läng′ər-häns′) Irregular clusters of endocrine cells that are scattered throughout the tissue of the pancreas and secrete insulin.

iso– A prefix that means "equal," as in *isometric,* having equal measurements.

isobar (ī′sə-bär′) A line drawn on a weather map connecting places having the same atmospheric pressure.

isoleucine (ī′sə-lo͞o′sēn′) An essential amino acid. *See more at* **amino acid.**

isomer (ī′sə-mər) One of two or more compounds composed of the same chemical elements in the same proportions but having a different arrangement of atoms. Isomers differ from one another in at least one physical or chemical property. Lactose and sucrose are isomers.

isometric (ī′sə-mĕt′rĭk) *See* **cubic** (sense 3).

isosceles (ī-sŏs′ə-lēz′) Having at least two sides of equal length: *an isosceles triangle.*

isotherm (ī′sə-thûrm′) A line drawn on a map connecting places having the same temperature or the same average temperature.

isotope (ī′sə-tōp′) One of two or more atoms that have the same number of protons but a different number of neutrons. Carbon-12, the most common form of carbon, has six protons and six neutrons, whereas carbon-13 has six protons and seven neutrons.

isthmus (ĭs′məs) A narrow strip of land connecting two larger masses of land.

–ite 1. A suffix used to form the names of minerals, such as *hematite* and *malachite.* **2.** A suffix used to form the name of a salt, ester, or anion of an acid whose name ends in *-ous.* Such compounds or ions have one oxygen atom fewer than corresponding compounds or ions with names ending in *-ate.* For example, a nitrite is a salt of nitrous acid and contains the group NO_2, while a nitrate contains NO_3. *Compare* **–ate.**

–itis A suffix meaning "inflammation," as in *bronchitis,* inflammation of the bronchial tubes.

IU Abbreviation of **international unit.**

IVF Abbreviation of **in vitro fertilization.**

ivory (ī′və-rē) A hard, smooth, yellowish-white substance that forms the tusks of elephants or the tusks or teeth of certain other animals, such as hippopotamuses, walruses, and whales.

J

j Abbreviation of **joule.**

Jacob (zhä-kôb′), **François** 1920–2013. French geneticist who studied how genes control cellular activity by directing the synthesis of proteins. With Jacques Monod, he theorized that there are genes that regulate the activity of other, neighboring genes. They also proposed the existence of messenger RNA.

jade (jād) Either of two hard minerals that are typically green or white and are often used as gemstones. Jade usually forms within metamorphic rocks.

jasper (jăs′pər) A reddish, brown, or yellow variety of opaque quartz.

jaundice (jôn′dĭs) Yellowish discoloration of the whites of the eyes, mucous membranes, and often the skin. Jaundice occurs as a symptom of diseases like hepatitis that interfere with the normal processing of bile.

jaw (jô) **1.** Either of two structures made of bone or cartilage that in most vertebrate animals form the framework of the mouth, hold the teeth, and are used for biting and chewing food. The lower, movable part of the jaw is called the mandible. The upper, fixed part is called the maxilla. **2.** Any of various structures of invertebrate animals, such as the pincers of spiders or mites, that function similarly to the jaws of vertebrates.

jellyfish

The Pacific sea nettle, a common jellyfish, captures and paralyzes prey with its stinging tentacles.

Edward Jenner

jawless fish (jô′lĭs) A long thin fish that lacks a jaw and paired fins. Lampreys and hagfish are jawless fish. *Compare* **bony fish, cartilaginous fish.**

jejunum (jə-jo͞o′nəm) The middle part of the small intestine, connecting the duodenum and the ileum.

jellyfish (jĕl′ē-fĭsh′) Any of numerous invertebrate marine animals having a soft, often umbrella-shaped body with stinging tentacles around a central mouth. Jellyfish are cnidarians and are related to the hydras and corals. *See also* **medusa, polyp.**

Jenner (jĕn′ər), **Edward** 1749–1823. British physician who developed a vaccine for smallpox that involved injecting a person with a small amount of infected material from a cow with cowpox, a mild skin disease of cattle. People injected with cowpox would usually become immune to smallpox. Vaccination against smallpox was the first large-scale vaccination campaign. *See more at* **immunity, smallpox, vaccine.**

jet (jĕt) **1.** A rapid stream of liquid or gas forced through a small opening or nozzle under pressure: *A jet of water shot out of the hose.* **2.** An aircraft or other vehicle propelled by a jet engine. **3.** A jet engine.

jet engine An engine that develops thrust by

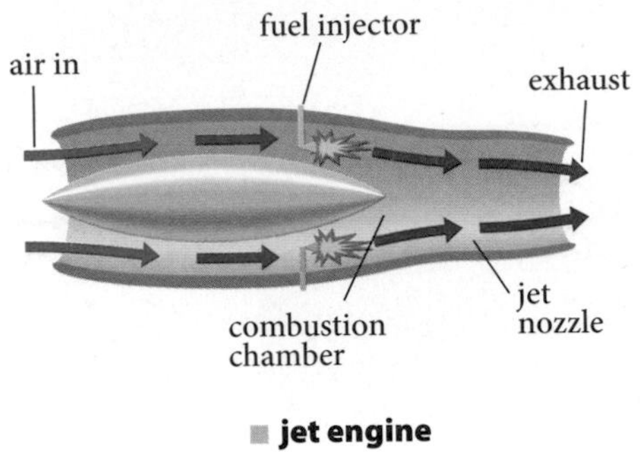

jet engine

ejecting a jet of hot gases from fuel burned in a combustion chamber. *See more at* **turbojet.**

jet propulsion 1. The driving of an aircraft by the powerful thrust developed when a jet of gas is forced out of a jet engine. **2.** Propulsion by means of any fluid that is forced out in a stream in the opposite direction. Squids, octopuses, and cuttlefish, for example, jet their way through the ocean by taking in and then quickly expelling water.

jet stream A narrow current of strong wind circling the Earth from west to east at altitudes of about 6 to 9 miles (10 to 15 kilometers) above sea level. There are usually four distinct jet streams, two each in the Northern and Southern Hemispheres.

joint (joint) **1.** A point in the skeleton of a vertebrate animal at which two bones are joined, usually connected by ligaments and other fibrous tissues and allowing motion. **2.** A point in the exoskeleton of an invertebrate at which movable parts join, as in an insect's leg.

Joliot-Curie (zhô-lyō′kyo͝or**′**ē), **Irène** 1897–1956. French physicist. With her husband, **Frédéric Joliot-Curie** (1900–1958), she made the first artificial radioactive isotope. They also contributed to the discovery of the neutron and the development of nuclear reactors.

joule (jo͞ol, joul) A unit used to measure energy or work. One joule is equal to the work done when a force of one newton acts over a distance of one meter.

Joule, James Prescott 1818–1889. British physicist. His work established the law of conservation of energy, stating that energy is never destroyed but may be converted from one form into another. The joule unit of energy is named for him.

jugular vein (jŭg**′**yə-lər) Any of several large veins in the neck that carry blood from the head into other veins that empty into the heart.

Julian (jo͞ol**′**yən), **Percy Lavon** 1899–1975. American chemist who developed an improved technique for synthesizing cortisone, a hormone used to treat arthritis and other forms of inflammation. He also developed a drug that is used to treat glaucoma and memory loss.

jumping gene (jŭm**′**pĭng) *See* **transposon.**

Jupiter (jo͞o**′**pĭ-tər) The fifth planet from the sun and the largest, with a diameter about 11 times that of Earth. It turns on its axis faster than any other planet in the solar system, taking less than ten hours to complete one rotation. *See Table at* **solar system,** pages 312–313.

Jurassic (jo͝o-răs**′**ĭk) The second and middle period of the Mesozoic Era, from about 200 to 146 million years ago, during which dinosaurs were the dominant form of land life and the earliest birds appeared. *See Chart at* **geologic time,** pages 146–147.

Just (jŭst), **Ernest Everett** 1883–1941. American biologist who investigated the processes of fertilization and embryonic development in animals.

juvenile (jo͞o**′**və-nīl′) An organism, especially an animal, that is not yet fully grown and mature.

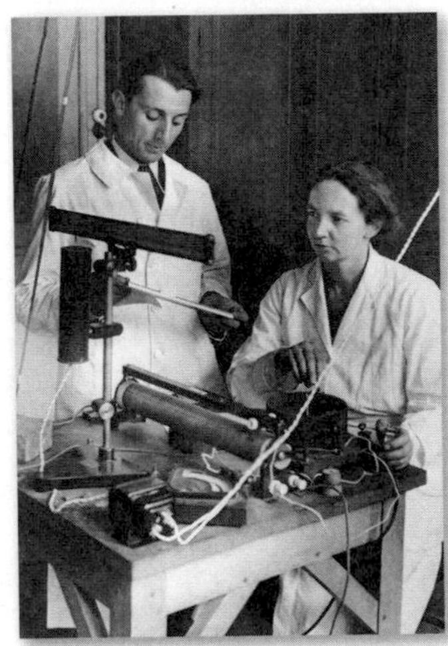

Irène and Frédéric Joliot-Curie

K 1. The symbol for **potassium. 2.** Abbreviation of **kelvin.**

kangaroo (kăng′gə-ro͞o′) Any of various plant-eating marsupials of Australia and nearby islands having short forelimbs, large hind limbs used for leaping, and a long tapered tail. A female kangaroo gives birth to a single offspring after a short gestation period of five to six weeks. The tiny newborn climbs into the mother's pouch, where it suckles and grows for several months.

kaolin (kā′ə-lĭn) A soft, fine, whitish sedimentary rock made of clay minerals, especially kaolinite. Kaolin forms from the weathering of other rocks that are rich in aluminum.

kaolinite (kā′ə-lĭ-nīt′) An aluminum-rich silicate mineral that is the main component of kaolin.

karyotype (kăr′ē-ə-tīp′) An organized visual profile of the chromosomes in the nucleus of a cell. Karyotypes are prepared using cells in the metaphase stage of cell division, when chromosomal strands have coiled together and duplicated, making them easily visible under a microscope after staining. The stained chromosomes are photographed, and the images are arranged in a standard format.

Kekulé von Stradonitz (kā′ko͞o-lā′ fôn shträ′dō-nĭts), **Friedrich August** 1829–1896. German chemist who was a founder of organic chemistry. His discovery of the structure of benzene was fundamental to understanding many other organic compounds.

■ **kangaroo**

■ **kelp**

kelp (kĕlp) Any of various brown or green seaweeds of ocean waters that can grow very long and are often found in large clusters. Kelp are algae, not plants.

kelvin (kĕl′vĭn) A unit of absolute temperature having the same value as one Celsius degree. It is used in the Kelvin scale. *See more at* **Celsius.** *See Table at* **measurement.**

Kelvin, First Baron. *Title of* **William Thomson.** 1824–1907. British mathematician and physicist known especially for his work on heat and electricity. In 1848 he proposed a scale of temperature independent of any physical substance, which became known as the Kelvin scale.

Kelvin scale A scale of temperature beginning at absolute zero (−273.15°C). Each degree, or kelvin, has the same value as one degree on the Celsius scale. On the Kelvin scale water freezes at 273.15 K and boils at 373.15 K. *See Note at* **Celsius.**

Kepler (kĕp′lər), **Johannes** 1571–1630. German astronomer and mathematician who was the first to accurately describe the elliptical orbits of Earth and the planets around the sun. He also demonstrated that planets move fastest when they are closest to the sun and that a planet's distance from the sun can be calculated if its period of revolution is known.

keratin (kĕr′ə-tĭn) Any of a group of tough, fi-

Did You Know...?

keratin

In the same way that a shed, a table, and a pencil can all be made of wood, varied structures in living things are often made of the same material. A good example is the group of closely related proteins collectively known as *keratin*. Most tough, hard structures of vertebrate animals are made of keratin. Your nails and hair are composed mostly of keratin, and so are a dog's claws, a bird's beak, a goat's horns, a turtle's shell, and the baleen that some whales have in their mouths. All proteins are strings of amino acids, and keratin is particularly rich in the amino acid cysteine. The sulfur atoms in one cysteine tend to form strong bonds with the sulfur atoms in other cysteines. Different kinds of keratin vary in hardness, depending on how many cysteine bonds are present. The bonds are what make the keratins tough as, well, nails.

brous proteins that are the main structural components of hair, nails, horns, feathers, and hooves.

kernel (kûr′nəl) **1.** A grain or seed, especially of a cereal plant such as corn or wheat, that is enclosed in a husk. **2.** The often edible seed inside the shell of a nut.

kerosene (kĕr′ə-sēn′) A thin, light-colored oil that is obtained from petroleum and used mainly as a fuel in lamps, home heaters and furnaces, and jet engines.

ketone (kē′tōn′) Any of a class of organic compounds, such as acetone, containing a CO group (a group consisting of a carbon and an oxygen atom) in which the carbon atom is attached to two hydrocarbon groups.

kettle (kĕt′l) A depression in the ground, often containing a pond or lake, formed by the melting of a chunk of ice that was left by a glacier and then partly or completely buried by deposited sediments.

kg Abbreviation of **kilogram.**

Khorana (kō-rä′nə), **Har Gobind** 1922–2011. Indian-born American biochemist. He was one of the first people to determine the sequence of nucleotides associated with each of the amino acids in the body, called the genetic code. He also developed one of the first artificial genes.

Khwarizmi (kwär′ĭz-mē), **al-** *Full name* **Muhammad ibn-Musa al-Khwarizmi.** 780?–850? Arab mathematician and astronomer. His work was widely translated into Latin, introducing Arabic numerals and algebraic concepts to Western mathematics. The word *algorithm* is derived from his name. *See Note at* **algebra.**

kidney (kĭd′nē) Either of a pair of organs that are located in the rear of the abdominal cavity of vertebrate animals and that regulate the amount of water in the body. They filter out wastes from the bloodstream and form urine, which travels from each kidney to the bladder through a muscular tube called the ureter.

killer whale (kĭl′ər) *See* **orca.**

kilo– **1.** A prefix that means "one thousand," as in *kilowatt,* one thousand watts. **2.** A prefix that means 2^{10} (that is, 1,024, which is the power of 2 closest to 1,000), as in *kilobyte,* 2^{10} bytes.

kilobit (kĭl′ə-bĭt′) *Computers* **1.** One thousand bits. **2.** 1,024 (2^{10}) bits. *See Note at* **megabyte.**

kilobyte (kĭl′ə-bīt′) **1.** A unit of computer memory or data storage capacity equal to 1,024 (that is, 2^{10}) bytes. **2.** One thousand bytes. *See Note at* **megabyte.**

kilocalorie (kĭl′ə-kăl′ə-rē) *See* **calorie** (sense 2a).

kilogram (kĭl′ə-grăm′) The basic unit of mass in

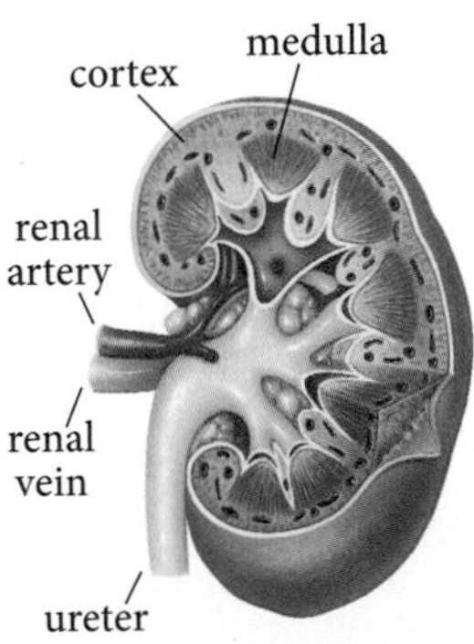

kidney

Blood that flows through a kidney is filtered to remove excess water and wastes, such as urea. The resulting liquid is urine, which travels through the ureter to the bladder, where it is stored until emptied by urination.

■ **kinetic energy**
A bowling ball has kinetic energy when it is moving. When it strikes the pins, some of that energy is passed on to the pins.

the metric system, equal to 1,000 grams (about 2.2 pounds). *See Table at* **measurement.** *See Note at* **weight.**

kilohertz (kĭl′ə-hûrts′) A unit of frequency equal to 1,000 cycles per second. It is used to express the frequency of radio waves.

kilometer (kĭ-lŏm′ĭ-tər, kĭl′ə-mē′tər) A unit of length in the metric system, equal to 1,000 meters (about 0.62 mile). *See Table at* **measurement.**

kilowatt (kĭl′ə-wŏt′) A unit of power equal to 1,000 watts.

kilowatt-hour A unit used to measure energy, especially electrical energy. One kilowatt-hour is equal to one kilowatt acting for a period of one hour.

kinematics (kĭn′ə-măt′ĭks) The branch of physics that deals with the motion of bodies without regard for the masses of the bodies or the forces affecting their motion. *Compare* **dynamics.**

kinetic energy (kə-nĕt′ĭk) The energy that an object possesses as a result of being in motion. The kinetic energy of an object depends on its mass, its velocity, and its rotational motion. *Compare* **potential energy.**

kingdom (kĭng′dəm) A broad classification into which organisms are grouped, ranking above a phylum and, in some systems, below a domain. One common system of classification divides life into five kingdoms: prokaryotes (bacteria and archaea), protists, fungi, plants, and animals. Other systems divide organisms into domains (bacteria, archaea, and eukaryotes) that replace or rank above kingdoms. *See Table at* **taxonomy.**

Klein bottle (klīn) A certain kind of smooth surface which has no inside or outside. It is often pictured in ordinary space as a tube that bends back upon itself, entering through the side and joining with the open end. A true Klein bottle, which cannot be constructed in ordinary three-dimensional space, would not actually intersect itself.

km Abbreviation of **kilometer.**

kneecap (nē′kăp′) *See* **patella.**

koala (kō-ä′lə) A tree-dwelling Australian marsupial having dense grayish fur, large ears, and sharp claws. Koalas feed almost exclusively on the leaves of eucalyptus trees.

Koch (kôk), **Robert** 1843–1910. German bacteriologist who developed techniques for growing bacteria in the laboratory and identified the bacteria that cause tuberculosis, cholera, and anthrax. He was one of the first scientists to propose that every specific infectious disease is caused by a specific microorganism.

Köhler (kŭ′lər), **Georges Jean Franz** 1946–1995. German scientist who investigated the immune system. With César Milstein he developed a method of producing antibodies that fight specific cells. The antibodies are used to diagnose and treat certain forms of cancer and other diseases.

Kovalevsky (kŏv′ə-lĕv′skē), **Sonya** 1850–1891. Russian mathematician. She made important contributions to calculus, and her mathematical description of the shape of Saturn's rings became a model for other scientists.

Kr The symbol for **krypton.**

Krebs (krĕbz), Sir **Hans Adolf** 1900–1981. German-born British biochemist who discovered the Krebs cycle in 1936.

Krebs cycle A series of chemical reactions that occur in most aerobic organisms and constitute the intermediate stage in cellular respiration, the process by which glucose and other molecules are broken down in the presence of oxygen to produce carbon dioxide, water, and energy in the form of ATP. Also called *citric acid cycle.*

krill (krĭl) Small crustaceans that are found in large numbers in the ocean. Krill resemble small shrimp and are usually less than 2 inches (5 centimeters) long. They are the principal food of certain whales and are also eaten by seals, fish, and other sea animals.

Stephanie Kwolek

krypton (krĭp′tŏn′) A colorless, odorless element that is a noble gas. It is used in certain fluorescent lamps and photographic flash lamps. *Symbol* **Kr.** *Atomic number* 36. *See* **Periodic Table,** pages 254–255.

Kuiper belt (kī′pər) A disk-shaped region in the solar system that is located beyond the orbit of the planet Neptune and contains thousands of small, icy celestial objects. This region is the source of comets that make one complete orbit of the sun in less than 200 years, and most of the orbit of the dwarf planet Pluto lies within it. *Compare* **Oort cloud.**

Kuiper belt object Any of the numerous small icy bodies orbiting the sun in the Kuiper belt. The dwarf planet Pluto is one of the largest Kuiper belt objects.

kwashiorkor (kwä′shē-ôr′kôr′) A disease, usually of children, caused by lack of protein in the diet and resulting in swelling of the limbs, enlargement of the liver, potbelly, reduced growth, and discoloration of the skin and hair.

Kwolek (kwŏl′ĕk′), **Stephanie** Born 1923. American chemist who developed the first liquid crystal polymer fiber, now used to make many products, including bulletproof vests.

L

l 1. Abbreviation of **length. 2.** or **L** Abbreviation of **liter.**

La The symbol for **lanthanum.**

laboratory (lăb′rə-tôr′ē) A room or building equipped for scientific research and for conducting experiments, especially under controlled conditions.

labyrinth (lăb′ə-rĭnth′) *See* **inner ear.**

lacrimal (lăk′rə-məl) Relating to or producing tears: *the lacrimal glands.*

lactase (lăk′tās′) An enzyme that catalyzes the breakdown of lactose into simpler sugars, such as glucose. It is found in the digestive tract of young mammals, where it functions to digest the lactose in milk. Lactase is not present in most adult humans except those of northern European ancestry.

lactation (lăk-tā′shən) The production and secretion of milk by the mammary glands, occurring in female mammals after they give birth.

lactic acid (lăk′tĭk) An organic acid produced when milk sours or various fruits ferment. It is used as a flavoring and preservative for foods. Lactic acid is also produced by muscle tissue during exercise, especially when oxygen supply is limited, and can cause cramping pains.

lactose (lăk′tōs′) A white crystalline sugar that is found in milk. It is used in infant formula and as an additive in various foods. ❖ The inability to properly digest lactose is called **lactose intolerance.** This condition is caused by a lack of the enzyme lactase and can cause stomach cramps and other symptoms.

lagoon
Bora Bora, French Polynesia

lahar
Mount St. Helens, Washington

lagoon (lə-go͞on′) **1.** A shallow body of salt water close to the sea but separated from it by a narrow strip of land, such as a barrier island, or by a coral reef. **2.** A shallow pond or lake close to a larger lake or river but separated from it by a barrier such as a levee.

Lagrange (lə-grānj′, lə-grănj′), Comte **Joseph Louis** 1736–1813. French mathematician and astronomer who made important contributions to algebra and calculus. His work on celestial mechanics extended scientific understanding of planetary and lunar motion.

lahar (lä′här′) A mudslide that moves rapidly down the side of a volcano and consists of ash and fragments of volcanic rock saturated with water. Lahars are usually caused by heavy rains, by the melting of snow or glacial ice in an eruption, or by the collapse of a crater wall which has a lake behind it.

lake (lāk) A large inland body of standing fresh or salt water.

lamina (lăm′ə-nə) **1.** *Botany* The expanded area of a leaf or petal; a blade. **2.** A thin layer of bone, membrane, or other tissue. **3.** *Geology* A thin layer of sediment.

laminar flow (lăm′ə-nər) Movement of a fluid

in which the motion of the particles of fluid is very orderly and all particles move along straight lines in the same direction. Laminar flow occurs especially in fluids that are moving slowly and have high viscosity. *Compare* **turbulent flow.**

lamprey (lăm′prē) Any of various fish having a long thin body, a jawless sucking mouth, and a skeleton made of cartilage. Lampreys attach to other fish and feed on their body fluids.

lancelet (lăns′lĭt) Any of various small, transparent, marine animals that have a long thin body and are usually found buried in sand. They have a structure similar to that of vertebrates, but with a notochord instead of a true spinal column. Also called *amphioxus.*

land bridge (lănd) A neck of land that connects two landmasses; an isthmus.

landfill (lănd′fĭl′) A disposal site where solid waste, such as paper, glass, and metal, is buried between layers of dirt and other materials in such a way as to reduce contamination of the surrounding land. Modern landfills are often lined with layers of absorbent material and sheets of plastic to keep pollutants from leaking into the soil and water. Also called *sanitary landfill.*

landform (lănd′fôrm′) Any recognizable, naturally formed feature on the Earth's surface. Landforms have a characteristic shape and can include such large features as plains, plateaus, mountains, and valleys, as well as smaller features such as hills, eskers, and gullies.

landmass (lănd′măs′) A large, continuous area of land, such as a continent or a very large island.

landslide (lănd′slīd′) **1.** The downward sliding of a relatively dry mass of earth and rock. **2.** The mass of soil and rock that moves in this way.

Landsteiner (lănd′stī′nər), **Karl** 1868–1943. Austrian-born American pathologist who discovered human blood types. *See Note at* **blood type.**

La Niña (lä nēn′yä) A climate event occurring every 2 to 7 years in which the surface water of the eastern and central Pacific Ocean becomes cooler than usual, affecting temperatures, storm tracks, and precipitation levels over much of the world. *Compare* **El Niño.**

lanolin (lăn′ə-lĭn) A yellowish-white, fatty substance obtained from wool and used in soaps, cosmetics, and ointments.

lanthanide (lăn′thə-nīd′) Any of a series of 15 naturally occurring metallic elements. The lanthanides include elements having atomic numbers 57 through 71. They are grouped apart from the rest of the elements in the periodic table because they all behave in a similar way in chemical reactions. The lanthanides, together with two other elements (yttrium and scandium) that have similar properties, make up a group of elements called the rare-earth elements. *See* **Periodic Table,** pages 254–255. *See Note at* **rare-earth element.**

lanthanum (lăn′thə-nəm) A soft, easily shaped, silvery-white metallic element of the lanthanide series. It is used to make glass for lenses and lights for movie and television studios. *Symbol* **La.** *Atomic number* 57. *See* **Periodic Table,** pages 254–255.

large calorie (lärj) *See* **calorie** (sense 2a).

large intestine The lower section of the intestine that extends from the end of the small intestine to the anus. In most vertebrate animals, it includes the cecum, colon, and rectum. It absorbs water and eliminates the waste matter that is left after food is digested.

larva (lär′və) *Plural* **larvae** (lär′vē) *or* **larvas 1.** An animal in an early stage of development that differs greatly in appearance from its adult stage. Larvae are adapted to a different environment and way of life than adults and go through a

WORD HISTORY

larva

The word *larva,* referring to the newly hatched form of insects before they undergo metamorphosis, comes from the Latin word *lārva,* meaning "evil spirit, ghost, demon." The Latin word also was used to mean "a terrifying mask," such as one that might have been worn by a Roman actor in the role of such an evil spirit. In the 1600s and 1700s, scientists began to use the Latin word to describe the stage in an insect's life during which its final form is still hidden — the larval stage is a mask, so to speak, that the insect will later remove to reveal its adult appearance.

Did You Know...?

laser

A *laser* emits a thin, intense beam of light that can travel long distances without spreading out very much. Most light beams consist of many waves traveling in roughly the same direction. But in laser light, the waves are all precisely in step with each other. Such light is called *coherent*. Lasers produce coherent light through a process called *stimulated emission*. A laser contains a chamber in which atoms of a medium such as a synthetic ruby rod or a gas are excited to a higher energy level by a flash of light from a flash tube. When one of those atoms drops to a lower energy level, it gives off the extra energy as a photon with a specific frequency. If this photon hits another excited atom, it stimulates that atom to drop to a lower energy level and release another photon that has the same frequency as the first and is in phase with it. The photons bounce back and forth between mirrors at both ends of the chamber, stimulating other atoms to emit still more coherent photons. One of the mirrors is partially transparent, allowing the laser beam to exit from the end of the chamber. Lasers have many applications. If the beam is focused and directed at an object, the light energy will be converted to heat energy that can be used for precision cutting.

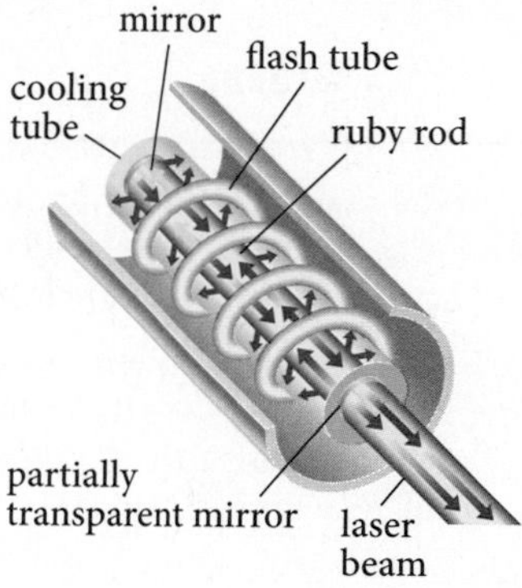

process of metamorphosis in changing to adults. Tadpoles are the larvae of frogs and toads. **2.** The immature, wingless, and usually wormlike feeding form of those insects that undergo complete metamorphosis, such as butterflies, moths, and beetles. Insect larvae hatch from eggs and later turn into pupae. *Compare* **imago, nymph, pupa.**

laryngitis (lăr′ĭn-jī′tĭs) Inflammation of the larynx, usually caused by a virus.

larynx (lăr′ĭngks) The upper part of the trachea in most vertebrate animals, containing the vocal cords. Air passes through the larynx on the way to the lungs. Also called *voice box.*

laser (lā′zər) A device that emits a very narrow and intense beam of light. Laser light is generated by exciting electrons in the atoms of some substance. As the electrons drop to their normal lower energy level, they give off photons of light that strike other excited electrons, which then drop as well and release more photons, producing light of a very precise frequency. Lasers are used for many purposes, such as cutting hard substances and destroying diseased tissue.

latent heat (lāt′nt) The quantity of heat absorbed or released by a substance undergoing a change of state, such as ice changing to water or water changing to ice, at constant temperature and pressure.

lateral line (lăt′ər-əl) A series of sensory pores along the head and sides of fish and some amphibians by which water currents, vibrations, and pressure changes are detected.

latex (lā′tĕks′) The milky or colorless sap of certain plants, such as the rubber tree and milkweeds, that hardens when exposed to air. ❖ Material made of such sap that comes from rubber trees is called **natural latex.** It is used to manufacture thin elastic products such as balloons, disposable gloves, and medical devices, and some people are allergic to it. ❖ A synthetic material that has similar properties to the latex of plants is made from petroleum and is called **synthetic latex.** It is used in paints, adhesives, mattresses, and other products.

latitude (lăt′ĭ-to͞od′) Distance north or south on the Earth's surface, measured in degrees from the equator, which has a latitude of 0°. The distance of a degree of latitude is about 69 statute miles (111

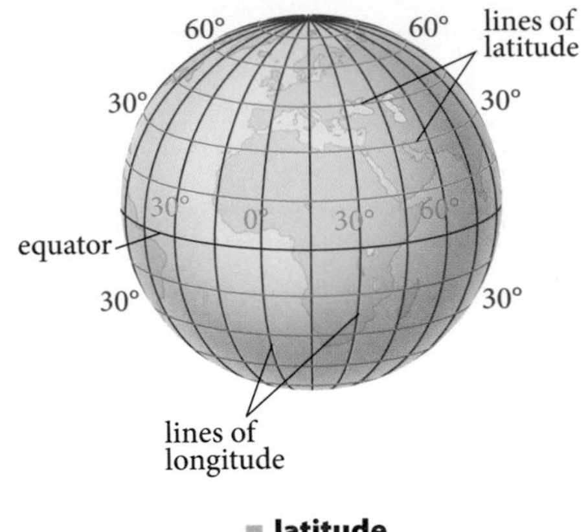

■ **latitude**

kilometers) or 60 nautical miles. Latitude and longitude are the coordinates used to identify any point on the Earth's surface. *Compare* **longitude.**

lattice (lăt′ĭs) An arrangement of objects separated in space, such as the pattern of intersecting lines on graph paper or the pattern of atoms in a crystal. *See more at* **crystal.**

laughing gas (lăf′ĭng) Nitrous oxide.

Laurasia (lô-rā′zhə) A supercontinent of the Northern Hemisphere made up of the landmasses that currently correspond to North America, Greenland, Europe, and Asia (except India). According to the theory of plate tectonics, Laurasia formed at the end of the Paleozoic Era and broke up in the middle of the Mesozoic Era. *Compare* **Gondwana.**

lava (lä′və) **1.** Molten rock that flows from a volcano or from a crack in the Earth. *See more at* **magma. 2.** The igneous rock formed when this substance cools and hardens.

Lavoisier (lä-vwä-zyā′), **Antoine Laurent** 1743–1794. French chemist who is regarded as one of the founders of modern chemistry. In 1778 he discovered that air consists of a mixture of two gases, oxygen and nitrogen. Lavoisier also discovered the law of conservation of mass and devised the modern method of naming chemical compounds. His wife, **Marie** (1758–1836), assisted him with his laboratory work and translated a number of important chemistry texts.

law (lô) A statement about the physical world that describes what will happen in all cases under a specified set of conditions. Laws describe an invariable relationship among phenomena. Boyle's law, for instance, describes what will happen to the volume of a gas if its pressure changes and its temperature remains the same.

law of conservation of energy The principle that energy can be converted from one form to another but cannot be created or destroyed. This principle is also known as the first law of thermodynamics. *See Note at* **thermodynamics.**

law of conservation of mass The principle that matter can neither be created nor be destroyed; it can only be rearranged. The principle does not apply in the case of nuclear reactions, such as fission and fusion, where some mass is converted to energy and vice versa.

law of universal gravitation *See* **Newton's law of gravitation.**

Lawrence (lôr′əns), **Ernest Orlando** 1901–1958. American physicist who built the first cyclotron, a type of particle accelerator, in 1930.

lawrencium (lô-rĕn′sē-əm) A synthetic, radioactive metallic element of the actinide series that can be produced by bombarding californium with boron ions. Its most stable isotope has a half-life of about 4 hours. *Symbol* **Lr.** *Atomic number* 103. *See* **Periodic Table,** pages 254–255.

laws of motion *See* **Newton's laws of motion.**

lb. Abbreviation of **pound.**

LCD (ĕl′sē-dē′) Short for *liquid-crystal display.* A display screen that produces images using a substance that has properties of both a liquid and a crystal. The rod-shaped molecules of this

■ **lava**

BIOGRAPHY

Antoine Lavoisier

Although Antoine Lavoisier made many fundamental contributions to the science of chemistry, one of his most important accomplishments was to collect and publish everything that was known about chemistry in his time. His *Elementary Treatise of Chemistry,* published in 1789, is regarded as the first textbook on modern chemistry. In it, Lavoisier presented a systematic and unified view of new theories and established a system for naming chemical compounds. Lavoisier also put to rest an important and long-standing theory about combustion, a mysterious process that had baffled the greatest minds since antiquity. It had long been believed that all combustible substances contained something called *phlogiston,* which was released during the process of combustion. By repeating the experiments of Joseph Priestley, Lavoisier demonstrated that when a combustible substance burns, the substance is not releasing phlogiston but is actually combining with a gas that is present in the air. He named this gas *oxygen.*

liquid crystal align to reflect or transmit light in response to an electric current.

leach (lēch) To remove the soluble materials from a substance, such as ash or rock, by passing a liquid through or over it: *Heavy rains leached minerals from the soil.*

lead (lĕd) A soft, easily shaped, heavy, bluish-gray metallic element that is extracted chiefly from galena. It is very durable and resistant to corrosion and is a poor conductor of electricity. Lead is used to make radiation shielding and containers for corrosive substances. *Symbol* **Pb.** *Atomic number* 82. *See* **Periodic Table,** pages 254–255. *See Note at* **element.**

leaf (lēf) *pl.* **leaves** (lēvz) A flat, usually green structure that grows on the stem of a plant and that functions mainly to manufacture food by photosynthesis. Leaves consist of an outer tissue layer (the epidermis) through which water vapor and gases are exchanged, a spongy inner layer of cells that contain chloroplasts, and veins that transport water and minerals into the leaf and carry food (in the form of carbohydrates) out to other parts of the plant. Some leaves are simple, while others are compound, consisting of multiple leaflets.

■ **LCD**
LCD clock with date and temperature display

leaflet (lē′flĭt) One of the separate segments of a compound leaf.

leafstalk (lēf′stôk′) The stalk by which a leaf is attached to a stem. Also called *petiole.*

Leakey (lē′kē) Family of British and Kenyan scientists. **Louis** (1903–1972) is known for fossil discoveries of early humans made in close collaboration with his wife, **Mary** (1913–1996). In 1959, while working in Tanzania, Africa, Mary Leakey uncovered skull and teeth fragments of a hominin species now thought to be about 1.75 million years old. The next year the Leakeys discovered remains of a larger-brained species, called *Homo habilis.* Their discoveries provided powerful evidence that human ancestors were of greater age than was previously thought, and that they had evolved in Africa rather than in Asia. Their son **Richard** (born 1944) and his wife,

Henrietta Swan Leavitt

Meave (born 1942), have continued the family's research and discoveries.

learning disability (lûr′nĭng) Any of various conditions that interfere with the ability to learn academic skills, such as reading or math. People with learning disabilities, such as dyslexia, are thought to process and store information differently.

least common denominator (lēst) *See* **lowest common denominator.**

Leavitt (lē′vĭt), **Henrietta Swan** 1868–1921. American astronomer who discovered over 2,400 variable stars and determined that there was a correlation between the brightness of these stars and the amount of time it took them to change from bright to dim. This discovery enabled astronomers to measure the distances to remote stars and galaxies.

lecithin (lĕs′ə-thĭn) Any of various fatty substances containing phosphorus, present in the cell membranes of plant and animal cells. Lecithin is extracted from seeds and used commercially in foods, cosmetics, paints, and plastics.

LED (ĕl′ē-dē′, lĕd) Short for *light-emitting diode.* An electronic semiconductor device that emits light when an electric current passes through it. LEDs are used in lamps, signs, and displays.

leech (lēch) Any of various segmented worms that live in water and suck blood from other animals, including humans. One species, the medicinal leech, was formerly used to remove blood from patients and today is used to help heal wounds and in plastic surgery. Leeches are annelids.

Leeuwenhoek (lā′vən-ho͝ok′), **Anton van** 1632–1723. Dutch naturalist. He constructed high-quality microscopes and made the first observations of many microscopic organisms and anatomical structures, including protozoans and red blood cells.

legume (lĕg′yo͞om′, lə-gyo͞om′) Any of a family of plants having seeds contained in pods that split along two sides. Most legumes have a symbiotic

BIOGRAPHY

Anton van Leeuwenhoek

Anton van Leeuwenhoek was a forty-year-old tradesman with little formal education when he began making optical lenses. Leeuwenhoek used a magnifying glass in his work as a cloth merchant, and he may also have been inspired by the book *Micrographia,* in which the English scientist Robert Hooke had illustrated tiny fleas, plant cells, and other items he had observed through a compound microscope. Leeuwenhoek began to grind lenses and build his own microscopes. Some of his instruments consisted of just a single lens held up to the eye, but the lenses were of such quality that they could magnify objects up to 200 times, whereas others had achieved magnifications of only 20 to 30 times. Leeuwenhoek examined everything around him: insects, blood, hair, semen, and plaque from teeth. He made the first known observations of bacteria, protozoans (then known as "animalcules"), sperm cells, and capillaries. By the time of his death at the age of ninety, Leeuwenhoek had constructed more than 400 microscopes.

relationship with bacteria that live in nodules in their roots and carry out nitrogen fixation, taking nitrogen from the air and converting it into compounds that the plant can use. Peas, beans, clover, and alfalfa are all legumes.

Leibniz (līb′nĭts), Baron **Gottfried Wilhelm von** 1646–1716. German philosopher and mathematician. He invented calculus independently of Newton, made important contributions to logic and probability theory, and designed a practical calculating machine.

lemur (lē′mər) Any of various small primates of the island of Madagascar that have large eyes, soft fur, and a long tail. Lemurs live in trees and are active chiefly at night.

lens (lĕnz) **1.** A transparent structure in the eye of a vertebrate or cephalopod (such as an octopus) that is located behind the iris and focuses light rays entering through the pupil to form an image on the retina. Some other invertebrates also have eyes with lenses. **2a.** A piece of glass or plastic shaped so as to focus or spread light rays that pass through it, often for the purpose of forming an image. **b.** A combination of two or more such lenses used to form an image, as in a camera or telescope. Also called *compound lens.*

Leo (lē′ō) A constellation in the Northern Hemisphere near Cancer and Virgo.

Leonardo da Vinci (lē′ə-när′dō də vĭn′chē) 1452–1519. Italian artist, scientist, and inventor whose notebooks show his careful observation of details of anatomy, geology, botany, hydraulics, optics, meteorology, and mechanics. He also drew speculative designs for various inventions, including gliders, a robot, and a helicopter-like device.

lepidopteran (lĕp′ĭ-dŏp′tər-ən) Any of numerous insects, including the butterflies and moths, that have four membranous wings covered with small scales. The larvae of lepidopterans are called caterpillars.

leprosy (lĕp′rə-sē) A mildly contagious disease caused by a bacterium that damages nerves, skin, and other organs. If untreated, leprosy eventually destroys the affected body tissues. Also called *Hansen's disease.*

leucine (lo͞o′sēn′) An essential amino acid. *See more at* **amino acid.**

leukemia (lo͞o-kē′mē-ə) Any of several cancers

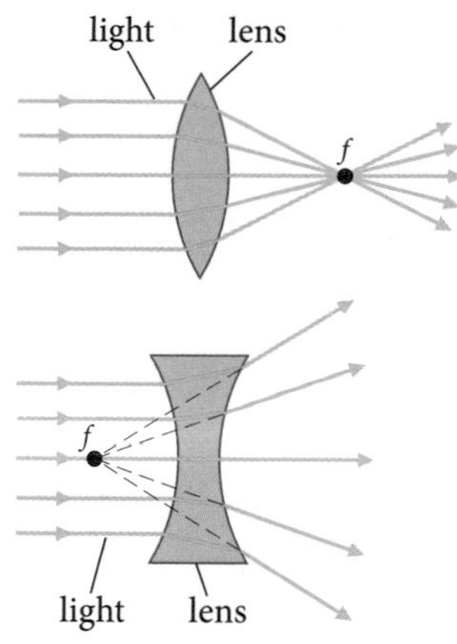

lens
top: *As light rays pass through a convex lens, they come together at the focal point (f).*
bottom: *As light rays pass through a concave lens, they spread apart.*

of the blood in which abnormal white blood cells multiply uncontrollably, eventually crowding out normal cells in the bone marrow.

leukocyte *also* **leucocyte** (lo͞o′kə-sīt′) *See* **white blood cell.**

levee (lĕv′ē) A long ridge consisting of sand, silt, and clay that were deposited by a river along its banks during past floods.

lever (lĕv′ər) A simple machine consisting of a bar that pivots on a support (called the fulcrum) and that changes the magnitude or direction of an applied force. For example, by pushing down on one end of a lever whose fulcrum lies between the two ends, one can raise or move a heavy weight at the other end. If the point where force is applied is further from the fulcrum than the load to be moved is, the lever will press on the load with more force than the force that is applied to the lever.

Leyden jar (līd′n) An early device for storing electric charge. It consists of a glass jar with one piece of conductive metal foil covering the outside of the jar and another piece covering the inside. The two pieces of foil act as conductors, with the glass jar as an insulator. A wire connected to the inner foil exits through an insulating stopper in the jar's neck. The wire can be charged by connecting the inner and outer foils to the two electrodes of a direct current power supply.

Li The symbol for **lithium.**

Libra (lē′brə) A constellation in the Southern Hemisphere near Scorpius and Virgo.

lichen (lī′kən) A composite organism that consists of a fungus and a green alga or a cyanobacterium living together in a symbiotic relationship. The alga or cyanobacterium supplies the fungus with nutrients produced by photosynthesis, while the fungus supplies water and provides a suitable environment for the alga or cyanobacterium. Lichens often live on rocks and tree bark and can thrive in extreme environments, such as deserts and arctic regions.

Liebig (lē′bĭg), Baron **Justus von** 1803–1873. German chemist who contributed to many areas of chemistry. He was one of the first to investigate organic compounds and to develop techniques for their analysis. Liebig also established one of the first teaching laboratories, where many 19th-century chemists were trained.

life (līf) **1.** The property or quality that distinguishes living organisms from dead organisms and nonliving matter. Living organisms have the ability to grow, carry on metabolism, respond to stimuli, and reproduce. **2.** Living organisms considered as a group: *plant life; marine life.*

life cycle The series of changes in the growth and development of an organism from its beginning as an independent life form to its mature state in which offspring are produced. In one-celled organisms, such as bacteria, the life cycle begins when an organism is produced by fission and ends when that organism in turn divides into two new ones. In sexually reproducing organisms, the life cycle starts with the fusion of sex cells to form a new organism and ends when that organism produces its own sex cells, which then begin the cycle again by fusing with other sex cells.

life science Any of several branches of science, such as biology, medicine, or ecology, that deal with living organisms and their organization, life processes, and relationships to each other and their environment. *Compare* **physical science.**

lift (lĭft) A force that acts on an object moving through a fluid such as air or water. Lift acts in a direction that is perpendicular to the object's direction of motion. Lift is the upward force acting on an airplane's wing during flight. The weight of the wing is the downward force. *See Note at* **aerodynamics.** *Compare* **drag.**

ligament (lĭg′ə-mənt) A sheet or band of tough fibrous tissue that connects two bones or holds an organ of the body in place.

light (līt) Electromagnetic radiation in the range of wavelengths (from red to violet) that can be perceived by the human eye. Light, like all forms of electromagnetic radiation, travels at a speed of about 186,282 miles (299,792 kilometers) per second in a vacuum. Electromagnetic radiation with shorter or longer wavelengths than visible light, especially infrared light or ultraviolet light, is sometimes also called light. *See Note at* **electromagnetic radiation.**

light-emitting diode *See* **LED.**

lightning (līt′nĭng) A flash of light in the sky

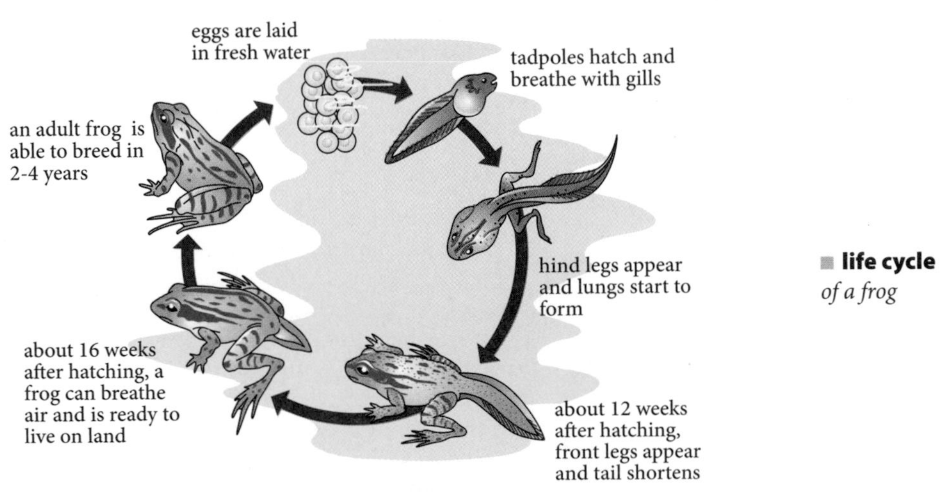

life cycle
of a frog

Did You Know...?

lightning

The energy within a bolt of *lightning* is so great that it heats the air around it to temperatures up to five times greater than that of the surface of the sun, or 55,000°F (30,000°C). The rapid expansion of this superheated air is what creates the sounds we call thunder. The sounds travel to us more slowly than the light from lightning, so it is possible to estimate how far away a lightning strike is by timing the gap between when you see the lightning and when you hear the thunder it has produced. Count the seconds from when you see the flash until you hear the thunder, and divide this number by five. The result will be the approximate number of miles you are from the point of the strike.

caused by an electrical discharge between clouds or between a cloud and the Earth's surface. The flash heats the air and usually causes thunder. Lightning usually appears as a jagged streak or (when there are clouds between it and the observer) as a bright sheet.

light year The distance that light travels in a vacuum in one year, equal to about 5.88 trillion miles (9.46 trillion kilometers).

lignin (lĭg′nĭn) A complex organic compound that binds to cellulose fibers and hardens and strengthens the cell walls of plants. It is the chief noncarbohydrate constituent of wood.

lignite (lĭg′nīt′) A soft, brownish-black form of coal having more carbon than peat has but less than bituminous coal has. Lignite is easy to mine but does not burn as well as other forms of coal. *Compare* **anthracite, bituminous coal.**

lime (līm) *See* **calcium oxide.**

limestone (līm′stōn′) A sedimentary rock consisting primarily of calcium carbonate, often in the form of the mineral calcite. Limestone can occur in many colors but is usually white, gray, or black. It often contains fossil shells and other marine organisms. *See Table at* **rock.**

limnology (lĭm-nŏl′ə-jē) The study of the physics, chemistry, geology, and biology of lakes and other inland waters.

USAGE

light year

It is important to remember that a *light year* is a measure of distance, not time. A light year is the length of empty space that light can traverse in a year, close to six trillion miles. When scientists calculate how many light years the stars are from Earth or from one another, they are calculating their distance, not their age.

line (līn) A geometric figure formed by a point moving in a fixed direction and in the reverse direction. The intersection of two planes is a line. ❖ The part of a line that lies between two points on the line is called a **line segment.**

linear (lĭn′ē-ər) Relating to or resembling a line. ❖ A **linear equation** is an algebraic equation, such as $y = 4x + 3$, in which the variables are of the first degree (that is, raised only to the first power). The graph of such an equation is a straight line.

linear accelerator A particle accelerator in which charged subatomic particles, such as protons and electrons, are accelerated in a straight line by a series of impulses from electric fields applied at radio frequencies, gradually increasing their speeds and energies. The high-energy particles that linear accelerators produce may be caused to collide with other particles in order to study the structure of subatomic particles. *Compare* **cyclotron, synchrotron.**

line of force A line used to show the direction of force and the strength of an electric or magnetic field. *See Note at* **magnetism.**

Linnaeus (lĭ-nē′əs, lĭ-nā′əs), **Carl** 1707–1778.

Carl Linnaeus

Swedish naturalist who founded the modern classification system for the naming of plants and animals, in which each organism is given a two-word name indicating what genus and species it belongs to. *See more at* **binomial nomenclature.**

lipase (lĭp′ās′, lī′pās′) An enzyme that catalyzes the breakdown of fats into glycerol and fatty acids.

lipid (lĭp′ĭd) Any of a large group of organic compounds, including fats, oils, waxes, and sterols, that are oily to the touch and insoluble in water. They are a source of stored energy and are a component of cell membranes.

lipoprotein (lĭp′ō-prō′tēn′) Any of various small particles made up of proteins and lipids. Lipoproteins transport cholesterol, triglycerides, and other lipids in the bloodstream. They are classified according to their density.

liquefaction (lĭk′wə-făk′shən) **1.** *Chemistry* The act or process of turning a gas into a liquid. **2.** *Geology* The process by which sediment that is very wet starts to behave like a liquid. Liquefaction is often caused by severe shaking, as in earthquakes.

liquid (lĭk′wĭd) One of the basic forms of matter, composed of atoms or molecules that can move short distances. Unlike a solid, a liquid has no fixed shape, but instead has a characteristic readiness to flow and therefore takes on the shape of any container. Unlike a gas, a liquid usually has a volume that remains constant or changes only slightly under pressure.

liquid-crystal display *See* **LCD.**

Lister (lĭs′tər), **Joseph.** First Baron Lister 1827–1912. British surgeon who introduced strict standards of hygiene to hospitals to help combat infection. As a young doctor, Lister observed that patients with compound fractures (fractures with bone protruding through the skin) often died of infection. He became convinced that infection was spread by contact with the air and demonstrated that keeping wounds clean and covered decreased infection. In 1865 he read about Pasteur's germ theory of disease and established a system of antiseptic measures that dramatically decreased the number of deaths caused by infection. Lister's practices were gradually adopted by hospitals throughout Europe.

liter (lē′tər) The basic unit of volume in the metric system, equal to about 1.06 liquid quarts or 0.91 dry quart. *See Table at* **measurement.**

lithium (lĭth′ē-əm) A soft, silvery metallic element that is an alkali metal and occurs in small amounts in some minerals. It is the lightest of all metals and is highly reactive. Lithium is used to make alloys, batteries, glass for large telescopes, and ceramics. *Symbol* **Li.** *Atomic number* 3. *See* **Periodic Table,** pages 254–255.

lithosphere (lĭth′ə-sfîr′) The outer part of the Earth, consisting of the crust and upper mantle. It is approximately 60 miles (100 kilometers) thick. *Compare* **asthenosphere, atmosphere, hydrosphere.**

litmus (lĭt′məs) A colored powder, obtained from certain lichens, that changes to red in an acid solution and to blue in an alkaline solution. ❖ Litmus is typically added to paper to make **litmus paper,** which is used to determine whether a solution is basic or acidic.

Little Dipper (lĭt′l) A group of seven stars in the constellation Ursa Minor that form the outline of a dipper.

littoral (lĭt′ər-əl) **1.** Relating to, growing in, or inhabiting the seashore, especially the zone between the limits of high and low tides. **2.** Relating to, growing in, or inhabiting the shallowest part of a lake or river, near the shore.

liver (lĭv′ər) **1.** A large organ located in the abdomen of vertebrate animals that is essential to many metabolic processes. The liver secretes bile, stores fats and carbohydrates as reserve energy sources, converts harmful substances to less toxic forms, and makes several blood proteins, including those that control clotting. **2.** A similar organ of invertebrate animals.

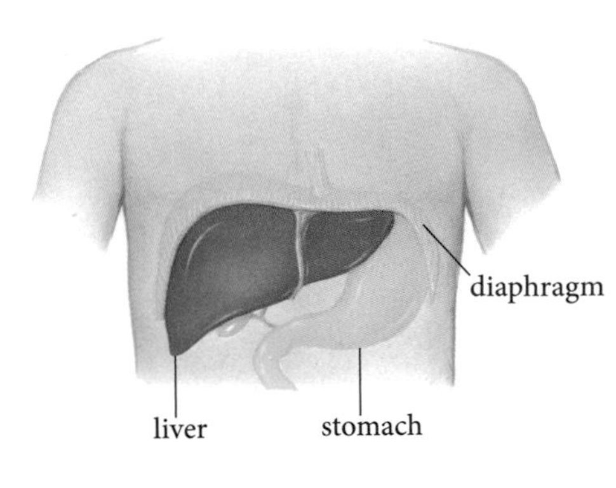

liver

livermorium (lĭv′ər-môr′ē-əm) An artificially produced radioactive element that has only been produced in trace amounts. Its most stable isotope has a half-life of about 53 milliseconds. *Symbol* **Lv.** *Atomic number* 116. *See* **Periodic Table,** pages 254–255.

liverwort (lĭv′ər-wûrt′, lĭv′ər-wôrt′) Any of numerous small green plants that lack vascular tissue and do not bear seeds. Liverworts are leafy or flat and usually grow in damp areas. They are closely related to the mosses.

lizard (lĭz′ərd) Any of numerous reptiles having a scaly, often slender body, a tapering tail, and usually four legs. Lizards typically have movable eyelids, unlike most other reptiles. Iguanas and chameleons are lizards.

load (lōd) **1.** The resistance that a machine must overcome in order to do work. **2.** The power output of a generator or power plant.

loam (lōm) Soil composed of approximately equal quantities of sand, silt, and clay. It typically also contains decayed plant matter.

Lobachevsky (lō′bə-chĕf′skē), **Nikolai Ivanovich** 1792–1856. Russian mathematician who developed (1826) a system of geometry that was not based on Euclid's axioms.

lobe (lōb) A rounded projection or part, as on a leaf or an organ of the body. The lobes of an organ, such as the liver, are often divided by fissures.

lobe-finned fish Any of various bony fish with fins that contain bone and muscle, unlike the fins of other fish. The lobe-finned fish first appeared in the Silurian Period and are extinct except for the coelacanth and lungfish. Ancient lobe-finned fish are thought to be the distant ancestors of land-dwelling vertebrate animals (amphibians, reptiles, birds, and mammals).

locomotion (lō′kə-mō′shən) The movement of an organism from place to place by its own power. Many animals move by the action of limbs, such as flippers or legs. Others, such as snakes, propel themselves by thrusting the body sideways against a hard surface. Fish move through the water by means of wavelike muscle contractions that course through the body from head to tail. Many protists use cilia or flagella to get around.

lodestone *also* **loadstone** (lōd′stōn′) A piece of the mineral magnetite that acts like a magnet.

loess (lō′əs, lĕs, lŭs) A fine-grained silt or clay, thought to consist of dust from deserts or rock dust that washed out from under Pleistocene glaciers and was picked up, carried, and deposited by the wind.

log (lôg) A logarithm.

logarithm (lô′gə-rĭ*th*′əm) The power to which some base number must be raised to produce a given number. For example, if the base is 10, then the logarithm of 1,000 (written $\log_{10}$ 1,000) is 3, because $10^3 = 1{,}000$. *See more at* **common logarithm, natural logarithm.**

logic (lŏj′ĭk) The study of the principles of reasoning.

longitude (lŏn′jĭ-to͞od′) Distance east or west on the Earth's surface, measured in degrees from a certain meridian, usually the prime meridian at Greenwich, England, which has a longitude of 0°. The distance of a degree of longitude is about 69 statute miles (111 kilometers) or 60 nautical miles at the equator, narrowing to zero at the poles. Longitude and latitude are the coordinates used to identify any point on the Earth's surface. *Compare* **latitude.**

longitudinal wave (lŏn′jĭ-to͞od′n-əl) A wave in which the particles of the medium move back and forth in the same direction as the wave travels through the medium. Sound waves are longitudinal waves. *See more at* **wave.** *Compare* **transverse wave.**

long ton (lông) *See* **ton** (sense 2).

louse (lous) *Plural* **lice** (līs) Any of numerous small, wingless insects that live as parasites on the bodies of many birds and mammals, including humans. Louse species are divided into two groups: one group has chewing mouthparts, and the other, which includes human lice, has sucking mouthparts used for feeding on blood.

Lovelace (lŭv′ləs), **Ada** *Full name* **Augusta Ada Byron King, Countess of Lovelace.** 1815–1852. British mathematician who is noted for her theoretical writings on the analytical engine, an early computer designed by Charles Babbage. She compiled detailed notations about how the machine could be programmed. *See Note on next page.*

lowest common denominator (lō′ĭst) The smallest common multiple of the denominators of a set of fractions. For example, the lowest com-

BIOGRAPHY

Ada Lovelace

Ada Lovelace was born Augusta Ada Byron, the daughter of the English poet George Gordon, Lord Byron. From her youth she displayed a wide-ranging curiosity as well as unusual mathematical abilities, and she kept up her intellectual life after marrying an English lord and giving birth to three children. She was in correspondence for many years with Charles Babbage, who had invented a mechanical device called the "analytical engine" that could be made to perform various calculations according to instructions encoded on a series of cards with holes punched in them. Though the analytical engine had not yet been constructed, Lovelace was fascinated by its potential. In 1846, with Babbage's encouragement, she translated an Italian scholar's paper on the device, adding to it a set of notes in which she described how the procedure for solving a complex mathematical problem could theoretically be encoded on the punched cards. This description is generally credited as the first published computer program. In her written letters, she also speculated about the analytical engine's capabilities for performing a broader range of tasks — not just solving mathematical problems but, for instance, engaging in more creative work such as composing music. More than a century later, with the development of electronic computers, her speculations have proven to be remarkably accurate: computers can indeed write music, in addition to their thousands of other uses, mostly unrelated to math. In 1980, the programming language Ada was named in her honor.

mon denominator of $\frac{1}{3}$ and $\frac{3}{4}$ is 12. Also called *least common denominator.*

low tide (lō) The time at which the tide reaches the lowest level in its regular rising and falling. There are usually two low tides per day.

Lr The symbol for **lawrencium.**

Lu The symbol for **lutetium.**

lumbar (lŭm′bər) Located at or near the part of the back lying between the lowest ribs and the hips: *lumbar vertebrae; the lumbar spine.*

lumen (lo͞o′mən) **1.** *Anatomy* The central space in a tubular organ, such as a blood vessel or intestine. **2.** *Physics* A unit used to measure the amount of light passing through a given portion of the space around a light source. One lumen is equal to $\frac{1}{4}\pi$ of the total amount of light given off each second by a light source with a brightness of one candela in all directions.

luminescence (lo͞o′mə-nĕs′əns) The giving off of light by a substance whose atoms have been excited by an energy source other than heat. Examples include bioluminescence, where the source is chemical energy, and fluorescence and phosphorescence, where the source is electromagnetic radiation. *Compare* **incandescence.**

lunar (lo͞o′nər) **1.** Relating to the moon: *a lunar mountain.* **2.** Measured by the revolution of the moon: *a lunar month.*

lunar eclipse *See under* **eclipse.**

lung (lŭng) **1.** Either of two spongy organs in the chest of air-breathing vertebrate animals that serve as the organs of gas exchange. Blood flowing through the lungs picks up oxygen from inhaled air and releases carbon dioxide, which is exhaled. Air enters and leaves the lungs through the bronchial tubes. **2.** A similar organ found in some invertebrate animals.

lungfish (lŭng′fĭsh′) Any of several tropical freshwater fish that, in addition to having gills, have lunglike organs for breathing air. Lungfish have a long, narrow body, and certain species can survive periods of drought by burrowing into mud and secreting a slimy, protective covering. Lungfish and the coelacanths are the only living lobe-finned fishes.

Luria (lo͝or′ē-ə), **Salvador Edward** 1912–1991. Italian-born American biologist who made discoveries about the process of genetic mutation in bacteria and the genetic structure of viruses as a result of his studies of viruses that infect bacteria.

luster (lŭs′tər) The shine from the surface of a mineral. Luster is important in describing different minerals. It is usually characterized using terms such as metallic, glassy, pearly, or dull.

lutetium (lo͞o-tē′shē-əm) A silvery-white metallic element of the lanthanide series that is used in nuclear technology. Its radioactive isotope is used to find the age of meteorites. *Symbol* **Lu.** *Atomic number* 71. *See* **Periodic Table,** pages 254–255.

lux (lŭks) A unit used to measure illumination. One lux is equal to one lumen per square meter.

Lv The symbol for **livermorium.**

L wave *See* **surface wave.** *See Note at* **earthquake.**

Lwoff (lwôf), **André Michel** 1902–1994. French microbiologist who studied viruses that infect bacteria. He showed how viruses replicate inside the cells they have infected and how a virus's genetic material can become incorporated into the DNA of an infected cell.

lye (lī) A strong alkaline solution of potassium hydroxide or sodium hydroxide, made by allowing water to wash through wood ashes. It is used to make soap.

Lyell (lī′əl), Sir **Charles** 1797–1875. British geologist who is considered one of the founders of modern geology. His *Principles of Geology* (1830–1833) had a powerful influence on the science of his day.

Lyme disease (līm) A disease caused by bacteria that are transmitted by deer ticks. It begins as a rash, followed by symptoms including fever, headache, and joint pain. If untreated, the disease can lead to chronic arthritis and damage other body tissues.

lymph (lĭmf) The clear fluid that flows through the vessels of the lymphatic system. Lymph carries waste from tissues and transports white blood cells. It collects fluid that has leaked out through the capillaries into the tissues.

lymphatic system (lĭm-făt′ĭk) A network of vessels, tissues, and organs in vertebrate animals that regulates fluid balance by draining excess fluid from the tissues and returning it to the blood and that also produces and carries cells that help the body fight disease. In humans the lymphatic system includes the bone marrow, thymus, spleen, and lymph nodes.

lymph node Any of the small, bean-shaped masses of tissue found along the vessels of the lymphatic system. Lymph nodes filter foreign substances from the blood and may become swollen during infection.

lymphocyte (lĭm′fə-sīt′) Any of various white blood cells that function in the body's immune system by recognizing and deactivating specific foreign substances called antigens. Certain lymphocytes (called B cells) act by stimulating the production of antibodies. Others (T cells) contain receptors on their cell surfaces that are capable of recognizing and binding to specific antigens.

Lyra (lī′rə) A constellation in the Northern Hemisphere near Cygnus and Hercules.

lysine (lī′sēn′) An essential amino acid. *See more at* **amino acid.**

lysis (lī′sĭs) The disintegration of a cell that results from destruction of the cell membrane, as by an antibody or enzyme.

lysosome (lī′sə-sōm′) A structure in animal cells that is surrounded by a membrane and contains enzymes. The enzymes break down cellular waste materials and food particles or other materials from outside the cell. *See more at* **cell.**

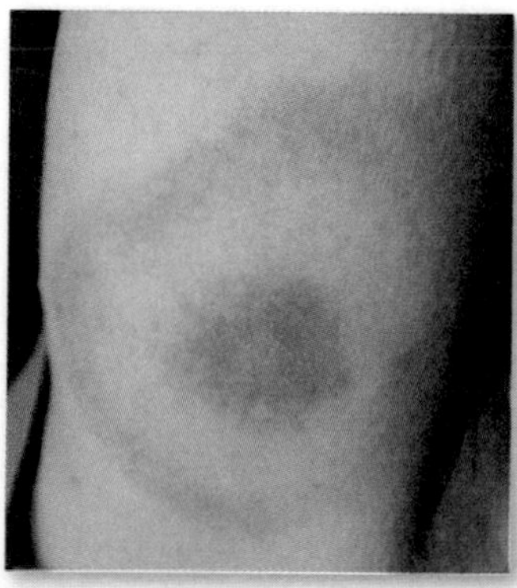

Lyme disease *the characteristic bull's-eye rash of Lyme disease*

M

m 1. Abbreviation of **mass. 2.** Abbreviation of **meter.**

machine (mə-shēn′) **1.** *See* **simple machine. 2.** A device usually having many moving parts and used to perform a task: *a washing machine.*

Mach number (mäk) The ratio of the speed of a body to the speed of sound in a particular medium. For example, an aircraft flying through air at twice the speed of sound has a Mach number of 2.

macro– A prefix that means "large," as in *macronucleus,* a large kind of nucleus.

macroclimate (măk′rō-klī′mĭt) The climate of a large geographic area.

macromolecule (măk′rō-mŏl′ĭ-kyo͞ol′) A large molecule, such as a polymer or protein, consisting of many smaller units linked together.

macrophage (măk′rə-fāj′) One of the large white blood cells that engulf and break down foreign particles and bacteria in blood or lymph. Macrophages develop from monocytes and are important in the body's defense against disease. They are found mainly in the spleen, lymph nodes, lungs, and liver.

macula (măk′yə-lə) An area near the center of the retina in vertebrate animals where vision is sharpest.

mad cow disease (măd) A disease of cattle in which the tissues of the brain deteriorate and take on a spongy appearance, resulting in abnormal behaviors and loss of muscle control. Mad cow disease is caused by agents called prions. A form of the disease can be transmitted to humans through the eating of infected meat. Also called *bovine spongiform encephalopathy.*

Magellanic Clouds (măj′ə-lăn′ĭk) Two small, irregularly shaped galaxies that are the galaxies closest to the Milky Way. They are faintly visible near the south celestial pole.

magma (măg′mə) The molten rock material that originates under the Earth's crust and forms igneous rock when it has cooled. When magma cools and solidifies beneath the Earth's surface, it forms what are known as intrusive rocks. When it reaches the Earth's surface, it flows out as lava and forms extrusive (or volcanic) rocks.

magnesia (măg-nē′zhə) *See* **magnesium oxide.**

magnesium (măg-nē′zē-əm) A lightweight, moderately hard, silvery-white metallic element that is an alkaline-earth metal and burns with an intense white flame. It is an essential component of chlorophyll and is used in lightweight alloys, flash photography, and fireworks. *Symbol* **Mg.** *Atomic number* 12. *See* **Periodic Table,** pages 254–255.

magnesium oxide A white powder, MgO, used in heat-resistant materials because of its very high melting point. It is also used as an ingredient in antacids and laxatives. Also called *magnesia.*

magnet (măg′nĭt) **1.** A material or object that produces a magnetic field and has the property of attracting iron and steel. Some objects, like lodestones (composed of magnetite), are natural magnets. Magnets can also be manufactured by inducing magnetism in steel or other metals or metal alloys. A magnet has two magnetic poles, called north and south. **2.** An electromagnet.

magnetic (măg-nĕt′ĭk) Having the properties of a magnet; showing magnetism.

magnetic declination The horizontal angle between true geographic north and magnetic north at a specific point on the Earth.

magnetic disk A memory device, such as a hard disk, that is covered with a magnetic coating. Digital information is stored on magnetic disks in the form of tiny magnetized regions.

magnetic field A region of space around a magnet or an electric current in which a magnetic force exists. A magnetic force causes charged particles to change their direction of motion. *See Note at* **magnetism.**

magnetic force The force of attraction or repulsion exerted on a magnet or on a moving electric charge by the magnetic field created by another magnet or by a moving electric charge. Opposite poles of two magnets (south and north) attract each other, whereas like poles (north and north or south and south) repel each other.

■ **magnetic field**
Iron filings show the magnetic field surrounding opposite poles.

magnetic induction The process by which a substance, such as iron, becomes magnetized by a magnetic field.

magnetic north The direction toward which the north-seeking arrow of a compass points. ❖ The **magnetic north pole** is the northern pole of the Earth's magnetic field and changes slightly in response to variations in the Earth's magnetism. The magnetic north pole is currently located in the Arctic Islands of Canada. *Compare* **geographic north.**

magnetic pole 1. Either of two areas of a magnet where the magnetic field is strongest. *See Note at* **magnetism. 2.** Either of two locations on the Earth's surface toward which a compass needle points; either the magnetic north pole or the magnetic south pole. The location of the magnetic poles, which are found near to but not exactly at the geographic poles, changes gradually over time.

magnetic resonance imaging The use of nuclear magnetic resonance to produce images of the molecules that make up a substance, especially the soft tissues of the human body. Magnetic resonance imaging is used in medicine to diagnose disorders of body structures that do not show up well on x-rays. *See more at* **nuclear magnetic resonance.**

magnetic storm A disturbance or fluctuation in the Earth's magnetic field, caused by streams of charged particles given off by solar flares.

magnetism (măg′nĭ-tĭz′əm) The properties of magnetic fields and the effects they produce.

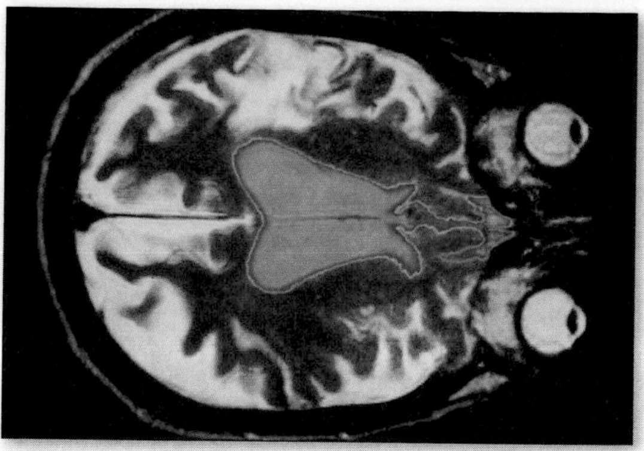

■ **magnetic resonance imaging**
image of a human head

magnetite (măg′nĭ-tīt′) A usually blackish, magnetic mineral composed of iron oxides. Magnetite occurs in many different types of rocks, commonly as small octahedral crystals. It is an important source of iron.

Did You Know...?

magnetism

Magnetism might not seem to have anything to do with electricity, but in fact, the two phenomena are intimately linked. A *magnetic field* is produced whenever electric charges are in motion, as when electrons move through a wire or around an atomic nucleus. In atoms, the invisible magnetic field consists of *lines of force* that surround and loop through the atom. The places where these lines of force come together, and where the magnetic field is strongest, are called the north and south *magnetic poles.* In substances in which the magnetic fields of each atom are aligned in the same direction, the entire substance acts like a magnet — with north and south poles and a surrounding magnetic field. These naturally magnetic substances are called *permanent magnets.* Other substances can be temporarily magnetized. You can magnetize a coil of wire, for example, by running an electric current through it. Electrically produced magnets, called *electromagnets,* are used in many industrial and everyday devices, such as motors and generators.

magnetize (măg′nĭ-tīz′) To cause an object to become a magnet. For example, you can magnetize an iron nail by placing it in a strong magnetic field, such as that produced inside a coil of wire carrying an electric current.

magnetometer (măg′nĭ-tŏm′ĭ-tər) An instrument for measuring the magnitude and direction of a magnetic field. Archaeologists use magnetometers to find buried objects and map ancient archaeological sites. Geologists use them to determine the ages of sediments and to study the motion of tectonic plates.

magnetron (măg′nĭ-trŏn′) An electron tube that produces microwave radiation by applying magnetic and electric fields to a stream of electrons emitted by a heated filament. Magnetrons are used in radar and in microwave ovens.

magnitude (măg′nĭ-to͞od′) **1.** The brightness of a celestial object as seen from the Earth, measured on a numerical scale in which lower numbers indicate greater brightness. A decrease of one unit of magnitude represents an increase in brightness by about 2.5 times. The dimmest stars visible to the unaided eye have magnitude 6, while the brightest star outside our solar system, Sirius, has magnitude −1.4. The moon has magnitude −12.7, and the sun has magnitude −26.8. **2.** A measure of the total amount of energy released by an earthquake, as indicated on the Richter scale.

maiasaura (mī′ə-sôr′ə) A duck-billed dinosaur of the late Cretaceous Period of North America. Remains of fossilized nests and juveniles suggest that the adults lived in herds and cared for their young in large nesting sites.

mainframe (mān′frām′) A large, powerful computer, often serving many terminals and usually used by large, complex organizations.

malachite (măl′ə-kīt′) A bright-green copper carbonate mineral found in copper veins and used as a copper ore. Malachite often occurs together with the mineral azurite.

malaria (mə-lâr′ē-ə) An infectious disease of tropical areas that is caused by a parasite transmitted by mosquitoes. It causes repeated attacks of chills, fever, and sweating.

male (māl) *Adjective* **1.** Relating to or being the sex that can fertilize egg cells and father offspring: *male frogs.* **2.** Relating to or being the sex cell that is smaller and more mobile than the other corresponding sex cell: *male gametes.* **3.** Relating to or being a reproductive organ that produces male sex cells: *male flower parts.* —*Noun* **4.** A male organism.

malignant (mə-lĭg′nənt) Likely to spread or get worse: *a malignant tumor.*

malleable (măl′ē-ə-bəl) Capable of being shaped or formed in its solid state, especially by pressure or hammering. Gold is a malleable metal.

malleus (măl′ē-əs) The largest and outermost of the three small bones, called ossicles, in the middle ear. It is also called the hammer.

malnutrition (măl′no͞o-trĭsh′ən) Poor nourishment caused by lack of essential foods or by disease.

malocclusion (măl′ə-klo͞o′zhən) A condition in which the upper and lower teeth do not meet properly; a faulty bite.

Malpighi (măl-pē′gē), **Marcello** 1628–1694. Italian anatomist who was a pioneer in using the microscope to study anatomy. He is noted for his descriptions of the structure of the kidney and other organs and for showing that the capillary system connects the arteries and veins.

maltose (môl′tōs′) A sugar made by the action of various enzymes on starch. It is formed in the body during digestion.

malware (măl′wâr′) Computer software that is designed to do harm by interfering with normal computer functions or by sending personal data about the user to unauthorized parties over the Internet.

mammal (măm′əl) Any of various warm-blooded vertebrate animals whose young feed on milk that is produced by the mother's mammary glands. Mammals usually have a covering of hair or fur on the skin, and all of them except the monotremes bear live young. Mice, dogs, kangaroos, whales, and humans are mammals.

mammary gland (măm′ə-rē) One of the milk-producing glands in a female mammal, consisting of a system of ducts that convey the milk to an external nipple or teat.

mammogram (măm′ə-grăm′) An x-ray image of the human breast, used to detect tumors or other abnormalities.

mammoth (măm′əth) Any of various extinct elephants that lived throughout the Northern Hemisphere during the Ice Age. Some mammoth species were very large and had long tusks and hair, but others were small, about the size of a baby modern elephant. One group of mammoths survived on an island in the Arctic Ocean until as recently as 4,000 years ago.

mandible (măn′də-bəl) **1.** The lower jaw of a vertebrate animal. *See more at* **skeleton. 2.** The upper or lower part of a bird's beak. **3.** An organ in the mouth of many invertebrate animals used for seizing and biting food, especially either of a pair of such organs in an insect or other arthropod.

manganese (măng′gə-nēz′) A grayish-white, hard, brittle metallic element that occurs in several different minerals. It is used to increase the hardness and strength of steel and other important alloys. *Symbol* **Mn.** *Atomic number* 25. *See* **Periodic Table,** pages 254–255.

manometer (mə-nŏm′ĭ-tər) An instrument that measures the pressure exerted by liquids and gases.

mantissa (măn-tĭs′ə) The part of a logarithm to the base ten that is to the right of the decimal point. For example, if 2.749 is a logarithm, 749 is the mantissa. *Compare* **characteristic.**

mantle (măn′tl) **1.** The layer of the Earth between the crust and the core. It consists mainly of silicate minerals and has an upper, partially molten part and a lower, solid part. The upper mantle is the source of magma and volcanic lava. **2.** The layer of soft tissue that covers the body of a clam, oyster, or other mollusk and secretes the material that forms the shell.

marble (mär′bəl) A metamorphic rock consisting primarily of calcite and dolomite. Marble is formed by the action of heat and pressure on limestone. Although it is usually white to gray in color, it often has irregularly colored marks due to impurities. *See Table at* **rock.**

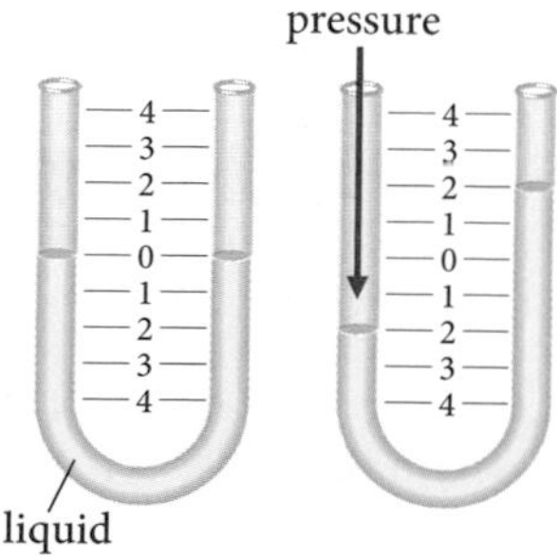

manometer
To calculate pressure in a U-tube manometer, add the values above and below zero. The manometer on the right shows a reading of 4 (2+2).

Guglielmo Marconi

Marconi (mär-kō′nē), **Guglielmo** 1874–1937. Italian physicist and inventor. In 1901 he used radio waves to transmit signals in Morse code across the Atlantic Ocean. Soon after his experiment, radio waves became established as a medium for communications.

mare (mä′rā) *Plural* **maria** (mä′rē-ə) Any of the large, dark areas on the moon or on Mars or other planets.

marine (mə-rēn′) Relating to or living in the sea: *marine biology; marine mammals.*

marine biology The scientific study of organisms living in or dependent on the oceans.

marrow (măr′ō) *See* **bone marrow.**

Mars (märz) The fourth planet from the sun and the second smallest, with a diameter about half that of Earth. Mars has seasons similar to but much longer than Earth's. *See Table at* **solar system,** pages 312–313.

mare
several maria on the moon

marsh (märsh) A wetland in which the vegetation consists mostly of grasses or grasslike plants.

marsupial (mär-so͞o′pē-əl) Any of various mammals whose young are very undeveloped when born and continue developing outside their mother's body while attached to one of her nipples. Most marsupials have longer hind legs than forelimbs, and the females usually have pouches in which they carry their young. Kangaroos, opossums, and koalas are marsupials.

maser (mā′zər) A device that works the same way as a laser but emits electromagnetic radiation having longer wavelengths than visible light, especially microwaves. *See Note at* **laser.**

mass (măs) A measure of the amount of matter contained in a physical body. Mass is independent of gravity and is therefore different from weight. *See Note at* **weight.**

mass-energy equivalence The principle that mass and energy can be converted into each other and that a particular quantity of mass is equivalent to a particular quantity of energy. The principle was stated mathematically by Albert Einstein as $E = mc^2$, where E is the energy in joules, m is the mass in kilograms, and c is the speed of light in meters per second.

mass number The total number of protons and neutrons in the nucleus of an atom. For example, nitrogen has 7 protons and 7 neutrons in its nucleus, giving it a mass number of 14.

mass spectrometry A technique used to determine the masses and the abundances of atoms or molecules in a sample. The atoms or molecules in the sample are ionized and then passed through electric and magnetic fields. The fields deflect the ions by different amounts depending on their masses, producing a spectrum that indicates the identity and abundance of each ion. ❖ The device used to perform mass spectrometry is called a **mass spectrometer.**

mastication (măs′tĭ-kā′shən) The chewing or grinding of food by the teeth.

mastodon (măs′tə-dŏn′) Any of several extinct mammals that resembled elephants but had differently shaped molar teeth. Mastodons disappeared from North America about 12,000 years ago, at the end of the Ice Age.

mastoid (măs′toid′) A protruding area of bone in the lower part of the skull that is located behind the ear in humans and many other vertebrates.

mathematics (măth′ə-măt′ĭks) The study of the measurement, relationships, and properties of quantities and sets, using numbers and symbols. Arithmetic, algebra, geometry, and calculus are branches of mathematics.

matrix (mā′trĭks) A substance within which something is contained or embedded. The mineral grains of a rock in which fossils are embedded make up a matrix. Bone cells are embedded in a matrix of collagen fibers and mineral salts.

matter (măt′ər) Something that occupies space and has mass. Matter is traditionally categorized as being in one of three states—solid, liquid, or gas—but plasma (a type of ionized gas) is sometimes considered a fourth state.

Maury (môr′ē), **Matthew Fontaine** 1806–1873. American naval officer and oceanographer who charted the currents of the Atlantic, Pacific, and Indian Oceans and wrote the pioneering book *Physical Geography of the Sea* (1855).

maxilla (măk-sĭl′ə) **1.** The upper part of the jaw in vertebrate animals. **2.** Either of a pair of appendages behind the mandibles in insects, spiders, crabs, and other arthropods.

maximum (măk′sə-məm) *Plural* **maxima 1.** The greatest known or greatest possible number, measure, quantity, or degree. **2.** *Mathematics* The greatest value of a function, if it has such a value.

Maxwell (măks′wĕl′), **James Clerk** 1831–1879. British physicist who united the concepts of electricity and magnetism into a comprehensive theory of electromagnetism and formulated four basic equations that describe the behavior of electric and magnetic fields. He also calculated the speed of light and showed that light is a form of electromagnetic radiation.

McClintock (mə-klĭn′tək), **Barbara** 1902–1992. American geneticist whose studies of kernel color in corn plants showed that certain genes, called transposons, can move from place to place on a single chromosome or from one chromosome to another. McClintock did other important research on the structure of chromosomes and on the history and genetics of cultivated corn.

Md The symbol for **mendelevium.**

mean (mēn) **1.** A number or quantity having a value that is intermediate between other numbers or quantities, especially an arithmetic mean or average. *See more at* **arithmetic mean. 2.** Either the second or third term of a proportion of four terms. In the proportion $\frac{2}{3} = \frac{4}{6}$, the means are 3 and 4. *Compare* **extreme.**

mean solar time Time measured with reference to an imaginary sun that lies in the same plane as the Earth's equator and that the Earth orbits at a constant speed. Using this convention results in equal, 24-hour days throughout the year. If days were measured by the actual movement of the Earth around the sun, they would vary slightly in length at different times of the year.

measles (mē′zəlz) A highly contagious disease that is caused by a virus and usually occurs in childhood. Symptoms include fever, coughing, and a rash that begins on the face and then spreads to other parts of the body.

measurement (mĕzh′ər-mənt) A method for determining quantity, capacity, or dimension. All systems of measurement use units whose amounts have been arbitrarily set and agreed upon by a group of people. Several systems of measurement are in common use, notably the United States Customary System and the metric system. The metric system has been officially adopted as the international standard for use in science, providing scientists all over the world with an efficient way of comparing the results of experiments conducted at different times and in different places. *See Table on page 208.*

mechanical advantage (mĭ-kăn′ĭ-kəl) The ratio of the output force produced by a simple machine to the applied input force.

■ **Barbara McClintock**

mechanical energy The sum of the kinetic energy and the potential energy of an object.

mechanical engineering The branch of engineering that deals with the design, production, and use of machines and mechanical devices.

mechanics (mĭ-kăn′ĭks) The branch of physics that deals with bodies at rest and in motion. The three traditional divisions of mechanics are dynamics, kinematics, and statics.

median (mē′dē-ən) **1.** In a sequence of numbers arranged from smallest to largest: **a.** The middle number, when such a sequence has an odd number of values. For example, in the sequence 3, 4, 14, 35, 280, the median is 14. **b.** The average of the two middle numbers, when such a sequence has an even number of values. For example, in the sequence 4, 8, 10, 56, the median is 9 (the average of 8 and 10). *Compare* **arithmetic mean, average, mode. 2.** A line joining a vertex of a triangle to the midpoint of the opposite side.

medicine (mĕd′ĭ-sĭn) **1.** The science and practice of diagnosing and treating disease or injury and maintaining health. **2.** A drug or other substance used to treat a disease or injury.

medium (mē′dē-əm) *Plural* **media** *or* **mediums 1.** A substance, such as agar, in which bacteria, other microorganisms, or cells are grown for scientific purposes. **2.** A substance through which energy is transmitted in the form of waves. Mechanical waves, like sound waves and ocean waves, need a medium to travel. Sound waves can travel through a solid (such as rock), a liquid (such as water), or a gas (such as air). In contrast, electromagnetic waves, such as light and x-rays, do not need a medium to travel. They can travel through a vacuum. *See more at* **wave.**

medulla (mĭ-dŭl′ə, mĭ-do͞o′lə) **1.** *See* **medulla oblongata. 2.** The central core of an anatomical structure, such as the adrenal gland or the kidney.

medulla oblongata (ŏb′lông-gä′tə) A mass of nerve tissue located at the base of the brain in humans and other vertebrates. It controls many involuntary functions, such as breathing, blood pressure, and heart rate.

medusa (mĭ-do͞o′sə) A cnidarian in its free-swimming stage. Medusas are bell-shaped, with tentacles hanging down around a central mouth. Jellyfish are medusas, while corals and sea

MEASUREMENT TABLE

INTERNATIONAL SYSTEM OF UNITS

The International System of Units (abbreviated SI for Système International d'Unités, the French name for the system) is an expanded and modified version of the metric system made up of seven base units from which all others in the system are derived. Larger or smaller multiples of any base unit are formed by adding a prefix to the unit and multiplying it by the appropriate factor. For example, to get a kilometer (multiplying factor = 10^3), you would multiply one meter by **1,000.** Similarly, to get a centimeter (multiplying factor = 10^{-2}), you would multiply one meter by **0.01.**

BASE UNITS

Unit	Quantity	Symbol
meter	length	m
kilogram	mass	kg
second	time	s
ampere	electric current	A
kelvin	temperature	K
mole	amount of matter	mol
candela	luminous intensity	cd

PREFIXES

Prefix	Symbol	Multiplying Factor	Prefix	Symbol	Multiplying Factor
tera-	T	10^{12} = 1,000,000,000,000	deci-	d	10^{-1} = 0.1
giga-	G	10^9 = 1,000,000,000	centi-	c	10^{-2} = 0.01
mega-	M	10^6 = 1,000,000	milli-	m	10^{-3} = 0.001
kilo-	k	10^3 = 1,000	micro-	µ	10^{-6} = 0.000,001
hecto-	h	10^2 = 100	nano-	n	10^{-9} = 0.000,000,001
deca-	da	10^1 = 10	pico-	p	10^{-12} = 0.000,000,000,001

US CUSTOMARY SYSTEM

Unit	Relation to Other US Customary Units	Unit	Relation to Other US Customary Units	Unit	Relation to Other US Customary Units
LENGTH		LIQUID VOLUME OR CAPACITY		WEIGHT	
inch	1/12 foot	ounce	1/16 pint	grain	1/7000 pound
foot	12 inches or 1/3 yard	gill	4 ounces	dram	1/16 ounce
yard	36 inches or 3 feet	pint	16 ounces	ounce	16 drams
rod	16½ feet or 5½ yards	quart	2 pints or ¼ gallon	pound	16 ounces
furlong	220 yards or 1/8 mile	gallon	128 ounces or 8 pints	ton (short)	2,000 pounds
mile	5,280 feet or 1,760 yards			ton (long)	2,240 pounds

CONVERSION BETWEEN METRIC AND US CUSTOMARY SYSTEMS

FROM US CUSTOMARY TO METRIC			FROM METRIC TO US CUSTOMARY		
When you know	**multiply by**	**to find**	**When you know**	**multiply by**	**to find**
inches	25.4	millimeters	millimeters	0.04	inches
	2.54	centimeters	centimeters	0.39	inches
feet	30.48	centimeters	meters	3.28	feet
yards	0.91	meters		1.09	yards
miles	1.61	kilometers	kilometers	0.62	miles
fluid ounces	29.57	milliliters	milliliters	0.03	fluid ounces
pints	0.47	liters	liters	1.06	quarts
quarts	0.95	liters		0.26	gallons
gallons	3.79	liters		2.11	pints
ounces	28.35	grams	grams	0.035	ounces
pounds	0.45	kilograms	kilograms	2.20	pounds

TEMPERATURE CONVERSION BETWEEN CELSIUS AND FAHRENHEIT

°C = (°F – 32) ÷ 1.8			°F = (°C × 1.8) + 32		
Condition	**Fahrenheit**	**Celsius**	**Condition**	**Fahrenheit**	**Celsius**
Boiling point of water	212°	100°	Freezing point of water	32°	0°
Normal body temperature	98.6°	37°	Lowest temperature Gabriel Fahrenheit could obtain mixing salt and ice	0°	–17.8°

USAGE

megabyte

Usually the prefix *kilo–* means "one thousand," and the prefix *mega–* means "one million." But in the calculation of data storage these prefixes have a different meaning. Data storage capacity (measured in bytes) is based on powers of 2 because of the binary nature of bits (1 byte is 8, or 2^3, bits). Here, the prefix *mega–* refers to the power of 2 closest to 1,000,000, which is 2^{20}, or 1,048,576. Thus, a *megabyte* is 1,048,576 bytes, although it is also used less technically to refer to a million bytes. Similarly, the prefix *kilo–* refers either to 1,000 or to 2^{10} (1,024). Measuring the transmission of data is somewhat different from measuring its storage. Since a bit of transmitted data is considered as one signal pulse rather than an either/or unit, it is natural to count transmitted bits using ordinary numbers instead of the binary system. Thus a megabit of transmitted data usually refers to a million (not 1,048,576) bits. Other prefixes for greater amounts, such as *giga–* and *tera–*, follow similar rules for data storage and transmission. There have been proposals to use different sets of prefixes to prevent confusion between the two systems, but none of them have yet been widely adopted.

anemones lack a medusa stage and exist only as polyps. *Compare* **polyp.**

mega– **1.** A prefix that means "large," as in *megavitamin,* a large dose of a vitamin. **2.** A prefix that means "one million," as in *megahertz,* one million hertz. **3.** A prefix that means 2^{20} (1,048,576), as in *megabyte,* 2^{20} bytes.

megabit (mĕg′ə-bĭt′) *Computers* **1.** One million bits. **2.** 1,048,576 (2^{20}) bits. *See Note at* **megabyte.**

megabyte (mĕg′ə-bīt′) **1.** A unit of computer memory or data storage capacity equal to 1,024 kilobytes (2^{20} bytes). **2.** One million bytes.

megafauna (mĕg′ə-fô′nə) Large or relatively large animals of a particular place or time period. The megafauna of the Pleistocene Epoch included saber-toothed tigers and mastodons.

megahertz (mĕg′ə-hûrts′) A unit of frequency equal to one million cycles per second, used to express the frequency of radio waves.

megatherium (mĕg′ə-thîr′ē-əm) A large, extinct ground sloth that lived from the Miocene through the Pleistocene Epochs, primarily in South America. It was as large as an elephant, had long curved claws, and ate plants.

megavitamin (mĕg′ə-vī′tə-mĭn) A dose of a vitamin that greatly exceeds the amount recommended for maintaining health.

megavolt (mĕg′ə-vōlt′) One million volts.

megawatt (mĕg′ə-wŏt′) One million watts.

meiosis (mī-ō′sĭs) The type of cell division that produces sex cells (or sometimes spores) in animals, plants, fungi, and many algae, in which the number of chromosomes is reduced to half the original number. The first division of meiosis involves replication of the chromosomes, followed by recombination, during which some genetic material is exchanged between pairs of chromosomes, and then separation of the paired chromosomes into two cells. In the second division, each of these two cells divides again, resulting in a total of four cells, each containing half the amount of genetic material as the original cell. Each division has four main phases: prophase, metaphase, anaphase, and telophase. *Compare* **mitosis.** *See A Closer Look, page 210.*

Meitner (mīt′nər), **Lise** 1878–1968. Austrian-born Swedish physicist who was the first to describe the process of nuclear fission. Her contributions to the field of nuclear fission led to the development of the atomic bomb and nuclear energy.

Lise Meitner

A CLOSER LOOK

Meiosis/Mitosis

In most animals and vascular plants, each body cell has two full sets of chromosomes. New cells are normally created by the type of cell division called **mitosis.** In mitosis, a cell first replicates its chromosomes and then divides, resulting in two daughter cells that are identical to the parent cell. By contrast, sex cells, or gametes, are created by **meiosis.** Meiosis also starts out with replication of the chromosomes, but there are two divisions instead of one, producing four daughter cells rather than two. Since the number of chromosomes is halved with each division, each daughter cell has just one set of chromosomes. In sexual reproduction, a female gamete unites with a male gamete, restoring the two full sets of chromosomes in a new organism.

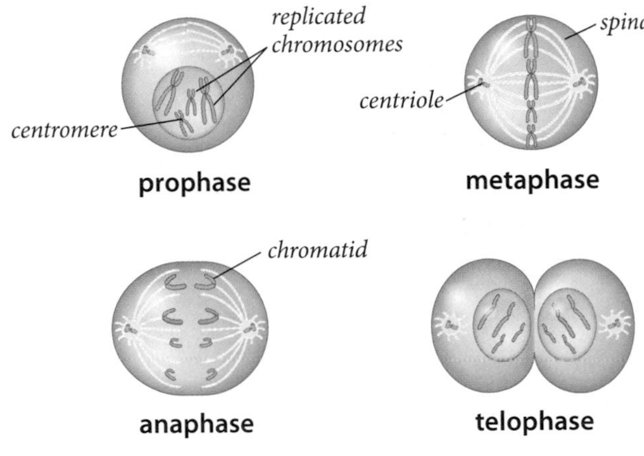

Mitosis

First, the chromosomes replicate. During prophase, the chromosomes thicken into chromatids, and centrioles move to opposite ends of the cell. In metaphase, a spindle is formed to which the centromeres attach, lining up the chromosomes at the center. In anaphase, the chromatids split, with each member of a pair moving to opposite ends of the spindle. In telophase, the spindle disappears and the cell divides.

Meiosis

First, the chromosomes replicate. During prophase I, chromosomes form homologous pairs, centrioles move toward opposite ends of the cell, and genetic material is exchanged in the process of recombination. During metaphase I, the chromosome pairs become attached to spindle fibers from opposite ends of the cell. In anaphase I, the chromatids from each chromosome pair separate and move toward opposite ends of the cell. During telophase I, the cell divides into two daughter cells. These two cells divide again during the second division of meiosis, resulting in four cells.

prophase I

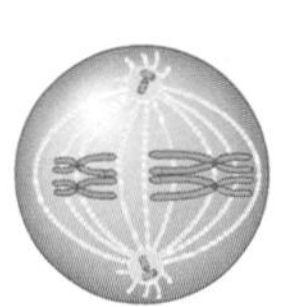

metaphase I

anaphase I

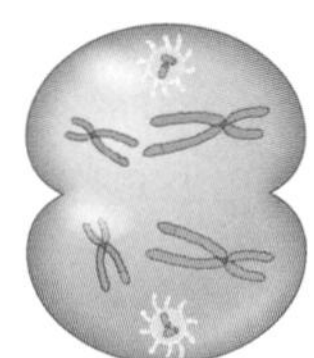

telophase I

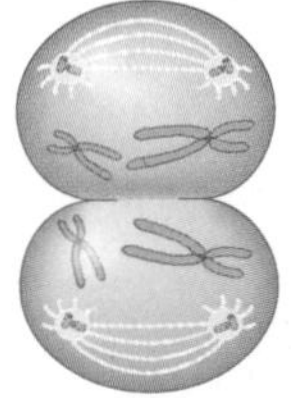

prophase II

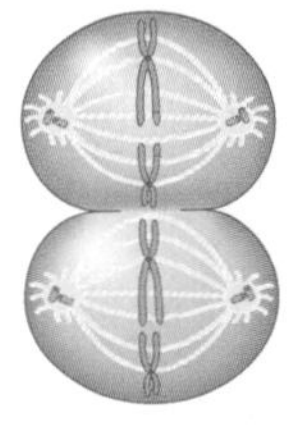

metaphase II

anaphase II

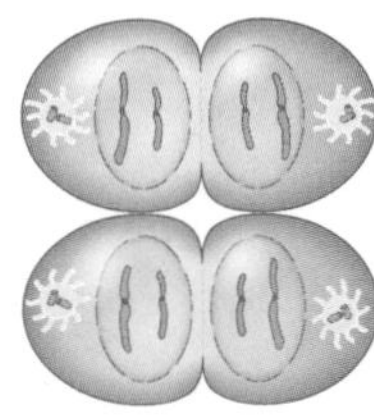

telophase II

meitnerium (mīt-nûr′ē-əm) A synthetic, radioactive element that can be produced by bombarding bismuth with iron ions. Its most stable isotope has a half-life of about 8 seconds. *Symbol* **Mt.** *Atomic number* 109. *See* **Periodic Table,** pages 254–255.

melanin (mĕl′ə-nĭn) A dark pigment that is found in most organisms. In humans it is present in the hair, skin, and eyes. It provides protection against the sun's rays by absorbing ultraviolet light.

melanoma (mĕl′ə-nō′mə) A type of skin cancer that arises from the cells that produce melanin, usually appearing as a dark-colored spot or mole.

melatonin (mĕl′ə-tō′nĭn) A hormone produced in the pineal gland that plays a role in regulating biological rhythms, including sleep and reproductive cycles.

melt (mĕlt) To change from a solid to a liquid state by heating or being heated to the melting point.

meltdown (mĕlt′doun′) Severe overheating of a nuclear reactor core, resulting in melting of the core and escape of radiation.

melting point (mĕl′tĭng) The temperature at which a solid becomes a liquid. For a given substance, the melting point of its solid form is the same as the freezing point of its liquid form. The melting point of ice is 32°F (0°C); that of iron is 2,800°F (1,538°C).

meltwater (mĕlt′wô′tər) Water that comes from melting snow or ice, especially from a glacier.

member (mĕm′bər) *Mathematics* **1.** A quantity that belongs to a set. **2.** The expression on either side of an equality sign.

membrane (mĕm′brān′) **1.** A thin, flexible layer of tissue that covers, lines, separates, or connects parts of an organism. **2.** A layer that surrounds a cell or organelle, typically consisting of molecules of lipids and proteins. **3.** *Chemistry* A thin sheet of natural or synthetic material that only certain substances in solution are able to pass through.

memory (mĕm′ə-rē) **1.** The ability to remember past experiences or learned information. **2a.** A unit of a computer in which data is stored for later use. **b.** A computer's capacity for storing information: *How much memory does this computer have?*

menarche (mə-när′kē) The first menstrual period.

Mendel (mĕn′dl), **Gregor Johann** 1822–1884. Moravian botanist who determined, through experiments on garden peas, the laws of heredity

BIOGRAPHY

Gregor Mendel

Gregor Mendel spent most of his life as a monk in a monastery in Brno (then in Moravia, now in the Czech Republic). He studied science and mathematics before entering the monastery and also at a university in Vienna after he became a monk. He became fascinated by heredity and decided to study inheritance in garden peas (after giving up initial plans to breed mice). First, Mendel developed true-breeding lines of peas that had distinctive characteristics such as flower color, height, and texture of the seeds. Then, he pollinated plants of one type with pollen from plants of another type to create hybrid offspring, and he crossed those offspring with each other. He kept careful records of the traits displayed by the offspring in each generation and analyzed the results. He introduced the idea of *dominant* and *recessive* factors (now called alleles) and developed what are now known as *Mendel's laws* of segregation and independent assortment. Long before the discovery of genes, Mendel found evidence that physical traits are passed from parent to child as pairs of discrete hereditary units.

that later became the foundation for the science of genetics. His work was published in 1865 but largely ignored until 1900, when it was rediscovered by several biologists.

Mendeleev (mĕn′də-lā′əf), **Dmitri Ivanovich** 1834–1907. Russian chemist. He devised the periodic table of the elements, which shows the relationships between the chemical elements. It was first published in 1869.

mendelevium (mĕn′də-lē′vē-əm) A synthetic, radioactive metallic element of the actinide series that can be produced by bombarding einsteinium with helium ions. Its most stable isotope has a half-life of about 52 days. *Symbol* **Md.** *Atomic number* 101. *See* **Periodic Table,** pages 254–255.

Mendel's laws (mĕn′dlz) Two principles first proposed by Gregor Mendel to describe the inheritance of traits passed from one generation to the next. The first law (also called the law of segregation) states that hereditary factors (now called genes) come in pairs (alleles), and these pairs separate during the formation of sex cells, with half the sex cells receiving one allele and half receiving the other, and each offspring receiving one allele from each parent. The second law (also called the law of independent assortment) states that different hereditary factors are distributed independently of each other into the sex cells. *See more at* **inheritance.**

meninges (mə-nĭn′jēz) The membranes enclosing the brain and spinal cord.

meningitis (mĕn′ĭn-jī′tĭs) Inflammation of the membranes, called meninges, that enclose the brain and spinal cord. It usually results from infection by a bacterium or virus.

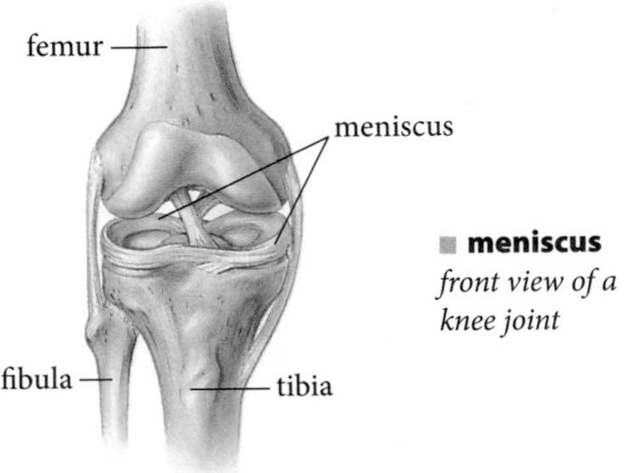

meniscus *front view of a knee joint*

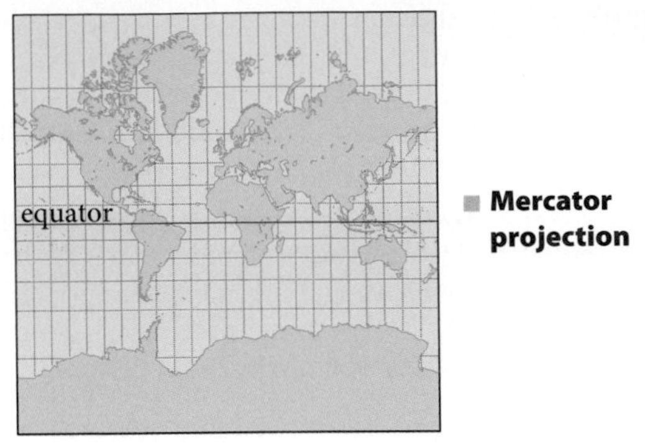

Mercator projection

meniscus (mə-nĭs′kəs) **1.** A piece of cartilage shaped like a crescent and located at the junction of two bones in a joint, such as the knee. **2.** The curved upper surface of a column of liquid. The surface is concave if the molecules of the liquid are attracted to the container walls and convex if they are not. **3.** A lens that is concave on one side and convex on the other.

menopause (mĕn′ə-pôz′) The time at which menstruation ceases, usually occurring between 45 and 55 years of age in humans.

menses (mĕn′sēz) *See* **menstruation.**

menstrual cycle (mĕn′stro͞o-əl) The series of bodily changes in women and certain other female primates in which the lining of the uterus thickens to allow for implantation of a fertilized egg. The cycle usually takes about a month to complete, with ovulation occurring around the midway point. If the egg produced is not fertilized, the lining of the uterus breaks down and is discharged during menstruation.

menstruation (mĕn′stro͞o-ā′shən) The cyclical flow of blood from the uterus that begins at puberty in female humans and certain other primates. Also called *menses.*

mental illness (mĕn′tl) Any of various disorders or diseases involving patterns of thought and behavior that severely limit a person's ability to work and to communicate with others.

menthol (mĕn′thôl′) A white, crystalline compound obtained from peppermint oil or produced synthetically. It is used as a flavoring and as a mild anesthetic.

Mercator projection (mər-kā′tər) A method of making a flat map of the Earth's surface so that the meridians and parallels appear as straight lines that cross at right angles. In a Mercator projection, areas farther from the equator appear larger, making the polar regions greatly distorted. *Compare* **conic projection, homolosine projection, sinusoidal projection.**

mercury (mûr′kyə-rē) A silvery-white, dense, poisonous metallic element that is a liquid at room temperature. It is used in some kinds of light bulbs and batteries. *Symbol* **Hg.** *Atomic number* 80. *See* **Periodic Table,** pages 254–255.

Mercury The planet that is the closest to the sun and the smallest, with a diameter about two-fifths that of Earth. Mercury's surface is covered with mountains, craters, ridges, and valleys. It orbits the sun once every 88 days, the shortest amount of time for any planet. *See Table at* **solar system,** pages 312–313.

mercury barometer A barometer consisting of a glass tube closed at one end and filled with mercury, with its open end immersed in a reservoir of mercury. The mercury in the tube falls until its weight is exactly balanced by the atmospheric pressure on the surface of the reservoir. Changes in atmospheric pressure are reflected in the varying height of the column of mercury in the tube.

WORD HISTORY

mercury

Like a few other elements, *mercury* has a chemical symbol, Hg, that bears no resemblance to its English name. This is because Hg is an abbreviation of *hydrargium,* the Latin name of the element. The Latin word came from a Greek word that meant "water-silver." With this name, the Greeks were referring to the fact that mercury is a silvery liquid at room temperature, rather than a solid like other metals. Mercury's ability to move like a living thing is the source of the old English name *quicksilver*: the word *quick* used to mean "alive," as in the Biblical phrase "the quick and the dead." The word *mercury,* which began to be used in England by the late 1300s, also refers to the element's ability to flow quickly; it was taken from the Roman god Mercury, who was the swift-footed messenger of the gods.

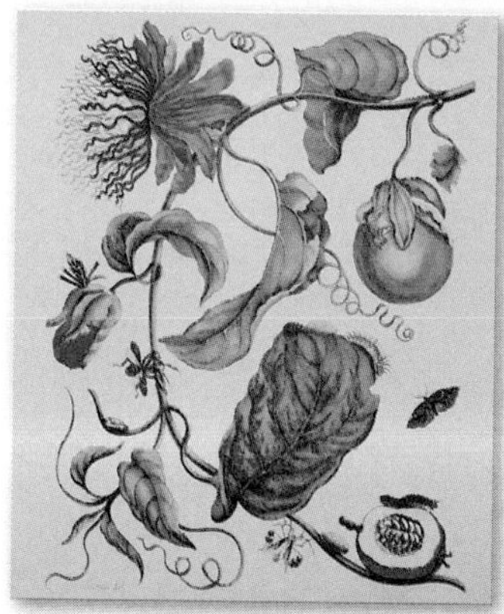

Maria Merian
watercolor of a passionflower plant and insects by Maria Merian

Merian (mā′rē-ən), **Maria Sibylla** 1647–1717. German naturalist and artist who published lavishly illustrated works based on her entomological and botanical studies in Europe and Suriname.

meridian (mə-rĭd′ē-ən) **1a.** An imaginary line forming a great circle that passes through the North and South Poles. **b.** Either half of such a circle from pole to pole. All the places on the same meridian have the same longitude. *See more at* **longitude. 2.** *Astronomy* A great circle passing through the poles of the celestial sphere and the point on the celestial sphere that is directly above the observer. *See more at* **celestial sphere.**

meristem (mĕr′ĭ-stĕm′) Plant tissue whose cells actively divide to produce new tissues that cause the plant to grow. The cells of the meristem are not specialized themselves, but they divide to

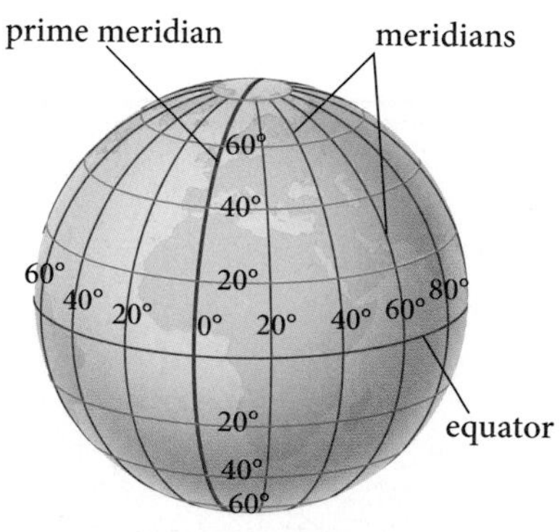

meridian

■ **mesa**
Colorado National Monument

form the specialized cells of the roots, leaves, and other plant parts. The growing tips of roots and stems and the tissue layer known as cambium are part of a plant's meristem.

mesa (mā′sə) An area of high land with a flat top and steep, clifflike sides. Mesas are larger than buttes and smaller than plateaus, and are common in the southwest United States.

mesic (mĕz′ĭk, mē′zĭk) Relating to, characterized by, or adapted to a moderately moist habitat.

Mesolithic (mĕz′ə-lĭth′ĭk) The cultural period of the Stone Age between the Paleolithic and the Neolithic, beginning at different times in different parts of the world, about 15,000 to 10,000 years ago. The Mesolithic is marked by the appearance of small-bladed stone tools and weapons and by the beginnings of settled communities. *Compare* **Neolithic, Paleolithic.**

mesophyll (mĕz′ə-fĭl′) The tissues of a leaf that carry on photosynthesis, consisting of the palisade layer and the spongy parenchyma.

mesosphere (mĕz′ə-sfîr′) The layer of the Earth's atmosphere lying above the stratosphere and below the thermosphere, from about 30 to 50 miles (50 to 80 kilometers) above the Earth's surface. In the mesosphere, temperatures decrease with increasing altitude.

Mesozoic (mĕz′ə-zō′ĭk) The era of geologic time from about 251 to 66 million years ago. The Mesozoic Era was characterized by the development of flowering plants and by the appearance and extinction of dinosaurs. *See Chart at* **geologic time,** pages 146–147.

messenger RNA (mĕs′ən-jər) *See under* **RNA.**

metabolism (mĭ-tăb′ə-lĭz′əm) The chemical processes taking place in a cell or organism that are needed to sustain life. As part of metabolism, organic compounds are broken down to provide the energy for cellular activities like growth and repair, while simple molecules are combined to make complex compounds like proteins and fatty acids. Many metabolic processes are brought about by the action of enzymes. —*Adjective* **metabolic.**

metacarpal (mĕt′ə-kär′pəl) Any of the bones of the hand lying between the carpals and the bones of the fingers (phalanges). *See more at* **skeleton.**

metal (mĕt′l) **1.** Any of a large group of elements, including iron, gold, copper, lead, and magnesium, that conduct heat and electricity well. Met-

USAGE

metal

We think of metals as hard, shiny materials used to make things like paper clips and cars. But for chemists, a *metal* is a chemical element that loses electrons in a chemical reaction. Metal atoms do this because of the structure of their electron shells—the layers in which electrons are arranged around an atom's nucleus. If an element's outermost electron shell is filled, the element is stable and does not react easily. But if the shell contains only a few electrons, the atom will try to share them with another atom in a chemical reaction, thereby becoming stable. Elements having only one electron in their outermost shell are the most reactive; all they have to do to become stable is lose this electron. Such elements are *alkali metals* like sodium and potassium, and they are listed in the left-hand column of the periodic table (pages 254–255). The metals farther toward the right side of the periodic table, such as tin and lead, have more electrons in their outermost shell and are not as reactive because sharing or losing all these electrons would require more energy. The elements that fall between these extremes are somewhat reactive and are called *transition elements.* They include elements like iron, copper, tungsten, and silver.

als can be hammered into thin sheets or drawn into wires. They are usually shiny and opaque. All metals except mercury are solid at room temperature. **2.** An alloy, such as steel or bronze, made of two or more metals.

metallic bond (mə-tăl′ĭk) The chemical bonding that holds the atoms of a metal together. This bond is formed from the attraction between mobile electrons and fixed, positively charged metallic ions. Whereas most chemical bonds are localized between specific neighboring atoms, metallic bonds extend over the entire molecular structure. *See more at* **bond.**

metalloid (mĕt′l-oid′) **1.** An element that is not a metal but that has some properties of metals. Arsenic, for example, is a metalloid that looks like a metal but is a poor conductor of electricity. **2.** A nonmetallic element, such as carbon, that can form alloys with metals.

metallurgy (mĕt′l-ûr′jē) The science and technology of extracting metals from their ores, refining them for use, and creating alloys and useful objects from them.

metamorphic (mĕt′ə-môr′fĭk) **1.** *Geology* Relating to metamorphism. Metamorphic rocks are formed when igneous, sedimentary, or other metamorphic rocks undergo a physical change due to extreme heat and pressure. These changes often produce folded layers and veins in the rocks, and they can also cause pockets of precious minerals to form. *See Table at* **rock. 2.** *Zoology* Relating to metamorphosis.

metamorphism (mĕt′ə-môr′fĭz′əm) The process by which rocks are changed in composition, texture, or structure by extreme heat and pressure.

metamorphosis (mĕt′ə-môr′fə-sĭs) Change in the form and habits of an animal during its development after birth or hatching. Examples of metamorphosis are the transformation of a maggot into an adult fly and a tadpole into an adult frog. ❖ Many insects, such as butterflies, bees, and flies, pass through four different stages during metamorphosis: egg, larva, pupa, and adult. The adult looks very different from the larva. This kind of metamorphosis is called **complete metamorphosis.** ❖ Some insects, such as grasshoppers, pass through only three different stages during metamorphosis: egg, larva, and adult. They have no pupal stage, and the adult insect looks very similar to the larva. This kind of metamorphosis is called **incomplete metamorphosis.**

metaphase (mĕt′ə-fāz′) The stage of cell division in which the spindle forms and chromosomes (or pairs of chromosomes in the first division of meiosis) line up along the center of the cell. Metaphase is preceded by prophase and followed by anaphase. *See more at* **meiosis, mitosis.**

metastasis (mə-tăs′tə-sĭs) The spread of cancerous cells from one area of the body to other areas. — *Verb* **metastasize.**

metatarsal (mĕt′ə-tär′səl) Any of the bones of the foot lying between the tarsals and the bones of the toes (phalanges). *See more at* **skeleton.**

meteor (mē′tē-ər) **1.** A bright trail or streak of light that appears in the night sky when a meteoroid enters the Earth's atmosphere. The friction with the air causes the rock to glow with heat. Also called *shooting star.* **2.** A rocky body that produces such light. Most meteors burn up before reaching the Earth's surface. *See Note on page 216. See Note at* **solar system.** ❖ A **meteor shower** occurs when a large number of meteors appear together and seem to come from the same area in the sky.

meteorite (mē′tē-ə-rīt′) A meteor that has reached the Earth's surface without completely burning up due to friction.

meteoroid (mē′tē-ə-roid′) A solid body that

■ **metamorphosis**
development of a monarch butterfly from egg to caterpillar to pupa to adult

USAGE

meteor/meteorite/meteoroid

Until the 1800s, the term *meteor* was applied to all sorts of atmospheric phenomena: rain was an *aqueous meteor,* winds were *airy meteors,* and streaks of light in the sky were *fiery meteors.* This general use of *meteor* survives in our word *meteorology,* the study of the weather and atmospheric phenomena. Nowadays, *meteor* has a more specific meaning: it refers to a rock from interplanetary space that has entered the Earth's atmosphere, giving off light as it is heated by friction with the atmosphere. A related word, *meteoroid,* refers to a rock in space that has the potential to enter the atmosphere. Most meteoroids are very small, typically ranging in size from specks of dust to the size of a pebble. A rock that has passed through the atmosphere as a meteor and landed on the ground is called a *meteorite.*

moves in space within our solar system and is smaller than an asteroid but at least as large as a speck of dust.

meteorology (mē′tē-ə-rŏl**′**ə-jē) The scientific study of the atmosphere and of atmospheric conditions, especially as they relate to weather.

meter (mē**′**tər) The basic unit of length in the metric system, equal to about 39.37 inches. *See Table at* **measurement.**

meter-kilogram-second Relating to a system of measurement in which the meter, the kilogram, and the second are the basic units of length, mass, and time.

methane (mĕth**′**ān′) A colorless, odorless, flammable gas that is the simplest of the hydrocarbons, having the formula CH_4. It is the major constituent of natural gas and is released during the decomposition of organic matter, as in marshes and landfills.

methanol (mĕth**′**ə-nôl′) A colorless, toxic, flammable liquid, CH_3OH, used as an antifreeze, a general solvent, and a fuel. Also called *methyl alcohol, wood alcohol.*

methionine (mə-thī**′**ə-nēn′) An essential amino acid. *See more at* **amino acid.**

methyl (mĕth**′**əl) The organic group CH_3, derived from methane and occurring as a radical, an ion, or a substituent in many important chemical compounds.

methyl alcohol *See* **methanol.**

metric (mĕt**′**rĭk) Relating to the meter or the metric system. *See Table at* **measurement.**

metric system A decimal system of weights and measures based on the meter as a unit of length, the kilogram as a unit of mass, and the liter as a unit of volume. *See Table at* **measurement.**

metric ton A unit of mass or weight equal to 1,000 kilograms (about 2,205 pounds). *See Table at* **measurement.**

mg Abbreviation of **milligram.**

Mg The symbol for **magnesium.**

MHz Abbreviation of **megahertz.**

mi. Abbreviation of **mile.**

mica (mī**′**kə) Any of a group of aluminum silicate minerals that can be split easily into thin, partly transparent sheets. Mica is common in igneous and metamorphic rocks. It is highly resistant to heat and is used in electric fuses and other electrical equipment.

Michelson (mī**′**kəl-sən), **Albert Abraham** 1852–1931. German-born American physicist. In a carefully conducted experiment in 1887, he and Edward Morley failed to find evidence of ether, the hypothetical medium of electromagnetic waves. The effort to explain this result eventually led to Einstein's development of the theory of relativity.

micro– **1.** A prefix that means "small," as in *microorganism,* a very small organism. **2.** A prefix that means "one millionth," as in *microgram,* one millionth of a gram.

microbe (mī**′**krōb′) A microorganism, especially a bacterium that causes disease. *See Note at* **germ.**

microbiology (mī′krō-bī-ŏl**′**ə-jē) The scientific study of microorganisms.

microclimate (mī**′**krō-klī′mĭt) The climate of a small, specific place within a larger area. An area as small as a yard or park can have several different microclimates depending on how much sunlight, shade, or exposure to the wind there is at a particular spot.

microcline (mī**′**krō-klīn′) A type of feldspar

consisting of potassium aluminum silicate. Microcline is white, pink, red-brown, or green.

micrograph (mī′krə-grăf′) A drawing or photograph of an object viewed through a microscope.

micrometer[1] (mī-krŏm′ĭ-tər) A device for measuring very small distances, angles, or objects.

micrometer[2] (mī′krō-mē′tər) *See* **micron.**

micron (mī′krŏn′) A unit of length in the metric system equal to one millionth (10^{-6}) of a meter. Also called *micrometer.*

micronutrient (mī′krō-no͞o′trē-ənt) A substance, such as a vitamin or mineral, that is essential in very small amounts for the proper growth and metabolism of a living organism.

microorganism (mī′krō-ôr′gə-nĭz′əm) An organism that can be seen only with the aid of a microscope. Microorganisms include bacteria, protozoans, and certain algae and fungi. *See Note at* **germ.**

microscope (mī′krə-skōp′) An instrument used to produce magnified images of objects or details too small for the naked eye to see. An optical microscope uses visible light to illuminate an object and a system of lenses to form an image. Other types of microscopes use other means to produce images.

microsecond (mī′krō-sĕk′ənd) A unit of time equal to one millionth (10^{-6}) of a second.

microtubule (mī′krō-to͞o′byo͞ol) Any of the tube-shaped structures that help cells maintain their shape and assist in forming the cell spindle during cell division. Microtubules are found in the cytoplasm of the cells of all organisms except bacteria and archaea.

microwave (mī′krō-wāv′) **1.** An electromagnetic wave having a wavelength longer than that of infrared waves and shorter than that of radio waves. Microwaves are used in telecommunications, radar, and microwave ovens. Microwaves are sometimes considered to be radio waves with the shortest wavelengths. *See more at* **electromagnetic spectrum. 2.** An oven in which food is cooked, warmed, or thawed by means of microwaves.

midbrain (mĭd′brān′) The middle part of the brain in vertebrate animals. In most animals except mammals, the midbrain processes sensory information. In mammals, it serves mainly to connect the forebrain with the hindbrain. *Compare* **forebrain, hindbrain.**

middle ear (mĭd′l) The part of the ear in most vertebrates that contains the eardrum and transmits sound vibrations to the inner ear. In mammals, it also contains three small bones called the ossicles. *See more at* **ear.**

mid-ocean ridge (mĭd′ō′shən) A long mountain range on the ocean floor, extending almost continuously through the North and South Atlantic Oceans, the Indian Ocean, and the South Pacific Ocean in places where tectonic plates are pulling away from each other. A deep rift valley is located at its center, from which magma flows and forms new oceanic crust. As the magma cools and hardens it becomes part of the mountain range. *See more at* **tectonic boundary.**

midrib (mĭd′rĭb′) The central or main vein of a leaf.

migraine (mī′grān′) A severe, throbbing headache, often accompanied by nausea, that usually affects only one side of the head and tends to recur.

migrate (mī′grāt′) To travel from one place to another at regular times of year, often over long distances. Salmon, whales, and swallows all migrate.

mil (mĭl) A unit of length equal to 0.001 of an inch (about 0.03 millimeter), used chiefly to measure the diameter of wires.

mildew (mĭl′do͞o′) Any of various fungi that form a white or grayish coating on surfaces, such

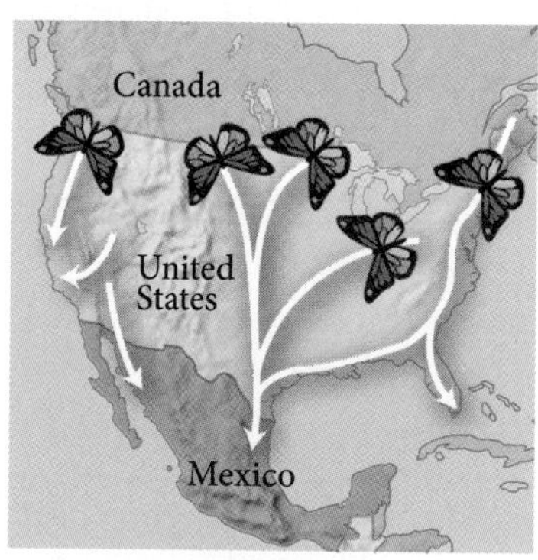

migrate
This map shows the paths that monarch butterflies take when they migrate south to a warmer climate for winter.

Milky Way

as plant leaves, cloth, or leather, especially under damp, warm conditions.

mile (mīl) **1.** A unit of length equal to 5,280 feet or 1,760 yards (about 1,609 meters). Also called *statute mile.* **2.** *See* **nautical mile.** *See Table at* **measurement.**

milk (mĭlk) A white liquid produced by the mammary glands of female mammals for feeding their young. Milk contains proteins, fats, vitamins, minerals, and sugars, especially lactose.

Milky Way (mĭl′kē) The galaxy containing the sun, the solar system, and all of the stars that are visible in the night sky. Our sun is in the outer part of the galaxy, and when we look toward its center we see a vast numbers of stars that cluster in a faint band that stretches across the night sky. This band is also called the Milky Way.

milli– A prefix that means "one thousandth," as in *millimeter,* one thousandth of a meter.

millibar (mĭl′ə-bär′) A unit of atmospheric pressure equal to 0.001 bar.

milligram (mĭl′ĭ-grăm′) A unit of mass in the metric system equal to 0.001 gram. *See Table at* **measurement.**

milliliter (mĭl′ə-lē′tər) A unit of fluid volume or capacity in the metric system equal to 0.001 liter. *See Table at* **measurement.**

millimeter (mĭl′ə-mē′tər) A unit of length in the metric system equal to 0.001 meter. *See Table at* **measurement.**

millipede (mĭl′ə-pēd′) Any of various small invertebrate animals having a cylindrical body composed of many narrow segments, most of which have two pairs of legs. Millipedes feed on plants and, unlike centipedes, are not venomous. *Compare* **centipede.**

Milstein (mĭl′stēn′), **César** 1927–2002. British-born Argentinian immunologist. With Georges Köhler he developed a method of producing antibodies that fight specific cells. The antibodies are used to diagnose and treat certain forms of cancer and other diseases.

milt (mĭlt) The sperm cells of male fish, together with the milky liquid containing them.

mimicry (mĭm′ĭ-krē) The resemblance of one organism to another or to an object in its surroundings, especially for concealment or protection.

mineral (mĭn′ər-əl) **1.** A naturally occurring, solid, inorganic element or compound having a uniform composition and a specific crystal structure. Minerals typically have a characteristic hardness and color, or range of colors, by which they can be recognized. **2.** A natural substance of commercial value, such as iron ore, coal, or petroleum, that is obtained by mining, quarrying, or drilling. **3.** An inorganic element, such as calcium, iron, potassium, sodium, or zinc, that is essential to the nutrition of animals and plants.

mineralogy (mĭn′ə-rŏl′ə-jē) The scientific study

Did You Know...?

mimicry

Have you ever seen a bug that looks like a leaf, or a butterfly with patterns on its wings that resemble the large eyes of an owl? Many animals, and even some plants and fungi, have evolved to imitate certain characteristics of other kinds of organisms. *Mimicry,* the name for this imitation of one species by another, is often a strategy for avoiding predation. Some harmless king snakes, for example, have a pattern of black, yellow, and red bands that is very similar to the pattern found in venomous coral snakes. This color pattern protects the king snakes — coyotes, hawks, and other predators avoid both the dangerous coral snakes and the tasty king snakes. Mimicry can be even more devious than this. One fungus species that infects plants causes the plant to make a structure that looks like a flower but is full of fungal spores. When an insect visits the fake flower looking for nectar, it picks up the spores and gives them a ride to another plant.

■ **mirage**
A distorted image of the sky creates the illusion of water on a highway.

of minerals, their composition and properties, and the places where they are likely to occur.

mineral oil A colorless, odorless, tasteless oil distilled from petroleum. It is used as a lubricant and, in medicine, as a laxative.

minimum (mĭn′ə-məm) **1.** The lowest known or lowest possible number, measure, quantity, or degree. **2.** *Mathematics* The lowest value of a function, if it has such a value.

minuend (mĭn′yo͞o-ĕnd′) A number from which another is subtracted. For example, in the numerical expression 100 – 23 = 77, the minuend is 100.

minute (mĭn′ĭt) **1.** A unit of time equal to $\frac{1}{60}$ of an hour, or 60 seconds. **2.** A unit of angular measurement equal to $\frac{1}{60}$ of a degree, or 60 seconds.

Miocene (mī′ə-sēn′) The fourth epoch of the Tertiary Period, from about 23 to 5 million years ago, characterized by the spread of grasses and grazing mammals. *See Chart at* **geologic time,** pages 146–147.

mirage (mĭ-räzh′) A phenomenon in which a distorted image of a distant object appears above or below the horizon. A mirage can occur when a layer of heated air immediately above a hot surface such as a highway or desert bends light upward, or when warmer air above a layer of much colder air bends light downward.

miscible (mĭs′ə-bəl) Relating to two or more substances, such as water and alcohol, that can be mixed together in any proportion without separating.

Mississippian (mĭs′ĭ-sĭp′ē-ən) The earlier of two subdivisions of the Carboniferous Period, from about 359 to 318 million years ago. During the Mississippian, shallow seas spread over many former land areas, and the first conifers appeared. In North America, the Mississippian and Pennsylvanian have traditionally been classified as full geologic periods rather than as subdivisions of the Carboniferous. *See Chart at* **geologic time,** pages 146–147.

Mitchell (mĭch′əl), **Maria** 1818–1889. American astronomer and educator noted for her study of sunspots and nebulae and for her discovery of a comet (1847).

mite (mīt) Any of numerous very small arachnids that often live as parasites on other animals or plants. Like ticks and unlike spiders, mites have no constriction between the cephalothorax and abdomen. Many mite species play an important ecological role as decomposers. Some species damage crops and stored food, and others transmit disease.

mitochondrial DNA (mī′tə-kŏn′drē-əl) DNA that is contained in the mitochondria of eukaryotic cells. Because it is inherited maternally, through the egg cell, it can be used for tracing maternal ancestry.

mitochondrion (mī′tə-kŏn′drē-ən) *Plural* **mitochondria** A structure in the cytoplasm of all cells except bacteria and archaea, where food molecules are broken down to produce usable energy in the form of ATP. *See more at* **cell.**

mitosis (mī-tō′sĭs) The type of cell division that occurs in the body cells (called somatic cells) of

■ **Maria Mitchell**

multicellular organisms, in which the cell divides to produce two new cells, each having the same number and type of chromosomes as the original. Early in mitosis, each chromosome replicates to form two identical strands (called chromatids), which line up along the center of the cell by attaching to the fibers of the cell spindle. The pairs of chromatids then separate, each half of a pair moving to an opposite end of the cell. When a new membrane forms around each of the two groups of chromosomes, division of the nucleus is complete. The four main phases of mitosis are prophase, metaphase, anaphase, and telophase. *See more at* **meiosis.**

mixed number (mĭkst) A number, such as $7\frac{3}{8}$, consisting of a whole number and a fraction.

mixture (mĭks′chər) A composition of two or more substances that are not chemically combined with each other and are capable of being separated.

ml or **mL** Abbreviation of **milliliter.**

mm Abbreviation of **millimeter.**

Mn The symbol for **manganese.**

Mo The symbol for **molybdenum.**

moa (mō′ə) Any of various large, wingless birds of New Zealand that resembled an ostrich and are thought to have become extinct before the year 1500. Most scientists believe that hunting by the early inhabitants of New Zealand caused the moas' extinction.

Möbius strip (mō′bē-əs) A continuous one-sided surface formed from a rectangular strip by rotating one end 180° and attaching it to the other end.

mode (mōd) The value that occurs most frequently in a data set. For example, in the set 125, 140, 172, 164, 140, 110, the mode is 140. *Compare* **arithmetic mean, average, median.**

model (mŏd′l) A representation of a system or of a set of observable events that accounts for its properties and is used to study its characteristics.

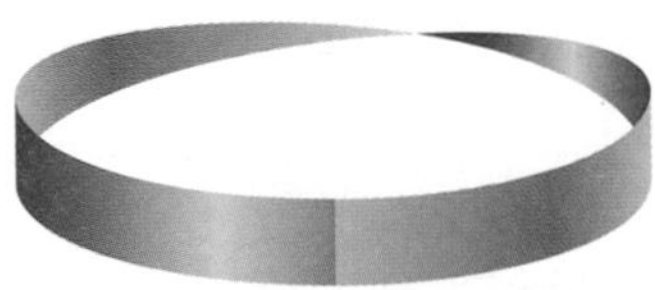

Möbius strip

modem (mō′dəm) A device that sends and receives digital data using an analog signal. Modems are used to establish network and Internet connections using telephone wires, television cables, and radio waves.

moderator (mŏd′ə-rā′tər) A substance, such as graphite or water, placed in a nuclear reactor to slow neutrons down to speeds at which they are likely to cause additional nuclear fission.

modulate (mŏj′ə-lāt′) To vary the amplitude, frequency, or some other characteristic of electromagnetic waves in a way that makes them correspond to a signal or to information that is to be transmitted.

Mohorovičić discontinuity (mō′hə-rō′və-chĭch) The boundary between the Earth's crust and mantle. The Mohorovičić discontinuity is located at an average depth of 5 miles (8 kilometers) under the oceans and 20 miles (32 kilometers) under the continents. Scientists discovered this boundary because they noticed that the velocity of seismic waves increases sharply as the waves pass from the Earth's crust into the mantle.

Mohs scale (mōz) A scale used to measure the relative hardness of a mineral by its resistance to scratching. There are ten standard minerals on this scale, ranging from talc, the softest (measuring 1 on the scale), to diamond, the hardest (measuring 10 on the scale).

molar[1] (mō′lər) *Chemistry* **1.** Relating to a mole. **2.** Containing one mole of solute per liter of solution.

molar[2] Any of the teeth located toward the back of

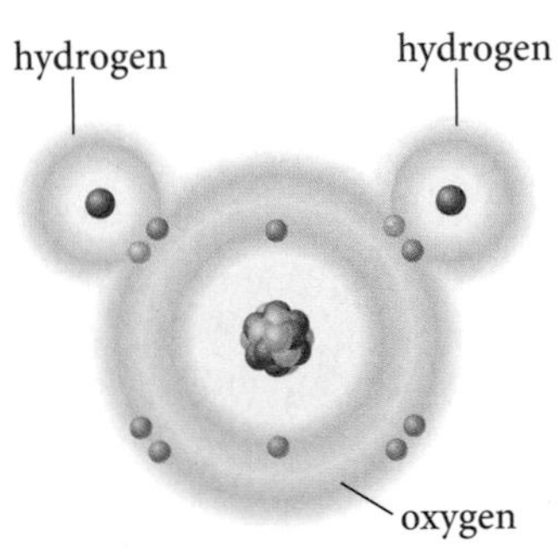

molecule

Two atoms of hydrogen and one atom of oxygen join together to form a molecule of water.

the jaws, having broad surfaces used for grinding food. Adult humans have 12 molars.

mold (mōld) Any of various fungi that often form a fuzzy growth on the surface of organic matter. Molds can cause food to spoil, but they are also used to make cheese and other foods, and many antibiotics are derived from molds.

mole[1] (mōl) A small, usually dark growth on the skin.

mole[2] Any of various small mammals that have silky fur, strong forefeet for burrowing, and poor vision. Moles usually live underground and eat insects and earthworms.

mole[3] A unit used in measuring amounts of chemical substances. One mole of a substance is defined as the amount of that substance that has the same number of atoms, molecules, ions, or other elementary units as the number of atoms in 12 grams of carbon-12. (That number is approximately 6.0221×10^{23}, or Avogadro's number.) A mole of a chemical has a mass in grams numerically equal to its molecular weight. For example, carbon dioxide, CO_2, has a molecular weight of 44; therefore, one mole of it weighs 44 grams.

molecular formula (mə-lĕk′yə-lər) A chemical formula that shows the total number and kinds of atoms in a molecule, but not their structural arrangement. For example, the molecular formula of aspirin is $C_9H_8O_4$. *Compare* **structural formula.**

molecular weight The sum of the atomic weights of all the atoms in a molecule. For example, since the atomic weight of hydrogen is 1 and the atomic weight of oxygen is 16, the molecular weight of water (H_2O) is 1 + 1 + 16, or 18.

■ **molt**
king penguin molting

molecule (mŏl′ĭ-kyo͞ol′) A group of two or more atoms linked together by sharing electrons in a chemical bond.

mollusk or **mollusc** (mŏl′əsk) Any of numerous invertebrate animals having a soft unsegmented body, a structure called the mantle that covers the internal organs, and usually a hard external shell. Mollusks include the gastropods (snails and slugs), bivalves (clams, oysters, and mussels), and cephalopods (octopuses, squids, and nautiluses).

molt (mōlt) To shed an outer covering, such as skin or feathers, for replacement by a new growth. Many snakes, birds, and arthropods molt.

molybdenum (mə-lĭb′də-nəm) A hard, silvery-white metallic element that resists corrosion and remains strong at high temperatures. It is used to harden and toughen steel and to make wire that can withstand high temperatures. Molybdenum is an essential trace element in plant metabolism. *Symbol* **Mo.** *Atomic number* 42. *See* **Periodic Table,** pages 254–255.

momentum (mō-mĕn′təm) A measure of the motion of matter, equal to the mass of the moving object times its velocity. If an object's mass, speed, or direction of motion changes, its momentum changes. The total momentum of a system of bodies will always remain constant unless the bodies are acted on by an outside force. *See more at* **angular momentum.**

mongoose (mŏng′go͞os′) Any of various mammals of Asia and Africa that resemble weasels and are noted for their ability to kill venomous snakes such as cobras.

monitor (mŏn′ĭ-tər) A device that accepts video signals from a computer and displays information on a screen.

monkey (mŭng′kē) Any of various primates that have tails and live in tropical or subtropical regions. Baboons, macaques, mandrills, and marmosets are monkeys. *Compare* **ape.**

mono– A prefix that means "one, only, single," as in *monochromatic,* having only one color. It is often found in chemical names, where it means "containing just one" of the specified atom or group, as in *carbon monoxide,* which is carbon attached to a single oxygen atom.

monochromatic (mŏn′ə-krō-măt′ĭk) **1.** Having

or appearing to have only one color: *monochromatic light.* **2.** Consisting of a single wavelength of light or other radiation: *monochromatic x-rays.*

monoclinic (mŏn′ə-klĭn′ĭk) Relating to a crystal having three axes of different lengths. Two of the axes are at oblique angles to each other, and the third axis is perpendicular to the plane that is made by the other two. The mineral gypsum has monoclinic crystals. *See more at* **crystal.**

monocotyledon (mŏn′ə-kŏt′l-ēd′n) or **monocot** (mŏn′ə-kŏt′) A flowering plant having a single cotyledon in the seed. Monocotyledons have leaves with parallel veins and flower parts in multiples of three. Grasses, palms, lilies, and irises are monocotyledons. *Compare* **dicotyledon.**

monocyte (mŏn′ə-sīt′) One of the large white blood cells that circulate in the blood and develop into macrophages, which engulf and break down microorganisms capable of causing infection.

Monod (mô-nō′), **Jacques Lucien** 1910–1976. French biochemist. With François Jacob, he proposed the existence of messenger RNA. They also studied how genes control cellular activity by directing the synthesis of proteins.

monoecious (mə-nē′shəs) Having separate male and female reproductive organs on the same plant. Corn plants and many conifers are monoecious. *Compare* **dioecious.**

monomer (mŏn′ə-mər) A molecule that can combine with others of the same kind to form a polymer. Glucose molecules, for example, are monomers that can combine to form the polymer cellulose.

monomial (mŏ-nō′mē-əl) An algebraic expression consisting of a single term having the form ax^n, where a is a number and n is an integer greater than or equal to 0. Examples of monomials are 27, $4x$, and x^2.

mononucleosis (mŏn′ō-no͞o′klē-ō′sĭs) A contagious disease caused by a virus and characterized by fever, sore throat, swollen lymph nodes, and fatigue. The symptoms may last for several weeks.

monosaccharide (mŏn′ə-săk′ə-rīd′) Any of a class of simple carbohydrates that cannot be broken down to simpler sugars by hydrolysis. Fructose is a monosaccharide.

monotreme (mŏn′ə-trēm′) Any of various mammals having a reproductive system in which the females lay eggs and have no teats but provide milk directly through the skin to their young. The only living monotremes are the platypus and the echidnas.

monounsaturated (mŏn′ō-ŭn-săch′ə-rā′tĭd) Relating to an organic compound, especially an oil or fatty acid, having only one double or triple bond per molecule. *See more at* **unsaturated.**

monoxide (mə-nŏk′sīd′) A compound consisting of two elements, one of which is a single oxygen atom. Carbon monoxide, for example, contains a carbon atom bound to a single oxygen atom.

monsoon (mŏn-so͞on′) **1.** A system of winds that influences the climate of a large area and that reverses direction with the seasons. Monsoons are caused primarily by the seasonal changes in temperature over large areas of land and water. **2.** In southern Asia, a wind that blows from the southwest in summer and usually brings heavy rains.

moon (mo͞on) **1.** Often **Moon** The natural satellite of Earth, visible by reflection of sunlight and

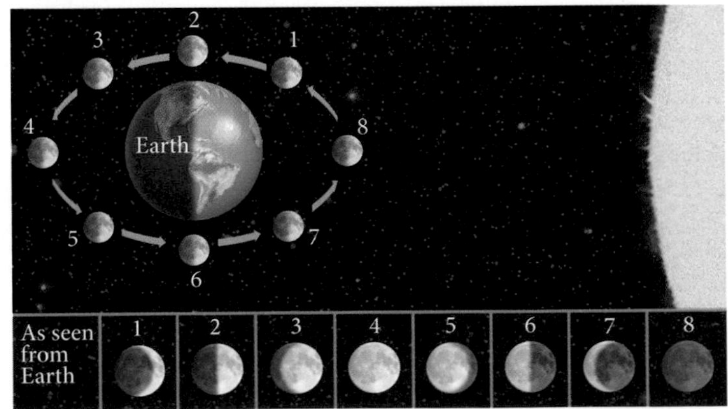

moon

The moon changes in appearance during its monthly cycle because as it orbits the Earth, different amounts of the side lit by the sun are visible from the Earth.

Did You Know...?

moons

We usually think of our moon as *the* moon, but any planet's natural satellites can be called moons. Jupiter and Saturn each have over 60 moons, and additional small ones around these and other planets are still being discovered. Many of the moons in our solar system are strikingly unlike Earth's moon. Our moon's surface is almost entirely rock, but one of Jupiter's moons, Europa, has an icy surface covering an ocean of liquid water that may support life. Io, another of Jupiter's moons, is covered with huge volcanoes that emit plumes of sulfur so enormous they can be seen by space telescopes orbiting Earth. Titan, Saturn's largest moon, has rivers and lakes on its surface, but the liquid in them is condensed methane, not water. Water on Titan is thought to play a role like that of magma on Earth, existing as a liquid beneath the surface and occasionally erupting in volcanos that form "lava flows" of ice.

traveling around Earth in a slightly elliptical orbit at an average distance of about 238,855 miles (384,400 kilometers). The moon's average diameter is 2,159 miles (3,475 kilometers), and its mass is about $\frac{1}{80}$ that of Earth. **2.** A natural satellite revolving around a planet: *the moons of Jupiter.* **3.** The moon as it appears at a particular time in its cycle of phases: *a half moon.*

moraine
at the front of the Briksdal Glacier, Norway

moraine (mə-rān′) A mass of boulders, pebbles, sand, and silt along the front or sides of a glacier, consisting mostly of material that fell onto the glacier from above or that was broken from the bedrock and carried along by the moving ice. This debris drops out from the ice when it melts at the edge of the glacier, forming a long ridge that can be pushed farther forward if the glacier advances or left behind if the glacier shrinks. ❖ A moraine that forms in front of a glacier is a **terminal moraine.** ❖ A moraine that forms along the side of a glacier is a **lateral moraine.**

Morgan (môr′gən), **Thomas Hunt** 1866–1945. American zoologist who investigated heredity. In experiments with fruit flies, he demonstrated that the genes that carry hereditary information are located on chromosomes, and he developed techniques for determining the location of a gene on a chromosome.

Morley (môr′lē), **Edward Williams** 1838–1923. American chemist and physicist noted for an 1887 experiment, conducted with Albert Michelson, that failed to find evidence of ether, the hypothetical medium of electromagnetic waves.

morphine (môr′fēn′) A drug extracted from opium, used in medicine to relieve severe pain and for its sedative effects. It can be highly addictive.

morphology (môr-fŏl′ə-jē) The size, shape, and structure of an organism or one of its parts. Biologists usually describe the morphology of an organism separately from its physiology.

Morse (môrs), **Samuel Finley Breese** 1791–1872. American inventor who developed a telegraphic code for transmitting messages, which became known as Morse code.

mosquito (mə-skē′tō) Any of numerous small flies, the females of which suck blood from animals through a slender organ called a proboscis. Some kinds transmit diseases such as malaria and yellow fever.

moss (môs) **1.** Any of numerous small green plants that lack vascular tissue and do not bear seeds. Mosses usually live in moist, shady areas and grow in clusters or mats on the ground, rocks, and tree trunks. **2.** Any of a number of plants that look like mosses but are not related to them. For instance, reindeer moss is a lichen, Irish moss is an alga, and Spanish moss is a flowering plant.

moth (môth) Any of numerous insects that are closely related to the butterflies but are usually nocturnal and have a stouter body and feathery or slender antennae. Unlike butterflies, moths tend to hold their wings out horizontally when at rest. *Compare* **butterfly.**

motherboard (mŭ*th*′ər-bôrd′) The main circuit board of a computer, usually containing the central processing unit and main system memory as well as circuitry that controls the drives, keyboard, monitor, and other peripheral devices.

mother-of-pearl (mŭ*th*′ər-əv-pûrl′) The hard, smooth, pearly layer on the inside of certain seashells, such as abalones and some kinds of oysters. It is used to make buttons and jewelry. Also called *nacre.*

motile (mōt′l, mō′tīl′) Moving or able to move by itself. Motile cells, such as sperm, often move by using flagella or cilia. —*Noun* **motility** (mō-tĭl′ĭ-tē).

motor (mō′tər) *Noun* **1.** A machine that uses a form of energy, such as electric energy or the explosive power of a fuel, to produce mechanical motion. —*Adjective* **2.** Involving the muscles or the nerves that are connected to them: *motor control; a motor nerve. Compare* **sensory.**

mountain (moun′tən) A large, usually steep-sided, raised portion of the Earth's surface. Mountains can occur as single peaks or as part of a long chain. They can form through volcanic activity, by erosion of the surrounding land, or by the collision of tectonic plates. The Himalayas, the highest mountains in the world, were formed when the plate carrying the landmass of India collided with the plate carrying the landmass of China.

mouse (mous) *Plural* **mice** (mīs) **1.** Any of numerous small rodents usually having a pointed snout, rounded ears, and a long narrow tail. Some kinds live in or near human dwellings. **2.** A movable hand-held device that is connected to a computer and is moved about on a flat surface to direct the cursor on a screen. A mouse also has buttons for activating computer functions. The plural form of this sense of *mouse* can be either **mice** or **mouses.**

mouthpart (mouth′pärt′) Any of the parts of the mouth of an insect or other arthropod that are used for feeding, usually occurring in pairs and often extending out from the head.

MRI Abbreviation of **magnetic resonance imaging.**

MRSA (mûr′sə) *See under* **staphylococcus.**

Mt The symbol for **meitnerium.**

mucous membrane (myo͞o′kəs) Any of the membranes lining the passages of the body that open onto the outside, such as those of the respiratory system and the digestive tract. Glands and cells in the mucous membranes secrete mucus, which lubricates the membranes and protects against infection.

mucus (myo͞o′kəs) The slippery substance secreted by the cells and glands of the mucous membranes to lubricate and protect them.

multi– A prefix that means "many" or "much," such as *multicellular,* having many cells.

multicellular (mŭl′tē-sĕl′yə-lər) Having or consisting of many cells: *multicellular organisms. Compare* **unicellular.**

multiple (mŭl′tə-pəl) A number that may be divided by another number with no remainder. For example, 4, 10, and 32 are multiples of 2.

multiple sclerosis (sklə-rō′sĭs) A disease of the central nervous system that gradually destroys the sheaths around nerve fibers. This nerve damage leads to weakness, loss of balance and coordination, and visual disturbances. Multiple sclerosis is thought to be an autoimmune disorder, in which the body's immune system attacks its own tissues.

multiple star A system of three or more stars that orbit a common center of mass. The group appears as a single star to the unaided eye. Alpha Centauri is a multiple star.

multiplicand (mŭl′tə-plĭ-kănd′) A number that is multiplied by another number.

multiplication (mŭl′tə-plĭ-kā′shən) A mathematical operation performed on a pair of numbers in order to derive a third number called a product. For positive integers, multiplication consists of adding a number (the multiplicand) to itself a specified number of times. Thus, multiplying 6 by 3 means adding 6 to itself 3 times: $6 \times 3 = 6 + 6 + 6 = 18$.

multiplier (mŭl′tə-plī′ər) The number by which another number is multiplied.

multiply (mŭl′tə-plī′) To perform multiplication on a pair of quantities.

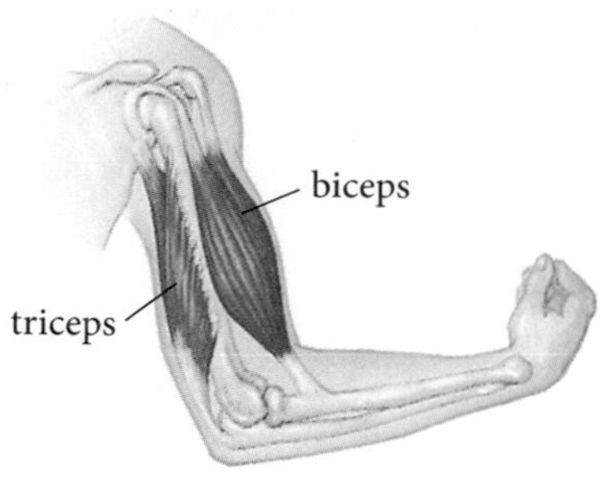

muscle
When the biceps contracts to bend the elbow, the triceps relaxes. When the triceps contracts to straighten the elbow, the biceps relaxes.

mumps (mŭmps) A contagious disease, usually affecting children, that is caused by a virus. Symptoms include inflammation of the salivary glands, especially those at the back of the jaw.

muscle (mŭs′əl) A body tissue composed of elongated cells (called muscle fibers) that contract to produce movement or exert force. In vertebrate animals, voluntary movement is produced by the action of muscles attached to bones. Movement of the muscles of the heart and other organs is involuntary and is controlled by the autonomic nervous system. —*Adjective* **muscular.**

muscovite (mŭs′kə-vīt′) A usually colorless to pale-gray mineral composed mostly of a silicate of potassium and aluminum. Muscovite is one of the most common forms of mica.

muscular dystrophy (mŭs′kyə-lər dĭs′trə-fē) Any of several hereditary diseases in which a person's muscles gradually deteriorate, causing progressive weakness.

mushroom (mŭsh′ro͞om′) Any of various fungi having a stalk topped by a fleshy, often umbrella-shaped cap. Some mushrooms are edible; others are poisonous.

muskeg (mŭs′kĕg′) A peat bog formed by an accumulation of sphagnum moss, leaves, and decayed matter, often with scattered small trees. Muskegs are found especially in northern North America.

mussel (mŭs′əl) Any of various saltwater or freshwater bivalve mollusks. Saltwater mussels often have narrow dark-blue shells, and several kinds are used for food. Freshwater mussels reach their greatest diversity in North America, where about 300 species are found. They were widely used by Native Americans for food and for making tools. ❖ The **zebra mussel** is a small freshwater mussel that has a shell with dark and light stripes. It is native to Eurasia but was introduced into the Great Lakes in the 1980s and has spread widely through other North American waterways. Zebra mussels often clog water-supply pipes and reduce levels of plankton on which native mussels and other aquatic species depend.

mutagen (myo͞o′tə-jən) An agent that can cause mutations in an organism's genes. Ultraviolet light, radioactive elements, and certain chemicals are mutagens.

mutation (myo͞o-tā′shən) A change in the structure of a gene or chromosome in a cell. A mutation occurs when there is a change in the DNA sequence of a gene or when part of a chromosome is duplicated, deleted, or moved to another location. Mutations occurring in the sex cells, such as an egg or sperm, can be passed from one generation to the next, but mutations occurring in the body cells cannot. Most mutations have harmful effects, but some can improve an organism's ability to survive. A mutation for a trait that benefits an individual may increase in frequency by means of natural selection until it is shared by all members of a species. *See Note at* **sickle cell anemia.**

mutualism (myo͞o′cho͞o-ə-lĭz′əm) A relationship between two organisms of different species in which each member benefits, as when an insect pollinates a plant while obtaining nectar from the plant's flowers.

mycelium (mī-sē′lē-əm) *Plural* **mycelia** The mass of fine branching filaments (called hyphae) that form the main growing structure of a fungus. The visible parts of a mushroom, the stalk and cap, are reproductive structures produced by the mycelium, which is located underground or within material such as a decaying tree trunk.

mycology (mī-kŏl′ə-jē) The scientific study of fungi.

myelin (mī′ə-lĭn) A whitish, fatty substance that forms a covering around many nerve fibers. Myelin insulates the nerves and permits nerve impulses to travel more rapidly. The white matter of the brain is composed of nerve fibers covered in myelin.

myopia (mī-ō′pē-ə) *See* **nearsightedness.**

N

N 1. Abbreviation of **newton. 2.** The symbol for **nitrogen.**

Na The symbol for **sodium.**

nacre (nā′kər) *See* **mother-of-pearl.**

nadir (nā′dər) The point on the celestial sphere that is directly below the observer. *Compare* **zenith.**

nano– 1. A prefix that means "one billionth," as in *nanosecond,* one billionth of a second. **2.** A prefix that means "extremely small," as in *nanotube.*

nanometer (năn′ə-mē′tər) A unit of length in the metric system equal to one billionth (10^{-9}) of a meter.

nanotechnology (năn′ə-tĕk-nŏl′ə-jē) The science and technology of materials and devices that are constructed on an extremely small scale, as small as individual atoms and molecules.

nanotube (năn′ə-to͞ob′) A type of carbon molecule in which the carbon atoms form a cylindrical or donutlike shape. *See Note at* **nanotechnology.**

naphtha (năf′thə) Any of several flammable liquids usually made by refining petroleum or by breaking down coal tar. Naphtha is used as a solvent and as an ingredient in gasoline. It is also used to make plastics.

naphthalene (năf′thə-lēn′) A white crystalline compound made from coal tar or petroleum and used to make dyes, moth repellents, explosives, and solvents.

narcotic (när-kŏt′ĭk) Any of a group of drugs used to relieve pain and cause drowsiness. Narcotics are highly addictive.

nasal (nā′zəl) Relating to the nose: *the nasal passages.*

natural gas (năch′ər-əl) A mixture of hydrocarbon gases that occurs naturally beneath the Earth's surface, often with or near petroleum deposits. Natural gas is composed mostly of methane but also contains varying amounts of ethane, propane, butane, and nitrogen. It is used as a fuel and to make fertilizer, plastics, and other products.

Did You Know...?

nanotechnology

There are many obvious advantages to making things smaller. Reducing the size of the circuits in a computer, for instance, makes the computer lighter and more compact. It also allows the computer to have more memory and to operate faster while using less power. But miniaturization isn't only about efficiency. When you start manufacturing objects that can be measured in nanometers (a billionth of a meter, or about 40 billionths of an inch), they are influenced by physical laws such as quantum mechanics which cause them to behave in some unexpected ways. *Nanotechnology,* which involves the science and technology of objects on this scale, has already resulted in the development of several useful new products. A nanotube, a tube-shaped fiber made of interlinked carbon atoms, is hundreds of times stronger than steel for its weight. Nanotubes also turn out to be excellent conductors of both heat and electricity. The same interlinked carbon atoms, if formed into a sheet rather than a tube, can be made into a membrane that lets water molecules pass through but blocks other molecules — a property that may be useful in constructing water filters and desalination plants. Thin sheets of other kinds of molecules, called nanofilms, can resist the growth of bacteria, repel water, or form a scratch-resistant coating for sunglasses or computer screens. But the potential applications of nanotechnology go far beyond simple fibers, membranes, and films. More complex molecules have been constructed that act as tiny motors, turning electrical energy into rotational motion. And researchers are designing other molecules for use in medicine — molecules that will aid in delivering drugs to the part of the body where they are needed or will identify and kill cancer cells.

■ **nautilus**

natural history The study and description of living things and natural objects, such as animals, plants, and rocks.

naturalist (năch′ər-ə-lĭst) A person who specializes in natural history, especially in the study of plants and animals in their natural surroundings.

naturalize (năch′ər-ə-līz′) To introduce and establish a plant or animal in a region that it is not native to. Eucalyptus trees are native to Australia but have become naturalized in many other parts of the world.

natural logarithm A logarithm whose base is the irrational number *e*. Natural logarithms are frequently used in calculus. Natural logarithms are usually written with the notation *ln*, where *ln(x)* means "the natural logarithm of *x*." *See more at* **e.** *Compare* **common logarithm.**

natural number A positive integer.

natural resource Something, such as a forest, a mineral deposit, or fresh water, that is found in nature and is necessary or useful to humans.

natural selection The process in nature by which organisms that are better adapted to their environment tend to survive longer and produce more offspring than organisms that are less well adapted, so that the genetic characteristics of the better-adapted individuals become more widespread in later generations. Biologists consider natural selection to be the main cause of evolution. *See Notes at* **adaptation, evolution.**

nature (nā′chər) **1.** The physical universe together with the events that occur in it and the laws that govern those events. **2.** Living organisms and their habitats.

nautical mile (nô′tĭ-kəl) A unit of length used in air and sea navigation, equal to about 6,076 feet (1,852 meters).

nautilus (nôt′l-əs) Any of several tropical sea mollusks having slender tentacles and a spiral shell divided into many partitions. Nautiluses are cephalopods, like octopuses and squids.

Nb The symbol for **niobium.**

Nd The symbol for **neodymium.**

Ne The symbol for **neon.**

Neanderthal (nē-ăn′dər-thôl′, nē-ăn′dər-tôl′) or **Neandertal** (nē-ăn′dər-tôl′) A species of extinct humans *(Homo neanderthalensis)* that lived throughout most of Europe and western and central Asia during the late Pleistocene Epoch until about 30,000 years ago. Members of this species had a large skull and stocky build and made stone tools.

neap tide (nēp) A tide in which the difference between high and low tide is the least. Neap tides occur in the first and third quarters of the moon, when the sun and moon are at right angles to the Earth. At these times, the total gravitational pull of the sun and the moon on the Earth's water is weakened because it comes from two different directions. *Compare* **spring tide.** *See more at* **tide.**

nearsightedness (nîr′sī′tĭd-nĭs) The ability to see objects at close range better than distant objects. Nearsightedness is caused by the eye focusing light in front of the retina instead of directly on it, usually as a result of an elongated eyeball

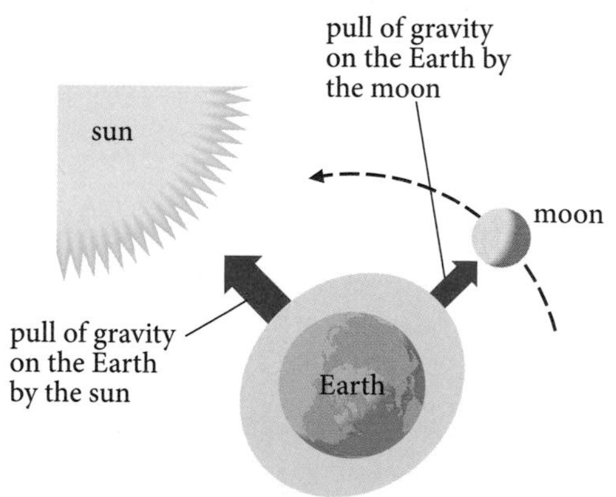

■ **neap tide**

Neap tides occur when the sun and the moon are at right angles to the Earth.

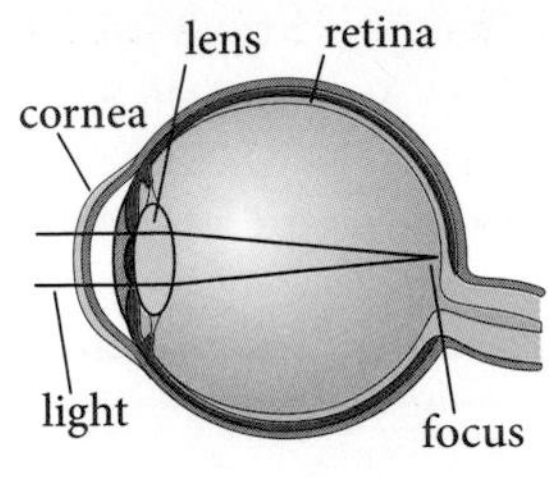

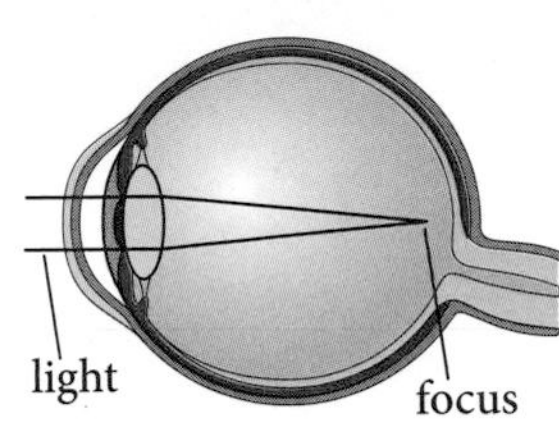

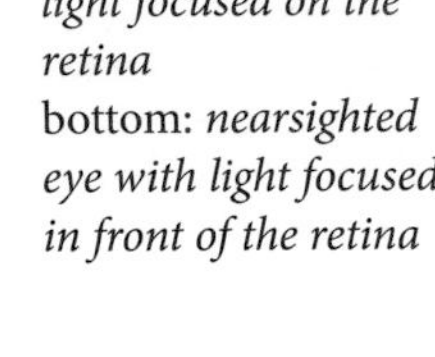

nearsightedness
top: *normal eye with light focused on the retina*
bottom: *nearsighted eye with light focused in front of the retina*

nebula
Orion Nebula (right) *and nebula NGC 1977, also known as the Running Man Nebula* (left), *both in the constellation Orion*

or a misshapen cornea. Also called *myopia. Compare* **farsightedness.**

nebula (nĕb′yə-lə) *Plural* **nebulae** (nĕb′yə-lē′) *or* **nebulas** A thinly spread cloud of interstellar gas and dust. It appears as a bright patch in the night sky if it reflects light from nearby stars, emits its own light, or re-emits ultraviolet radiation from nearby stars as visible light. If it absorbs light, the nebula appears as a dark patch. In dark nebulae, stars form from clumps of hydrogen gas. *See more at* **star.**

nebular hypothesis (nĕb′yə-lər) A hypothesis describing the formation of our solar system, which states that a rotating nebula collapsed in on itself, forming a star (the sun) in the center of a disk, while the dust particles in the outer part of the disk clumped together to form the planets, comets, and asteroids. Astronomers believe that this pattern of star formation occurs throughout the universe.

nectar (nĕk′tər) A sweet liquid that many plants secrete from special structures, usually inside flowers. Pollinating insects and birds feed on nectar, and bees use it to make honey.

needle (nēd′l) **1.** A narrow, stiff leaf, as of a pine, spruce, or other conifer. Needles are strong, and their thickness reduces their surface area, minimizing water loss during dry conditions. **2.** *See* **hypodermic needle.**

negative (nĕg′ə-tĭv) **1.** Less than zero. The number −3 is a negative number. **2.** Having the electric charge of an electron. The symbol for a negative charge is a minus sign. **3.** Having more electrons than protons. When a body such as an atom or molecule is negatively charged, it repels other negatively charged bodies but attracts positively charged bodies. **4.** Not showing the presence of a suspected disease or microorganism, as in a blood test.

nematocyst (nĕm′ə-tə-sĭst′, nĭ-măt′ə-sĭst′) One of the stinging cells in the tentacles of a jellyfish, coral, or related animal, used to capture prey and ward off attackers.

nematode (nĕm′ə-tōd′) Any of numerous slender, usually very small worms, having an unsegmented body that often narrows at each end. Some kinds of nematodes are abundant in soil and water, and others are parasites of plants and animals. Certain nematodes parasitize the human digestive tract, causing diseases such as trichinosis. Also called *roundworm.*

neodymium (nē′ō-dĭm′ē-əm) A shiny, silvery metallic element of the lanthanide series that reacts readily with air. It is used to make colored glass for welders' goggles, lasers, and lenses in optical instruments. *Symbol* **Nd.** *Atomic number* 60. *See* **Periodic Table,** pages 254–255.

Neogene (nē′ō-jēn′) The later of two divisions of the Tertiary Period, from 23 to 2.6 million years ago, including the Miocene and Pliocene Epochs.

Neolithic (nē′ə-lĭth′ĭk) The period of human culture that began around 10,000 years ago in the Middle East and later in other parts of the world. It is characterized by the beginning of farming, the domestication of animals, the development of crafts such as pottery and weaving, and the making of polished stone tools. *Compare* **Mesolithic, Paleolithic.**

neon (nē′ŏn′) A rare element that is a noble gas and occurs naturally in extremely small amounts in the atmosphere. It is colorless but glows reddish orange when electricity passes through it, such as in a tube in an electric sign. Neon is also used for refrigeration. *Symbol* **Ne.** *Atomic number* 10. *See* **Periodic Table,** pages 254–255.

neoprene (nē′ə-prēn′) A tough synthetic rubber that is resistant to the effects of oils, solvents, heat, and weather.

nephritis (nə-frī′tĭs) Inflammation of the kidneys.

nephron (nĕf′rŏn) One of the units of the kidney that filter waste products from the blood and produce urine.

Neptune (nĕp′to͞on′) The eighth planet from the sun and the fourth largest, with a diameter almost four times that of Earth. Neptune has a very active weather system with extremely long and powerful storms. It is the coldest planet in the solar system, with an average surface temperature of −330°F (−201°C). *See Table at* **solar system,** pages 312–313.

neptunium (nĕp-to͞o′nē-əm) A silvery, radioactive metallic element of the actinide series. It occurs naturally in minute amounts in uranium ores and is produced artificially as a byproduct of plutonium production. The most stable isotope of neptunium has a half-life of 2.1 million years. *Symbol* **Np.** *Atomic number* 93. *See* **Periodic Table,** pages 254–255.

nerve (nûrv) Any of the bundles of fibers made up of nerve cells that carry information in the form of electrical impulses throughout the body. Nerves send sensory information to the brain and spinal cord and carry impulses to the muscles, organs, and glands.

nerve cell Any of the cells of the nervous system. Nerve cells consist of a cell body, one or more dendrites that carry electrical impulses toward the cell body, and an axon, which carries impulses away from the cell body. Also called *neuron. See more at* **cell.**

nerve fiber *See* **axon.**

nervous system (nûr′vəs) The system of nerve cells and tissues that regulates the actions and responses of vertebrate and many invertebrate animals. The nervous system of vertebrates consists mainly of the brain, spinal cord, and nerves. The nervous systems of invertebrates vary from a simple nerve net to a complex nerve network under the control of a central brain. *See also* **autonomic nervous system, central nervous system, peripheral nervous system.**

Neumann (noi′män′), **John von** 1903–1957. Hungarian-born American mathematician who contributed to mathematical theories about numbers and games. He was a leader in the design and development of high-speed electronic computers and also pioneered the field of cybernetics.

neural (no͝or′əl) Relating to the nerves or the nervous system.

neurology (no͞o-rŏl′ə-jē) The branch of medicine that deals with the diagnosis and treatment of disorders of nerves and the nervous system.

neuron (no͝or′ŏn′) *See* **nerve cell.**

neurotransmitter (no͝or′ō-trănz′mĭt-ər) A chemical substance that transmits nerve impulses from one nerve cell to another nerve cell, a muscle cell, or a gland cell. Dopamine and serotonin are neurotransmitters.

neutral (no͞o′trəl) **1.** Neither acid nor alkaline. **2.** Having no electric charge or having positive electric charges exactly balanced by negative electric charges.

neutralize (no͞o′trə-līz′) To cause to be neither acid nor alkaline: *neutralize a solution.*

neutrino (no͞o-trē′nō) An electrically neutral subatomic particle that has extremely small mass

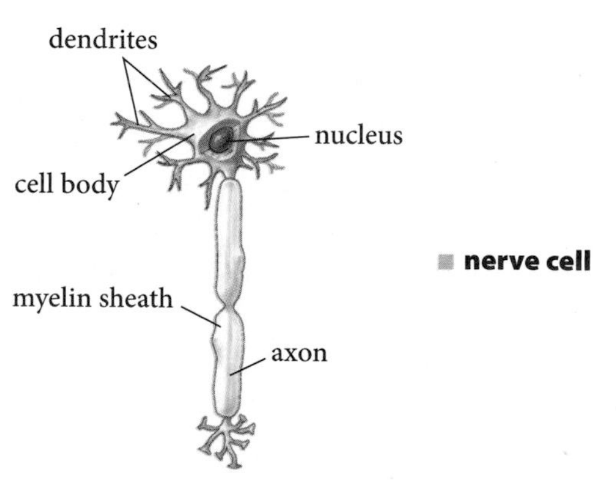

nerve cell

Did You Know...?

neutrinos

Neutrinos were first observed in 1956, 26 years after the physicist Wolfgang Pauli first proposed that they should exist. While studying a form of radioactive decay, Pauli noticed that a certain amount of energy that was lost could not be accounted for. He suggested that the energy was being carried away by a very small electrically neutral particle that had not been detected. (He wanted to name the particle *neutron,* but he did not publish his suggestion, and a few years later that name was used for a much more massive particle that forms part of the atomic nucleus. The Italian physicist Enrico Fermi then coined the term *neutrino,* which means "little neutral one" in Italian.) Neutrinos are hard to detect because they interact very weakly with other forms of matter, but scientists have developed special methods to find evidence of them. Neutrinos are produced in nuclear reactors and are generated by the fusion reactions that power the sun and other stars. Every second, billions of neutrinos from the sun pass through every square centimeter of the Earth's surface. Most of them pass right through the Earth and go out the other side.

and travels at very high speed, close to the speed of light. Three kinds of neutrinos are known.

neutron (no͞o′trŏn′) An electrically neutral subatomic particle that has a mass slightly greater than that of a proton and is part of every atomic nucleus except that of protium, an isotope of hydrogen whose nucleus consists of a single proton. Beams of neutrons from nuclear reactors are used to bombard the nuclei of various elements to cause fission and other nuclear reactions and to determine the structure of molecules. *See more at* **atom.**

neutron star A celestial object consisting of an extremely dense mass of neutrons, formed by the forcing together of protons and electrons during the collapse of a massive star. Most neutron stars rotate very rapidly. Many have powerful magnetic fields that cause radio waves, light, and other radiation to be emitted in two beams that point outward from the magnetic poles. *See more at* **star.**

Newcomen (no͞o′kə-mən), **Thomas** 1663–1729. English inventor who developed an early steam engine (c. 1711) that was used successfully to pump water.

new moon (no͞o) The phase of the moon in which it is not visible at all or is visible as only a thin crescent at sunset. This phase occurs when the moon passes between Earth and the sun. *See more at* **moon.** *Compare* **full moon.**

newton (no͞ot′n) A unit used to measure force. One newton is equal to the force needed to accelerate a mass of one kilogram one meter per second per second.

Newton, Sir **Isaac** 1642–1727. English mathematician and scientist. He developed the basic techniques of calculus and formulated the law of universal gravitation and three basic laws of motion, which he presented in the treatise *Principia Mathematica* (1687). He also built the first working reflecting telescope.

Newton's law of gravitation A physical law stating that two bodies attract each other with a force that increases as their masses increase and as the distance between them decreases. In mathematical terms, the gravitational force equals the gravitational constant multiplied by the product of the two masses and divided by the square of the distance. Also called *law of universal gravitation. See Note at* **gravity.**

Newton's laws of motion The three laws proposed by Sir Isaac Newton that describe how the motion of a body is affected by the forces acting on it. These laws form the basis of classical mechanics. The first law states that when no external force is acting on it, a body at rest remains at rest and a body in motion continues in motion at the same speed in the same direction. The second law states that when a force acts on a body, it accelerates by an amount equal to the force divided by its mass: $a = \frac{F}{m}$ or $F = ma$. The third law, known as the law of action and reaction, states that when one body exerts a force on another body, the second body exerts a force on the first body that is equal in magnitude but opposite in direction.

Ni The symbol for **nickel.**

niacin (nī′ə-sĭn) A vitamin belonging to the vitamin B complex that is important in carbohydrate and fat metabolism. It is found in meat, fish, legumes, and whole-grain foods.

niche (nĭch, nēsh) The function or position of a species within an ecological community. A species' niche includes the physical environment to which it is adapted as well as the other species with which it interacts.

nickel (nĭk′əl) A silvery, hard, easily shaped metallic element that occurs in ores along with iron or magnesium. It resists oxidation and corrosion and is used to make alloys such as stainless steel. It is also used as a coating for other metals. *Symbol* **Ni.** *Atomic number* 28. *See* **Periodic Table,** pages 254–255.

BIOGRAPHY

Isaac Newton

Isaac Newton's studies at Cambridge University were interrupted in 1665 when the university temporarily closed because of an outbreak of the plague. Returning to his family's farm, Newton continued his research on his own. He was especially interested in light. His experiments with prisms demonstrated that sunlight contains all the colors of the spectrum. During this time he also made his famous observation of an apple falling from a tree. Hypothesizing that the force acting on the apple was the same force that held the moon in orbit around the Earth, Newton derived a single formula that could describe the effects of gravity anywhere in the universe. He also explored and defined new concepts of mass, weight, force, inertia, and acceleration, demonstrating the mathematical relationships between them. These concepts still have great power to predict how matter will behave under many different conditions.

nicotine (nĭk′ə-tēn′) A poisonous compound occurring naturally in the tobacco plant. It is the substance in tobacco that people who smoke cigarettes or chew tobacco become addicted to.

nictitating membrane (nĭk′tĭ-tā′tĭng) A transparent inner eyelid in many vertebrate animals that closes to protect and moisten the eye without blocking vision.

nimbostratus (nĭm′bō-străt′əs) A low, gray, dark cloud formation often covering the entire sky. Nimbostratus clouds usually produce steady rain, sleet, or snow.

nimbus (nĭm′bəs) A rain cloud.

niobium (nī-ō′bē-əm) A soft, silvery, easily shaped metallic element that usually occurs in nature together with the element tantalum. It is used to build nuclear reactors, to make steel alloys, and to allow magnets to conduct electricity with almost no resistance. *Symbol* **Nb.** *Atomic number* 41. *See* **Periodic Table,** pages 254–255.

nipple (nĭp′əl) **1.** A small projecting body part near the center of the mammary gland in female humans and most other mammals that contains the outlets of the milk ducts. **2.** A corresponding but undeveloped projecting body part in male humans and most other mammals.

nitrate (nī′trāt′) A salt or ester of nitric acid; a compound containing the group NO_3. Nitrates dissolve extremely easily in water and are an important component of the nitrogen cycle. *Compare* **nitrite.**

nitric (nī′trĭk) Containing nitrogen, especially with a valence of 5. *Compare* **nitrous.**

nitric acid A clear, colorless to yellow liquid, HNO_3. It is very corrosive and is used to make fertilizers, explosives, dyes, and rocket fuels. Nitric acid can dissolve most metals.

nitrification (nī′trə-fĭ-kā′shən) The process by which bacteria in soil oxidize ammonia and form nitrites and nitrates. Because nitrates can be absorbed by the roots of green plants, nitrification is an important step in the nitrogen cycle.

nitrifying bacterium (nī′trə-fī′ĭng) Any of various bacteria in soil or water that obtain energy by converting ammonium compounds into nitrites or by converting nitrites into nitrates as part of the nitrogen cycle.

nitrite (nī′trīt′) A salt or ester of nitrous acid; a compound containing the group NO_2. Nitrites are an important component of the nitrogen cycle and are used as food preservatives. *Compare* **nitrate.**

nitrogen (nī′trə-jən) A nonmetallic element that makes up about 78 percent of the atmosphere by volume, occurring as a colorless, odorless gas. It is a component of all proteins, making it essential for life, and it is also found in various minerals. Nitrogen is used to make ammonia, nitric acid, TNT, and fertilizers, and it is also used in refrigeration. *Symbol* **N.** *Atomic number* 7. *See* **Periodic Table,** pages 254–255.

nitrogen cycle The continuous process by which nitrogen is exchanged between organisms and the environment. Some of the atmosphere's free nitrogen combines with other elements to form compounds that are deposited in soil, partially through the action of nitrogen-fixing bacteria. These compounds are then converted by nitrifying bacteria into nutrients that are absorbed by the roots of green plants. Nitrogen is then passed into the food chain and returned to the soil by the metabolism and decay of plants and animals. A similar process occurs in aquatic environments.

nitrogen fixation The process by which free nitrogen from the air is combined with other elements to form organic compounds that plants can use as nutrients. Nitrogen fixation occurs through some nonbiological processes, like lightning, but it occurs chiefly through the action of bacteria, especially those that live in the roots of legumes, where they convert gaseous nitrogen into organic compounds.

nitroglycerin (nī′trō-glĭs′ər-ĭn) A thick, pale-yellow, explosive liquid formed by treating glycerin with nitric and sulfuric acids. It is used to make dynamite, and in medicine to dilate blood vessels.

nitrous (nī′trəs) Containing nitrogen, especially with a valence of 3. *Compare* **nitric.**

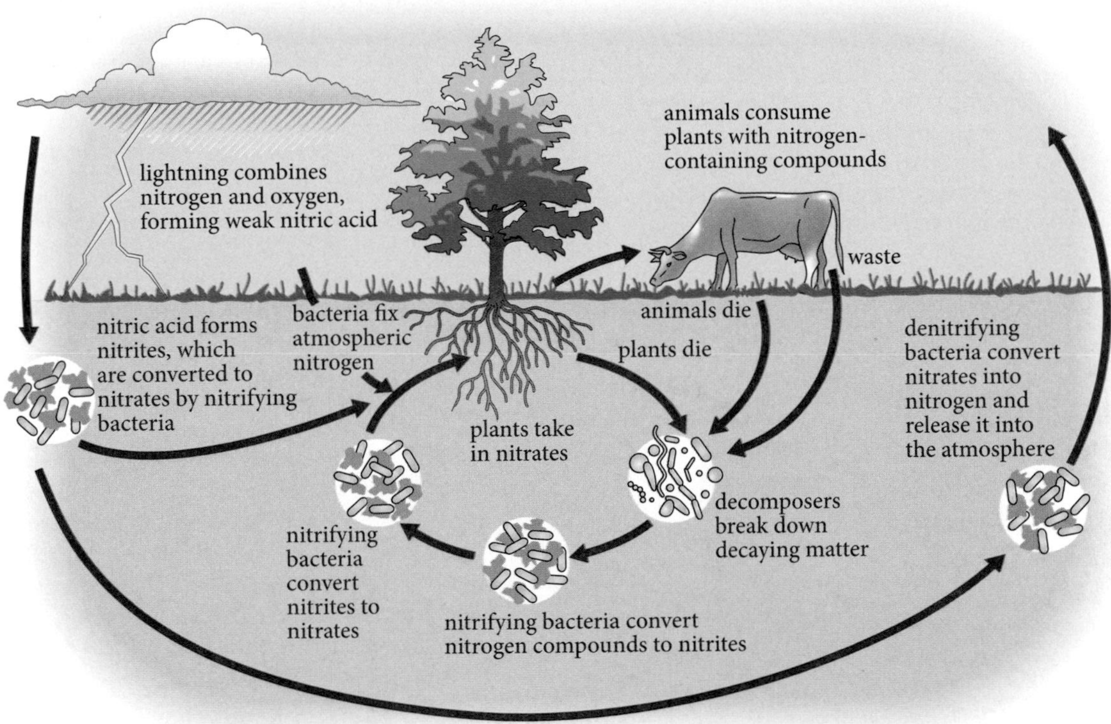

■ **nitrogen cycle**

Emmy Noether

nitrous acid A weak acid, HNO_2, that exists only in solution or in the form of nitrite salts.

nitrous oxide A colorless, sweet-smelling gas, N_2O. Nitrous oxide results from agricultural and waste management processes and also occurs naturally in the atmosphere. It is one of the greenhouse gases. When used as an anesthetic, nitrous oxide is sometimes called laughing gas.

No The symbol for **nobelium.**

nobelium (nō-bĕl′ē-əm) A synthetic, radioactive metallic element in the actinide series that can be produced by bombarding curium with carbon ions. Its most stable isotope has a half-life of about three minutes. *Symbol* **No.** *Atomic number* 102. *See* **Periodic Table,** pages 254–255.

noble gas (nō′bəl) Any of the six gases helium, neon, argon, krypton, xenon, and radon. Because the outermost electron shell of atoms of these gases is full, they do not react chemically with other substances except under certain special conditions. *See* **Periodic Table,** pages 254–255.

nocturnal (nŏk-tûr′nəl) **1.** Occurring at night. **2.** Most active at night rather than during the daytime. Owls, bats, and many other animals are nocturnal. **3.** Opening during the night and closing at daylight. Nocturnal flowers are often pollinated by moths or bats. *Compare* **diurnal.**

node (nōd) **1.** *Anatomy* A small mass of tissue in the body, such as a lymph node. **2.** *Botany* A point on a stem where a leaf is attached. **3.** *Physics* In a standing wave, the point at which the amplitude is zero. *Compare* **antinode. 4.** *Astronomy* **a.** Either of the two points on the celestial sphere at which the path of an orbiting celestial object, such as the moon, a planet, or a comet, intersects the ecliptic. **b.** Either of the two points at which the orbit of an artificial satellite intersects the equatorial plane of the planet it is orbiting.

nodule (nŏj′o͞ol) **1.** *Anatomy* A small, usually hard mass of tissue. **2.** *Botany* A small knoblike outgrowth found on the roots of many plants that are legumes. *See more at* **legume. 3.** *Geology* A small rounded lump that is made of one or more minerals and that is harder than the surrounding rock or sediment.

Noether (nŭ′tər), **Amalie** *Known as* **Emmy.** 1882–1935. German mathematician who contributed to the development of modern algebra and geometry.

nonrenewable (nŏn′rĭ-no͞o′ə-bəl) Relating to a natural resource, such as oil or iron ore, that cannot be replaced once it has been used. *Compare* **renewable.**

normal fault (nôr′məl) A geologic fault in which the block above the plane of the fault has slid downward relative to the lower block as the two blocks are pulled in opposite directions. *See more at* **fault.**

norovirus (nôr′ō-vī′rəs) Any of a group of viruses that are spread primarily through contaminated food or water and cause stomach pain, vomiting, and diarrhea.

Northern Hemisphere (nôr′*th*ərn) **1.** The half of the Earth north of the equator. **2.** *Astronomy* The half of the celestial sphere north of the celestial equator.

northern lights *See* **aurora borealis.**

north pole (nôrth) The pole of a magnet that tends to point north.

North Pole The northern end of the Earth's axis of rotation, a point in the Arctic Ocean.

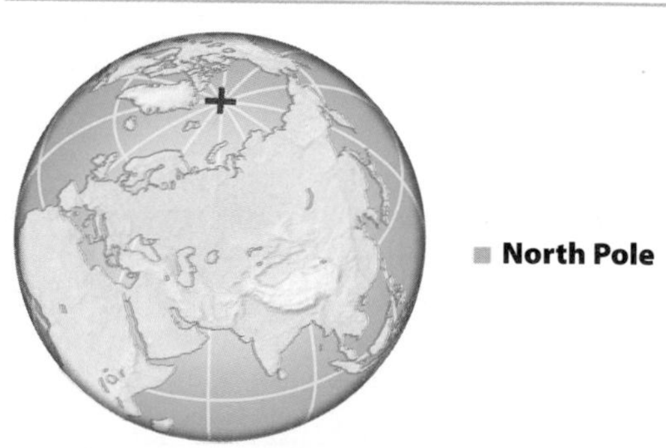

North Pole

North Star *See* **Polaris.**

notochord (nō′tə-kôrd′) A firm rodlike structure that extends along the length of the embryo in all vertebrates and certain related animals, such as the lancelets, the tunicates, and the hagfishes. In most vertebrates, the notochord develops into the spinal column in the adult. Animals that have a notochord during some stage of their development are called chordates.

nova (nō′və) *Plural* **novae** (nō′vē) *or* **novas** A sudden increase in the brightness of a star that lasts for weeks or years. A nova occurs when the surface of a white dwarf star accumulates material, mostly hydrogen, that its gravitational field has pulled from a nearby star, and the material heats up so much that it explodes. *Compare* **supernova.**

Np The symbol for **neptunium.**

nuclear (no͞o′klē-ər) **1.** Relating to a cell nucleus. **2.** Relating to atomic nuclei. **3.** Using energy derived from the nuclei of atoms: *a nuclear power plant.*

nuclear energy 1. The energy released during a nuclear reaction. **2.** Electricity generated by a nuclear reactor.

nuclear magnetic resonance The absorption of energy (as specific frequencies of radio waves) by the nuclei of atoms that are placed within a strong magnetic field. Because certain atoms absorb specific frequencies, nuclear magnetic resonance is used to analyze substances in spectroscopy and to examine soft body tissues in magnetic resonance imaging (MRI).

nuclear physics The scientific study of the properties of atomic nuclei, including their composition, structure, and reactions.

nuclear reaction A process in which an atomic nucleus changes in composition, structure, or energy. Fission, fusion, and radioactive decay are examples of nuclear reactions. *See more at* **fission, fusion.**

nuclear reactor A device in which a nuclear chain reaction is started and controlled, producing heat that is usually used to generate electricity.

nuclear weapon A weapon whose destructive power comes from the release of nuclear energy; an atomic bomb or a hydrogen bomb.

nucleic acid (no͞o-klē′ĭk) Any of a group of organic compounds that are found in living cells and viruses. Nucleic acids constitute the genetic material of a particular cell or virus and control the synthesis of proteins. The two main nucleic acids are DNA and RNA.

nucleolus (no͞o-klē′ə-ləs) A small structure within the nucleus of a cell that contains RNA and protein and is the site where ribosomes are formed. *See more at* **cell.**

nucleon (no͞o′klē-ŏn′) A proton or a neutron, especially as part of an atomic nucleus.

nucleotide (no͞o′klē-ə-tīd′) Any of a group of organic compounds composed of one of several nitrogen-containing bases (purines and pyrimidines) linked to a sugar and a phosphate group. The nucleic acids DNA and RNA are made up of chains of nucleotides. *See Note at* **DNA.**

nucleus (no͞o′klē-əs) *Plural* **nuclei** (no͞o′klē-ī′) **1.** *Biology* A structure within a living cell that is surrounded by a membrane and contains the cell's DNA. Almost all the cells of eukaryotes contain nuclei, unlike the cells of prokaryotes, such as bacteria, which do not contain nuclei. *See more at* **cell. 2.** *Chemistry* The positively charged central region of an atom, composed of protons and neutrons and containing most of the mass of the atom. *See more at* **atom. 3.** *Astronomy* The solid central part of a comet, composed of ice, frozen gases, and dust.

nudibranch (no͞o′də-brăngk′) *See* **sea slug.**

number (nŭm′bər) **1.** A positive integer; one of a set of symbols in a fixed order that have unique meaning and that can be derived by counting. **2.** A mathematical object, such as a negative integer or a real number, that can be derived from the positive integers.

numeral (no͞o′mər-əl) A symbol or mark used to represent a number.

numerator (no͞o′mə-rā′tər) The number above or to the left of the line in a fraction, indicating the number of parts of the whole. For example, in the fraction $\frac{2}{7}$, 2 is the numerator.

nutrient (no͞o′trē-ənt) A substance that an organism takes in and uses for growth and metabolism. Plants absorb nutrients mainly from the soil in the form of minerals and other inorganic compounds. Animals obtain nutrients from the foods they eat or take in. The three most important nu-

Did You Know...?

nuclear reactor

A *nuclear reactor* uses a nuclear chain reaction to produce energy. The core of a nuclear reactor usually consists of *fuel rods* containing pellets of fissionable material, such as uranium-235 or plutonium-239. The unstable nuclei of these isotopes undergo fission, splitting into two smaller nuclei and releasing free neutrons, which strike other such nuclei and cause them to undergo fission too, thus starting a nuclear *chain reaction*. *Control rods,* which are made of a material (usually boron or cadmium) that absorbs neutrons, are placed among the fuel rods to control the reaction. Inserting the control rods partially into the reactor core slows the chain reaction down, and inserting them completely stops it. The nuclear chain reaction creates enormous amounts of heat, which is used to generate electricity.

In a common type of reactor, water constantly circulates through the reactor and becomes heated (and radioactive). The heat from that water is transferred through a heat exchanger to nonradioactive water, which is used to produce high-pressure steam. The pressurized steam drives turbines that turn generators, producing electricity. Nuclear reactors are highly efficient at generating electric power. But nuclear power remains controversial because of safety concerns. When accidents happen, radioactive material can be spread over a huge area. Even under normal operating conditions, the reactor vessel itself, as well as the spent fuel rods and the coolant liquid, remain radioactive for thousands of years. There is no agreement yet about how to store these materials.

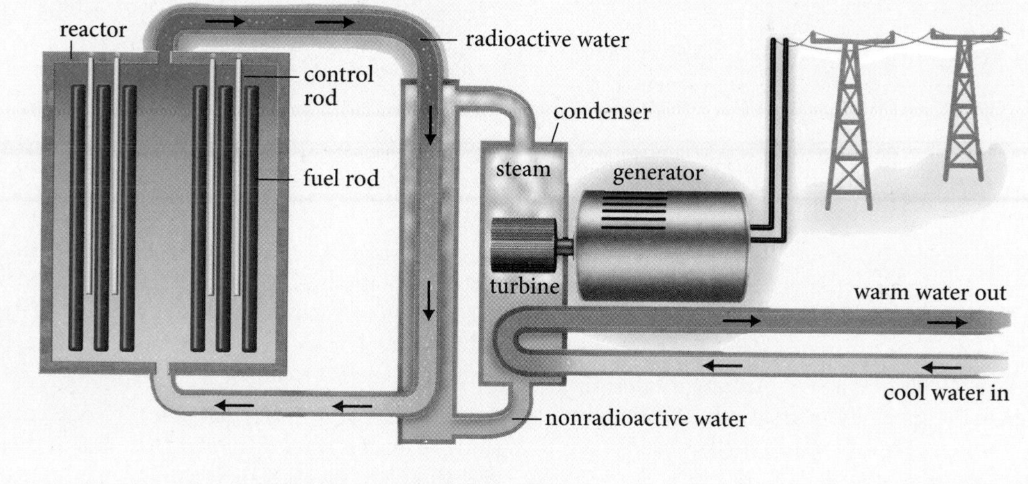

trients for animals are proteins, carbohydrates, and fats.

nutrition (no͞o-trĭsh′ən) **1.** The process of obtaining the nutrients that are needed to maintain health. **2.** The scientific study of food and nourishment, especially in connection with health and disease.

nylon (nī′lŏn′) Any of various very strong, elastic, synthetic polymers. Nylon can be formed into fibers, sheets, or bristles, and is used to make fabrics and plastics.

nymph (nĭmf) The immature form of certain insects, such as grasshoppers, that do not pass through a pupal stage during metamorphosis. Nymphs resemble adults but are smaller and lack fully developed wings. The eight-legged immature forms of ticks and mites are also called nymphs. *Compare* **imago, larva, pupa.**

O

O The symbol for **oxygen.**

oak (ōk) Any of numerous trees that bear thick-walled nuts called acorns and that often have lobed or notched leaves. Oaks are native to the Northern Hemisphere.

oasis (ō-ā′sĭs) *Plural* **oases** (ō-ā′sēz) A small area in a desert that has a supply of water and is able to support vegetation. An oasis forms when groundwater lies close enough to the surface to form a spring or to be reached by wells.

objective (əb-jĕk′tĭv) The lens or group of lenses that first receives light from the object in an optical instrument such as a telescope.

obsidian (ŏb-sĭd′ē-ən) A shiny, usually black, volcanic glass. Obsidian forms when lava cools so quickly that crystals do not have a chance to form.

obstetrics (ŏb-stĕt′rĭks) The branch of medicine that deals with the care of women during pregnancy and childbirth.

obtuse angle (ŏb-to͞os′) An angle whose measure is between 90° and 180°. *Compare* **acute angle.**

occipital lobe (ŏk-sĭp′ĭ-tl) The part of each cerebral hemisphere that is in the back of the brain and is responsible for processing visual information.

occlusion (ə-klo͞o′zhən) **1.** An obstruction in a passageway, especially of the body. **2.** The manner in which the upper and lower sets of teeth fit together.

occultation (ŏk′ŭl-tā′shən) The passage of a celestial object between an observer and another celestial object, blocking the second object from view. An occultation occurs when the moon moves between Earth and the sun in a solar eclipse.

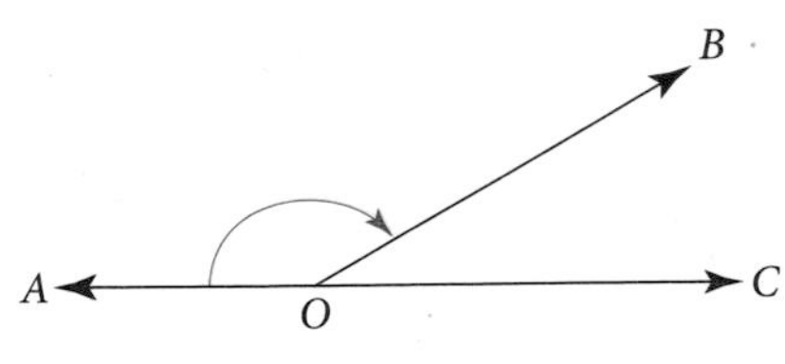

obtuse angle
Angle AOB is an obtuse angle.

USAGE

ocean/sea

The word *ocean* refers to one of the Earth's four distinct, large areas of salt water, the Atlantic, Pacific, Indian, and Arctic Oceans. The word can also mean the entire network of water that covers almost three-quarters of our planet. It comes from the Greek *Okeanos,* a river believed to circle the globe. The word *sea* can also mean the vast ocean covering most of the world. But it more commonly refers to large landlocked or almost landlocked bodies of salt water smaller than the great oceans, such as the Mediterranean Sea or the Bering Sea. Sailors have long referred to all the world's waters as *the seven seas,* but the origin of this phrase is not known for certain. Different cultures have had different lists of which seven seas the ocean was divided into.

ocean (ō′shən) **1.** The continuous saltwater body that covers about 72 percent of the surface of the Earth. **2.** Any of the principal divisions of this body of water, including the Atlantic, Pacific, Indian, and Arctic Oceans.

oceanography (ō′shə-nŏg′rə-fē) The scientific study of oceans, the organisms that inhabit them, and their physical characteristics, including the movement and chemical makeup of ocean waters and the topography and composition of the ocean floors.

ocellus (ō-sĕl′əs) *Plural* **ocelli** (ō-sĕl′ī′) **1.** A simple eye, found in many invertebrate animals, composed of sensory cells and often a single lens. **2.** A marking that resembles an eye, as on a peacock's tail feathers.

octagon (ŏk′tə-gŏn′) A polygon having eight sides.

octahedron (ŏk′tə-hē′drən) A three-dimensional geometric figure with eight triangular faces.

octane (ŏk′tān′) Any of several hydrocarbon compounds having the formula C_8H_{18}. It is often a component of gasoline, and one isomer of octane is known for exceptionally even burning in internal-combustion engines.

octopus (ŏk′tə-pəs) *Plural* **octopuses** *or* **octopi** (ŏk′tə-pī) Any of various soft-bodied sea mollusks having eight arms bearing suckers used for grasping and holding, a large head, and a mouth with a strong beak. Octopuses have large and highly complex eyes.

ocular (ŏk′yə-lər) Of or having to do with the eye or the sense of vision.

odd (ŏd) Divisible by 2 with a remainder of 1, such as 17 or −103.

odd-toed ungulate *See* **perissodactyl.**

Oersted (ûr′stĕd′), **Hans Christian** 1777–1851. Danish physicist who founded the science of electromagnetism with his discovery (1820) of the magnetic effect produced by an electric current.

ohm (ōm) A unit used to measure the electrical resistance of a material. One ohm is equal to the resistance of a conductor through which a current of one ampere flows when an electric potential difference of one volt is applied to it.

Ohm, Georg Simon 1789–1854. German physicist who discovered the relationship between voltage, current, and resistance in an electric circuit. His discovery is now known as Ohm's law. The unit of electrical resistance is named for him.

Ohm's law A law stating that the current in an electric circuit is equal to the voltage divided by the resistance. The current increases as the voltage increases, but decreases as the resistance increases.

-oid A suffix meaning "like" or "resembling," as in *ellipsoid,* a geometric solid that resembles an ellipse.

oil (oil) **1.** Any of a large class of liquid or easily melted substances that are typically very slippery and greasy. Oils are flammable, do not mix with water, and include animal and vegetable fats as well as substances of mineral or synthetic origin. They are used in food, soap, and candles, and make good lubricants and fuels. **2.** Petroleum.

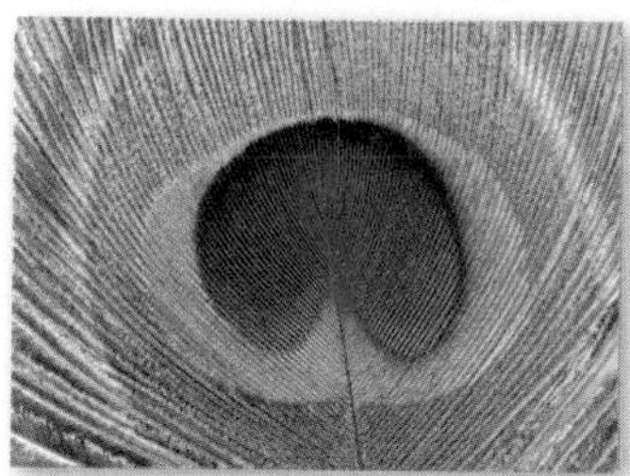

ocellus *on a peacock feather*

-ol A suffix used to form the names of chemical compounds having a hydroxyl (OH) group, such as *ethanol.*

olefin (ō′lə-fĭn) *See* **alkene.**

olfactory (ŏl-făk′tə-rē, ōl-făk′tə-rē) Relating to the sense of smell or the organs of smell.

olfactory nerve The nerve that carries sensory information relating to smell from the nose to the brain. The olfactory nerve is a cranial nerve.

Oligocene (ŏl′ĭ-gō-sēn′) The third epoch of the Tertiary Period, from about 34 to 23 million years ago, characterized by the continued development of modern mammalian groups and the rise of the first cats, dogs, and related mammals. *See Chart at* **geologic time,** pages 146–147.

olivine (ŏl′ə-vēn′) An olive-green to brownish-green mineral consisting primarily of iron, magnesium, and silica. Olivine is a common mineral in the igneous rocks, such as basalt and gabbro, that make up most of the Earth's crust beneath the oceans.

omasum (ō-mā′səm) The third compartment of the stomach in ruminant animals. It removes excess water from food and further reduces the size of food particles before passing them to the abomasum for digestion by enzymes. *See more at* **ruminant.**

ommatidium (ŏm′ə-tĭd′ē-əm) *Plural* **ommatidia** One of the many small light-sensitive units that make up the compound eye of an insect or crustacean. Each ommatidium contains photoreceptors and usually one or more lenses. *See more at* **compound eye.**

omnivore (ŏm′nə-vôr′) An organism that eats food of any kind, including both animals and plants. —*Adjective* **omnivorous.**

oncogene (ŏn′kə-jēn) A gene containing a mutation in its DNA that causes normal cells to turn into cancerous ones.

oncology (ŏn-kŏl′ə-jē) The branch of medicine that deals with the diagnosis and treatment of cancer.

opal

onyx (ŏn′ĭks) A type of quartz that occurs in bands of different colors, often black and white.

Oort cloud (ôrt, ōrt) A sphere-shaped mass of comets that makes up the outer edge of the solar system, surrounding the Kuiper belt and the planets. The more than 100 billion comets in this region orbit the sun at a distance of one to two light years. Comets from this area that come into the inner solar system take more than 200 years to make one complete orbit. *Compare* **Kuiper belt.**

opacity (ō-păs′ĭ-tē) The quality or condition of being opaque.

opal (ō′pəl) A usually transparent form of hydrous silica. Opal can occur in almost any color, but it is often pinkish white with a milky or pearly appearance. It typically forms within cracks in igneous rocks, in limestone, and in mineral veins. It also occurs in the silica-rich shells of certain marine organisms.

opaque (ō-pāk′) Not letting light pass through; neither transparent nor translucent. Metals and many minerals are opaque.

open circuit (ō′pən) An electric circuit through which current cannot flow because the path is broken or interrupted by an opening.

open cluster A loose group of stars that were all formed at the same time from a nebula in the Milky Way or another spiral galaxy. The Pleiades is an open cluster. *Compare* **globular cluster.**

open universe A model of the universe in which there is not enough matter, and therefore not enough gravitational force, to stop the expansion started by the Big Bang. *See Note at* **Big Bang.**

operating system (ŏp′ə-rā′tĭng) Software designed to control the hardware of a specific data-processing system in order to allow users and programs to make use of the system.

operculum (ō-pûr′kyə-ləm) A lid or flap covering an opening. Some examples of operculums are the flap covering the opening of a snail shell, the thin plate protecting the gills of many fish, and the cover on the spore capsule of a moss plant.

ophthalmology (ŏf′thəl-mŏl′ə-jē, ŏp′thəl-mŏl′ə-jē) The branch of medicine that deals with the eye, its diseases, and their treatment.

opium (ō′pē-əm) A highly addictive drug obtained from the pods of a variety of poppy, from which other drugs, such as morphine, are prepared.

opossum (ə-pŏs′əm) Any of various marsupials that have thick fur, a long snout, and a long, hairless, prehensile tail that can grasp objects such as tree branches. Baby opossums are carried in the mother's pouch for about two months after birth. The Virginia opossum is the only marsupial found in North America.

Oppenheimer (ŏp′ən-hī′mər), **J(ulius) Robert** 1904–1967. American physicist who made discoveries in the field of quantum theory. Oppenheimer also directed the laboratory at Los Alamos, New Mexico, during the development of the first atomic bomb (1942–1945).

opposable thumb (ə-pō′zə-bəl) A thumb that is capable of moving opposite to and touching the fingers of the same hand. Opposable thumbs allow the fingers to grasp and handle objects,

J. Robert Oppenheimer

and are characteristic of humans and many other primates.

optic (ŏp′tĭk) Relating to the eye or vision.

optical (ŏp′tĭ-kəl) **1.** Relating to sight; visual. **2.** Relating to optics. **3.** Relating to or using visible light: *optical astronomy.*

optical disc or **optical disk** A plastic-coated disk that stores digital data, such as text, music, or video, as tiny regions that vary by how much light is reflected. Optical discs are read by scanning the surface with a laser.

optical fiber A very thin, transparent fiber made of pure glass or plastic that is used to carry light signals. Optical fibers are used in telecommunications and in medical instruments to see inside hollow body structures. *See more at* **fiber optics.**

optic nerve The nerve that carries sensory information relating to vision from the retina of the eye to the brain. The optic nerve is a cranial nerve.

optics (ŏp′tĭks) The scientific study of the properties and behavior of light. Optics includes the study of optical devices and of how organisms perceive light.

oral (ôr′əl) Relating to the mouth.

orangutan (ô-răng′ə-tăn′) Either of two species of large, tree-dwelling apes of the islands of Borneo and Sumatra. Orangutans have long arms and a reddish-brown coat.

orbit (ôr′bĭt) *Noun* **1a.** The path of a celestial object or an artificial satellite as it revolves around another celestial object. **b.** One complete revolution of such an object. *See Note at* **solar system. 2.** The path of a body in a field of force surrounding another body; for example, the path of an electron in relation to the nucleus of an atom. **3.** Either of two bony hollows in the skull containing the eye and its associated structures. — *Verb* **4.** To move in an orbit around another body.

orbital (ôr′bĭ-tl) A region in an atom where an electron is most likely to be found. Each electron shell is composed of one or more orbitals.

orca (ôr′kə) A marine mammal that has a black body with a white underside and a tall, triangular dorsal fin. Orcas grow up to 30 feet (9.1 meters) in length and feed on large fish, squid, and other marine mammals. Also called *killer whale.*

■ **orca**

orchid (ôr′kĭd) Any of numerous tropical and subtropical plants that grow on the ground or in trees as epiphytes. Orchids have bilaterally symmetrical flowers with one distinctively shaped petal.

order (ôr′dər) A taxonomic category of organisms that share certain characteristics, ranking above a family and below a class. *See Table at* **taxonomy.**

ordinal number (ôr′dn-əl) A number, such as 3rd, 11th, or 412th, used in counting to indicate position in a series but not quantity. *Compare* **cardinal number.**

ordinate (ôr′dn-ĭt) The distance of a point from the *x*-axis on a graph in the Cartesian coordinate

■ **orchid**

ORGANIC COMPOUNDS

Chemical compounds containing one or more carbon atoms are called **organic compounds.** Hundreds of thousands of organic compounds are found in nature or have been artificially made. They range from the very simple, like methane, with its five atoms, to the very complex, like DNA, which has millions of atoms.

A very common class of organic compounds, called the **alkanes,** all have one or more carbon atoms arranged in a row, or chain. Atoms are attached to each other in a molecule by sharing electrons; these attachments are called **bonds.** Because of its particular structure, a carbon atom (C) must share a total of four electrons with other atoms. In an alkane, each carbon in the chain shares one electron with its neighboring carbon, forming what are called **single bonds** (indicated by single lines between the element symbols in the diagrams below). The remaining electrons are shared with hydrogen atoms (H). Below are illustrated the first four compounds in the alkane series—methane, ethane, propane, and butane:

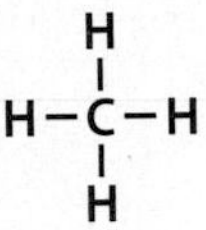

```
  H            H H            H H H              H H H H
  |            | |            | | |              | | | |
H-C-H        H-C-C-H        H-C-C-C-H          H-C-C-C-C-H
  |            | |            | | |              | | | |
  H            H H            H H H              H H H H
```

methane
CH_4

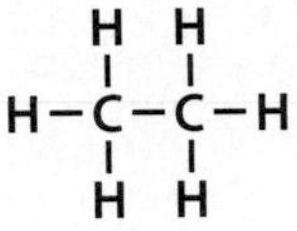

ethane
C_2H_6

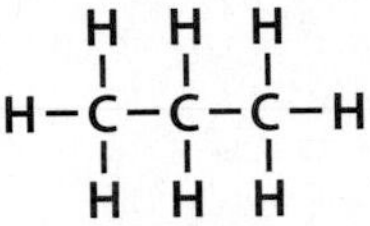

propane
C_3H_8

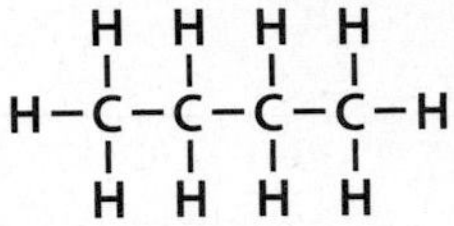

butane
C_4H_{10}

A large number of compounds can be created by modifying these basic alkanes. For example, replacing one of the hydrogen atoms at the end of an ethane molecule with a group containing an oxygen atom and a hydrogen atom (OH) produces ethanol, the most familiar form of alcohol:

```
  H H
  | |
H-C-C-O-H
  | |
  H H
```

ethanol
C_2H_6O

A slightly more complicated modification of a basic alkane, shown below, produces acetic acid, the acid occurring in vinegar. The double line between the carbon and the upper oxygen atom indicates that the carbon and oxygen atoms each share two electrons (rather than one) with each other, forming what is called a **double bond:**

```
  H    O
  |   //
H-C-C
  |   \
  H    O
        \
         H
```

acetic acid
$C_2H_4O_2$

The carbon atoms in organic molecules can also be joined to each other by double bonds, or (more rarely) **triple bonds,** in which each atom shares three electrons with the other. Two such molecules are ethylene, with a double bond between the carbon atoms, and acetylene, with a triple bond:

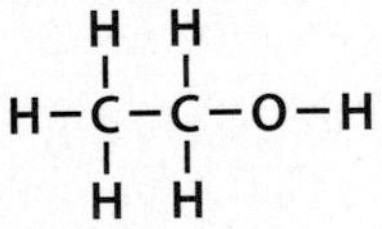

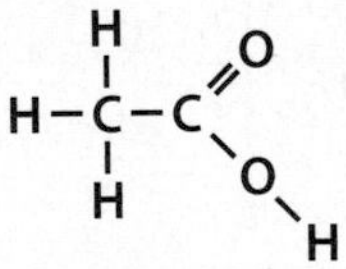

```
H     H
 \   /
  C=C
 /   \
H     H
```

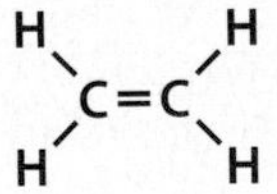

ethylene
C_2H_4

```
H-C≡C-H
```

acetylene
C_2H_2

Very often, chains of carbon atoms loop to form rings. One basic ring compound in organic chemistry is benzene, which has six carbon and six hydrogen atoms. The carbon atoms are joined to each other by alternating single and double bonds:

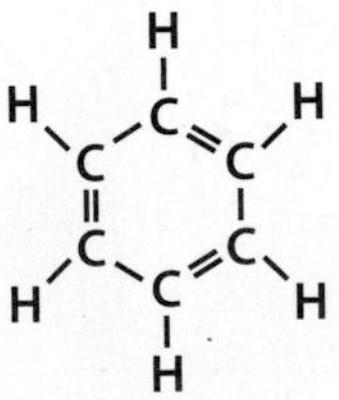

```
      H
      |
H     C     H
 \  /   \\ /
  C       C
  ||      |
  C       C
 /  \   // \
H     C     H
      |
      H
```

benzene
C_6H_6

system. It is measured parallel to the *y*-axis. For example, a point having coordinates (2,3) has 3 as its ordinate. *Compare* **abscissa.**

Ordovician (ôr′də-vĭsh′ən) The second period of the Paleozoic Era, from about 488 to 444 million years ago, characterized by a diversity of marine invertebrates and the appearance of fish. *See Chart at* **geologic time,** pages 146–147.

ore (ôr) A mineral or rock from which a valuable or useful substance, especially a metal, can be extracted at a reasonable cost.

organ (ôr′gən) A distinct part of an organism that performs one or more particular functions. Examples of organs are the eyes, ears, lungs, and heart of an animal, and the roots, stem, and leaves of a plant.

organelle (ôr′gə-nĕl′) A structure in a cell that is enclosed within its own membrane and serves a particular function. Organelles are found only in eukaryotic cells and are absent from the cells of prokaryotes like bacteria. Nuclei, mitochondria, and chloroplasts are examples of organelles.

organic (ôr-găn′ĭk) **1.** Involving organisms or the products of their life processes. **2.** Relating to chemical compounds containing carbon, especially hydrocarbons. **3.** Grown or raised without the use of synthetic fertilizers or pesticides, antibiotics, hormones, irradiation, or genetically modified organisms, or made from plants or animals grown or raised in this way.

organic chemistry The branch of chemistry that deals with carbon and carbon compounds.

organism (ôr′gə-nĭz′əm) An individual form of life, such as a bacterium, fungus, plant, or animal, that consists of one or many cells in which the cell parts or organs work together to carry out the processes of life.

origin (ôr′ə-jĭn) The point at which the axes of a Cartesian coordinate system intersect. The coordinates of the origin are (0,0) in two dimensions and (0,0,0) in three dimensions.

Orion (ō-rī′ən) A constellation in the region of the celestial equator near Gemini and Taurus. It contains the bright stars Betelgeuse and Rigel.

ornithischian (ôr′nə-thĭs′kē-ən) One of the two main types of dinosaurs. Ornithischians were plant eaters and had a pelvis similar to that of modern birds. Many of them had a horny beak or bill. The stegosaurus is an example of an ornithischian. *Compare* **saurischian.**

ornithology (ôr′nə-thŏl′ə-jē) The scientific study of birds.

orthoclase (ôr′thə-klās′) A type of feldspar consisting of potassium aluminum silicate. Orthoclase is typically white, pink, yellow, or brown, but it can also be colorless. It is especially common in igneous rocks.

orthopedics (ôr′thə-pē′dĭks) The branch of medicine that deals with the correction or treatment of disorders or injuries of the bones, joints, and associated muscles and ligaments.

orthorhombic (ôr′thō-rŏm′bĭk) Relating to a crystal having three axes of different lengths intersecting at right angles. The mineral topaz has orthorhombic crystals. *See more at* **crystal.**

Os The symbol for **osmium.**

oscillation (ŏs′ə-lā′shən) **1.** Continuous motion back and forth through a central position. **2.** A single cycle of variation between two extremes, especially one that repeats at regular time intervals.

oscilloscope (ə-sĭl′ə-skōp′) An electronic instrument used to measure changing electric volt-

oscillation

Oscillation of a clock pendulum takes it from point **a** *to point* **b** *and back to* **a**. *The dashed red line shows the position of the pendulum at rest.*

ages. It displays the waveforms of electric oscillations on a screen.

-ose A suffix used to form the chemical names of carbohydrates, such as *glucose.*

-osis 1. A suffix that means: "diseased or abnormal condition," as in *scoliosis.* **2.** A suffix that means "condition or process," as in *metamorphosis.*

osmium (ŏz′mē-əm) A hard, brittle, bluish-white metallic element. Osmium is the densest naturally occurring element. It is used to make very hard alloys for fountain pen points and electrical contacts. *Symbol* **Os.** *Atomic number* 76. *See* **Periodic Table,** pages 254–255.

osmosis (ŏz-mō′sĭs) The movement of a solvent through a membrane separating two solutions of different concentrations. The solvent from the side of weaker concentration usually moves to the side of the stronger concentration, diluting it, until the concentrations of the solutions are equal on both sides of the membrane. ❖ The pressure of the solution exerted on the membrane when solvent flow is equalized in both directions is called **osmotic pressure.** The tendency to reach this equilibrium is the energy driving osmosis and is important for all living organisms because it allows water and nutrients dissolved in water to pass through cell membranes.

ossicle (ŏs′ĭ-kəl) A small bone, especially one of the three (the incus, malleus, and stapes) located in the middle ear that transmit sound vibrations from the eardrum to the inner ear in mammals. Most other vertebrates have only one ossicle in the ear.

ossification (ŏs′ə-fĭ-kā′shən) The process of bone formation, brought about by the action of specialized bone cells called osteoblasts.

osteoarthritis (ŏs′tē-ō-är-thrī′tĭs) A form of arthritis that is characterized by wearing down of the cartilage of the joints.

osteoblast (ŏs′tē-ə-blăst′) A cell that produces new bone by secreting collagen and other proteins. As new bone grows and hardens, osteoblasts become embedded in the bone matrix. Once embedded, they are called osteocytes and are no longer bone-producing.

osteoclast (ŏs′tē-ə-klăst′) A cell that absorbs bone, allowing for the deposition of new bone and maintenance of bone strength.

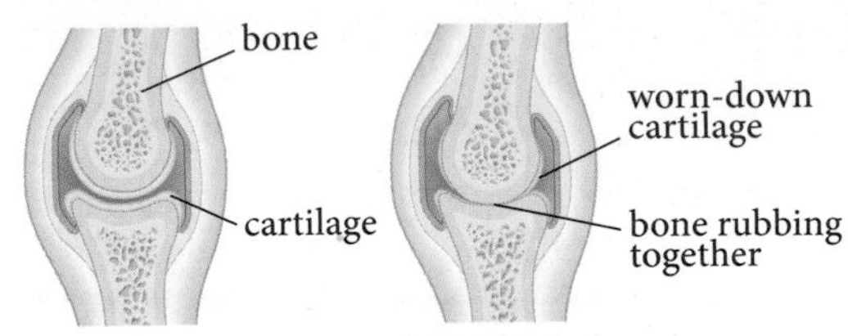

osteoarthritis
left: *normal joint*
right: *joint affected by osteoarthritis*

osteocyte (ŏs′tē-ə-sīt′) A cell that is embedded in the matrix of bone and has branching extensions that connect with other cells of the same type. Osteocytes, which develop from osteoblasts, help to maintain healthy bone and to control the formation of new bone.

osteopathy (ŏs′tē-ŏp′ə-thē) A form of medical practice that involves a variety of therapeutic practices, with an emphasis on the manipulation of bones and muscles.

osteoporosis (ŏs′tē-ō-pə-rō′sĭs) A condition in which the bones become porous and weak from loss of minerals, especially calcium. People with osteoporosis are at increased risk of breaking or fracturing a bone.

ostrich (ŏs′trĭch) Either of two large African birds having a small head, a long neck, and long legs. Ostriches can run fast but cannot fly. They are the largest living birds.

otter (ŏt′ər) Any of various mammals having a long slim body, webbed feet, and thick dark-

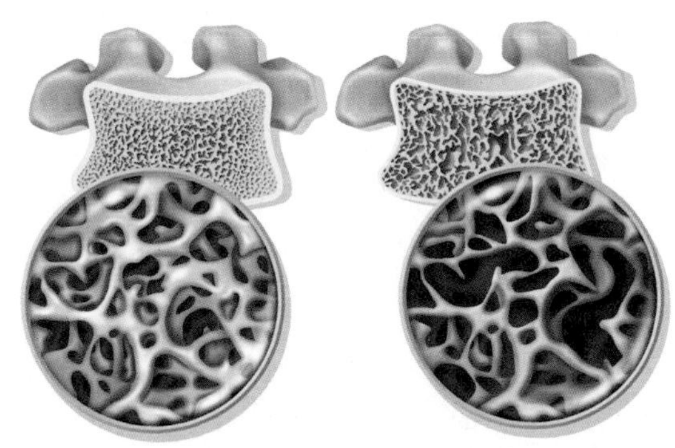

osteoporosis
left: *healthy vertebra*
right: *vertebra affected by osteoporosis*

brown fur. Some kinds of otters live in the ocean, and others live mostly in and near rivers.

ounce (ouns) **1.** A unit of weight equal to $\frac{1}{16}$ of a pound and containing 16 drams or 437.5 grains (about 28.35 grams). *See Table at* **measurement. 2.** A unit of volume or capacity used to measure liquids, equal to $\frac{1}{16}$ of a pint and containing 8 fluid drams or about 1.8 cubic inches (about 29.57 cubic centimeters). *See Table at* **measurement.**

outbreeding (out′brē′dĭng) The mating or breeding of distantly related or unrelated individuals, especially over several generations. Outbreeding often produces offspring with fewer harmful genetic mutations because it reduces the chances that an individual will inherit the same mutation from both parents. *Compare* **inbreeding.**

outcrop (out′krŏp′) An area of visible bedrock that is not covered with soil.

outer ear (ou′tər) The outermost part of the ear in mammals and some other vertebrates, consisting of the passage leading to the eardrum and often an external, protruding structure. The outer ear gathers and focuses incoming sound waves and transmits them to the middle ear. *See more at* **ear.**

outer space The region of space beyond Earth's atmosphere.

output (out′po͝ot′) **1.** The energy, power, or work produced by a system or device: *the output of an engine.* **2.** The information that a computer produces by processing a specific input.

outcrop

ovary (ō′və-rē) **1.** The usually paired reproductive organs in female vertebrates that produce eggs and the sex hormones estrogen and progesterone. Some invertebrates, such as mollusks and annelids, have a similar egg-producing organ. **2.** The part of a flower pistil that contains ovules. The ovary is located at the base of the pistil and ripens into a fruit after fertilization of one or more of the ovules. *See more at* **flower.** —*Adjective* **ovarian** (ō-vâr′ē-ən).

oviduct (ō′vĭ-dŭkt′) A tube through which eggs travel after they leave an ovary. The fallopian tubes in mammals are oviducts.

oviparous (ō-vĭp′ər-əs) Producing eggs that hatch outside the body. Amphibians, birds, and most reptiles, fish, and insects are oviparous. Monotremes are the only oviparous mammals. *Compare* **ovoviviparous, viviparous.**

ovipositor (ō′və-pŏz′ĭ-tər) **1.** A tube in many female insects that extends from the end of the abdomen and is used to lay eggs. **2.** A similar organ of certain other animals, such as turtles.

ovoviviparous (ō′vō-vī-vĭp′ər-əs) Producing eggs that hatch within the female's body. Certain fish, reptiles, and invertebrates are ovoviviparous. *Compare* **oviparous, viviparous.**

ovulation (ŏv′yə-lā′shən) The release an egg cell (ovum) from the ovary in a female animal, regulated in mammals by hormones of the pituitary gland. In humans and most other primates, ovulation usually occurs midway through the menstrual cycle.

ovule (ŏv′yo͞ol) A small structure in the ovary of a seed plant that develops into a seed after fertilization. *See more at* **flower.**

ovum (ō′vəm) *Plural* **ova.** *See* **egg** (sense 1).

owl (oul) Any of various birds of prey that are usually active at night and have a large head, large forward-facing eyes, a short hooked bill, and a flat round face.

oxalic acid (ŏk-săl′ĭk) A poisonous, crystalline acid, $C_2H_2O_4$, found in a number of plants. It is used for many industrial purposes, including rust removal and bleaching.

oxbow

oxbow (ŏks′bō′) A sharp, U-shaped bend in a river. ❖ When a river changes its course and cuts through the strip of land in the middle of an oxbow, the water that remains in the former oxbow loop is called an **oxbow lake.**

oxidation (ŏk′sĭ-dā′shən) **1.** The chemical combination of a substance with oxygen. **2.** A chemical reaction in which an atom or ion loses electrons, thus undergoing an increase in valence. Removing an electron from an iron atom having a valence of +2 changes the valence to +3. *Compare* **reduction.**

oxidation-reduction A chemical reaction in which electrons are lost by one atom or ion and gained by another atom or ion.

oxide (ŏk′sīd′) A compound of oxygen and another element. Water (H_2O) and rust are examples of oxides.

oxidize (ŏk′sĭ-dīz′) To undergo or cause to undergo oxidation.

oxygen (ŏk′sĭ-jən) A nonmetallic element that exists in its free form as a colorless, odorless gas and makes up about 21 percent of the Earth's atmosphere. It is the most abundant element in the Earth's crust and occurs in many compounds, including water, carbon dioxide, and iron ore. Oxygen combines with most elements, is required for combustion, and is essential for life in most organisms. *Symbol* **O.** *Atomic number* 8. *See* **Periodic Table,** pages 254–255.

oxygenate (ŏk′sĭ-jə-nāt′) To combine or mix with oxygen, as in a physical, chemical, or biological system. Blood is oxygenated in the lungs, for example.

oxyhemoglobin (ŏk′sē-hē′mə-glō′bĭn) The compound formed when a molecule of hemoglobin binds with a molecule of oxygen. In vertebrate animals, oxyhemoglobin forms in the red blood cells as they take up oxygen in the lungs.

Did You Know...?

oxidation

If you've ever seen rust, you've seen *oxidation.* If you've ever watched a candle burn, you've seen oxidation. Actually, your own body is engaging in oxidation at this very moment! In all these examples, oxygen is added to another substance. Rust is oxygen reacting with iron. The burning of the candle and your body's process of carbohydrate metabolism both involve oxygen reacting with carbon and hydrogen. These reactions release heat energy as the oxygen atoms form chemical bonds with the other atoms. (Rust can be thought of as burning that happens incredibly slowly — so slowly that the heat it releases isn't noticeable.) Because the oxygen in these reactions takes electrons from the atoms it is oxidizing, chemists also use the word oxidation to describe what happens to any substance that loses electrons to another substance.

oxytocin (ŏk′sĭ-tō′sĭn) A hormone released by the pituitary gland that stimulates contraction of the uterus during childbirth and secretion of milk from the mammary glands.

oyster (oi′stər) Any of several bivalve mollusks of shallow waters, having a rough, irregularly shaped, hinged shell. Many kinds of oysters are used as food, and some kinds produce pearls inside their shells.

Did You Know...?

ozone

Ozone can be a lifesaver or a threat to health, depending on how high it is in the atmos-phere. In the lower atmosphere, ozone is a pollutant and contributes to respiratory diseases like asthma. But the ozone in the upper atmosphere is beneficial. The region of the atmosphere where ozone is most concentrated, known as the *ozone layer,* lies about 10 to 20 miles (16 to 32 kilometers) above the Earth. Because ozone absorbs certain wavelengths of harmful ultraviolet radiation from sunlight, this layer acts as an important protection for life on Earth. In the 1980s, scientists noticed that the ozone layer was thinning, especially in the polar regions, creating an *ozone hole* that let in dangerous amounts of ultraviolet radiation. In response to this threat, certain industrial chemicals that cause the breakdown of atmospheric ozone have been banned internationally, but the ozone layer is not expected to recover completely for decades.

oz. Abbreviation of **ounce.**

ozone (ō′zōn′) A poisonous, blue form of oxygen that has three atoms per molecule rather than the usual two. It is produced by electricity passing through air, as in a lightning strike, and also by the sun's radiation reacting with ordinary oxygen or with the pollutants in smog. Ozone is used commercially in water purification, as a disinfectant, and as a bleach.

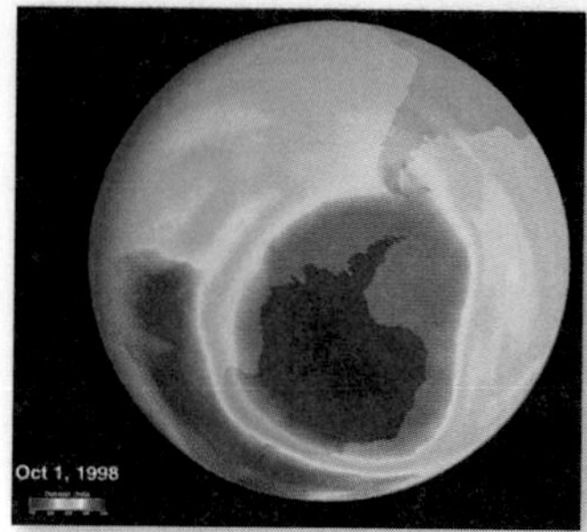

ozone hole
An image of Antarctica (dark purple) generated by a satellite instrument that measures infrared radiation from the Earth. The light purple and blue areas indicate an ozone hole, where the ozone layer is thin.

ozone hole A severe decrease in the amount of ozone in a region of the ozone layer, caused by the destruction of ozone by chlorofluorocarbons and other compounds, especially those containing chlorine or bromine. The largest ozone hole forms annually over Antarctica, during the Southern Hemisphere spring.

ozone layer A region of the atmosphere lying mostly in the stratosphere, containing relatively high levels of ozone. The ozone absorbs large amounts of solar ultraviolet radiation, preventing it from reaching the Earth's surface.

P 1. The symbol for **phosphorus. 2.** Abbreviation of **pressure.**

Pa 1. Abbreviation of **pascal. 2.** The symbol for **protactinium.**

pacemaker (pās′mā′kər) An electronic device that is surgically implanted to regulate the heartbeat.

pachycephalosaurus (păk′ĭ-sĕf′ə-lə-sôr′əs) A medium-sized, plant-eating dinosaur of the late Cretaceous Period having a domed skull up to 10 inches (25.4 centimeters) thick.

pack ice (păk) A large area of floating ice consisting of a mixture of ice fragments packed or squeezed ogether.

pahoehoe (pə-hoi′hoi′, pə-hō′ē-hō′ē) Lava with a smooth, swirled surface. It is highly fluid and spreads out in shiny sheets. *Compare* **aa.** *See Table at* **rock.**

palate (păl′ĭt) The roof of the mouth in vertebrate animals, separating the mouth from the passages of the nose. ❖ The bony part of the palate is called the **hard palate.** ❖ A soft, flexible, rear portion of the palate, called the **soft palate,** is present in mammals only and serves to close off the mouth from the nose during swallowing.

Paleocene (pā′lē-ə-sēn′) The earliest epoch of the Tertiary Period, from about 66 to 56 million years ago, characterized by the appearance of placental mammals and the formation of the Rocky Mountains. *See Chart at* **geologic time,** pages 146–147.

Paleogene (pā′lē-ə-jēn′) The earlier of two divisions of the Tertiary Period, from about 66 to about 23 million years ago, and including the Paleocene, Eocene, and Oligocene Epochs.

Paleolithic (pā′lē-ə-lĭth′ĭk) The cultural period of the Stone Age that began with the earliest chipped stone tools, about 2.4 million years ago, and ended with the beginning of the Mesolithic Period, about 15,000 to 10,000 years ago. *Compare* **Mesolithic, Neolithic.**

paleontology (pā′lē-ŏn-tŏl′ə-jē) The scientific study of life in the geologic past, especially through the study of animal and plant fossils.

Paleozoic (pā′lē-ə-zō′ĭk) The era of geologic time from about 542 to 251 million years ago. The Paleozoic Era is characterized by the appearance of marine invertebrate animals, fish and reptiles, and land plants. *See Chart at* **geologic time,** pages 146–147.

palisade layer (păl′ĭ-sād′) A layer of cells just below the upper surface of most leaves, consisting of cylindrical cells that contain many chloroplasts and are arranged perpendicular to the leaf

WORD HISTORY

pahoehoe and aa

The islands that make up Hawaii were created by volcanoes, and volcanoes remain an important part of the Hawaiian landscape and environment, so it is not surprising that the language of the native Polynesian people of Hawaii includes various words to distinguish different types of lava. English-speaking scientists have borrowed two such words from Hawaiian. One, *pahoehoe,* refers to lava with a smooth, shiny, or swirled surface and comes from the Hawaiian verb *hoe,* "to paddle" (since paddles make swirls in the water). The other, *aa,* refers to lava having a rough surface and comes from the Hawaiian verb meaning "to burn."

■ **pahoehoe**

surface. Also called *palisade parenchyma. See more at* **photosynthesis.**

palladium (pə-lā′dē-əm) An easily shaped, grayish-white metallic element that occurs naturally with platinum. Because it can absorb large amounts of hydrogen, it is used as a catalyst in reactions involving hydrogen. Palladium and its alloys are used to make electrical contacts and jewelry. *Symbol* **Pd.** *Atomic number* 46. *See* **Periodic Table,** pages 254–255.

palm (päm) Any of various evergreen trees or shrubs of tropical and subtropical regions, usually having a branchless trunk with a group of large feather-shaped or fan-shaped leaves at the top.

palmate (păl′māt′, päl′māt′) **1.** Shaped or arranged somewhat like a hand with the fingers extended. In a palmate leaf, like that of a maple, the veins radiate out from a single point. **2.** Having the front toes joined by a web; web-footed.

palp (pălp) One of a pair of appendages extending from the mouth of an invertebrate organism such as a mollusk, crustacean, or insect. Palps are often segmented and are used for feeding and sensing.

pampa (păm′pə) An extensive, treeless grassland of southern South America.

pancreas (păng′krē-əs) A long, irregularly shaped gland in vertebrate animals that is located behind the stomach. It secretes insulin into the blood and produces enzymes needed for digestion, which are secreted into the beginning part of the small intestine (the duodenum).

pandemic (păn-dĕm′ĭk) An epidemic that spreads over a very wide area, such as a whole country or continent.

Pangaea (păn-jē′ə) A supercontinent made up of all the world's present landmasses as they are thought to have been joined during the Permian and Triassic Periods. According to the theory of plate tectonics, Pangaea later broke up into Laurasia and Gondwana, which eventually broke up into the continents we know today.

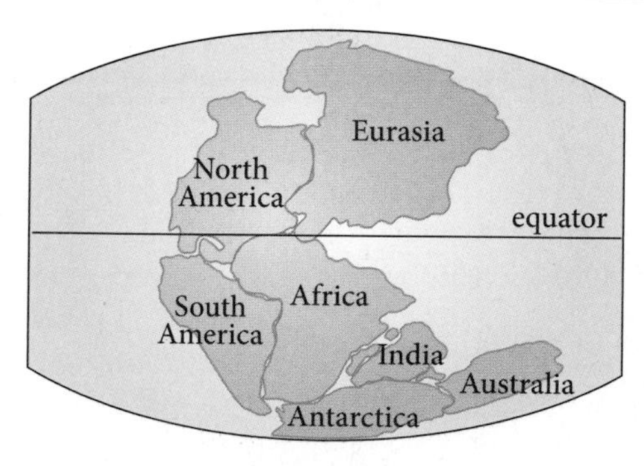

Pangaea

panicle (păn′ĭ-kəl) A loosely branched cluster of flowers, especially one in which the branches are racemes. Lilac flowers are arranged in panicles.

pantothenic acid (păn′tə-thĕn′ĭk) A vitamin belonging to the vitamin B complex that is important in the metabolism of fats, proteins, and carbohydrates. It is found in chicken, fish, legumes, dairy products, and certain vegetables.

papilla (pə-pĭl′ə) *Plural* **papillae** (pə-pĭl′ē) A small projection from a body surface, especially a taste bud on the tongue.

parabola (pə-răb′ə-lə) The curve formed by the set of points in a plane that are all equally distant from both a given line (called the directrix) and a given point (called the focus) that is not on the line.

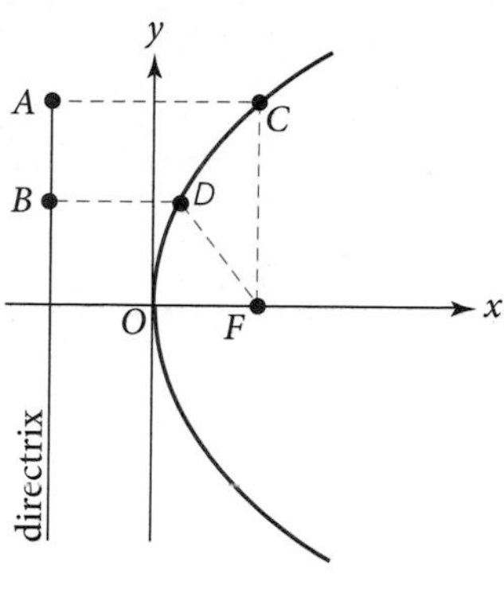

parabola

Any point on a parabola is the same distance from the directrix as it is from the focus (F). AC equals CF, and BD equals DF.

paraffin (păr′ə-fĭn) A waxy, white or colorless solid mixture made from petroleum and used to make candles, wax paper, lubricants, and waterproof coatings.

parallax (păr′ə-lăks′) A change in the apparent position of an object, such as a star, in relation to more distant objects, caused by a change in the observer's line of sight toward the object. The parallax of nearby stars caused by observing them from opposite points in Earth's orbit around the

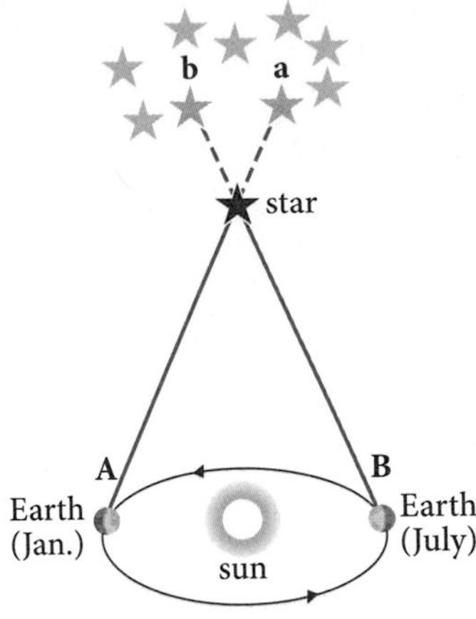

■ **parallax**

Viewed from point **A**, *a nearby star appears to occupy position* **a** *against a background of more distant stars. Six months later, from point* **B**, *the star appears to occupy position* **b**.

sun is used in estimating the stars' distance from Earth.

parallel (păr′ə-lĕl′) *Adjective* **1.** Relating to lines or surfaces that are separated everywhere from each other by the same distance. —*Noun* **2.** Any of the imaginary lines encircling the Earth's surface parallel to the plane of the equator, used to represent degrees of latitude.

parallel circuit *See under* **circuit.**

parallel computing *See* **parallel processing.**

parallelepiped (păr′ə-lĕl′ə-pī′pĭd) A three-dimensional geometric figure having six faces, each one being a parallelogram.

parallelogram (păr′ə-lĕl′ə-grăm′) A four-sided plane figure in which each pair of opposite sides is parallel.

parallel processing The processing of computing tasks by two or more processors working together at the same time. Tasks may be divided up among multiple processors in a single computer or among multiple computers connected together in a network. Also called *parallel computing.*

paramecium (păr′ə-mē′sē-əm) *Plural* **paramecia** *or* **parameciums** Any of various freshwater protozoans that are usually oval in shape and that move by means of cilia.

parameter (pə-răm′ĭ-tər) A quantity whose value can vary in general but is fixed when the quantity is used in a specific mathematical expression involving one or more other variables. For example, in finding the area of a circle, one needs to know the length of the circle's radius; that length is a parameter that will have different values for circles of different sizes.

paraplegia (păr′ə-plē′jē-ə) Paralysis of the lower part of the body, caused by injury to the spinal cord.

parasite (păr′ə-sīt′) An organism that lives in or on a different species of organism (called the host) from which it gets some or all of its nourishment. Parasites sometimes kill their hosts, but often the damage they do is minor. Bedbugs, lice, and tapeworms are all parasites of humans.

parasitism (păr′ə-sĭ-tĭz′əm) A relationship between two organisms of different species in which one of the organisms causes harm to the other, as when a tapeworm lives inside the digestive tract of a cow.

parasympathetic nervous system (păr′ə-sĭm′pə-thĕt′ĭk) The part of the autonomic nervous system that tends to act in opposition to the sympathetic nervous system, as by slowing down the heart and dilating the blood vessels. It also regulates the function of many glands, such as those that produce tears and saliva.

parathyroid gland (păr′ə-thī′roid) Any of four small kidney-shaped glands located behind or within the thyroid gland of many vertebrate animals. The parathyroid glands secrete a hormone (called parathyroid hormone) that regulates the amount of calcium in the blood.

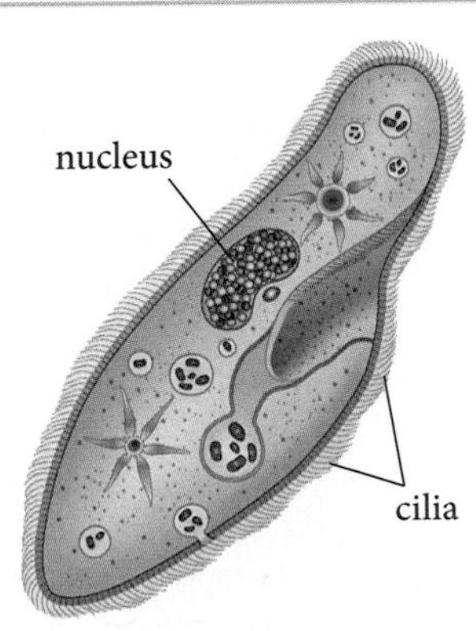

■ **paramecium**

parenchyma (pə-rĕng′kə-mə) A basic plant tissue, consisting of thin-walled cells that are usually unspecialized but sometimes take on specialized roles. The internal layers of leaves, the cortex and pith of the stem, and the soft parts of fruits are made of parenchyma. Parenchyma cells store water and food, and many of them contain chloroplasts where photosynthesis takes place.

parietal lobe (pə-rī′ĭ-təl) The middle portion of each cerebral hemisphere, where sensory information from the body is processed.

Parkinson's disease (pär′kĭn-sənz) A disease characterized by muscle tremors, slowed movement, and rigid muscles. The disease is associated with low levels of the neurotransmitter dopamine in the brain. It usually affects older people and worsens over time.

parsec (pär′sĕk′) A unit of astronomical length equal to 3.26 light years. It is based on the distance from Earth at which a star would have a parallax of one second of arc.

parthenogenesis (pär′thə-nō-jĕn′ĭ-sĭs) Reproduction in which an unfertilized egg develops into a new individual, occurring primarily in insects. Aphids, for example, typically reproduce parthenogenetically during the summer. A female aphid produces several female offspring every day, and those offspring can mature in a week and start producing their own young. —*Adjective* **parthenogenetic** (pär′thə-nō-jə-nĕt′ĭk).

partial product (pär′shəl) A product formed by multiplying the multiplicand by one digit of the multiplier when the multiplier has more than one digit. For example, the product of 67 multiplied by 12 is 134 (that is, 67 × 2) + 670 (that is, 67 × 10), or 804. In this example 134 and 670 are partial products.

particle (pär′tĭ-kəl) **1.** A very small piece of solid matter; a speck: *particles of dust.* **2.** A subatomic particle, such as a proton, an electron, or a quark.

particle accelerator Any of several machines, such as a linear accelerator, cyclotron, or synchrotron, that greatly increase the speed of protons, electrons, and other charged subatomic particles and cause them to collide with each other or with a target. Studying the results of these collisions can lead to the discovery of new subatomic particles. Particle accelerators are also used to bombard atomic nuclei with neutrons to create isotopes that are used in medicine and industry. *See Note at* **subatomic particle.**

particle detector A device that can detect charged particles, such as ions, electrons, or positrons. Examples include Geiger counters, which also count the number or the rate of detected particles, and cloud chambers and bubble chambers, which also record the tracks of detected particles.

particulate (pər-tĭk′yə-lĭt) *Adjective* **1.** Formed of very small, separate particles. Dust and soot are forms of particulate matter. —*Noun* **2.** A very small particle, as of dust or soot. Particulates that are given off by the burning of oil, gasoline, and other fuels are a major component of air pollution and smog.

pascal (pă-skăl′, pä-skäl′) A unit used to measure pressure. One pascal is equal to one newton per square meter.

Pascal, Blaise 1623–1662. French mathematician, physicist, and philosopher. He invented the mechanical calculator and the syringe. With Pierre de Fermat, he developed the mathematical theory of probability.

Pascal's law A physical law stating that for a fluid in a closed container, the pressure is the same throughout the fluid. If the pressure increases at one point, that increase is transmitted equally to every other point.

Pasteur (păs-tûr′), **Louis** 1822–1895. French chemist who was one of the founders of modern microbiology. He did research on fermentation, investigated the cause of infectious diseases, and developed vaccines for anthrax and rabies. *See Note on next page.*

pasteurization (păs′chər-ĭ-zā′shən) A process in which an unfermented liquid, such as milk, or a partially fermented one, such as beer, is heated to a specific temperature for a certain amount of time in order to kill harmful microorganisms or prevent further fermentation. During pasteurization, the liquid is not allowed to reach its boiling point so as to avoid changing its molecular structure.

patella (pə-tĕl′ə) The small, flat, movable bone at the front of the knee in most mammals. Also called *kneecap. See more at* **skeleton.**

pathogen (păth′ə-jən) An agent that causes infection or disease, especially a microorganism,

BIOGRAPHY

Louis Pasteur

In the mid-1800s, most people believed that diseases developed in the body from a combination of internal imbalances and unhealthy environmental conditions. Although tiny microorganisms were sometimes seen in diseased tissue, they were generally thought to be the result rather than the cause of the illness. In the 1860s, Louis Pasteur demonstrated in a series of experiments that the process of fermentation that converts sugar to alcohol in wine production was caused by living agents, and that these agents originated from the external environment rather than developing directly from the fermenting material by spontaneous generation. He contended that similar agents were responsible for spoiling wine, and he showed that they could be killed with heat—a technique that came to be called "pasteurization." Pasteur became convinced that many diseases were also caused by agents that entered the body from outside and multiplied within it. His work on the deadly animal disease anthrax confirmed this theory, and he developed a successful vaccine for the disease. Later he developed a vaccine for rabies, although the causative agent, a virus, could not be seen with the microscopes of the day. The discoveries of Pasteur and other microbiologists had immense influence on the theory and treatment of infectious diseases.

such as a bacterium or protozoan, or a virus. *See Note at* **germ.**

pathology (pə-thŏl′ə-jē) **1.** The scientific study of disease and its causes, processes, and effects. **2.** The physical changes in the body and its functioning as a result of illness or disease.

Pauli (pou′lē), **Wolfgang** 1900–1958. Austrian-born American physicist. He formulated a principle stating that no two electrons in an atom can have identical energy, mass, and angular momentum at the same time. This principle is known as the Pauli Exclusion Principle.

Pauling (pô′lĭng), **Linus Carl** 1901–1994. American chemist noted for his work on the structure and nature of chemical bonding. After studying in Europe with Niels Bohr and other physicists, Pauling applied quantum physics to chemistry. He discovered the structure of many molecules found in living tissue, especially proteins and amino acids. While studying the structure of hemoglobin, Pauling discovered the genetic defect that causes sickle cell anemia.

Pavlov (păv′lôv′, păv′lôf′), **Ivan Petrovich** 1849–1936. Russian physiologist who studied digestion and behavior in dogs. His experiments showed that if a bell is rung whenever food is presented to a dog, the dog will eventually salivate when it hears the bell, even if no food is presented. Pavlov contrasted this learned response (salivation in response to the bell) with the dog's natural, innate response (salivation in response to food). His research has been influential in subsequent studies of human and animal behavior.

Pb The symbol for **lead.**

PCB (pē′sē-bē′) Any of a family of compounds containing chlorine that were formerly used in many industrial applications. PCBs were banned in the United States in 1979 because of their toxic effects on humans and other animals. PCB is short for *polychlorinated biphenyl.*

Pd The symbol for **palladium.**

pearl (pûrl) A smooth, slightly iridescent, white or grayish rounded growth inside the shells of some mollusks. A pearl, which forms as a reaction to the presence of a foreign particle, consists of thin layers of mother-of-pearl that are deposited around the particle. The pearls of oysters are often valued as gems.

peat (pēt) Partially decayed vegetable matter, especially mosses, found in bogs. Peat is burned as a fuel and is also used as a fertilizer.

pectin (pĕk′tĭn) Any of a group of substances that are found in ripe fruits and can be made to form gels. Pectins are derived from carbohydrates. They are used in certain medicines and cosmetics and in making jellies.

pectoral (pĕk′tər-əl) Located in or attached to the chest: *a pectoral muscle; the pectoral fins.*

pediatrics (pē′dē-ăt′rĭks) The branch of medicine that deals with the care and treatment of infants, children, and adolescents.

pedicel (pĕd′ĭ-səl) A small stalk supporting a single flower in a plant.

peduncle (pĭ-dŭng′kəl, pē′dŭng′kəl) **1.** *Botany* The stalk of a single flower or flower cluster. *See more at* **flower. 2.** *Zoology* A stalk supporting an animal organ, such as the eyestalk of a lobster.

Pegasus (pĕg′ə-səs) A constellation in the Northern Hemisphere near Aquarius and Andromeda.

pegmatite (pĕg′mə-tīt′) Any of various coarse-grained igneous rocks that often occur as wide veins cutting across other types of rock. Pegmatites form from magma that is rich in water and cools slowly, allowing the crystals to grow to large sizes.

pelagic (pə-lăj′ĭk) Relating to or living in the open ocean: *pelagic birds.*

pelican (pĕl′ĭ-kən) Any of various large, web-footed waterbirds of warm regions, having a large expandable pouch under the lower bill. The pouch is used for catching and holding fish.

pellagra (pə-lăg′rə, pə-lā′grə) A disease caused by a lack of niacin in the diet. It causes skin and digestive disorders and mental deterioration.

pelvis (pĕl′vĭs) The basin-shaped structure in most vertebrate animals that joins the spine with the lower or hind limbs. In primates, the pelvis is composed of the two hipbones joined to the sacrum. It supports and protects the intestines, bladder, and internal reproductive organs.

pendulum (pĕn′jə-ləm) A mass hung from a fixed support so that it is able to swing freely under the influence of gravity. Pendulums are often used to regulate the action of various devices, especially clocks.

penguin (pĕng′gwĭn) Any of various flightless sea birds of the Southern Hemisphere, having flipperlike wings, webbed feet used for swimming

BIOGRAPHY

Linus Pauling

After devoting two decades to investigating chemical bonding, Linus Pauling made one of his most important discoveries one day while he was sick in bed. He lay there playing with pieces of paper, imagining them as molecules, and in a few hours he had figured out how amino acids are arranged in proteins. For this and related work he won the Nobel Prize in Chemistry in 1954. But Pauling also worked tirelessly on behalf of world peace. He studied the harmful effects of fallout from nuclear weapons and concluded that they should be banned, a position that got him into trouble. He was accused of being a Communist and was prevented from traveling abroad for a while, almost missing the award ceremony for the Nobel Prize. Pauling did not give in, however. He helped get a petition signed by thousands of scientists calling for an end to nuclear testing. In 1962 he won the Nobel Peace Prize for his efforts. He is the only person ever to receive two unshared Nobel Prizes. Pauling devoted much of his later life to researching the possible health benefits of large doses of vitamins and minerals, especially vitamin C.

penicillium
penicillium fungus growing on an orange

and diving, short scalelike feathers, and white underparts with a dark back. Penguins feed on fish, squid, and crustaceans such as krill.

penicillin (pĕn′ĭ-sĭl′ĭn) Any of a group of antibiotics that are either obtained directly from penicillium molds or prepared by a chemical process. They are used to treat or prevent infections caused by a wide variety of bacteria.

penicillium (pĕn′ĭ-sĭl′ē-əm) Any of various blue-green fungi that grow as molds on citrus fruits, cheeses, and bread, and are used to produce antibiotics, especially penicillin.

peninsula (pə-nĭn′syə-lə) A piece of land that projects into a body of water and is connected with a larger landmass.

penis (pē′nĭs) **1.** The male sex organ that releases sperm during sexual reproduction in mammals, most reptiles, and certain birds. It is composed largely of erectile tissue. In mammals, the penis also contains the urethra, which carries urine from the bladder. **2.** A similar organ found in the males of certain invertebrates, such as insects and some mollusks.

Pennsylvanian (pĕn′səl-vān′yən) The later of two subdivisions of the Carboniferous Period, from about 318 to 299 million years ago, characterized by rock deposits that are rich in coal and the appearance of the first reptiles. In North America, the Mississippian and Pennsylvanian have traditionally been classified as full geologic periods rather than as subdivisions of the Carboniferous. *See Chart at* **geologic time,** pages 146–147.

Penrose (pĕn′rōz′), **Roger** Born 1931. British mathematician and physicist. With Stephen Hawking he studied the physics of black holes.

pentagon (pĕn′tə-gŏn′) A polygon having five sides.

penumbra (pĭ-nŭm′brə) **1.** A partial shadow between regions of complete shadow and complete illumination, especially as cast by Earth, the moon, or another object during an eclipse. **2.** The lighter-colored outer part of a sunspot. *Compare* **umbra.**

pepsin (pĕp′sĭn) An enzyme that is produced in the stomach of vertebrate animals and acts as a catalyst in the breakdown of proteins.

peptic (pĕp′tĭk) Relating to the process of digestion or the secretions associated with it.

peptide (pĕp′tīd′) A chemical compound that is composed of a chain of two or more amino acids and is usually smaller than a protein. Some hormones and antibiotics are peptides.

percent *also* **per cent** (pər-sĕnt′) One part in a hundred. For example, 62 percent (also written 62%) means 62 parts out of 100.

percentile (pər-sĕn′tīl′) Any of the 100 equal parts into which the range of the values of a set of data can be divided to show the distribution of those values. The percentile of a given value is approximately equal to the percentage of the values that are smaller than that value. For example, a test score that is higher than 95 percent of the other scores is in the 95th percentile.

perchlorate (pər-klôr′āt′) A salt of perchloric acid; a compound containing the group ClO_4.

perchloric acid (pər-klôr′ĭk) A clear, colorless

peninsula
Kaikoura Peninsula, New Zealand

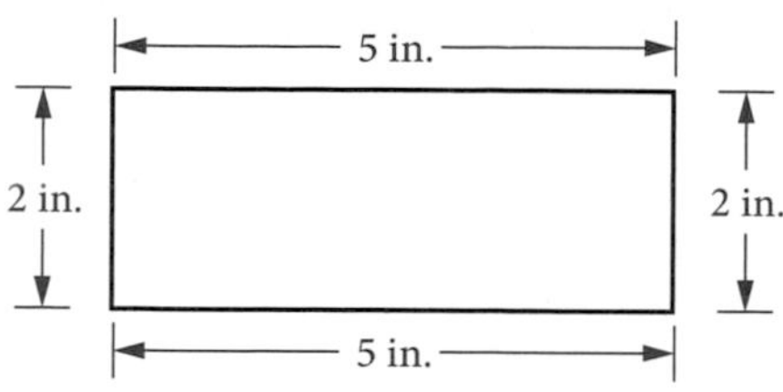

perimeter
The perimeter of this rectangle measures 14 inches.

liquid, $HClO_4$, that is very corrosive and, under some conditions, extremely explosive. It is a powerful oxidant and is used as a catalyst and in explosives.

perennial (pə-rĕn′ē-əl) *Botany. Adjective* **1.** Living for three or more years. —*Noun* **2.** A perennial plant. Peonies, irises, and asparagus are some examples of perennials.

perfect number (pûr′fĭkt) A positive integer that equals the sum of all of its divisors other than itself. An example is 28, whose divisors (not counting itself) are 1, 2, 4, 7, and 14, which added together give 28.

peri– **1.** A prefix that means: "around," as in *pericardium,* the membrane around the heart. **2.** A prefix that means "near," as in *perihelion,* the point at which a planet is nearest the sun.

perianth (pĕr′ē-ănth′) The part of a flower outside the reproductive structures, usually consisting of the sepals and the petals.

pericardium (pĕr′ĭ-kär′dē-əm) The membrane sac that encloses the heart in vertebrate animals.

periderm (pĕr′ĭ-dûrm′) The outer, protective layers of tissue of woody roots and stems, consisting of the cork cambium and the tissues produced by it. *See more at* **cork cambium.**

perigee (pĕr′ə-jē) The point in an orbit around Earth where the orbiting body is nearest to Earth. Sometimes this term is used informally to describe an analogous point in an orbit around a celestial object other than Earth. *Compare* **apogee.**

perihelion (pĕr′ə-hē′lē-ən) The point nearest the sun in the orbit of a body, such as a planet or comet, that travels around the sun.

perimeter (pə-rĭm′ĭ-tər) **1.** The sum of the lengths of the segments that form the sides of a polygon. **2.** The total length of any closed curve, such as the circumference of a circle.

period (pîr′ē-əd) **1.** *Geology* A division of geologic time, longer than an epoch and shorter than an era. **2.** The time it takes for a regularly recurring action or event to be repeated; a cycle. **3.** *Biology* An instance or occurrence of menstruation. **4.** *Chemistry* In the periodic table, any of the seven horizontal rows that contain elements arranged in order of increasing atomic number. All the elements in a particular period have the same number of electron shells in their atoms. *See* **Periodic Table,** pages 254–255.

periodic table (pîr′ē-ŏd′ĭk) A table in which the chemical elements are arranged in order of increasing atomic number. Elements with similar properties are arranged in the same column (called a group), and elements with the same number of electron shells are arranged in the same row (called a period). *See Table,* pages 254–255.

peripheral nervous system (pə-rĭf′ər-əl) In vertebrate animals, the part of the nervous system that lies outside the brain and spinal cord. It includes the nerves that extend to the limbs. *Compare* **central nervous system.**

periscope (pĕr′ĭ-skōp′) Any of several optical instruments in which mirrors or prisms allow

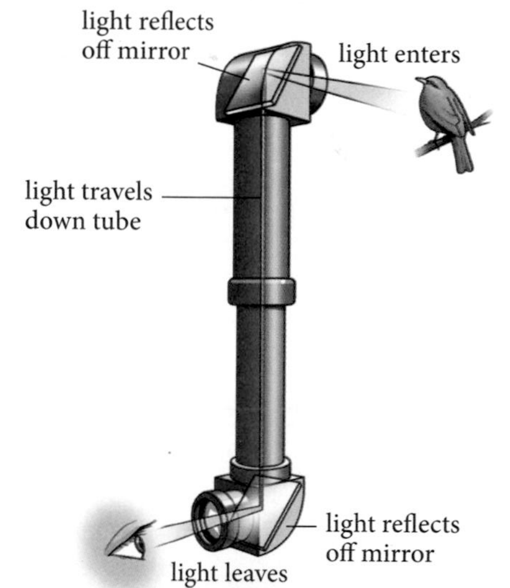

periscope
Light enters the top lens, reflects off a mirror set at a 45° angle, travels down the periscope tube, reflects off a second mirror also set at a 45° angle, and exits through the bottom lens.

PERIODIC TABLE OF THE ELEMENTS

The periodic table is a systematic arrangement of the chemical elements according to their atomic structure. The elements are arranged so that their **atomic numbers**—the number of protons in each element's nucleus—increase as you read across each row from left to right. Thus hydrogen (atomic number 1) comes first in the table, helium (atomic number 2) comes second, lithium (atomic number 3) comes third, and so on.

The first periodic table was designed by Dmitri Mendeleev in 1869. At that time only 63 of the elements were known. Today we know a total of 118. When Mendeleev made the first table he knew that other elements would eventually be discovered, and he left empty spaces so that the new elements could be added as they were found.

Key	
1	atomic number
H	symbol
Hydrogen 1.00794	atomic weight (or mass number of most stable isotope if in parentheses)

	Group 1	Group 2	Group 3	Group 4	Group 5	Group 6
Period 1	1 **H** Hydrogen 1.00794					
Period 2	3 **Li** Lithium 6.941	4 **Be** Beryllium 9.0122				
Period 3	11 **Na** Sodium 22.9898	12 **Mg** Magnesium 24.305				
Period 4	19 **K** Potassium 39.098	20 **Ca** Calcium 40.08	21 **Sc** Scandium 44.956	22 **Ti** Titanium 47.87	23 **V** Vanadium 50.942	24 **Cr** Chromium 51.996
Period 5	37 **Rb** Rubidium 85.47	38 **Sr** Strontium 87.62	39 **Y** Yttrium 88.906	40 **Zr** Zirconium 91.22	41 **Nb** Niobium 92.906	42 **Mo** Molybdenum 95.96
Period 6	55 **Cs** Cesium 132.905	56 **Ba** Barium 137.33	57–71 * Lanthanides	72 **Hf** Hafnium 178.49	73 **Ta** Tantalum 180.948	74 **W** Tungsten 183.84
Period 7	87 **Fr** Francium (223)	88 **Ra** Radium (226)	89–103** Actinides	104 **Rf** Rutherfordium (261)	105 **Db** Dubnium (262)	106 **Sg** Seaborgium (266)

* LANTHANIDES	57 **La** Lanthanum 138.91	58 **Ce** Cerium 140.12	59 **Pr** Praseodymium 140.908	60 **Nd** Neodymium 144.24
** ACTINIDES	89 **Ac** Actinium (227)	90 **Th** Thorium 232.038	91 **Pa** Protactinium 231.036	92 **U** Uranium 238.03

PERIODS

The elements are placed into seven rows, or **periods,** according to the number of electron shells in their atoms. Each atom consists of a nucleus of neutrons and protons surrounded by one or more energy levels, or shells, in which electrons are continuously orbiting. The smallest atoms have only one electron shell. Larger atoms have as many as seven shells, each one successively larger than the one inside it. Hydrogen and helium have only one electron shell and are therefore placed in Period 1, while sodium and chlorine have three shells and are placed in Period 3. By noting the period in which an element is located, you can immediately know how many electron shells it has.

LANTHANIDES AND ACTINIDES

The elements of the **lanthanide series** (elements 57–71) and the **actinide series** (elements 89–103) all behave in a manner similar to that of the elements in Group 3. But since they have different atomic numbers, they are separated from the main periodic table to make it easier to read.

GROUPS

The elements are organized into 18 separate columns, or **groups,** primarily according to the number of electrons occupying their outermost shell. This number is important because it strongly affects the way an element will behave in a chemical reaction. Since the elements in each group have the same number of electrons in their outer shell, they share certain chemical behaviors such as the ability to combine with other elements to form compounds. In the case of the larger elements in Periods 4 through 7, the number of electrons in some of the inner shells also affects their behavior and thus determines where their groups are placed in the table.

Group 7	Group 8	Group 9	Group 10	Group 11	Group 12	Group 13	Group 14	Group 15	Group 16	Group 17	Group 18
											2 **He** Helium 4.0026
						5 **B** Boron 10.811	6 **C** Carbon 12.011	7 **N** Nitrogen 14.0067	8 **O** Oxygen 15.9994	9 **F** Fluorine 18.9984	10 **Ne** Neon 20.18
						13 **Al** Aluminum 26.9815	14 **Si** Silicon 28.086	15 **P** Phosphorus 30.9738	16 **S** Sulfur 32.066	17 **Cl** Chlorine 35.453	18 **Ar** Argon 39.948
25 **Mn** Manganese 54.938	26 **Fe** Iron 55.845	27 **Co** Cobalt 58.9332	28 **Ni** Nickel 58.69	29 **Cu** Copper 63.546	30 **Zn** Zinc 65.38	31 **Ga** Gallium 69.72	32 **Ge** Germanium 72.64	33 **As** Arsenic 74.9216	34 **Se** Selenium 78.96	35 **Br** Bromine 79.904	36 **Kr** Krypton 83.80
43 **Tc** Technetium (98)	44 **Ru** Ruthenium 101.07	45 **Rh** Rhodium 102.905	46 **Pd** Palladium 106.4	47 **Ag** Silver 107.868	48 **Cd** Cadmium 112.41	49 **In** Indium 114.82	50 **Sn** Tin 118.71	51 **Sb** Antimony 121.76	52 **Te** Tellurium 127.60	53 **I** Iodine 126.9045	54 **Xe** Xenon 131.29
75 **Re** Rhenium 186.2	76 **Os** Osmium 190.2	77 **Ir** Iridium 192.22	78 **Pt** Platinum 195.08	79 **Au** Gold 196.967	80 **Hg** Mercury 200.59	81 **Tl** Thallium 204.38	82 **Pb** Lead 207.2	83 **Bi** Bismuth 208.98	84 **Po** Polonium (209)	85 **At** Astatine (210)	86 **Rn** Radon (222)
107 **Bh** Bohrium (264)	108 **Hs** Hassium (277)	109 **Mt** Meitnerium (268)	110 **Ds** Darmstadtium (281)	111 **Rg** Roentgenium (280)	112 **Cp** Copernicium (285)	113† (284)	114 **Fl** Flerovium (289)	115† (288)	116 **Lv** Livermorium (293)	117† (293)	118† (294)

61 **Pm** Promethium (145)	62 **Sm** Samarium 150.36	63 **Eu** Europium 151.96	64 **Gd** Gadolinium 157.25	65 **Tb** Terbium 158.925	66 **Dy** Dysprosium 162.50	67 **Ho** Holmium 164.930	68 **Er** Erbium 167.26	69 **Tm** Thulium 168.934	70 **Yb** Ytterbium 173.05	71 **Lu** Lutetium 174.97
93 **Np** Neptunium (237)	94 **Pu** Plutonium (244)	95 **Am** Americium (243)	96 **Cm** Curium (247)	97 **Bk** Berkelium (247)	98 **Cf** Californium (251)	99 **Es** Einsteinium (252)	100 **Fm** Fermium (257)	101 **Md** Mendelevium (258)	102 **No** Nobelium (259)	103 **Lr** Lawrencium (262)

† Elements 113, 115, 117, and 118 have been isolated experimentally but not yet officially named.

Alkali metals	Alkaline-earth metals	Transition metals	Other metals
Nonmetals	Noble gases	Lanthanide series	Actinide series

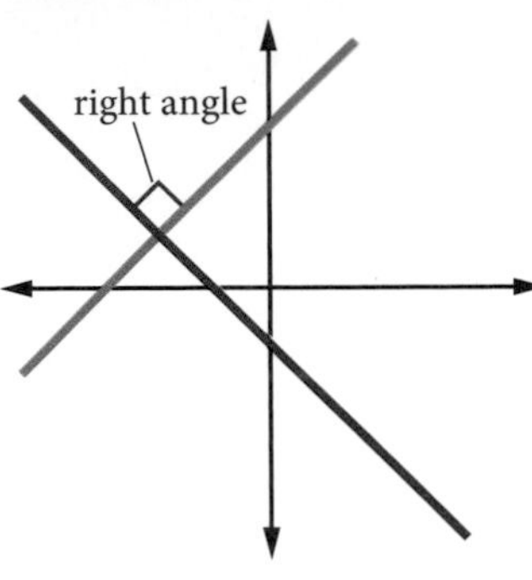

perpendicular
The purple line is perpendicular to the green line.

observation of objects that are not in a direct line of sight.

perissodactyl (pə-rĭs′ō-dăk**′**təl) Any of various hoofed mammals having an odd number of toes, either one or three, on each foot. Perissodactyls include the horses, tapirs, and rhinoceroses. Also called *odd-toed ungulate. Compare* **artiodactyl.**

peristalsis (pĕr′ĭ-stôl**′**sĭs) The wavelike muscle contractions in the organs of the digestive tract that push food into the stomach and then to the intestines. Peristalsis starts in the esophagus and ends when digested food is eliminated as waste.

peritoneum (pĕr′ĭ-tn-ē**′**əm) The membrane that lines the inside of the abdomen and encloses the abdominal organs.

permafrost (pûr**′**mə-frôst′) A layer of permanently frozen subsoil and bedrock, reaching depths up to about 4,900 feet (1,500 meters). Permafrost is found throughout most of the polar regions.

permeable (pûr**′**mē-ə-bəl) Capable of being passed through or permeated, especially by liquids or gases: *a permeable membrane.*

Permian (pûr**′**mē-ən) The last period of the Paleozoic Era, from about 299 to 251 million years ago. The Permian Period was characterized by the formation of the supercontinent Pangaea, the rise of modern conifers, and the diversification of reptiles. It ended with the largest known mass extinction in the history of life. *See Chart at* **geologic time,** pages 146–147.

peroxide (pə-rŏk**′**sīd′) **1.** The anion O_2^{2-} or a compound containing this ion, such as Na_2O_2. Peroxides are extremely reactive and are commonly used in bleaching and oxidation processes. **2.** Hydrogen peroxide.

perpendicular (pûr′pən-dĭk**′**yə-lər) *Adjective* **1.** Intersecting at or forming a right angle or right angles. —*Noun* **2.** A line or plane that is perpendicular to a given line or plane.

Perseus (pûr**′**sē-əs) A constellation in the Northern Hemisphere near Andromeda and Taurus.

pertussis (pər-tŭs**′**ĭs) *See* **whooping cough.**

Perutz (pə-ro͞ots**′**, pĕr**′**əts), **Max Ferdinand** 1914–2002. Austrian-born British biochemist who determined the structure of hemoglobin, demonstrating that it is composed of four subunits, each of which consists of a chain of amino acids folded around an iron-containing molecule called a heme.

pesticide (pĕs**′**tĭ-sīd′) A substance used to kill unwanted or harmful organisms. Fungicides, herbicides, and insecticides are examples of pesticides.

petal (pĕt**′**l) One of the often brightly colored parts of a flower surrounding the reproductive organs. Petals may be separate or joined at their bases. As a group, the petals are called the corolla. *See more at* **flower.**

petiole (pĕt**′**ē-ōl′) *See* **leafstalk.**

petri dish (pē**′**trē) A shallow, circular dish with a loose cover, used especially for growing bacterial cultures.

petrifaction (pĕt′rə-făk**′**shən) *also* **petrification** (pĕt′rə-fĭ-kā**′**shən) The process by which organic materials are turned into rock. Petrifaction occurs when water that is rich with inorganic minerals, such as calcium carbonate or silica, passes slowly through organic matter, such as wood, replacing its cellular structure with minerals.

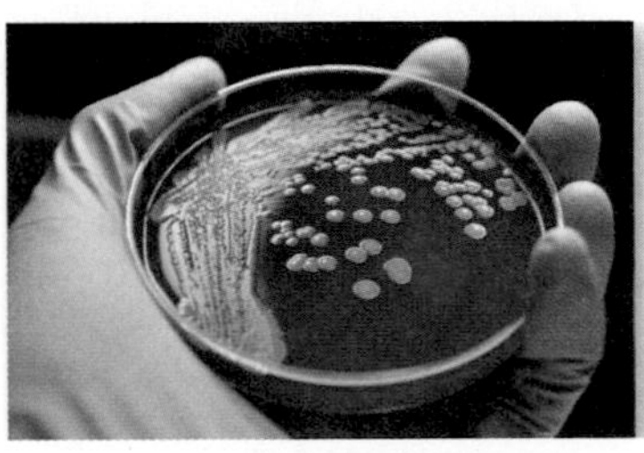

petri dish
staphylococcus bacteria growing in a petri dish

petrochemical (pĕt′rō-kĕm′ĭ-kəl) Any of a large number of chemicals made from petroleum or natural gas. Important petrochemicals include benzene, ammonia, acetylene, and polystyrene. Petrochemicals are used to produce a wide variety of materials, such as plastics, explosives, fertilizers, and synthetic fibers.

petroleum (pə-trō′lē-əm) A thick, black to yellow, flammable mixture of gaseous, liquid, and solid hydrocarbons. Petroleum occurs naturally beneath the Earth's surface, where it formed millions of years ago when the remains of organisms were buried under sediment, compressed, and heated. It is the source of petrochemicals and is used to make gasoline, lubricating oils, plastics, and many other products.

petrology (pə-trŏl′ə-jē) The scientific study of the origin, composition, and structure of rocks.

pH (pē′āch′) A numerical measure of the acidity or alkalinity of a solution, usually measured on a scale of 0 to 14. Neutral solutions have a pH of 7, acidic solutions have a pH lower than 7, and alkaline solutions have a pH higher than 7.

phagocyte (făg′ə-sīt′) A cell that has the ability to engulf and ingest other cells or particles. Several kinds of white blood cells in vertebrate animals, such as the macrophages, are phagocytes. They protect against disease by ingesting and killing bacteria, and they also break down debris from dead cells. ❖ The process by which cells engulf and break down other cells or particles is called **phagocytosis** (făg′ə-sī-tō′sĭs). Amoebas and many other single-celled organisms ingest food by the process of phagocytosis.

phalanges (fə-lăn′jēz) The small bones of the fingers or toes. *See more at* **skeleton.**

Phanerozoic (făn′ər-ə-zō′ĭk) The period of geologic time from about 542 million years ago to the present, including the Paleozoic, Mesozoic, and Cenozoic Eras. The Phanerozoic Eon is marked by an abundance of fossil evidence of life, especially more complex forms. *See Chart at* **geologic time,** pages 146–147.

pharmacology (fär′mə-kŏl′ə-jē) The scientific study of drugs and their effects, especially in the treatment of disease.

pharynx (făr′ĭngks) The passage that leads from the cavities of the nose and mouth to the larynx (voice box) and esophagus.

phase (fāz) **1.** Any of the forms, recurring in cycles, in which the moon or a planet appears. **2.** *See* **state of matter. 3.** A measure of how far some cyclic process, such as wave motion, has proceeded through its cycle. Two waves are said to be "in phase" when their crests and troughs line up. They are said to be "out of phase" when the crest of one wave lines up with the trough of the other. *See more at* **wave.**

phellem (fĕl′əm) *See* **cork** (sense 1).

phelloderm (fĕl′ə-dûrm′) The tissue produced on the inside of the cork cambium in woody plants. *See more at* **cork cambium.**

phellogen (fĕl′ə-jən) *See* **cork cambium.**

phenol (fē′nôl′, fē′nōl′) A poisonous, white, crystalline compound used as a disinfectant and to make plastics and drugs. Also called *carbolic acid.*

phenology (fĭ-nŏl′ə-jē) The scientific study of cyclical biological events, such as flowering and migration, in relation to climatic conditions.

phenolphthalein (fē′nōl-thăl′ēn′) A white or pale-yellow, crystalline powder used as an indicator for acid and basic solutions. It is also used in making dyes and was formerly used in medicine as a laxative.

phenotype (fē′nə-tīp′) The physical appearance of an organism, as distinguished from its genetic makeup. The phenotype of an organism depends on which genes are dominant and on how the genes are affected by the environment (both inside and outside the organism). *Compare* **genotype.**

phenyl (fĕn′əl, fē′nəl) The organic group C_6H_5, derived from benzene and occurring as a radical, as an ion, or as a component of many compounds.

phenylalanine (fĕn′əl-ăl′ə-nēn′) An essential amino acid. *See more at* **amino acid.**

pheromone (fĕr′ə-mōn′) A chemical that is secreted by an animal and influences the behavior or physiology of other animals of the same species. For example, ants use pheromones to mark trails, and aphids that are attacked by a predator release a pheromone that causes neighboring aphids to move away or drop off the plant.

phlegm (flĕm) Mucus produced by the mucous membranes of the respiratory tract.

phloem (flō′ĕm′) A tissue in vascular plants that conducts food in the form of dissolved

A CLOSER LOOK

Photosynthesis

A leaf is a plant's food factory. It makes food by photosynthesis, a two-stage process that converts the energy of sunlight into chemical energy. In the first stage, light from the sun strikes leaf cells that contain special structures called chloroplasts. The chloroplasts contain chlorophyll, a pigment that makes photosynthesis possible. Supplied with water brought up from the soil, the chloroplasts convert the light energy into chemical energy in the form of ATP. The water is split into hydrogen and oxygen, with the oxygen being given off as a waste product. In the second stage, which does not require light, the chloroplasts use the chemical energy stored in the ATP to combine the hydrogen with carbon dioxide from the air to make carbohydrates. The carbohydrates are then distributed throughout the plant as food.

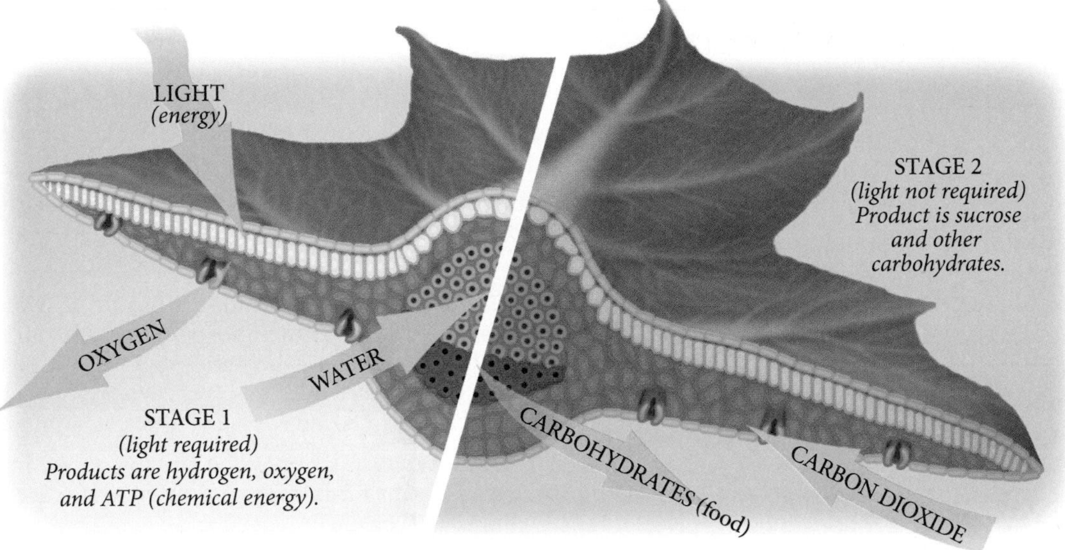

Photosynthesis takes place in the column-like cells of the palisade layer and in the irregularly shaped cells of the spongy parenchyma. Chloroplasts are present in both kinds of cells, but are especially numerous in the palisade layer. The cells receive carbon dioxide from air that enters the leaf through pores called stomata. The stomata also allow oxygen produced by photosynthesis to escape. Water from the roots is supplied by the vascular tissue known as xylem. Carbohydrates made by the leaf are distributed to the rest of the plant by the vascular tissue known as phloem.

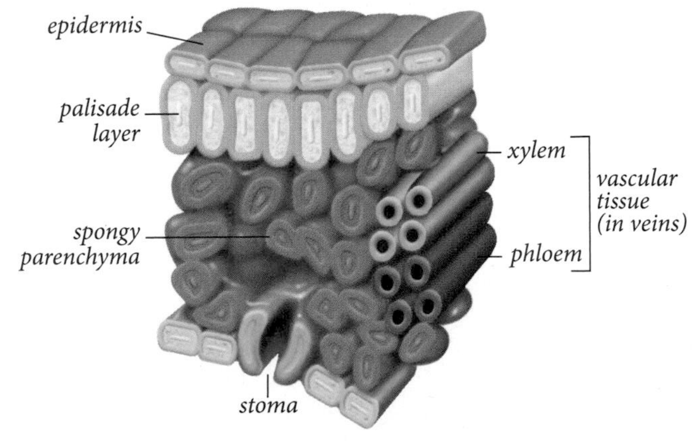

sugars from the leaves to the other plant parts. Phloem consists primarily of tubelike cells that have porous openings. In mature woody plants it forms a sheathlike layer of tissue in the stem that makes up the inner bark. *See more at* **cambium, photosynthesis.** *Compare* **xylem.**

phlogiston (flō-jĭs′tən) A hypothetical substance once thought to be the combustible part of all flammable substances and to be given off as flame during burning. In the late 1700s, a new theory of combustion was developed, and phlogiston was no longer believed to exist. *See Note at* **Lavoisier.**

phosphate (fŏs′fāt′) A salt or ester of phosphoric acid; a compound containing the group PO_4. Phosphates are important in metabolism and are frequently used in fertilizers.

phospholipid (fŏs′fō-lĭp′ĭd) Any of a class of molecules consisting of a lipid (a fat-like compound that does not dissolve in water) that contains phosphorus. Cell membranes are made of two layers of phospholipids.

phosphor (fŏs′fər) A substance that emits light after absorbing some form of radiation. The inside of a fluorescent light is coated with phosphors.

phosphorescence (fŏs′fə-rĕs′əns) The giving off of light by a substance while it is exposed to electromagnetic radiation, such as ultraviolet light or x-rays, and for a short time after the source of radiation has been removed. *Compare* **fluorescence.**

phosphorus (fŏs′fər-əs) A highly reactive, poisonous nonmetallic element occurring naturally in phosphates and existing in white (or sometimes yellow), red, and black forms. It is an essential component of living things. Phosphorus is used to make matches, fireworks, and fertilizers and to protect metal surfaces from corrosion. *Symbol* **P.** *Atomic number* 15. *See* **Periodic Table,** pages 254–255. —*Adjective* **phosphoric.**

photo– A prefix that means "light," as in *phototropism,* movement toward or away from light.

photodegradable (fō′tō-dĭ-grā′də-bəl) Capable of being chemically decomposed by light. For example, photodegradable plastic becomes brittle and breaks into smaller pieces when exposed to sunlight, helping reduce litter and environmental damage.

photoelectric (fō′tō-ĭ-lĕk′trĭk) Relating to the electrical effects of light. Light can cause the generation of an electric current, as in a photoelectric cell, or a change in the electrical resistance of a material, as in a photoresistor. ❖ The emission of electrons from a material, such as a metal, as a result of being struck by light is called the **photoelectric effect.**

photometry (fō-tŏm′ĭ-trē) The measurement of the intensity, brightness, or other properties of light.

photomicrograph (fō′tō-mī′krə-grăf′) A photograph made through a microscope.

photon (fō′tŏn′) The smallest unit of light or other electromagnetic energy, having no mass and no electric charge. Photons behave both as particles and as waves. *See Note at* **electromagnetic radiation.**

photoreceptor (fō′tō-rĭ-sĕp′tər) **1.** A specialized structure, cell, or molecule that is sensitive to light. In vertebrate animals, the primary photoreceptors are the rods and cones of the eye's retina. *See Note at* **circadian rhythm. 2.** An electronic device that converts light energy into electrical signals.

photosphere (fō′tə-sfîr′) The visible layer on the outer surface of the sun or another star, just inside the chromosphere.

photosynthesis (fō′tō-sĭn′thĭ-sĭs) The process by which green plants, algae, and certain forms of bacteria make carbohydrates from carbon dioxide and water using energy from light, which is captured by chlorophyll or other pigments. Photosynthesis normally releases oxygen as a byproduct. *See Note at* **transpiration.**

phototropism (fō-tŏt′rə-pĭz′əm) Growth or movement of an organism, especially a plant, toward or away from light. —*Adjective* **phototropic** (fō′tə-trō′pĭk).

photovoltaic cell (fō′tō-vōl-tā′ĭk, fō′tō-vŏl-tā′ĭk) *See* **solar cell.**

phylum (fī′ləm) *Plural* **phyla** A taxonomic category of organisms that share certain characteristics, ranking above a class and below a kingdom. *See Table at* **taxonomy.**

physical chemistry (fĭz′ĭ-kəl) The branch of chemistry that is concerned with the physical structure of atoms and molecules, the ways in which they react and bond, and the amount of energy they have.

physical science Any of several branches of science, such as physics, chemistry, or geology, that deal with the nature and properties of energy and nonliving matter. *Compare* **life science.**

physics (fĭz′ĭks) The scientific study of matter and energy and the relations between them.

physiology (fĭz′ē-ŏl′ə-jē) The scientific study of an organism's vital functions, such as circulation, respiration, and digestion.

phytoplankton (fī′tō-plăngk′tən) Plankton consisting of photosynthetic organisms, including algae, dinoflagellates, and cyanobacteria. Phytoplankton are a major source of food for aquatic animals and play an important role in carbon fixation, taking up carbon dioxide from the water and converting it into organic compounds.

pi (pī) An irrational number that has a numerical value of 3.141592653589. . . and is represented by the symbol π. It expresses the ratio of the circumference to the diameter of a circle and appears in many mathematical expressions.

piezoelectric effect (pī-ē′zō-ĭ-lĕk′trĭk) The generation of an electric charge in certain nonconducting materials, such as quartz crystals and ceramics, when they are subjected to mechanical stress (such as pressure or vibration), or the generation of vibrations in such materials when they are subjected to an electric field. These effects have many applications, as in microphones and quartz watches.

pigment (pĭg′mənt) **1.** An organic compound that gives a characteristic color to plant or animal tissues and is involved in vital processes. Chlorophyll and hemoglobin are examples of pigments. **2.** A substance or material used as coloring.

pincers (pĭn′sərz) A grasping claw, as of a lobster or scorpion, or a pair of appendages used for grasping, as in certain insects.

pine (pīn) Any of various evergreen trees that bear cones and have clusters of needle-shaped leaves. Pines are native to the Northern Hemisphere and are widely planted for timber.

pineal gland (pĭn′ē-əl, pī′nē-əl) A small gland that is located in the brain of many vertebrate animals. The pineal gland secretes the hormone melatonin, which controls daily and seasonal biological rhythms.

pinnate (pĭn′āt′) Having parts or divisions arranged on each side of a common axis in the manner of a feather. Ash, hickory, and walnut trees have pinnate leaves.

pinniped (pĭn′ə-pĕd′) Any of various carnivorous, aquatic mammals having flippers that are used for swimming and for moving on land. Pinnipeds include the seals and walruses.

pint (pīnt) **1.** A unit of volume or capacity used in liquid measure, equal to 16 fluid ounces or about 28.88 cubic inches (0.47 liter). **2.** A unit of volume or capacity used in dry measure, equal to $\frac{1}{2}$ of a quart or about 34.6 cubic inches (0.55 liter). *See Table at* **measurement.**

pipette (pī-pĕt′) A narrow tube that is open at both ends and often marked to show volume. It is used for transferring liquids.

Pisces (pī′sēz) A constellation in the Northern Hemisphere near Aries and Pegasus.

pistil (pĭs′təl) The female reproductive organ of a flower, consisting of the ovary, style, and stigma. *See more at* **flower.**

pistillate (pĭs′tə-lāt′) Having pistils but no stamens. Female flowers are pistillate.

piston (pĭs′tən) A solid cylinder or disk that fits snugly into a hollow cylinder and moves back and forth under the pressure of a fluid, as in many engines, or moves or compresses a fluid, as in a pump or compressor.

pit (pĭt) The hard, central part of certain fruits, such as a peach or cherry, usually containing a single seed.

pitchblende (pĭch′blĕnd′) A brown to black, often crusty mineral that is a principal ore of uranium. It is highly radioactive.

pith (pĭth) The soft, spongy tissue in the center of the stems and roots of most vascular plants.

pituitary gland (pĭ-to͞o′ĭ-tĕr′ē) A gland at the base of the brain in vertebrate animals that releases hormones that regulate the function of most of the body's other hormone-producing glands and organs, including the thyroid and adrenal glands. The pituitary gland also produces hormones that directly affect certain tissues, such as one that controls overall body growth.

pixel (pĭk′səl) The basic unit of a digital image, representing a single color or level of brightness. Display screens, camera sensors, and image files are all composed of pixels. Pixel is a shortening of *picture element.*

placebo (plə-sē′bō) A substance resembling a drug but containing only inactive ingredients, used especially in scientific experiments to test the effectiveness of a drug. Researchers give one group of people a real drug and another group a placebo and then determine whether the people taking the drug get better results than the people taking the placebo.

placenta (plə-sĕn′tə) **1.** A spongy organ that forms in the uterus of most female mammals during pregnancy and supplies oxygen and nutrients to the developing embryo or fetus through the umbilical cord. It is expelled after birth. **2.** The part of the ovary of a flowering plant to which the ovules are attached. —*Adjective* **placental.**

placental mammal Any of a large group of mammals in which the female bears live young that are nourished before birth by means of a placenta. All mammals except the marsupials and the monotremes are placental mammals.

placer (plăs′ər) A deposit of minerals, such as gold or magnetite, left in sediments, as of a riverbed or beach. The minerals are usually concentrated in one area because they are relatively heavy and therefore settle out of the water more quickly than lighter sediments such as silt and sand. When mineral prospectors pan for gold, they look for placer deposits.

plagioclase (plā′jē-ə-klās′) Any of a series of common feldspar minerals, consisting of mixtures of sodium and calcium aluminum silicates. Plagioclase is typically white, yellow, or reddish-gray, but it can also be blue to black. It is especially common in igneous rocks.

plague (plāg) **1.** Any highly infectious, usually fatal epidemic disease. **2.** An often fatal disease caused by a bacterium transmitted to humans usually by fleas that have bitten infected rats or other rodents. The most common form of plague is bubonic plague, though plague can also exist as a highly contagious form infecting the lungs and as an extremely severe form infecting the blood.

plain (plān) **1.** An extensive, level, usually treeless area of land. **2.** A broad, level expanse, such as an area of the sea floor or a lunar mare.

Planck (plängk), **Max Karl Ernst Ludwig** 1858–1947. German physicist who formulated quantum theory (1900), which explained and predicted certain phenomena that could not be accounted for in classical physics. Planck's theory was essential to the work of Albert Einstein, Niels Bohr, and many other modern physicists.

plane (plān) *Noun* **1.** A two-dimensional surface, any two of whose points can be joined by a straight line that lies entirely in the surface. —*Adjective* **2.** Lying in a plane: *a plane curve.*

plane geometry The mathematical study of geometric figures whose parts lie in the same plane, such as polygons, circles, and lines.

planet (plăn′ĭt) A large, nearly spherical celestial object that orbits a star, does not produce

Did You Know...?

planet

In 1930, the astronomer Clyde Tombaugh discovered Pluto, and Pluto was classified as our solar system's ninth planet. In 2006, the International Astronomical Union voted to change the definition of *planet.* They stated that in order for an object in space to be called a planet, it must have enough mass to form a round shape and "clear the neighborhood around its orbit." This means that it must be the only significant object orbiting the sun at that distance, except for smaller objects that the planet's gravity has captured, such as moons that revolve around it. Because many other objects are now known to orbit the sun in the vicinity of Pluto, astronomers declared that Pluto has not cleared its own orbit and is therefore not a planet. To describe objects like Pluto, they created a new category, the *dwarf planet.* A dwarf planet orbits the sun and forms a nearly round shape, like a regular planet, but it does not orbit a planet (as our moon does) or clear the neighborhood around its orbit. Astronomers have identified four other dwarf planets in our solar system, including one named Eris that is about the same size as Pluto.

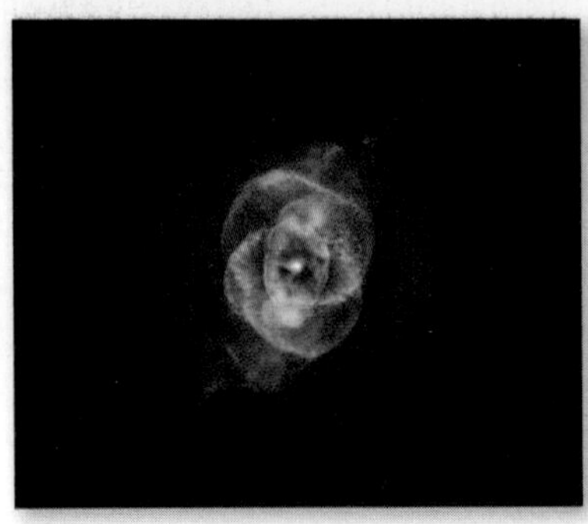

planetary nebula
Cat's Eye nebula

its own light, is not a satellite of another planet, and is massive enough to clear away neighboring objects from its orbit. In our solar system there are eight planets: Mercury, Venus, Earth, Mars, Jupiter, Saturn, Uranus, and Neptune. Pluto was considered a planet until 2006, when it was reclassified as a dwarf planet. —*Adjective* **planetary.**

planetary nebula (plăn′ĭ-tĕr′ē) A circular or ring-shaped nebula formed by the ejection of the outer layers of a star of relatively low mass during a late stage in its evolution. *See more at* **star.**

plankton (plăngk′tən) Small organisms that drift or swim weakly in great numbers in bodies of salt or fresh water. Plankton is a primary food source for many animals and is made up of bacteria, algae, protozoans, small crustaceans such as copepods, and the larvae of aquatic invertebrates.

plant (plănt) Any of a large group of multicellular organisms that usually have chloroplasts and manufacture their own food by means of photosynthesis. Plants have cell walls made of cellulose, cannot move about under their own power, and have no nervous system. Trees, ferns, and mosses are examples of plants. Plants are grouped as a separate kingdom in taxonomy. *See Table at* **taxonomy.**

plant kingdom The category of living organisms that includes all plants. *See Table at* **taxonomy.**

plaque (plăk) **1.** A film of mucus and bacteria on the surface of the teeth. **2.** A deposit of fatty material on the inner lining of an artery wall, characteristic of atherosclerosis.

plasma (plăz′mə) **1.** *Biology* The clear, liquid part of the blood, composed mainly of water and proteins, in which the red and white blood cells are suspended. The plasma of mammals also contains platelets. Also called *blood plasma.* **2.** *Physics* A form of matter that is similar to a gas except that the electrons have been detached from their atoms, so that it contains positively charged ions and negatively charged electrons rather than electrically neutral atoms. The plasma as a whole is electrically neutral, however, because the concentrations of negative and positive charge are the same. Plasmas are produced by very high temperatures, as in the sun and other stars, and also by electrical discharge through a gas, as in a flash of lightning or a fluorescent light bulb. Plasma is often considered a fourth state of matter, in addition to solid, liquid, and gas.

plasma cell A cell that produces antibodies as part of an immune response. B cells develop into plasma cells. *See Note at* **antibody.**

plasmodial slime mold (plăz-mō′dē-əl) *See under* **slime mold.**

plasmodium (plăz-mō′dē-əm) *Plural* **plasmodia** **1.** A mass of protoplasm that has many cell nuclei, is capable of moving and ingesting food, and is characteristic of one phase of certain slime molds. **2.** Any of various protozoans that exist as parasites in vertebrate animals. One species of plasmodium causes malaria.

plastic (plăs′tĭk) *Noun* **1.** Any of numerous artificial compounds formed by linking simple chemical units into giant molecules called polymers. Plastics are soft or liquid when heated. They can be molded into objects, pressed into thin layers, and drawn into fibers for use in textiles. —*Adjective* **2.** Capable of being molded or formed into a shape.

plastic surgery Surgery to repair, restore, or remodel the appearance or sometimes the function of body parts.

plastid (plăs′tĭd) Any of several structures, such as chloroplasts, that are found in the cells of plants and algae and are surrounded by two membranes. Plastids have various functions, including the synthesis and storage of food, and they often contain pigments.

plate (plāt) *Noun* **1.** A thin, flat sheet of metal or other material, especially one used as an electrode in a storage battery or capacitor. **2.** In plate tectonics, one of the sections of the Earth's lithosphere (crust and upper mantle) that is in constant motion relative to other sections. *See more at* **tectonic boundary.** — *Verb* **3.** To coat or cover with a thin layer of metal.

plateau (plă-tō′) An elevated, comparatively level expanse of land.

platelet (plāt′lĭt) Any of numerous small cell fragments that are found in the blood of mammals and function in blood clotting. Platelets are formed in the bone marrow. When a blood vessel is injured, platelets clump together to form a sticky mass that prevents bleeding.

plate tectonics In geology, a theory that the Earth's lithosphere (crust and upper mantle) is divided into a number of large, platelike sections that move as distinct masses. *See more at* **tectonic boundary.** *See Notes at* **fault, Gondwana.**

Did You Know...?

plate tectonics

Have you ever noticed that the Earth's continents seem to fit together like pieces of a puzzle? This observation led the German meteorologist Alfred Wegener to propose the theory of continental drift in 1915. Since rocks and fossils were found to match up in parts of different continents, it seemed that they must have once been joined, but no one could explain how such large landmasses could move so far apart. This problem was not solved until the 1960s, when the theory of *plate tectonics* was proposed. According to this theory, the continents move by riding piggyback on plates—huge slabs of the Earth's lithosphere—that are much larger than the continents themselves. The plates move like parts of a conveyor belt powered by huge convection currents of molten rock that many geologists believe is heated by the decay of radioactive elements deep within the Earth. Although they only move a few inches per year, over hundreds of millions of years the continents are carried thousands of miles. Along their boundaries, the plates crumple, scrape, or pull apart from one another, giving rise to volcanoes and earthquakes and creating and destroying rock on the ever-changing surface of the planet.

platform (plăt′fôrm′) The basic technology of a computer system's hardware and software, defining how a computer is operated and determining what other kinds of software can be used. Additional software or hardware must be compatible with the platform.

platinum (plăt′n-əm) A soft, easily shaped, silver-white metallic element that occurs worldwide with similar metals. It has a high melting point and does not corrode in air. Platinum is used as a catalyst and in making jewelry, electrical contacts, and dental crowns. *Symbol* **Pt.** *Atomic number* 78. *See* **Periodic Table,** pages 254–255.

platypus (plăt′ĭ-pəs) An egg-laying mammal of Australia and Tasmania that spends much of its life in water. Platypuses have a broad flat tail, webbed feet, and a snout resembling a duck's bill.

playa (plī′ə) A dry lake bed at the bottom of a desert basin, sometimes temporarily covered with water. Playas have no vegetation and are among the flattest geographical features in the world.

Pleiades (plē′ə-dēz′) A loose collection of several hundred stars in the constellation Taurus, at least six of which are visible to the unaided eye.

Pleistocene (plī′stə-sēn′) The earlier of the two epochs of the Quaternary Period, from about 2.6 million to 12,000 years ago. The Pleistocene Epoch was characterized by the formation of widespread glaciers in the Northern Hemisphere and by the appearance of humans. Many large animals, including saber-toothed cats and mastodons, went extinct at the end of the Pleistocene. *See Chart at* **geologic time,** pages 146–147.

pleura (plo͝or′ə) A thin membrane that encloses each lung and lines the chest cavity.

Pliocene (plī′ə-sēn′) The fifth and last epoch of the Tertiary Period, from about 5.3 to 2.6 million years ago, characterized by the appearance of distinctly modern animals. *See Chart at* **geologic time,** pages 146–147.

plumage (plo͞o′mĭj) The covering of feathers on a bird.

plume (plo͞om) **1.** A feather, especially a large one. **2.** A body of magma that rises from the Earth's mantle into the crust. If a plume rises to the Earth's surface, it erupts as lava. If it remains below the Earth's surface, it eventually solidifies into a body of rock known as a pluton. **3.** An area of air, water, or soil containing pollutants released

plume
left: *smoke from an oil refinery*
right: *water pollutants discharging into the sea*

from a single source. A plume often spreads in the environment due to the action of wind, currents, or gravity.

plumule (plo͞om′yo͞ol) The young shoot of a plant embryo, situated just above the cotyledons and often containing immature leaves. *See more at* **germination.**

plutino (plo͞o-tē′nō) *Plural* **plutinos** A Kuiper belt object that orbits the sun in the same time period as Pluto, making two complete orbits in the time that it takes Neptune to make three complete orbits.

Pluto (plo͞o′tō) A dwarf planet that until 2006 was classified as the ninth planet in our solar system. It has a diameter about one-sixth that of Earth. It orbits the sun once every 248 years, and its orbit crosses that of Neptune. It has an average surface temperature of −378°F (−228°C). *See Note at* **planet.**

plutoid (plo͞o′toid′) A dwarf planet that orbits the sun at a greater distance on average than Neptune.

pluton (plo͞o′tŏn′) A large body of igneous rock formed when a plume of magma cools underground. Although most plutons are deep within the Earth's crust, some become exposed at the surface due to plate-tectonic processes.

plutonium (plo͞o-tō′nē-əm) A silvery, radioactive metallic element of the actinide series that has the highest atomic number of all naturally occurring elements. It can be found in tiny amounts in uranium ores and is produced artificially by bombarding uranium with neutrons. It is absorbed by bone marrow and is highly poisonous. Plutonium is used in nuclear weapons and as a fuel in nuclear reactors. Its most stable isotope has a half-life of 80 million years. *Symbol* **Pu.** *Atomic number* 94. *See* **Periodic Table,** pages 254–255.

Pm The symbol for **promethium.**

pneumatic (no͞o-măt′ĭk) **1.** Relating to air or another gas: *pneumatic pressure.* **2.** Filled with or operated by compressed air: *a pneumatic drill.*

pneumonia (no͞o-mōn′yə) A disease in which the lungs become inflamed and irritated, often resulting in coughing, fever, and difficulty breathing. It is usually caused by infection with a bacterium or virus.

Po The symbol for **polonium.**

pod (pŏd) A fruit or seed case that splits along two seams to release its seeds when it matures. Legumes, such as peas and beans, produce pods.

-pod A suffix meaning "foot" or "footlike part." It is used in the names of many groups of organisms, such as *arthropod,* an organism having jointed feet, and *decapod,* a crustacean having ten legs.

point (point) A geometric object having no dimensions and no property other than its location. The intersection of two lines is a point.

polar bond (pō′lər) A type of covalent bond between two atoms in which electrons are shared unequally. Because of this, one end of the molecule has a slightly negative charge and the other a slightly positive charge. *See more at* **covalent bond.**

polar cap 1. The mass of ice that covers either of the Earth's polar regions. **2.** The mass of frozen carbon dioxide and water that covers either of Mars's polar regions.

polar circle The Arctic Circle or the Antarctic Circle.

polar coordinate system A system of coordinates in which the location of a point is determined by its distance from a fixed point at the center of the coordinate space (called the pole) and by the measurement of the angle formed by a fixed line (the polar axis, corresponding to the x-axis in Cartesian coordinates) and a line from the pole through the given point. The polar coordinates of a point are given as (r, θ), where r is the distance of the point from the pole, and θ

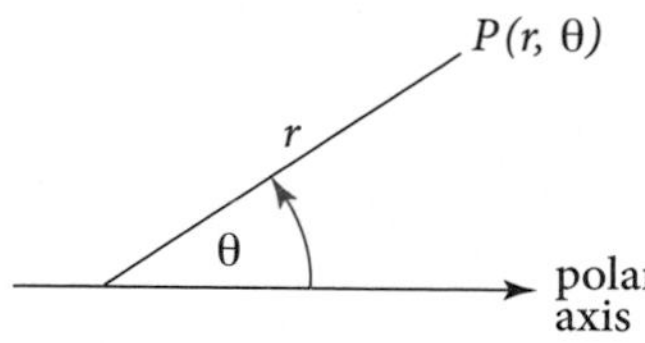

polar coordinate system
The polar coordinates of point P are (r, θ).

is the measure of the angle. *Compare* **Cartesian coordinate system.**

Polaris (pə-lăr′ĭs) A bright star at the end of the handle of the Little Dipper and almost at the north celestial pole. Also called *North Star.*

polarity (pō-lăr′ĭ-tē) The condition of having separate poles, especially magnetic or electric poles.

polarize (pō′lə-rīz′) **1.** To cause the positive and negative electric charges in an object, such as an atom, to become separate from each other, or to cause electric charges that are already separate to align with an electric field. **2.** To control the direction of vibration of transverse waves, such as electromagnetic waves. When light is polarized, for example, it vibrates in only one direction instead of in all directions, as in ordinary light.

pole (pōl) **1.** *Mathematics* **a.** Either of the points at which an axis that passes through the center of a sphere intersects the surface of the sphere. **b.** The fixed point used as a reference in a system of polar coordinates. It corresponds to the origin in the Cartesian coordinate system. **2.** *Geography* **a.** Either of the points at which the Earth's axis of rotation intersects the Earth's surface; the North Pole or South Pole. **b.** Either of the two similar points on another planet. **3.** *Physics* A magnetic pole. **4.** *Electricity* Either of two oppositely charged terminals, such as the two electrodes of an electrolytic cell or the electric terminals of a battery. —*Adjective* **polar.**

Did You Know...?

pollination

A plant cannot produce seeds until it undergoes *pollination.* For that to happen, a pollen grain (which contains the male sex cell) must reach an ovule (which contains the female sex cell). In the case of *self-pollination,* pollination occurs within a single flower or plant; in *cross-pollination,* the pollen travels to a different plant. Pollen grains disperse by different means. Some are blown by the wind. Some are carried by birds or insects. Certain clues can help you guess what mode of pollination a plant uses. Wind-pollinated plants, like ragweed and pine trees, usually have drab-colored flowers or cones and produce large amounts of pollen. Flowers pollinated by hummingbirds are often bright red. Moths and bats visit flowers that open at night. If a flower smells like rotting flesh, it's probably fly-pollinated. The fly lands on what appears to be delicious decaying meat, unaware that the plant has lured it in to provide pollination services.

polio (pō′lē-ō′) A contagious disease, caused by a virus, that mainly affects the nerve cells of the spinal cord and brainstem, often leading to muscle weakness and paralysis. The name is a shortening of **poliomyelitis** (pō′lē-ō-mī′ə-lī′tĭs).

pollen (pŏl′ən) Powdery grains that contain the male sex cells of seed plants. In flowering plants, pollen is produced by the anthers of stamens.

pollen tube A slender tube that is formed by a pollen grain of a seed plant during pollination. It releases the male gametes that fertilize the egg.

pollination (pŏl′ə-nā′shən) The process by which plant pollen is transferred from the male

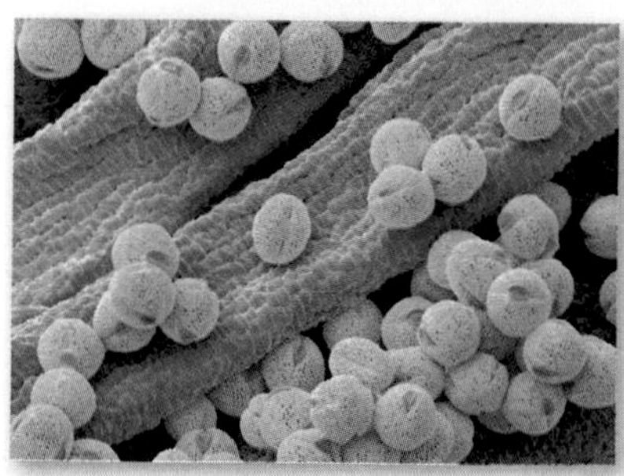

pollen
left: *photomicrograph of bellflower pollen*
right: *photomicrograph of sunflower pollen*

reproductive organs to the female reproductive organs to form seeds. In flowering plants, pollen is transferred from the anther to the stigma. In cone-bearing plants, male cones release pollen that is usually borne by the wind to the ovules of female cones. — *Verb* **pollinate.**

pollutant (pə-lo͞ot′nt) A substance, especially a waste material, that contaminates air, water, or soil.

pollution (pə-lo͞o′shən) The contamination of air, water, or soil by substances that are harmful to living things. ❖ Light from cities and towns at night that interferes with astronomical observations is known as **light pollution.** It can also disturb natural rhythms of growth in plants and other organisms. ❖ Continuous noise that is loud enough to be annoying or physically harmful is known as **noise pollution.** ❖ Heat from hot water that is discharged from a factory into a river or lake, where it can kill or endanger aquatic life, is known as **thermal pollution.**

polonium (pə-lō′nē-əm) A very rare, radioactive, silvery-gray or black metallic element. It is produced in extremely small amounts by the radioactive decay of naturally occurring radium or the bombardment of bismuth or lead with neutrons. *Symbol* **Po.** *Atomic number* 84. *See* **Periodic Table,** pages 254–255.

poly– A prefix meaning "many," as in *polygon,* a figure having many sides.

polychromatic (pŏl′ē-krō-măt′ĭk) **1.** Of or having many colors. **2.** Consisting of radiation of more than one wavelength.

polyester (pŏl′ē-ĕs′tər) Any of various synthetic resins that are light, strong, and resistant to weather. Polyesters are long chains of esters and are used to make plastics and fibers.

polyethylene (pŏl′ē-ĕth′ə-lēn′) An artificial resin that is easily molded and is resistant to other chemicals. It can be repeatedly softened and hardened by heating and cooling, and it is used for many purposes, such as making containers, tubes, and packaging.

polygon (pŏl′ē-gŏn′) A closed plane figure having three or more sides. Triangles, rectangles, and octagons are all examples of polygons.

polyhedron (pŏl′ē-hē′drən) A three-dimensional geometric figure whose sides are polygons. A tetrahedron, for example, is a polyhedron having four triangular sides.

polymer (pŏl′ə-mər) Any of various chemical compounds made of smaller, identical molecules (called monomers) linked together. Some polymers, like cellulose, occur naturally, while others, like nylon, are artificial. Polymers have extremely high molecular weights, make up many of the tissues of organisms, and are used to make such materials as plastics, concrete, glass, and rubber. ❖ The process by which molecules are linked together to form polymers is called **polymerization** (pə-lĭm′ər-ĭ-zā′shən).

polymorphism (pŏl′ē-môr′fĭz′əm) **1.** *Biology* **a.** The existence of two or more different forms

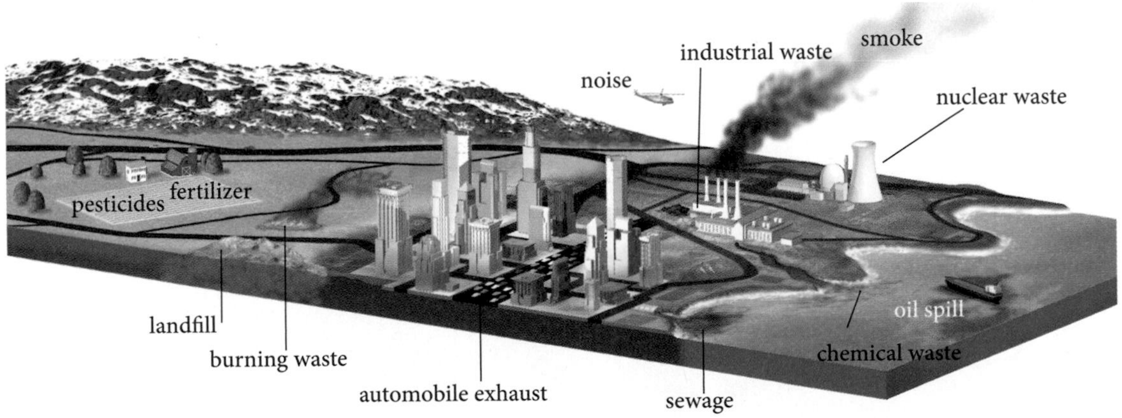

pollution

Pollution can affect air, water, or land and can threaten the health of humans, wildlife, and plants.

of individuals of a species, such as winged and wingless forms of an insect. Differences between juveniles and adults and between males and females are not considered examples of polymorphism. **b.** The existence within a population of two or more different DNA sequences at a particular location on a chromosome. **2.** *Chemistry* The crystallization of a compound in at least two distinct forms. Diamond and graphite, for example, are polymorphs of the element carbon. They both consist entirely of carbon but have different crystal structures and different physical properties.

polynomial (pŏl′ē-nō**′**mē-əl) An algebraic expression that consists of a monomial or the sum or difference of any number of monomials.

polyp (pŏl**′**ĭp) **1.** A cnidarian in its sedentary stage. Polyps have hollow, tube-shaped bodies with a central mouth on top surrounded by tentacles. Some cnidarians, such as corals and sea anemones, live as polyps for their entire lives, while others, like jellyfish, live as polyps when young and as medusas when mature. *Compare* **medusa. 2.** An abnormal growth protruding from the mucous lining of an organ such as the nose, bladder, or intestine.

polysaccharide (pŏl′ē-săk**′**ə-rīd′) Any of a class of carbohydrates that are made of long chains of simple carbohydrates (called monosaccharides). Starch and cellulose are polysaccharides.

polystyrene (pŏl′ē-stī**′**rēn) A plastic polymer that is transparent, hard, and rigid. It can be molded into objects or made into a white foam that is used for cups, packaging, and insulation.

polyunsaturated (pŏl′ē-ŭn-săch**′**ə-rā′tĭd) Relating to an organic compound, especially a fat, in which more than one pair of carbon atoms are joined by double or triple bonds. *See more at* **unsaturated.**

polyurethane (pŏl′ē-yo͝or**′**ə-thān′) Any of various synthetic resins used to make tough resistant coatings, adhesives, and electrical insulation.

pond (pŏnd) An inland body of standing water that is smaller than a lake.

pons (pŏnz) A part of the brainstem in mammals that links the medulla oblongata and the cerebellum with the upper portions of the brain.

population (pŏp′yə-lā**′**shən) All of the organisms of a species that live in a particular area: *the population of turtles in a pond.*

pore (pôr) **1.** A tiny opening, as one in an animal's skin or on the surface of a plant leaf or stem, through which liquids or gases may pass. **2.** A space in soil, rock, or loose sediment that is not occupied by mineral matter and allows the passage or absorption of fluids, such as water, petroleum, or air.

poriferan (pə-rĭf**′**ər-ən) *See* **sponge** (sense 1).

porous (pôr**′**əs) Having many pores or other small spaces that allow a gas or liquid to pass through. —*Noun* **porosity** (pə-rŏs**′**ĭ-tē).

porphyry (pôr**′**fə-rē) A fine-grained igneous rock containing some relatively large crystals, especially of feldspar.

porpoise (pôr**′**pəs) Any of several marine mammals having a blunt snout and a triangular dorsal fin. Porpoises, like whales and dolphins, are cetaceans.

positive (pŏz**′**ĭ-tĭv) **1.** Greater than zero. The number 12 is a positive number. **2.** Having the electric charge of a proton. The symbol for a positive charge is a plus sign. **3.** Having more protons than electrons. When a body such as an atom or molecule is positively charged, it repels other positively charged bodies but attracts negatively charged bodies. **4.** Showing the presence of a suspected disease or microorganism, as in a blood test.

positron (pŏz**′**ĭ-trŏn′) The subatomic particle that is the antiparticle of the electron.

post– **1.** A prefix that means "after," as in *postoperative,* after an operation. **2.** A prefix that means "behind," as in *postnasal,* behind the nose or nasal passages.

postulate (pŏs**′**chə-lĭt) A principle that is accepted as true without proof; an axiom.

potash (pŏt**′**ăsh′) Any of several chemical compounds that contain potassium, especially potassium carbonate (K_2CO_3), which is a strongly alkaline material obtained from wood ashes and used in fertilizers.

potassium (pə-tăs**′**ē-əm) A soft, highly reactive, silvery-white metallic element that is an alkali metal and occurs in nature only in compounds. It is essential for the growth and function of living

■ **potential energy**
top: *The unstretched exercise band has no potential energy.*
bottom: *The effort used to stretch the exercise band is stored as potential energy. This energy causes the exercise band to snap back to its normal shape when it is released.*

things and is used especially in fertilizers and soaps. *Symbol* **K.** *Atomic number* 19. *See* **Periodic Table,** pages 254–255.

potassium hydroxide A white, corrosive, solid compound, KOH, used in bleaches and to make soaps and detergents. It is soluble in water and in alcohol. In solution, it forms lye.

potassium nitrate A white or colorless crystalline compound and strong oxidizing agent, KNO_3. It is used as a preservative and in making glass, fireworks, matches, and fertilizers. Also called *saltpeter.*

potential energy (pə-tĕn**′**shəl) The energy that an object possesses as a result of its position or condition rather than its motion. A raised weight, a compressed spring, and a positive charge separated from a negative charge all have potential energy. *Compare* **kinetic energy.**

potentiometer (pə-tĕn′shē-ŏm**′**ĭ-tər) **1.** An adjustable resistor used to control the magnitude of the voltage that is applied to an electric circuit. Potentiometers are used in the volume controls of radios and televisions. **2.** An instrument for measuring an unknown voltage by comparison with a known voltage, such as that of a generator.

pound (pound) A unit of weight equal to 16 ounces (about 453.6 grams). *See Table at* **measurement.** *See Note at* **weight.**

power (pou**′**ər) **1.** The form of energy supplied to a machine or other device for it to operate: *trains that run on steam power; ships that use nuclear power.* **2.** *Physics* The rate (per unit time) at which work is done or energy is converted from one form to another. Power is measured in watts or horsepower. *Compare* **energy, work. 3.** *Mathematics* The number of times a number or an expression is multiplied by itself, as shown by an exponent. Thus, ten to the sixth power, or 10^6, equals one million. **4.** A number that represents the magnification of an optical instrument, such as a microscope or telescope. A 500-power microscope can magnify something 500 times.

Pr The symbol for **praseodymium.**

prairie (prâr**′**ē) An extensive area of flat land or rolling hills covered by grasses and other low vegetation, especially in central North America.

praseodymium (prā′zē-ō-dĭm**′**ē-əm) A soft, silvery, easily shaped metallic element of the lanthanide series that develops a green tarnish in air. It is used to color glass and ceramics yellow and to make glass used in goggles for welders. *Symbol* **Pr.** *Atomic number* 59. *See* **Periodic Table,** pages 254–255.

pre– A prefix that means "earlier, before," or "in advance," as in *prenatal,* before birth.

Precambrian (prē-kăm**′**brē-ən, prē-kām**′**brē-ən) The span of geologic time between Hadean Time and the Phanerozoic Eon, from about 3.8 billion to 542 million years ago. During the Precambrian Eon, which is divided into the Archean and Proterozoic, primitive forms of life first appeared on Earth. *See Chart at* **geologic time,** pages 146–147.

precession (prē-sĕsh**′**ən) **1.** The motion of the axis of a spinning body, such as the wobbling of a spinning top, that arises when an external force acts on the axis. **2.** The motion of this kind made by the Earth's axis, caused mainly by the gravitational pull of the sun, moon, and other planets. ❖ The **precession of the equinoxes** is the slow westward shift of the equinoxes along the ecliptic, resulting from precession of the Earth's

■ **precipitate**
When a solution of potassium iodide is added to a solution of lead nitrate, a precipitate of lead iodide (yellow) forms.

axis. The equinoxes circle all the way around the ecliptic once every 25,800 years.

precipitate (prĭ-sĭp′ĭ-tāt′) *Verb* **1.** To fall from the air as a form of water, such as rain or snow. **2.** To separate chemically from a solution in the form of a solid. —*Noun* **3.** A solid material separated from a solution by chemical means: *an insoluble precipitate.*

precipitation (prĭ-sĭp′ĭ-tā′shən) A form of water, such as rain, snow, or sleet, that condenses from the atmosphere and falls to the Earth's surface.

precocial (prĭ-kō′shəl) Hatched or born with the eyes open and the ability to move around and search for food. The offspring of chickens, horses, and sheep are precocial. *Compare* **altricial.**

predator (prĕd′ə-tər) An animal that lives by capturing and eating other animals.

pregnancy (prĕg′nən-sē) The condition of carrying developing offspring within the body; gestation.

prehensile (prē-hĕn′səl) Able to seize, grasp, or hold, especially by wrapping around an object. Many monkeys have prehensile tails, and elephants have prehensile trunks.

premolar (prē-mō′lər) Any of eight bicuspid teeth in mammals, arranged in pairs on both sides of the upper and lower jaws between the canines and molars. Premolars are used to tear and grind food.

■ **prehensile**
Opossums have prehensile tails.

pressure (prĕsh′ər) Force exerted per unit area, as by an object resting on the ground or by a liquid or gas pressing against the sides of a container. Pressure is usually measured in pascals, atmospheres, or pounds per square inch.

Priestley (prēst′lē), **Joseph** 1733–1804. British chemist who discovered oxygen (1774) and ten other gases, including hydrogen chloride, sulfur dioxide, and ammonia.

primary color (prī′mĕr′ē) Any of a group of colors from which colors of any hue can be made by mixing. *See more at* **color.**

primary growth Growth in vascular plants that occurs in the tips of roots and shoots, causing the plant to grow lengthwise. *Compare* **secondary growth.**

primary wave An earthquake wave in which rock particles vibrate parallel to the direction of wave travel. Primary waves can travel through both solids and liquids. Also called *P wave. See Note at* **earthquake.**

■ **Joseph Priestley**

primate (prī′māt′) Any of various mammals belonging to a group that includes the lemurs, monkeys, and apes (including humans). Primates have a large brain, a short snout, and forward-facing eyes. Their hands and feet have nails instead of claws and can be used for grasping objects. Because the human species has evolved to walk upright, the ability to grasp with the toes has largely been lost.

prime meridian (prīm) The meridian with a longitude of 0°, used as a reference line from which longitude east and west is measured. It passes through Greenwich, England.

prime number An integer greater than 1 that can be divided only by itself and 1 without leaving a remainder. Examples of prime numbers are 7, 23, and 67. *Compare* **composite number.**

primitive (prĭm′ĭ-tĭv) **1.** Relating to an early or original stage: *primitive computer software.* **2.** Being in an early stage of development or evolution: *fossils of primitive mammals.*

prion (prē′ŏn) An infectious agent consisting of a misshapen protein. Scientists believe that prions are normal body proteins that have become misfolded and transmit their shape to other proteins, causing the proteins to form clumps. Prions cause mad cow disease and other neurological diseases.

prism (prĭz′əm) **1.** A three-dimensional geometric figure whose bases are congruent polygons lying in parallel planes and whose sides are parallelograms. **2.** A solid of this type, often made of glass with triangular ends, used to disperse light and break it up into a spectrum.

probability (prŏb′ə-bĭl′ĭ-tē) A number expressing the likelihood of the occurrence of a given event, especially a fraction expressing how many times the event will happen in a given number of tests or experiments. For example, when rolling a six-sided die, the probability of rolling a particular side is 1 in 6, or $\frac{1}{6}$.

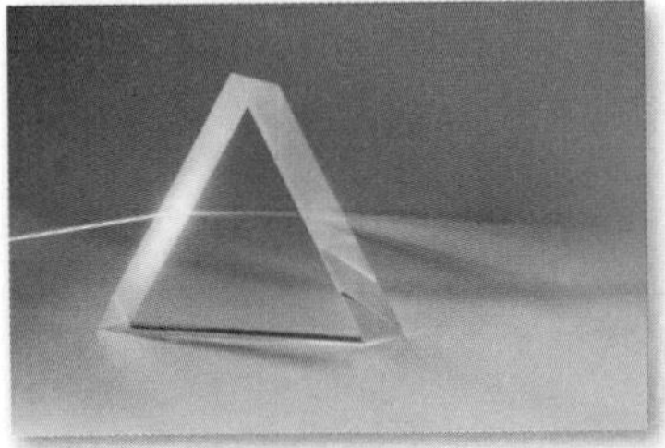

prism
White light passing through a prism is split into the colors of the spectrum.

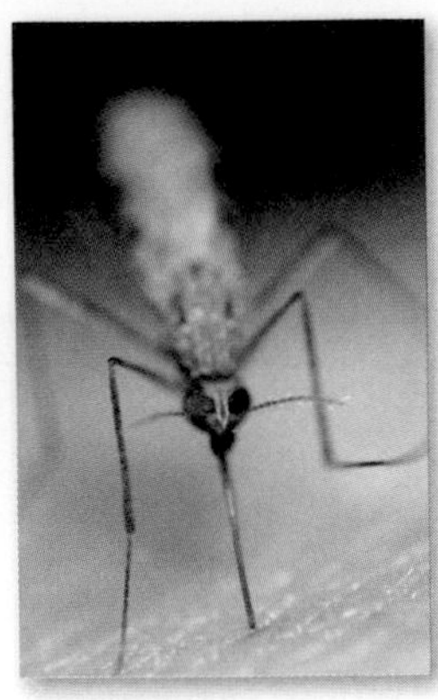

proboscis
left: *of an African elephant*
right: *of a mosquito*

proboscis (prō-bŏs′ĭs) **1.** A long, flexible snout or trunk, as of an elephant. **2.** The slender, tubular feeding and sucking organ of certain invertebrates, such as butterflies and mosquitoes.

Procyon (prō′sē-ŏn′) A very bright binary star in the constellation Canis Minor.

producer (prə-do͞o′sər) An organism that produces its own food and serves as a source of food for other organisms. Producers include green plants, which produce food through photosynthesis, and certain bacteria that are capable of converting inorganic substances into food through chemosynthesis. *Compare* **consumer.**

product (prŏd′əkt) A number or quantity obtained by multiplication. For example, the product of 3 and 7 is 21.

progesterone (prō-jĕs′tə-rōn′) A steroid hormone that prepares the uterus for pregnancy, maintains pregnancy, and promotes development of the mammary glands. The main sources of progesterone are the ovary and the placenta.

progestin (prō-jĕs′tĭn) Any of several synthetic substances that produce effects similar to those of progesterone. Progestins are used in many oral contraceptives, often in combination with estrogen.

Did You Know...?

program

Computer *programs* are coded in an artificial language called a *programming language.* The most elemental programming language in a computer is machine language, in which each instruction takes the form of a sequence of ones and zeros that is interpreted directly by the computer's central processing unit (CPU). Most programming, however, is done in more abstract, or high-level, programming languages that are easier for programmers to use. Programs in high-level languages are written with letters, numbers, and other characters, according to rules that allow them to be translated into machine language.

program (prō′grăm′) A set of coded instructions that enables a machine, especially a computer, to perform a desired sequence of operations.

prokaryote (prō-kăr′ē-ōt′) Any of numerous one-celled organisms that lack a distinct cell nucleus or other structures bound by a membrane and that have DNA that is not organized into chromosomes. Prokaryotes include the bacteria and archaea. *Compare* **eukaryote.** *See Note at* **archaeon.**

proline (prō′lēn′) A nonessential amino acid. *See more at* **amino acid.**

promethium (prə-mē′thē-əm) A radioactive metallic element of the lanthanide series. Promethium does not occur in nature, but it can be found as a product of the fission of uranium. It has 35 known isotopes, one of which can be used to make miniature batteries that work at extreme temperatures for up to five years. *Symbol* **Pm.** *Atomic number* 61. *See* **Periodic Table,** pages 254–255.

prominence (prŏm′ə-nəns) A tonguelike cloud of flaming gas that erupts from the surface of the sun. During a total solar eclipse, prominences are visible as part of the corona.

proof (pro͞of) A demonstration of the truth of a mathematical or logical statement, based on axioms and theorems derived from these axioms.

propagation (prŏpə-gā′shən) **1.** *Physics* The process by which energy travels from one place to another, such as sound traveling through air or light traveling through air or through a vacuum. **2.** *Biology* Natural or artificial reproduction of an organism or organisms. Gardeners and horticulturalists undertake plant propagation, for example, through processes such as growing seeds, taking cuttings, and making grafts.

propane (prō′pān′) A colorless, gaseous hydrocarbon, C_3H_8, found in petroleum and natural gas. It is widely used as a fuel.

propeller (prə-pĕl′ər) A device consisting of a series of twisted blades mounted around a shaft and spun to force air or water in a specific direction and thereby move an aircraft or boat.

proper fraction (prŏp′ər) A fraction in which the numerator is less than the denominator, such as $\frac{1}{2}$. *Compare* **improper fraction.**

prophase (prō′fāz′) The first stage of cell division. Before prophase begins in mitosis or the first division of meiosis, the DNA in the nucleus replicates. In the second division of meiosis, no DNA replication occurs. During prophase itself, the replicated pairs of chromosomes form long, thin strands called chromatids that are joined together at the centromere, and the nuclear membrane disappears. Prophase is followed by metaphase. *See more at* **meiosis, mitosis.**

prosimian (prō-sĭm′ē-ən) Any of various small primates that usually have large eyes and ears and are active at night. Lemurs are prosimians.

prostaglandin (prŏs′tə-glăn′dĭn) Any of a group of substances that are produced in the body from fatty acids and have a wide range of effects. Prostaglandins influence the contraction of the muscles lining many internal organs and can lower or raise blood pressure.

propeller
airplane propeller

prostate gland (prŏs′tāt′) A gland in male mammals surrounding the urethra at the base of the bladder. The prostate gland controls release of urine from the bladder and secretes a fluid which is a major constituent of semen.

protactinium (prō′tăk-tĭn′ē-əm) A rare, extremely toxic, radioactive metallic element of the actinide series that occurs in uranium ores. Its most common isotope has a half-life of 32,760 years. *Symbol* **Pa.** *Atomic number* 91. *See* **Periodic Table,** pages 254–255.

protease (prō′tē-ās′) Any of various enzymes that bring about the breakdown of proteins into peptides or amino acids by hydrolysis. Pepsin is an example of a protease.

protein (prō′tēn′) Any of a large class of complex organic chemical compounds that form the basis of living tissues and play a central role in biological processes. Proteins consist of chains of smaller compounds called amino acids and are usually folded in a characteristic three-dimensional structure. They contain carbon, hydrogen, oxygen, nitrogen, and usually sulfur atoms. Enzymes, antibodies, and hemoglobin are examples of proteins.

Proterozoic (prŏt′ər-ə-zō′ĭk) The later of the two divisions of the Precambrian Eon, from about 2.5 billion to 542 million years ago. The Proterozoic was characterized by the buildup of oxygen in the atmosphere and the appearance of the first multicellular organisms. *See Chart at* **geologic time,** pages 146–147.

protist (prō′tĭst) Any of a large variety of organisms that are usually one-celled or colonial and are not fungi, plants, or animals. Protists, unlike bacteria, are eukaryotes (that is, they have cell nuclei). Protists include protozoans, many algae, and slime molds. They have traditionally been grouped together as a kingdom in taxonomy, but some scientists believe that they should be divided into several different kingdoms. *See Table at* **taxonomy.**

protium (prō′tē-əm, prō′shē-əm) The most abundant isotope of hydrogen, having an atomic mass of 1. Its nucleus consists of a single proton. *See more at* **hydrogen.**

protocol (prō′tə-kôl′) A standard procedure for regulating data transmission between computers.

proton (prō′tŏn′) A stable subatomic particle that is part of the nucleus of an atom and has a positive electric charge. Its charge is opposite to that of an electron but is equal in magnitude. The mass of a proton is about 1,836 times that of an electron. *See more at* **atom.**

protoplasm (prō′tə-plăz′əm) A substance resembling jelly that forms the living matter inside cells. Protoplasm is made up of proteins, fats, and other substances suspended in water.

protostar (prō′tə-stärz′) A celestial object that is in the process of developing into a star. A protostar is formed when a dense interstellar cloud collapses into a spherical core that has a luminous surface but is not yet dense enough to sustain nuclear reactions.

protozoan (prō′tə-zō′ən) *Plural* **protozoans** *or* **protozoa** Any of a large group of one-celled organisms that take in food and move about freely, often using appendages called cilia or flagella. Protozoans are usually classified as protists and include the amoebas, the paramecia, and many species that live as parasites in other organisms.

Proxima Centauri (prŏk′sə-mə) *See under* **Alpha Centauri.**

pseudopod (so͞o′də-pŏd′) also **pseudopodium** (so͞o′də-pō′dē-əm) *Plural* **pseudopods** *or* **pseudopodia** A temporary footlike extension of the cell body of a one-celled organism, such as an amoeba, used for moving about and for surrounding and taking in food.

psychiatry (sĭ-kī′ə-trē) The branch of medicine that deals with the study and treatment of mental and emotional disorders.

psychology (sī-kŏl′ə-jē) The scientific study of mental processes and behavior.

psychosis (sī-kō′sĭs) *Plural* **psychoses** (sī-kō′sēz) A mental state in which a person loses the ability to think clearly, understand what is real, and communicate with others. Sometimes people with a psychosis think they see or hear things that others do not perceive. Psychoses may occur in people with schizophrenia or other mental or physical disorders. *—Adjective* **psychotic** (sī-kŏt′ĭk).

Pt The symbol for **platinum.**

pteranodon (tə-răn′ə-dŏn′) Any of several large, extinct, flying reptiles of the Cretaceous Period, having a long crested head, no teeth, and a wingspan of 20 feet (6.1 meters) or more.

pterodactyl

pterodactyl (tĕr′ə-dăk′təl) Any of various small, extinct, flying reptiles of the late Jurassic Period. The pterodactyls were about the size of a large bird, such as an eagle.

pterosaur (tĕr′ə-sôr′) Any of various extinct flying reptiles of the Mesozoic Era, having wings consisting of a membrane of skin extending from the side of the body to an elongated fourth digit on the forelimb. Pterosaurs had wingspans ranging from less than a foot (0.3 meter) to about 30 feet (10.7 meters). Pteranodons and pterodactyls were types of pterosaurs.

Ptolemaic system (tŏl′ə-mā′ĭk) The astronomical system of Ptolemy, in which the Earth is at the center of the universe with the sun, moon, planets, and stars revolving about it in circular orbits at increasing distance. The planets, according to this system, orbited in small circles around a point that itself was moving in a circle around the Earth. This hypothesis explained why the planets appear to periodically reverse direction and move from east to west in the sky before returning to their usual west to east movement.

Ptolemy (tŏl′ə-mē) Second century AD. Greek astronomer and mathematician who based his astronomy on the belief that all heavenly bodies revolve around Earth. *See more at* **Copernicus.**

Pu The symbol for **plutonium.**

puberty (pyo͞o′bər-tē) The stage in the development of humans and other mammals marked by maturing of the reproductive organs and by the start of ovulation in females and sperm production in males. During puberty in humans, the production of sex hormones causes other physical changes, including breast development in females and deepening of the voice in males.

pubis (pyo͞o′bĭs) The forwardmost of the three bones that fuse together to form each of the hipbones. *See more at* **skeleton.** —*Adjective* **pubic.**

pulley (po͝ol′ē) A simple machine consisting of a wheel over which a pulled rope or chain runs to change the direction of the pull used for lifting a load. Combinations of two or more pulleys working together reduce the force needed to lift a load. *See more at* **block and tackle.**

pulmonary (po͝ol′mə-nĕr′ē) Relating to the lungs: *a pulmonary infection.*

pulmonary artery An artery that carries blood with low levels of oxygen from the right ventricle of the heart to the lungs.

pulmonary vein A vein that carries blood with high levels of oxygen from the lungs to the left atrium of the heart.

pulsar (pŭl′sär′) A spinning neutron star that emits radio waves or other electromagnetic radiation in narrow beams that stream outward from its magnetic poles. Because a pulsar's magnetic poles do not align with the poles of its axis, these beams sweep around like the beacon of

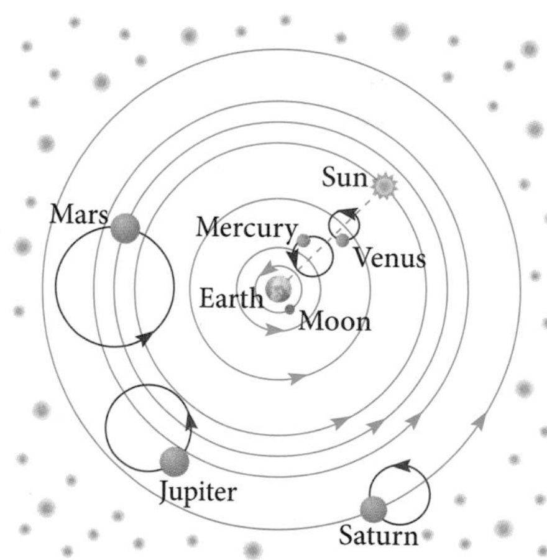

Ptolemaic system

Ptolemy believed that Earth was at the center of the universe and that the sun and planets orbited Earth (with the planets also moving in smaller circles called epicycles). In this system, the centers of Mercury's and Venus's epicycles always lie on the line shown in the diagram between Earth and the sun.

Did You Know...?

pulsar

It's not every day that a graduate student discovers a new kind of astronomical object in the universe. But that's just what Jocelyn Bell Burnell did in 1967. Bell Burnell, a student at Cambridge University, was analyzing data from a radio telescope designed by her adviser, Anthony Hewish, when she noticed a curious pulsing signal on the paper charts produced by the telescope. The intense pulses of radio waves occurred every 1.3 seconds and didn't match the characteristics of any known type of celestial object. She and Hewish joked that the signal was from extraterrestrial aliens and called it LGM, for "little green men." In the next few months, though, Bell Burnell and others found more such pulsing signals coming from different parts of the sky. Could the pulsing be caused by a white dwarf whose intensity was rapidly varying? Or by two stars revolving around each other? Astronomers eventually concluded that these signals came from rapidly spinning neutron stars that were emitting beams of radiation. They named them *pulsars* for "pulsating stars." Since Bell Burnell identified the first pulsar, over 1,800 have been discovered, with rates of rotation ranging from every 4 seconds to more than 1,000 times per second.

a lighthouse and are observed on Earth as short, regular bursts.

pulse (pŭls) The rhythmical expansion and contraction of the arteries as blood is pumped through them by the beating of the heart.

pumice (pŭm′ĭs) A usually light-colored, porous, lightweight rock of volcanic origin. The pores form when water vapor and other gases escape from the lava during its quick solidification into rock.

pump (pŭmp) A machine for raising or transferring fluids. Most pumps function either by compression or suction.

pupa (pyo͞o′pə) *Plural* **pupae** (pyo͞o′pē) An insect in the stage of development between the larva and the adult form, during which it changes shape dramatically while inside a protective covering such as a cocoon. Only insects that undergo complete metamorphosis, such as moths, butterflies, ants, and beetles, go through a pupal stage. *Compare* **imago, larva, nymph.** —*Adjective* **pupal.**

pupil (pyo͞o′pəl) The opening in the center of the iris through which light enters the eye.

purine (pyo͝or′ēn′) Any of a group of organic compounds containing two rings of alternating single and double bonds between carbon and nitrogen atoms. Purines include caffeine and uric acid, as well as the two bases adenine and guanine, which are components of DNA and RNA.

pus (pŭs) A thick, yellowish-white liquid that forms in infected body tissues. It consists mainly of dead white blood cells.

P wave *See* **primary wave.** *See Note at* **earthquake.**

pyridoxine (pĭr′ĭ-dŏk′sēn) *See under* **vitamin B complex.**

pyrimidine (pī-rĭm′ĭ-dēn′) Any of a group of organic compounds having a single ring with alternating single and double bonds between carbon and nitrogen atoms. Pyrimidines include the bases cytosine, thymine, and uracil, which are components of DNA and RNA.

pyrite (pī′rīt′) A silver to yellow, metallic mineral consisting of iron and sulfur. Pyrite often crystallizes in cubes or octahedrons but also occurs as shapeless masses of grains. It is used as a source of iron and in making sulfur dioxide. Because of its shiny look and often yellow color, it is sometimes mistaken for gold and for this reason is also called *fool's gold.*

pupa
of a ladybug

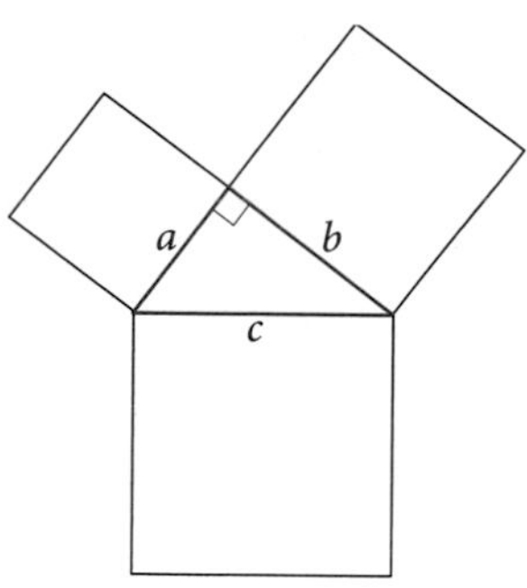

■ **Pythagorean theorem**
The Pythagorean theorem is $a^2 + b^2 = c^2$.

pyroclastic (pī′rō-klăs′tĭk) Composed chiefly of volcanic rock fragments or particles, such as pumice, obsidian, or ash. ❖ A cloud of very hot gas and pyroclastic particles traveling quickly down the slope of the volcano during an eruption is known as a **pyroclastic flow.**

pyroxene (pī-rŏk′sēn′) Any of a series of rock-forming minerals consisting of mixtures of calcium, sodium, magnesium, or iron silicates. Pyroxenes vary in color from white to dark green or black and are characterized by a rectangular-shaped cross section. They occur in igneous and metamorphic rocks.

pyruvic acid (pī-rōō′vĭk) A colorless organic liquid formed by the breakdown of carbohydrates and sugars during cell metabolism. It is the final product of the process known as glycolysis and has the formula $C_3H_4O_3$.

Pythagoras (pĭ-thăg′ər-əs) Sixth century BC. Greek philosopher who is said to have developed the Pythagorean theorem and to have theorized that numbers constitute the essence of all natural things.

Pythagorean theorem (pĭ-thăg′ə-rē′ən) A theorem stating that the square of the length of the hypotenuse (the longest side) of a right triangle is equal to the sum of the squares of the lengths of the other sides. It is mathematically stated as $c^2 = a^2 + b^2$, where c is the length of the hypotenuse and a and b the lengths of the other two sides.

python (pī′thŏn′) Any of various very large and colorful snakes of Africa, Asia, and Australia. Pythons are not venomous, but coil around and suffocate their prey.

qt. Abbreviation of **quart.**

quadrant (kwŏd**′**rənt) **1.** An arc equal to one quarter of the circumference of a circle; an arc of 90°. **2.** Any of the four regions into which a plane is divided by the axes of a Cartesian coordinate system. The quadrants are numbered counterclockwise one through four, beginning with the quadrant in which both the x- and y-coordinates are positive (usually the upper right quadrant). **3.** An early navigational instrument consisting of a 90° arc with a movable arm for measuring angles. The observer's latitude can be determined based on the angle between a celestial object (such as the sun or Polaris) and the horizon.

quadratic (kwŏ-drăt**′**ĭk) Relating to a mathematical expression containing a term of the second degree, such as $x^2 + 2$. ❖ A **quadratic equation** is an equation having the general form $ax^2 + bx + c = 0$, where *a, b,* and *c* are constants. ❖ The **quadratic formula** is

$$x = \frac{-b \pm \sqrt{(b^2 - 4ac)}}{2a}$$

It is important in algebra, where it is used to calculate the roots of quadratic equations.

quadriceps (kwŏd**′**rĭ-sĕps′) The large, four-part muscle at the front of the thigh that acts to extend the leg.

quadrilateral (kwŏd′rə-lăt**′**ər-əl) A polygon that has four sides, such as a rectangle or rhombus.

quadriplegia (kwŏd′rə-plē**′**jē-ə) Paralysis of the body from the neck down, caused by injury to the spinal cord.

quadrumanous (kwŏ-dro͞o**′**mə-nəs) Having opposable first digits on both the feet and the hands, used for gripping and climbing. Many primates are quadrumanous.

quadruped (kwŏd**′**rə-pĕd′) An animal having four feet, such as most reptiles and mammals.

quantitative analysis (kwŏn**′**tĭ-tā′tĭv) The act of testing a substance or mixture to find out the amounts and proportions of its chemical components.

quantity (kwŏn**′**tĭ-tē) *Mathematics* Something, such as a number or a symbol that represents a number, on which a mathematical operation is performed.

quantum (kwŏn**′**təm) *Plural* **quanta** The smallest amount of a physical property that can exist. A quantum of electromagnetic energy is called a photon.

quantum mechanics The branch of physics that deals with physical properties that come in discrete units called quanta. Quanta have properties of both particles and waves. For example, a photon, the quantum of electromagnetic energy, is emitted and absorbed as a particle but propagates as a wave. In quantum mechanics, as opposed to classical mechanics, the behavior of matter and energy is described in terms of probability. Quantum mechanics is mainly used for describing phenomena at the scale of atoms and subatomic particles. Also called *quantum physics.*

quantum physics *See* **quantum mechanics.**

quark (kwôrk, kwärk) Any of a group of six elementary particles that combine in groups of three to form protons, neutrons, and certain other subatomic particles. *See Note at* **subatomic particle.**

quart (kwôrt) A unit of volume or capacity used in liquid measure, equal to $\frac{1}{4}$ of a gallon or 32 ounces (about 0.95 liter). *See Table at* **measurement.**

quartz (kwôrts) A hard, transparent mineral composed of silicon dioxide. Quartz is the most common of all minerals. It occurs as a component of rocks such as sandstone and granite, and separately in a variety of forms such as rock crystal, flint, and agate. Some crystalline forms,

quartz
geode lined with amethyst

Did You Know...?

quasar

In the 1960s, astronomers observed a new kind of object in the night sky and called such objects *quasars,* short for *quasi-stellar radio sources*—that is, star-like objects that emit radio waves. These objects were puzzling because the particular wavelengths of radiation coming from them didn't match those of any other known objects. The mystery was solved when astronomers realized that quasars were extremely distant and were moving rapidly away from our galaxy. Now the observed wavelengths made sense; they corresponded to known patterns that had been modified by the quasars' rapid movement (an effect called the *red shift*). Tens of thousands of quasars have now been identified, and they are among the most distant celestial objects known. Some of them are more than ten billion light years away, which means that it has taken ten billion years for the radiation they emit to reach Earth. In order for us to be able to see something that far away, it must be extraordinarily bright—and, in fact, a single quasar can be a trillion times brighter than the sun. But what is a quasar? The current theory is that a quasar is made up of material surrounding a black hole at the center of a young galaxy. As the material falls into the black hole, it emits extremely large amounts of radiation. Astronomers are especially interested in quasars because they enable us to see what the universe was like when it was very young, only a few billion years after the Big Bang.

such as amethyst, are considered gemstones. Quartz is the mineral used to represent a hardness of 7 on the Mohs scale.

quartzite (kwôrt′sīt′) A metamorphic rock consisting entirely of quartz. Quartzite forms when quartz crystals in sandstone or chert are heated during metamorphism and grow into larger crystals.

quasar (kwā′zär′) A compact, extremely bright celestial object whose power output can be hundreds to several thousand times that of the entire Milky Way galaxy. Quasars are among the most distant objects in the universe.

Quaternary (kwŏt′ər-nĕr′ē) The second and last period of the Cenozoic Era, from about 2.6 million years ago to the present, characterized by the appearance of humans. *See Chart at* **geologic time,** pages 146–147.

queen (kwēn) The fertile, mature female in a colony of social insects such as bees, ants, or termites. The queen's sole function is to lay eggs. Usually there is only one queen in a colony.

quicksand (kwĭk′sănd′) A deep bed of loose sand mixed with water, forming a soft, shifting mass into which objects or people can easily sink and become stuck.

quill (kwĭl) **1.** The hollow, main shaft of a feather. **2.** One of the sharp hollow spines of a porcupine or hedgehog.

quinine (kwī′nīn′) A bitter-tasting, colorless drug derived from cinchona bark, used to treat malaria. *See Note at* **aspirin.**

quotient (kwō′shənt) The number that results when one number is divided by another. If 6 is divided by 3, the quotient can be represented as 2, or as $6 \div 3$, or as the fraction $\frac{6}{3}$.

R

r 1. *Mathematics* Abbreviation of **radius. 2.** or **R** *Electricity.* Abbreviation of **resistance.**

Ra The symbol for **radium.**

rabies (rā′bēz) A usually fatal viral disease of warm-blooded animals that causes inflammation of the brain and spinal cord. It is transmitted by the bite of an infected animal and can be prevented in humans by a vaccine.

race (rās) **1a.** A usually geographically isolated population of organisms that differs from other populations of the same species in certain heritable traits. **b.** A breed or strain, as of domestic animals. **2.** A group of people identified as distinct from other groups because of supposed physical or genetic traits shared by the group. Most biologists and anthropologists do not recognize race as a biologically valid classification, in part because there is more genetic variation within groups than between them.

raceme (rā-sēm′) A flower cluster in which each flower grows on its own stalk from a common stem. Wisteria flowers are arranged in racemes.

rad (răd) A unit used to measure energy absorbed by a material from radiation. One rad is equal to 100 ergs per gram of material. Many scientists now measure this energy in grays rather than in rads.

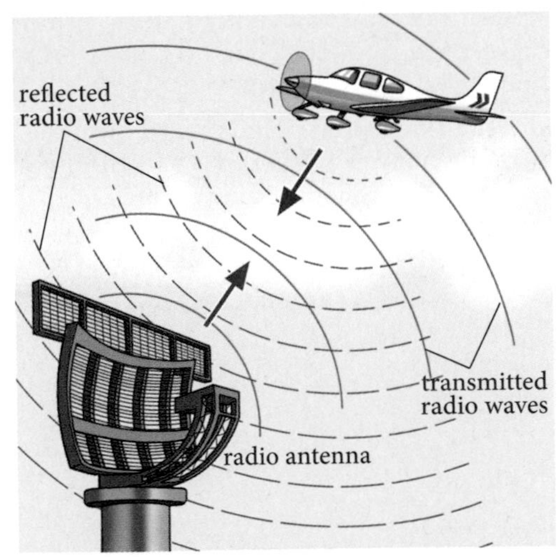

radar

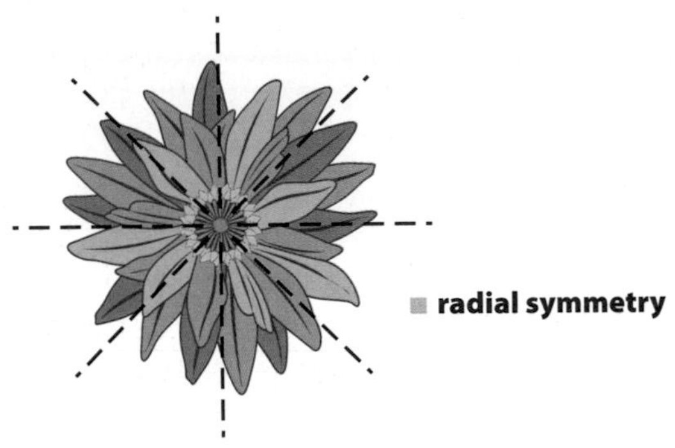

radial symmetry

radar (rā′där) **1.** A method of detecting and determining the location and velocity of distant objects by sending out radio waves and then analyzing the waves that are reflected back from the objects. The information obtained by radar can be represented in visual form, as in a weather map. **2.** The equipment used in doing this.

radial symmetry (rā′dē-əl) An arrangement of parts, such as the structures of an organism, around a central axis, such that there is more than one way to divide the organism into similar halves that are mirror images of each other. The bodies of echinoderms, such as starfish and sea urchins, are radially symmetrical. *Compare* **bilateral symmetry.**

radian (rā′dē-ən) A unit of angular measure equal to a little more than 57°. This is the measure of an angle whose vertex is the center of a circle and whose two rays intersect the circle so as to form an arc with the same length as the circle's radius.

radiant (rā′dē-ənt) **1.** Sending forth light, heat, or other radiation: *a radiant star.* **2.** Consisting of or transmitted as radiation.

radiant energy Energy in the form of electromagnetic waves. Radio waves, visible light, and x-rays are all forms of radiant energy.

radiation (rā′dē-ā′shən) **1a.** Energy in the form of electromagnetic waves or streams of particles. Radiation in the form of alpha and beta particles is released during radioactive decay. Thermal radiation involves the giving off of radiation in the infrared part of the electromagnetic spectrum. **b.** The giving off or movement of such energy.

See Notes at **conduction, electromagnetic radiation. 2.** The use of such energy, especially x-rays and gamma rays, in medical diagnosis and treatment.

radiative zone (rā′dē-ə-tĭv) An interior layer of a star just outside the core. The radiative zone absorbs photons that originate in the core and reradiates them outward, thereby transporting energy from the core outward.

radical (răd′ĭ-kəl) **1.** A root, such as $\sqrt{2}$, especially as indicated by a radical sign ($\sqrt{\ }$). **2.** An atom or group of atoms that is very reactive and not stable except as part of a molecule. The hydroxyl, ethyl, and phenyl radicals are examples.

radicand (răd′ĭ-kănd′) The number or expression written under a radical sign, such as the 3 in $\sqrt{3}$.

radio (rā′dē-ō) *Noun* **1.** The equipment used to generate, alter, transmit, and receive radio waves so that they carry information. —*Adjective* **2.** Involving the emission of radio waves: *radio frequency.*

radioactive decay (rā′dē-ō-ăk′tĭv) The spontaneous breakdown of a radioactive nucleus into a lighter nucleus. Radioactive decay causes the release of radiation in the form of alpha particles, beta particles, or gamma rays. The end result of radioactive decay is the creation of a stable atomic nucleus.

radioactivity (rā′dē-ō-ăk-tĭv′ĭ-tē) The phenom-

Did You Know...?

radioactivity

In the nuclei of stable atoms, such as those of lead, the force binding the protons and neutrons to each other individually is great enough to hold together each nucleus as a whole. In the nuclei of other atoms, especially of heavy ones such as uranium atoms, this energy is not great enough, and the nuclei are unstable. An unstable nucleus gives off particles and energy in a process known as *radioactive decay.* The term *radioactivity* refers to this phenomenon. When enough particles and energy have been given off to create a new, stable nucleus (often the nucleus of an entirely different element), radioactive decay ceases. For example, uranium-238, a very unstable element, goes through 18 different stages of decay before finally turning into a stable isotope of lead, lead-206. (Some of the intermediate stages include the heavier elements thorium, radium, radon, and polonium.) All known elements with an atomic number greater than 83 (bismuth) are radioactive, and many isotopes of elements with lower atomic numbers (such as carbon-14) are radioactive, too.

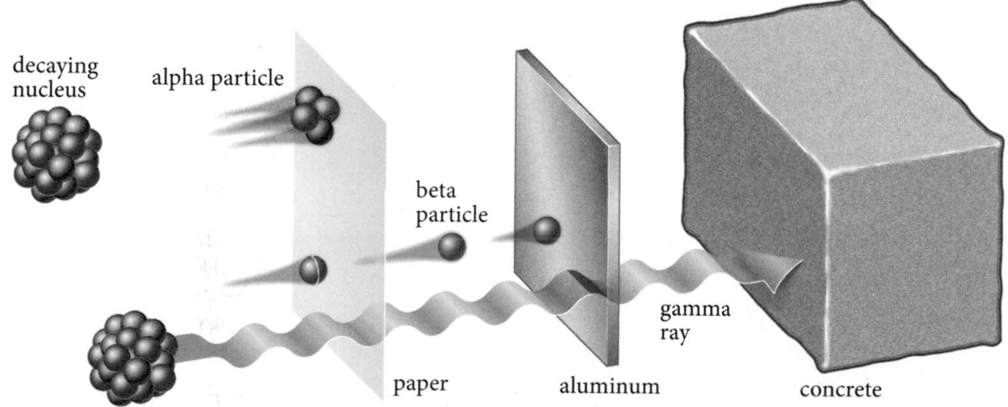

radioactive decay

As the nucleus of a radioactive element decays, it releases alpha particles, beta particles, or gamma rays. Alpha particles (composed of two protons and two neutrons) are the weakest form of radiation and can be stopped by paper. Beta particles (high-speed electrons) are able to pass through paper but not aluminum. Gamma rays (a form of electromagnetic radiation) are the strongest. They are able to pass through paper and aluminum, but not through a block of lead or concrete.

enon by which unstable atomic nuclei emit radiation when they undergo radioactive decay.

radio astronomy The branch of astronomy that uses observations of emissions in the radio wave region of the electromagnetic spectrum to study stars, planets, galaxies, interstellar gas, dust clouds, and other celestial objects.

radiocarbon (rā′dē-ō-kär′bən) A radioactive isotope of carbon, especially carbon-14.

radiocarbon dating A technique for measuring the age of organic remains based on the rate of decay of carbon-14. The carbon-14 present in an organism at the time of its death decays at a steady rate, and so the age of the remains can be calculated from the amount of carbon-14 that is left.

Did You Know...?

radiocarbon dating

The cells of all living things contain carbon that they take in from their environment. Back in the 1940s, the American chemist Willard Libby used this fact to determine the ages of organisms long dead. Most carbon atoms have six protons and six neutrons in their nuclei and are called carbon-12. Carbon-12 is very stable. But a tiny percentage of carbon is made of carbon-14, or *radiocarbon,* which has six protons and eight neutrons and is not stable: half of any sample of it decays into other atoms after 5,700 years. Carbon-14 is continually being created in the Earth's atmosphere by the interaction of nitrogen and gamma rays from outer space. Since atmospheric carbon-14 arises at about the same rate that the atom decays, the Earth's levels of carbon-14 have remained relatively constant. In living organisms, which are always taking in carbon, the levels of carbon-14 reflect the level of carbon-14 in the atmosphere. But in a dead organism, no new carbon is coming in, and its carbon-14 gradually begins to decay. By measuring carbon-14 levels in an organism that died long ago, it is possible to calculate how long ago it died. The procedure of radiocarbon dating can be used for remains that are up to about 50,000 years old.

radio frequency A frequency in the radio wave region of the electromagnetic spectrum.

radioisotope (rā′dē-ō-ī′sə-tōp′) A radioactive isotope of a chemical element.

radiology (rā′dē-ŏl′ə-jē) The branch of medicine that deals with the use of x-rays and other forms of radiation in diagnosis and treatment.

radiometer (rā′dē-ŏm′ĭ-tər) A device used to detect and measure electromagnetic radiation. One simple radiometer consists of a glass bulb containing a partial vacuum in which four vanes are mounted on a central axis. Each vane is black on one side and silvery on the other. When light or infrared radiation strikes them, the black side absorbs radiation and the silvery side reflects it, resulting in a temperature difference between the two sides that causes the vanes to spin. The greater the intensity of radiation, the faster the vanes spin.

radiometric dating (rā′dē-ō-mĕt′rĭk) A method for determining the age of an object based on the concentration of a particular radioactive isotope contained within it. The amount of the isotope in the object is compared to the amount of the isotope's decay products. The object's approximate age can then be figured out using the known rate of decay of the isotope. Radiocarbon dating is one kind of radiometric dating, used for determining the age of organic remains that are less than 50,000 years old. For inorganic matter and for older materials, isotopes of other elements, such as potassium, uranium, and strontium, are used.

radiosonde (rā′dē-ō-sŏnd′) An instrument that is carried into the atmosphere, usually by balloon, to gather and transmit information about the weather.

radio telescope An instrument that consists of a radio receiver and antenna system mounted on a wide, bowl-shaped reflector, used to detect radio waves coming from celestial objects.

radio wave An electromagnetic wave having a long wavelength. Radio waves have the longest wavelengths of all forms of electromagnetic radiation. They are used to transmit radio, television, and other telecommunication signals. The microwaves used for cooking are sometimes considered to be radio waves with the shortest wavelengths. Many celestial objects, such as the sun and other stars, pulsars, and quasars, emit radio waves. *See more at* **electromagnetic spectrum.**

radium (rā′dē-əm) A rare, bright-white, highly radioactive element that is an alkaline-earth metal and gives off its own light. It occurs naturally in very small amounts in ores and minerals containing uranium. Radium is used as a neutron source for scientific research and was formerly widely used in medicine and as an ingredient in luminescent paints. The most common of its several isotopes has a half-life of about 1,600 years. *Symbol* **Ra.** *Atomic number* 88. *See* **Periodic Table,** pages 254–255.

radius (rā′dē-əs) *Plural* **radii** (rā′dē-ī′) *or* **radiuses 1.** *Mathematics* A line segment that joins the center of a circle or sphere with any point on the circumference of the circle or the surface of the sphere. It is half the length of the diameter. **2.** *Anatomy* The shorter and thicker of the two bones of the forearm in humans, or the corresponding bone in other vertebrates. *See more at* **skeleton.**

radon (rā′dŏn) A colorless, odorless, radioactive element that is a noble gas. It is produced by the radioactive decay of radium and occurs in small amounts in soil, rocks, and the air near the ground. If inhaled, radon can cause lung cancer and other diseases. Its most stable isotope has a half-life of about four days. *Symbol* **Rn.** *Atomic number* 86. *See* **Periodic Table,** pages 254–255.

rain (rān) Water that condenses from vapor in the atmosphere and falls to earth as separate drops from clouds.

rainbow (rān′bō′) An arc-shaped spectrum of color seen in the sky opposite the sun, especially before or after rain, caused by the refraction and reflection of sunlight by droplets of water in the air.

rainforest (rān′fôr′ĭst) A dense forest with an annual rainfall of at least 60 inches (150 centimeters) and vegetation that stays green all year round. Most of the world's rainforests lie near the equator and have tropical climates, but there are also cooler rainforests, such as the one in the Pacific Northwest region of the United States and Canada.

RAM (răm) Short for *random access memory.* The main memory of a computer, in which data can be accessed by the central processing unit in any order without having to go through other data first. The random access of data greatly increases processing speed and efficiency.

Ramsay (răm′zē), Sir **William** 1852–1916. British chemist who discovered the noble gases argon, neon, xenon, and krypton.

random-access memory (răn′dəm-ăk′sĕs) *See* **RAM.**

range (rānj) **1a.** The set of all values that a given function may have. *Compare* **domain. b.** The difference between the smallest and largest values in a set of data. If the lowest test score of a group of students is 54 and the highest is 94, the range is 40. **2.** The geographic region in which a plant, animal, or other organism normally lives or grows.

rapid eye movement (răp′ĭd) *See* **REM.**

raptor (răp′tər) **1.** A bird of prey, such as a hawk, eagle, or owl. **2.** Any of several small meat-eating dinosaurs of the Cretaceous Period that walked on two legs and had sharp teeth and claws, with one especially long, curved claw on each hind foot. Velociraptors were raptors.

rare-earth element (râr′ûrth′) Any of 17 naturally occurring metallic elements consisting of the 15 elements with atomic numbers 57 through 71 (the lanthanides) plus scandium and yttrium. The rare-earth elements often occur together in certain widely dispersed minerals, and they are

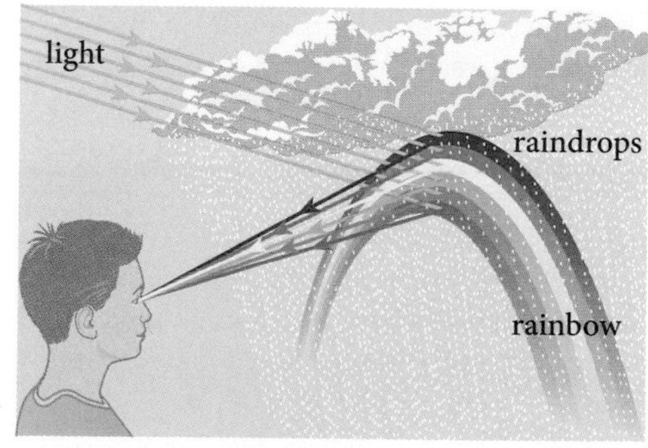

rainbow
Raindrops act like mirrors that reflect sunlight back toward the observer. They also act like prisms that refract the sunlight into the colors of the spectrum.

Did You Know...?

rare-earth elements

The *rare-earth elements* (that is, those elements having atomic numbers 21, 39, and 57 through 71) are actually not especially rare. They are widespread in the Earth's crust, but they mostly occur in low concentrations and are not easy to extract from the surrounding rock—mining and refining them is difficult and often results in harm to the environment. But these elements have physical properties that make them essential in much modern technology: fluorescent bulbs, smartphone screens, solar panels, computer chips, and lasers all incorporate rare-earth elements. As a result, worldwide demand for these elements has increased steadily in the past few decades and is expected to keep increasing in coming years. But the supply will run out eventually, so scientists and engineers are searching for materials and technologies that will make it possible to reduce our society's dependence on rare-earth elements in the future.

essential to many modern electronic and magnetic devices, catalysts, and lasers.

rat (răt) Any of various long-tailed rodents that resemble mice but are larger. The most common species, the brown rat, is probably native to Asia but is now found worldwide in populated areas. It is a destructive pest of crops and stored food and a carrier of disease.

rate (rāt) **1.** A quantity measured with respect to another quantity, usually time. For example, the rate of speed of a person who walks 8 miles in 2 hours is 4 miles per hour. **2.** A measure of a part with respect to a whole; a proportion: *the mortality rate of polar bears.*

ratio (rā′shō, rā′shē-ō′) A relationship between two quantities, normally expressed as the quotient of one divided by the other. For example, if a box contains six red marbles and four blue marbles, the ratio of red marbles to blue marbles is 6 to 4, also written 6:4. A ratio can also be expressed as a decimal or percentage.

rational number (răsh′ə-nəl) A number that can be expressed as an integer or a quotient of integers. For example, 2, –5, and $\frac{1}{2}$ are rational numbers.

rattlesnake (răt′l-snāk′) Any of various venomous snakes of the Western Hemisphere having at the end of the tail several hard, hollow segments that make a rattling sound when the tail is shaken and the segments knock against each other. Rattlesnakes have a small pit below each eye that senses heat and helps in finding prey. Their fangs are hollow and are folded back in the mouth when not being used.

ray (rā) **1.** *Physics* A narrow beam of light or other radiation. **2.** *Mathematics* A geometric figure consisting of the part of a line that is on one side of a point on the line.

Rb The symbol for **rubidium.**

Re The symbol for **rhenium.**

reactant (rē-ăk′tənt) A substance participating in a chemical reaction, especially one present at the start of the reaction.

reaction (rē-ăk′shən) **1.** A change or transformation in which a substance decomposes, combines with one or more other substances, or exchanges atoms or groups of atoms with other substances. Chemical reactions occur when electrons of one substance interact with those of another, and they result in the formation of one or more new substances. The reaction of an acid with a base, for example, often results in the formation of a salt and water. Some reactions can be reversed. **2.** A change to the structure of an atomic nucleus; a nuclear reaction. **3.** An equal but opposite force exerted by one body on a second body when the second body is exerting a force on the first. For example, if two people on ice skates are facing one another and skater A reaches out and pushes skater B, not only will A produce a force on B, causing B to move away, but B will produce a force on A that will cause A to move away in the opposite direction. *See more at* **Newton's laws of motion.**

reactive (rē-ăk′tĭv) Tending to participate readily in reactions: *a highly reactive element.*

read-only memory (rēd′ōn′lē) *See* **ROM.**

reagent (rē-ā′jənt) Any substance involved in a chemical reaction, especially one used to detect, measure, or produce another substance. *Compare* **agent.**

real number (rē′əl) A number that is rational or irrational and not imaginary. The numbers 2, −12.5, $\frac{3}{7}$, and pi are all real numbers.

receiver (rĭ-sē′vər) A device that converts incoming radio or microwave signals into sound or light signals that humans can perceive. Radios, televisions, and telephones all have receivers.

Recent (rē′sənt) *See* **Holocene.**

receptacle (rĭ-sĕp′tə-kəl) The expanded upper end of a stalk or stem that bears a flower or group of flowers. *See more at* **flower.**

receptor (rĭ-sĕp′tər) **1.** A specialized cell or group of nerve endings that senses or receives stimuli. Skin receptors respond to stimuli such as heat and pressure and send signals to the nervous system. Photoreceptors in the eye sense light. **2.** A protein located within a cell membrane or inside a cell that binds with a chemical substance such as a hormone, antigen, or neurotransmitter and activates a specific cell response.

recessive (rĭ-sĕs′ĭv) Relating to an allele (a form of a gene) that does not produce its characteristic effect if a dominant allele is present at the same position on the other of a pair of chromosomes. For example, if a plant has one allele for purple flowers and one allele for white flowers, and the white allele is recessive, then that plant will have all purple flowers, with no white flowers. *See more at* **inheritance.** *Compare* **dominant.**

reciprocal (rĭ-sĭp′rə-kəl) Either of a pair of numbers whose product is 1. For example, the number 3 is the reciprocal of $\frac{1}{3}$.

recombinant DNA (rē-kŏm′bə-nənt) DNA that has been produced by splicing genetic material from one organism into the genome of another organism of a different species. Recombinant DNA is used, for example, to produce human insulin from bacterial cells into which insulin-making genes have been inserted.

recombination (rē′kŏm-bə-nā′shən) The rearrangement of genetic material in living organisms or viruses, especially the interchange of segments between paired chromosomes during meiosis.

rectangle (rĕk′tăng′gəl) A four-sided plane figure with four right angles. A rectangle whose sides are equal is a square.

rectilinear (rĕk′tə-lĭn′ē-ər) Relating to, consisting of, or moving in a straight line or lines: *a rectilinear path.*

rectum (rĕk′təm) The lower end of the digestive tract, extending from the colon to the anus.

recycle (rē-sī′kəl) To collect and usually reprocess discarded materials for reuse, often in another form. For example, newspaper and other paper waste can be reprocessed to make cardboard or insulation, and plastics can be melted down and molded into new products. Recycling helps reduce pollution and conserve natural resources.

red blood cell (rĕd) Any of the disc-shaped cells

Did You Know...?

red blood cells

The distinctive red color of human blood comes from the abundant *red blood cells* that it contains. The red blood cells, in turn, are red because they are full of an iron-containing protein called *hemoglobin* that appears bright red (because it doesn't absorb red light) when bound to oxygen. Hemoglobin is like a sophisticated dump truck. When hemoglobin is in the lungs it picks up oxygen molecules, which bind to the iron atoms. Blood vessels carry the hemoglobin throughout the body, where the oxygen is released for use by muscle, nerve, and other cells. The oxygen-depleted hemoglobin (now dark red) then returns to the lungs to pick up another load. All animals have some oxygen distribution system, but only vertebrate animals have red blood cells. Earthworms have hemoglobin that floats freely in the blood rather than being contained in cells. Certain animals do not use hemoglobin at all. Horseshoe crabs and many mollusks, such as octopuses, use a copper-containing molecule to transport oxygen, making their blood bluish instead of red.

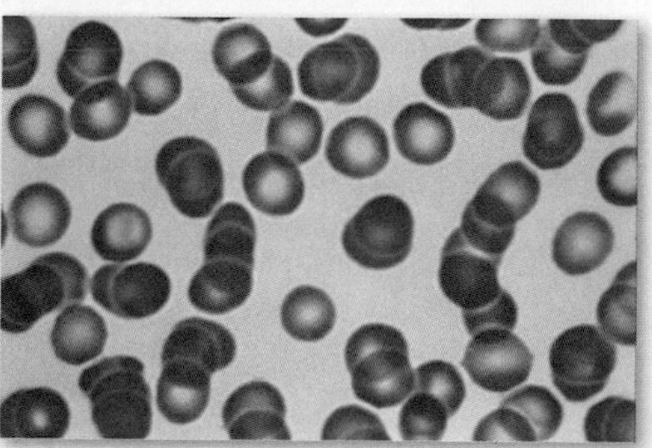

in the blood of vertebrate animals that contain hemoglobin and give blood its red color. The hemoglobin binds to oxygen, which is then transported to all of the tissues of the body. Red blood cells are formed in the bone marrow. The red blood cells of mammals have no nucleus. Also called *erythrocyte*. *See more at* **cell.**

red dwarf A star that is cool, small, and very faint. Red dwarfs burn very slowly and live for about 100 billion years. Although they are difficult to see, they are likely the most abundant type of star. Proxima Centauri is a red dwarf. *See more at* **star.** *See Note at* **dwarf star.**

red giant A very large and bright star that has relatively low surface temperature compared with other stars, making it appear red or orange. The sun will become a red giant in several billion years. *See more at* **star.** *See Note at* **dwarf star.**

red shift An increase in the wavelength of radiation emitted by a receding celestial object as a consequence of the Doppler effect. Red light has longer wavelengths than blue light, so this shift is toward the red end of the electromagnetic spectrum. *See Note at* **Doppler effect.**

red tide A growth of plankton, especially dinoflagellates, that gives a reddish color to coastal ocean waters. Toxins produced by the plankton can contaminate shellfish, making them unsafe to eat, and can kill fish.

reduction (rĭ-dŭk′shən) **1.** *Mathematics* The changing of a fraction into a simpler form, especially by dividing the numerator and denominator by a common factor. For example, the fraction $\frac{8}{12}$ can be reduced to $\frac{4}{6}$, which can be further reduced to $\frac{2}{3}$, in each case by dividing both the numerator and denominator by 2. **2.** *Chemistry* A chemical reaction in which an atom or ion gains electrons, thus undergoing a decrease in valence. If an iron atom having a valence of +3 gains an electron, the valence decreases to +2. If a chlorine atom having a valence of 0 gains an electron, the valence decreases to −1. *Compare* **oxidation.**

red tide

redwood (rĕd′wo͝od′) A very tall, cone-bearing evergreen tree that grows along the coast of northwest California and southern Oregon. Redwoods can grow to a height of over 300 feet (91.4 meters).

Reed (rēd), **Walter** 1851–1902. American physician and army surgeon who demonstrated that yellow fever is transmitted by the *Aedes aegypti* mosquito.

reef (rēf) An irregular mass of rock or coral that rises up to or near the surface of a body of water. *See more at* **coral reef.**

refinery (rĭ-fī′nə-rē) An industrial plant for purifying a substance, such as petroleum or sugar, or converting it to a form that is more useful.

reflecting telescope (rĭ-flĕk′tĭng) A telescope in which light from an object is gathered and focused by a concave mirror. The resulting image is magnified by the eyepiece. *See more at* **telescope.**

reflection (rĭ-flĕk′shən) **1.** The bending or turning back of a wave, such as a light or sound wave, when it encounters a boundary between two media. The reflected wave returns to the original medium and does not pass through the boundary into the other medium. According to the **law of reflection,** the angle of reflection is equal to the angle of incidence. *See more at* **wave.** *Compare* **refraction. 2.** Something, such as sound or light, that is reflected.

reflex (rē′flĕks′) An automatic, involuntary response to a stimulus. Pulling your hand away from a fire is an example of a reflex.

refracting telescope (rĭ-frăk′tĭng) A telescope in which light from an object is gathered and focused by a lens. The resulting image is magnified by the eyepiece. *See more at* **telescope.**

refraction (rĭ-frăk′shən) **1.** The bending or turning of a wave when its speed is altered, as by passing from one medium into another. *See more at* **wave.** *Compare* **reflection. 2.** The apparent

refraction
Light waves bend as they pass from one substance to another. This pencil appears to be broken because the light from the bottom part of the pencil is refracted when it passes from the water to the air (via the glass).

change in position of a celestial object caused by the bending of light as it enters the Earth's atmosphere.

refrigerant (rĭ-frĭj′ər-ənt) A substance, such as ice or ammonia, used to cool something by absorbing heat from it. Refrigerants used in modern times are usually substances that evaporate quickly. In the process of evaporation they draw heat from surrounding substances.

regeneration (rĭ-jĕn′ə-rā′shən) Regrowth of damaged or destroyed parts or organs. Certain lizards, for example, can regenerate their tails if they lose them to a predator, and a number of invertebrate animals, such as starfish, can be cut into several pieces that will each regenerate into a whole new organism.

regolith (rĕg′ə-lĭth′) The layer of soil and loose rock resting on bedrock, constituting the surface of most land.

regular (rĕg′yə-lər) Having all sides or faces equal. A square is a regular polygon, and a cube is a regular polyhedron.

regurgitate (rē-gûr′jĭ-tāt′) To bring undigested food back up from the stomach to the mouth.

relative humidity (rĕl′ə-tĭv) The ratio of the actual amount of water vapor present in the air at a given temperature to the maximum amount that the air could hold at that temperature. Relative humidity is expressed as a percentage. *Compare* **absolute humidity.**

USAGE

refraction/reflection

The words *refraction* and *reflection* describe two different ways that a wave can change its direction when it encounters a boundary between two different substances, between one substance and a vacuum, or between regions of a single substance that are in different states, such as regions of warmer and cooler air. Reflection occurs when a wave hits the boundary and bounces back. Refraction occurs when a wave speeds up or slows down in passing through the boundary and is bent; that is, the wave deviates from the straight-line path it would have otherwise followed. For example, light passing through a prism bends when it enters the prism and again when it leaves the prism. The light is therefore *refracted.* Light striking a mirror bounces off the silver backing without entering it. The light is therefore *reflected.* A boundary does not have to be abrupt for reflection or refraction to occur. On a hot day, when the air close to the surface of an asphalt road is warmer than the air above it, the road in the distance may appear to shimmer because light waves bend as they pass through moving bodies of air of different temperatures.

relativity (rĕl′ə-tĭv′ĭ-tē) The two-part theory of physical laws developed by Albert Einstein. The first part, called the **theory of special relativity,** is based on two postulates about motion in frames of reference that are not accelerating (such as a car moving at a constant speed): first, the laws of physics are the same in all of these frames; and second, the speed of light (in a vacuum) is the same in all of these frames, even if the light source is moving relative to the observer. From these two postulates it follows that measurements of length, time, and simultaneity are not absolute; they all depend on the relative motion of the observer. The theory also predicts the equivalence of mass and energy, states that mass increases with speed, and shows that no object with mass can move at the speed of light. The second part, the **theory of general relativity,** extends the first part to

Did You Know...?

relativity

The laws of Newtonian mechanics that had been the cornerstone of physics for 200 years were fundamentally altered by Einstein's theory of *relativity.* Although Newton's laws work for most everyday situations, they do not accurately describe the behavior of objects that are moving extremely fast or are subject to very strong gravitational fields. Einstein's theory of special relativity is based on simple assumptions, but it leads to some seemingly bizarre consequences concerning length and time measurement. Imagine two people moving relative to each other: person A is traveling in a very fast train past person B, who is standing next to the railroad track. If A holds up a foot-long ruler and B measures it as the train zooms past, B will get a measurement of less than a foot. If A is holding a clock with a hand that moves every second, B will claim that the hand is moving more slowly than once per second. This effect is taken into account in setting the clocks in satellites that control GPS systems. Einstein's theory of general relativity deals with frames of reference undergoing acceleration, as in cases involving gravity. Gravity is now regarded as a curvature in space-time itself. In cases where Newton's and Einstein's theories of gravity produce different predictions, those based on Einstein's theory have so far been confirmed.

accelerating systems and states that acceleration and gravity are equivalent. According to this theory, gravitational effects are caused by the curvature of the fabric of four-dimensional space-time. *See Notes at* **Einstein, gravity, space-time.**

relay (rē′lā) An electrical switch that is operated by an electromagnet, such as a solenoid. When a small current passes through the electromagnet's coiled wire, it causes a movable iron bar to pivot and open or close the switch.

REM (rĕm) Short for *rapid eye movement.* A stage of sleep characterized by twitching movements of the muscles of the eyes, faster heartbeat, and increased circulation to the brain. REM sleep occurs in humans and other warm-blooded vertebrates, including birds.

remainder (rĭ-mān′dər) *Mathematics* In division, the difference between the dividend and the product of the quotient and divisor.

remission (rĭ-mĭsh′ən) A lessening or disappearance of the symptoms of a disease, especially cancer.

renal (rē′nəl) Relating to the kidneys: *renal disease.*

renewable (rĭ-no͞o′ə-bəl) Relating to a natural resource, such as solar energy or wood, that is never used up or that can be replaced by new growth. *Compare* **nonrenewable.**

repetitive strain injury (rĭ-pĕt′ĭ-tĭv) Damage to muscles, tendons, ligaments, and nerves caused by excessive repetition of specific motions. Carpal tunnel syndrome is a repetitive strain injury.

replication (rĕp′lĭ-kā′shən) **1.** The process by which genetic material, a virus, or a single cell makes an exact copy of itself. **2.** In scientific research, the repetition of an experiment to confirm findings or to ensure accuracy.

reproduction (rē′prə-dŭk′shən) The process by which organisms produce other organisms of the same kind. ❖ The reproduction of organisms by the union of male and female sex cells (gametes) is called **sexual reproduction.** Most animals, plants, and other multicellular organisms reproduce sexually, and sexual reproduction also occurs in many single-celled organisms. ❖ Reproduction in which offspring are produced by a single parent, without the union of sex cells, is called **asexual reproduction.** The fission (splitting) of bacterial cells is a form of asexual reproduction. Many plants and fungi are capable of reproducing both sexually and asexually, as are some animals, such as sponges and aphids.

reproductive cell (rē′prə-dŭk′tĭv) *See* **sex cell.**

reproductive system The system of organs involved with the reproduction of an organism, especially sexual reproduction. In flowering plants, the reproductive system consists of pistils and stamens. In mammals, it consists mainly of the ovaries, uterus, and vagina in females and the testes and penis in males.

reptile (rĕp′tīl′) Any of various cold-blooded vertebrate animals that are covered with scales or horny plates, lay eggs, and breathe by means of

■ **reptile**
a lizard, a turtle, and a snake

lungs. Crocodiles, turtles, snakes, and lizards are reptiles.

reservoir (rĕz′ər-vwär′) **1.** A natural or artificial pond or lake used for the storage of water. **2.** An underground mass of rock or sediment that is porous and permeable enough to allow oil or natural gas to accumulate in it.

resin (rĕz′ĭn) **1.** Any of numerous clear or translucent, yellowish or brownish substances that ooze from conifer trees and other plants. Resins are used in products such as varnishes, lacquers, adhesives, and plastics. *See Note at* **amber. 2.** Any of various artificial substances, such as polyurethane, that have similar properties to natural resins and are used to make plastics.

resistance (rĭ-zĭs′təns) **1.** A force, such as friction, that prevents or slows down motion: *a car shaped to lessen wind resistance.* **2.** The ability of a material or object to slow down the free flow of electrons of an electric current. Good conductors, such as copper, have low resistance. Good insulators, such as rubber, have high resistance. Resistance results in a change of electric energy into heat. **3.** A lack of response by a cell, tissue, or organism to a disease agent or to a drug, hormone, or chemical. A plant might be resistant to a fungal disease, for example, or a bacterium can develop resistance to an antibiotic.

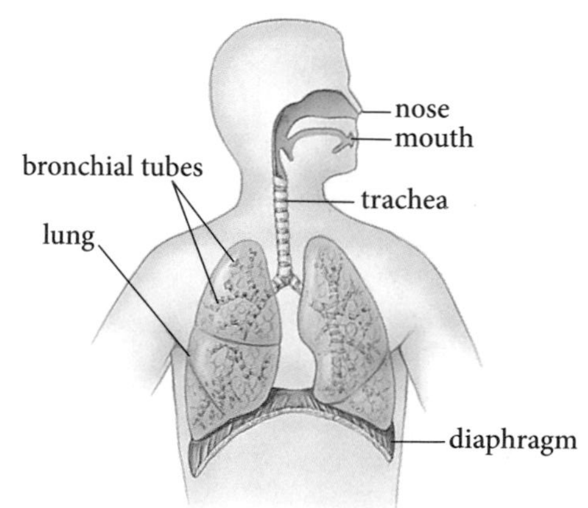

■ **respiratory system**

resistor (rĭ-zĭs′tər) A device used to control current in an electric circuit by providing resistance.

resonance (rĕz′ə-nəns) The phenomenon whereby an oscillating system, such as a swing, oscillates more strongly when it is exposed to a periodic force that is applied with the same frequency as that of the oscillating system. For example, a swing will swing to greater heights if each consecutive push on it is timed to be in rhythm with the initial swing. To tune a radio, you adjust the frequency of the receiver so that it matches the frequency of the incoming radio waves.

respiration (rĕs′pə-rā′shən) **1.** The action or process of inhaling and exhaling; breathing. **2.** The process by which organisms exchange gases, especially oxygen and carbon dioxide, with the environment. In air-breathing vertebrates, respiration takes place in the lungs. In fish and many invertebrates, respiration takes place through the gills. ❖ The biochemical process by which cells obtain energy in the form of ATP is called **cellular respiration.** This process usually involves the use of oxygen to break down nutrients (such as glucose) and the release of carbon dioxide and water as byproducts.

respiratory system (rĕs′pər-ə-tôr′ē) The system of organs and structures in which gas exchange takes place, consisting of the lungs and airways in air-breathing vertebrates, gills in fish and many invertebrates, and air-filled tubes (called tracheae) in insects.

reticulum (rĭ-tĭk′yə-ləm) The second compartment of the stomach in ruminant animals, which together with the rumen contains microorganisms that digest fiber. The reticulum's contents are regurgitated for further chewing as part of the cud. *See more at* **ruminant.**

retina (rĕt′n-ə) The light-sensitive membrane that lines the inside of the back of the eyeball and is connected to the brain by the optic nerve. The retina of a vertebrate animal contains specialized photoreceptor cells called rods and cones.

retinol (rĕt′n-ôl′) *See* **vitamin A.**

retort (rĭ-tôrt′, rē′tôrt′) A glass laboratory vessel in the shape of a bulb with a long, downward-pointing outlet tube. It is used for distillation or decomposition by heat.

retrograde (rĕt′rə-grād′) Relating to the revolution in an orbit or rotation about an axis of a celestial object that moves clockwise from east to west, in the direction opposite to the movement of most celestial objects.

USAGE

revolution/rotation

We use the words *revolution* and *rotation*—or the verbs *revolve* and *rotate*—to indicate cyclic patterns. We talk of *crop rotation* to refer to the successive planting of different crops on the same land, or of a *revolving door* to refer to a door turning about a central pivot. In everyday speech *revolution* and *rotation* are often used as synonyms, but in science they are not synonyms and have distinct meanings. The difference between the two terms lies in the location of the central axis that the object turns about. If the axis is outside the body itself—that is, if the object is orbiting about another object—then one complete orbit is called a *revolution.* But if the object is turning about an axis that passes through itself, then one complete cycle is called a *rotation.* This difference is often summed up in this statement: "Earth *rotates* on its axis and *revolves* around the sun."

retrovirus (rĕt′rō-vī′rəs) Any of a group of viruses containing RNA in which the RNA is copied as DNA after the virus enters a cell. The DNA is then incorporated into the host cell's genome and used to make more viruses. The virus that causes AIDS is a retrovirus.

reverse fault (rĭ-vûrs′) A geologic fault in which the block above the plane of the fault has slid upward relative to the lower block as the two blocks are pushed together from opposite directions. *See more at* **fault.**

revolution (rĕv′ə-lo͞o′shən) **1.** The cyclic motion of an object around a point, especially circular or elliptical motion around another object or a center of mass. **2.** A single complete cycle of such motion.

Rf The symbol for **rutherfordium.**

Rg The symbol for **roentgenium.**

Rh The symbol for **rhodium.**

rhenium (rē′nē-əm) A rare, dense, silvery-white metallic element with a very high melting point. It is used to make catalysts and electrical contacts. *Symbol* **Re.** *Atomic number* 75. *See* **Periodic Table,** pages 254–255.

rheostat (rē′ə-stăt′) A resistor whose resistance can be varied between two extremes, used to control the flow of current in an electric circuit.

rheumatic fever (ro͞o-măt′ĭk) A disease characterized by inflammation of the joints, skin, and heart, resulting from infection by certain bacteria. It occurs mainly in children and can cause permanent damage to the heart valves.

rheumatoid arthritis (ro͞o′mə-toid′) A chronic

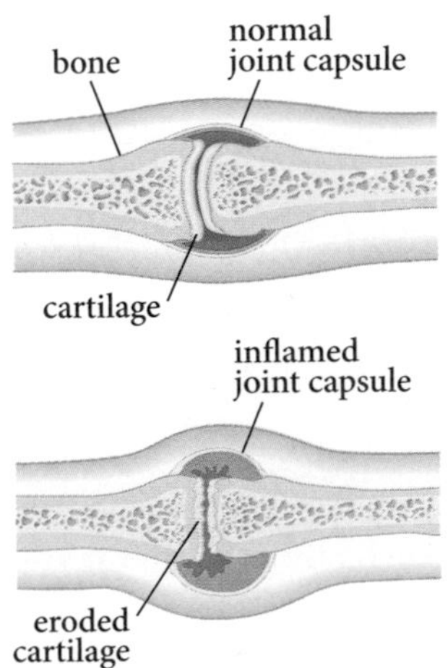

rheumatoid arthritis
top: *normal finger joint*
bottom: *arthritic finger joint*

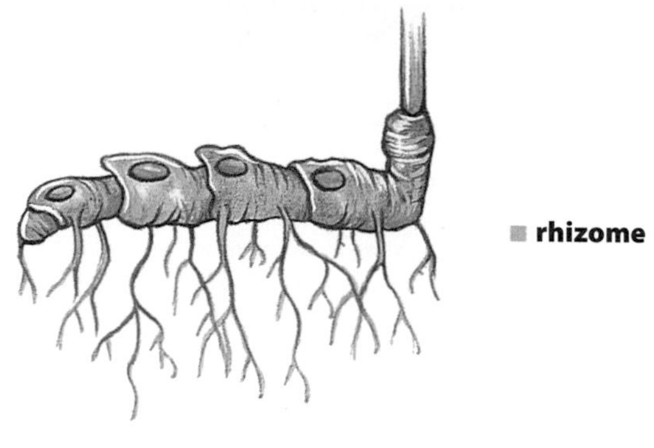
■ rhizome

disease in which the joints, especially of the hands and feet, become inflamed, leading to stiffness, weakness, and loss of movement.

Rh factor (är′āch′) An antigen present in red blood cells, used in the classification of human blood. The blood cells of most people contain an Rh factor. For a blood transfusion to be successful, the blood of the donor must match that of the recipient — both must have or must be missing the Rh factor. RH factor is short for *Rhesus factor.* ❖ The Rh factor was first discovered in the **rhesus monkey,** a kind of monkey native to Asia that has been widely used in scientific research.

rhinoceros (rī-nŏs′ər-əs) Any of several large African or Asian mammals having short legs, thick tough skin, and one or two upright horns on the snout. Rhinoceroses eat plants.

rhizoid (rī′zoid′) A slender, rootlike filament that grows from an alga, fungus, moss, liverwort, or fern, used for attachment and nourishment.

rhizome (rī′zōm′) A plant stem that grows horizontally under or along the ground and sends out roots and shoots that develop into new plants. Ginger, irises, and violets have rhizomes. *Compare* **bulb, corm, runner, tuber.**

rhodium (rō′dē-əm) A rare, silvery-white metallic element that is hard, durable, and resistant to acids. It is used as a permanent plating for jewelry and is added to platinum to make hard alloys that can withstand high temperatures. *Symbol* **Rh.** *Atomic number* 45. *See* **Periodic Table,** pages 254–255.

rhombus (rŏm′bəs) A parallelogram having four equal sides. A square is a rhombus with 90-degree angles.

rib (rĭb) **1.** Any of a series of long, curved bones

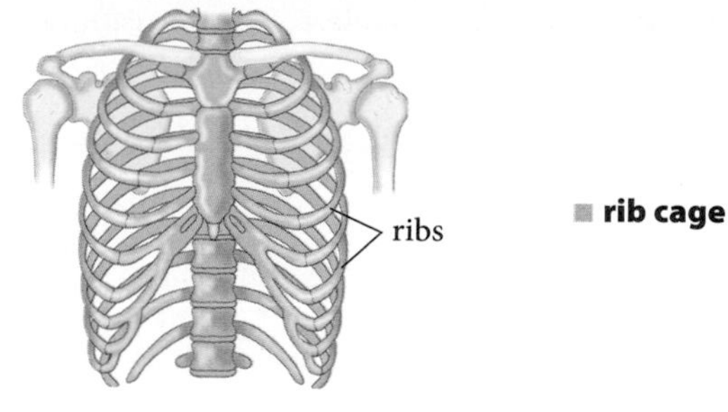

■ rib cage

extending from the spine and enclosing the chest cavity. In mammals, reptiles, and birds, the ribs curve toward the center of the chest and in most cases attach to the sternum (breastbone). There are 12 pairs of ribs in humans. *See more at* **skeleton. 2.** One of the main veins of a leaf.

rib cage The bony structure in the chest formed by the ribs and sternum (breastbone) that encloses and protects the heart and lungs.

riboflavin (rī′bō-flā′vĭn) A vitamin belonging to the vitamin B complex (B_2) that is important especially for carbohydrate metabolism and iron absorption. It is found in dairy products, meat, fish, almonds, leafy green vegetables, and whole grains.

ribonucleic acid (rī′bō-no͞o-klē′ĭk) *See* **RNA.**

ribosome (rī′bə-sōm′) A sphere-shaped structure within the cytoplasm of a cell that is composed of RNA and protein and is the site of protein synthesis. Ribosomes are often attached to the membrane of the endoplasmic reticulum. *See more at* **cell.**

Richards (rĭch′ərdz), **Ellen Swallow** 1842–1911. American chemist and educator. Her survey of water quality in Massachusetts led to the establishment of the first water quality standards

■ Ellen Swallow Richards

in the US and the first modern sewage treatment plant.

Richter scale (rĭk′tər) A scale used to rate the strength or total energy of earthquakes. The scale has no lower or upper limit but usually ranges from 1 to 9. Each increase in whole number represents a tenfold increase in magnitude, so that an earthquake rated as 5 is ten times as powerful as one rated as 4. An earthquake with a magnitude of 1 is detectable only by instruments (seismographs); one with a magnitude of 7 is a major earthquake. *See Note at* **earthquake.**

rickets (rĭk′ĭts) A bone disorder in children that is caused by lack of vitamin D, either in the diet or from lack of exposure to sunlight. In a child with rickets, the bones do not grow properly and become soft and misshapen.

rift (rĭft) **1.** A fault along the border of a rift valley. **2.** A narrow break, crack, or other opening in a rock, usually made by cracking or splitting.

rift valley **1.** A long, narrow valley having normal geologic faults on either side. A rift valley usually forms where a tectonic plate is pulled apart under tension. *See more at* **tectonic boundary.** **2.** The deep undersea valley located along the center of the mid-ocean ridge.

rift zone An area of the Earth's crust in which there are numerous rifts and rift valleys. *See more at* **tectonic boundary.**

Rigel (rī′jəl) A bright binary star in the constellation Orion.

right angle (rīt) An angle having a measure of 90°.

right ascension The position of a celestial object on the celestial sphere, measured in terms of the angle eastward from the vernal equinox to the point on the celestial equator nearest to the object in question. Right ascension and declination are used as coordinates to map objects on the celestial sphere. These measurements are expressed in degrees or hours. *See more at* **celestial sphere.**

right triangle A triangle having a right angle.

rigor mortis (rĭg′ər môr′tĭs) Stiffening of the muscles after death. It occurs because the energy needed to interrupt the contraction of muscle fibers is no longer being produced.

ringworm (rĭng′wûrm′) Any of a number of contagious skin diseases caused by a fungus and resulting in ring-shaped, scaly, itching patches on the skin.

WORD HISTORY

Rigel and star names

The history of astronomy owes much to Arabic scientists of the Middle Ages, who preserved the astronomical learning of ancient Greece and made improvements on it. The English names of many of the brightest stars in the heavens are Arabic in origin. The name of the supergiant star *Rigel,* for example, comes from the Arabic word for "foot" (the foot of the constellation Orion, that is). Some other important stars whose names are Arabic include *Aldebaran,* "the one following (the Pleiades)"; *Betelgeuse,* "hand of Orion"; *Deneb,* "tail" (of the constellation Cygnus, the swan); and *Altair,* "the flying eagle" (in the constellation Aquila, the eagle). The names of other stars are usually Greek or Latin, such as Antares or Sirius, as are the names of the constellations.

rip current (rĭp) A strong, narrow surface current flowing rapidly away from the shore. Rip currents form where water that has been brought to shore by wind and breaking waves runs back to deeper waters through a channel such as a break in a sandbar. Also called *rip tide.*

river (rĭv′ər) A large, natural stream of fresh water that flows into an ocean, a lake, or another body of water, usually fed by smaller streams that flow into it.

Rn The symbol for **radon.**

RNA (är′ĕn-ā′) Short for *ribonucleic acid.* A nucleic acid that is found in all living cells and many viruses and is involved in protein synthesis.

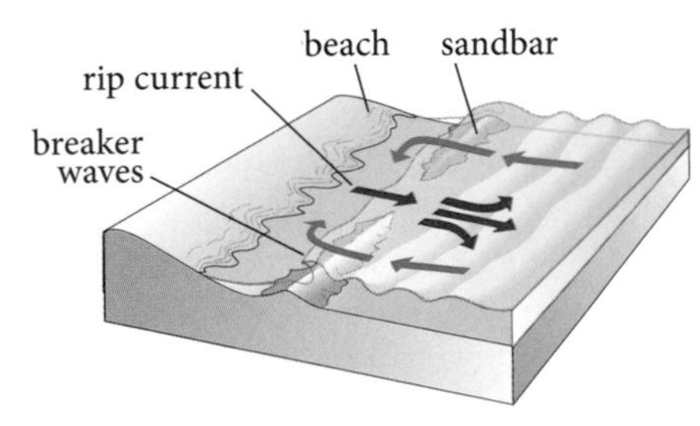

rip current

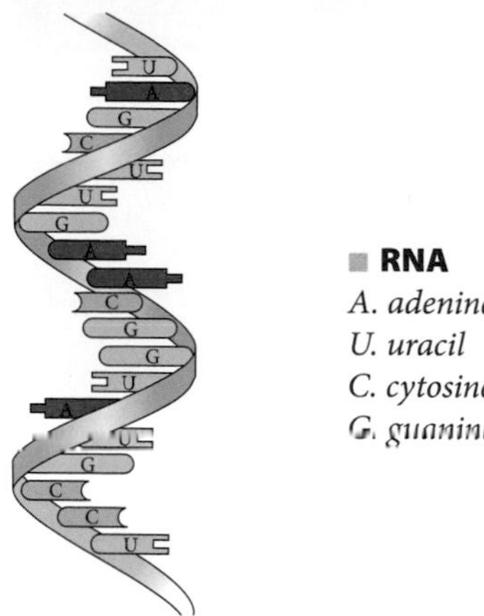

■ **RNA**
A. adenine
U. uracil
C. cytosine
G. guanine

Unlike double-stranded DNA, RNA consists of a single strand of nucleotides. RNA also differs from DNA in having uracil instead of thymine as one of its bases, and in having a different sugar component (ribose instead of deoxyribose). ❖ **Messenger RNA** is RNA that carries genetic information from the DNA to the structures in the cytoplasm (known as ribosomes) where protein synthesis takes place. In animals, plants, and other eukaryotes, the DNA is in the nucleus, and the ribosomes are in the cytoplasm. ❖ **Transfer RNA** is RNA that delivers the amino acids necessary for protein synthesis to the ribosomes. *Compare* **DNA.**

robot (rō′bŏt′) A machine that can perform a variety of tasks either on command or by being programmed in advance.

rock (rŏk) **1.** A relatively hard, naturally occurring mineral material. Rock can consist of a single mineral or of several minerals that are either tightly compacted or held together by a cementlike mineral matrix. The three main types of rock are igneous, sedimentary, and metamorphic. **2.** A fairly small piece of such material; a stone. *See Table on* **page 292.**

rocket (rŏk′ĭt) A vehicle or device propelled by one or more rocket engines, especially such a vehicle designed to travel through space.

rocket engine An engine that contains all the substances necessary for its operation and is propelled by a jet of hot gases produced by burning fuel. Since they do not rely on the oxygen in the atmosphere, rocket engines can operate in space.

Rocky Mountain spotted fever A severe infection caused by bacteria and characterized by fever, extreme exhaustion, muscle pains, and skin rash. It is transmitted by the bite of infected ticks.

rod (rŏd) One of the rod-shaped cells in the retina of the eye of many vertebrate animals. Rods are responsible for the ability to see in dim light. *Compare* **cone.**

rodent (rōd′nt) Any of numerous mostly small mammals having large front teeth used for gnawing. The teeth grow throughout the animal's life but are continuously worn away at the tips. Over 2,000 species of rodents are known. They include rats, mice, beavers, squirrels, shrews, porcupines, and hamsters.

roe (rō) The eggs of a fish, often together with the membrane of the ovary in which they are held.

Roentgen (rĕnt′gən, rĕnt′jən), **Wilhelm Conrad** 1845–1923. German physicist who discovered x-rays and developed x-ray photography, revolutionizing medical diagnosis.

roentgenium (rĕnt-gĕn′ē-əm, rĕnt-jĕn′ē-əm) An artificially produced radioactive element that has only been produced in trace amounts. Its most stable isotope has a half-life of 3.6 seconds. *Symbol* **Rg.** *Atomic number* 111. *See* **Periodic Table,** pages 254–255.

ROM (rŏm) Short for *read-only memory.* Computer hardware that holds permanently stored data. After the data is installed in ROM, it cannot be added to, modified, or deleted. ROM usually contains instructions that enable the computer's operating system to communicate with other hardware.

rookery (ro͝ok′ə-rē) A place where certain birds or mammals, such as crows, herons, penguins, or seals, gather in large numbers to breed.

■ **rookery**
penguin rookery on South Georgia Island, Antarctica

ROCK TYPES

IGNEOUS ROCKS	METAMORPHIC ROCKS	SEDIMENTARY ROCKS

HOW THEY FORM		
Igneous rocks form from cooling of magma (underground) or lava (at the Earth's surface). Many of the rocks that we see on the surface today actually formed deep down in the Earth and were later pushed upward by the processes of plate tectonics and then exposed by erosion. Lava forms when magma from deep within the Earth comes up to the surface.	Metamorphic rocks form when igneous, sedimentary, or other metamorphic rocks are subjected to great pressure or high temperatures deep within the Earth. This can happen on a very small scale where only the rocks in direct contact with a source of heat or pressure become metamorphosed, or it can happen on a regional scale, as along a mountain chain.	Sedimentary rocks form underwater or at the surface of the Earth, through the transport and deposition of sediments by water, wind, or ice. The sediments can be fragments of fossils or sea shells, or small pieces of igneous, metamorphic, or other sedimentary rocks. Some sedimentary rocks take the form of crystals, such as salt crystals, that precipitate out as water evaporates.
EXAMPLES		
granite, basalt, gabbro, pahoehoe	slate, schist, gneiss, marble	sandstone, limestone, shale, conglomerate
CHARACTERISTICS		
The crystals of the minerals that make up igneous rocks are tightly locked together because they form close to each other when the magma or lava becomes solid. Individual crystals often have sharp edges and distinctive geometric forms. Because new magma can form underground and move through fractures in rock, igneous rocks often have fractures filled with different types of igneous rock; these magma-filled fractures are called veins or dikes.	The crystals of minerals in metamorphic rocks have been stretched, folded, or changed by the pressure or high temperature to which they have been exposed. Often the crystals have been reorganized into layers. Sometimes, if a mass of rock becomes very hot, partial melting of the original rock occurs, and new minerals form. These minerals are often of gem quality.	Sediment grains are often rounded because they have been eroded by water, wind, or ice. But they can also be sharp, especially in high mountainous areas, where rocks are mechanically broken down into sediments by the forces exerted by the formation and melting of ice. Sediment grains can be small, like sand, or they can consist of large cobbles and boulders. Often sedimentary rocks are layered, because their sediments were deposited over a long course of time. Sedimentary rocks often contain fossils.
A SLICE OF ROCK SEEN THROUGH A MICROSCOPE		
IGNEOUS ROCKS	METAMORPHIC ROCKS	SEDIMENTARY ROCKS
	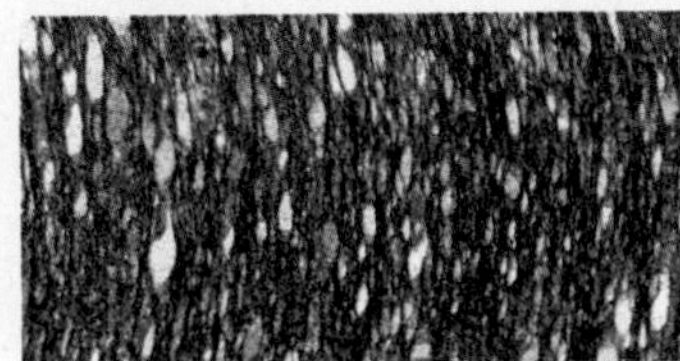	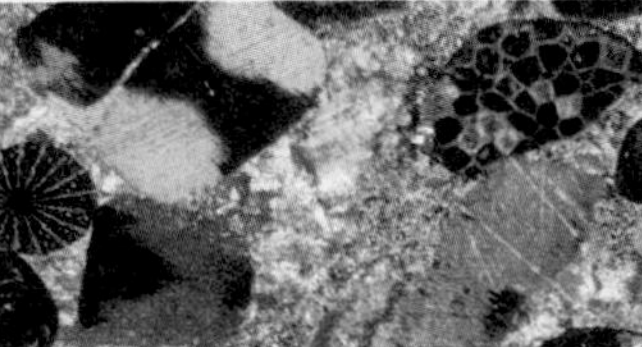

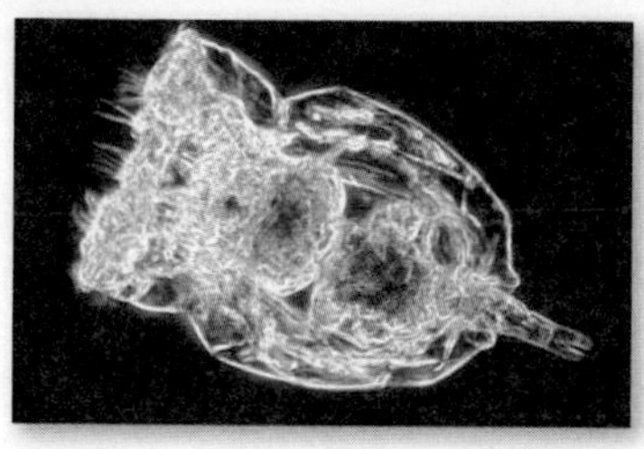

rotifer

root (ro͞ot) **1.** A plant part that usually grows underground and that secures the plant in place, absorbs minerals and water, and stores food manufactured by leaves and other plant parts. In certain plants, such as mangroves, additional roots grow out from the stem above ground, bending down into the soil, to provide more support. **2.** Any of various other plant parts that grow underground, especially an underground stem such as a corm, rhizome, or tuber. **3.** The part of a tooth that is embedded in the jaw and not covered by enamel. **4.** *Mathematics* **a.** A number that, when multiplied by itself a given number of times, produces a specified number. For example, since $2 \times 2 \times 2 \times 2 = 16$, 2 is a fourth root of 16. **b.** A solution to an equation. For example, a root of the equation $x^2 - 4 = 0$ is 2, since $2^2 - 4 = 0$.

root hair A thin, hairlike outgrowth of a plant root that absorbs water and minerals from the soil.

rotation (rō-tā′shən) **1.** The cyclic motion of an object around its own axis: *the daily rotation of the Earth.* **2.** A single complete cycle of such motion. *See Note at* **revolution.**

rotator cuff (rō′tā′tər) A group of muscles and tendons attaching the shoulder to the scapula (shoulder blade) that provide stability to the shoulder joint and act to rotate the arm. Injuries to the rotator cuff often happen when the arm is repeatedly moved over the head with great force, as when pitching a baseball.

rotifer (rō′tə-fər) Any of various very small aquatic animals that move and take in food by means of a ring of cilia around the mouth opening.

roundworm (round′wûrm′) *See* **nematode.**

Ru The symbol for **ruthenium.**

rubber (rŭb′ər) **1.** An elastic material prepared from the milky sap of certain tropical plants, especially the rubber tree, and used after processing in a great variety of products, including electric insulation and tires. **2.** Any of various synthetic materials having properties that are similar to those of natural rubber.

rubella (ro͞o-bĕl′ə) *See* **German measles.**

rubidium (ro͞o-bĭd′ē-əm) A soft, silvery-white element that is an alkali metal. It ignites spontaneously in air and reacts violently with water. Rubidium is used in photoelectric cells and in making vacuum tubes. *Symbol* **Rb.** *Atomic number* 37. *See* **Periodic Table,** pages 254–255.

ruby (ro͞o′bē) A deep-red, transparent form of the mineral corundum that is valued as a precious stone.

rumen (ro͞o′mən) The first and largest compartment of the stomach in ruminant animals, in which the food is fermented by microorganisms. *See more at* **ruminant.**

ruminant (ro͞o′mə-nənt) Any of various hoofed, even-toed, usually horned mammals that have a stomach divided into four compartments (called the rumen, reticulum, omasum, and abomasum) and chew a cud consisting of regurgitated, partially digested food. Cattle, sheep, goats, deer, giraffes, and antelopes are ruminants.

runner (rŭn′ər) A creeping plant stem that puts forth roots at intervals along its length, thus producing new plants. Strawberries spread by runners. Also called *stolon. Compare* **bulb, corm, rhizome, tuber.**

Russell (rŭs′əl), **Henry Norris** 1877–1957. American astronomer who studied binary stars and developed methods to calculate their mass and distances. He also demonstrated the relationship between types of stars and their brightness.

rust (rŭst) *Noun* **1.** Any of the various reddish-brown oxides of iron that form on iron and many

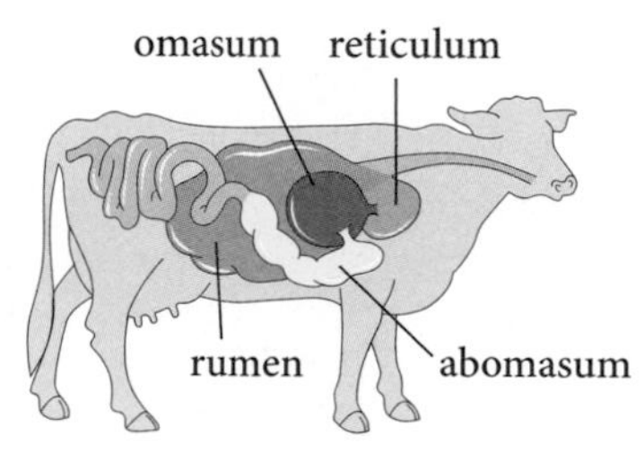

ruminant

of its alloys when they are exposed to oxygen in the presence of moisture. *See Note at* **oxidation. 2.** Any of various plant diseases caused by fungi that produce reddish or brownish spots on leaves. —*Verb* **3.** To become corroded or oxidized.

ruthenium (ro͞o-thē′nē-əm) A rare, silvery-gray metallic element that is hard, brittle, and very resistant to corrosion. It is used to harden alloys of platinum and palladium for jewelry and electrical contacts. *Symbol* **Ru.** *Atomic number* 44. *See* **Periodic Table,** pages 254–255.

Rutherford (rŭ*th*′ər-fərd), **Ernest**. First Baron Rutherford of Nelson. 1871–1937. New Zealand-born British physicist who was a pioneer of subatomic physics. He discovered the atomic nucleus and named the proton. Rutherford demonstrated that radioactive elements give off three kinds of radiation: alpha particles, beta particles, and gamma rays. He also invented the term *half-life,* which is used to describe the rate of radioactive decay.

Ernest Rutherford

rutherfordium (rŭ*th*′ər-fôr′dē-əm) A synthetic, radioactive element that can be produced by bombarding plutonium with neon ions. Its most stable isotope has a half-life of 65 seconds. *Symbol* **Rf.** *Atomic number* 104. *See* **Periodic Table,** pages 254–255.

s Abbreviation of **second.**

S The symbol for **sulfur.**

saber-toothed tiger (sā′bər-to͞otht′) Any of various large extinct cats of the late Pleistocene Epoch having very long upper canine teeth. Also called *smilodon.*

Sabin (sā′bĭn), **Albert Bruce** 1906–1993. American microbiologist and physician who developed a live-virus vaccine against polio that contained an active form of the polio virus (1957). This replaced the vaccine, invented by Jonas Salk, that contained an inactivated (and less effective) form of the virus.

sac (săk) A baglike part in an organism, often containing fluid.

saccharin (săk′ər-ĭn) A white, crystalline powder used as a calorie-free sweetener. It tastes about 500 times sweeter than sugar.

sacrum (sā′krəm, săk′rəm) A triangular bone at the base of the spine, above the coccyx (tailbone), that forms the rear section of the pelvis. In humans it is made up of five vertebrae that fuse together by adulthood. *See more at* **skeleton.**

Sagittarius (săj′ĭ-târ′ē-əs) A constellation in the Southern Hemisphere near Scorpius and Capricornus.

salamander (săl′ə-măn′dər) Any of various small amphibians that have a long tail and smooth moist skin.

salicylic acid (săl′ĭ-sĭl′ĭk) A white, crystalline acid used to make aspirin, to treat certain skin conditions, and to preserve foods.

■ **Albert Sabin**

saline (sā′lēn′) Relating to or containing salt; salty. —*Noun* **salinity** (sə-lĭn′ĭ-tē).

saliva (sə-lī′və) The watery fluid that is secreted into the mouth by the salivary glands. Saliva helps to moisten food as it is chewed, serves to protect against infections, and contains enzymes that begin the digestion of carbohydrates.

salivary gland (săl′ə-vĕr′ē) A gland that secretes saliva, especially any of three pairs of large glands in humans that secrete saliva into the mouth.

Salk (sôlk), **Jonas Edward** 1914–1995. American microbiologist who developed the first effective vaccine against polio (1954).

salmon (săm′ən) Any of various large food fish native to northern waters, having pinkish flesh. Salmon swim from salt to fresh water to spawn. Most salmon harvested for food are now raised in fish farms.

salmonella (săl′mə-nĕl′ə) A rod-shaped bacterium that causes food poisoning in humans.

salt (sôlt) Any of a large class of chemical compounds formed when one or more hydrogen ions of an acid are replaced by metal ions or other cations. Because salts are composed of ions, they conduct electricity when melted or when dissolved in water. ❖ One of the most abundant salts is NaCl, also called **sodium chloride** or **common salt.** It is found in all animal fluids, in seawater, and in underground deposits. It is widely used as a food seasoning and preservative.

saltpeter (sôlt′pē′tər) *See* **potassium nitrate.**

saltwater (sôlt′wô′tər) Consisting of or living in salty water, especially seawater: *saltwater fish.*

samarium (sə-mâr′ē-əm) A silvery-white metallic element of the lanthanide series. It is used to make lasers, glass that absorbs infrared light, and permanent magnets. It is also used to absorb neutrons in nuclear reactors. *Symbol* **Sm.** *Atomic number* 62. *See* **Periodic Table,** pages 254–255.

sand (sănd) **1.** Small, often rounded grains or particles of disintegrated rock, larger than particles

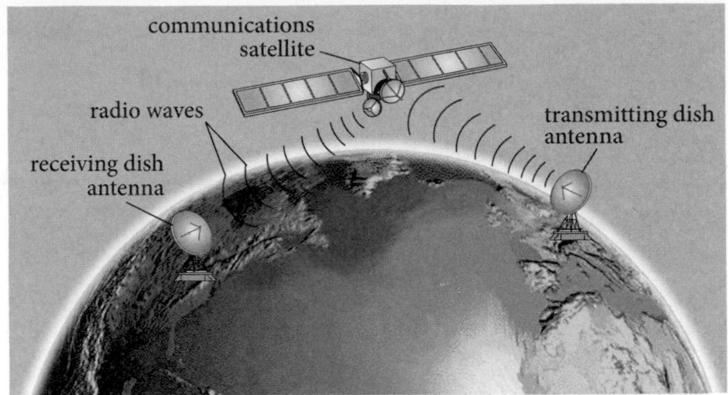

■ **satellite**
Communications satellites receive, amplify, and transmit radio signals between dish antennas that may be hundreds of miles apart.

of silt. Although sand often consists of quartz, it can consist of any other mineral or rock fragment as well. Coral sand, for example, consists of limestone fragments. **2.** A loose collection or deposit of sand grains.

sandbar (sănd′bär′) A long, low ridge of sand deposited in shallow water by waves or currents, as in a river or offshore from a beach.

sandstone (sănd′stōn′) A sedimentary rock formed of fine to coarse sand-sized grains that have been either compacted or cemented together. Although sandstone usually consists primarily of quartz, it can also consist of other minerals. Sandstone varies in color from yellow or red to gray or brown. *See Table at* **rock.**

Sanger (săng′ər), **Frederick** 1918–2013. British biochemist. He determined the order of amino acids in the insulin molecule, thereby making it possible to manufacture synthetic insulin. Sanger also developed methods for decoding DNA sequences.

sanitary landfill (săn′ĭ-tĕr′ē) *See* **landfill.**

sap (săp) Watery fluid that circulates through the xylem and phloem of vascular plants. Xylem sap usually contains water and minerals, while phloem sap contains sugars.

sapphire (săf′īr′) Any of several fairly pure forms of the mineral corundum, especially a blue form valued as a gem.

saprophyte (săp′rə-fīt′) An organism, such as a mushroom or other fungus, that lives on and gets its nourishment from decaying organic material. ❖ Because the suffix *-phyte* often means "plant," and fungi are not plants, some scientists prefer to describe fungi as *saprotrophs* or *saprobes.* —*Adjective* **saprophytic** (săp′rə-fĭt′ĭk).

sarcoma (sär-kō′mə) A malignant tumor that usually arises in bone or in soft tissues such as cartilage, muscle, or fat.

satellite (săt′l-īt′) **1.** A celestial object, such as a moon, planet, or comet, that orbits a larger celestial object. *See Note at* **moon. 2.** An object that is launched to orbit Earth or another celestial object. Satellites are used for research, communications, weather information, and navigation.

saturated (săch′ə-rā′tĭd) **1.** Relating to an organic compound that contains only single bonds between the carbon atoms and therefore has the maximum number of hydrogen atoms. Propane and saturated fatty acids are examples of saturated compounds. *Compare* **unsaturated. 2.** Relating to a solution that is unable to dissolve more of a solute. **3.** Containing as much water vapor as is possible at a given temperature. Air

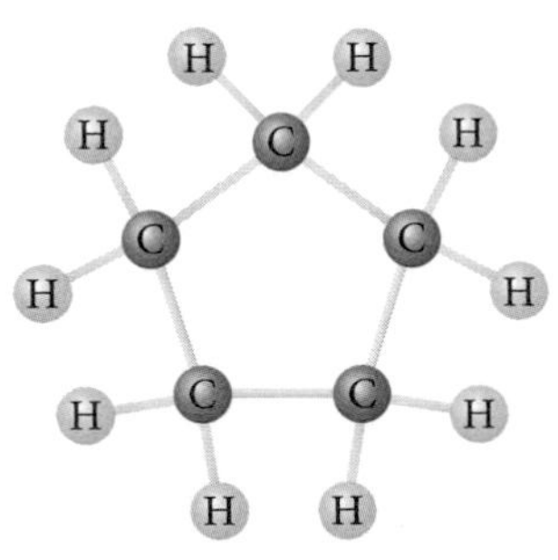

■ **saturated**
a cyclopentane molecule (C_5H_{10}), with only single bonds between the carbon atoms

savanna

that is saturated has a relative humidity of 100 percent.

saturated fat A fat containing fatty acids that are saturated (having only single bonds between the carbon atoms). Most fats derived from animal sources (such as butter and lard) are saturated fats, as are fats from some plants (such as palm oil and coconut oil). Saturated fats are usually solid at room temperature. Eating foods high in saturated fats is associated with a higher risk of heart disease. *Compare* **trans fat, unsaturated fat.**

saturation (săch′ə-rā′shən) The vividness of a color's hue. Saturation measures the degree to which a color differs from a gray of the same brightness or lightness. *See more at* **color.**

saturation point The point at which a substance can receive no more of another substance in solution under given conditions.

Saturn (săt′ərn) The sixth planet from the sun and the second largest, with a diameter about ten times that of Earth. Saturn is encircled by a large, flat system of rings that are made up mostly of tiny particles of ice. *See Table at* **solar system,** pages 312–313.

saurischian (sô-rĭs′kē-ən) One of the two main types of dinosaurs. Saurischians had a pelvis similar to that of modern reptiles. They included the theropods, such as *Tyrannosaurus rex,* and the sauropods, such as the apatosaurus. *Compare* **ornithischian.**

sauropod (sôr′ə-pŏd′) One of the two types of saurischian dinosaurs, widespread during the Mesozoic Era. Sauropods were plant-eaters and had a long neck and tail, a small head, and four stout legs. Some of them grew to tremendous size. The apatosaurus and brachiosaurus were sauropods. *Compare* **theropod.**

savanna also **savannah** (sə-văn′ə) A flat grassland of warm regions, often with scattered trees.

Sb The symbol for **antimony.**

Sc The symbol for **scandium.**

scalar (skā′lər) A quantity, such as mass, length, or speed, whose only property is magnitude; a number. *Compare* **vector.**

scale¹ (skāl) **1.** One of the small, thin plates forming the outer covering of fish, reptiles, and certain other animals. **2.** A similar part in other animals, such as one of the thin, flat, overlapping structures that cover the wings of butterflies and moths. **3.** A small, thin, often flattened plant structure, such as one of the modified leaves that cover a tree bud or one of the structures that bear the reproductive organs on the cones of a conifer. **4.** A plant disease caused by scale insects.

scale² **1.** A system of numbering used as a standard in measurement, with each number corresponding to a physical quantity. Some scales, such as temperature scales, have equal intervals; other scales, such as the Richter scale, are arranged as a geometric progression. **2.** A set of marks at regular intervals, as on a ruler or protractor, used for measuring. **3.** The ratio between distances in a representation such as a map or model and the corresponding distances in

scale¹
top: *fish scales*
bottom: *pine cone scales*

the object being represented. **4.** An instrument or a machine for weighing.

scale insect Any of various small insects that feed on plant sap. Scale insects secrete a waxy substance that covers the body, and some are agricultural pests.

scalene (skā′lēn′) Having three unequal sides, as a triangle that is neither equilateral nor isosceles.

scandium (skăn′dē-əm) A soft, silvery, very lightweight metallic element that is often found in minerals with other rare-earth elements and is a byproduct in the processing of certain uranium ores. It has a high melting point and is used to make high-intensity lights. *Symbol* **Sc.** *Atomic number* 21. *See* **Periodic Table,** pages 254–255. *See Note at* **rare-earth element.**

scanning electron microscope (skăn′ĭng) An electron microscope that creates an image of the three-dimensional surface of an object by moving a beam of electrons back and forth across the object and detecting the electrons that are scattered by or knocked loose from the object.

scanning tunneling microscope A microscope used to make images of individual atoms on the surface of a material. The microscope has a probe ending in a tiny sharp tip that moves along the material's surface while emitting a stream of electrons. The flow of electrons is constant so long as the distance between the tip and the material's surface atoms is held constant. An image is formed based on the continual adjustments made to the height of the tip to keep the electron flow constant over the "bumps" that are the atoms.

scapula (skăp′yə-lə) Either of two flat, triangular bones forming part of the shoulder. In humans and other primates, they lie on the upper part of the back on either side of the spine. Also called *shoulder blade. See more at* **skeleton.**

scarlet fever (skär′lĭt) A severe contagious bacterial disease that is characterized by a high fever, sore throat, and rough scarlet-red or dark rash on the skin. It mainly occurs in children.

scattering (skăt′ər-ĭng) The spreading out in many directions of a stream of particles or a wave as it passes through a medium and collides with particles in the medium.

scavenger (skăv′ən-jər) An animal that feeds on organisms that have already died or that have been killed by another animal. Vultures and hyenas are scavengers.

Scheele (shā′lə), **Carl Wilhelm** 1742–1786. German-born Swedish chemist who discovered a number of compounds and elements. He discovered oxygen around 1772, but because his results were not published until 1777, Joseph Priestley is usually credited with the discovery. Scheele made extensive investigations of plant and animal materials, and his work was fundamental to the development of organic chemistry.

schist (shĭst) A metamorphic rock characterized by a very fine alignment of its minerals, which allows it to be easily split into flakes or slabs. Because schist often contains abundant mica, it usually has a shiny, gray appearance. *See Table at* **rock.**

schistosomiasis (shĭs′tə-sə-mī′ə-sĭs) A disease caused by any of several flatworm parasites that infest the blood of humans and other mammals. Symptoms include severe diarrhea and the gradual destruction of vital organs. Schistosomiasis occurs chiefly in tropical areas and is transmitted through contact with contaminated water.

schizophrenia (skĭt′sə-frē′nē-ə, skĭt′sə-frĕn′ē-ə) A severe mental disorder in which a person loses touch with reality. People with schizophrenia also experience disorganized thinking that usually interferes with their ability to work and communicate with others. Schizophrenia is associated with chemical and structural abnormalities of the brain and is thought to be caused by a combination of genetic and environmental factors.

Schrödinger (shrō′dĭng-ər, shrā′dĭng-ər), **Erwin** 1887–1961. Austrian physicist who was a founder of the study of wave mechanics. He developed a mathematical equation that describes the wavelike behavior of subatomic particles. Schrödinger's equation was fundamental to the development of quantum mechanics.

sciatic nerve (sī-ăt′ĭk) A thick nerve that arises in the lower part of the spine and passes through the pelvis on its way to the back of the leg. It carries sensory information from the leg to the spine and controls the action of many muscles. The sciatic nerve is the largest nerve in the body.

science (sī′əns) The investigation of natural phenomena through observation, experimentation, and theoretical explanation. ❖ Science makes

sea cucumber

use of the **scientific method**, which includes the careful observation of natural phenomena, the formulation of a hypothesis, the conducting of one or more experiments to test the hypothesis, and the drawing of a conclusion that confirms or modifies the hypothesis.

scientific name (sī′ən-tĭf**′**ĭk) A name used by scientists, especially the taxonomic name of an organism that consists of a genus name and a second name identifying the species. Scientific names usually come from Latin or Greek. An example is *Didelphis virginiana,* the scientific name for the opossum.

scientific notation A method of expressing numbers in terms of a decimal number between 1 and 10 multiplied by a power of 10. The scientific notation for 10,492, for example, is 1.0492×10^4.

sclera (sklîr**′**ə) The tough, white, fibrous tissue that covers all of the eyeball except the cornea.

scoliosis (skō′lē-ō**′**sĭs) Abnormal sideways curvature of the spine.

scoria (skôr**′**ē-ə) Rough, crusty, solidified lava containing numerous cavities that originated as gas bubbles in the lava while it was still molten.

Scorpius (skôr**′**pē-əs) A constellation in the Southern Hemisphere near Libra and Sagittarius.

scrotum (skrō**′**təm) The external sac of skin that encloses the testes in most mammals.

scurvy (skûr**′**vē) A disease caused by lack of vitamin C in the diet. It is characterized by bleeding of the gums, rupture of capillaries under the skin, loose teeth, and weakness of the body.

Se The symbol for **selenium.**

sea (sē) **1.** The continuous body of salt water that covers most of the Earth's surface. *See Note at* **ocean. 2.** A region of water within an ocean and partly enclosed by land, such as the North Sea. **3.** A large body of water, especially salt water, that is completely enclosed by land, such as the Caspian Sea. **4.** A mare of the moon.

sea anemone Any of numerous often brightly colored marine animals having a flexible, cylindrical body that attaches to an underwater surface, and a mouth surrounded by stinging tentacles. Sea anemones, like jellyfish and corals, are cnidarians.

Seaborg (sē**′**bôrg′), **Glenn Theodore** 1912–1999. American chemist who led the team that discovered plutonium (1940). In 1944 they discovered americium and curium. By bombarding these two elements with alpha particles, Seaborg produced the elements berkelium and californium.

seaborgium (sē-bôr**′**gē-əm) An artificially produced, radioactive element that can be produced by bombarding californium with oxygen ions or bombarding lead with chromium ions. Its most stable isotope has a half-life of about 21 seconds. *Symbol* **Sg.** *Atomic number* 106. *See* **Periodic Table,** pages 254–255.

sea cucumber Any of various invertebrate sea animals having a rough or spiny cucumber-shaped body and a mouth surrounded by tentacles. Sea cucumbers are echinoderms.

seahorse (sē**′**hôrs′) Any of several small ocean fish having a head resembling that of a horse, a body covered with bony ridges, and a tail that can be curled around a supporting object. Females transfer their eggs to a pouch on the male's belly, where they are fertilized and develop until they hatch.

seal (sēl) Any of various meat-eating sea mammals having a streamlined body, thick fur or hair, and limbs in the form of flippers.

sea level The level of the surface of the ocean, used as a standard in determining land elevation or sea depths.

seam (sēm) *Geology* A thin layer or stratum, as of coal or rock.

sea slug Any of various colorful ocean mollusks

sea slug

that lack a shell and gills but have fringelike projections that serve as respiratory organs. Also called *nudibranch.*

season (sē′zən) **1.** One of four natural divisions of the year — spring, summer, autumn, and winter — in the North or South Temperate Zones. The seasons are often defined as beginning and ending on the solstices and equinoxes. **2.** In some tropical climates, either of the two parts — rainy and dry — into which the year is divided.

sea squirt Any of various sea animals having a sac-shaped body with two siphons. Sea squirts pump water through the siphons and filter it with gill-like structures to catch food particles. Sea squirts belong to the group known as tunicates.

sea urchin Any of various invertebrate sea animals having a soft body enclosed in a rounded shell covered with movable spines. Sea urchins are echinoderms.

seaweed (sē′wēd′) Any of various algae that live in ocean waters. Some species are free-floating, while others are attached to the ocean bottom. Kelp is a kind of seaweed.

sebaceous gland (sĭ-bā′shəs) Any of the small glands in the skin of humans and other mammals that secrete an oily material (called sebum) into the hair follicles.

sebum (sē′bəm) The fatty substance secreted by the sebaceous glands in the skin of mammals. It protects and lubricates the skin and hair.

sec Abbreviation of **secant.**

secant (sē′kănt′) **1.** A straight line or ray that intersects a curve, especially a circle, at two or more points. **2.** The ratio of the length of the hypotenuse in a right triangle to the side adjacent to an acute angle; the inverse of the cosine.

second (sĕk′ənd) **1.** A unit of time equal to $\frac{1}{60}$ of a minute. **2.** A unit of angular measurement equal to $\frac{1}{60}$ of a minute of arc.

secondary color (sĕk′ən-dĕr′ē) A color produced by mixing two primary colors in equal proportions. *See more at* **color.**

secondary growth Growth in woody plants that results from the production of new tissues by cambium, causing the stem, branches, and roots to become wider. *Compare* **primary growth.**

secondary sex characteristic Any of the physical traits in a sexually mature animal that differ between the sexes and are not directly involved in the act of reproducing. They include the breasts of female humans and the facial hair of male humans, the antlers of male moose, and the differing plumage of many female and male birds. The development of secondary sex characteristics is controlled by the sex hormones.

secondary wave An earthquake wave in which rock particles vibrate at right angles to the direction of wave travel. Secondary waves can travel through solids but not through liquids. Also called *S wave. See Note at* **earthquake.**

secrete (sĭ-krēt′) To produce and release a substance from a cell or gland. For example, the endocrine glands secrete hormones.

sector (sĕk′tər) The part of a circle bounded by two radii and the arc between them.

sedative (sĕd′ə-tĭv) A drug or other substance that has a calming or quieting effect.

sediment (sĕd′ə-mənt) **1.** *Geology* Silt, sand, rocks, fossils, and other matter carried and deposited by water, wind, or ice. **2.** *Chemistry* Particles of solid matter that settle out of a suspension to the bottom of the liquid.

seaweed
sea beech (left), *bladder wrack* (center), *and kelp* (right)

■ **sedimentary**
sandstone rock formation, Paria Canyon–Vermilion Cliffs Wilderness, Utah

sedimentary (sĕd′ə-mĕn′tə-rē) Relating to rocks formed when sediment, such as sand or mud, is deposited and becomes tightly compacted. Sandstone, conglomerate, and limestone are examples of sedimentary rocks. *See Table at* **rock.**

seed (sēd) *Noun* **1.** A part of a gymnosperm or flowering plant that contains an embryo and the food it will need to grow into a new plant. A seed is a mature fertilized ovule. —*Verb* **2.** To plant seeds in soil. **3.** To attempt to produce rain by cloud seeding. *See more at* **cloud seeding.**

seed coat The outer protective covering of a seed.

seed leaf *See* **cotyledon.**

seedling (sēd′lĭng) A young plant, especially one that grows from a seed, rather than from a cutting or bulb, for example.

seed plant Any of numerous plants that bear seeds. The seed plants include the gymnosperms, such as pines and spruces, and the angiosperms (flowering plants). Ferns and mosses are not seed plants.

segment (sĕg′mənt) **1.** The portion of a line between any two of its points. **2.** The region bounded by an arc of a circle and the chord that connects the endpoints of the arc. **3.** The portion of a sphere included between a pair of parallel planes that intersect it or are tangent to it.

seismic (sīz′mĭk) Relating to an earthquake or to other tremors of the Earth, such as those caused by large explosions: *a seismic disturbance.*

seismograph (sīz′mə-grăf′) An instrument that detects and records vibrations and movements in the Earth, especially during an earthquake. By comparing the records produced by seismographs located in three or more locations across the Earth, geologists can determine the location and strength of an earthquake. ❖ The record produced by a seismograph is called a **seismogram.**

seismology (sīz-mŏl′ə-jē) The scientific study of earthquakes, including their origin, geographic distribution, effects, and possible prediction.

selenium (sĭ-lē′nē-əm) A nonmetallic element that can exist as a gray crystal, a red powder, or a black glassy material. It can convert light directly into electricity, and its ability to conduct electricity increases as light striking it becomes more intense. Because of this, selenium is used in copy machines, photography, and solar cells. *Symbol* **Se.** *Atomic number* 34. *See* **Periodic Table,** pages 254–255.

semen (sē′mən) A whitish fluid that is produced by the reproductive organs of male mammals and carries sperm cells.

semi– **1.** A prefix that means "half," as in *semicircle,* half a circle. **2.** A prefix that means "partly," "somewhat," or "less than fully," as in *semiconscious,* partly conscious.

semiarid (sĕm′ē-ăr′ĭd) Having low rainfall but able to support grassland and scrubby vegetation; not completely arid.

semicircular canal (sĕm′ĭ-sûr′kyə-lər) Any of the three looped tubes of the inner ear that together work to maintain the sense of balance of the body.

semiconductor (sĕm′ē-kən-dŭk′tər) A solid material, such as silicon or germanium, that conducts electricity more easily than an insulator but less easily than a conductor. In a semiconductor, a small number of electrons have escaped from the atoms to which they were bound, leaving spaces, called holes, that can be filled with other electrons. An electric current is created by the movement of these electrons and electron holes. Semiconductors are used in computers and many electronic devices.

semipalmate (sĕm′ē-păl′māt′, sĕm′ē-päl′māt′)

Having partially webbed feet or toes, as many wading and shore birds do.

semipermeable (sĕm′ē-pûr′mē-ə-bəl) Allowing passage of certain, especially small, molecules or ions but acting as a barrier to others. Many biological and synthetic membranes are semipermeable.

Semmelweis (zĕm′əl-vīs′), **Ignaz Philipp** 1818–1865. Hungarian physician who was a pioneer of antiseptic medical practices. He demonstrated that fatal infections in the obstetric clinic where he worked were caused by doctors and students going directly from performing autopsies to examining pregnant women. The death rate dropped after Semmelweis required staff members to disinfect their hands before examinations.

sense organ (sĕns) In animals, an organ or part that is sensitive to a stimulus, as of sound, touch, or light. Examples of sense organs include the eye, ear, and nose, as well as the taste buds on the tongue.

sensor (sĕn′sər) A device that responds to a physical stimulus and converts the stimulus into a signal conveyed to another device. For example, a sensor in a printer detects that the paper tray is empty and sends a signal to the digital display that the tray is out of paper.

sensory (sĕn′sə-rē) Involving the sense organs or the nerves that relay messages from them: *sensory receptors; a sensory nerve. Compare* **motor.**

sepal (sē′pəl) One of the usually green leaflike structures that make up the outermost part of a flower and usually enclose the flower bud before it opens. As a group, the sepals are called the calyx. *See more at* **flower.**

sepsis (sĕp′sĭs) Infection of the blood by disease-causing microorganisms, especially bacteria. —*Adjective* **septic.**

septum (sĕp′təm) *Plural* **septa** A thin partition or membrane between two cavities or soft masses of tissue in an organism. The chambers of the heart are separated by septa.

sequence (sē′kwəns) *Noun* **1.** *Mathematics* A set of quantities ordered in the same manner as the positive integers. A sequence can be finite, such as $\{1, 3, 5, 7, 9\}$, or it can be infinite, such as $\{1, \frac{1}{2}, \frac{1}{3}, \frac{1}{4}, \ldots \frac{1}{n}\}$. **2.** *Chemistry* The order of subunits that make up a large chemical compound, especially the order of nucleotides in a nucleic acid or of amino acids in a protein. —*Verb* **3.** To determine the order of subunits in a chemical compound, especially a nucleic acid or a protein molecule.

series (sîr′ēz) *Mathematics* The sum of a sequence of terms, for example $2 + 2^2 + 2^3 + 2^4 + 2^5 + \ldots$

series circuit *See under* **circuit.**

serine (sĕr′ēn′) A nonessential amino acid. *See more at* **amino acid.**

serotonin (sĕr′ə-tō′nĭn) A chemical compound that is formed from the amino acid tryptophan and is found in many animals and plants. In humans it acts as a neurotransmitter and is involved in the control of pain perception, the sleep-wake cycle, and mood.

serum (sîr′əm) *Plural* **serums** *or* **sera 1.** *See* **blood serum. 2.** Blood serum extracted from an animal that has immunity to a particular disease. The serum contains antibodies to specific antigens and can transfer immunity to humans or other animals by means of injection.

server (sûr′vər) A computer that controls a central storage area of data that can be downloaded or manipulated by another computer.

sessile (sĕs′īl′) *Biology* **1.** Permanently attached or fixed; not free-moving: *Adult barnacles are*

sessile
left: *sessile sponge*
right: *sessile acorn*

sessile. **2.** Stalkless and attached directly at the base: *sessile leaves.*

set (sĕt) A collection of distinct elements that have something in common. In mathematics, sets are commonly represented by enclosing the members of a set in curly braces, as {1, 2, 3, 4, 5}, the set of all positive integers from 1 to 5.

sex (sĕks) **1.** Either of the two divisions, designated female and male, into which most organisms are grouped on the basis of their reproductive organs and functions. **2.** Sexual intercourse. —*Adjective* **sexual.**

sex cell A cell whose nucleus unites with that of a cell of the opposite sex to form a new organism. A sex cell contains only a single set of chromosomes. Egg and sperm cells are sex cells. Also called *gamete, reproductive cell.*

sex chromosome Either of a pair of chromosomes, usually called X and Y, that determine the sex of an individual and are found in most animals. In humans, individuals with two X chromosomes develop ovaries, and individuals with one X chromosome and one Y chromosome develop testes.

sex hormone Any of several steroid hormones in vertebrate animals that regulate the development and function of the sex organs and the secondary sex characteristics and that influence reproductive behavior. Testosterone and estrogen are sex hormones.

sex-linked Relating to a gene carried on a sex chromosome or to a trait transmitted by a sex chromosome. Colorblindness in humans is a sex-linked trait.

sextant (sĕk′stənt) A navigational instrument consisting of a 60° arc with a movable arm and two small mirrors that allows precise measurement of the angle between a celestial object and the horizon. This angle can then be used to calculate the observer's latitude and longitude.

sexual intercourse (sĕk′sho͞o-əl) The process by which sperm from the male is deposited in the female during sexual reproduction in many animals.

sexually transmitted disease (sĕk′sho͞o-ə-lē) Any of various diseases, such as chlamydia, gonorrhea, and syphilis, that are transmitted through sexual intercourse or other intimate sexual contact. Also called *sexually transmitted infection* or *venereal disease.*

shale

sexual reproduction *See* under **reproduction.**

Sg The symbol for **seaborgium.**

shale (shāl) A fine-grained sedimentary rock consisting of compacted and hardened clay, silt, or mud. Shale forms in many distinct layers and splits easily into thin sheets or slabs. It varies in color from black or gray to brown or red. *See Table at* **rock.**

shark (shärk) Any of numerous ocean fish that have tough skin and a skeleton made of cartilage rather than bone. Most sharks are meat-eating, but whale sharks, which can reach lengths of 40 feet (12 meters), feed on plankton.

shelf (shĕlf) *See* **continental shelf.**

shell (shĕl) **1.** *Biology* **a.** The usually hard outer covering of certain animals, such as insects, turtles, and most mollusks and crustaceans. **b.** The hard outer covering of a bird's or reptile's egg. **c.** The hard outer covering of a seed or nut. **2.** *Physics* Any of the spherical regions in which electrons are considered to be concentrated around the nucleus of an atom. An atom can have up to seven shells, depending on the number of protons in its nucleus. The innermost shell can hold only 2 electrons, but outer shells hold more, up to a maximum of 32. Electrons in outer shells have more energy than those in inner shells. If an electron in an inner shell gains energy, it can jump to an unfilled outer shell. Similarly, if an electron gives off energy, it can drop to an unfilled inner shell. The energy gained or lost is usually in the form of a photon of light or other electromagnetic radiation. *See more at* **atom.** *See Note at* **metal.**

shoal (shōl) A sandy elevation of the bottom of a body of water; a sandbar.

shock (shŏk) **1.** A life-threatening condition marked by a severe drop in blood pressure, resulting from serious injury or illness. **2.** An instance of the passage of an electric current through the body. The amount of injury caused by electric shock depends on the type and strength of the current, the length of time the current is applied, and the route the current takes once it enters the body.

Shockley (shŏk′lē), **William Bradford** 1910–1989. American physicist who co-developed the transistor.

shock wave A large-amplitude wave formed by the sudden compression of the medium through which the wave moves. Shock waves are caused by explosions or by objects moving through a fluid at a speed greater than the speed of sound in that medium. Because the waves generated by the object move more slowly than the object, they become compressed and pile up. Sonic booms are produced by shock waves.

shoot (sho͞ot) A young plant or plant part, such as a stem or leaf, that has just begun to sprout or grow.

shooting star (sho͞o′tĭng) *See* **meteor** (sense 1).

short circuit (shôrt) A path that allows most of the current in an electric circuit to flow around or away from the principal elements or devices in the circuit. Short circuits can cause too much current to flow through one part of the circuit, leading to damage of the circuit's components because of overheating.

short ton *See* **ton** (sense 1).

shoulder blade (shōl′dər) *See* **scapula.**

shrub (shrŭb) A woody plant that is smaller than a tree, usually having several stems rather than a single trunk; a bush.

Si The symbol for **silicon.**

SI Abbreviation of **International System of Units.** SI is short for *Système International d'Unités.*

sickle cell anemia (sĭk′əl) A hereditary disease characterized by red blood cells that are sickle-shaped instead of round because of an abnormality in the hemoglobin, the protein that carries oxygen in the blood. The cells deteriorate more quickly than normal and, because of their shape, they can block small blood vessels, reducing the amount of oxygen available to body tissues and causing pain, organ damage, and infections.

sidereal (sī-dîr′ē-əl) **1.** Relating to the stars or constellations. **2.** Relating to sidereal time: *a sidereal day.*

sidereal time Time based on the rotation of the Earth with respect to the distant stars. A sidereal day lasts from when a particular star is directly overhead until the next time it is directly overhead. *Compare* **solar time.**

SI-derived unit (ĕs′ī′-dĭ-rīvd′) Any of various units of measurement, such as the newton and joule, that are derived from the base units in the International System of Units.

sierra (sē-ĕr′ə) A high, rugged range of mountains having an irregular outline somewhat like the teeth of a saw.

sievert (sē′vərt) A unit representing an amount of radiation producing the same effect on living tissue as one gray of high-penetration x-rays.

significant digits (sĭg-nĭf′ĭ-kənt) The digits in a decimal number that are warranted by the accuracy of the means of measurement. Significant digits are all the numbers beginning with the leftmost nonzero digit, or beginning with the first digit after the decimal point if there are no nonzero digits to the left of the decimal point, and extending to the right. For example, 302, 3.20, and 0.023 all have three significant digits. Also called *significant figures.*

silica (sĭl′ĭ-kə) Silicon dioxide, SiO_2, a compound that occurs widely in rocks and mineral forms, such as quartz and flint, and is used to make glass, concrete, and other materials. —*Adjective* **siliceous** (sĭ-lĭsh′əs).

silicate (sĭl′ĭ-kāt′) Any of a large class of chemical compounds composed of silicon and oxygen, often bonded to at least one metal. The most common minerals, such as quartz, are silicates. One important subset of silicates are those that include the group SiO_4 in their crystal lattice, such as mica and feldspar.

silicon (sĭl′ĭ-kŏn′) A nonmetallic element that occurs in both gray crystalline and brown noncrystalline forms. It is the second most abundant element in the Earth's crust and can be found only in silica and silicates. Silicon is used in glass, semiconductors, concrete, and ceramics.

Did You Know...?

sickle cell anemia

When scientists discovered that *sickle cell anemia* is caused by an inherited genetic mutation, they wondered why it was so common. If people with the mutation died young and had fewer children than people without the mutation, then the mutation should have become rare long ago. It is now believed that the mutation remains widespread because of malaria, a serious disease transmitted by mosquitoes. What is the connection? It turns out that people become very sick with sickle cell anemia only when they have two copies of the defective gene (one from each parent). People with only one copy of the gene have few symptoms, but their blood does contain some abnormal hemoglobin. This abnormal hemoglobin has been found to provide protection against malaria parasites, which infect red blood cells. The final piece of the puzzle is that sickle cell anemia is most common in regions where malaria is prevalent, such as parts of tropical Africa. Scientists have concluded that the mutation persists in these regions because a person with one copy of the defective gene has the highest likelihood of survival (a person with two copies of the normal gene is likely to die of malaria, while a person with two copies of the mutated form is likely to die of sickle cell anemia). Thus, the mutation continues to be passed down from generation to generation.

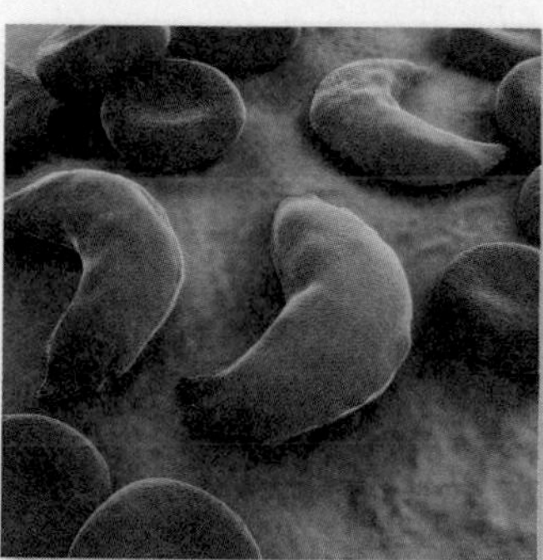

photomicrograph showing normal red blood cells (top left) *and sickle-shaped cells* (center)

Symbol **Si.** *Atomic number* 14. *See* **Periodic Table,** pages 254–255.

silicone (sĭl′ĭ-kōn′) Any of a class of chemical compounds consisting of long chains of alternating oxygen and silicon atoms, with two organic groups attached to each silicon atom. Silicones are used to make adhesives, lubricants, and synthetic rubber.

silk (sĭlk) **1.** A strong, flexible fiber composed of protein that is produced by certain insect larvae to form cocoons. The silk from a silkworm cocoon is composed of two long, continuous filaments that are stuck together with a gummy substance. Silk is used to make thread and fabric. **2.** A similar substance produced by spiders and used to make webs and other structures.

silkworm (sĭlk′wûrm′) Any of various caterpillars that produce silk cocoons, especially the larva of a moth native to Asia. The fiber of silkworm cocoons is the source of commercial silk.

sill (sĭl) A sheet of igneous rock formed when magma is squeezed between existing layers of rock.

silt (sĭlt) Small grains or particles of disintegrated rock, smaller than sand and larger than clay. Silt is often found at the bottom of bodies of water, such as lakes, where it accumulates slowly by settling through the water.

siltstone (sĭlt′stōn′) A fine-grained sedimentary rock consisting primarily of compacted and hardened silt. It varies in color from black or gray to brown or red. *See Table at* **rock.**

Silurian (sĭ-lo͝or′ē-ən) The third period of the Paleozoic Era, from about 444 to 416 million years ago, characterized by the appearance of

■ **sill**

jawed fish and the rise of the first land plants and invertebrate land animals. *See Chart at* **geologic time,** pages 146–147.

silver (sĭl′vər) A soft, shiny, white metallic element that is found in many ores, especially together with copper, lead, and zinc. It conducts heat and electricity better than any other metal. Silver is used in photography and in making electrical circuits and conductors. *Symbol* **Ag.** *Atomic number* 47. *See* **Periodic Table,** pages 254–255. *See Note at* **element.** ❖ An alloy of silver that contains up to 7.5 percent copper or another metal is called **sterling silver,** from which jewelry and silverware are made.

silver iodide A pale-yellow, odorless powder, AgI, that darkens when it is exposed to light. It is used in photography, as an antiseptic in medicine, and in cloud seeding.

silver nitrate A poisonous, clear, crystalline compound, $AgNO_3$, that darkens when exposed to light. It is used in photography and silver plating, and as an external antiseptic.

simple fraction (sĭm′pəl) A fraction in which both the numerator and denominator are whole numbers, such as $\frac{5}{7}$.

simple machine A simple device, such as a lever or pulley, that changes the magnitude or direction of an applied force.

sin Abbreviation of **sine.**

sine (sīn) The ratio of the length of the side opposite an acute angle in a right triangle to the length of the hypotenuse.

sinus (sī′nəs) A cavity or hollow space in a bone of the skull, especially one that connects with the nose.

sinusoidal projection (sī′nə-soid′l) A method of making a flat map of the Earth so that the relative areas of the landmasses are correct and the parallels and the prime meridian are straight lines, while the other meridians curve outward from the prime meridian. *Compare* **conic projection, homolosine projection, Mercator projection.**

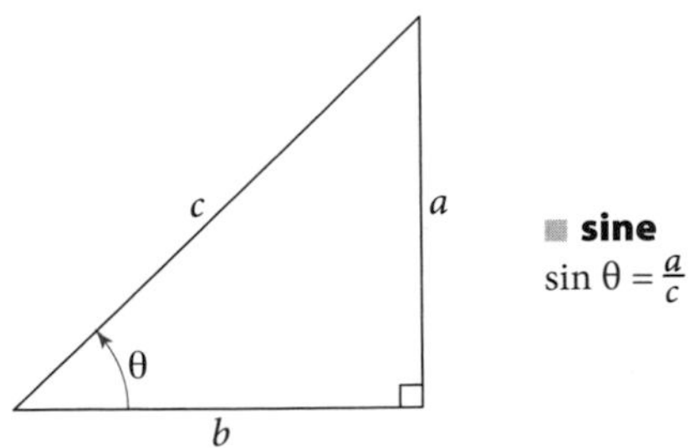

sine
$\sin\theta = \frac{a}{c}$

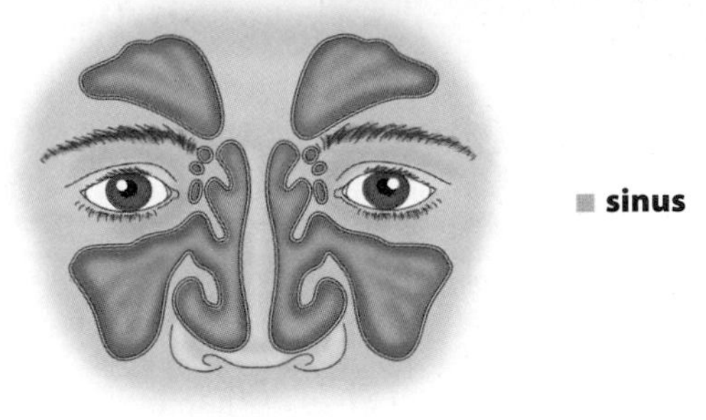

sinus

siphon (sī′fən) **1.** A tube that carries a liquid from a higher level up and over a barrier and then down to a lower level, with the flow maintained by gravity and atmospheric pressure as long as the tube remains filled. **2.** A tubular animal part, as of a clam, through which water is taken in or expelled.

Sirius (sĭr′ē-əs) The brightest star seen in the night sky. It is in the constellation Canis Major.

SI unit Any of the seven base units of measure in the International System of Units: the meter, the kilogram, the second, the ampere, the kelvin, the mole, and the candela. *See Table at* **measurement.**

skeleton (skĕl′ĭ-tn) **1.** The internal structure of vertebrate animals, usually composed of bone and cartilage, that supports the body, serves as a framework for the attachment of muscles, and protects the vital organs and associated structures. **2.** The hard protective covering or supporting structure of many invertebrate animals, such as crustaceans and insects. *See also* **endoskeleton, exoskeleton.** —*Adjective* **skeletal.**

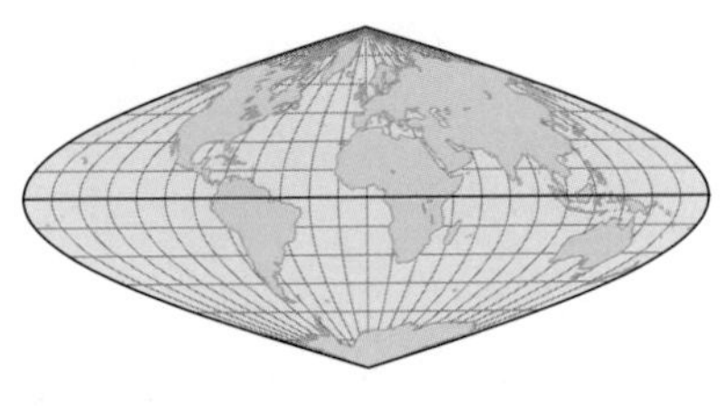

sinusoidal projection

A CLOSER LOOK

Skeleton

The human skeleton has 206 bones. It provides a stable framework for the attachment of hundreds of muscles, tendons, and ligaments. In addition, the bones of the skull and chest protect the brain and vital internal organs. The spinal column, or backbone, houses the delicate spinal cord, which transmits sensory and motor impulses between the limbs and the brain. Bones come together at flexible joints, which are acted on by a finely balanced system of muscles to produce coordinated movement.

Action of a muscle on a joint

The muscles of the skeleton often work in opposition to one another. For example, when the biceps—the muscle that bends the elbow—contracts, the triceps, which straightens it, must relax. (Similarly, for the triceps to straighten the elbow, the biceps must relax.)

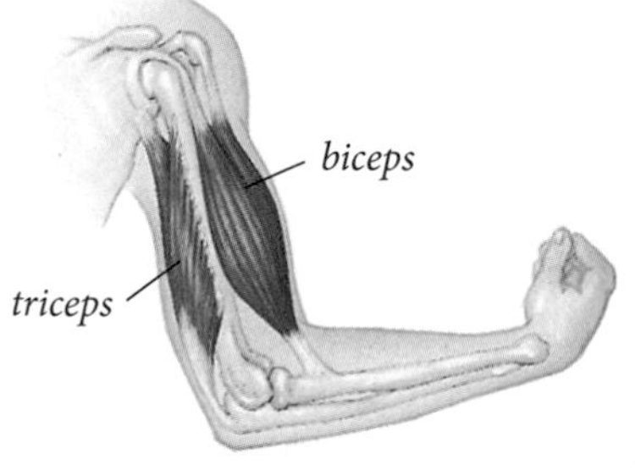

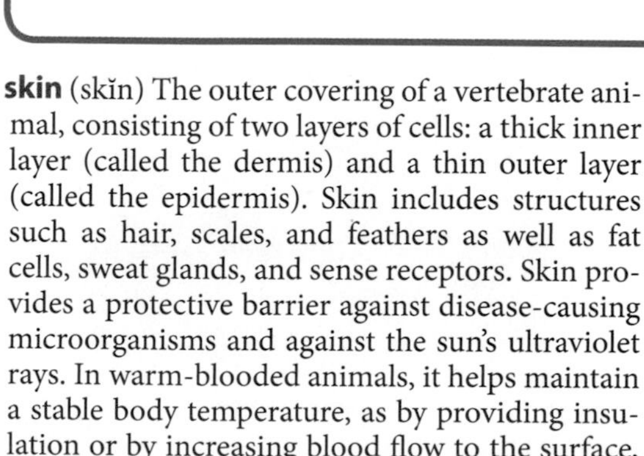

skin (skĭn) The outer covering of a vertebrate animal, consisting of two layers of cells: a thick inner layer (called the dermis) and a thin outer layer (called the epidermis). Skin includes structures such as hair, scales, and feathers as well as fat cells, sweat glands, and sense receptors. Skin provides a protective barrier against disease-causing microorganisms and against the sun's ultraviolet rays. In warm-blooded animals, it helps maintain a stable body temperature, as by providing insulation or by increasing blood flow to the surface,

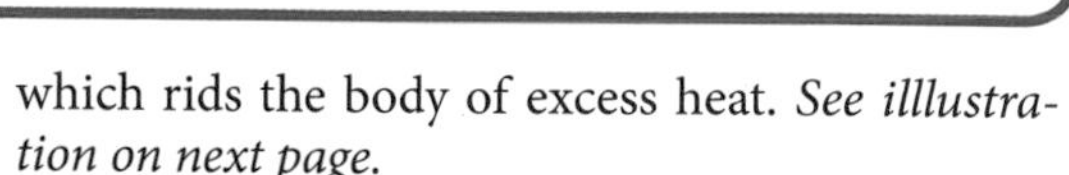

which rids the body of excess heat. *See illustration on next page.*

skull (skŭl) The framework of bone or cartilage in vertebrates that supports and protects the brain and the sense organs of the head. It includes the cranium and the mandible (jaw).

slate (slāt) A fine-grained metamorphic rock that forms when shale undergoes metamorphosis. Slate splits into thin layers with smooth surfaces. It ranges in color from gray to black or from red

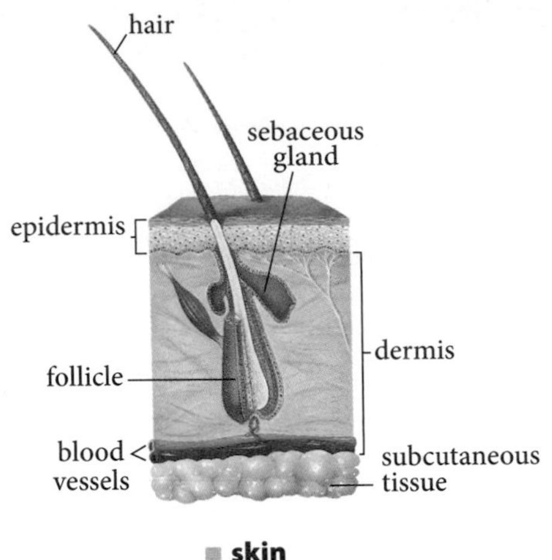

skin
cross section of human skin

to green, depending on the minerals contained in the shale from which it formed. *See Table at* **rock.**

sleep (slēp) A natural state of rest, occurring at regular intervals, in which the eyes usually close, the muscles relax, and responsiveness to external events decreases. Growth and repair of the tissues of the body are thought to occur during sleep, and energy is conserved and stored. In humans and some other animals, scientists have identified one phase of sleep (called REM sleep) as the phase in which dreams occur.

sleeping sickness (slē′pĭng) An often fatal disease that occurs in sub-Saharan Africa and causes fever and extreme sluggishness. It is caused by infection with protozoans that are spread by the bite of tsetse flies.

sleet (slēt) Water that falls to earth in the form of frozen or partially frozen raindrops.

slide (slīd) A thin, usually rectangular, glass plate on which something, such as a sample of rock or a microorganism, is placed for examination under a microscope.

slime (slīm) A slippery or sticky mucous substance secreted by certain animals, such as slugs or snails.

slime mold Any of various amoebalike organisms that exist in both unicellular and multicellular stages and are found on decaying plant matter. ❖ **Cellular slime molds** usually live as single cells that move about and feed on bacteria. When food becomes scarce, large numbers mass together to form a colony that develops into a single multicellular, stalked, spore-producing structure. ❖ **Plasmodial slime molds** exist as single cells or as a mass of protoplasm (called a plasmodium) that contains many nuclei within a single cell membrane. The slimy mass moves along ingesting bacteria and other food. When food grows scarce, the plasmodium stops moving and forms numerous multicellular, stalked, spore-producing structures that look similar to those produced by fungi.

slough (slŭf) *Noun* **1.** The dead outer skin shed by a reptile or an amphibian. — *Verb* **2.** To shed an outer layer of skin.

Sm The symbol for **samarium.**

small calorie (smôl) *See* **calorie** (sense 1).

small intestine The long, narrow, coiled section of the intestine that extends from the stomach to the beginning of the large intestine and in mammals is made up of the duodenum, jejunum, and ileum. Nutrients are absorbed into the bloodstream from the small intestine.

smallpox (smôl′pŏks′) A highly infectious and often fatal disease caused by a virus and characterized by fever, headache, and severe pimples that result in extensive scarring. Smallpox was once a dreaded killer of children and caused the deaths of millions of Native Americans after the arrival of European settlers in North and South America. Following a worldwide vaccination campaign, smallpox was declared eradicated in 1980, although samples have been preserved in laboratories in the United States and Russia. *See Note at* **vaccine.**

small solar system body Any of various celestial objects, such as asteroids and comets, that orbit the sun and are not classified as either planets or dwarf planets.

slime mold
spore-producing structures of a plasmodial slime mold

smelt (smĕlt) To melt ores in order to extract the metals they contain.

smilodon (smī′lə-dŏn′) *See* **saber-toothed tiger.**

smog (smŏg) **1.** A form of air pollution produced when sunlight reacts with hydrocarbons and nitrogen compounds released into the atmosphere, especially from automobile exhaust. Smog is common in many large cities, especially during hot, sunny weather. It appears as a brownish haze and can irritate the eyes and lungs. **2.** Fog that has become polluted with smoke, especially smoke from burning coal.

smoke (smōk) A mixture of gases, such as carbon dioxide and water vapor, and small particles of soot or other solids, produced by the burning of carbon-containing materials such as wood and coal.

smut (smŭt) Any of various plant diseases caused by parasitic fungi that form black, powdery masses of spores on the affected parts. Smut chiefly affects cereal grasses like corn and wheat.

Sn The symbol for **tin.**

snake (snāk) Any of numerous meat-eating reptiles having a long narrow body with no legs, a forked tongue used for detecting chemical signals, and no eyelids or external ears. A snake's jaws are flexible, allowing it to swallow prey larger than itself. Many snakes kill their prey with venom injected through sharp fangs.

snout (snout) The projecting nose, jaws, or front part of the head of an animal.

snow (snō) Crystals of ice that form from water vapor in the atmosphere and fall to earth.

soap (sōp) A substance used for cleaning, consisting of a mixture of sodium or potassium salts of naturally occurring fatty acids. Like detergents, soaps work by surrounding otherwise insoluble particles of grease or dirt with their molecules, making them soluble in water and allowing them to be washed away. Unlike detergents, soaps react with the minerals common in most water, forming an insoluble residue on fabrics and other surfaces. For this reason, soap is not as efficient a cleaner as most detergents. *Compare* **detergent.**

smut *on a corn plant*

soapstone (sōp′stōn′) A soft metamorphic rock composed mostly of the mineral talc.

social science (sō′shəl) Any of various academic disciplines dealing with human society or the relationships of individuals within society, including sociology, psychology, anthropology, economics, political science, and history.

sociobiology (sō′sē-ō-bī-ŏl′ə-jē) The study of the biological underpinnings of social behavior in humans and other animals, based on the theory that many social behaviors, such as altruism, are genetically based and have developed through the process of evolution.

sociology (sō′sē-ŏl′ə-jē) The scientific study of human social behavior and its origins, development, organizations, and institutions.

soda (sō′də) *See* **sodium carbonate.**

Soddy (sŏd′ē), **Frederick** 1877–1956. British chemist who was a pioneer in the study of radioactivity. With Ernest Rutherford, he explained the atomic disintegration of radioactive elements. Soddy also coined the word *isotope* to describe forms of an element that are chemically identical but have different atomic weights.

sodium (sō′dē-əm) A soft, lightweight, silvery-white metallic element that reacts violently with water. It is the most abundant alkali metal on Earth, occurring especially in common salt. Sodium is very easily shaped, and its compounds have many important uses in industry. Sodium ions are essential to numerous biological processes in animals. *Symbol* **Na.** *Atomic number* 11. *See* **Periodic Table,** pages 254–255.

sodium bicarbonate The chemical name for baking soda. Also called *bicarbonate of soda.*

sodium carbonate A white powdery compound, Na_2CO_3, used in making baking soda, sodium nitrate, glass, ceramics, detergents, and soap. Also called *soda.*

Did You Know...?

solar cell

How can light make electricity? By causing electrons to break free from their atoms. A *solar cell* has an upper layer of negatively charged silicon, with free-flowing electrons, and a lower layer of positively charged silicon, with atoms that are missing some electrons. A weak electric field is created at the surface where the two layers meet. When light penetrates the solar cell and reaches the positively charged layer, its energy is absorbed by some of the electrons, which break away from their atoms. The electric field pushes these electrons into the negative layer. Meanwhile, other electrons in the positive layer move into the spaces that the first electrons left behind. In the negatively charged silicon layer, the electrons pile up, increasing the electric charge. When the two layers of a solar cell are connected to a circuit, the electrons flow out of the negative layer, through the circuit, and back to the positive layer, producing an electric current. Many solar cells are connected together in solar panels that can be used to provide electricity for homes and businesses.

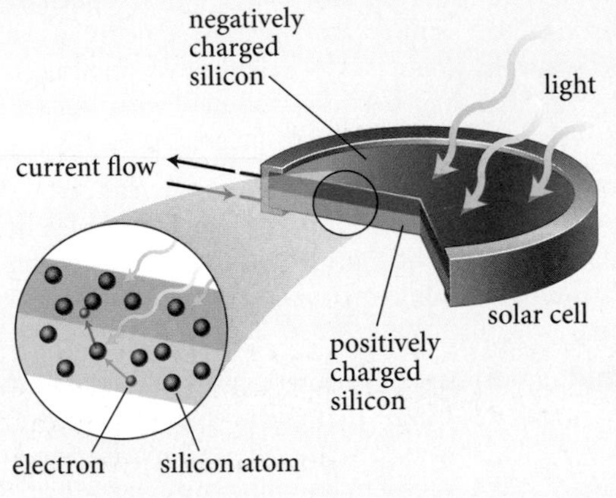

sodium chloride *See under* **salt.**

sodium fluoride A colorless, crystalline salt, NaF, used to fluoridate water and treat tooth decay. It is also used as an insecticide and a disinfectant.

sodium hydroxide A strongly alkaline compound, NaOH, used in making chemicals and soaps, in refining petroleum, and as a cleansing agent. In solution, it forms lye.

sodium nitrate A poisonous, white, crystalline compound, $NaNO_3$, used in solid rocket propellants, as a fertilizer, and in small amounts for curing meat.

soft palate (sôft) *See under* **palate.**

software (sôft′wâr′) The programs, programming languages, and data that direct the operations of a computer system. Word processing programs and Internet browsers are examples of software. *Compare* **hardware.**

soil (soil) The loose top layer of the Earth's surface, consisting of rock and mineral particles mixed with decayed organic matter (known as humus). Soil provides the support and nutrients that many plants need to grow.

solar (sō′lər) **1.** Relating to the sun: *solar radiation.* **2.** Using or operated by energy from the sun: *a solar heating system.* **3.** Relating to solar time: *a solar day.*

solar cell An electric cell that converts the energy of visible light, usually from the sun, into electrical energy. Solar cells are used as sources of electricity especially in remote locations and in satellites and space vehicles. Also called *photovoltaic cell.*

solar eclipse *See under* **eclipse.**

solar energy 1. The energy produced or radiated by the sun. **2.** Energy derived from the sun's radiation. Solar energy is used on Earth in various ways. It is used as a passive source of energy, for example, in the form of sunlight that comes through a window and heats up a room, or as an active source, as in the conversion of sunlight to electrical energy in solar cells.

solar flare A sudden release of magnetic energy on or near the surface of the sun, usually associated with sunspots and accompanied by bursts of electromagnetic radiation. Ultraviolet and x-ray radiation from solar flares often cause electromagnetic disturbances in the Earth's atmosphere.

solar system 1. *Often* **Solar System.** The sun

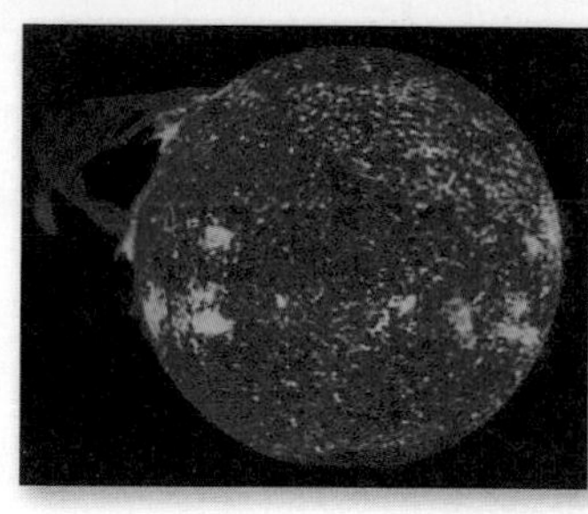

■ **solar flare**

together with the eight planets and their moons and all other celestial objects that orbit the sun, including asteroids and comets. *See more at* **nebular hypothesis.** *See Table,* pages 312–313. **2.** A system of planets or other celestial objects orbiting another star.

solar time Time based on the rotation of the Earth with respect to the sun. A solar day lasts from when the sun is directly overhead until the next time it is directly overhead. *Compare* **sidereal time.**

solar wind A stream of high-speed, charged atomic particles flowing outward from the sun's corona.

Did You Know...?

solar system

We usually think of our *solar system* as including just the sun and the eight planets. Sometimes we remember the moons that revolve around most of the planets. But in fact, the solar system contains billions of other objects as well. Several hundred thousand asteroids have been discovered, and there are countless bits of debris formed during collisions between larger bodies. These smaller particles often come near Earth—millions of meteors, most no bigger than a speck of dust, cross through our planet's atmosphere each day. Astronomers have also recorded more than a thousand comets passing through the inner part of the solar system. All of these objects travel around the sun at high speeds in paths called orbits. Some of these orbits, like those of the planets, are almost circular. Other orbits, like those of comets, are stretched out into long ellipses.

soldier (sōl′jər) A sterile or sexually immature ant or termite that has a large head and powerful jaws and defends the colony against attack. Ant soldiers are females, but termite soldiers can be either females or males.

solenoid (sō′lə-noid′) A coil of wire that acts as a magnet when an electric current passes through it.

solid (sŏl′ĭd) **1.** *Physics* One of the basic forms of matter, composed of atoms or molecules that are closely spaced and tightly bound to one another. Unlike gases and liquids, a solid has a fixed shape, and unlike gases, a solid also has a fixed volume. **2.** *Mathematics* A geometric figure that has three dimensions.

solid solution A uniform mixture of substances in solid form. Solid solutions consist of two or more types of atoms or molecules in a single crystal lattice structure, as in many metal alloys. For example, most of the steel used in construction is a solid solution of iron and carbon. The carbon atoms fit neatly into the iron crystal lattice and increase the strength of the structure.

solid-state drive A device that uses transistors to store data and that allows data to be erased and rewritten many times. Solid-state drives can be used in place of hard drives.

solid-state physics The branch of physics that specializes in the study of solids, especially in the electric and magnetic properties of solid crystalline materials, such as semiconductors.

solstice (sŏl′stĭs, sōl′stĭs) **1.** Either of the two moments of the year when the sun is farthest north or south of the celestial equator. In the Northern Hemisphere, the summer solstice occurs on or about June 21, and the winter solstice occurs on or about December 21. **2.** Either of the two points on the celestial sphere where the apparent path of the sun (known as the ecliptic) reaches its greatest distance from the celestial equator. *Compare* **equinox.**

soluble (sŏl′yə-bəl) Capable of being dissolved. Salt, for example, is soluble in water.

solute (sŏl′yo͞ot) A substance that is dissolved in another substance, forming a solution.

solution (sə-lo͞o′shən) **1.** *Chemistry* A mixture in which particles of one or more substances are distributed uniformly throughout another

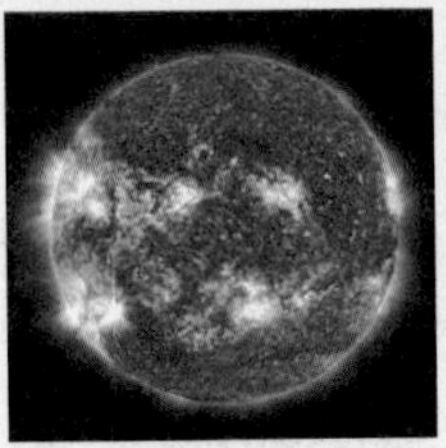
SUN

MERCURY

VENUS

EARTH

MARS

PHYSICAL PROPERTIES OF THE PLANETS

Listed below are the planets that have been identified in our solar system. The **orbital period** is the amount of time it takes for a planet to make one complete revolution around the sun. This is usually measured in relation to the fixed stars. The orbital period of Earth is exactly one year. The **rotational period** is the amount of time it takes for a body to make one complete rotation about its own axis, usually also measured relative to the stars. Earth rotates about its axis in about one day. Earth rotates from west to east, coun-

PLANET	DIAMETER (AT EQUATOR)		MASS	ORBITAL PERIOD
	miles	*kilometers*	*× 10^{24} kilograms*	*days*
Mercury	3,032	4,879	0.33	87.97
Venus	7,521	12,104	4.87	224.70
Earth	7,926	12,756	5.97	365.26
Mars	4,220	6,792	0.64	686.98
Jupiter	88,846	142,984	1,898.60	4,332.59
Saturn	74,897	120,536	568.46	10,759.22
Uranus	31,763	51,118	86.83	30,685.40
Neptune	30,775	49,528	102.43	60,189.00

PHYSICAL PROPERTIES OF THE SUN

The sun is hottest at its core, with a temperature of more than 28 million degrees Fahrenheit (15 million degrees Celsius). On its surface the sun is much cooler, only about 10,000 degrees Fahrenheit (6,000 degrees Celsius). Further out, in the corona, an irregular layer of gas that surrounds the sun, the temperature rises again (to more than 2 million degrees Fahrenheit, or 1 million degrees Celsius). The sun is

	DIAMETER		MASS
	miles	*kilometers*	*× 10^{24} kilograms*
Sun	865,000	1,392,000	1,989,100

JUPITER

SATURN

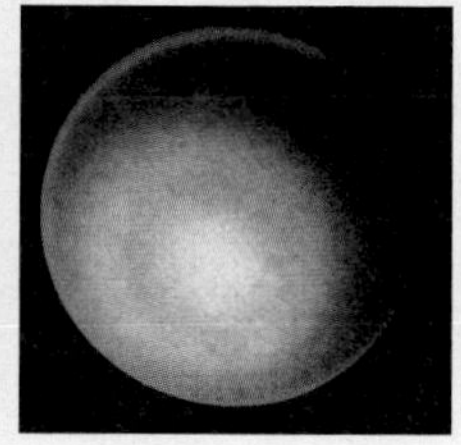

URANUS

NEPTUNE

terclockwise when seen from above the North Pole. If a planet rotates about its axis clockwise from east to west (the manner opposite to that of Earth), the rotation is called **retrograde** and a minus sign (–) appears in front of the planet's rotational period. Pluto was considered to be a planet until 2006, when the International Astronomical Union created the category of *dwarf planet*. Pluto was placed in that category along with other celestial objects such as the asteroid Ceres.

ROTATIONAL PERIOD	AVERAGE SURFACE TEMPERATURE		AVERAGE DISTANCE FROM SUN (*in millions*)	
days	*degrees Fahrenheit*	*degrees Celsius*	*miles*	*kilometers*
58.65	333	167	36.0	57.9
–243.02	867	464	67.2	108.2
0.997	59	15	93.0	149.6
1.03	–81	–63	141.6	227.9
0.41	–162	–108	483.8	778.6
0.44	–218	–139	890.8	1,433.5
–0.72	–323	–197	1,784.9	2,872.5
0.67	–330	–201	2,793.1	4,495.1

more than 330,000 times more massive than Earth and contains more than 99.8 percent of the mass of the entire solar system. Because the sun is not a solid body like Earth, its rotational period is not the same everywhere on its surface. Its outer layers rotate at different rates in different places, taking a longer time at the poles. The sun's core, on the other hand, does rotate as a solid body.

ROTATIONAL PERIOD (OUTER LAYERS)		TEMPERATURE		
	days		*degrees Fahrenheit*	*degrees Celsius*
Equator:	26.8	*Surface:*	9,941	5,505
Poles:	36	*Core:*	28,278,500	15,710,000

Did You Know...?

solution

A *solution* is a homogeneous mixture of two substances—that is, it has the same distribution of particles throughout. Technically speaking, a solution consists of a mixture of one or more *solutes* dissolved in a *solvent*. The particles of solute and solvent are molecules or ions, with one or more solvent molecules bound to each solute particle. Both the solvent and the solute can be solid, liquid, or gas, but the solvent is usually liquid. We use solutions every day without realizing it. The ammonia with which we clean windows and floors is a solution of ammonia gas in water. The vinegar we sometimes put on salads is a solution of acetic acid (a liquid) and water. And seawater is a solution of sodium chloride (a solid) and water. Other common solutions are gasoline and metal alloys, including the solution of copper and nickel that is found in dimes, nickels, and quarters.

substance, so that the mixture is homogeneous at the molecular or ionic level. The particles in a solution are smaller than those in either a colloid or a suspension. *Compare* **colloid, suspension.** **2.** *Mathematics* A value or values which, when substituted for a variable in an equation, make the equation true. For example, the solutions to the equation $x^2 = 4$ are 2 and −2.

solvent (sŏl′vənt) A substance that can dissolve another substance, or in which another substance is dissolved, forming a solution.

somatic (sō-măt′ĭk) Relating to the body. ❖ The cells of the body with the exception of the sex cells (gametes) are known as **somatic cells.**

Somerville (sŭm′ər-vĭl′), **Mary Fairfax Greig** 1780–1872. British astronomer and mathematician whose writings, particularly on astronomy, helped make science understandable to the general public.

Mary Somerville

sonar (sō′när′) **1.** A method of detecting and determining an object's location by sending out sound waves and then analyzing the waves that are reflected back from the object. Sonar is most often used to detect underwater objects, such as submarines or schools of fish. Because the speed of sound in water is constant, the time it takes for a transmitted signal to reach an object and return can be used to calculate the object's distance. **2.** The equipment used in doing this.

sonic barrier (sŏn′ĭk) *See* **sound barrier.**

sonic boom The shock wave of compressed air caused by an aircraft traveling faster than the

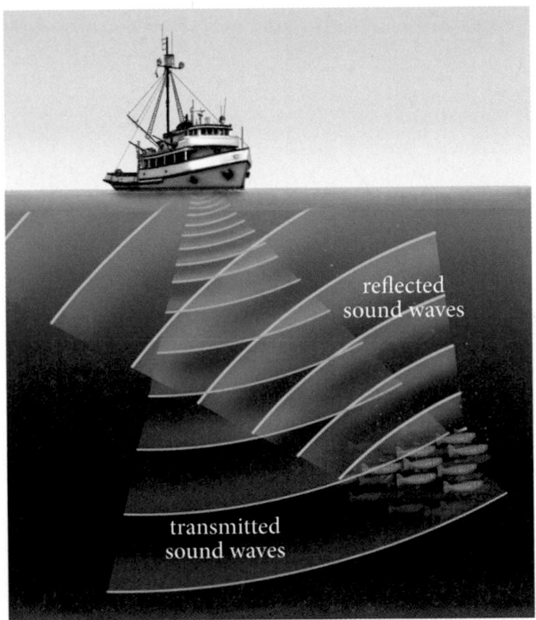

sonar

Sonar equipment on a ship emits sound waves underwater. The sound waves reflect off a school of fish and return to the ship, where the sonar equipment calculates how far away the fish are.

speed of sound. It is often audible as a loud, explosive sound, and it sometimes causes damage to structures on the ground.

soot (so͝ot) A black, powdery compound consisting mainly of carbon. Soot forms through the incomplete combustion of wood, coal, oil, or other materials.

sorption (sôrp′shən) The taking up and holding of one substance by another. Sorption is used especially as a general term for absorption and adsorption.

sound[1] (sound) A longitudinal wave that originates as the vibration of a medium (such as a person's vocal cords or a guitar string) and travels through gases, liquids, and elastic solids as variations of pressure and density. The loudness of a sound perceived by the ear is determined by the amplitude of the sound wave and is measured

Did You Know...?

sound[1]

The form of energy called *sound* is produced when matter moves or vibrates. The vibrations are transferred to another medium, usually the air, and travel through the medium as sound waves. You hear a sound when its vibrations reach your eardrum and cause it to vibrate. The pitch of a sound is directly related to the frequency of its waves' vibrations. Humans can hear sounds with frequencies of 20 to 20,000 hertz. (One hertz is equal to one vibration per second.) Other animals can detect sounds that are inaudible to us. Bats and dolphins, for instance, can hear high-frequency sounds of over 100,000 hertz, while elephants communicate with very low-frequency sounds. The loudness, or intensity, of sound is measured in decibels. For each increase of 10 decibels, the sound wave has 10 times as much energy—a sound of 20 decibels is twice as loud as one of 10 decibels, but it has 10 times as much energy. A moderate conversation has a loudness of about 60 decibels. Prolonged exposure to levels above 85 decibels, the sound of a lawnmower, can lead to hearing loss.

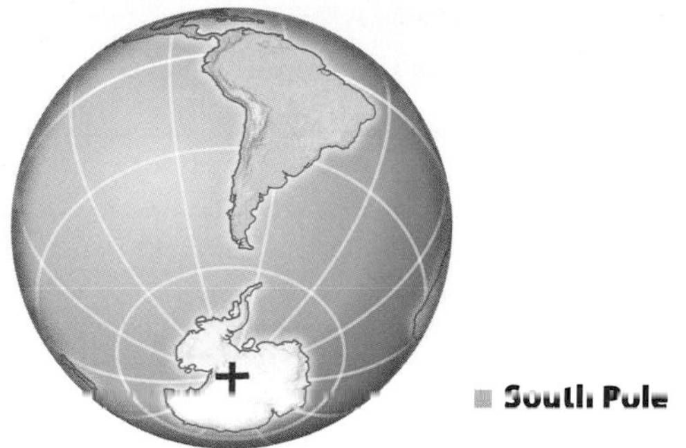

South Pole

in decibels, while the pitch is determined by its frequency and is measured in hertz. *See Note at* **ultrasound.**

sound[2] **1.** A long body of water, wider than a strait, that connects larger bodies of water. **2.** A long, wide inlet of the ocean, often parallel to the coast. Long Island Sound, between Long Island and the coast of New England, is an example.

sound barrier The sudden, sharp increase in drag experienced by aircraft approaching the speed of sound. Also called *sonic barrier.*

Southern Cross (sŭ*th*′ərn) A constellation in the polar region of the Southern Hemisphere near Centaurus.

Southern Hemisphere 1. The half of the Earth south of the equator. **2.** *Astronomy* The half of the celestial sphere south of the celestial equator.

southern lights *See* **aurora australis.**

south pole The pole of a magnet that tends to point south.

South Pole The southern end of the Earth's axis of rotation, a point in Antarctica.

space (spās) **1.** A set of points that satisfies some set of geometric rules: *a space of five dimensions.* **2.** The familiar three-dimensional region or field of everyday experience. **3a.** The expanse in which the solar system, stars, and galaxies exist; the universe. **b.** The part of this expanse beyond the Earth's atmosphere.

space-time A four-dimensional frame of reference, consisting of three dimensions of space (for example, length, width, and height) and one dimension of time. Space-time is used in relativity theory for identifying the location and timing of objects and events. According to the theory of

Did You Know...?

space-time

In Einstein's theory of relativity, space and time are so closely linked that physicists developed the concept of *space-time* for describing the position and time of an event. An object's location in space is indicated by three dimensions, which you can think of as length, width, and height, and a fourth dimension indicates the time at which the object is in that location. Because motion affects measurement, the space and time dimensions cannot be separated. An essential feature of space-time is that it is curved by any mass located within it. You can roughly visualize this curved space by imagining a bowling ball placed on a trampoline, causing a depression in its surface. If an ant tried to walk straight across the trampoline, it would end up taking a curved path because of the curved surface of the trampoline. In the same way, an apple that detaches from a branch accelerates toward the Earth because of the way it is affected by the curving of space-time created by the Earth's mass. This acceleration is what we call gravity. Einstein predicted that the curvature of space-time would affect even light, which has no mass. This prediction was confirmed by a famous observation in 1919 during a solar eclipse, when astronomers showed that the light coming from distant stars was bent when it passed near the sun, by the exact amount predicted.

general relativity, space-time is curved by the presence of mass. *See more at* **relativity.**

spadix (spā′dĭks) A fleshy spike bearing tiny flowers, often surrounded by a part (the spathe) resembling a leaf or petal, as in the jack-in-the-pulpit.

spathe (spā*th*) A plant part that resembles a leaf or petal and surrounds a fleshy flower spike (the spadix), as in the jack-in-the-pulpit.

spawn (spôn) *Noun* **1.** Eggs that are released into water, including those of fish, amphibians, and most mollusks. **2.** Offspring produced in large numbers. — *Verb* **3.** To lay eggs; produce spawn.

speciation (spē′shē-ā′shən) The formation of new biological species through the process of evolution. All existing species are thought to have arisen from the speciation of earlier organisms.

species (spē′shēz, spē′sēz) A taxonomic category of closely related organisms that are very similar to each other and are usually capable of producing fertile offspring when they breed with each other. The species is the fundamental category of taxonomic classification, ranking below a genus. Every species has a unique scientific name with two parts, such as *Homo sapiens. See Table at* **taxonomy.**

specific gravity (spĭ-sĭf′ĭk) **1.** An amount equal to the density of a solid or liquid divided by the density of an equal volume of water that is at a temperature of 4°C (about 39°F). **2.** An amount equal to the density of a gas divided by the density of an equal volume of air or hydrogen that is at a specified temperature and pressure.

specific heat The amount of heat required to raise the temperature of a unit mass of a substance by one degree Celsius. Specific heat is usually measured in joules per kilogram per degree Celsius. Different substances have different specific heats because they are composed of molecules that have different masses. The greater the specific heat of a substance, the more energy is needed to raise the temperature of a certain amount of the substance by a given number of degrees.

spectrograph (spĕk′trə-grăf′) A spectroscope fitted with a camera or other device to record the spectrum produced. ❖ The image of a spectrum produced by a spectrograph is called a **spectrogram** (spĕk′trə-grăm′).

spectrometer (spĕk-trŏm′ĭ-tər) A spectroscope equipped with devices for measuring the wavelengths of the radiation detected by it. ❖ The technique of using a spectrometer to analyze spectra is called **spectrometry** (spĕk-trŏm′ĭ-trē).

spectroscope (spĕk′trə-skōp′) An instrument used to split up electromagnetic radiation into a spectrum of different wavelengths that can then be analyzed. In a simple spectroscope, light passes through a narrow slit and then through a prism that spreads it out into a spectrum. ❖ The technique of using a spectroscope to analyze spectra is called **spectroscopy** (spĕk-trŏs′kə-pē). Spectroscopy is used especially in astronomy to determine the chemical composition and temperature of stars and other celestial objects.

spectrum (spĕk′trəm) *Plural* **spectra** (spĕk′trə) *or* **spectrums 1.** The entire range of values of a property, arranged in order of magnitude. For example, the electromagnetic spectrum consists of all wavelengths of electromagnetic radiation, from gamma rays (with the shortest wavelengths) to radio waves (with the longest wavelengths). **2.** A particular subset of such values. For example, when white light passes through a prism, it is spread out into a spectrum (a small portion of the entire electromagnetic spectrum) that we see as a range of colors from red (with the shortest wavelengths) through orange, yellow, green, blue, indigo, and violet (with the longest wavelengths).

speed (spēd) The ratio of the distance an object moves (regardless of direction) to the time taken to move that distance. *See Note at* **velocity.**

speleology (spē′lē-ŏl′ə-jē) The exploration and scientific study of caves.

sperm (spûrm) **1.** In male animals, the sex cell whose nucleus is capable of fusing with the nucleus of an egg cell to form a new organism; a spermatozoon. A sperm has half as many chromosomes as the other cells of the body and moves to unite with the egg. **2.** In plants and most algae, the sex cell whose nucleus is capable of fusing with the nucleus of a female reproductive cell to form a new organism. A sperm has half as many chromosomes as the other cells of the organism and moves to unite with the egg. In seed plants, the sperm are contained within the pollen grains.

spermaceti (spûr′mə-sē′tē) A white, waxy substance obtained from the head of the sperm whale and formerly used to make candles, ointments, and cosmetics.

spermatophyte (spər-măt′ə-fīt′) A plant that produces seeds, such as a conifer or flowering plant.

spermatozoon (spər-măt′ə-zō′ŏn′) *Plural* **spermatozoa** A sperm cell of an animal.

Sperry (spĕr′ē), **Roger Wolcott** 1913–1994. American neurobiologist who established that the right and left hemispheres of the brain each control specific functions.

sphagnum (sfăg′nəm) Any of various mosses that grow in bogs and decompose to form a type of peat.

sphere (sfîr) A three-dimensional geometric surface having all of its points the same distance from a given point.

spheroid (sfîr′oid′) A three-dimensional geometric surface generated by rotating an ellipse on or about one of its axes.

spider (spī′dər) Any of numerous small arachnids having fangs that produce venom and spinnerets that spin the silk that is used to make webs for trapping insects. Unlike mites and ticks, spiders have a constriction between the cephalothorax and abdomen.

spike (spīk) **1.** An ear of grain, such as wheat. **2.** A long cluster of flowers lacking or nearly lacking stalks, as in the gladiolus.

spina bifida (spī′nə bĭf′ĭ-də) A congenital defect in which the spinal column is not fully closed, causing part of the spinal cord to bulge out. Spina bifida often results in damage to the spinal cord.

spinal canal (spī′nəl) The passage formed by successive openings in the bones of the spinal column, containing the spinal cord and the membranes that enclose it.

spinal column The series of vertebrae extending from the base of the skull to the coccyx (tailbone) that forms the supporting axis of the body in vertebrate animals. It encloses and protects the spinal cord and provides a stable attachment for the muscles of the trunk. Also called *backbone, spine, vertebral column.*

spinal cord The part of the central nervous sys-

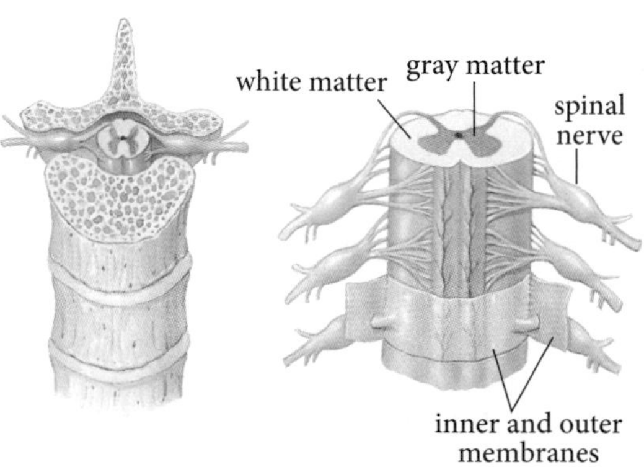

spinal cord
left: *section of vertebral column showing the spinal cord within the column*
right: *segment of spinal cord with nerve fibers arising from it*

tem that extends from the brain along the length of the spinal canal, branching to form smaller nerves that convey impulses to and from the tissues of the body.

spindle (spĭn′dl) A network of cell fibers that forms during cell division. Chromosomes attach to the spindle fibers in the center of the cell and then are pulled to opposite ends as the cell divides. *See more at* **meiosis, mitosis.**

spine (spīn) **1.** *See* **spinal column. 2.** A sharp-pointed projection on an animal, such as a sea urchin. **3.** A sharp-pointed projection on a plant, especially one derived from a leaf, as on a cactus. *See Note at* **cactus.**

spinneret (spĭn′ə-rĕt′) One of the small organs from which a spider or silk-producing insect larva secretes sticky fluid that dries into the silk used to spin a web or cocoon.

spinosaurus (spī′nō-sôr′əs) A very large meat-eating dinosaur of the Cretaceous Period, having a long narrow snout and long spines on the back that may have formed a sail-like structure.

spiracle (spĭr′ə-kəl, spī′rə-kəl) An opening through which certain animals breathe, such as the blowhole of a whale or one of the openings in the exoskeleton of an insect.

spirillum (spī-rĭl′əm) *Plural* **spirilla** Any of various bacteria that are shaped like a spiral.

spirochete (spī′rə-kēt′) Any of a group of spiral-shaped bacteria that have a long, coiled form. Lyme disease, syphilis, and several other diseases are caused by spirochetes.

spirogyra (spī′rə-jī′rə) Any of various freshwater green algae having spiral-shaped bands of chloroplasts.

spleen (splēn) An organ in vertebrate animals that in humans is located on the left side near the stomach. Mainly composed of lymphatic tissue and blood vessels, the spleen filters the blood, stores red blood cells, destroys old red blood cells, and produces white blood cells called lymphocytes.

splice (splīs) To join together genes or gene fragments or to insert them into a cell or other structure, such as a virus. In genetic engineering, scientists splice together genetic material to produce new genes or to alter a genetic structure.

sponge (spŭnj) **1.** Any of numerous invertebrate animals that live chiefly in the ocean, where they attach to underwater surfaces and often form colonies. Sponges do not have organs or specialized tissues. They filter food particles out of water by drawing the water in through pores in their bodies and releasing it through a larger opening. Also called *poriferan.* **2.** The soft, porous, absorbent skeleton of certain of these animals, used for bathing, cleaning, and other purposes.

spongy parenchyma (spŭn′jē) A leaf tissue consisting of loosely arranged, irregularly shaped cells that have chloroplasts. The spongy parenchyma has many spaces between cells that facilitate the circulation of air and the exchange of gases. It lies just below the palisade layer. Also called *spongy mesophyll. See more at* **photosynthesis.**

spontaneous combustion (spŏn-tā′nē-əs) The bursting into flame of organic matter, such as a pile of oily rags or damp hay, as a result of heat generated by slow oxidation.

spontaneous generation The supposed development of living organisms from nonliving matter, as maggots from rotting meat or bacteria from broth. The theory of spontaneous generation was discredited by the late 1800s.

sporangium (spə-răn′jē-əm) *Plural* **sporangia** A cell or structure in which reproductive spores are produced. Ferns, fungi, mosses, and algae release spores from sporangia.

spore (spôr) **1.** A usually one-celled reproductive body that can grow into a new organism

sponge

Sponges exhibit a variety of growth forms, including vase-shaped (left) *and tubular* (right).

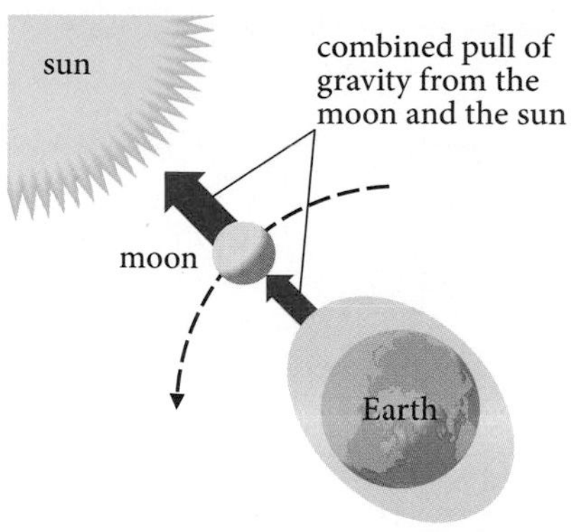

spring tide
Spring tides occur when the sun and the moon are directly in line with the Earth.

without uniting with another cell. Fungi, algae, non-seed-bearing plants such as mosses, and certain protozoans produce spores. **2.** A similar one-celled body in seed plants that develops into either the embryo sac or a pollen grain. **3.** A rounded, inactive form that certain bacteria assume under conditions of extreme temperature, dryness, or lack of food. The bacterium develops a waterproof cell wall that protects it from being dried out or damaged.

sporophyte (spôr′ə-fīt′) In plants and most algae, the phase or generation that produces spores. The sporophyte is diploid (each cell has two sets of chromosomes). The spores produced by the sporophyte develop into the gametophyte, which in turn produces sex cells (gametes) that unite to form the sporophyte. In seed plants (flowering plants and gymnosperms) and ferns, the main plant form is the sporophyte. In mosses and other nonvascular plants, the sporophyte is often a small stalked structure that grows from the gametophyte, which is the main plant form. *Compare* **gametophyte.**

spreading zone (sprĕd′ĭng) *See* **divergent plate boundary.**

spring (sprĭng) **1.** A device, such as a coil of wire, that returns to its original shape after being compressed or stretched. Because of their ability to return to their original shape, springs are used to store energy, as in mechanical clocks, and to absorb or lessen energy, as in the suspension system of vehicles. **2.** A small stream of water flowing naturally from the earth.

spring tide A tide in which the difference between high and low tide is the greatest. Spring tides occur when the moon is either new or full, and the sun, the moon, and the Earth are aligned. At these times, the effects of the gravitational pulls of the sun and the moon on the Earth's water reinforce each other. *Compare* **neap tide.** *See more at* **tide.**

spruce (spro͞os) Any of various evergreen trees having short needles, drooping cones, and soft wood often used for paper pulp. Spruces are found chiefly in cool or high altitude regions of the Northern Hemisphere.

squall (skwôl) A brief, sudden, violent windstorm, often accompanied by rain or snow.

square (skwâr) *Noun* **1.** A rectangle having four equal sides. **2.** The product that results when a number or quantity is multiplied by itself. The square of 8, for example, is 64. —*Adjective* **3.** Relating to, being, or using units that express the measure of area: *square miles.* —*Verb* **4.** To multiply a number, quantity, or expression by itself.

square root A number that, when squared, yields a given number. For example, since $5 \times 5 = 25$, the square root of 25 (written $\sqrt{25}$) is 5.

Sr The symbol for **strontium.**

stable (stā′bəl) **1.** Not likely to break down by radioactive decay into a nucleus or atomic particle with less mass. For example, the most common isotope of carbon, carbon-12, is stable. **2.** Relating to a substance that does not easily decompose or change into other compounds or into elements. Water is an example of a stable compound. **3.** Relating to an atom or chemical element that is unlikely to share electrons with another atom or element; unreactive.

stainless steel (stān′lĭs) Any of various steel alloys that are resistant to rusting and corrosion because they contain chromium and nickel.

stalactite (stə-lăk′tīt′) A cylindrical or conical mineral deposit projecting downward from the roof of a cave or cavern, formed by dripping water saturated with minerals. Stalactites form gradually as the minerals precipitate out of the saturated water. They usually consist of calcite, but can also consist of other minerals.

stalagmite (stə-lăg′mīt′) A cylindrical or coni-

USAGE

stalactite/stalagmite

If you find it hard to remember the difference between stalagmites and stalactites, you're not alone. Both words refer to mineral deposits in caves. The source of both words is the Greek word *stalassein,* which means "to drip." This is appropriate, since both kinds of deposit are formed by the dripping of mineral-rich water. The difference is in their orientation: a *stalactite* points down, and a *stalagmite* points up. If you get confused about which is which, try remembering that stala**c**tites hang from the **c**eiling of a cave, while stala**g**mites rise up from the **g**round.

cal mineral deposit, similar to a stalactite, but built up from the floor of a cave or cavern.

stalk (stôk) **1a.** The main stem of a plant. **b.** A slender structure that supports a plant part, such as a flower or leaf. **2.** A slender supporting or connecting part of an animal, such as the eyestalk of a lobster.

stamen (stā′mən) The male reproductive organ of a flower, usually consisting of a slender stalk (the filament) with a pollen-bearing anther at its tip. *See more at* **flower.**

staminate (stā′mə-nĭt) Having stamens but no pistils. Male flowers are staminate.

standard time (stăn′dərd) The time in any of the 24 time zones into which the Earth's surface is divided, usually the mean solar time at the central meridian of the given zone. In the continental United States, there are four standard time zones: Eastern, using the 75th meridian; Central, using the 90th meridian; Mountain, using the 105th meridian; and Pacific, using the 120th meridian. *See more at* **time zone.**

standing wave (stăn′dĭng) A wave that appears not to travel but rather to vibrate in place. A standing wave occurs when two identical waves travel in opposite directions, forming nodes (points were no vibration occurs) and antinodes (points where the maximum amount of vibration occurs). Standing waves may be transverse waves, like those on a guitar string, or longitudinal waves, like sound waves in a flute. Also called *stationary wave.*

stalactite and stalagmite

stannic (stăn′ĭk) Containing tin, especially tin with a valence of 4.

stannous (stăn′əs) Containing tin, especially tin with a valence of 2.

stapes (stā′pēz) The innermost of the three small bones, called ossicles, of the middle ear. The stapes is also called the stirrup.

staphylococcus (stăf′ə-lō-kŏk′əs) *Plural* **staphylococci** (stăf′ə-lō-kŏk′sī, stăf′ə-lō-kŏk′ī) Any of various bacteria that are normally found on the skin and mucous membranes of warm-blooded animals. One kind of staphylococcus can cause infections in humans, especially in wounds. ❖ One strain of staphylococcus, called **MRSA,** has become resistant to many antibiotics. MRSA causes serious infections and can spread easily in hospitals. It stands for methicillin-resistant *Staphylococcus aureus.*

star (stär) A celestial object that generates light and other radiant energy and consists of a mass of gas held together by its own gravity. Nuclear fusion in the core of a star is the source of its energy. The stars that we see from Earth in the night sky appear as twinkling points of light, some of which are binary stars or multiple stars.

A CLOSER LOOK

Star

A star is a giant sphere of gas that produces its own light by making its own energy. It generates this energy through nuclear fusion in its core, using as fuel the elements that make it up. Fusion in a star combines atoms of lighter elements, such as hydrogen, into different, heavier elements, such as helium. A massive star can burn its fuel into elements as heavy as iron. Nuclear fusion begins when a star is fully formed out of a nebula and ends when a smaller star burns out and becomes a white dwarf or when a massive star's iron core collapses in a supernova. Because a star's composition changes as it burns its fuel, it goes through a series of stages during the course of its life, which may be hundreds of millions or billions of years long.

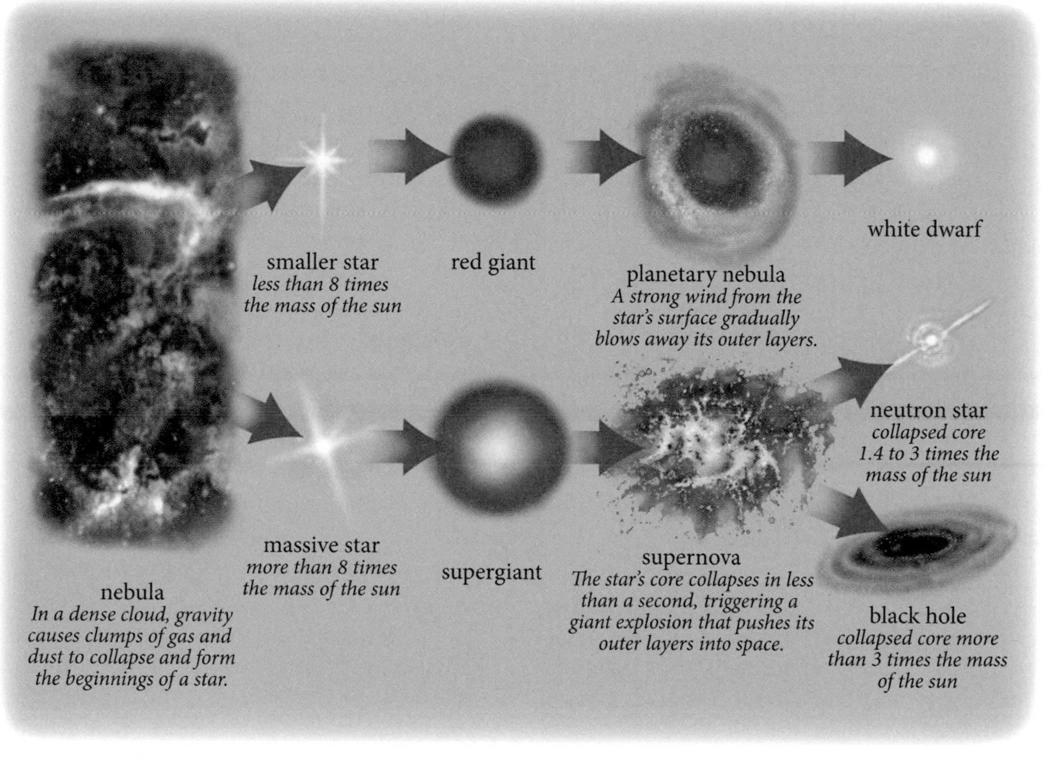

starburst (stär′bûrst′) An unusually rapid and intense burst of star formation in a galaxy. ❖ In a **starburst galaxy,** thousands of stars may form per year, a rate tens to hundreds of times greater than in an ordinary galaxy. The resulting stars are massive but short-lived.

starch (stärch) A carbohydrate that is the chief form of stored energy in plants, especially wheat, corn, rice, and potatoes. Starch is a kind of polysaccharide and forms a white, tasteless powder when purified. It is an important source of nutrition for humans and many other animals and is also used to stiffen fabrics and in making adhesives and paper.

starfish (stär′fĭsh′) Any of various invertebrate sea animals having a star-shaped body usually with five arms. The arms have rows of little suckers on the undersides, called tube feet, with which the animal moves around and grasps prey. Starfish are echinoderms.

state of matter (stāt) One of the principal conditions in which matter exists, depending on temperature and pressure. Matter is traditionally divided into three basic states: solid, liquid, and gas. Ice, liquid water, and steam, for example, are three states of matter of the same substance. Plasma, which is found in stars, is often considered a fourth state of matter.

static (stăt′ĭk) *Adjective* **1.** Having no motion; being at rest. *Compare* **dynamic. 2.** Relating to or producing static electricity. —*Noun* **3.** Distortion or interruption of a broadcast signal, such as crackling in a receiver or specks on a television screen, produced when static electricity or electricity in the atmosphere disturbs signal reception.

static electricity 1. Electric charge that accumulates on an object rather than flowing through it as a current. Static electricity forms especially when two objects that are not good electrical conductors are rubbed together, so that electrons from one of the objects rub off onto the other. This happens, for example, when you comb your hair or take off a sweater. *See Note at* **charge. 2.** An electric discharge, such as lightning, resulting from the accumulation of such a charge.

statics (stăt′ĭks) The branch of physics that deals with bodies that are at rest or in steady motion and with the forces acting on them, which are in equilibrium (because opposing forces balance each other).

stationary wave (stā′shə-nĕr′ē) *See* **standing wave.**

statistics (stə-tĭs′tĭks) **1.** *Used with a singular verb.* The branch of mathematics that deals with the collection, organization, analysis, and interpretation of numerical data. Statistics is especially useful in drawing general conclusions about a set of data from a sample of it. **2.** *Used with a plural verb.* Numerical data used in drawing general conclusions from a sample of it.

statute mile (stăch′o͞ot) *See* **mile** (sense 1).

STD Abbreviation of **sexually transmitted disease.**

steady state (stĕd′ē) A stable condition that does not change over time or in which any one change is continually balanced by another.

steady state universe A model of the universe in which the ratio of matter to volume always remains the same. Because the universe is expanding, this model requires the continuous creation of matter to maintain a constant density. This model was largely abandoned in favor of the Big Bang theory after scientists discovered microwave radiation that permeates cosmic space and is thought to be a remnant of the Big Bang. *Compare* **Big Bang.**

steam (stēm) **1.** Water in its gaseous state when it is at a temperature equal to or above its boiling point (100°C, or 212°F, at sea level). **2.** In informal usage, the mist that forms when hot water vapor cools and condenses into tiny droplets, as on a bathroom mirror.

steam engine An engine in which the energy of hot steam is converted into mechanical power, especially an engine in which the steam expands in a closed cylinder and drives a piston.

steel (stēl) Any of various hard, strong, and flexible alloys of iron and carbon. Often, other metals are added to give the steel a particular property. Chromium and nickel, for example, are added to steel to make it stainless. Steel is widely used in many kinds of tools and as a structural material in building.

stegosaurus (stĕg′ə-sôr′əs) A plant-eating dinosaur of the Jurassic Period. Stegosauruses had a small head with a beaked mouth, a double row of large upright plates along the back, and sharp spikes on the tail.

stellar (stĕl′ər) Relating to or consisting of stars: *stellar clusters.*

stem (stĕm) **1.** The main, often long or slender part of a plant that usually grows upward above the ground and supports other parts, such as branches and leaves. Some underground plant structures, such as rhizomes and corms, are stems rather than roots. **2.** A slender stalk supporting or connecting another plant part, such as a leaf or flower.

STEM Abbreviation of science, technology, engineering, and mathematics.

stem cell An unspecialized cell that has the potential to develop into one or more different types of specialized cells, such as blood cells or nerve cells. Embryos have stem cells that can develop into almost any kind of body cell. Many tissues in adults also have stem cells, but the range of cells that they can develop into is limited. Stem cells are widely used in scientific research.

steppe (stĕp) A vast, semiarid, grassy plain, as

found in southeast Europe, Siberia, and central North America.

stereochemistry (stĕr′ē-ō-kĕm′ĭ-strē) The branch of chemistry that is concerned with the spatial arrangements of atoms in molecules and with the chemical and physical effects of these arrangements.

sterile (stĕr′əl, stĕr′īl′) **1.** Not able to produce offspring, seeds, or fruit; unable to reproduce. **2.** Free from disease-causing microorganisms: *a sterile bandage.* —*Noun* **sterility** (stə-rĭl′ĭ-tē).

sterling silver (stûr′lĭng) *See under* **silver.**

sternum (stûr′nəm) A long, flat bone located in the center of the chest, serving as a support for the clavicles (collarbones) and ribs. Also called *breastbone. See more at* **skeleton.**

steroid (stĕr′oid′) **1.** Any of a class of organic compounds having as a basis 17 carbon atoms arranged in four rings. Steroids include the sex hormones, such as testosterone, and hormones produced by the adrenal glands. They also include sterols, such as cholesterol, and certain forms of vitamins. **2.** Any of various hormones having the structure of a steroid that are made synthetically and are used to treat certain medical conditions. The sale of such substances without a prescription, for example to improve athletic performance, is illegal in the United States.

sterol (stîr′ôl′) Any of various alcohols having the structure of a steroid, including cholesterol. Sterols are found in the tissues of animals, plants, and fungi.

Stevens (stē′vənz), **Nettie Maria** 1861–1912. American biologist who identified the role of X and Y chromosomes in determining the sex of many organisms. Stevens showed that in certain insects, the cells of females have two X chromosomes, while the cells of males have one X and one Y chromosome. She also showed that these chromosomes separate during meiosis, so that in males, half the sperm cells contain an X chromosome and produce a female offspring, while the other half contain a Y chromosome and produce a male offspring.

Nettie Stevens

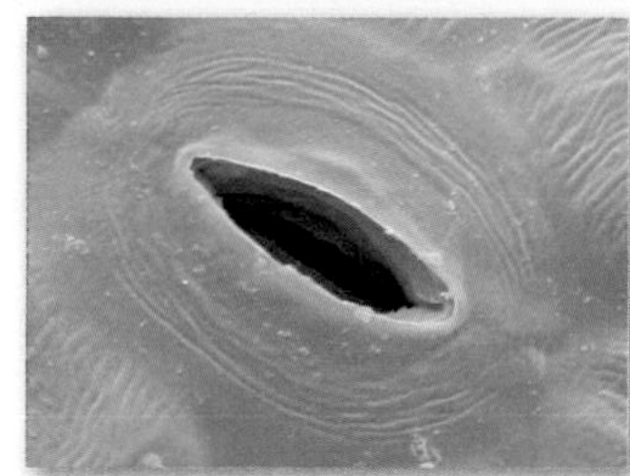

stoma *of an iceberg lettuce leaf*

stigma (stĭg′mə) The sticky tip of a flower pistil, on which pollen grains are deposited during pollination. *See more at* **flower.**

stimulant (stĭm′yə-lənt) A drug or other substance, such as caffeine, that speeds up or excites a body system, especially the nervous system.

stimulus (stĭm′yə-ləs) *Plural* **stimuli** (stĭm′yə-lī′) Something that causes a response in a body part or organism. A stimulus may be internal or external. Sense organs, such as the ear, and sensory receptors, such as those in the skin, are sensitive to external stimuli such as sound and touch.

stinger (stĭng′ər) A sharp stinging organ, such as that of a bee, scorpion, or stingray. Stingers usually inject venom. Also called *sting.*

stipule (stĭp′yo͞ol) One of the usually small, paired parts resembling leaves at the base of a leafstalk in certain plants, such as roses and beans.

stolon (stō′lŏn′) *See* **runner.**

stoma (stō′mə) *Plural* **stomata** (stō′mə-tə) One of the tiny openings in the outer surface of a plant leaf or stem, through which gases and water vapor pass. Most stomata are on the underside of leaves.

stomach (stŭm′ək) **1.** A hollow, muscular organ in vertebrate animals that stores and digests food. It is located between the esophagus and the small intestine. In ruminants, like cattle and sheep, it is divided into four separate compartments: the rumen, reticulum, omasum, and abomasum. **2.** A similar digestive structure of many invertebrates.

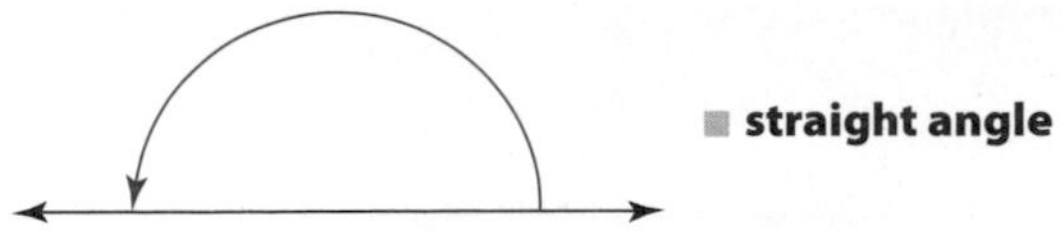

■ straight angle

stone (stōn) **1.** *Geology* A general term for rock, especially as used in construction. **2.** *Botany* A seed with a hard covering in certain fruits, such as a plum or cherry; a pit. **3.** *Medicine* A hard mass of minerals or other substance, such as cholesterol, that forms in a body part or organ: *kidney stones.*

Stone Age The earliest known period of human culture, marked by the use of stone tools. *See* **Mesolithic, Neolithic, Paleolithic.**

straight angle (strāt) An angle having a measure of 180°.

strain (strān) **1.** *Biology* A group of bacteria or viruses that are genetically distinct from others of the same species. **2.** *Physics* The extent to which a body is distorted when it is subjected to a deforming force, such as stress. The distortion can involve a change in both shape and size. ❖ In **elastic strain** the distorted body returns to its original shape and size when the force is removed. ❖ In **plastic strain** the distorted body does not return to its original shape and size even after the force has been removed. *Compare* **stress.** *See more at* **Hooke's law.**

strait (strāt) A narrow waterway joining two larger bodies of water. The Strait of Gibraltar, for example, connects the Mediterranean Sea with the Atlantic Ocean.

stratification (străt′ə-fĭ-kā′shən) Formation or deposition of layers, as of rock or sediments.

stratocumulus (străt′ō-kyo͞om′yə-ləs) A low-lying, often patchy cloud formation occurring in extensive horizontal layers with distinct, rounded tops.

stratosphere (străt′ə-sfîr′) The layer of the Earth's atmosphere lying above the troposphere and below the mesosphere, from the tropopause to about 30 miles (50 kilometers) above the Earth's surface. In the stratosphere, temperatures rise slightly with altitude.

stratum (strā′təm, străt′əm) *Plural* **strata** *or* **stratums 1.** A layer of rock whose composition is more or less the same throughout. A particular rock stratum is visibly different from the rock strata above and below it. **2.** Any of the regions of the atmosphere, such as the troposphere, that occur as layers.

stratus (străt′əs) *Plural* **strati** A low-lying, grayish cloud layer that sometimes produces drizzle. A stratus cloud that is close to the ground or water is called fog.

streak (strēk) The characteristic color of a mineral after it has been ground into a powder. Because the streak of a mineral is not always the same as its natural color, it is a useful tool in mineral identification.

streamline (strēm′līn′) To design or construct something so that it offers the least resistance to the flow of a fluid, especially air or water.

strep throat (strĕp) Infection of the throat caused by streptococcus bacteria. Symptoms include fever, redness of the throat, and inflammation of the tonsils.

streptococcus (strĕp′tə-kŏk′əs) *Plural* **streptococci** (strĕp′tə-kŏk′sī, strĕp′tə-kŏk′ī) Any of various bacteria that are normally found on the skin and mucous membranes and in the digestive tract of mammals. Certain kinds of streptococcus bacteria can cause severe infections in humans, including strep throat, scarlet fever, pneumonia, and blood infections.

stress (strĕs) **1.** A force that tends to distort or deform something by compressing or stretching it. *Compare* **strain.** *See more at* **Hooke's law. 2.** A physiological reaction by an organism to a harmful or threatening situation. In humans and many other animals, the body's initial response to stress includes a rise in heart rate and blood pressure and a heightened state of alertness. In plants, stress from factors such as drought or disease can reduce

■ **stratum**
sedimentary strata in a rockface

the rate of growth. **3.** A psychological response to a disturbing situation. People who experience this type of stress may feel irritable and have difficulty sleeping.

striation (strī-ā′shən) One of a number of parallel lines or grooves on the surface of a rock. Striations form when pieces of rock frozen into the base of a glacier move across the bedrock and scratch it, or when two blocks of rock along opposite sides of a fault plane slide past each other, scratching the rocks' outer surfaces.

strike-slip fault (strīk′slĭp′) A geologic fault in which the blocks of rock on either side of the fault slide horizontally in opposite directions along the line of the fault plane. *See more at* **fault.**

string theory (strĭng) A theory about elementary particles and fundamental forces that is based on a mathematical model in which elementary particles are represented as tiny vibrating stringlike objects that exist in a space-time with more than the four dimensions of space-time in the theory of relativity. Scientists have not yet found experimental evidence to support this theory.

strobe light (strōb) A device that produces very short, intense flashes of light by means of an electric discharge in a gas. The ability of strobe lights to "freeze" the motion of rapidly moving objects makes them very useful in photography and in making measurements of vibration or other types of high-speed motion.

stroke (strōk) A sudden interruption in the normal functioning of the brain, often resulting in slurred speech and loss of muscle control and feeling on one side of the body. Strokes occur when a blood vessel in the brain bursts or when a blood clot or other particle blocks the flow of blood to the brain.

strong nuclear force (strông) The force that binds quarks together to form protons and neutrons and also binds protons and neutrons together to form the nuclei of atoms. The strong nuclear force is the strongest of the four basic forces of nature, being stronger than the electromagnetic force, the weak nuclear force, and gravity. Also called *strong force* or *strong interaction.*

strontium (strŏn′chē-əm, strŏn′tē-əm) A soft, silvery metallic element that is an alkaline-earth metal and occurs naturally only as a sulfate or carbonate. One of its isotopes is used in the radiometric dating of rocks. Because strontium salts burn with a red flame, they are used to make fireworks and signal flares. *Symbol* **Sr.** *Atomic number* 38. *See* **Periodic Table,** pages 254–255.

strontium-90 A radioactive isotope of strontium having a mass number of 90 and a half-life of 29 years. Strontium-90 is the most dangerous component of the fallout from nuclear explosions because it can be absorbed by the body. It is also used in industrial gauges and in certain medical treatments.

structural formula ([illegible]) A chemical formula that shows how the atoms in a molecule are arranged or connected. Structural formulas are usually two-dimensional representations, with lines connecting the atoms and showing the location and nature of the bonds. They can also be condensed or abbreviated in various ways. For example, a condensed structural formula of ethane may be given as CH_3CH_3, indicating that it consists of two methyl groups (CH_3) attached to each other. Even condensed structural formulas can get quite long (such as the one for aspirin: $CH_3COOC_6H_4COOH$), so formulas are often given as molecular formulas, with all the similar atoms totaled up (for ethane, C_2H_6; for aspirin, $C_9H_8O_4$). *Compare* **molecular formula.**

strychnine (strĭk′nīn′) An extremely poisonous, white crystalline compound derived from certain plants. It is used as a rat poison and was formerly used in medicine to stimulate the nervous system.

style (stīl) The slender part of a flower pistil, extending from the ovary to the stigma. *See more at* **flower.**

sub– **1.** A prefix that means "underneath" or "lower," as in *subsoil.* **2.** A prefix that means "a subordinate or secondary part of something else," as in *subspecies.* **3.** A prefix that means "less than completely," as in *subtropical.*

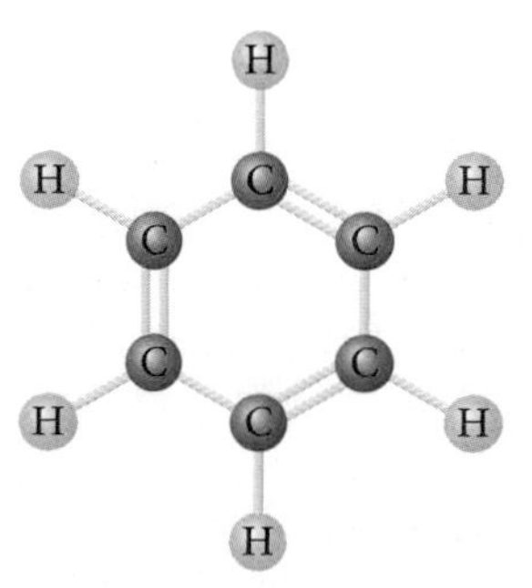

structural formula

structural formula of benzene (C_6H_6)

Did You Know...?

subatomic particles

Imagine what would happen if you cut an apple in half, then cut that half apple in half, then the quarter apple in half, and so on. Would you eventually arrive at some kind of particle that couldn't be divided any more? This question has intrigued people for thousands of years. Ancient Greeks used the word *atomos* to refer to a hypothetical, indivisible bit of matter, and until the late 1800s, physicists believed that atoms were the smallest units of matter. This view started to change in 1897 when the British physicist J. J. Thomson proposed that cathode rays consisted of streams of negatively charged particles that were smaller than atoms. These particles, later named *electrons,* were the first known kind of *subatomic particle.* Since atoms are electrically neutral, scientists believed that they must contain a positively charged substance or particle to balance the negatively charged electron. In 1911 Ernest Rutherford found evidence that this positive charge resided in the center, or nucleus, of an atom, in a particle he called the *proton.* Further experiments by James Chadwick in 1932 showed that the nucleus also contains another kind of subatomic particle, the *neutron.* Since that time, scientists have come to believe that protons and neutrons themselves can be divided into a host of even smaller particles, called *elementary particles.* Protons, for example, are thought to be made up of three quarks.

subatomic particle (sŭb′ə-tŏm**′**ĭk) Any of various units of matter that are components of atoms. Protons, neutrons, and electrons are subatomic particles. Elementary particles such as neutrinos, quarks, and photons are also subatomic particles. *See Note at* **neutrino.**

subcutaneous (sŭb′kyo͞o-tā**′**nē-əs) Located or placed just beneath the skin.

subduction zone (səb-dŭk**′**shən) A convergent plate boundary where one plate sinks (subducts) beneath the other, usually because it is denser. *See more at* **tectonic boundary.**

sublimation (sŭb′lə-mā**′**shən) The process of changing from a solid to a gas without passing through an intermediate liquid phase. An example of a substance that undergoes sublimation is solid carbon dioxide (dry ice). *Compare* **deposition.**

subset (sŭb**′**sĕt′) A set whose members are all contained in another set. The set of positive integers, for example, is a subset of the set of integers.

subsoil (sŭb**′**soil′) The layer of earth below the surface soil.

subspecies (sŭb**′**spē′shēz, sŭb**′**spē′sēz) A subdivision of a species of organisms having distinctive characteristics, usually located in a specific geographic region.

substrate (sŭb**′**strāt′) **1.** The molecule on which a certain enzyme acts. The substrate usually binds to a special site on the enzyme. *See Note at* **enzyme. 2.** The surface on which an organism grows or to which it is attached. Barnacles, for example, are usually attached to a rocky substrate.

subtraction (səb-trăk**′**shən) The act, process, or operation of subtracting one number or quantity from another to compute their difference.

subtractive (səb-trăk**′**tĭv) **1.** Being any of the primary colors cyan, magenta, or yellow, which can be combined using overlapping filters to produce all other colors. The filters absorb certain wavelengths and allow others to pass through. *See more at* **color. 2.** *Mathematics* Marked by or involving subtraction.

subtrahend (sŭb**′**trə-hĕnd′) A number subtracted from another. For example, in the expression 4 – 3, 3 is the subtrahend.

subtropical (sŭb-trŏp**′**ĭ-kəl) Relating to the regions of the Earth bordering on the tropics, just north of the Tropic of Cancer or just south of the Tropic of Capricorn. Subtropical regions are the warmest parts of the two Temperate Zones.

succession (sək-sĕsh**′**ən) The gradual replacement of one type of ecological community by another, involving a series of changes especially in the vegetation. For example, after a forest fire, grasses will grow back first on the burnt-over land, followed by shrubs, and then trees. *See more at* **climax community.**

succulent (sŭk′yə-lənt) A plant having thick, fleshy leaves or stems that store water. Cacti are succulents.

sucker (sŭk′ər) **1.** *Zoology* A part that an animal uses for clinging by suction to something or for sucking blood or other liquids from another animal. Leeches use suckers for feeding, and octopuses and squid use suckers to grab and hold on to prey. **2.** *Botany* A shoot growing from the base or root of a tree or shrub and giving rise to a new plant.

sucrose (so͞o′krōs′) A crystalline sugar having the formula $C_{12}H_{22}O_{11}$, found in many plants, especially sugar cane, sugar beets, and sugar maple. Sucrose is used widely as a sweetener.

suction (sŭk′shən) A force acting on a fluid caused by a difference in pressure between two regions, tending to make the fluid flow from the region of higher pressure to the region of lower pressure.

Suess (zo͞os), **Eduard** 1831–1914. Austrian geologist who was the first to propose the existence of the early supercontinent Gondwana. He also investigated the origin of the Alps.

sugar (sho͝og′ər) **1.** Any of a class of crystalline carbohydrates, such as sucrose, glucose, or lactose, that dissolve in water and have a characteristic sweet taste. **2.** Sucrose.

sulfate (sŭl′fāt′) A chemical compound made from sulfuric acid and containing the group SO_4.

sulfide (sŭl′fīd′) A compound of sulfur and another element, such as hydrogen sulfide.

sulfur also **sulphur** (sŭl′fər) A pale-yellow, brittle nonmetallic element that occurs widely in nature, especially in volcanic deposits, many common minerals, natural gas, and petroleum. It is used to make gunpowder and fertilizer, to vulcanize rubber, and to produce sulfuric acid. *Symbol* **S.** *Atomic number* 16. *See* **Periodic Table,** pages 254–255.

sulfur dioxide A colorless, poisonous gas or liquid, SO_2, that has a strong odor. It is formed naturally by volcanic activity, and is a waste gas produced by burning coal and oil and by many industrial processes, such as smelting. It is also a hazardous air pollutant and a major contributor to acid rain.

sulfuric acid (sŭl-fyo͝or′ĭk) A very corrosive acid, H_2SO_4. It combines very easily with water, making it a good drying agent, and is the most widely used acid in industry.

sum (sŭm) The result of adding numbers or quantities. The sum of 6 and 9, for example, is 15, and the sum of $4x$ and $5x$ is $9x$.

summer solstice (sŭm′ər) The solstice that occurs on or about June 21 in the Northern Hemisphere and on or about December 21 in the Southern Hemisphere, marking the beginning of summer and the day of the year with the longest period of sunlight. *Compare* **winter solstice.**

sun (sŭn) **1.** Often **Sun.** The star that is orbited

Did You Know...?

sublimation

We've all seen a solid heated to a liquid and a liquid heated to a gas. Ice, for instance, melts to become liquid water, and liquid water can be boiled away as steam. However, under the right conditions of pressure and temperature something else can happen: a solid can turn directly into a gas. This strange process is called *sublimation*. The most familiar example of a solid turning into a gas is probably that of dry ice, as seen in the photograph to the right. Solid carbon dioxide, dry ice, seems to give off smoke at room temperature. This "smoke" is actually carbon dioxide gas. Dry ice is useful for packing certain materials that need to stay cold, since it doesn't melt and get everything wet.

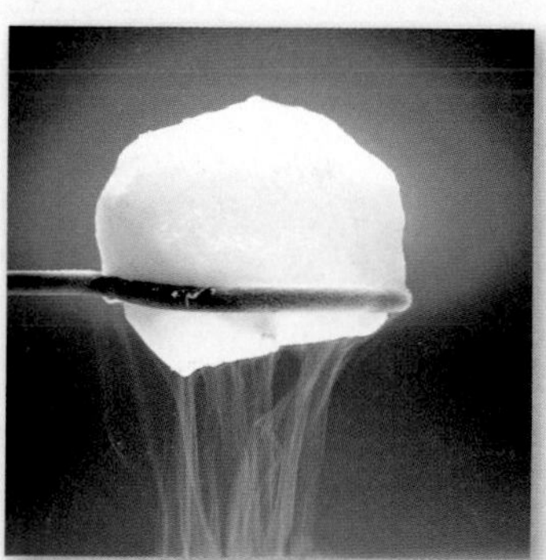

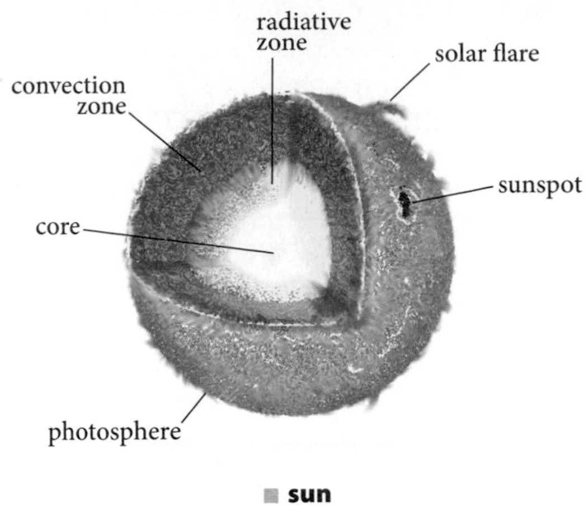

sun

by all of the planets and other celestial objects of our solar system and that supplies the heat and light that sustain life on Earth. It has a diameter of about 864,000 miles (1,391,000 kilometers), an average distance from Earth of about 93 million miles (150 million kilometers), and a mass about 333,000 times that of Earth. *See Table at* **solar system,** pages 312–313. *See Note at* **dwarf star. 2.** A star that is the center of a system of planets.

sunspot (sŭn**′**spŏt′) Any of the relatively cool dark spots that appear in groups on the surface of the sun. Sunspots are associated with strong magnetic fields.

supercell (so͞o**′**pər-sĕl′) A severe, usually isolated thunderstorm with a rotating current of rising air at its center. Supercells often give rise to damaging winds, flooding, large hail, and tornadoes.

superconductor (so͞o′pər-kən-dŭk**′**tər) A metal or alloy that conducts electric current with no resistance when at a very low temperature. Most superconductors work only at temperatures near absolute zero (–459.67°F; –273.15°C), but certain alloys become superconductors at higher temperatures, around –225°F (–143°C).

supercell

supercontinent (so͞o**′**pər-kŏn′tə-nənt) A large continent that, according to the theory of plate tectonics, is thought to have split into smaller continents in the geologic past. Pangaea and Gondwana are supercontinents. *See Note at* **Gondwana.**

supergiant (so͞o**′**pər-jī′ənt) A star that is larger, brighter, and more massive than a giant star. Supergiants, such as Betelgeuse or Rigel, are thousands of times brighter than the sun. A supergiant ultimately explodes as a supernova and then develops into either a neutron star or a black hole. *See more at* **star.**

supernova (so͞o′pər-nō**′**və) *Plural* **supernovae** (so͞o′pər-nō**′**vē) *or* **supernovas** The explosion of a massive star, resulting in a very bright, short-lived object that gives off enormous amounts of energy. The explosion may result in a neutron star or a black hole, or the star may be completely destroyed, leaving behind only glowing remnants. *See more at* **star.** *Compare* **nova.**

supersonic (so͞o′pər-sŏn**′**ĭk) Relating to or traveling at a speed greater than the speed of sound in a given medium, especially air: *supersonic jets.*

supersymmetry (so͞o**′**pər-sĭm′ĭ-trē) A theory about elementary particles and fundamental forces in which every elementary particle has an associated particle (called its superpartner) that is identical except in one property. This theory would allow the four basic forces of nature — the electromagnetic force, the strong nuclear force, the weak nuclear force, and gravity — to be unified under one overall theory. Scientists have not yet found experimental evidence to support this theory.

supplementary angles (sŭp′lə-mĕn**′**tə-rē) Two angles whose sum is 180°.

surface tension (sûr**′**fəs) A property of liquids whereby their surfaces behave as though covered by a thin elastic film. Surface tension is caused by forces of attraction between molecules of the liquid. Compared with molecules below the surface, the molecules at or near the surface have fewer neighboring molecules but are more strongly attracted to them. Surface tension causes drops to be shaped like spheres and allows small objects, like an insect on a pond, to be supported on the surface of a liquid without sinking.

surface wave An earthquake wave in which rock particles vibrate at right angles to the direction of wave travel. Surface waves travel only on the Earth's surface, and not through it. Also called *L wave. See Note at* **earthquake.**

surfactant (sər-făk′tənt) **1.** A substance that is added to a liquid to reduce its surface tension or increase its ability to mix with other materials. Soaps and detergents act as surfactants. **2.** A substance produced by the tiny air-filled sacs of the lung that reduces the surface tension of the fluids coating the lung. Surfactant helps keep the tiny air sacs from collapsing during normal breathing.

suspension (sə-spĕn′shən) A mixture in which small particles of a substance are dispersed throughout a gas or liquid. If left undisturbed, the particles are likely to settle to the bottom. The particles in a suspension are larger than those in either a colloid or a solution. Muddy water is an example of a suspension. *Compare* **colloid, solution.**

swallow (swŏl′ō) Any of various small, swift-flying birds having narrow pointed wings, a forked or notched tail, and a large mouth for catching flying insects. Some species of swallows migrate thousands of miles every year. A barn swallow, for example, might breed in Iowa and spend the winter in Brazil.

swamp (swŏmp) A wetland in which much of the vegetation consists of trees or other woody plants.

S wave *See* **secondary wave.** *See Note at* **earthquake.**

sweat (swĕt) The salty liquid given off by glands in the skin of mammals. As sweat evaporates, the skin cools, resulting in a reduction of body heat.

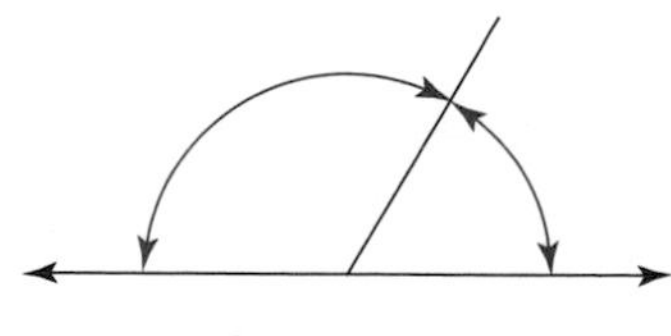

supplementary angles

Each of the two angles shown is a supplementary angle to the other one.

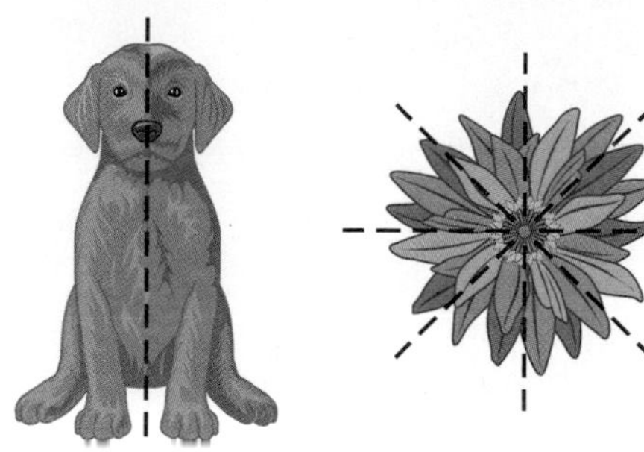

symmetry

left: *bilateral symmetry*
right: *radial symmetry*

❖ The glands in the skin that secrete sweat are called **sweat glands.**

swim bladder (swĭm) A gas-filled structure in many fish that functions to maintain buoyancy and, in some species, to aid in respiration or to produce sound. Also called *air bladder.*

symbiosis (sĭm′bē-ō′sĭs) A close association between two or more different organisms of different species, often but not necessarily benefiting each member. Three different kinds of symbioses are commensalism, mutualism, and parasitism. —*Adjective* **symbiotic** (sĭm-bē-ŏt′ĭk).

symmetry (sĭm′ĭ-trē) An exact matching of form and arrangement of parts on opposite sides of a boundary, such as a plane or line, or around a central point or axis. ❖ Most organisms display either **bilateral symmetry** or **radial symmetry.** —*Adjective* **symmetric** (sĭ-mĕt′rĭk), **symmetrical** (sĭ-mĕt′rĭ-kəl).

sympathetic nervous system (sĭm′pə-thĕt′ĭk) The part of the autonomic nervous system that tends to act in opposition to the parasympathetic nervous system, as by speeding up the heart and contracting the blood vessels. It also regulates the function of glands, particularly the sweat glands. The sympathetic nervous system is activated especially under conditions of stress.

synapse (sĭn′ăps′) The gap across which a nerve impulse passes from one nerve cell to another nerve cell, a muscle cell, or a gland cell.

synchrotron (sĭng′krə-trŏn′) A particle accelerator in which charged subatomic particles, such as protons and electrons, are accelerated repeatedly around a large circular path. The synchrotron gradually increases the speeds and energies

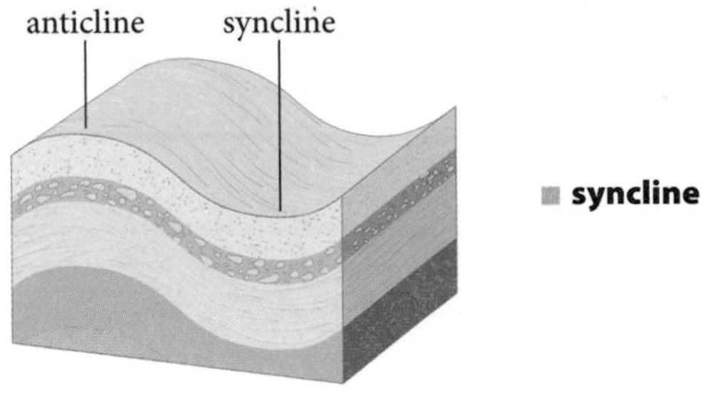

■ **syncline**

of these particles to high values. The high-energy particles that are produced can be caused to collide with other particles so that scientists can study their structure. *Compare* **cyclotron, linear accelerator.**

syncline (sĭn′klīn′) A fold of rock layers that slope upward on both sides of a common low point. Synclines form when rocks are compressed by plate-tectonic forces. *Compare* **anticline.**

syndrome (sĭn′drōm′) A group of signs and symptoms that together characterize a specific physical or psychological disease, disorder, or condition.

synthesis (sĭn′thĭ-sĭs) The formation of a chemical compound by combining simpler compounds or elements. — *Verb* **synthesize.**

synthetic (sĭn-thĕt′ĭk) Produced by chemical synthesis, especially in a laboratory or other artificial environment.

synthetic biology The branch of biology that involves altering the existing DNA sequence of an organism or creating a new DNA sequence in order to perform a specific function or produce a desired compound, such as a medical drug or biofuel.

syphilis (sĭf′ə-lĭs) A sexually transmitted disease caused by a bacterial infection that is characterized in its early stages by sores on the genitals. If untreated, skin ulcers develop, followed by often fatal infection of major organs of the body.

syringe (sə-rĭnj′) A medical instrument used to inject fluids into the body or draw them from it.

system (sĭs′təm) A group of elements or parts that function together to form a complex whole. For example, the mouth, stomach, and other structures that enable an animal to ingest and break down food form its *digestive system*. A *weather system* is made up of the different masses of warmer and cooler air that are present in a region, along with any winds, clouds, and rain or snow that they produce.

systole (sĭs′tə-lē) The period during the normal beating of the heart in which contraction of the ventricles occurs, forcing blood into the aorta and the arteries that lead to the lungs. *Compare* **diastole.**

Szilard (zĭl′ərd), **Leo** 1898–1964. Hungarian-born American physicist and biologist who developed the concept of the nuclear chain reaction and was instrumental in the creation of the first atomic bomb. Szilard was later opposed to the manufacture and use of all nuclear weapons and devoted himself to studying molecular biology.

T

T 1. Abbreviation of **temperature. 2.** Abbreviation of **thymine.**

Ta The symbol for **tantalum.**

tactile (tăk′təl, tăk′tīl′) Used for or sensitive to touch: *tactile organs.*

tadpole (tăd′pōl′) The aquatic larva of a frog or toad, having gills, a long tail, and in early stages, no legs. During the metamorphosis of a tadpole into an adult, legs and lungs develop, and the tail gradually disappears.

taiga (tī′gə) A forested area of far northern regions, consisting mainly of cone-bearing evergreens, such as firs, pines, and spruces, and some deciduous trees, such as larches, birches, and aspens. The taiga is found just south of the tundra.

tail (tāl) **1.** The rear, elongated part of many animals, extending beyond the main part of the body. **2.** The long, bright stream of gas and dust forced from the head of a comet when it is close to the sun.

tailbone (tāl′bōn′) *See* **coccyx.**

talc (tălk) A white, greenish, or gray mineral that is a silicate of magnesium, usually occurring as massive micalike flakes. It has a soft, soapy texture, and is used in face powder and talcum powder, for coating paper, and as a filler in paints and plastics. Talc is the mineral used to represent a hardness of 1 on the Mohs scale.

WORD HISTORY

tadpole

The word *tadpole,* which first appeared in English in the 1400s, is an old compound word whose meaning is no longer obvious. *Tad* is a variant of *toad,* while *pole* is simply an alternative spelling of *poll,* whose original meaning was "head." *Tadpole* thus means "a toad that is all head," so to speak. The most common senses of *poll* today are "a survey of public opinion" and "the place where votes are cast." These senses probably derive at least partly from the notion of the head as the most prominent part of each individual in a crowd — the part that can be counted.

■ talon

talon (tăl′ən) A sharp, curved claw of a bird of prey, such as a hawk or owl.

talus[1] (tā′ləs) The bone that forms a joint with the tibia and fibula, making up the main bone of the ankle. *See more at* **skeleton.**

talus[2] A sloping mass of rock fragments at the base of a cliff.

tan Abbreviation of **tangent.**

tangent (tăn′jənt) **1.** A line, curve, or surface touching but not intersecting another. **2.** The ratio of the length of the side opposite an acute angle in a right triangle to the side adjacent to the angle.

tantalum (tăn′tə-ləm) A hard, heavy, gray metallic element that is highly resistant to corrosion at temperatures below 300°F (149°C). It is used to make light-bulb filaments, surgical instruments, and glass for camera lenses. *Symbol* **Ta.** *Atomic number* 73. *See* **Periodic Table,** pages 254–255.

tapeworm (tāp′wûrm′) Any of various long flatworms that live as parasites in the intestines of humans and other animals.

tar (tär) **1a.** A thick, oily, dark substance consisting mainly of hydrocarbons, made by heating plant material such as wood or peat in the absence of air. **b.** *See* **coal tar. 2.** A solid, sticky substance that is the residue of tobacco smoke. Tar contains numerous chemical compounds, many of which are known to cause cancer.

tarantula (tə-răn′chə-lə) Any of various large, hairy, mostly tropical spiders that have a bite that is painful but usually not dangerous to humans. They live in burrows in the ground and eat insects, other spiders, and sometimes small mammals or lizards.

tar pit An accumulation of natural bitumen at the Earth's surface, especially one that traps animals and preserves their bones.

tarsal (tär′səl) Any of the bones of the foot lying between the ankle and metatarsals. *See more at* **skeleton.**

taste bud (tāst) Any of numerous sense organs that are located in the mouth, usually on the tongue, of vertebrate animals and that are sensitive to different kinds of tastes, such as salty and sweet.

Taurus (tôr′əs) A constellation in the Northern Hemisphere near Orion and Aries.

taxonomy (tăk-sŏn′ə-mē) The science of classifying and naming organisms based on shared characteristics and natural relationships.

Tay-Sachs disease (tā′săks′) An inherited disease in which the products of fat metabolism accumulate in the nervous system, especially the brain, causing a steady decline in mental and physical function and resulting in death by the age of 4. It mostly affects children of Eastern European Jewish descent.

Tb The symbol for **terbium.**

TB Abbreviation of **tuberculosis.**

Tc The symbol for **technetium.**

T cell Any of various lymphocytes whose cell surfaces have receptors that bind to foreign antigens, thus deactivating the antigens and defending the body against disease. T cells also regulate the function of B cells.

Te The symbol for **tellurium.**

tear (tîr) A drop of the clear salty liquid secreted by glands (lacrimal glands) in the eyes. Tears wet the membrane covering the eye and help rid the eye of substances that cause irritation.

teat (tēt) The part of a mammary gland of a female mammal that contains the outlets of the milk ducts.

technetium (tĕk-nē′shē-əm) A silvery-gray, radioactive metallic element that is produced naturally in extremely small amounts during the radioactive decay of uranium. It was the first element to be artificially made. Technetium is used as a medical tracer and to prevent corrosion in steel. *Symbol* **Tc.** *Atomic number* 43. *See* **Periodic Table,** pages 254–255.

technology (tĕk-nŏl′ə-jē) **1.** The use of scientific knowledge to solve practical problems, especially in industry and commerce. **2.** The specific methods, materials, and devices used to solve practical problems: *aerospace technology.*

tectonic boundary (tĕk-tŏn′ĭk) In the theory of plate tectonics, a boundary between two or more plates. The plates can be moving toward each other (at convergent plate boundaries), away from each other (at divergent plate boundaries), or past each other (at transform faults). Maps of seismic and volcanic activity across the Earth indicate that most earthquakes and volcanic eruptions occur along or near tectonic boundaries. Scientists believe this is due to the scraping, pushing, pulling, and melting of the Earth's outer layer (the lithosphere) along these boundaries. *See A Closer Look, on page 334.*

tectonic plate In the theory of plate tectonics, one of the sections of the Earth's lithosphere, constantly moving relative to the other sections.

tektite (tĕk′tīt′) Any of numerous dark-brown to green glassy objects, usually small and round, composed of silica and various oxides and found in several parts of the world. They are thought to have come from the moon or to have resulted from impacts of large meteorites with the Earth's surface.

tele– A prefix that means "at a distance," as in *telemetry.*

telecommunication (tĕl′ĭ-kə-myo͞o′nĭ-kā′shən) The science and technology of sending messages over long distances by electronic transmission of impulses, as by telephone, radio, television, or computer network.

telegraph (tĕl′ĭ-grăf′) A communications system in which a message in the form of electric impulses is sent, either by wire or radio, to a receiving station.

telemetry (tə-lĕm′ĭ-trē) The automatic measurement and transmission of data from a distant source to a receiving station. Telemetry is used, for example, to track the movements of wild animals that have had radio transmitters attached to them.

TAXONOMY

Taxonomy is the scientific classification of life. The most widely used system today is based on a system developed in the 1700s by the Swedish botanist Carl Linnaeus, who divided all forms of life into two large groups—animals and plants. Since Linnaeus's time, biologists have discovered new forms of life and have developed new techniques, such as the ability to view microscopic structures and to determine DNA sequences. Although modern taxonomy is a rapidly changing field, many modern biologists use a system that divides life into three **domains** and recognizes four **kingdoms** within the domain of the eukaryotes, as shown in the following table:

DOMAIN KINGDOM	TYPES OF ORGANISMS
Archaea	one-celled organisms without a nucleus that often live in extreme environments
Bacteria	one-celled organisms without a nucleus that live in soil, water, and other organisms
Eukaryotes	
Protista	one-celled organisms such as amoebas, euglenas, and paramecia; also dinoflagellates, slime molds, and most algae
Fungi	mushrooms, yeasts, and molds
Plantae	plants
Animalia	multicellular animals

Below the kingdom are six major lower levels, arranged hierarchically. From highest to lowest these are **phylum** (or **division,** in the plant kingdom), **class, order, family, genus,** and **species.** These categories indicate how closely or distantly organisms are related to each other, based on structural and genetic similarities. By convention, taxonomic categories are capitalized except for the second part of a species name. Species (and genus) names are written in italic, as in *Homo sapiens.* The chart below compares the taxonomy of three species: the human, the blue whale, and the albacore tuna.

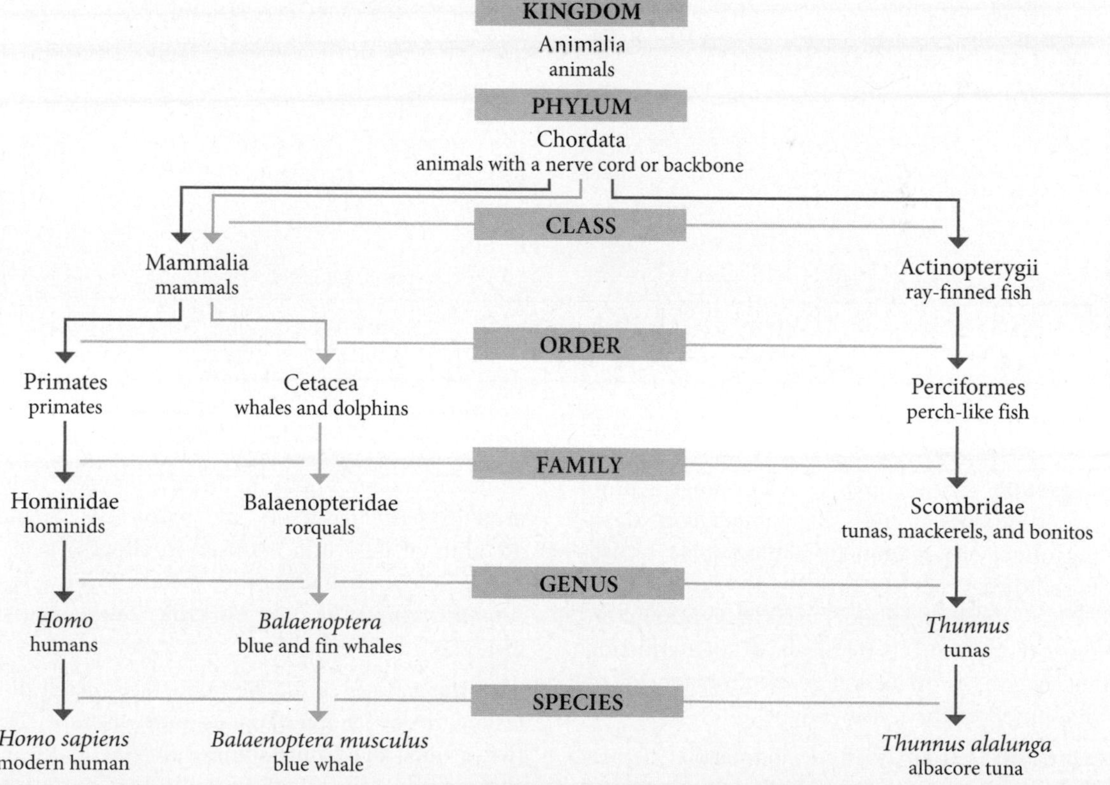

A CLOSER LOOK

Tectonic Boundaries

Subduction Zones

Two tectonic plates collide. The denser plate sinks below the other, and a deep trench forms where the two plates meet. The downgoing plate heats up with depth and begins to melt. A chain of volcanoes forms in the overriding plate, creating an island arc in the ocean or a mountain range along the edge of a continent. The Aleutian Islands and the Andes formed in this way.

Hot Spots

A volcano forms over a hot spot—an area within the Earth where hot material is rising through the mantle toward the crust. The Hawaiian Islands formed in this way.

Spreading Zones

As plates spread apart, new lava rises to the surface from deep within the Earth and cools to form new rock. The island of Iceland formed in this way. When a single plate begins to break into two, a rift valley forms. Sometimes sea water flows into it. This is how the Red Sea formed.

Collision Zones

Two equally dense plates collide. Neither plate sinks below the other, and as the two push against each other a mountain chain forms. The Himalayas formed in this way.

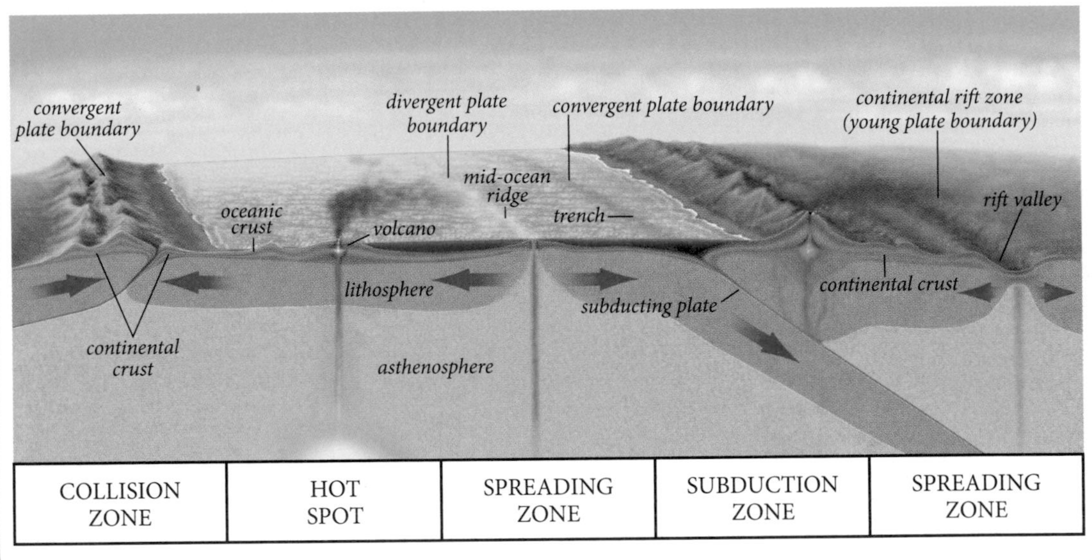

telescope (tĕl′ĭ-skōp′) **1.** An arrangement of lenses, mirrors, or both that gathers light, allowing direct observation or photographic recording of distant objects. **2.** Any of various devices, such as a radio telescope, used to detect and observe distant objects by their emission, absorption, or reflection of electromagnetic radiation other than visible light.

tellurium (tĕ-lo͝or′ē-əm) A nonmetallic element that occurs as either a brittle, shiny, silvery-white crystal or a gray or brown powder. It is used in semiconductors and solar cells. Small amounts of tellurium are used in alloys of copper, stainless steel, and other metals. *Symbol* **Te.** *Atomic number* 52. *See* **Periodic Table,** pages 254–255.

telophase (tĕl′ə-fāz′) The final stage of cell division, in which membranes form around the two groups of chromosomes, each at opposite ends of the cell, to produce the two nuclei of

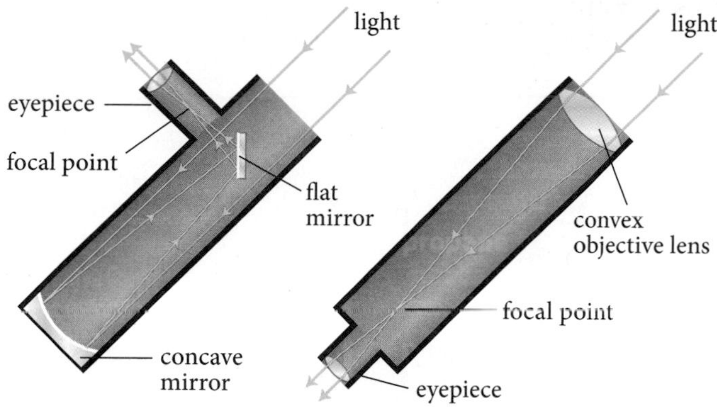

telescope

In a reflecting telescope (left), *light is gathered by reflecting off a concave mirror. It is then reflected off an angled flat mirror toward the eyepiece. In a refracting telescope* (right), *light is gathered by being refracted through a convex objective lens. It then exits through the eyepiece.*

the daughter cells. Telophase is preceded by anaphase. *See more at* **meiosis, mitosis.**

temperate (tĕm′pər-ĭt) Marked by moderate temperatures, weather, or climate; neither hot nor cold.

Temperate Zone Either of two zones of the Earth of intermediate latitude, the **North Temperate Zone,** between the Arctic Circle and the Tropic of Cancer, or the **South Temperate Zone,** between the Antarctic Circle and the Tropic of Capricorn.

temperature (tĕm′pər-ə-cho͝or′) **1.** A measure of the average kinetic energy of the atoms or molecules of an object. The higher the temperature of an object, the higher the average kinetic energy of its molecules. Temperature is usually measured on one of three standard scales: Fahrenheit, Celsius, or Kelvin. *See Note at* **Celsius. 2.** An abnormally high body temperature; a fever. *See Note on page 336.*

temporal lobe (tĕm′pər-əl) The portion of each cerebral hemisphere lying to the side and rear of the frontal lobe. In humans, it contains the main speech and language centers of the brain.

tendon (tĕn′dən) A band of tough fibrous tissue that connects a muscle to a bone.

tendril (tĕn′drəl) A twisting, slender structure by which a plant twines around and often climbs an object or another plant. Grapes, cucumbers, and peas produce tendrils.

tensile strength (tĕn′səl, tĕn′sīl′) A measure of the ability of an object or a material to withstand a force that tends to pull it apart. The tensile strength of an object is the greatest force that can be applied without breaking it.

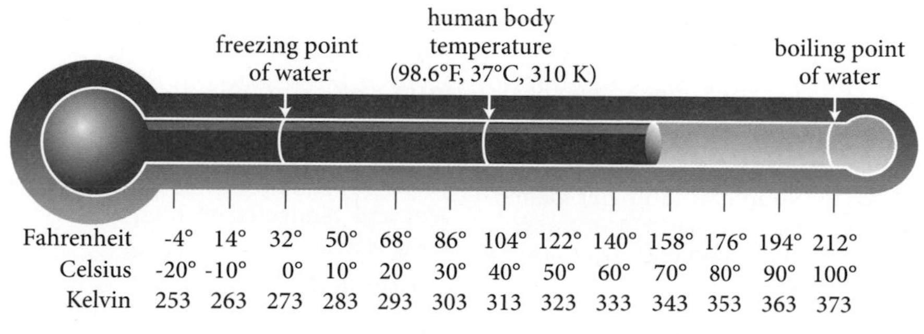

temperature

USAGE

temperature/heat

Temperature and *heat* are closely related but distinct ideas. Heat is simply transferred thermal energy — most commonly, the kinetic energy of molecules making up a substance, vibrating and bouncing against each other. A substance's temperature, on the other hand, is a measure of its ability to transfer heat, rather than the amount of heat transferred. When two bodies of different temperatures are in thermal contact, heat flows from the higher-temperature body into the lower-temperature body until the temperatures of the two bodies are the same. When you hold a glass of milk, your hand feels cold because energy is being transferred from your hand (the hotter object) to the glass (the cooler object). Adding heat to a system usually raises its temperature, but not always; for example, ice at zero degrees Celsius requires considerable additional heat in order to melt into water at zero degrees Celsius.

tension (tĕn′shən) **1.** *Physics* A force that tends to stretch or elongate something. **2.** *Electricity* A difference of electric potential; voltage: *high-tension wires.*

tentacle (tĕn′tə-kəl) A narrow, flexible, unjointed part extending from the body of certain animals, such as a jellyfish or sea anemone. Tentacles are used for feeling, grasping, or moving.

tephra (tĕf′rə) Solid matter, such as ash, dust, and cinders, that is ejected into the air by an erupting volcano.

tera– **1.** A prefix that means "one trillion," as in *terahertz,* one trillion hertz. **2.** A prefix that means 2^{40} (that is, 1,099,511,627,776, which is the power of two closest to a trillion), as in *terabyte.*

terabit (tĕr′ə-bĭt′) *Computers* **1.** One trillion bits. **2.** 1,099,511,627,776 (2^{40}) bits. *See Note at* **megabyte.**

terabyte (tĕr′ə-bīt′) **1.** A unit of computer memory or data storage capacity equal to 1,024 gigabytes (2^{40} bytes). **2.** One trillion bytes. *See Note at* **megabyte.**

terbium (tûr′bē-əm) A soft, easily shaped, silvery-gray metallic element of the lanthanide series. It is used in x-ray machines and lasers. *Symbol* **Tb.** *Atomic number* 65. *See* **Periodic Table,** pages 254–255.

term (tûrm) *Mathematics* **1.** Each of the quantities or expressions that form the parts of a ratio or the numerator and denominator of a fraction. **2.** Any of the quantities in an equation that are connected to other quantities by a plus sign or a minus sign.

terminal (tûr′mə-nəl) **1.** *Computers* A device, often equipped with a keyboard and a video display, by which one can read, enter, or manipulate information in a computer system. **2.** *Electricity* A position in a circuit or device at which a connection can be made or broken. *See Note at* **battery.**

termite (tûr′mīt′) Any of numerous pale-colored, soft-bodied insects that live in large colonies and feed on wood. Reproductive individuals often have wings, but workers and soldiers, which forage for food, tend the eggs, and protect the nest, do not. Termites can destroy houses and other wooden structures. *See also* **queen, soldier, worker.**

terrestrial (tə-rĕs′trē-əl) **1.** Relating to the Earth or its inhabitants. **2.** Living or growing on land or in the ground.

territory (tĕr′ĭ-tôr′ē) An area occupied by a single animal, mating pair, or group. Animals usually defend their territory vigorously against intruders, especially of the same species. Different animals use different methods for communicating territorial information. Some animals, such as foxes, leave scent markings along the territory's boundaries, and many birds use special calls to announce the location of their territory.

Tertiary (tûr′shē-ĕr′ē) The first period of the Cenozoic Era, from about 66 to 2.6 million years ago, characterized by the appearance of most modern classes of plants and mammals. *See Chart at* **geologic time,** pages 146–147.

Tesla (tĕs′lə), **Nikola** 1856–1943. Serbian-born American electrical engineer and physicist. He developed improved technologies for generating, transmitting, and making use of alternating current and pioneered techniques for transmitting radio waves.

testicle (tĕs′tĭ-kəl) Either of the testes of a male mammal, usually contained within a scrotum.

testis (tĕs′tĭs) *Plural* **testes** (tĕs′tēz) The paired reproductive organs of male vertebrates, in which sperm and the sex hormones (androgens) are produced. In most vertebrates the testes are contained inside the body, but in many mammals they lie outside the body and are enclosed by the scrotum. Some invertebrates, such as mollusks and annelids, have a similar sperm-producing organ.

testosterone (tĕs-tŏs′tə-rōn′) A steroid hormone produced primarily in the testes and responsible for the development of the male reproductive system and male secondary sex characteristics. Testosterone is one of the hormones called androgens.

BIOGRAPHY

Nikola Tesla

When Nikola Tesla went to work for George Westinghouse's electrical company in the 1880s, most commercially generated electricity was distributed over a low-voltage direct current (DC) system. Such a system was very expensive to maintain, in part because at low voltage more electricity is lost to resistance and wasted as heat in the wires. The alternating current (AC) system Tesla developed could be transmitted over long distances at high voltages by using transformers, and it was cheaper and easier to maintain than the DC system. Tesla gave public demonstrations of electricity to ease peoples' fears about the safety of the system (even having currents passed through his body to ignite flames). Tesla's invention of motors and generators to use with the AC system helped make it the standard for power distribution throughout the country.

test tube (tĕst) A cylindrical tube of clear glass, usually open at one end and rounded at the other, used as a container for small amounts of a substance in laboratory tests and experiments.

tetanus (tĕt′n-əs) A serious disease caused by bacteria that usually enter the body through a wound. Tetanus is characterized by painful contractions of the muscles, especially of the jaw, and can be fatal if untreated.

tetragonal (tĕ-trăg′ə-nəl) Relating to a crystal having three axes, two of which are of the same length and are at right angles to each other. The third axis is perpendicular to these. The mineral zircon has tetragonal crystals. *See more at* **crystal.**

tetrahedron (tĕt′rə-hē′drən) A three-dimensional geometric figure with four triangular faces.

Th The symbol for **thorium.**

thalamus (thăl′ə-məs) The part of the brain in vertebrate animals that lies under the cerebrum and above the brainstem. It relays sensory information to the cerebral cortex and regulates the perception of touch, pain, and temperature.

Thales (thā′lēz) 624?–546? BC. Greek philosopher who was a founder of geometry and abstract astronomy.

thallium (thăl′ē-əm) A soft, easily shaped, very poisonous metallic element that has a low melting temperature. It is used in photography, in making low-melting and highly refractive glass, and in treating skin infections. *Symbol* **Tl.** *Atomic number* 81. *See* **Periodic Table,** pages 254–255.

thallus (thăl′əs) *Plural* **thalli** (thăl′ī) A part of certain plants and plantlike organisms that is a single cell or a mass of cells and cannot be distinguished as a leaf, stem, or root. Fungi, lichens, liverworts, and most algae have thalli.

theorem (thē′ər-əm, thîr′əm) A mathematical statement whose truth can be proved on the basis of a given set of axioms or assumptions.

theory (thē′ə-rē, thîr′ē) A set of statements or principles devised to explain a group of facts or phenomena. In science, a theory is usually not accepted until it has been tested experimentally and used to make accurate predictions about natural phenomena.

thermal (thûr**′**məl) *Adjective* **1.** Relating to heat. —*Noun* **2.** A current of warm air that rises because it is less dense than the air around it.

thermal vent *See under* **hydrothermal vent.**

thermion (thûr**′**mī′ən) An electrically charged particle, especially an electron, given off by a conductor that has been heated.

thermo– or **therm–** A prefix that means "heat," as in *thermometer.*

thermocline (thûr**′**mə-klīn′) A layer of water in the ocean or a lake that is between the warm surface layer and the cold bottom layer and in which the temperature decreases rapidly with depth.

thermocouple (thûr**′**mə-kŭp′əl) A thermoelectric device consisting of two wires made of different metals that are connected in a circuit and are welded together at a junction point. When the junction is heated, the difference between the high temperature at the junction and the lower temperature at the other end of each wire, combined with the fact that each wire responds differently to the temperature change, causes an electric current to flow. Because the amount of voltage generated depends on the temperature difference, thermocouples can be used to make accurate temperature measurements. They can also be used to convert heat energy into electric energy.

Did You Know...?

thermodynamics

Think about what happens when a car is driven. To generate the power to make the car move, energy must come from fuel (such as gas) or from electricity generated by a battery. After the car has been driven for a while, the engine will be hot. But after the car is parked, the engine will cool off. These everyday events illustrate the first two laws of *thermodynamics.* The first law, also called the *law of the conservation of energy,* states that energy cannot be created or destroyed—it can only be converted from one form to another. In this case, the energy in the car's fuel is converted into the energy of the moving car. The second law states that disorder in a system, also known as *entropy,* always tends to increase. A system in which thermal energy is equally spread out is considered to be at maximum entropy. The second law thus implies that heat can flow spontaneously from a hot object (such as the car) to a cold object (such the surrounding air), but not the other way around. The car has converted some of the chemical energy in its fuel or battery to mechanical energy, but in the process some of the energy has been lost in the form of waste heat, with an overall increase in the disorder of the car-air system as the car cools off and the air around it warms up.

thermodynamics (thûr′mō-dī-năm**′**ĭks) The branch of physics that deals with the conversion of energy, especially heat, from one form to another.

thermoelectric (thûr′mō-ĭ-lĕk**′**trĭk) Relating to electric energy produced by heat or to heat produced by electric energy. The flow of electricity through a thermoelectric device can be used to cause heat to flow from a cool region to a warm region, and the natural flow of heat from a warm region to a cool region can be used to create an electric current.

thermometer (thər-mŏm**′**ĭ-tər) An instrument used to measure temperature. There are many types of thermometers, each of which makes use of a physical effect of temperature to indicate the temperature of the medium being measured. One simple type of thermometer consists of a closed, graduated glass tube in which a liquid expands or contracts as the temperature increases or decreases. Other thermometers work by detecting changes in the volume of an enclosed gas or by registering changes in the electrical resistance of a conducting material at different temperatures.

thermonuclear (thûr′mō-no͞o**′**klē-ər) **1.** Derived from the fusion of atomic nuclei at high temperatures or the energy produced in this way. **2.** Relating to weapons based on nuclear fusion, especially as distinguished from those based on nuclear fission.

thermosphere (thûr**′**mə-sfîr′) The outermost layer of the Earth's atmosphere, lying above the mesosphere and extending hundreds of miles into outer space. In the thermosphere, which includes most of the ionosphere, temperatures increase steadily with altitude.

thermostat (thûr**′**mə-stăt′) A device that automatically controls heating or cooling equipment in such a way as to keep the temperature nearly constant.

theropod (thîr′ə-pŏd′) One of the two types of saurischian dinosaurs, widespread during the Mesozoic Era. Theropods walked on two legs and had short forelimbs and a large skull with long jaws and sharp teeth. Most of them were meat eaters. Velociraptors and *Tyrannosaurus rex* were theropods. *Compare* **sauropod.**

thiamine (thī′ə-mĭn) A vitamin belonging to the vitamin B complex (B_1) that is important in carbohydrate metabolism and normal activity of the nervous system. It is found in whole grains, beans, yeast, and meat.

Thompson (tŏmp′sən, tŏm′sən), **Benjamin.** Count Rumford. 1753–1814. American-born British physicist who conducted numerous experiments on heat and friction, which led him to discover that heat is produced by moving particles.

Thomson (tŏm′sən), Sir **Joseph John** 1856–1940. British physicist who discovered the electron. While experimenting with cathode rays, he deduced that the particles he observed were smaller than an atom. Thomson went on to study the ability of gases to conduct electricity.

thoracic (thə-răs′ĭk) Relating to or located in or near the thorax: *thoracic vertebrae.*

thorax (thôr′ăks′) **1.** The upper part of the body below the neck in vertebrate animals. The thorax includes the rib cage, which encloses the heart and lungs. In humans and other mammals, the thorax lies above the abdomen. **2.** The middle region of the body of many arthropods, including the insects and crustaceans. The thorax lies between the head and the abdomen. In insects, the legs and wings are attached to the thorax. In crustaceans, the thorax and head are usually joined together in a structure called the cephalothorax.

thorium (thôr′ē-əm) A silvery-white, radioactive metallic element of the actinide series. It is used in gas and electric lamps, for fuel in some nuclear reactors, and for improving the high-temperature strength of magnesium alloys. The only naturally occurring isotope of thorium is also its most stable, having a half-life of 14.1 billion years. *Symbol* **Th.** *Atomic number* 90. *See* **Periodic Table,** pages 254–255.

thorn (thôrn) A sharp, hard projection on a plant, especially a woody one on a branch or stem.

threonine (thrē′ə-nēn′) An essential amino acid. *See more at* **amino acid.**

thrust (thrŭst) The force that causes an object to move forward. Thrust in a jet or rocket engine develops as a reaction to the ejection of exhaust gases from the rear of the engine. Thrust in a propeller results from the spinning of the propeller blades that pushes air or water in a certain direction.

thulium (tho͞o′lē-əm) A soft, easily shaped, silver-gray metallic element of the lanthanide series. An artificial radioactive isotope of thulium is used as a radiation source in small, portable x-ray machines. *Symbol* **Tm.** *Atomic number* 69. *See* **Periodic Table,** pages 254–255.

thunder (thŭn′dər) The explosive noise that accompanies a stroke of lightning. Thunder is a series of sound waves produced by the rapid expansion of the air through which the lightning passes. *See Note at* **lightning.**

thunderstorm (thŭn′dər-stôrm′) A storm of heavy rain accompanied by lightning and thunder and sometimes hail.

thymine (thī′mēn′) A base that is a component of DNA, forming a base pair with adenine.

thymus (thī′məs) An organ in vertebrate animals located behind the top of the sternum (breastbone) where lymphocytes called T cells develop. In humans, the thymus stops growing in early childhood and gradually shrinks in size through adulthood.

thyroid gland (thī′roid′) A two-lobed gland located at the base of the neck in vertebrate

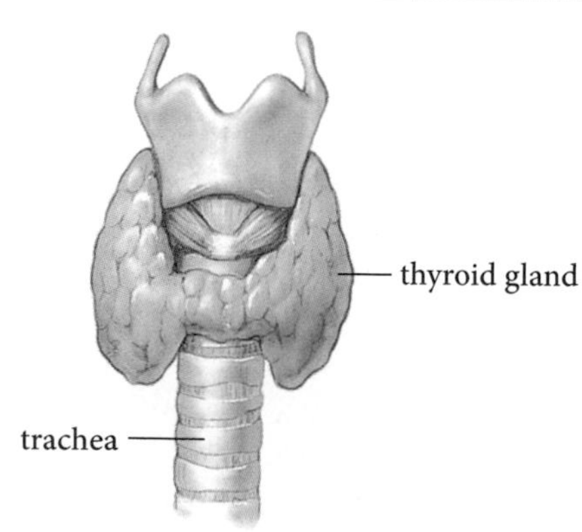

thyroid gland
front view of a human thyroid gland

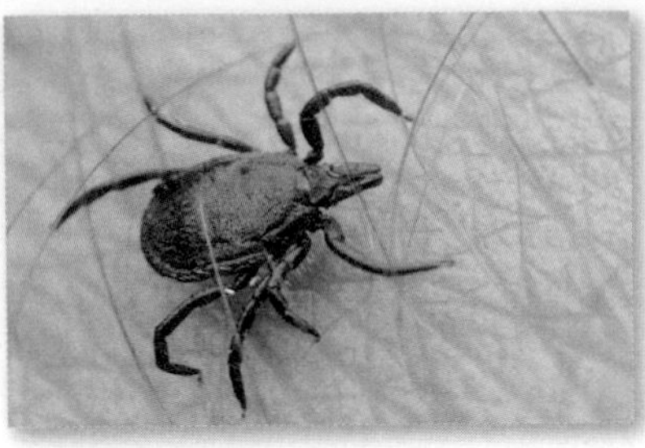

■ **tick**

animals. It secretes hormones that regulate body metabolism and the amount of calcium in the blood.

Ti The symbol for **titanium.**

tibia (tĭb′ē-ə) The larger of the two bones of the lower leg in humans, or the corresponding bone in other vertebrates. *See more at* **skeleton.**

tick (tĭk) Any of numerous small arachnids that attach themselves to the skin of humans and other vertebrate animals and suck their blood. They sometimes carry microorganisms that cause diseases, such as Lyme disease. Like mites and unlike spiders, ticks have no constriction between the cephalothorax and abdomen.

tidal wave (tīd′l) **1.** The swell or crest of surface ocean water created by the tides. **2.** An unusual rise in the level of water along a seacoast, as from a storm or a combination of wind and tide. **3.** A tsunami.

tide (tīd) **1.** The regular rise and fall in the surface level of the Earth's oceans, seas, and bays caused by the gravitational attraction of the moon and to a lesser extent the sun. **2.** A particular occurrence of such a variation. Most coastal locations experience either one low tide and one high tide or two low tides and two high tides during a 24-hour period. *See also* **ebb tide, flood tide, neap tide, spring tide.**

tide pool A pool of water remaining after a tide has retreated. Also called *tidal pool.*

till (tĭl) A mass of boulders, pebbles, sand, and silt scraped up by a moving glacier and eventually deposited by the melting of the ice.

timberline (tĭm′bər-līn′) A geographic boundary beyond which trees cannot grow. On the Earth as a whole, the timberline is the northernmost or southernmost latitude at which trees can survive; in a mountainous region, it is the highest elevation at which trees can survive. Also called *tree line.*

time (tīm) **1.** A continuous, measurable quantity in which events occur in a sequence proceeding from the past through the present to the future. *See Note at* **space-time. 2a.** An interval separating two points of this quantity; a duration. **b.** A system by which such intervals are measured or such numbers are calculated: *standard time; daylight-saving time.*

time zone Any of the divisions of the Earth's surface used to determine the time in a given locality. Most time zones are roughly 15° of longitude in width, with the time in each time zone being one hour ahead of the time in the time zone to its west and one hour behind the time in the time zone to its east. So, for example, when it is 11:00 AM in Chicago, it is 10:00 AM in Denver and noon in New York City. *See more at* **International Date Line.**

tin (tĭn) A silvery crystalline metallic element that occurs in igneous rocks. It has two crystal forms, one of which is easily shaped and very useful and the other of which occurs at low temperatures and is very brittle. It is used

■ **tide**
high tide (top) *and low tide* (bottom)

■ tombolo

to coat other metals to prevent corrosion and is a part of numerous alloys, including pewter and bronze. *Symbol* **Sn.** *Atomic number* 50. *See* **Periodic Table,** pages 254–255. *See Note at* **element.**

tissue (tĭsh′o͞o) A large collection of similar cells that together perform a specific function in an organism. Examples of tissues are cartilage and muscle in animals, and xylem in plants.

titanium (tī-tā′nē-əm) A shiny, white metallic element that occurs widely in all kinds of rocks and soils. It is lightweight, strong, and highly resistant to corrosion. Titanium alloys are used to make artificial joints and parts for aircraft and ships. *Symbol* **Ti.** *Atomic number* 22. *See* **Periodic Table,** pages 254–255.

Tl The symbol for **thallium.**

Tm The symbol for **thulium.**

TNT (tē′ĕn-tē′) Short for *trinitrotoluene.* A yellow, crystalline compound used mainly as an explosive.

toad (tōd) Any of numerous frogs that have thick, rough, often bumpy skin that sometimes secretes toxic substances. Toads usually do not live in water as adults but prefer cool, moist places on the ground. *See more at* **frog.**

toluene (tŏl′yo͞o-ēn′) A colorless liquid aromatic hydrocarbon, C_7H_8, that is poisonous and burns easily. It is used in fuels, explosives, dyes, medicines, and many industrial chemicals.

Tombaugh (tŏm′bô′), **Clyde William** 1906–1997. American astronomer who discovered Pluto in 1930.

tombolo (tŏm′bə-lō′) A sandbar that connects an island to the mainland or to another island.

tomography (tō-mŏg′rə-fē) Any of several techniques for creating three-dimensional images of the internal structure of a solid object by analyzing how waves of energy, such as x-rays or seismic waves, move through the object. CT scans are made from cross-sectional images created by tomography that uses x-rays.

ton (tŭn) **1.** A unit of weight equal to 2,000 pounds. Also called *short ton.* **2.** A unit of weight equal to 2,240 pounds. Also called *long ton.* **3.** *See* **metric ton.**

tongue (tŭng) **1.** A muscular organ in most vertebrate animals that is usually attached to the bottom of the mouth. In some reptiles, such as snakes, the tongue is mainly used as a sense organ, while in some other animals, such as frogs, chameleons, and anteaters, it is used to capture prey. The tongue is the main organ of taste in mammals, and it is used to aid in chewing and swallowing. In humans, it is also used to produce speech sounds. **2.** A similar organ in certain invertebrate animals.

tonsils (tŏn′səlz) The two oval-shaped tissues at the back of the throat in mammals that lie between the mouth and the pharynx. The tonsils are thought to help prevent the body from respiratory infections. ❖ Inflammation of the ton-

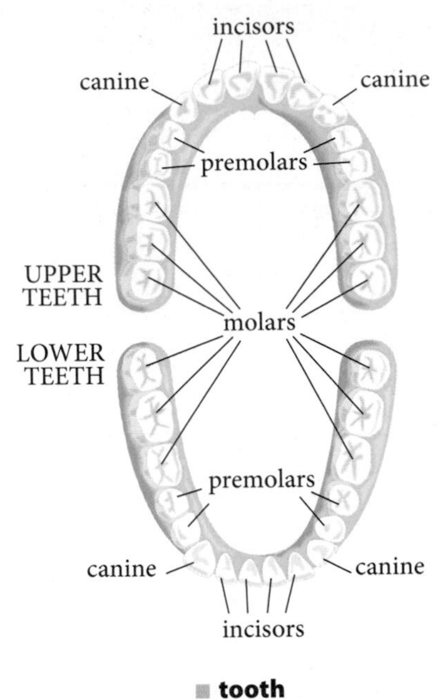

tooth
a full set of adult human teeth

sils is called **tonsillitis** (tŏn′sə-lī′tĭs). ❖ Surgical removal of the tonsils is called a **tonsillectomy** (tŏn′sə-lĕk′tə-mē).

tooth (to͞oth) *Plural* **teeth** (tēth) **1a.** Any of a set of hard bony structures inside the mouth of most vertebrate animals, used to grasp, hold, and chew and as weapons of attack and defense. In mammals and certain reptiles, the teeth are set in sockets in the jaw. In many other vertebrates, they are attached to the sides or crest of the jawbone or are located on the roof of the mouth. *See also* **dentition. b.** A similar structure in certain invertebrate animals, such as snails. **2.** A small, notched projection along a margin, especially of a leaf.

topaz (tō′păz′) A colorless, blue, yellow, brown, or pink mineral consisting largely of aluminum silicate and valued as a gem. Topaz is often found in pegmatites and is the mineral used to represent a hardness of 8 on the Mohs scale.

topography (tə-pŏg′rə-fē) **1.** The shape, height, and depth of the land surface in a place or region. Physical features that make up the topography of an area include mountains, valleys, plains, and bodies of water. Manmade features such as roads, railroads, and landfills are also often considered part of a region's topography. **2.** The detailed description or drawing of the physical features of a place or region, especially in the form of contour maps. *See more at* **gradient.**

topology (tə-pŏl′ə-jē) The mathematical study of the geometric properties that are not normally affected by changes in the size or shape of geometric figures. In topology, a donut and a coffee cup with a handle are equivalent shapes, because each has a single hole.

tornado (tôr-nā′dō) A violently rotating column of air ranging in width from a few yards to more than a mile and whirling at speeds of up to 300 miles (483 kilometers) an hour. A tornado usually takes the form of a funnel-shaped cloud extending downward out of a cumulonimbus cloud. Where the funnel touches the ground, it can cause enormous destruction.

torque (tôrk) The tendency of a force to cause an object to rotate about an axis. Torque is equal to the radius between the point where the force is applied and the axis around which the object rotates, multiplied by the strength of the portion of the force that is directed at right angles to the radius and the axis.

Torricelli (tō′rə-chĕl′ē), **Evangelista** 1608–1647. Italian mathematician and physicist who discovered that the atmosphere exerts pressure. He demonstrated that this pressure affected the level

tornado

of mercury in a tube, thereby inventing the mercury barometer.

Torrid Zone (tôr′ĭd) The zone of the Earth of central latitude, between the Tropic of Cancer and the Tropic of Capricorn. Because the sun's rays hit the Torrid Zone at a high angle or even from directly overhead, the region has a very warm climate.

torsion (tôr′shən) The stress that an object undergoes when one of its ends is twisted out of line with the other end.

tortoise (tôr′tĭs) Any of various turtles that live on land.

tourmaline (to͝or′mə-lĭn, to͝or′mə-lēn′) A silicate mineral consisting of aluminum, boron, and other elements. Tourmaline occurs in many different colors, usually in crystals shaped like 3-, 6-, or 9-sided prisms. It is especially common in pegmatites.

toxic (tŏk′sĭk) Poisonous.

toxicology (tŏk′sĭ-kŏl′ə-jē) The scientific study of poisons, of their effects and detection, and of the treatment of poisoning.

toxin (tŏk′sĭn) **1.** A poisonous substance produced by a living organism. Toxins can be products of ordinary metabolism (such as lactic acid), can be produced to kill or immobilize prey (such as the toxins in snake venom), or can be produced for self-defense (such as the cyanide produced by several plants). Toxins produced by bacteria cause disease. **2.** A poisonous or harmful nonbiological substance. Such toxins include environmental pollutants such as formaldehyde, mercury, and many chemical pesticides.

trace element (trās) **1.** An element that is present in very small amounts in a particular location or substance. Aluminum is a common trace element in drinking water, for example. **2.** An element that is essential in very small amounts for the normal functioning of an organism. Iodine and cobalt, for example, are trace elements required by humans.

tracer (trā′sər) An identifiable substance, such as a dye or radioactive isotope, that can be followed through the course of a mechanical, chemical, or biological process. Tracers are used to provide information about details of the process or about the distribution of the substances involved in it.

trachea (trā′kē-ə) *Plural* **tracheae** (trā′kē-ē′) *or* **tracheas 1.** The tube-shaped structure in vertebrate animals that leads from the larynx to the bronchi and carries air to the lungs. In mammals, the trachea is strengthened by rings of cartilage. Also called *windpipe.* **2.** One of the internal respiratory tubes of insects and some other terrestrial arthropods, which are connected to the spiracles (openings in the exoskeleton) and are used for gas exchange.

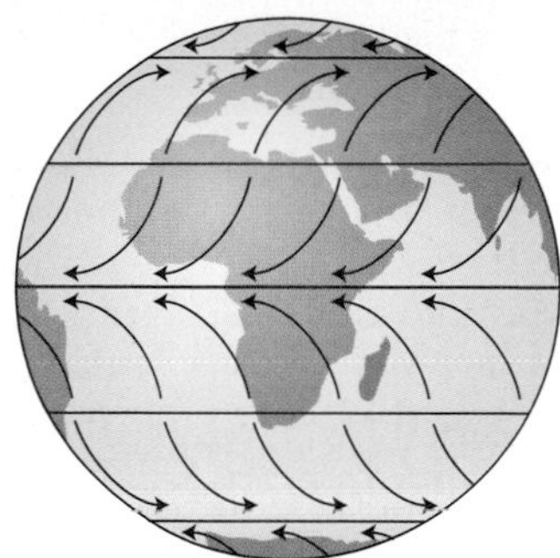

trade winds

As warm, moist air rises along the equator, surface air moves in to take its place, creating trade winds.

tract (trăkt) A system of body organs and connected parts that work together to perform a specialized function, such as digestion.

trade winds (trād) Winds that blow steadily from east to west and toward the equator over most of the Torrid Zone. The trade winds blow from the northeast in the Northern Hemisphere and from the southeast in the Southern Hemisphere, converging on the doldrums.

trait (trāt) A physical or behavioral feature of an organism, especially one that is determined largely by the organism's genes. Examples of traits are the shape of a plant's leaves and the nesting behavior of a bird.

trajectory (trə-jĕk′tə-rē) **1.** *Physics* The path that a moving object, such as an arrow or a baseball, traces through space over time. **2.** *Geometry* A curve or surface that passes through a given set of points or intersects a given series of curves or surfaces at a constant angle.

transcription (trăn-skrĭp′shən) The process in a cell by which genetic material is copied from a strand of DNA to a complementary strand of RNA (called messenger RNA). In eukaryotes, transcription takes place in the nucleus. The messenger RNA is then transported to the ribosomes, where proteins are made.

transducer (trăns-do͞o′sər) A device that converts one form of energy into another. For example, the transducer in a microphone converts sound waves into electrical signals, whereas the transducer in a loudspeaker converts electrical signals into sound waves.

trans fat (trăns) A fat that is artificially produced by adding hydrogen atoms to unsaturated vegetable oils in a process called partial hydrogenation, which makes the fat more solid. Trans fats are found in margarine and in many commercial baked and fried foods. Eating foods high in trans fats is associated with a higher risk of heart disease. *Trans* refers to the position of the hydrogen atoms attached to the carbon atoms that are linked by a double bond: the hydrogen atoms are located across from each other rather than next to each other.

transfer RNA (trăns′fər) *See under* **RNA.**

transformer (trăns-fôr′mər) A device used to change the voltage of an alternating current in one circuit (the primary circuit) to a different voltage in a second circuit (the secondary circuit). A transformer consists of a frame of an easily magnetized material, such as iron, with two coils of wire wound around it. Each coil is connected to one of the two circuits. An alternating current in the primary coil produces a magnetic field in the frame that induces an alternating current in the secondary coil. ❖ If there are more turns on the secondary coil than on the primary coil, the voltage in the secondary circuit will be greater than in the primary circuit. This is called a **step-up transformer.** In a **step-down transformer,** there are fewer turns on the secondary coil, and the voltage in the secondary circuit is less than in the primary circuit.

transform fault (trăns′fôrm′) A type of strike-slip fault that is common along the edges of tectonic plates in mid-ocean ridge regions. *See more at* **fault.**

transfusion (trăns-fyo͞o′zhən) The transfer of blood from one person to another. *See more at* **Rh factor.** *See Note at* **blood type.**

transistor (trăn-zĭs′tər) An electronic device that controls the flow of an electric current and is used as an amplifier or switch. Transistors consist of three layers of semiconductor material connected to an electric circuit. In some transistors, the outer layers have an excess of electrons; in others, the middle layer has more electrons. Transistors work like gates, allowing or closing off the flow of electrons when an electric current or voltage is applied to a particular layer. Because of their tiny size and increased efficiency, transistors have replaced electron tubes in most electronic devices.

transition element (trăn-zĭsh′ən) Any of the metallic elements within Groups 3 through 12 in the periodic table. All the transition metals have two electrons in their outermost shell, and all but zinc, cadmium, and mercury have an incompletely filled inner electron orbital just beneath the outer orbital. Transition elements have more than one valence because of their incomplete inner shells, and many form alloys easily. *See* **Periodic Table,** pages 254–255. *See Note at* **metal.**

translation (trăns-lā′shən) The process in a cell by which a strand of messenger RNA directs the assembly of a sequence of amino acids to make a protein. Translation takes place in the ribosomes, where molecules of transfer RNA deliver specific amino acids based on the three-base sequences of the genetic code.

translucent (trăns-lo͞o′sənt) Transmitting light, but not clearly enough to be transparent. A translucent object causes enough diffusion of light that an object or image on the other side of it can only be seen indistinctly. Frosted glass is translucent. *Compare* **transparent.**

transmission (trăns-mĭsh′ən) **1.** The process of allowing energy to move from one place to another through a medium or, in the case of electromagnetic radiation, through a vacuum. **2.** The sending out of energy; emission: *the transmission of radio waves by an antenna.*

transmitter (trăns′mĭt-ər) A device that generates radio or microwave signals, changes their amplitude or frequency so that they can carry information (such as spoken words), and radiates the resulting wave by means of an antenna.

transmutation (trăns′myo͞o-tā′shən) The changing of one chemical element into another. Transmutations occur naturally through radio-

Did You Know...?

transpiration

For a plant to carry out photosynthesis, it has to take in carbon dioxide from the atmosphere and release oxygen. This gas exchange takes place through tiny openings in the leaves, called stomata. A consequence of this process is that water vapor, coming from the moist surfaces of the cells inside the plant, is released through the stomata. This loss of water vapor is called *transpiration*. Plants need much more water than animals do because they are constantly losing so much through their leaves. It is estimated that ten percent of the water vapor in the atmosphere comes from transpiration. Plants can control this process to some extent, though; during dry periods, stomata close tightly to reduce the amount of water vapor that escapes.

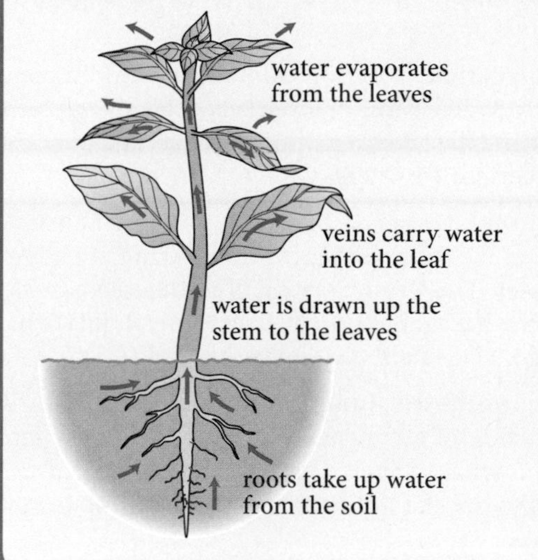

active decay, or artificially by bombarding the nucleus of a substance with subatomic particles.

trans-Neptunian object (trăns′nĕp-to͞o′nē-ən) A celestial object that orbits the sun at a greater distance on average than Neptune.

transparent (trăns-pâr′ənt) Transmitting light so as to be seen through clearly. The glass in windows is usually transparent. *See Note at* **glass.** *Compare* **translucent.**

transpiration (trăn′spə-rā′shən) The process of giving off water vapor through small openings in a plant part, such as a leaf.

transplant (trăns-plănt′) *Verb* **1.** To uproot and replant a growing plant. **2.** To transfer tissue or an organ from one body or body part to another. —*Noun* (trăns′plănt′) **3.** A plant that has been uprooted and replanted. **4.** An operation in which tissue or an organ is transplanted: *a kidney transplant; a stem cell transplant.*

transpose (trăns-pōz′) To move a term or quantity from one side of an algebraic equation to the other by adding or subtracting that term to or from both sides. By subtracting 2 from both sides of the equation $2 + x = 4$, one can transpose the 2 to the other side, yielding $x = 4 - 2$, and thus determine that x equals 2.

transposon (trăns-pō′zŏn) A segment of DNA that is capable of moving into a new position within the same chromosome or to another chromosome. Also called *jumping gene.*

transverse wave (trăns-vûrs′, trăns′vûrs′) A wave in which the particles of the medium move at right angles to the direction that the wave travels through the medium. For example, the waves on a taut string or the ripples on a surface of standing water are transverse waves. Electromagnetic waves are also transverse waves. *See more at* **wave.** *Compare* **longitudinal wave.**

trapezium (trə-pē′zē-əm) A four-sided figure having no parallel sides.

trapezoid (trăp′ĭ-zoid′) A four-sided figure having two parallel sides.

tree (trē) A perennial plant that typically has a single woody stem and increases in width by producing new layers of vascular tissues during every growing season.

treeline or **tree line** (trē′līn′) *See* **timberline.**

tremor (trĕm′ər) A shaking or vibrating movement, as from a small earthquake.

T. rex (tē′ rĕks′) *See under* **tyrannosaur.**

triangle (trī′ăng′gəl) A closed geometric figure consisting of three sides.

triangulation (trī-ăng′gyə-lā′shən) **1.** A method used to determine distances and directions of a region of land. The region is divided into a set of triangles based on a line of known length. The triangles are then measured using trigonometry. **2.**

A method of determining the location of a boat or aircraft by means of trigonometry.

Triassic (trī-ăs′ĭk) The earliest period of the Mesozoic Era, from about 251 to 200 million years ago. During the Triassic Period, land life diversified, dinosaurs arose, and the earliest mammals appeared. *See Chart at* **geologic time,** pages 146–147.

tributary (trĭb′yə-tĕr′ē) A stream that flows into a river or larger stream.

triceps (trī′sĕps′) The muscle at the back of the upper arm that straightens the elbow. The triceps has three points of origin.

triceratops (trī-sĕr′ə-tŏps′) A large, plant-eating dinosaur of the late Cretaceous Period, measuring up to 25 feet (7.6 meters) in length. The triceratops had three horns: one long horn above each eye and a short horn on the beaklike snout. A wide, bony plate extended from the back of the skull.

trichinosis (trĭk′ə-nō′sĭs) A disease caused by a parasitic worm found in raw or undercooked meat, especially pork. It is characterized by mild to severe intestinal upset, fever, and pain.

triclinic (trī-klĭn′ĭk) Relating to a crystal having three axes of different lengths intersecting at oblique angles. The mineral microcline (a type of feldspar) has triclinic crystals. *See more at* **crystal.**

WORD HISTORY

triceratops

The name of the dinosaur known as the *triceratops* is made out of three Greek roots. The first part, *tri–*, means "three," and appears in other English words, such as *triangle* and *tripod.* The *–cerat–* part is from the Greek word for "horn," *keras.* This Greek word was also used to name the hard protein that horns and hair are made of, *keratin.* The *–ops* at the end of the dinosaur's name means "face," and is related to other Greek words meaning "eye" and "to see." These words are the source of such English terms as *optics* and *autopsy* (which once meant "personal inspection"). So the triceratops is simply a dinosaur having "three horns on the face."

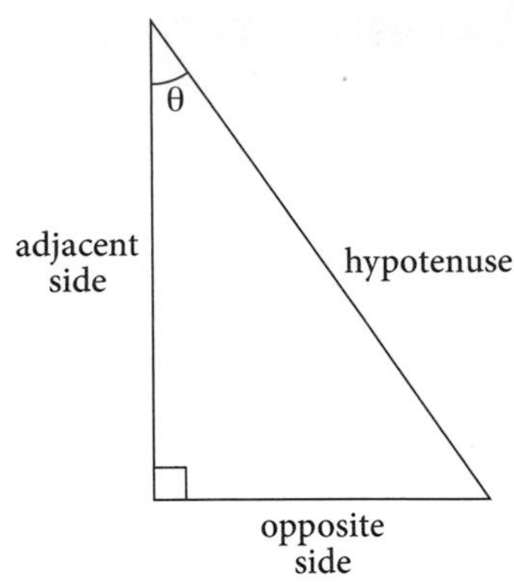

■ **trigonometric function**

In a right triangle, the trigonometric functions are:

$$\textit{sine}\ \theta = \frac{\textit{opposite}}{\textit{hypotenuse}} \qquad \textit{cosine}\ \theta = \frac{\textit{adjacent}}{\textit{hypotenuse}}$$

$$\textit{tangent}\ \theta = \frac{\textit{opposite}}{\textit{adjacent}}$$

tricuspid (trī-kŭs′pĭd) A tooth having three points or cusps, especially a molar.

triglyceride (trī-glĭs′ə-rīd′) Any of various compounds consisting of three fatty acids and glycerol that are the chief constituents of fats and oils. Triglycerides are esters.

trigonal (trī-gō′nəl) Relating to a crystal having three axes of equal length intersecting at oblique angles. This crystal system is considered a subset of the hexagonal system. The mineral quartz has trigonal crystals. *See more at* **crystal.**

trigonometric function (trĭg′ə-nə-mĕt′rĭk) A function of an angle, as the sine, cosine, or tangent, whose value is expressed as a ratio of two of the sides of the right triangle that contains the angle.

trigonometry (trĭg′ə-nŏm′ĭ-trē) The study of the properties and uses of trigonometric functions.

trilobite (trī′lə-bīt′) Any of numerous extinct sea animals that had a body with a hard outer covering divided by grooves into three lengthwise sections. Trilobites were arthropods. They lived during the Paleozoic Era and are often found as fossils.

trinitrotoluene (trī-nī′trō-tŏl′yo͞o-ēn′) *See* **TNT.**

triple bond (trĭp′əl) A chemical bond in which

three covalent bonds are formed between two atoms. *See more at* **covalent bond.**

tritium (trĭt′ē-əm, trĭsh′ē-əm) A radioactive isotope of hydrogen whose nucleus has one proton and two neutrons and whose atomic mass is about 3. Tritium is rare in nature but can be made artificially in nuclear reactions. It is used in thermonuclear weapons and sometimes as a tracer. *See more at* **hydrogen.**

trivalent (trī-vā′lənt) *Chemistry* Having a valence of three.

trophic (trŏf′ĭk) Relating to the feeding habits of different organisms in a food chain or web: *trophic interactions between mammals and parasitic insects.* ❖ A position that a group of organisms occupies in a food chain is called a **trophic level.** Producers, such as plants, are in the lowest trophic level.

tropic (trŏp′ĭk) **1.** Either of the two parallels of latitude representing the points farthest north and south at which the sun can shine directly overhead. The northern tropic is the Tropic of Cancer, and the southern one is the Tropic of Capricorn. **2. tropics.** The region of the Earth lying between these latitudes; the Torrid Zone. The tropics are generally the warmest and most humid region of the Earth. —*Adjective* **tropical.**

Tropic of Cancer The parallel of latitude 23°26' north of the equator. It forms the boundary between the Torrid Zone and the North Temperate Zone.

Tropic of Capricorn The parallel of latitude 23°26' south of the equator. It forms the boundary between the Torrid Zone and the South Temperate Zone.

■ **trilobite**

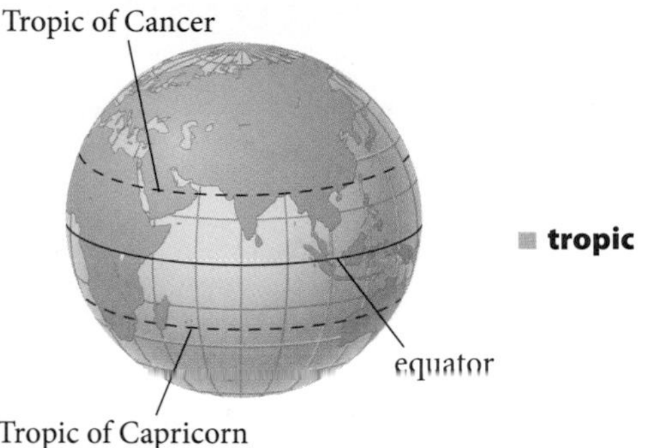

■ **tropic**

tropism (trō′pĭz′əm) Growth or movement of a plant or animal toward or away from an external stimulus, such as light, heat, or gravity.

tropopause (trō′pə-pôz′, trŏp′ə-pôz′) The boundary between the upper troposphere and the lower stratosphere, varying in altitude from about 5 miles (8 kilometers) at the poles to about 11 miles (18 kilometers) at the equator.

troposphere (trō′pə-sfîr′, trŏp′ə-sfîr′) The lowest region of the atmosphere, bounded by the Earth's surface and the tropopause and characterized by temperatures that decrease with increasing altitude. Weather and most cloud formations occur in the troposphere.

trough (trôf) The lowest part of a wave. *See more at* **wave.**

true north *See* **geographic north.**

trypanosome (trĭ-păn′ə-sōm′) Any of various parasitic protozoans that are transmitted to the bloodstream of humans and other vertebrate animals by the bite of certain insects. They can cause serious diseases such as sleeping sickness.

trypsin (trĭp′sĭn) An enzyme that aids digestion by breaking down proteins. It is produced by the pancreas and secreted into the small intestine.

tryptophan (trĭp′tə-făn′) An essential amino acid. *See more at* **amino acid.**

tsetse fly (tsĕt′sē) Any of several bloodsucking African flies that often carry and transmit the protozoans that cause sleeping sickness.

tsunami (tso͞o-nä′mē) A very large ocean wave that is caused by an underwater geological event

tsunami

such as an earthquake, volcanic eruption, or landslide and often causes extreme destruction when it strikes land.

tuber (to͞o′bər) A thick, fleshy, usually underground outgrowth of the stem or rhizome of a plant, bearing buds from which new plants grow. Potatoes are tubers. *Compare* **bulb, corm, rhizome, runner.**

tubercle (to͞o′bər-kəl) A small rounded projection or swelling, as on the roots of legumes or on skin, on a bone, or in an organ.

tuberculosis (to͝o-bûr′kyə-lō′sĭs) A contagious disease caused by a bacterium and characterized by abnormal growths, called tubercles, in affected body tissues. Tuberculosis most commonly affects the lungs, causing coughing, fever, weight loss, and chest pain. It is usually transmitted by breathing contaminated air.

tufa (to͞o′fə) A rock formed of minerals such as calcium carbonate deposited during the evaporation of lake water, spring water, or groundwater.

tuff (tŭf) A rock made up of particles of volcanic ash, varying in size from fine sand to coarse gravel.

tumor (to͞o′mər) An abnormal growth of tissue resulting from uncontrolled growth of specific cells. Tumors can be benign (unlikely to spread to other body parts) or malignant (likely to spread). *See Note at* **cancer.**

tundra (tŭn′drə) A cold, treeless, usually lowland area of far northern regions. The subsoil of tundras is permanently frozen, but in summer the top layer of soil thaws and can support low-growing mosses, lichens, grasses, and small shrubs.

tungsten (tŭng′stən) A hard, gray to white metallic element that is very resistant to corrosion. It has the highest melting point of all elements. Tungsten remains very strong at high temperatures and is used to make light-bulb filaments and to increase the hardness and strength of steel. Also called *wolfram. Symbol* **W.** *Atomic number* 74. *See* **Periodic Table,** pages 254–255.

tunicate (to͞o′nĭ-kĭt) Any of various marine

tufa
tufa formations in Mono Lake, California

tundra
Dovrefjell National Park, Norway

Alan Turing

chordate animals, including the sea squirts, having a rounded or cylindrical body enclosed in a tough outer covering. Tunicate larvae are free-swimming and have a notochord (a stiff structure along the back), but most species lose the notochord and become fixed to rocks or other objects when mature.

turbine (tûr′bĭn, tûr′bīn′) Any of various mechanical devices in which the kinetic energy of a moving fluid, such as water, steam, or gas, is converted to rotary motion. Turbines are used in boat propulsion systems, hydroelectric power generators, and jet aircraft engines.

turbojet (tûr′bō-jĕt′) **1.** A jet engine in which the exhaust gas operates a turbine that in turn drives a compressor that forces air into the intake of the engine. **2.** An aircraft powered by an engine or engines of this type.

turbulent flow (tûr′byə-lənt) Movement of a fluid in which the individual particles of fluid move in irregular patterns even though the overall flow is in one direction. Turbulent flow is common in fluids that are moving rapidly and have low viscosity. *Compare* **laminar flow.**

turf (tûrf) A surface layer of earth containing a dense growth of grass and its matted roots.

Turing (tŏŏr′ĭng), **Alan Mathison** 1912–1954. British mathematician. In 1937 he formulated a precise mathematical concept for a theoretical

Did You Know...?

turbojet

Fully loaded, a fighter aircraft can weigh over 60,000 pounds. Yet its *turbojet* engines are powerful enough to enable it to lift into the air, climb to altitudes over 60,000 feet, and fly at speeds over 1,500 miles an hour. Where does this power come from? From the movement of air itself. Every turbojet has a compressor, a series of small rotating fan blades. These blades draw in air and pressurize it, driving it back into a combustion chamber where fuel (such as kerosene) is injected and ignited. The burning of the fuel causes the air to expand, adding to the already high pressure and causing the mixture of hot air and gas to rush over turbines with enormous speed. This causes the turbine blades to turn, and they spin a drive shaft that rotates the compressor fans. The hot pressurized air then blasts out the rear opening of the engine, forcing the plane forward and generating aerodynamic lift.

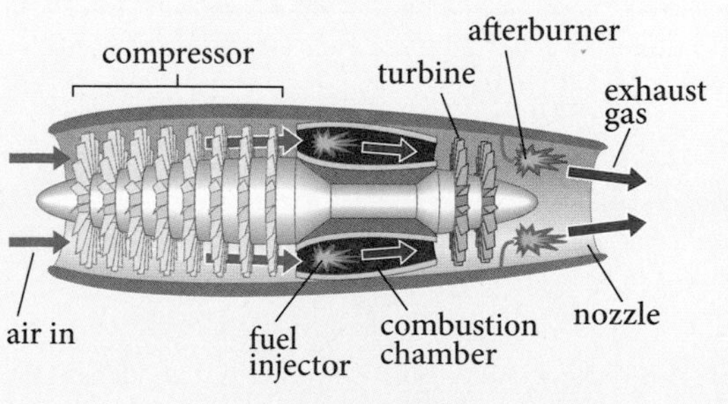

computing machine, a key step in the development of the first computer. During World War II Turing did important work on breaking German codes.

turpentine (tûr′pən-tīn′) **1.** A thin, easily vaporized oil, $C_{10}H_{16}$, that is distilled from the wood or resin of certain pine trees. It is used as a paint thinner and solvent. **2.** The sticky mixture of resin and oil from which this oil is distilled.

turtle (tûr′tl) Any of various egg-laying reptiles having a bony or leathery shell into which the head, legs, and tail can be pulled for protection. Turtles that live on land rather than in water are often called tortoises.

tusk (tŭsk) A long, pointed tooth, usually one of a pair, projecting from the mouth of certain animals, such as elephants, walruses, and wild pigs.

tympanic membrane (tĭm-păn′ĭk) *See* **eardrum.**

typhoid fever (tī′foid′) A life-threatening disease caused by bacteria and characterized by high fever, intestinal bleeding, and often pink spots on the skin. It is transmitted through contaminated food and water.

typhoon (tī-fo͞on′) A powerful tropical cyclone occurring in the western Pacific Ocean. *See Note at* **cyclone.**

typhus (tī′fəs) Any of several diseases transmitted by lice, fleas, or mites and characterized by high fever and skin rash. Typhus carried by lice can cause epidemics of the disease, which may be fatal in people with weakened immune systems.

tyrannosaur (tĭ-răn′ə-sôr′) Any of various large meat-eating dinosaurs of the Cretaceous Period. Tyrannosaurs had short deep jaws with large teeth, long hind limbs, and short forelimbs. ❖ The best-known tyrannosaur is **Tyrannosaurus rex,** often abbreviated **T. rex.** Over 40 *T. rex* skeletons have been found, all of them in western North America.

tyrosine (tī′rə-sēn′) A nonessential amino acid. *See more at* **amino acid.**

U **1.** Abbreviation of **uracil. 2.** The symbol for **uranium.**

udder (ŭd′ər) A bag-shaped part of cows and certain other female mammals, such as sheep, goats, and camels, in which milk is formed and stored. Udders contain the mammary glands and have teats from which the young suckle.

ulcer (ŭl′sər) An inflamed sore on the skin or on a mucous membrane, as of the mouth or stomach.

ulna (ŭl′nə) The larger of the two bones of the forearm in humans, or the corresponding bone in other vertebrates. *See more at* **skeleton.**

ultrasound (ŭl′trə-sound′) **1.** Sound waves that have frequencies higher than 20,000 hertz, which are too high for humans to hear. **2.** The medical use of ultrasound waves to produce images of the inside of the body or to provide deep heat or vibration to a specific region of the body. *—Adjective* **ultrasonic** (ŭl′trə-sŏn′ĭk).

ultraviolet (ŭl′trə-vī′ə-lĭt) Relating to electromagnetic radiation having wavelengths shorter than those of visible light but longer than those of x-rays. Ultraviolet radiation is emitted by the sun, and some of it is absorbed by ozone in the atmosphere. Too much exposure to ultraviolet light can lead to sunburn, skin cancer, or cataracts. *See more at* **electromagnetic spectrum.** *See Notes at* **infrared, ozone.**

umbel (ŭm′bəl) A flat or rounded flower cluster in which the individual flower stalks arise from about the same point on the stem. Milkweed flowers are arranged in umbels.

umbilical cord (ŭm-bĭl′ĭ-kəl) The flexible cordlike structure connecting a fetus at the abdomen to the placenta. It contains blood vessels that supply nourishment to the fetus and remove its wastes.

umbra (ŭm′brə) **1.** The darkest part of a shadow, especially the completely dark portion of the shadow cast by Earth, the moon, or another object during an eclipse. **2.** The darkest region of a sunspot. *Compare* **penumbra.**

uncertainty principle (ŭn-sûr′tn-tē) A principle in quantum mechanics stating that for certain pairs of observable properties of a particle, the more precisely one property is measured, the less precisely the other property can be measured. For example, it is impossible to measure a particle's exact position and exact momentum (that is, its mass multiplied by its velocity) at the same time. The principle was formulated in the 1920s by Werner Heisenberg.

Did You Know...?

ultrasound

Any sound whose frequency is higher than the upper end of the normal range of human hearing (higher than about 20,000 hertz) is called *ultrasound.* (Sound at frequencies too low to be audible—lower than about 20 hertz—is called *infrasound.*) Medical ultrasound images (of a fetus in the womb, for example) are made by directing ultrasonic waves into the body, where they bounce off internal organs and are reflected back to a detector. Because ultrasonic waves have very short wavelengths, they can be used to create images of very small objects. Ultrasound can also be used to focus large amounts of energy into very small spaces, making it possible, for example, to break up kidney stones without surgical incision and without disturbing surrounding tissue. Ultrasound's industrial uses include measuring the thickness of materials, welding, and testing for cracks in pipelines.

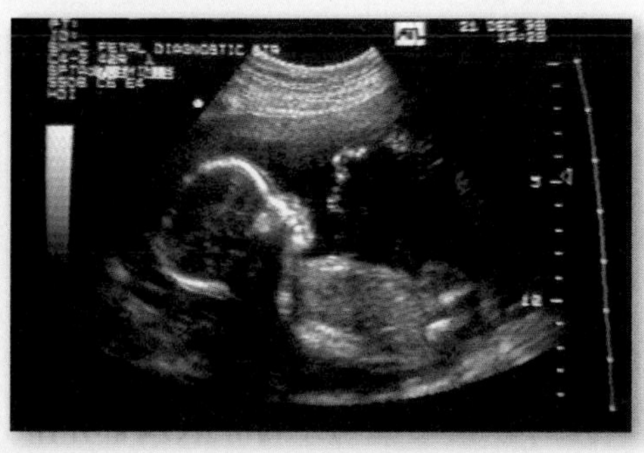

undergrowth (ŭn′dər-grōth′) Low-growing plants, shrubs, and young trees that grow under the taller trees in a forest.

undertow (ŭn′dər-tō′) An underwater current flowing strongly away from shore. Undertows are generally caused by the seaward return of water from waves that have broken against the shore.

ungulate (ŭng′gyə-lĭt) A hoofed mammal. Ungulates with an even number of toes are called artiodactyls, and those with an odd number of toes are called perissodactyls.

unicellular (yo͞o′nĭ-sĕl′yə-lər) Having or consisting of a single cell; one-celled: *unicellular organisms. Compare* **multicellular.**

union (yo͞on′yən) A set whose members belong to at least one of a group of two or more given sets. The union of the sets {1,2,3} and {3,4,5} is the set {1,2,3,4,5}, and the union of the sets {6,7} and {11,12,13} is the set {6,7,11,12,13}.

United States Customary System The main system of weights and measures used in the United States and a few other countries. The system is based on the yard as a unit of length, the pound as a unit of weight, the gallon as a unit of liquid volume, and the bushel as a unit of dry volume. *See Table at* **measurement.**

univalent (yo͞o′nĭ-vā′lənt) *Chemistry* Having a valence of one.

univalve (yo͞o′nĭ-vălv′) Any of numerous mollusks, such as a snail, having a single shell. All univalves are gastropods. *Compare* **bivalve.**

universe (yo͞o′nə-vûrs′) All matter, energy, and space-time, including our solar system, the stars and galaxies, and the contents of the space between the galaxies, regarded as a whole.

unsaturated (ŭn-săch′ə-rā′tĭd) **1.** Relating to an organic compound that contains one or more double bonds or triple bonds between carbon atoms and therefore tends to combine easily with additional atoms or radicals. Acetylene and unsaturated fatty acids are examples of unsaturated compounds. *Compare* **saturated.** *See also* **monounsaturated, polyunsaturated. 2.** Relating to a solution that is capable of dissolving more solute than it already contains.

unsaturated fat A fat containing fatty acids that are unsaturated (having some double bonds between the carbon atoms). Most fats derived from plants (such as olive oil, peanut oil, and canola oil) are unsaturated, as are fats from certain fish. Unsaturated fats are usually liquid at room temperature. Eating foods high in unsaturated fats is associated with a lower risk of heart disease. *Compare* **saturated fat, trans fat.**

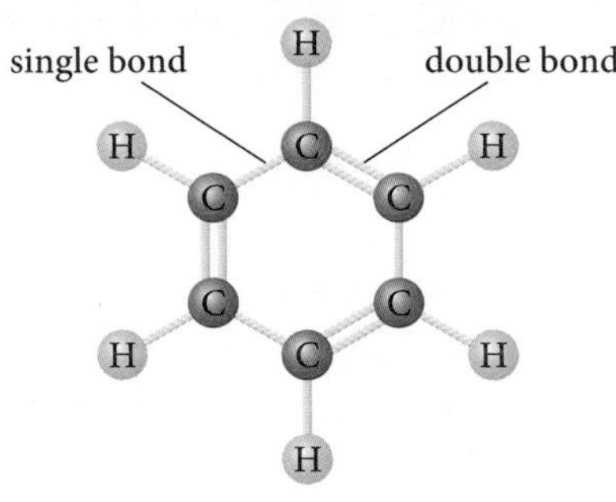

unsaturated
a benzene molecule (C_6H_6), with three double bonds

unstable (ŭn-stā′bəl) **1.** Liable to change spontaneously into a nucleus or atomic particle with less mass. For example, the nucleus of uranium-238 is unstable and changes by radioactive decay into the nucleus of thorium-234, a lighter element. **2.** Relating to a chemical compound that easily decomposes or changes into other compounds or into elements. Such reactions are often rapid and explosive. Potassium, for example, reacts violently with water to form combustible hydrogen and potassium hydroxide. **3.** Relating to a substance that is likely to share electrons; reactive.

uracil (yo͝or′ə-sĭl) A base that is a component of RNA, forming a base pair with adenine during transcription.

uranium (yo͝o-rā′nē-əm) A heavy, silvery-white, highly toxic, radioactive metallic element of the actinide series. It occurs in several minerals and ores, such as pitchblende. Uranium is used as a fuel for nuclear reactors to generate electricity. *Symbol* **U.** *Atomic number* 92. *See* **Periodic Table,** pages 254–255.

Uranus (yo͝or′ə-nəs, yo͝o-rā′nəs) The seventh planet from the sun and the third largest, with a diameter about four times that of Earth. Uranus is composed mainly of hydrogen and helium gases and is encircled by a thin system of rings. *See Table at* **solar system,** pages 312–313.

urea (yo͝o-rē′ə) The chief nitrogen-containing waste product excreted in the urine of mammals, most amphibians, and certain fish. It is produced by the breakdown of amino acids in the liver and is also made artificially for use in fertilizers and medicine.

ureter (yo͝o-rē′tər, yo͝or′ĭ-tər) Either of two long, narrow ducts that carry urine from the kidneys to the urinary bladder.

urethra (yo͝o-rē′thrə) The duct through which urine passes from the bladder to the outside of the body in mammals and some fish and birds. In male mammals, semen is discharged through the urethra during sexual intercourse.

uric acid (yo͝or′ĭk) The chief nitrogen-containing waste product excreted by birds, most reptiles, and insects. It is produced by the breakdown of amino acids.

urinary system (yo͝or′ə-nĕr′ē) The system of organs involved in the formation and excretion of urine. In mammals, the urinary system consists of the kidneys, ureters, bladder, and urethra. Also called *urinary tract.*

urine (yo͝or′ĭn) A liquid or semisolid substance containing waste products of metabolism that are filtered from the blood by the kidneys. In most vertebrates except birds and some reptiles, urine is stored in the bladder and discharged from the body through the urethra.

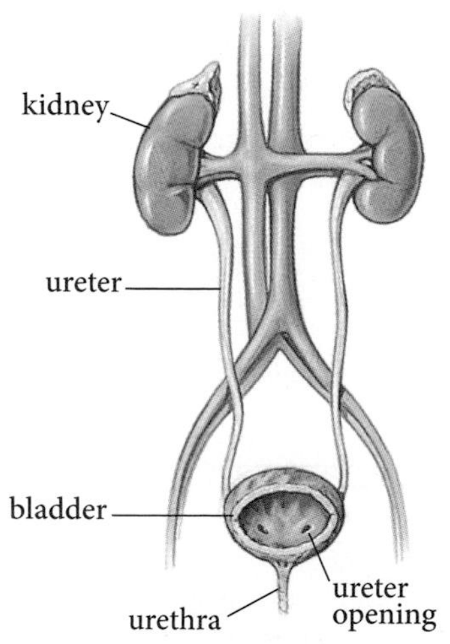

urinary system
human urinary system

Ursa Major (ûr′sə) A constellation in the polar region of the Northern Hemisphere near Draco and Leo. It contains the seven stars that form the Big Dipper.

Ursa Minor A constellation very near the north celestial pole, containing the ladle-shaped grouping of seven stars called the Little Dipper. Polaris, the North Star, is at the end of the dipper's handle.

uterus (yo͞o′tər-əs) A hollow, muscular organ of female mammals in which a fertilized egg implants and develops. In most mammals the uterus is divided into two parts, but in humans and certain other primates, it is a single structure. The embryo develops in the uterus until birth, when it passes to the outside through the vagina. Also called *womb. See more at* **menstrual cycle.**

UV Abbreviation of **ultraviolet.**

UVA (yo͞o′vē′ā′) Ultraviolet radiation that is found in sunlight, has a wavelength between 320 and 400 nanometers, and after long-term exposure can cause damage to the skin, including premature aging and cancer. Unlike UVB, UVA can pass through clouds and glass. The letter *A* designates the first of the categories based on wavelength in which ultraviolet radiation is classified.

UVB (yo͞o′vē′bē′) Ultraviolet radiation that is found in sunlight, has a wavelength between 290 and 320 nanometers, and can cause damage to the skin, including sunburn, premature aging, and cancer. The letter *B* designates the second of the categories based on wavelength in which ultraviolet radiation is classified.

UV index (yo͞o′vē′) A scale ranging from zero to eleven or above, used to estimate the risk for sunburn on a given day in a specific location. The UV index takes into account conditions, such as the amount of cloud cover and ozone in the atmosphere, that affect the amount of ultraviolet light at the Earth's surface.

uvula (yo͞o′vyə-lə) The small cone-shaped mass of fleshy tissue that hangs from the end of the soft palate above the tongue in the back of the mouth.

v Abbreviation of **velocity.**

V 1. The symbol for **vanadium. 2.** Abbreviation of **volt. 3.** Abbreviation of **volume.**

vaccine (văk-sēn′) A substance that stimulates cells in the immune system to recognize and attack disease-causing agents such as bacteria and viruses, especially through the production of antibodies. Most vaccines are given by injection or in a form that can be swallowed. Vaccines usually contain a killed or weakened form of the agent or a component of it such as a DNA fragment.

vacuole (văk′yo͞o-ōl′) A small cavity in the cytoplasm of most cells, especially plant cells, surrounded by a membrane and filled with a watery fluid and dissolved substances such as sugars, enzymes, and amino acids. Vacuoles act as storage sites for food or waste. *See more at* **cell.**

vacuum (văk′yo͞om) A region in which there is no matter or almost no matter, as in outer space or within a vacuum tube.

vacuum bottle A small container with a double wall and a partial vacuum in the space between the two walls. Vacuum bottles are used to minimize the transfer of heat between the inside and the outside and thus keep the contents at a desired temperature.

vacuum tube An electron tube from which all air has been removed so that the moving electrons do not collide with any gas particles and can move more efficiently from one electrode to the other. Cathode-ray tubes, found in older televisions, are a type of vacuum tube. *Compare* **electron tube.**

vagina (və-jī′nə) The passage leading from the uterus to the outside of the body in female mammals. Offspring pass through the vagina during birth.

vagus nerve (vā′gəs) A long nerve that passes from the brain to the face, trunk, and abdomen. It controls the muscles of the larynx (voice box), stimulates digestion, and regulates the heartbeat. The vagus nerve is a cranial nerve.

valence (vā′ləns) A whole number that represents the ability of an atom or a group of atoms to combine with other atoms or groups of atoms. The valence is determined by the number of electrons that an atom can lose, add, or share. A carbon atom, for example, can share four electrons with other atoms and therefore has a valence of 4.

valine (văl′ēn′) An essential amino acid. *See more at* **amino acid.**

valley (văl′ē) A long, narrow region of low land between ranges of mountains, hills, or other high areas, often having a river or stream running along the bottom. Valleys are most commonly formed through the erosion of land by rivers or

Did You Know...?

vaccine

The first *vaccine* was developed for a deadly disease that no longer exists: smallpox. For centuries, smallpox was a leading cause of death all over the world. If victims survived, they often had terrible scars. Various methods for inducing immunity to smallpox had long been used in parts of Africa and Asia, but they had a high risk of causing fatal smallpox infections. Smallpox was declared to be eradicated in 1980, following a massive campaign that involved vaccinating millions of people using a technique first developed by Edward Jenner, a British surgeon, in the late 1700s. Jenner observed that people who got cowpox, a mild disease contracted from milking infected cows, did not get smallpox. To test his theory that cowpox provided protection against smallpox, Jenner did an experiment: he took liquid from the cowpox sores of a milkmaid and injected a young boy with it. Two months later, he exposed the boy to smallpox (something that would be considered unethical by today's standards). Luckily, as Jenner expected, the boy remained healthy. The injected material became known as a *vaccine,* after the Latin name Jenner used for cowpox: *variolae vaccinae* ("smallpox of a cow").

glaciers. They also form where large regions of land are lowered because of geological faults.

value (văl′yo͞o) **1.** *Mathematics* An assigned or calculated numerical quantity. **2.** The relative darkness or lightness of a color. *See more at* **color.**

valve (vălv) **1a.** Any of various mechanical devices that control the flow of liquids, gases, or loose material through pipes or channels by blocking and uncovering openings. **b.** The movable part or element of such a device. **2.** Any of various structures that prevent the backward flow of a body fluid. Examples include the valves between the chambers of the heart and the valves in the veins. **3.** One of the paired hinged shells of certain mollusks, such as clams and oysters.

vanadium (və-nā′dē-əm) A soft, bright-white metallic element that occurs naturally in several minerals. It has good structural strength and is used especially to make strong varieties of steel. *Symbol* **V.** *Atomic number* 23. *See* **Periodic Table,** pages 254–255.

Van Allen belt (văn ăl′ən) Either of the two zones surrounding the Earth in which atomic particles with very high energies are trapped by Earth's magnetic field. The inner belt lies between about 300 and 4,000 miles (500 to 6,500 kilometers) above Earth's equator and consists mostly of a mix of protons and electrons. The upper belt lies between about 9,300 and 18,600 miles (15,000 to 30,000 kilometers) and consists mostly of protons.

Van de Graaff (văn′ də grăf′), **Robert Jemison** 1901–1967. American physicist. In 1929, he invented an electrical generator (later called the Van de Graaff generator) that was adapted for use as a particle accelerator and became an important research tool for atomic physicists. The generator was also used to produce x-rays used for cancer treatment.

Van de Graaff generator A device used to build up static electrical charge of very high voltages by means of a rapidly moving belt that transfers electric charge from a power supply to a spherical metal terminal. When an object touches the terminal, the accumulated charge is transferred to the object.

van der Waals force (văn′ dər wôlz′) A weak force of attraction between electrically neutral molecules that are very close to each other. It is caused by the temporary attraction between a slightly positively charged region of one molecule with a slightly negatively charged region of another molecule. This force is much weaker than a hydrogen bond or an ionic or covalent bond.

vapor (vā′pər) The gaseous state of a substance that can be condensed to a liquid or a solid by increasing the pressure while keeping the temperature constant. At room temperature, water in its gaseous state is referred to as a vapor because it can also exist as a liquid at that temperature, but oxygen is referred to as a gas, not a vapor, because it cannot exist as a liquid at that temperature. Oxygen will not liquefy (and form vapor) at any pressure at temperatures above −181°F (−119°C). The term *vapor* is sometimes used for substances that are actually aerosols (particles suspended in a vapor or gas). — *Verb* **vaporize.**

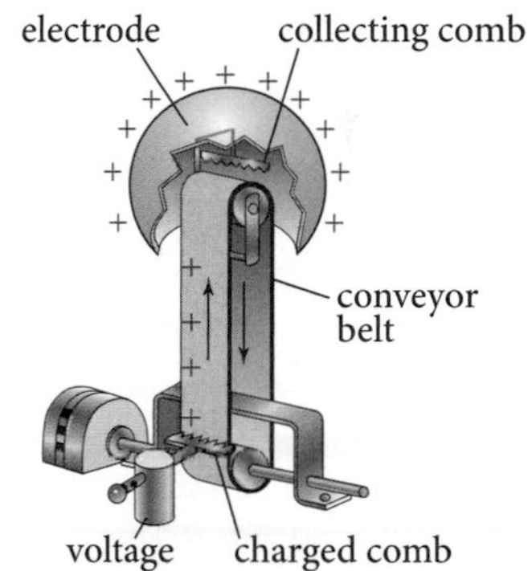

Van de Graaff generator

top: *The charged comb continuously pulls electrons from the conveyor belt. The belt, now positively charged, pulls electrons from the collecting comb, transferring a positive charge to the electrode.*
bottom: *Touching the electrode causes a person's hair to stand straight up as the positive charge spreads to the tips of the strands of hair, which then repel each other.*

vapor pressure 1. The pressure exerted by a vapor that is in equilibrium with its liquid or solid phase. At a given temperature, different substances have different vapor pressures depending on how tightly their atoms or molecules are bound to each other. For example, alcohol has a higher vapor pressure than water and consequently evaporates more quickly. Heating a liquid increases its vapor pressure. **2.** The pressure exerted by water vapor in the atmosphere.

variable (vârʹē-ə-bəl) **1.** A quantity that can take on any of a set of values. **2.** A symbol that represents such a quantity, such as x in the expression $3x + 2$.

variable star A star whose brightness changes periodically. The variation can be caused in several different ways, such as by internal changes in a single star or by the periodic eclipsing of a brighter star by a darker star in a binary star system.

varicella (vărʹĭ-sĕlʹə) *See* **chickenpox.**

vascular (văsʹkyə-lər) Relating to or containing cells or vessels that transport or circulate liquids such as blood, lymph, or water within an animal or plant.

vascular cambium The cambium that produces the vascular tissues xylem and phloem in woody plants. *See more at* **cambium.**

vascular plant Any of numerous plants, including the seed plants and the ferns, that have well-developed vascular tissues consisting of phloem to transport sugars and other organic nutrients and xylem to transport water and minerals. *See more at* **phloem, xylem.**

vas deferens (văsʹ dĕfʹə-rĕnzʹ) Either of two ducts through which sperm passes from a testis to the urethra.

vector (vĕkʹtər) **1.** *Physics* A quantity, such as velocity or change of position, that has both magnitude and direction. *Compare* **scalar. 2.** *Biology* An organism, such as a mosquito or tick, that spreads disease-causing agents from one host to another without harm to itself.

Vega (vēʹgə, väʹgə) A star in the constellation Lyra. It is the fifth brightest star in the night sky.

vegetable (vĕjʹtə-bəl) **1.** A plant part that is used for food and usually comes from the roots (such as carrots), leaves (such as lettuce), or stems (such as celery). Some seeds and fruits, such as beans, peas, and squash, are also called vegetables. **2.** A plant from which such parts are harvested. *See Note at* **fruit.**

USAGE

velocity/speed

We normally think of *velocity* as the speed at which an object is traveling. But in physics, velocity and speed are not the same. Like speed, velocity refers to the rate at which an object is moving—the distance per unit of time. But velocity in physics also includes the direction in which the object is moving, whereas direction has no bearing on an object's speed. For example, if two cars were driving at a rate of 50 miles per hour, and both headed due north, you could rightly say that they were both traveling at the same speed and at the same velocity. But if one of the cars turned west at a certain point, continuing at the same rate of 50 miles per hour, you could only say that they were traveling at the same speed, not at the same velocity. A car traveling around a curve may maintain the same speed throughout, but its velocity is constantly changing. A change in velocity over time is called acceleration.

vein (vān) **1.** Any of the blood vessels that carry blood toward the heart. Veins are thin-walled and contain valves that prevent the backflow of blood. All veins except the pulmonary vein (which returns to the heart from the lungs) carry blood having low levels of oxygen. **2.** One of the strands of vascular tissue that form the supporting framework of a leaf. **3.** One of the thickened ribs of cuticle that form the supporting network of the wing of an insect and that often carry a circulatory fluid called hemolymph. **4.** A band of mineral or rock within a different type of rock, formed when a solution of hot water and minerals flowed through fractures in bedrock. —*Adjective* **venous** (vēʹnəs).

veldt also **veld** (vĕlt, fĕlt) An extensive, treeless grassland of southern Africa.

velociraptor (və-lŏsʹə-răpʹtər) A small meat-eating dinosaur of the Cretaceous Period. It had curved claws, a long flat snout with sharp teeth, and feathers on its forelimbs.

velocity (və-lŏsʹĭ-tē) The rate at which a moving object's position is changing, defined in terms of both the object's speed and the direction it is moving. Because it has both magnitude (the speed) and direction, an object's velocity is a vector.

vena cava (vē′nə kā′və) Either of two large veins that carry blood with low levels of oxygen to the right atrium of the heart. The lower one, called the inferior vena cava, is the largest vein in the body.

venation (vē-nā′shən) **1.** The distribution or arrangement of a system of veins, as in a leaf blade or the wing of an insect. **2.** The veins of such a system considered as a group.

venereal disease (və-nîr′ē-əl) *See* **sexually transmitted disease.**

Venn diagram (věn) A diagram that uses circles to represent sets. Relations between the sets can be indicated by the arrangement of the circles, as for example by drawing one circle within another to indicate that the first set is a subset of a second set.

venom (věn′əm) A poisonous substance that is secreted by certain snakes, spiders, scorpions, and insects. It can be transmitted to prey or to an attacker by a bite or sting.

ventral (věn′trəl) Of or on the front or lower surface of an animal.

ventricle (věn′trĭ-kəl) **1.** A chamber of the heart that receives blood from one or more atria and pumps it into the arteries. Mammals, birds, and reptiles have two ventricles; amphibians and fish have one. **2.** Any of four fluid-filled cavities in the brain of vertebrate animals. —*Adjective* **ventricular** (věn-trĭk′yə-lər).

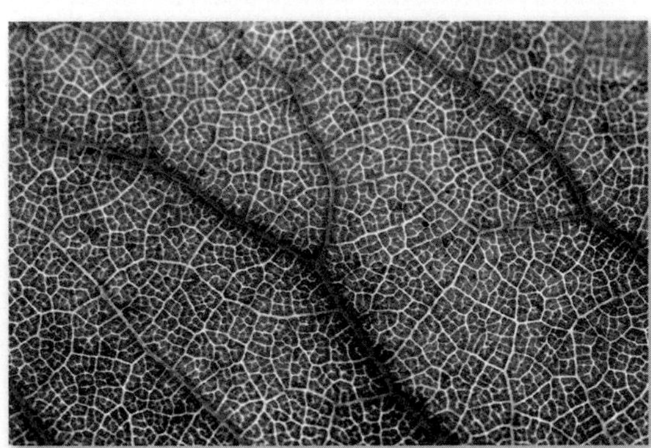

venation
of a leaf

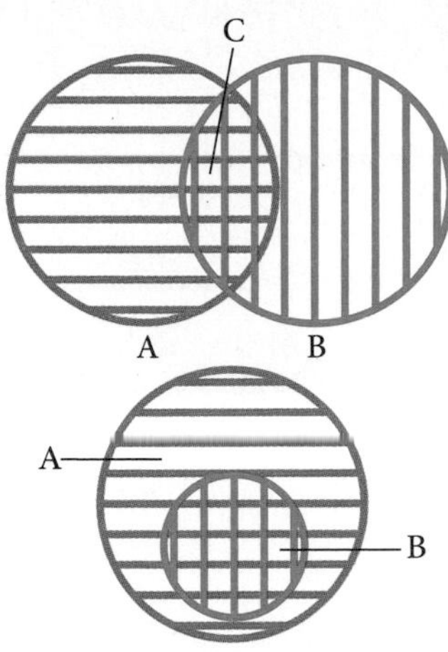

Venn diagram
top: *Sets A and B intersect to form set C. All members of C are also members of A and B.*
bottom: *Set B is a subset of set A. All members of B are also members of A.*

Venus (vē′nəs) The second planet from the sun and the third smallest, with a diameter about 400 miles less than that of Earth. Venus comes nearer to Earth than any other planet and is the brightest object in the night sky aside from Earth's moon. It is the hottest planet in the solar system, with an average surface temperature of 867°F (464°C). *See Table at* **solar system,** pages 312–313.

vernal equinox (vûr′nəl) **1.** The moment of the year when the sun crosses the celestial equator while moving from south to north. It occurs on or about March 20. In the Northern Hemisphere, this marks the beginning of spring. **2.** The point on the celestial sphere where this crossing occurs. *Compare* **autumnal equinox.**

Vernier (věr-nyā′), **Pierre** 1580–1637. French mathematician and maker of scientific instruments who invented a device that allows highly precise readings to be made from the scale of a tool such as a caliper.

vertebra (vûr′tə-brə) *Plural* **vertebrae** (vûr′tə-brā′, vûr′tə-brē′) *or* **vertebras** Any of the bones or, in some animals, segments of cartilage, that make up the spinal column. Humans usually have 33 vertebrae, and snakes can have over 300. Each

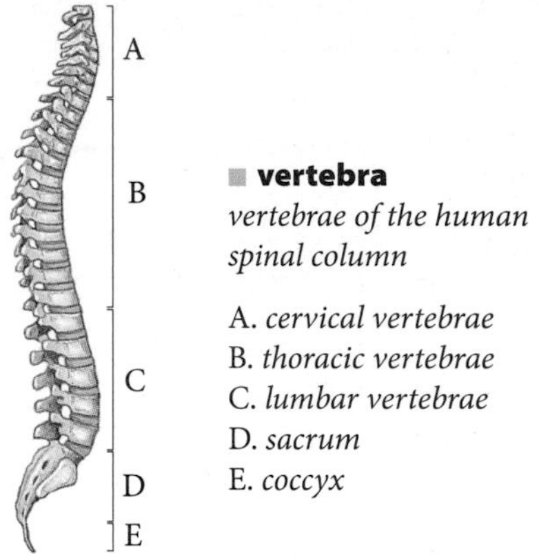

vertebra
vertebrae of the human spinal column

A. *cervical vertebrae*
B. *thoracic vertebrae*
C. *lumbar vertebrae*
D. *sacrum*
E. *coccyx*

Vesalius

vertebra contains a hollow section through which the spinal cord passes. *See more at* **skeleton.**

vertebral column (vûr**′**tə-brəl) *See* **spinal column.**

vertebrate (vûr**′**tə-brĭt, vûr**′**tə-brāt′) Any of a large group of animals having a spinal column (backbone), including fish, amphibians, reptiles, birds, and mammals. Vertebrates are bilaterally symmetrical and have an internal skeleton of bone or cartilage, a nervous system along the back that is divided into brain and spinal cord, and not more than two pairs of limbs.

vertex (vûr**′**tĕks′) *Plural* **vertices** (vûr**′**tĭ-sēz′) *or* **vertexes 1.** The point at which the sides of an angle intersect. **2.** The point of a triangle, cone, or pyramid that is opposite to and farthest away from its base; the apex. **3.** A point of a polyhedron at which three or more of the edges intersect.

vertical angles (vûr**′**tĭ-kəl) Two angles formed by two intersecting lines and lying on opposite sides of the point of intersection.

Vesalius (vĭ-sā**′**lē-əs), **Andreas** 1514–1564. Flemish anatomist and surgeon who is considered the founder of modern anatomy. His major work, *On the Structure of the Human Body* (1543), contains numerous illustrations based on meticulous dissection of cadavers that he performed while teaching at the university in Padua (a city in what is now Italy).

vesicle (vĕs**′**ĭ-kəl) **1.** A small fluid-filled sac in the body. **2.** A small structure in a cell in which materials such as enzymes are transported or stored.

vestigial (vĕ-stĭj**′**ē-əl) Relating to a body part that had a useful function in an early form of an organism but has lost its function and usually become smaller during the course of evolution. Certain fish and salamanders that live in dark caves and cannot see, for example, have vestigial, nonfunctioning eye-like structures that they have inherited from their sighted ancestors.

veterinary medicine (vĕt**′**ər-ə-nĕr′ē) The science and practice of diagnosing and treating disease or injury in animals and maintaining their health.

vibration (vī-brā**′**shən) A rapid oscillation of a particle or an elastic solid back and forth through a central position. *See Note at* **sound**[1].

villus (vĭl**′**əs) *Plural* **villi** (vĭl**′**ī) A small projection on the surface of a mucous membrane, especially that of the small intestine.

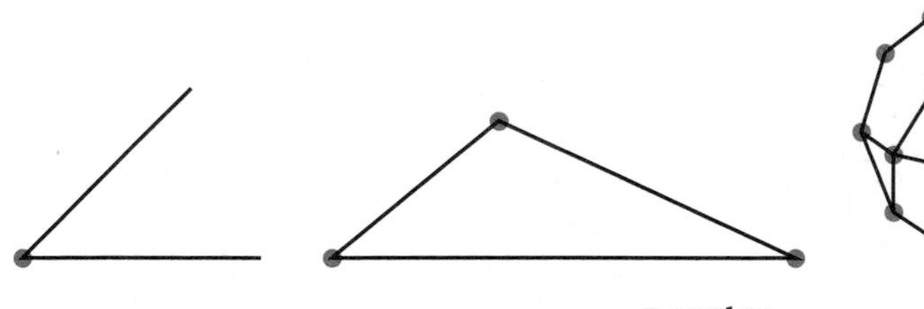

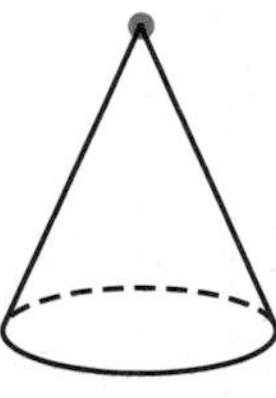

vertex
from left to right: *vertices of intersecting lines, a triangle, a polyhedron, and a cone*

vinyl (vī′nəl) A univalent hydrocarbon group containing two carbon atoms linked by a double bond or a compound containing this group. Vinyl compounds are easily polymerized and are used in plastics, fabrics, and paints.

Virgo (vûr′gō) A constellation in the region of the celestial equator near Leo and Libra.

virology (vī-rŏl′ə-jē) The scientific study of viruses and viral diseases.

virus (vī′rəs) **1.** Any of a large group of disease-causing agents consisting of a molecule of RNA or DNA within a protein shell. Viruses can only replicate after they have entered a living cell. They are too small to see with a standard microscope and are usually not considered living organisms. **2.** *Computers* A computer program that can make copies of itself and spread from one computer to another. Viruses usually have a harmful effect, as in erasing all the data on a drive. —*Adjective* **viral.**

viscosity (vĭ-skŏs′ĭ-tē) The resistance of a substance to flow. The more easily a substance flows, the lower its viscosity. For example, the viscosity of water is lower than that of molasses.

viscous (vĭs′kəs) Having relatively high resistance to flow. As the molecules of a viscous fluid, such as honey, slide past each other, the friction between them causes the fluid to flow very slowly.

vitamin (vī′tə-mĭn) Any of various complex organic compounds that are needed in small amounts for normal growth and activity of the body. Bacteria and plants make vitamins themselves, while humans and other animals obtain them chiefly from their food.

vitamin A A vitamin important for normal vision, tissue growth, and healthy skin. It is found in fish-liver oils, fortified milk, green leafy vegetables, and yellow and orange vegetables and fruits. Also called *retinol.*

vitamin B complex Any of a group of related vitamins important for normal cell growth and metabolism. The vitamins of the vitamin B complex include thiamine (vitamin B_1), riboflavin (vitamin B_2), pantothenic acid, niacin, biotin, and folic acid. ❖ The complex also includes **vitamin B_6** (also called *pyridoxine*), which is important in protein metabolism and in healthy nerve function. It is found in liver, poultry and fish, potatoes, and noncitrus fruits. ❖ Another vitamin in this complex, **vitamin B_{12}** (also called *cobalamin*), is important in the function of the nervous system and the formation of red blood cells. It is found in meat, fish, shellfish, dairy products, certain yeasts, and some fortified foods.

Did You Know...?

vitamins

Although it has long been known that certain diseases can be treated with specific foods, the scientific link between *vitamins* and good health wasn't made until the early 1900s. The biochemist Casimir Funk was studying beriberi, a disease that causes nerve and heart damage, when he discovered an organic compound in rice husks that prevents the illness. He named the compound *vitamine,* from *vita,* the Latin word for "life," and *amine,* a kind of chemical compound. (It was later discovered that not all vitamins are amines.) Funk's compound is now known as thiamine, or vitamin B_1. Other diseases, such as scurvy and rickets, were also found to be caused by vitamin deficiencies. Thirteen essential vitamins are now known, and most of them cannot be produced by the body. A diet that includes a variety of foods, sometimes supplemented with vitamin pills, usually supplies all the vitamins you need.

vitamin C A vitamin important for healthy skin, teeth, bones, and blood vessels. It is found especially in citrus fruits, tomatoes, red peppers, and broccoli. Also called *ascorbic acid.*

vitamin D Any of a group of vitamins necessary for normal bone growth. Vitamin D is found in fish, eggs, and fortified milk and is produced in the skin on exposure to sunlight.

vitamin E A vitamin important for normal cell growth and function. It is found in vegetable oils, nuts, green leafy vegetables, and avocados.

vitamin K Any of a group of vitamins important for normal clotting of the blood. Vitamin K is found in green leafy vegetables and vegetable oils.

vitreous (vĭt′rē-əs) Relating to or resembling glass; glassy.

vitreous humor The jellylike substance that fills the area of the eyeball between the retina and the lens.

A CLOSER LOOK

Volcanoes

When magma from deep within the Earth rises to the surface, a volcano is born. But volcanoes take many different forms. If the magma has a low viscosity (that is, if it's more liquid), it tends to spill out on the surface in broad lava flows that build up into a broad, gently sloped mound. Such a volcano is called a **shield volcano.** Since magma that is low in silica tends to have lower viscosity, and since silica is much less common in the parts of the Earth's crust that lie under the oceans than it is in the parts of the crust that form the continents, most shield volcanoes are found on islands. Well-known shield volcanoes include Kilauea and Mauna Loa on the island of Hawaii.

Stratovolcanoes typically form at subduction zones where oceanic crust has been forced down under continental crust. Their magma contains high levels of dissolved gases and water. Magma can build up within a stratovolcano for years, slowly increasing in pressure, until suddenly the top of the volcano is blown off in an explosive eruption, often scattering particles of the magma for miles in the form of airborne ash. At other times, the magma in a stratovolcano may escape in the form of lava flows. Since these flows tend to be more viscous than those of shield volcanoes, they pile up into a steeper-sided cone. Well-known stratovolcanoes include Vesuvius in Italy, which destroyed the Roman city of Pompeii in AD 79, and Mount Saint Helens in the United States, which erupted violently in 1980.

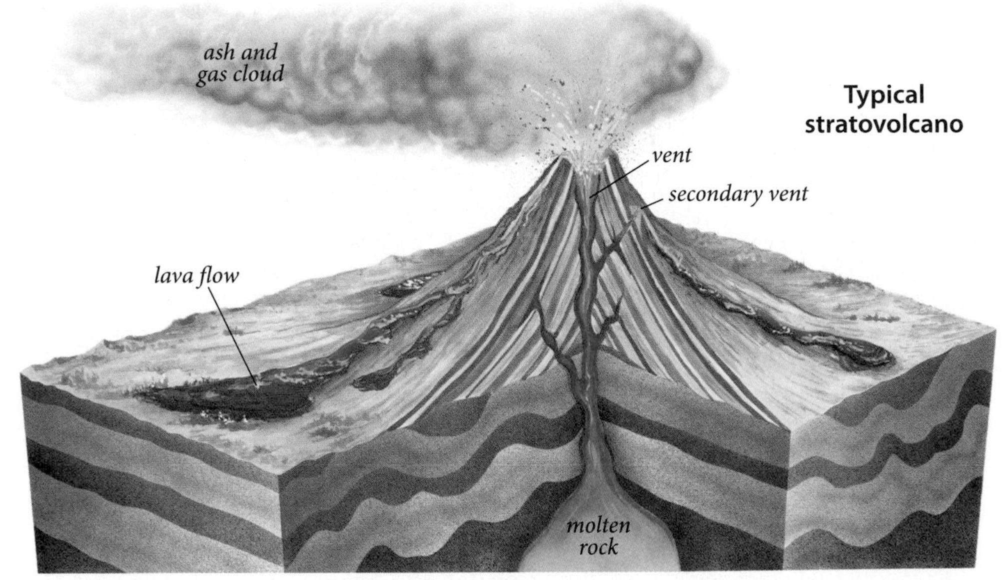

Typical stratovolcano

viviparous (vī-vĭp′ər-əs) Giving birth to living young that develop within the mother's body rather than hatching from eggs. Most mammals are viviparous. *Compare* **oviparous, ovoviviparous.**

vivisection (vĭv′ĭ-sĕk′shən) The practice of cutting into or dissecting a living animal for the purpose of scientific research.

vocal cords (vō′kəl) A pair of muscular bands or folds in the larynx that vibrate when air from the lungs is forced between them, thereby producing the sound of the voice.

voice box (vois) *See* **larynx.**

volatile (vŏl′ə-tl) Changing easily from liquid to vapor at normal temperatures and pressures.

volcanic arc (vŏl-kăn′ĭk) A usually curved chain

of volcanoes located on the margin of the overriding plate at a convergent plate boundary.

volcano (vŏl-kā′nō) **1.** An opening in the Earth's crust from which lava, ash, and hot gases flow or are thrown out during an eruption. **2.** A usually cone-shaped mountain formed by the materials that flowed or were thrown out from such an opening. *See more at* **tectonic boundary.**

volt (vōlt) A unit used to measure electromotive force. One volt is equal to the force that carries one ampere of current through a conductor that has a resistance of one ohm.

Volta (vōl′tə), Count **Alessandro** 1745–1827. Italian physicist who invented the electric battery (1800). Called the voltaic pile, it was the first device to produce a steady stream of electric current. The volt unit of electromotive force is named for him.

voltage (vōl′tĭj) A difference in electric potential between two points, as in an electric circuit, expressed in volts.

voltaic cell (vōl-tā′ĭk, vŏl-tā′ĭk) An electric cell containing two electrodes immersed in an electrolyte, used to produce electricity. As a result of chemical reactions occurring at the electrodes, ions flow through the electrolyte from one electrode to the other, and at the same time, electrons flow through a wire connecting the electrodes, producing an electric current. Most batteries are made of voltaic cells. *Compare* **electrolytic cell.**

voltmeter (vōlt′mē′tər) An instrument used for measuring voltage between two points in an electric circuit.

■ **vortex**

volume (vŏl′yo͞om) **1.** The amount of space occupied by a three-dimensional object or region of space. **2.** A measure of the loudness or intensity of a sound.

volumetric (vŏl′yo͞o-mĕt′rĭk) Relating to measurement by volume or to a unit that is used to measure volume.

voluntary (vŏl′ən-tĕr′ē) Under conscious control. The muscles attached to the skeleton are voluntary muscles because they can be moved at will.

vortex (vôr′tĕks′) *Plural* **vortices** (vôr′tĭ-sēz′) *or* **vortexes** A whirling current of fluid, such as water or air, that tends to draw the fluid toward its center. Eddies and whirlpools are examples of vortexes.

vulcanize (vŭl′kə-nīz′) To harden rubber by heating it and combining it with sulfur. Vulcanization increases rubber's strength and elasticity.

vulva (vŭl′və) The external genital organs of female mammals.

W

w Abbreviation of **width.**

W 1. The symbol for **tungsten. 2.** Abbreviation of **watt.**

wadi (wä′dē) A gully or streambed in northern Africa and southwest Asia that remains dry except during the rainy season.

Wallace (wŏl′ĭs), **Alfred Russel** 1823–1913. British naturalist who traveled widely in South America and Southeast Asia and formulated a theory of evolution by natural selection independently of Charles Darwin. Wallace corresponded with Darwin, and the two men's theories were presented jointly at a scientific meeting in London in 1858.

walrus (wôl′rəs) A large sea mammal of Arctic regions having tough, wrinkled skin and large tusks.

Walton (wôl′tən), **Ernest Thomas Sinton** 1903–1995. Irish physicist. With the physicist John Cockcroft, he developed the particle accelerator. Their experiments with it led to the first successful splitting of an atom in 1932.

warm-blooded (wôrm′blŭd′ĭd) Having a warm body temperature that does not vary much and is maintained by heat generated internally. Birds and mammals are warm-blooded.

warm front The forward edge of an advancing mass of warm air that rises over a mass of cold air. A warm front is often accompanied by a prolonged period of steady rain. *See more at* **front.**

wart (wôrt) A small growth on the skin caused by a virus, occurring typically on the hands or feet.

wasp (wŏsp) Any of numerous insects having a hairless body with a constriction of the abdomen, two pairs of wings, biting or sucking mouthparts, and in the females of many species, a stinger extending from the abdomen that is used to deliver venom to kill or paralyze prey. Wasps are related to ants and bees and can be solitary or live in colonies.

water (wô′tər) A clear, colorless, odorless liquid compound of hydrogen and oxygen, H_2O. Water covers about three-quarters of the Earth's surface and also occurs in solid form as ice and in gaseous form as steam. It is an essential component of all organisms, and it is necessary for most biological processes. Water freezes at 32°F (0°C) and boils at 212°F (100°C).

water cycle The continuous process by which water is circulated throughout the Earth and its atmosphere. Energy from the sun causes water to evaporate from oceans and other bodies of water and from soil surfaces. Plants and animals also release water vapor into the air. As it rises into the atmosphere, the water vapor condenses to form clouds. Rain and other forms of precipitation return water to the Earth, where it flows into bodies of water and into the ground, beginning the cycle over again.

watershed (wô′tər-shĕd′) **1.** The entire region that is drained by a river system. **2.** A ridge forming a boundary between two different river systems.

water table The level at which the ground beneath the surface is saturated with water. The water table usually rises after heavy rainfall and the melting of snow and falls during drier periods.

water vapor Water in its gaseous state, especially when it is in the atmosphere and at a temperature below the boiling point.

Watson (wŏt′sən), **James Dewey** Born 1928. American biologist who with Francis Crick identified the structure of DNA. By analyzing the

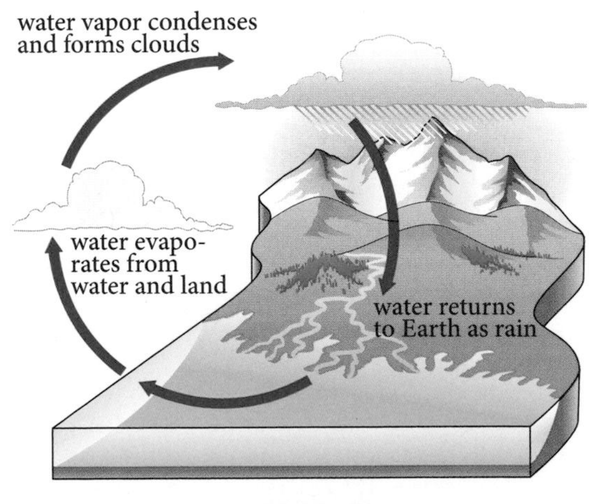

water cycle

patterns cast by x-rays striking DNA molecules, they discovered that DNA has the structure of a double helix, two spirals linked together by bases in ladderlike rungs. Their discovery formed the basis of molecular genetics.

Watson-Watt (wŏt′sən-wŏt′), Sir **Robert Alexander** 1892–1973. British physicist who pioneered the development of radar. In 1919 he produced a system for locating thunderstorms by tracking their radio emissions. In the 1930s Watson-Watt led the team that developed radar into a practical system for locating aircraft.

watt (wŏt) A unit used to measure power, equal to one joule of work per second. In electricity, a watt is equal to the amount of current (in amperes) multiplied by the amount of potential (in volts).

Watt, James 1736–1819. British engineer, inventor, and scientist. He invented a greatly improved steam engine (1769) and devised the unit of horsepower. The watt unit of power is named for him.

wattage (wŏt′ĭj) An amount of power, especially electrical power, expressed in watts or kilowatts.

watt-hour A unit of power, especially electrical power, equal to the work done by one watt acting for one hour. It is equivalent to 3,600 joules.

wave (wāv) A disturbance or oscillation that travels from one point to another and transports energy. When a wave, such as a sound wave, travels through a medium, the medium remains unchanged. Electromagnetic waves can travel through a vacuum. *See also* **longitudinal wave, transverse wave.** *See Note at* **refraction.** *See A Closer Look, on next page.*

wavelength (wāv′lĕngkth′) The distance over which the shape of a periodic wave repeats, especially the distance between one crest and the next crest or between one trough and the next trough.

wave mechanics A theory in quantum mechanics that uses mathematical equations relating to waves to describe the behavior of subatomic particles. Wave mechanics describes the location of particles, such as electrons moving around the nucleus of an atom, in terms of probability.

wax (wăks) Any of various solid, usually whitish or yellowish substances that melt or soften easily when heated. Waxes are produced in nature by various animals and plants, or are made artificially. They are similar to fats, but are less greasy and more brittle.

weak nuclear force (wēk) The force that causes certain subatomic particles to decay—to break up into smaller particles and give off energy as radiation. For example, it is responsible for beta decay, the process that occurs when a neutron changes into a proton. The weak nuclear force is one of the four basic forces of nature. It is weaker than the strong nuclear force and the electromagnetic force but stronger than gravity. Also called *weak force* or *weak interaction.*

weather (wĕ*th*′ər) The state of the atmosphere at a particular time and place. Weather is described by variable conditions such as temperature, humidity, wind velocity, precipitation, and barometric pressure.

web (wĕb) **1.** A structure of fine silky strands woven by spiders or by certain insect larvae. Spiders use their webs to catch insects. **2.** A fold of skin or thin tissue connecting the toes of certain animals,

USAGE

weight/mass

You may have been taught to convert pounds into kilograms by multiplying the number of pounds by 0.45 (or, for greater precision, by 0.4536). But this technique is misleading, because a pound is a unit of *force,* while a kilogram is a unit of *mass.* A pound is a measure of the force that a gravitational field exerts on an object. The magnitude of this force is the object's *weight,* not its mass. An object's mass is its ability to resist changes in the speed or direction of its motion, and it is always the same regardless of what forces are acting upon it. If you were walking on the moon, for example, your mass would be the same as it is on the Earth, but your weight would be one sixth of what it is on the Earth because of the lower gravitational pull of the moon. If this is so, you might ask, how can my science teacher ask me to convert pounds into kilograms? The reason we can make such conversions is that we assume the object in question is on the Earth, at sea level, where objects with a mass of 0.4536 kg do weigh approximately 1 lb.

A CLOSER LOOK

Waves

Sound, light, x-rays, and other types of energy spread outward in the form of waves. Many waves travel through what is known as a medium: the medium of a sound wave consists of the atoms making up any form of matter, for example, and the medium of a wave in the ocean is the ocean water. Other waves, such as electromagnetic waves, can travel without a medium. Waves have a characteristic structure and fall into two basic types: longitudinal and transverse. They also have other properties that are illustrated below.

Structure of a Wave

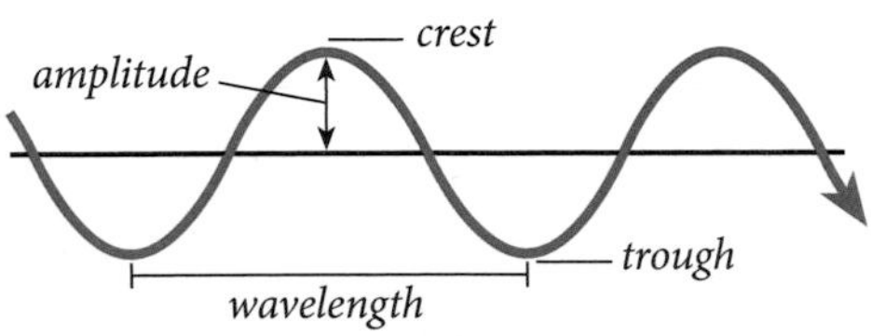

Frequency and Wavelength

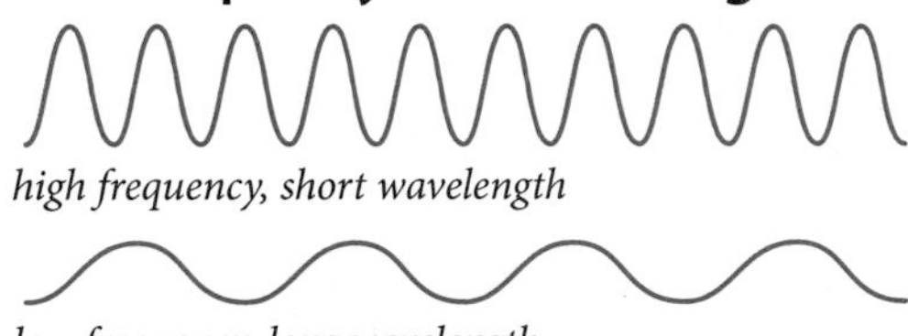

Types of Waves (as illustrated by a stretched spring)

Longitudinal (disturbance in same direction as direction of wave)

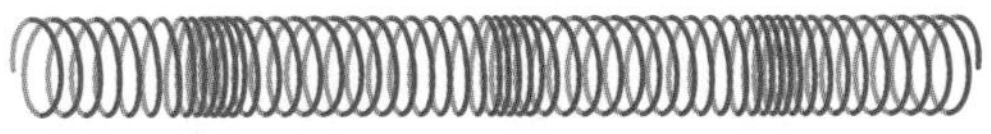

Transverse (disturbance at right angles to direction of wave)

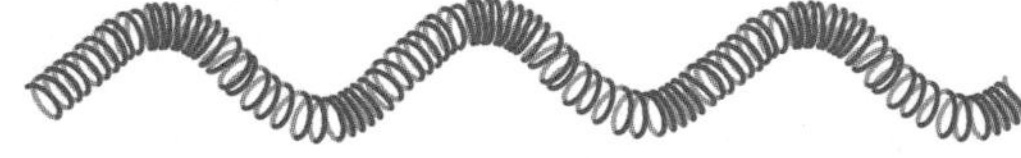

Interference

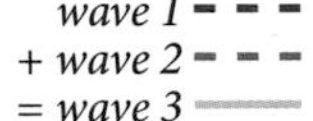

Constructive (waves 1 and 2 in phase)

Destructive (waves 1 and 2 out of phase)

Reflection, Refraction, and Diffraction

Reflection
The two angles are equal.

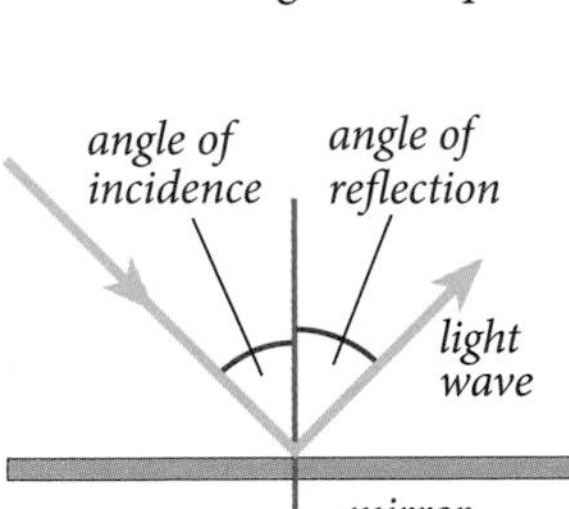

Refraction
The two angles are not equal.

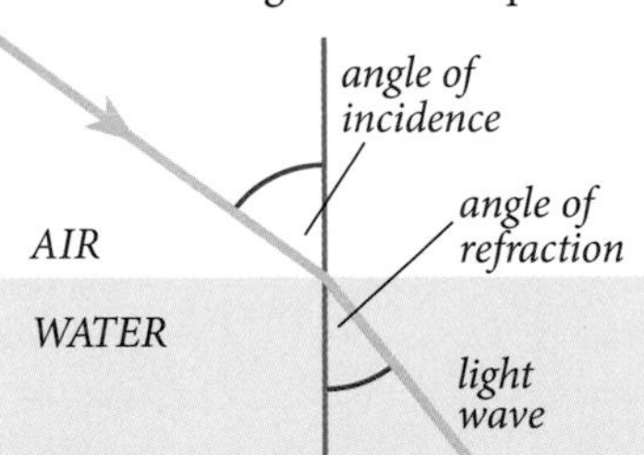

Diffraction

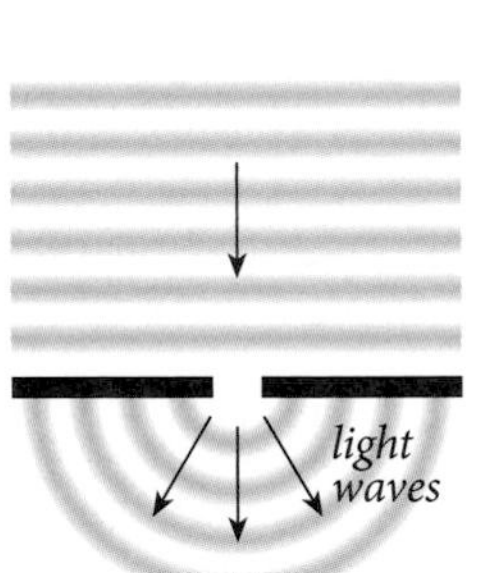

especially ones that swim, such as water birds and otters. The web improves the ability of the foot to push against water. **3.** also **Web** The World Wide Web.

Wegener (vā′gə-nər), **Alfred Lothar** 1880–1930. German physicist, meteorologist, and explorer who introduced the theory of continental drift in 1915. His hypothesis was controversial and remained so until the 1960s, when new scientific understanding of the structure of the ocean floors provided evidence that his theory was correct. *See more at* **plate tectonics.**

weight (wāt) **1.** The force with which an object near the Earth or another celestial body is attracted toward the center of the body by gravity. An object's weight depends on its mass (the amount of matter it consists of) and the strength of the gravitational pull. On Earth, for example, an object weighs less at the top of a very high mountain than it does at sea level, simply because the gravitational pull at the top of the mountain is lower than it is at sea level. **2.** A unit used as a measure of gravitational force: *a table of weights and measures.* **3.** A system of such measures: *avoirdupois weight; troy weight. See Note on page 363.*

Weinberg (wīn′bûrg′), **Steven** Born 1933. American nuclear physicist who helped develop important theories explaining the relationship between the electromagnetic force and the weak nuclear force, two of the four basic forces of nature.

Western Hemisphere (wĕs′tərn) The half of the Earth that includes North America, Central America, and South America.

Did You Know...?

wetland

A *wetland* is just what it sounds like—a piece of land that is usually very wet. Wetlands are soggy enough that you wouldn't want to go camping in them, but they have enough soil that grasses, shrubs, and sometimes even trees can take root and grow. In the past, many wetlands in the United States were drained or filled in to make farmland or to develop the area for housing. Scientists have discovered, however, that wetlands can act like huge filters, removing pollutants from the waters of an area before those substances can do harm. They also help in flood control by holding excess water and releasing it slowly. And wetlands provide habitat for many different plant and animal species that have evolved to live in their unique conditions. Federal and state regulations now protect many kinds of wetlands from development.

wetland
top to bottom: *marsh in Maine, swamp in Louisiana, and bog in the United Kingdom*

Westinghouse (wĕs′tĭng-hous′), **George** 1846–1914. American engineer and manufacturer who introduced the high-voltage alternating current system for the transmission of electricity in the United States. A prolific inventor, Westinghouse received 361 patents in his lifetime, including the air brake, automated train-switching signals, and devices for the transmission of natural gas. His inventions made an important contribution to the growth of railroads.

wet cell (wĕt) An electric cell in which the chemicals producing the current are in the form of a liquid rather than a paste (as in a dry cell). A car battery consists of a series of wet cells.

wetland (wĕt′lănd′) A low-lying area of land that is saturated with moisture, especially when regarded as the natural habitat of wildlife. Marshes, swamps, and bogs are examples of wetlands.

whale (wāl) Any of various large marine mammals that have a streamlined body resembling that of a fish, forelimbs modified to form flippers, a tail with horizontal flukes, and one or two blow-

Did You Know...?

whale

You can descend thousands of feet underwater in a submarine. But if you swam out of the vessel, you would immediately be crushed by the pressure of the water. Amazingly, there are many animals that happily exist in such conditions. Sperm whales, for instance, can dive to depths of over a mile with no ill effects. Many adaptations allow these whales, and other deep-sea organisms, to survive at great depths. One of these adaptations is a flexible ribcage: the whale's ribcage is not rigid, like ours, but collapses in a controlled way as the pressure increases. The lungs collapse, too, reducing gas exchange and keeping whales from being affected by the *bends*—the formation of nitrogen bubbles in the blood and tissues when returning to the surface, which is a serious risk for human deep-sea divers. With their lungs collapsed, whales use oxygen stored in their muscles and blood when they dive. These adaptations enable sperm whales to swim up and down as fast as they like, diving down to hunt for giant squid and then ascending to the surface to replenish their store of oxygen.

holes for breathing. Some whales have teeth, and others have baleen, which is used to filter small organisms from the water. Whales, like dolphins and porpoises, are cetaceans.

whalebone (wāl′bōn′) *See* **baleen.**

whirlpool (wûrl′po͞ol′) A rapidly rotating current of water or other liquid, such as one produced by the meeting of two tides.

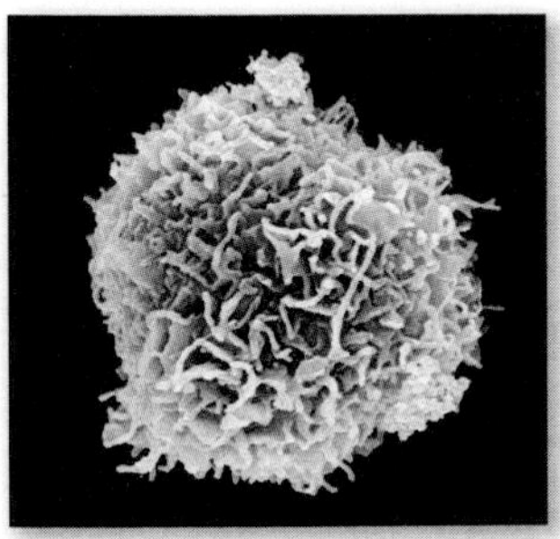

■ **white blood cell**

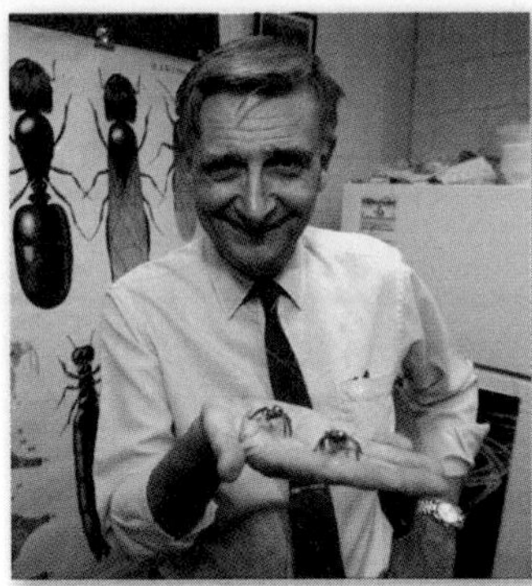

■ **E.O. Wilson**

white blood cell (wīt) Any of various whitish or colorless cells in the blood of vertebrate animals that act to protect the body against infection and to repair tissues after injury. White blood cells have a nucleus, unlike red blood cells, and are formed mainly in the bone marrow. The major types of white blood cells are granulocytes, lymphocytes, and monocytes. Also called *leukocyte.*

white dwarf The collapsed core of a star of relatively low mass that has ejected its outer layers and can no longer sustain nuclear fusion. White dwarfs are very small, about the size of the Earth, and extremely dense. *See more at* **star.** *See Note at* **dwarf star.**

white matter The whitish tissue of the brain and spinal cord in vertebrate animals, made up chiefly of nerve fibers covered in myelin sheaths. *Compare* **gray matter.**

whole number (hōl) A positive integer or zero.

whooping cough (ho͞o′pĭng, ho͝op′ĭng, wo͞o′pĭng, wo͝op′ĭng) A bacterial infection of the airways and lungs that causes spasms of coughing ending in loud gasps. It occurs mostly in children. Also called *pertussis.*

Wilkins (wĭl′kĭnz), **Maurice Hugh Frederick** 1916–2004. British biophysicist who contributed to the discovery of the structure of DNA. He worked with Rosalind Franklin to produce x-ray studies of DNA that helped to establish its structure as a double helix.

Wilson (wĭl′sən), **Edmund Beecher** 1856–1939. American zoologist who did important work on the structure of cells and the role of chromosomes in heredity. He and the biologist Nettie Stevens independently discovered that sex in many organisms is determined by the sex chromosomes.

Wimshurst machine

Wilson, E(dward) O(sborne) Born 1929. American biologist whose research on ants led to the development of a new scientific discipline outlined in his 1975 book *Sociobiology.*

Wimshurst machine (wĭmz′hûrst′) A device used to generate static electricity, consisting of rotating disks made of an insulator such as glass and partially covered with thin metal plates. When the disks are rotated in opposite directions, the metal plates become charged, and the charge can be transferred to capacitors. Wimshursts machines are used in science education to demonstrate high-voltage electric discharges.

wind (wĭnd) A current of air, especially a natural one that moves along or parallel to the ground.

wind-chill factor The temperature of motionless air that would make a person feel as cold as a particular combination of wind speed and air temperature. As the wind blows faster, heat is lost more quickly from exposed skin, making a person feel colder even though the air temperature remains the same.

windpipe (wĭnd′pīp′) *See* **trachea** (sense 1).

wind tunnel A chamber through which air can be forced at controlled speeds so its effect on an object, such as an aircraft, can be studied.

wing (wĭng) **1.** One of a pair of specialized parts used for flying, as in birds, bats, or insects. **2.** A thin projection on certain fruits that are dispersed by the wind, such as the fruits of ash, elm, and maple trees. **3.** A part extending from the side of an aircraft, such as an airplane, having a curved upper surface that causes the pressure of air rushing over it to decrease, thereby providing lift.

winter solstice (wĭn′tər) The solstice that occurs on or about December 21 in the Northern Hemisphere and on or about June 21 in the Southern Hemisphere, marking the beginning of winter and the day of the year with the shortest period of sunlight. *Compare* **summer solstice.**

wireless (wīr′lĭs) Relating to the transmission of information between electronic devices by means of electromagnetic waves, usually radio waves.

wisdom tooth (wĭz′dəm) One of four molars, the last on each side of both jaws in humans, usually appearing in young adulthood.

wishbone (wĭsh′bōn′) The forked bone in front of the breastbone in most birds, consisting of the two collarbones partly fused together. It serves as a spring, capturing some of the energy during the downward stroke of the wings for release on the upward stroke. Also called *furcula.*

wolfram (wo͝ol′frəm) *See* **tungsten.**

womb (wo͞om) *See* **uterus.**

wood (wo͝od) The tough, fibrous substance lying beneath the bark of trees and shrubs, consisting of vascular tissue known as xylem. The inner part of a tree trunk is composed of old, nonfunctional xylem, while the outer part is composed of new, living xylem. The main components of wood are cellulose and lignin.

wood alcohol *See* **methanol.**

work (wûrk) The transfer of energy from one object to another, especially when force is applied to move a body in a certain direction. Work is equal to the amount of force multiplied by the distance over which it is applied. If a force of 10 newtons, for example, is applied over a distance of 3 meters, the work is equal to 30 newton-meters (30 joules). *Compare* **energy, power.**

worker (wûr′kər) A member of a colony of social insects, such as ants, bees, or termites, that performs specialized work such as building the nest, collecting and storing food, and feeding other members of the colony. Workers are usually sterile or sexually immature females, but in termites, workers include both females and males.

World Wide Web (wûrld) The complete set of electronic documents stored on computers that are connected over the Internet and are made available by the process known as HTTP (Hypertext Transfer Protocol). The World Wide Web makes up a large part of the Internet. *See more at* **Internet.**

worm (wûrm) **1.** Any of numerous invertebrate

Did You Know...?

worm

Although there are many kinds of *worms* of all shapes and sizes, we usually think of *earthworms* when someone mentions worms. Earthworms do not get much respect, but Charles Darwin wrote an entire book explaining how important they are. "Long before [the plow] existed," he said, "the land was in fact regularly plowed, and still continues to be thus plowed by earthworms. It may be doubted whether there are many other animals which have played so important a part in the history of the world." As they tunnel in the soil, earthworms open channels that allow in air and water. These channels improve drainage and make it easier for plants to send down roots. Earthworms eat and digest soil and the organic wastes it contains, and their own wastes provide nourishment for plants and other organisms. We enjoy the fruits of the earthworm's labor in the form of rich soil and healthy vegetation.

animals having a soft, long body that is round or flattened and usually lacks limbs. Nematodes and earthworms are examples of worms. **2.** *Computers* A destructive computer program that copies itself over and over until it fills all of the storage space on a computer's hard drive or on a network. ❖ A person or a dog, cat, or other animal is said to have **worms** when infested with tapeworms, hookworms, or other parasitic worms.

Wu (wo͞o), **Chien-Shiung** 1912–1997. Chinese-born American physicist. Her research on electron emission in the decay of radioactive elements helped to disprove the widely held principle that the laws of nature always display symmetry.

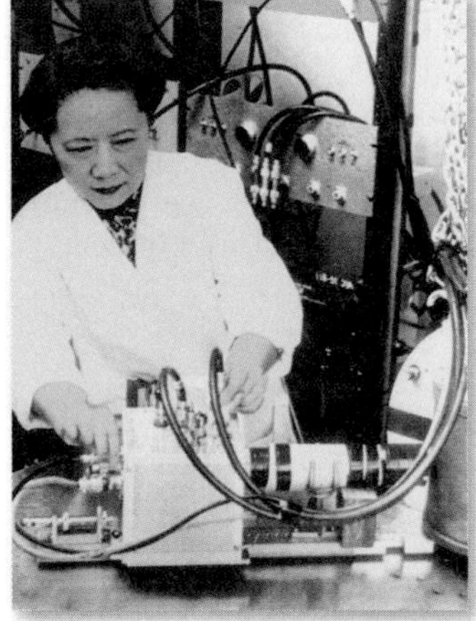

Chien-Shiung Wu

x-axis (ĕks′ăk′sĭs) **1.** The horizontal axis of a two-dimensional Cartesian coordinate system. **2.** One of the three axes of a three-dimensional Cartesian coordinate system.

X chromosome The sex chromosome that in most mammals is paired with another X chromosome in females and is paired with a Y chromosome in males.

Xe The symbol for **xenon.**

xenon (zē′nŏn′) A colorless, odorless element that is a noble gas and occurs in extremely small amounts in the atmosphere. It was the first noble gas found to form compounds with other elements. Xenon is used to make lamps that make intense flashes, such as strobe lights and flashbulbs for photography. *Symbol* **Xe.** *Atomic number* 54. *See* **Periodic Table,** pages 254–255.

xeric (zîr′ĭk) Relating to, characterized by, or adapted to an extremely dry habitat.

xerophyte (zîr′ə-fīt′) A plant that can grow in an environment with very little water. Cacti are xerophytes.

X-linked (ĕks′lĭngkt′) Relating to an inherited trait controlled by a gene on an X chromosome.

x-ray (ĕks′rā′) **1.** A stream of electromagnetic radiation having wavelengths shorter than those of ultraviolet light but longer than those of gamma rays. Because x-rays are able to penetrate materials, they are used in medicine and industry to produce images of the insides of objects. They are also used to determine the structure of crystals by the method of x-ray diffraction. *See more at* **electromagnetic spectrum. 2.** An image of an internal structure, such as a body part, taken with x-rays. — *Verb* **x-ray.**

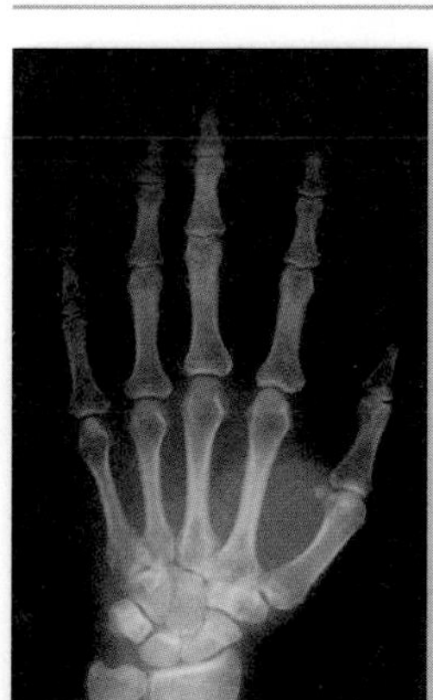

x-ray
of a human hand

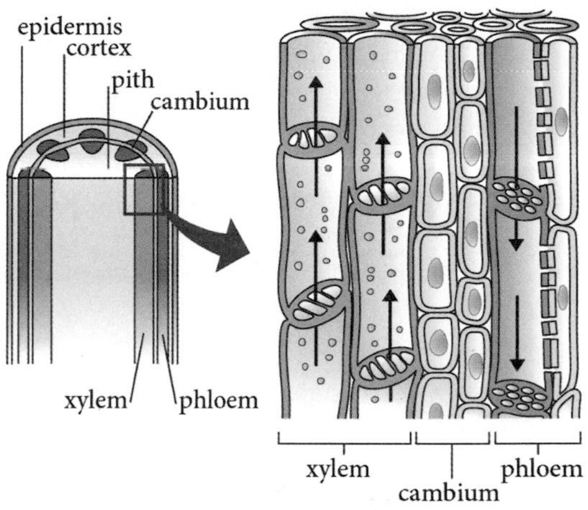

xylem
Xylem cells in a stem carry water from a plant's roots to its leaves. The phloem distributes food that is made in the plant's leaves to other parts of the plant. The cambium cells divide into either xylem or phloem cells. The cortex and pith provide structural support.

x-ray diffraction The scattering (diffraction) of x-rays as they pass through crystal atoms, used to produce wave interference patterns that yield information about the molecular and atomic structure of the crystal.

xylem (zī′ləm) A tissue in vascular plants that carries water and dissolved minerals up from the roots through the stem to the leaves and also provides support. Xylem consists primarily of dead, elongated cells that function as tubes. In a tree trunk, the innermost part of the wood is nonfunctional but structurally strong xylem, while the outer part consists of functional xylem. Outside the xylem lie the vascular cambium and the phloem. *See more at* **cambium, photosynthesis.** *Compare* **phloem.**

Y The symbol for **yttrium.**

Yalow (yăl′ō), **Rosalyn Sussman** 1921–2011. American medical physicist who developed the radioimmunoassay, an extremely sensitive technique for measuring very small quantities of substances such as hormones, enzymes, and drugs in the blood.

yard (yärd) A unit of length equal to 3 feet or 36 inches (about 0.91 meter). *See Table at* **measurement.**

y-axis (wī′ăk′sĭs) **1.** The vertical axis of a two-dimensional Cartesian coordinate system. **2.** One of the three axes of a three-dimensional Cartesian coordinate system.

Yb The symbol for **ytterbium.**

Y chromosome The sex chromosome that in most mammals is paired with an X chromosome in males.

yd. Abbreviation of **yard.**

yeast (yēst) **1.** Any of various one-celled fungi that usually reproduce asexually by budding and can cause the fermentation of carbohydrates, producing carbon dioxide and alcohol. **2.** A commercial preparation in either compressed or powdered form that contains yeast cells. It is used to make bread dough rise and in the production of alcoholic beverages. ❖ Yeasts of a type called candida live harmlessly on and in humans, but sometimes they grow too much, especially on the skin or mucous membranes, causing a **yeast infection.**

Rosalyn Yalow

yellow fever (yĕl′ō) A life-threatening disease caused by a virus and characterized by fever and internal bleeding and often by jaundice. Yellow fever occurs mainly in tropical regions of Africa and Latin America and is transmitted by mosquitoes.

yolk (yōk) The yellow part inside the egg of a fish, bird, reptile, or egg-laying mammal (monotreme). The yolk contains proteins, fats, and minerals and supplies food to the developing embryo.

yolk sac A membranous sac attached to the embryo and enclosing the yolk in egg-laying vertebrates. In humans and other placental mammals, it functions as the circulatory system for the embryo before the placenta develops.

ytterbium (ĭ-tûr′bē-əm) A soft, silvery-white, easily shaped metallic element of the lanthanide series that is used in solar cells, laser materials, and as a radiation source for portable x-ray machines. *Symbol* **Yb.** *Atomic number* 70. *See* **Periodic Table,** pages 254–255.

yttrium (ĭt′rē-əm) A silvery, easily shaped metallic element that is found in the same ores as other rare-earth elements. Yttrium is used to strengthen magnesium and aluminum alloys, and as a component of various optical and electronic devices. *Symbol* **Y.** *Atomic number* 39. *See* **Periodic Table,** pages 254–255. *See Note at* **rare-earth element.**

Z

z-axis (zē′ăk′sĭs) One of the three axes of a three-dimensional Cartesian coordinate system.

zebra (zē′brə) Any of several African mammals resembling and closely related to the horse, having the entire body marked with white and black or brown stripes.

zebra mussel *See under* **mussel.**

zenith (zē′nĭth) The point on the celestial sphere that is directly above the observer. *Compare* **nadir.**

zero (zîr′ō) **1.** A number that when added to another number leaves that number unchanged. **2.** The numerical symbol 0, representing this number.

zero gravity The condition of apparent weightlessness that occurs when the force of gravity acting on a body meets with no resistance, and the body is allowed to accelerate freely. A body falling freely toward the Earth or in orbit around the Earth is in a state of zero gravity. A body at rest on the Earth's surface is not, since the gravitational force acting downward on it is counterbalanced by the force of the supporting surface acting upward.

zinc (zĭngk) A shiny, bluish-white metallic element that is brittle at room temperature but is easily shaped when heated. It is widely used in alloys such as brass and bronze, as a coating for iron and steel, and in various household objects. US pennies minted after 1982 consist of a zinc core plated with copper. Zinc is an essential element for humans and other living organisms. *Symbol* **Zn.** *Atomic number* 30. *See* **Periodic Table,** pages 254–255.

zebra

Did You Know...?

zero

Zero may seem to be nothing at all, but it is important in two ways. First, it is important as a quantity: once mathematicians realized that "nothing" could be thought of as a number like any other, they were able to use it in arithmetic operations — to add it, subtract it, multiply it, and so on. This innovation, in turn, made possible the concept of negative numbers and eventually the development of algebra. Secondly, zero is important as a digit: by acting as a place holder in decimal notation, zero helps to indicate the value of nonzero numerals to its left or right. For instance, in the number 203, the zero helps to indicate that the numeral 2 stands for the quantity 200, not for 2 or 20.

zinc oxide A white or yellowish powdery compound, ZnO, used in paints and in various medicines and skin cosmetics.

zircon (zûr′kŏn′) A brown, reddish to bluish, gray, green, or colorless mineral that is a silicate of zirconium and occurs in igneous, metamorphic, and sedimentary rocks, and especially in sand. The colorless varieties are valued as gems.

zirconium (zûr-kō′nē-əm) A shiny, grayish-white metallic element that occurs primarily in zircon. It is used to build nuclear reactors because it is not damaged from bombardment by neutrons and remains strong at high temperatures. Zirconium is also highly resistant to corrosion, making it a useful component of pumps, valves, and alloys. *Symbol* **Zr.** *Atomic number* 40. *See* **Periodic Table,** pages 254–255.

Zn The symbol for **zinc.**

zodiac (zō′dē-ăk′) A band of the celestial sphere that extends about eight degrees both north and south of the ecliptic. It represents the path of the planets, the sun, and the moon.

zoology (zō-ŏl′ə-jē, zo͞o-ŏl′ə-jē) The scientific study of animals, including their growth, anatomy, and behavior.

zooplankton (zō′ə-plăngk′tən) Plankton that consists of tiny animals and certain protozoans, including copepods, rotifers, jellyfish, and the larvae of corals and sea anemones.

zooxanthella (zō′ə-zăn-thĕl′ə) *Plural* **zooxanthellae** (zō′ə-zăn-thĕl′ē) Any of various yellow-brown photosynthetic algae that live symbiotically within the tissues of other organisms, especially certain corals and other marine invertebrates. Most zooxanthellae are dinoflagellates.

Zr The symbol for **zirconium.**

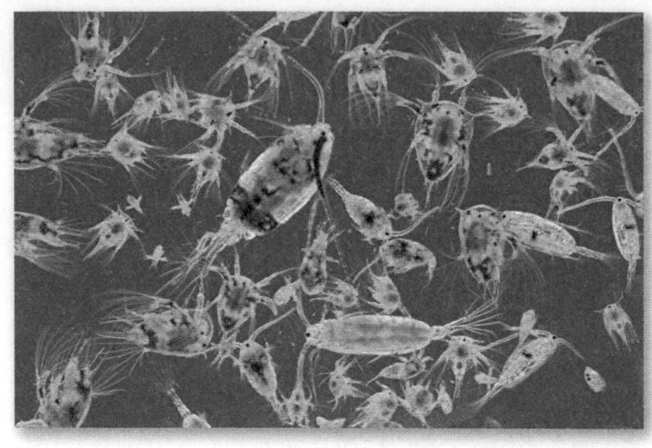

zooplankton

zygote (zī′gōt′) The cell formed by the union of two sex cells (gametes), especially a fertilized egg cell.

Did You Know...?

zooxanthellae

You might think that the beautiful color of coral reefs comes from the coral itself, but you'd be wrong. The color actually comes from single-celled algae called *zooxanthellae* that live inside the coral's tissue. Zooxanthellae carry out photosynthesis and live symbiotically within various aquatic species, including giant clams, jellyfish, and most notably, reef-building corals. The zooxanthellae in coral share with their hosts the oxygen and carbohydrates produced through photosynthesis. In return, the coral supplies carbon dioxide, nitrogen, and phosphorus—necessary nutrients for the algae, but metabolic waste for the coral—as well as shelter. This efficient relationship supports the building of immense reefs. If light intensity or water temperature becomes too high, however, the zooxanthellae are ejected from the coral. This may occur because of damage to the photosynthetic systems of the zooxanthellae, causing them to release molecules that are toxic to the coral. Following the expulsion, the coral reverts to its natural white coloring, a phenomenon called *coral bleaching.* Without its zooxanthellae, the coral starves and may die. Incidents of coral bleaching have been increasing, and scientists believe that global warming is to blame. Research continues on the exact nature of the delicate relationship between coral and zooxanthellae and how to protect the world's coral reefs.

The following source abbreviations are used throughout the credits: AA/Academy Artworks; AG/age fotostock; CL-AA/Clarinda-Academy Artworks; CI/Carlyn Iverson; EM/Elizabeth Morales; GI-/Getty Images; PG/Precision Graphics; RS/Robin Storesund; and SS/SuperStock.

A-Z TEXT

abacus HMH **abscissa** AA **acid rain** GI-Richard Packwood, Oxford Scientific **acoustics** UG/GGS **acupuncture** SS-Tetra Images **acute angle** AA **adsorption** AA **aerodynamics** AA **Agassiz** Alamy-Photo Researchers **agate** GI Edward Kinsman **Agnesi** SS-DeAgostini **alluvial fan** Alamy-Tony Waltham, Robert Harding Picture Library Ltd. **alternate angle** CL-AA **altocumulus** Corbis-Image Source **ammonite** SS-Mauritius **amoeba** Alamy-Melba Photo Agency **Ampère** The Bridgeman Art Library-Musée André Marie Ampère, Poleymieux au Mont d'Or, France, Archives Charmet **amphibian (frog)** SS-imagebroker.net **amphibian (salamander)** Cutcaster-Jason Ross **anadromous** GI-Fuse **anemometer** Alamy-matthiasengelien.com **aneroid barometer** PG **aneurysm** EM **Antarctic Circle** Thom Gillis **antenna (insect)** GI-Kees Smans **antenna (tv)** Shutterstock-Igorsky **antibody** CI **anticline** PG **aphid** SS-age fotostock **archaeopteryx** GI-Jason Edwards, National Geographic **Archimedes** Alamy-bilwissedition Ltd & Co. KG **Arctic Circle** Thom Gillis **artesian well** RS **asthma** Garth Glazier **asymptote** AA **atmosphere** AA **atoll** AA **atomic bomb** SS-Photri Images **Audubon** Corbis **aurora australis** GI-Photodisc **azimuth** PG

bacterium (sphere) Fotolia-Sebastian Kaulitzki **bacterium (rod)** Alamy-Jezper **bacterium (spiral)** GI-CMSP **Baily's beads** SS-Belinda Images **bamboo** Cutcaster-Phil Morley **Banneker** North Wind Picture Archives **baobab** SS-imagebroker.net **basalt** SS-imagebroker.net **battery** UG/GGS **beak** EM **bedbug** Photo Researchers, Inc.-Science Source **Bell** Library of Congress-Harris & Ewing **benzene ring** RS **Berners-Lee** AP Images-Martial Trezzini **Bethe** Alamy-Keystone Pictures USA **bilateral symmetry** PG **binoculars** PG **bioluminescence** Shutterstock-Narchuk **biome (desert)** Cutcaster-Frank Bach **biome (rainforest)** Alamy-Douglas Peebles Photography **biome (taiga)** Shutterstock-Aibolit **Blackwell** US National Library of Medicine **block and tackle** PG **blowhole** Photo Researchers, Inc.-Christopher Swann **Bohr** GI-Hulton Archive **bond** RS **brain** CI **bromeliad** SS-age fotostock **Bunsen burner** Photo Researchers, Inc.-Charles D. Winters, Science Source **butte** Corbis-moodboard **Byrd** SS-Everett Collection

cactus Shutterstock-CBH **camouflage** Alamy-Michael Stubblefield **capacitor** UG/GGS **carbon cycle** EM **Carson** AP Images **Cartesian coordinate system** AA **Carver** AP Images **cave** Wendy Smith **celestial sphere** Jerry Malone **centripetal force** PG **chameleon** Cutcaster-Emmanuelle Bonzami **chromosome** Photo Researchers, Inc.-Biophoto Associates, Science Source **circle** RS **circulatory system** CI **cloud** PG **colony** SS-Phanie **compass (directional)** HMH Digital Studio **compass (drawing tool)** GI-Comstock **complementary angles** AA **compound eye** Cutcaster-gewoldi **cone (solid)** RS **cone (eye)** PG **conic section** EM **continent** Joe LeMonnier **contour map** HMH Digital Studio **convection** Ken Batelman **Copernicus** The Bridgeman Art Library-Private Collection **corona (solar)** GI-Photodisc **corona (daffodil)** Cutcaster-Manuela Schueler **corrosion** Corbis-Ocean **cosecant** CL-AA **cosine** CL-AA **cotangent** CL-AA **covalent bond** RS **crater** Alamy-Images & Stories **crevasse** Shutterstock-Steve Faber **crinoid** GI-Comstock **crystal** RS **culm** Dreamstime-Barak Tal **cumulonimbus** SS-Dave Reede, All Canada Photos **Curie** GI-Science Source **cyclone** NASA-Jeff Schmaltz, MODIS Rapid Response Team, Goddard Space Flight Center **cyclotron** PG

Darwin The Bridgeman Art Library-English Heritage Photo Library **decibel** EM **delta** GI-Peter Adams **desalination** PG **desert (Antarctica)** Alamy-Eric Carr **desert (western US)** SS-James Mattil **dewlap** GI-Jeremy Woodhouse **diatom** GI-Jan Hinsch **diffusion** EM **digestive tract** CI **dihedral** AA **distillation** PG **DNA** AA **Doppler effect** UG/GGS **drumlin** EM **du Châtelet** akg-images - Archives CDA, St-Genès **dune (Canyon de Chelly)** Alamy-Douglas Peebles Photography **dune (desert sand)** GI-in salah

ear[1] CI **earthquake** RS **eclipse (solar)** PG **ecosystem** Bob Novak **Einstein** AG-Everett Collection **electromagnetic spectrum** PG **El Niño** EM **emission** Corbis-Larry Lee Photography **emphysema** EM **endocrine gland** CI **enzyme** EM **equator** Thom Gillis **equinox** RS **esker** SS-Grambo Photography, All Canada Photos **Euclid** GI-Science Source **exterior angle** AA **eye (anatomy)** CI **eye (hurricane)** SS-StockTrek, Purestock

Fahrenheit EM **farsightedness** EM **fault** RS **Fermi** AP Images **fin** EM **Fleming** AP Images **fog** Geoff McCormack **food web** Michael Rothman **fractal** GI-Images Etc Ltd **Franklin** SS-National Portrait Gallery **frequency** PG **front (cold)** UG/GGS **front (warm)** UG/GGS **fulcrum** PG **fullerene** ShutterStock-Leonid Andronov

galaxy NASA-Gemini Observatory, GMOS Team **Galileo Galilei** SuperStock **generator** UG/GGS **germination** Tom Connell **gill** EM **Goodall** SS-NHPA **graft** Patrice Rossi Calkin **graph** UG/GGS **greenhouse effect** PG **Gulf Stream** NASA-Liam Grumley, MODIS Atmosphere Team, University of Wisconsin-Madison **gyroscope** Alamy-Tony Cordoza

hair CI **halo** GI-Martin Ruegner **Harvey** Corbis-Bettmann **Hawking** AP Images-The Canadian Press, Dave Chidley **heart** CI **heat exchanger** PG **Herschel (William)** The Bridgeman Art Library-National Maritime Museum, **Herschel (Caroline)** Alamy-The Art Gallery Collection London, UK **Hodgkin** GI-Mondadori Portfolio **holography** UG/GGS **homolosine projection** Jerry Malone **Hopper** US Navy-James S. Davis **hurricane** Barb Cousins **hydroelectric** UG/GGS **hyperbola** AA

incandescent light PG **induction** PG **inheritance** UG/GGS **insect** EM **intercept** CL-AA **interior angle** AA **internal-combustion engine** PG

jellyfish Corbis-Image Source **Jenner** Photo Researches, Inc.-Jean-Loup Charmet, Science Source **jet engine** PG **Joliot-Curie** GI-AFP

kelp GI-Karen Gowlett-Holmes **kidney** CI **kinetic energy** EM **Kwolek** Copyright © Dupont

lagoon SS-Nordic Photos **lahar** USGS-Tom Casadevall **laser** PG **latitude** Jerry Malone **lava** GI-Stockbyte **Lavoisier** SS-DeAgostini **LCD** Alamy-studiomode **Leavitt** Photo Researchers, Inc.-Science Photo Library, Science Source **Leeuwenhoek** SS-Pantheon **lens** PG **life cycle** EM **Linnaeus** SS-Fine Art Images **liver** CI **Lovelace** AG-Universal History Arc **Lyme disease** SS-Kallista Images

magnetic field Alamy-Alchemy **magnetic resonance imaging** Corbis **manometer** PG **Marconi** AG-Image Asset Management **mare** GI-Photodisc **McClintock** Alamy-Science Source **Meitner** GI-Science Source **Mendel** Photo Researchers, Inc.-Science Source **meniscus** CI **Mercator projection** Jerry Malone **Merian** Alamy-INTERFOTO **meridian** Jerry Malone **mesa** iStockphoto.com **metamorphosis** EM **migrate** Joe LeMonnier **Milky Way** Alamy-Design Pics Inc. **mirage** GI-Jeremy Woodhouse **Mitchell** GI-NYPL **Möbius strip** PG **molecule** RS **molt** AG -DLILLC, Corbis RF **moon** Tony Randazzo **moraine** SS-Eye Ubiquitous **muscle** CI

nautilus Corbis-Imagemore Co., Ltd. **neap tide** PG **nearsightedness** EM **nebula** Corbis-Stocktrek Images **nerve cell** AA **Newton** The Bridgeman Art Library-National Portrait Gallery, London, UK **nitrogen cycle** EM **Noether** Photo Researchers, Inc.-Science Source **North Pole** Joe LeMonnier **nuclear reactor** PG

PICTURE CREDITS

obtuse angle CL-AA **ocellus** Cutcaster-Oleksiy Fedorov **opal** ShutterStock-Tomas Pavelka **Oppenheimer** GI-Marie Hansen, Time Life Pictures **orca** SS-Gerard Lacz Images **orchid** SS-Design Pics **oscillation** PG **osteoarthritis** PG **osteoporosis** Photo Researchers, Inc.-BSIP, Science Source **outcrop** iStockphoto.com-Black Beck Photographic **oxbow** Alamy-Melba Photo Agency **oxidation** Cutcaster-Yali Shi **ozone** GI-SSPL

pahoehoe GI-Karl Weatherly, Photodisc **Pangaea** EM **parabola** CL-AA **parallax** PG **paramecium** Garth Glazier **Pasteur** AG-Pixtal **Pauling** Alamy-World History Archive **penicillium** SS-NHPA **peninsula** SS-age fotostock **perimeter** Pronk&Associates **periscope** Graham White **perpendicular** Pronk&Associates **petri dish** GI-R. Parulan, Jr. **planetary nebula** NASA-x-ray(NASA, CXC, SAO), optical (NASA, STScI) **plume (air pollution)** SS-Pixtal **plume (water pollution)** Alamy-Suzanne Long **polar coordinate system** CL-AA **pollen (bellflower)** Alamy-Science Photo Library **pollen (sunflower)** Alamy, Medical-on-Line **pollution** David Mackay Ballard **potential energy** EM **precipitate** GI-Charles D. Winters **prehensile** Corbis **Priestley** The Bridgeman Art Library, Collection of the New-York Historical Society, USA p**rism** Getty Images, Dimitri Vervitsiotis, Photographer's Choice RF **proboscis (elephant)** GI-HPH Image Library **proboscis (mosquito)** Photo Researchers, Inc. -Sinclair Stammers, Science Source **propeller** Alamy-Zoonar GmbH, Harald Richter **pterodactyl** Corbis-Jonathan Blair **Ptolemaic system** RS **pupa** Shutterstock-D. Kucharski & K. Kucharska **Pythagorean theorem** CL-AA

quartz GI-Photodisc, Siede Preis

radar Graham White **radial symmetry** PG **radioactive decay** PG **rainbow** PG **red blood cell** Photo Researchers, Inc.-Biophoto Associates, Science Source **red tide** AG-Photoshot **refraction** Jerry Malone **reptile** Patrick Gnan **respiratory system** CI **rheumatoid arthritis** PG **rhizome** EM **rib cage** EM **Richards** Library of Congress-Bain News Service **rip current** EM **RNA** EM **rookery** SS-Radius **rotifer** GI-M. I. Walker **ruminant** EM **Rutherford** Library of Congress-Bain News Service

Sabin Corbis-Bettmann **satellite** UG/GGS **saturated** RS **savanna** GI-Joseph Sohm, Visions of America, Photodisc **scale[1] (fish)** Alamy-imagebroker **scale[1] (cone)** GI-Photodisc **sea cucumber** SS-age fotostock **sea slug** Cutcaster-Cigdem Cooper **seaweed (sea beech)** SS-NHPA **seaweed (bladderwort)** Photo Researchers, Inc. -D.P. Wilson, FLPA, Science Source **seaweed (kelp)** GI-Justin Lewis **sedimentary** Cutcaster-mdphot **sessile (sponge)** GI-Franco Banfi **sessile (oak)** Alamy-imagebroker **shale** Photo Researchers, Inc.-James Steinberg **sickle cell anemia** SS-Science Picture Co, SF **sill** Photo Researchers, Inc.-Catherine Ursillo **sine** CL-AA **sinus** EM **sinusoidal projection** Jerry Malone **skin** CI **slime mold** GI-National Geographic, Paul Zahl **smut** Alamy-blickwinkel **solar cell** PG **solar flare** GI-Digital Vision **Somerville** The Bridgeman Art Library-Private Collection **Sonar** PG **South Pole** Joe LeMonnier **spinal cord** CI **sponge (vase-shaped)** iStockphoto.com **sponge (tubular)** GI-Photodisc **spring tide** PG **stalactite/stalagmite** Alamy-Chris Howes, Wild Places Photography **Stevens** Courtesy Carnegie Institution for Science **stoma** GI-Scimat Scimat **straight angle** CL-AA **stratum** Alamy-David R. Frazier Photolibrary, Inc. **structural formula** RS **sublimation** GI-Charles D. Winters **sun** AA **supercell** Shutterstock-Minerva Studio **supplementary angles** CL-AA **symmetry** PG **syncline** PG

talon Eva Vagreti Cockrille **telescope** PG **temperature** EM **Tesla** AG-Everett Collection **thyroid gland** CI **tick** Shutterstock-D. Kucharski & K. Kucharska **tide (high)** Alamy-Laszlo Podor **tide (low)** Alamy-Laszlo Podor **tombolo** Shutterstock-Tramont_ana **tooth** Jerry Malone **tornado** Geoff McCormack **trade winds** EM **transpiration** EM **trigonometric function** RS **trilobite** Photo Researchers, Inc.-Sinclair Stammers **tropic** Jerry Malone **tsunami** Geoff McCormack **tufa** Ardea-Bob GI-bbons **tundra** Ardea-Steffen & Alexandra Sailer **turbojet** PG **Turing** Photo Researchers, Inc.-Science Source

ultrasound SS-Nordic Photos **unsaturated** RS **urinary system** CI

Van de Graaff generator CL-AA **Van de Graaff generator** Photo Researchers, Inc.-Ted Kinsman, Science Source **venation** Alamy-Fabrizio Troiani **Venn diagram** EM **vertebra** CI **vertex** Pronk&Associates **Vesalius** AG-Image Asset Management **vortex** GI-Yamada Taro, Digital Vision

water cycle EM **wetland (marsh)** AG-Brian Jannsen **wetland (swamp)** AG-Robert Francis **wetland (bog)** Alamy-Chris Howes, Wild Places Photography **white blood cell** Alamy-Science Photo Library **Wilson** AP Images **Wimshurst machine** SS-Science and Society **Wu** GI-Science Source

x-ray GI-Photodisc **xylem** EM

Yalow Corbis-Bettmann

zebra GI-Photodisc **zooplankton** Photo Researchers, Inc.-M.I. Walker, Science Source

A CLOSER LOOK

Atoms PG **Cells (animal and plant)** PG; **(nerve)** GI-Photodisc; **(blood)** Science Source-Power & Syred; **(guard)** Science Source-Biophoto Associates **Color** PG **Fission/Fusion** PG **Flowers** EM **Meiosis/Mitosis** PG **Photosynthesis** PG **Skeleton** CI **Star** PG **Tectonic Boundaries** PG **Volcanoes (photo)** Alamy-Marco Regalia Sell; **(diagram)** Patrice Rossi Calkin **Waves (structure, longitudinal, transverse, reflection, refraction, diffraction)** RS; **(frequency, wavelength)** PG

CHARTS & TABLES

Geologic Time PG and Symmetry, Inc. **Organic Compounds** Symmetry, Inc. **Periodic Table of the Elements** Cathy Hawkes and Symmetry, Inc. **Rock (igneous)** Corbis-Ocean; **(metamorphic)** Corbis-Frank Krahmer; **(sedimentary)** SS-Biosphoto; **(igneous slice)** Corbis-Pantafos, Science Photo Library; **(metamorphic slice)** Alamy-Melba Photo Agency; **(sedimentary slice)** GI-M. I. Walker **Solar System (sun)** NASA/SDO; **(Mercury)** GI-Photodisc; **(Venus)** GI-Photodisc; **(Earth)** Corbis-L. Clarke; **(Mars)** NASA/JPL **(Jupiter)** NASA/JPL/University of Arizona; **(Saturn)** Corbis; **(Uranus)** NASA/JPL/USGS; **(Neptune)** GI-StockTrek, Photodisc **Taxonomy** PG and Symmetry, Inc.